ATLAS

CONTENTS

HOW TO USE THE ATLAS 4   AZEROTH WORLD MAP 6

REGION MAPS

Alterac Mountains 8	Eastern Plaguelands 40	Stormwind 72
Arathi Highlands 10	Elwynn Forest 42	Stranglethorn Vale 74
Ashenvale 12	Felwood 44	Swamp of Sorrows 76
Azshara 14	Feralas 46	Tanaris 78
Badlands 16	Hillsbrad Foothills 48	Teldrassil 80
Barrens 18	Hinterlands 50	Thousand Needles 82
Blasted Lands 20	Ironforge 52	Thunder Bluff 84
Burning Steppes 22	Loch Modan 54	Tirisfal Glades 86
Darkshore 24	Moonglade 56	Undercity 88
Darnassus 26	Mulgore 58	Un'Goro Crater 90
Deadwind Pass 28	Orgrimmar 60	Western Plaguelands 92
Desolace 30	Redridge Mountains 62	Westfall 94
Dun Morogh 32	Searing Gorge 64	Wetlands 96
Durotar 34	Silithus 66	Winterspring 98
Duskwood 36	Silverpine Forest 68	
Dustwallow Marsh 38	Stonetalon Mountains 70	

TOWN & CAMP MAPS

Aerie Peak 100	Ghost Walker Post 111	Raven Hill: Cemetery 122
Agamand Mills 100	Goldshire 112	Razor Hill 122
Astranaar 101	Grom'Gol Base Camp 112	Sen'jin Village 123
Auberdine 101	Hammerfall 113	Sentinel Hill 123
Bloodhoof Village 102	Hillsbrad Fields 113	The Sepulcher 124
Booty Bay 103	Kargath 114	Shadowglen 124
Brackenwall Village 104	Kharanos 114	Shadowprey Village 125
Brill 104	Lakeshire 115	Southshore 125
Camp Mojache 105	Light's Hope Chapel 116	Splintertree Post 126
Camp Narache 105	Marshal's Refuge 116	Stonard 126
Camp Taurajo 106	Menethil Harbor 117	Stromgarde Keep 127
Coldridge Valley 106	Mirage Raceway 118	Sun Rock Retreat 127
The Crossroads 107	Morgan's Vigil 118	Tarren Mill 128
Darkshire 108	Nethergarde Keep 119	Thelsamar 129
Deathknell 109	Nijel's Point 119	Theramore 130
Dolanaar 109	Nighthaven 120	Valley of Trials 131
Everlook 110	Northshire Valley 120	Zoram Strand 131
Feathermoon Stronghold 110	Ratchet 121	Zoram'gar Outpost 131
Gadgetzan 111	Raven Hill 121	

INDICES

Main Index 132	Profession Trainers 184
Flight Masters, Innkeepers,	Resources 186
Mount Trainers and Weapon Masters 181	Rare Mobs 188
Class Trainers 182	Skill Trainers and Specialty Vendors 191

HOW TO USE THE ATLAS

This project began when we rediscovered Azeroth through new eyes in **World of Warcraft**. The lush regions, vast population of players and the abundance of in-game characters provided the impetus to begin development.

This section explains how each section can be used, both alone and with other sections, and how best to tackle the massive amount of information in the indices.

AZEROTH WORLD MAP

Azeroth is a vast landmass currently broken apart into 40 playable regions. Each region has points of interest including flight points, cities and dungeons. The Azeroth world map shows all this and more. However, to see a more detailed map of the regions, you'll need to refer to those specific maps. The world map is meant to give you an overall view of the world and give you a better understanding about where regions are located in relation to the continents and other regions throughout Azeroth.

FLIGHT POINTS & PATHS

The available flight/travel paths are indicated by faction-specific colors. (See the Azeroth Map Legend.) The points themselves are numbered and correspond to the legends on either side of the map. These legends give you a specific city, town or camp in which the flight points are located. If you're trying to find the Alliance flight point in the Hinterlands (Page 50) for example, you'll see that it's #12 on the Alliance Travel Point legend and can be found at Aerie Peak (Page 100).

Obviously, not every flight point connects to every other. This map also indicates which paths are available from each location. If, for example, there's no mage around to offer a port and your hearthstone's still got some cooldown, but you're trying to fly from Booty Bay to Light's Hope Chapel, just check out the map and plot the course. This is the best method to find your way around, discover the shortest routes and learn how to get anywhere in Azeroth.

WORLD DUNGEONS

World Dungeons (a.k.a. Instances) are some of the most sought after locations in Azeroth. Dungeons are scattered across both continents and they're marked on the world map with numbered triangles that refer to a corresponding list of dungeon names. (See the Azeroth Map and Continent Instance legends.) The best way to find out exactly where an instance dungeon is within a region is to refer to the region map itself, but the world map offers the perfect start to your search.

ZEPPELINS AND SHIPS

Both types of alternate (often intercontinental) travel are indicated on the map with dotted lines. (See Azeroth Map Legend.)

REGION MAPS

Maps make up the bulk of the atlas and the region maps are going to be used more often than any others. They have been modified from those that you see in game to a) mark all of the mini-regions and b) include a grid. The grid is a component to be used in conjunction with the various indices and serves as a tool to help people find NPCs, monsters, and bosses. (For more information, check out the **Indices** section farther along in this section.)

These maps are listed in alphabetical order. (See the Table of Contents [Page 3] for a complete list.) The major city maps aren't broken out in any special form and are listed alphabetically as well. Region-specific legends border the map and highlight any Flight Masters, Trainers, and Vendors in the region. For ease, Innkeepers are listed under the "Vendors" heading. This is the fastest option to use when trying to discover whether there's a flight point or inn in the region.

Quick reference lists appear at the bottom of the page. These show the corresponding page numbers of any connecting regions and/or associated town/camp maps in the atlas. If you're having a tough time finding a character in one of the towns or camps, take advantage of the quick reference list to pinpoint their location.

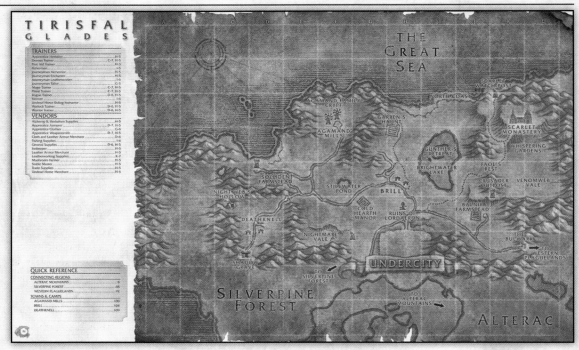

TOWN & CAMP MAPS

This section includes maps that detail some of the more interesting and/or complex areas that often include important NPCs. This section is organized in alphabetical order by the name of the town or encampment, **not** the region from which the maps are drawn.

The region in which the town or encampment can be found is indicated underneath the legend for that specific map, along with the page number of that region.

Callouts on each map correspond to the associated legend. All of the NPCs in the area are marked as are the mobs that may appear. (Some areas have various spawning points of the same type of mob and they're listed with the same number throughout the map.)

 In the legend, a mailbox icon shows whether the area has a mailbox and where it is located.

INDICES

These indices were created for use with the maps included in this atlas. They're cross-referenced with the regions, and the town/camp maps in some cases, and tie into the grids placed onto each region map.

THE MAIN INDEX

This is the exhaustive index in which all the NPCs, mobs (or creeps if you're a **Warcraft** player), and bosses appear. Here's the basic information that you'll find in a single entry.

Aayndia Floralwind
Ashenvale (12), Astranaar (101), E-5, Expert Leatherworker, Left as you enter southwest building

Name: Aayndia Floralwind
Region: Ashenvale (Page 12)
Sub-Region: Astranaar (Page 101)
Grid: E-5 on the Ashenvale map
Title/Description: Expert Leatherworker
Note: A note on the location of the subject, what may be of interest about the subject, or the rarity of the subject

Many mobs and NPCs appear in multiple grids. The easiest type of grid entry is the simplest, a single vertical and horizontal coordinate: e.g. E-5. If an NPC appears in two adjacent grids, that would be listed in two ways. First, if it spawns in two horizontally adjacent grids, the grid locations are separated by a comma: e.g. E-5, F-5. If it's two vertically adjacent grids, it's shown with parenthesis: e.g. E:(5, 6). Lastly, if a mob appears in a few vertical grid locations, it's separated with a hyphen: e.g. E:(5-9).

There are many mobs that appear throughout a given map. The Angerclaw Grizzly in Felwood is a great example. Here's the grid entry for that mob: G:(2, 3), H:(1-3), I-2.

That mob is in the following grid locations: G-2, G-3, H-1, H-2, H-3, and I-2.

Here are a few things to keep in mind about the index entries.

- A subject may roam outside of the mentioned Grid, Sub-Region, and occasionally the Region. The information given in the listing only shows where it **spawns**.
- The page numbers in the Region and Sub-Region entries relate to pages in the Atlas where any associated maps are located. Many Sub-Regions don't have maps.
- Many entries don't have Sub-Regions or Titles/Descriptions. A few won't have Grid locations since they spawn throughout a Region (normally a city).

SUPPLEMENTAL INDICES

These indices were created to offer other ways to look up specific types of NPCs. For example, if you're looking for the enchanting trainers of the world, look in the table listing those trainers. The same rule applies for class trainers.

Class Trainer Listings

This is where to look to find trainers for your specific class. However, they're not broken down by faction, just region. If you're a Night Elf Priest, you can be sure that Aelthalyste (a Priest Trainer in the Undercity) won't be helping you any time soon.

Profession Trainer Listings

These lists show where all the trainers are for each profession and secondary skill and their level: Journeyman, Expert, Artisan, or Master.

Faction Flight Point Listings

This is a simple list for each faction showing all the flight points and in which Regions/Mini-Regions they appear.

Resource Listings

These tables are quick references to discover where to find specific resources. The Herb and Ore tables cross-reference each type of resource with each of the regions. To discover whether there's Tin Ore to be found in a region, just look across the table. Vice versa, if you want to discover which herbs are available in Felwood, that table shows all the available herbs in the region.

The Leather table explains which mobs to hunt for each type of leather. The general leather list is broken down by skill level, but the specialty leather list shows exactly which mobs to hunt for specific types of leather.

Vendor Listings

These lists break down each type of vendor and where to find them. General and Trade Goods vendors are excluded from this list since they appear all over the world and in almost every city or town. The vendors that many players are interested in are the unique and rare vendors scattered across the world of Azeroth.

Rare Spawn Listings

There are rare spawning mobs throughout the world and they often have better drops than regular mobs—that's why they're so sought after. This list shows all of the rare mobs, their levels, and their rarity. Use the corresponding table to decipher how often certain mobs spawn.

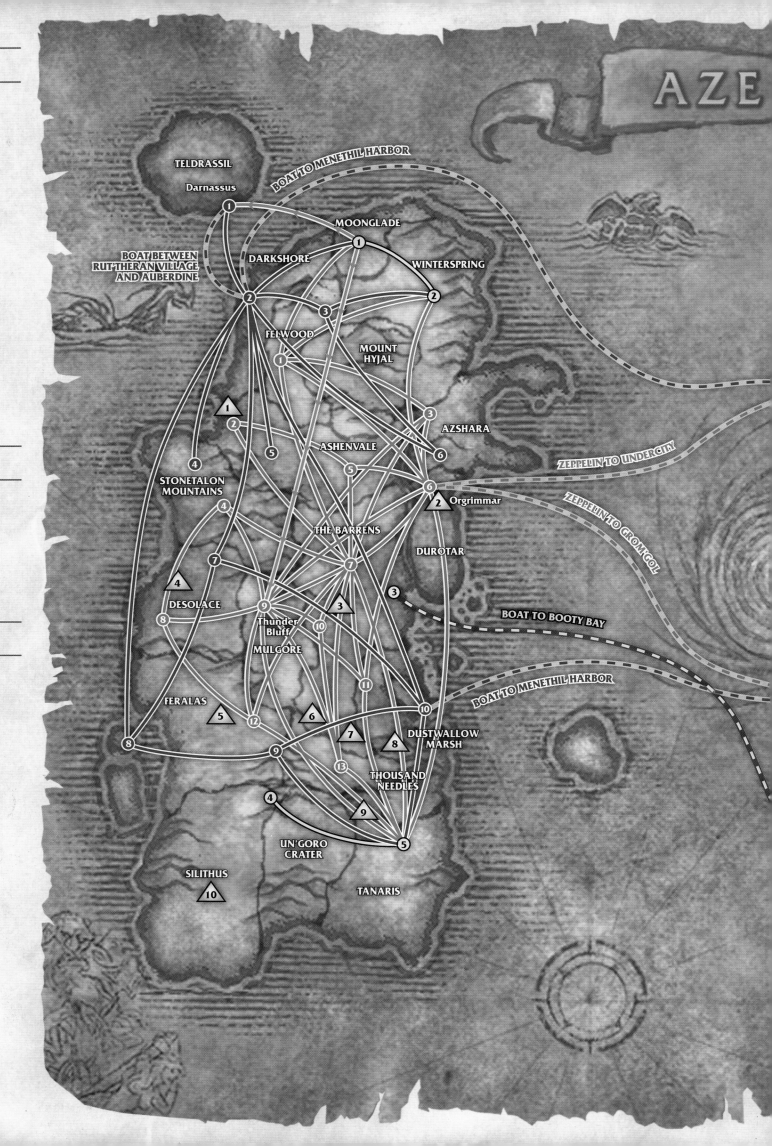

HORDE TRAVEL POINTS

1 Bloodvenom Post
2 Zoram'gar Outpost
3 Valormok
4 Sunrock Retreat
5 Splintertree Post
6 Orgrimmar
7 Crossroads
8 Shadowprey Village
9 Thunder Bluff
10 Camp Taurajo
11 Brackenwall Village
12 Camp Mojache
13 Freewind Post
14 Undercity
15 The Sepulcher
16 Tarren Mill
17 Hammerfall
18 Revantusk Village
19 Kargath
20 Ruins of Thaurissan
21 Grom'Gol Base Camp
22 Stonard

NEUTRAL TRAVEL POINTS

1 Moonglade
2 Everlook
3 Ratchet
4 Valor's Rest
5 Gadgetzan
6 Light's Hope Chapel
7 Thorium Point
8 Booty Bay

KALIMDOR INSTANCES

1 Blackfathom Deeps
2 Ragefire Chasm
3 The Wailing Caverns
4 Maraudon
5 Dire Maul
6 Razorfen Kraul
7 Razorfen Downs
8 Onyxia's Lair
9 Zul'Farrak
10 Ahn'Qiraj

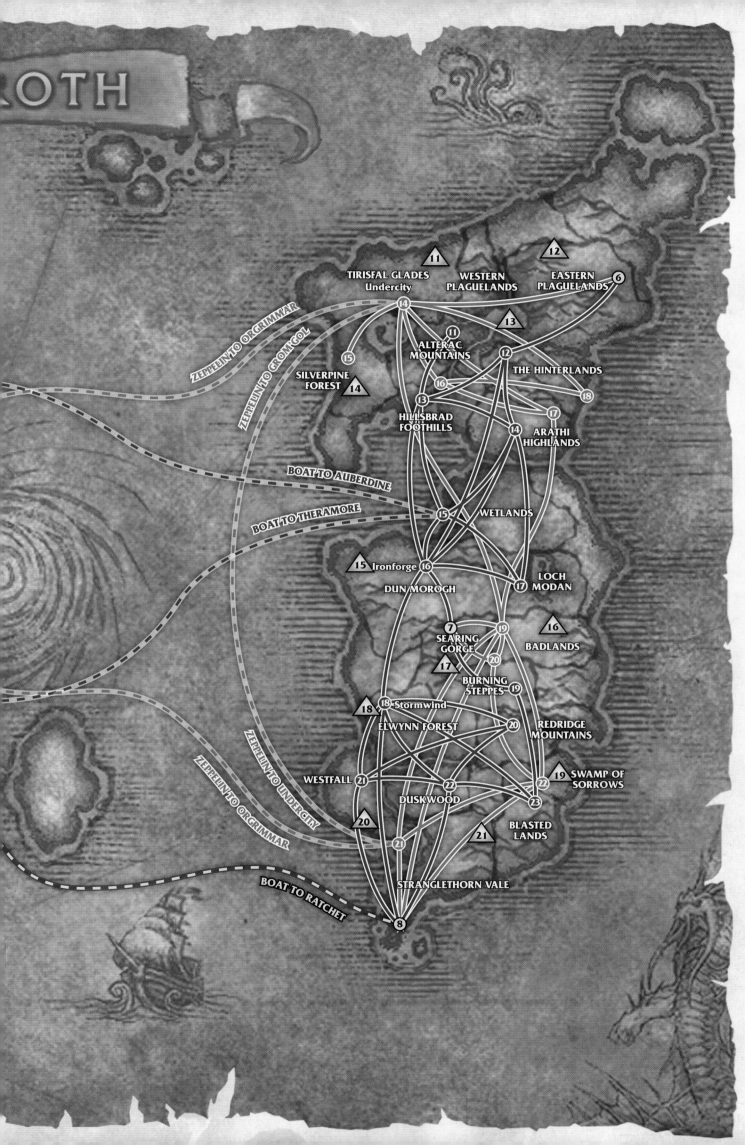

ROTH

ALLIANCE TRAVEL POINTS

1 Rut'Theran Village
2 Auberdine
3 Talonbranch Glade
4 Stonetalon Peak
5 Astranaar
6 Talrendls Point
7 Nijel's Point
8 Feathermoon Stronghold
9 Thalanaar
10 Theramore Isle
11 Chillwind Pointe
12 Aerie Peak
13 Southshore
14 Refuge Point
15 Menethil Harbor
16 Ironforge
17 Thelsamar
18 Stormwind
19 Morgan's Vigil
20 Lakeshire
21 Sentinel Hill
22 Darkshire
23 Nethergarde Keep

EASTERN KINGDOMS INSTANCES

11 Scarlet Monastery
12 Stratholme
13 Scholomance
14 Shadowfang Keep
15 Gnomeregan
16 Uldaman
17 Blackrock Mountain
  Blackrock Depths
  Blackrock Spire
  Blackwing Lair
  The Molten Core
18 The Stockade
19 The Temple of Atal'Hakkar
20 The Deadmines
21 Zul'Gurub

MAP LEGEND

△ Instance
● Horde Travel Point
━ Horde Flight Path
┅ Horde Zeppelin Path
◓ Alliance Flight Point
═ Alliance Flight Path
┄ Alliance Boat Path
○ Neutral Travel Point
═ Neutral Flight Path
═ Neutral Boat Path
═ Druid-Only Flight Path
   (One Way)

ALTERAC
MOUNTAINS

WESTERN
PLAGUELANDS

TO
WESTERN
PLAGUELANDS

NBRAD

CHILLWIND
POINT

TO
WESTERN
PLAGUELANDS

QUICK REFERENCE

ARATHI HIGHLANDS

FLIGHT MASTERS

Gryphon Master	F-5
Wind Rider Master	J-3

TRAINERS

Superior Butcher	J-3
Trauma Surgeon (First Aid)	J-4

VENDORS

Alchemy Supplies	F-5
Bowyer	J-3
Butcher	F-4, J-3
General Goods	F-5, J-3
Innkeeper	J-3
Leatherworking Supplies	F-5, J-3
Scrolls and Potions	C-6
Stable Master	J-3
Superior Macecrafter	F-5
Superior Tradesman	F-5
Tailoring Supplies	J-4
Trade Goods	J-3

QUICK REFERENCE

CONNECTING REGIONS

HILLSBRAD FOOTHILLS	48
WETLANDS	96

CITY & CAMPS

HAMMERFALL	113
STROMGARDE KEEP	127

ASHENVALE

FLIGHT MASTERS

Hippogryph Master	E-5
Wind Rider Master	B-4

TRAINERS

Expert Alchemist	G-6
Expert Leatherworker	E-5
Fisherman	B-4
Herbalist	G-6
Hunter Trainer	C-6, F-6, G-6
Pet Trainer	C-6, F-6
Skinner	F-6

VENDORS

Alchemy Supplies	G-6
Baker	E-5
Bowyer	G-6
Clothier	E-5
Fish Merchant & Supplies	B-4
Food & Drink Vendor	E-5
General Goods	E-5
Heavy Armor Merchant	I-6
Innkeeper	E-5, I-6
Leather Armor Merchant	E-5
Leatherworking Supplies	C-6, E-5
Reagent Supplies	E-5
Silverwing Supply Officer	H-8
Stable Master	E-5
Tools & Supplies	E-5
Trade Goods	E-5, F-6
Weaponsmith	E-5

QUICK REFERENCE

CONNECTING REGIONS

AZSHARA	14
BARRENS	18
DARKSHORE	24
FELWOOD	44
STONETALON MOUNTAINS	70

TOWNS & CAMPS

ASTRANAAR	101
SPLINTERTREE POST	126
ZORAM STRAND	131
ZORAM'GAR OUTPOST	131

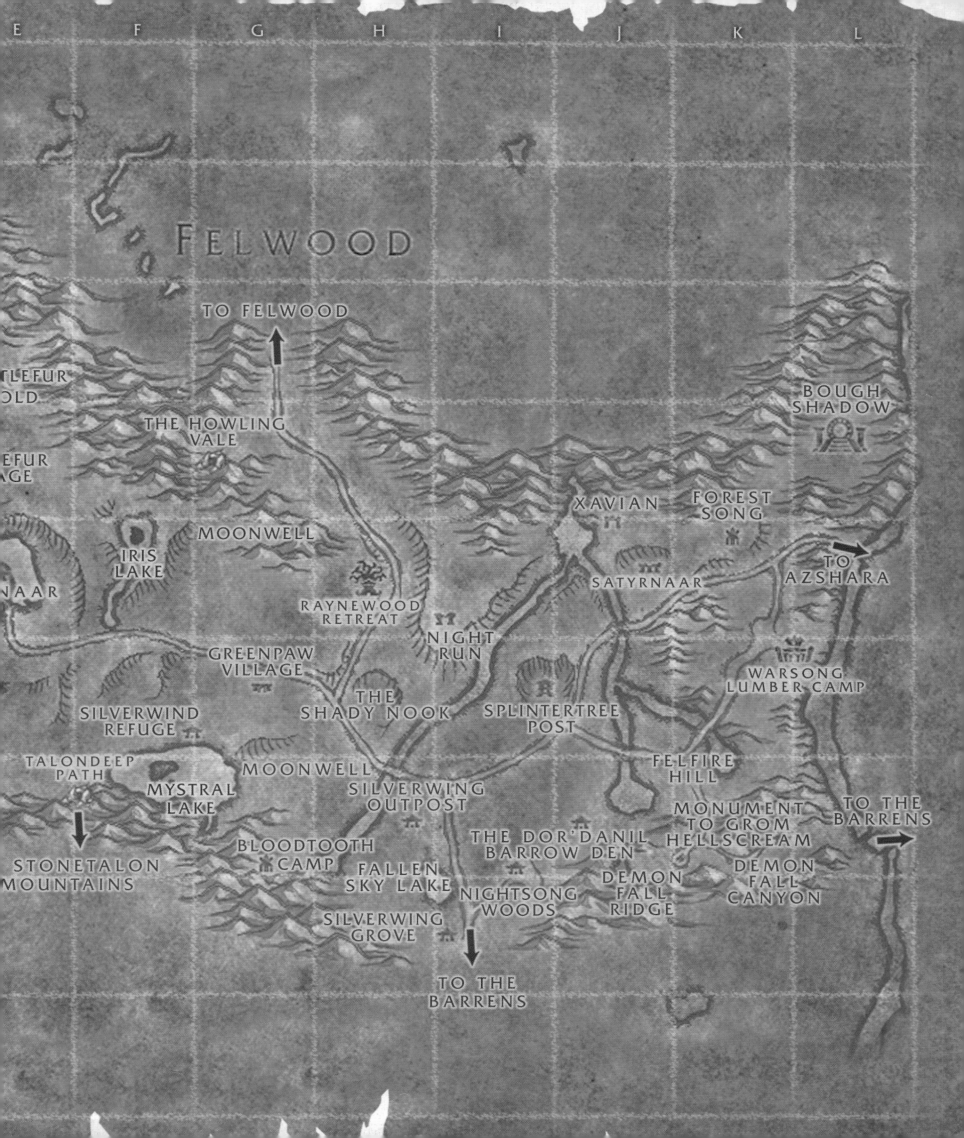

NTERSPRING

JAGGED REEF

LEGASH
ENCAMPMENT

URSOLAN

THALASSIAN
BASE CAMP

TIMBERMAW
HOLD

THE SHATTERED
STRAND

BEAR'S
HEAD   TEMPLE OF
ZIN-MALOR

HETAERA'S
CLUTCH

VALORMOK

RUINS OF
ELDARATH

SOUTHFURY
RIVER

THE
BAY OF STORM

HALDARR
ENCAMPMENT

TO ASHENVALE

THE
FORLORN RIDGE

SOUTHRIDGE
BEACH

SHADOWSONG
SHRINE

LAKE
MENNAR

THE RU
REACH

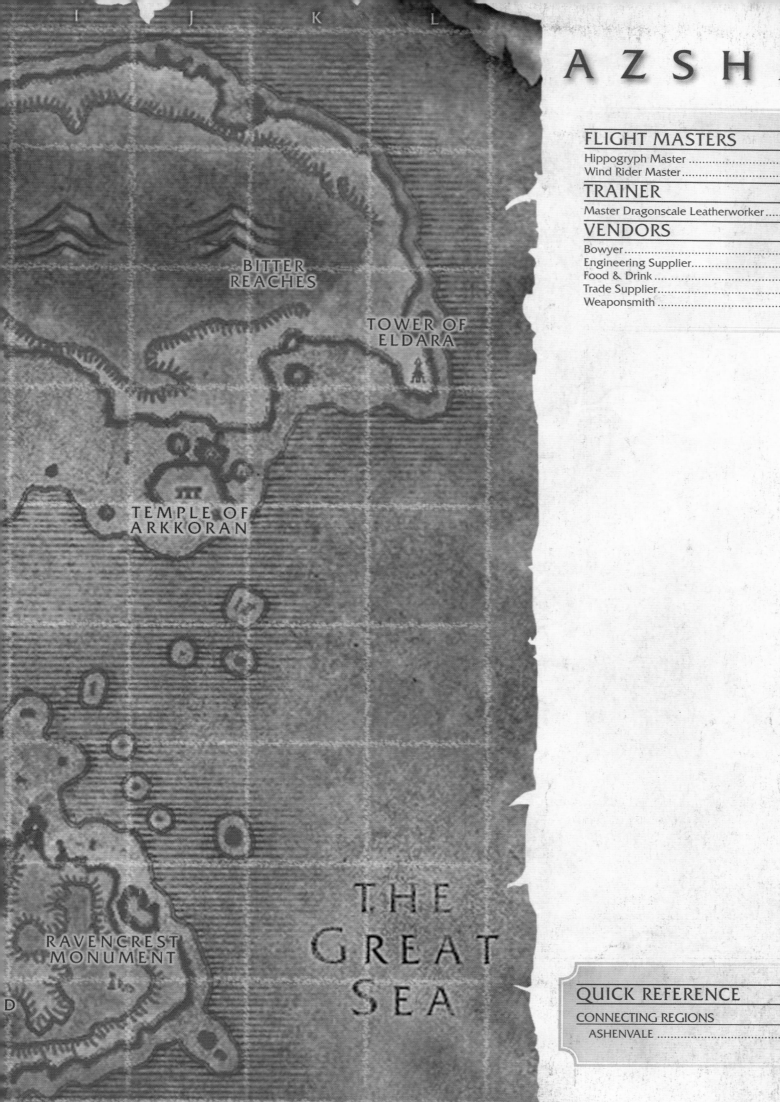

AZSHARA

BITTER
REACHES

TOWER OF
ELDARA

TEMPLE OF
ARKKORAN

RAVENCREST
MONUMENT

THE
GREAT
SEA

FLIGHT MASTERS

Hippogryph Master A-8
Wind Rider Master B-5

TRAINER

Master Dragonscale Leatherworker D-6

VENDORS

Bowyer A-8
Engineering Supplier E-9
Food & Drink B-5
Trade Supplier E-9
Weaponsmith B-5

QUICK REFERENCE

CONNECTING REGIONS

ASHENVALE 12

15

BADLANDS

LOCH MOD

A   B   D

1

2

3

4

KARGATH

5   CAMP WURG

THE DUS

TO SEARING
GORGE

6

APOCRYPHAN'S
REST

MIRAG

7

CAMP CAGG

8

DUSTBELCH
GROTTO

9

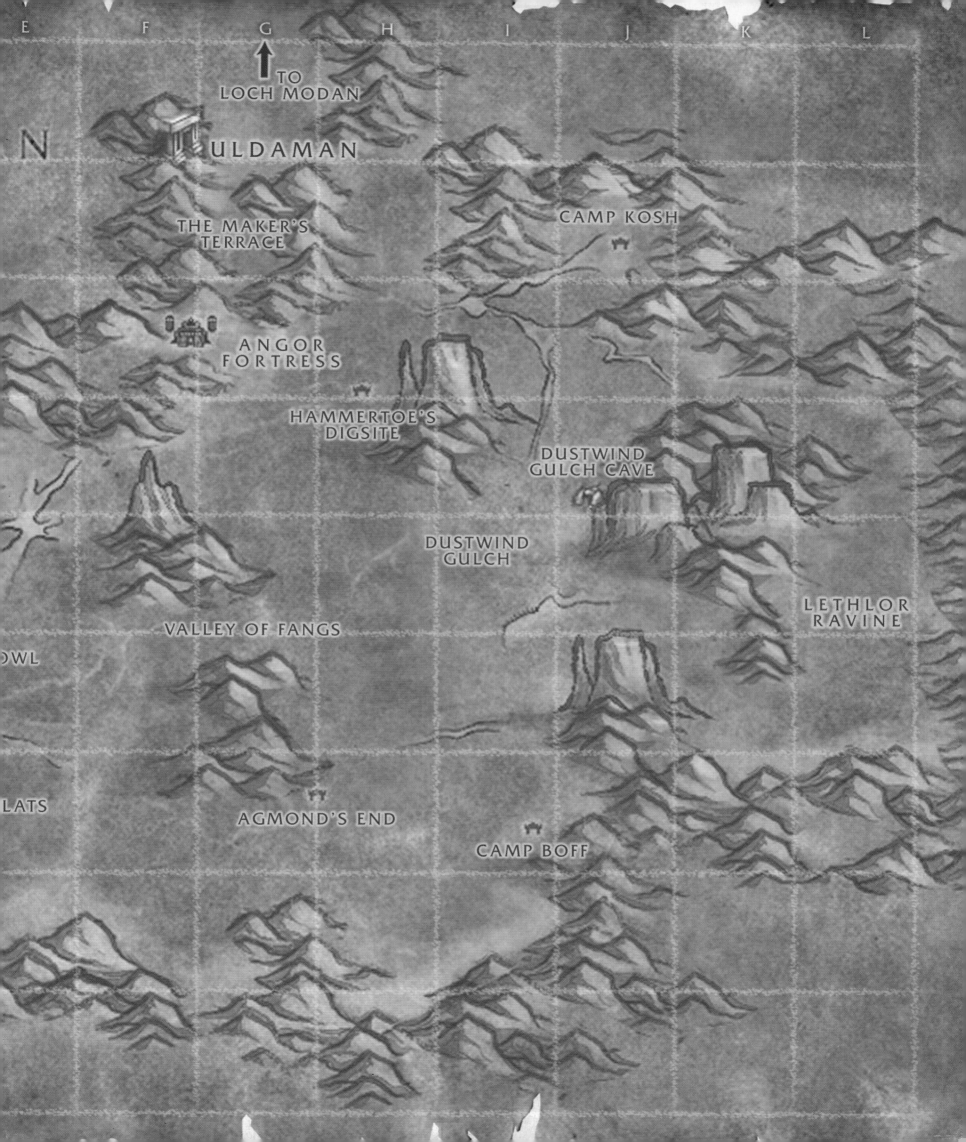

E   F   G   H   I   J   K   L

↑
TO
LOCH MODAN

ULDAMAN

N

THE MAKER'S
TERRACE

CAMP KOSH

ANGOR
FORTRESS

HAMMERTOE'S
DIGSITE

DUSTWIND
GULCH CAVE

DUSTWIND
GULCH

VALLEY OF FANGS

LETHLOR
RAVINE

OWL

LATS

AGMOND'S END

CAMP BOFF

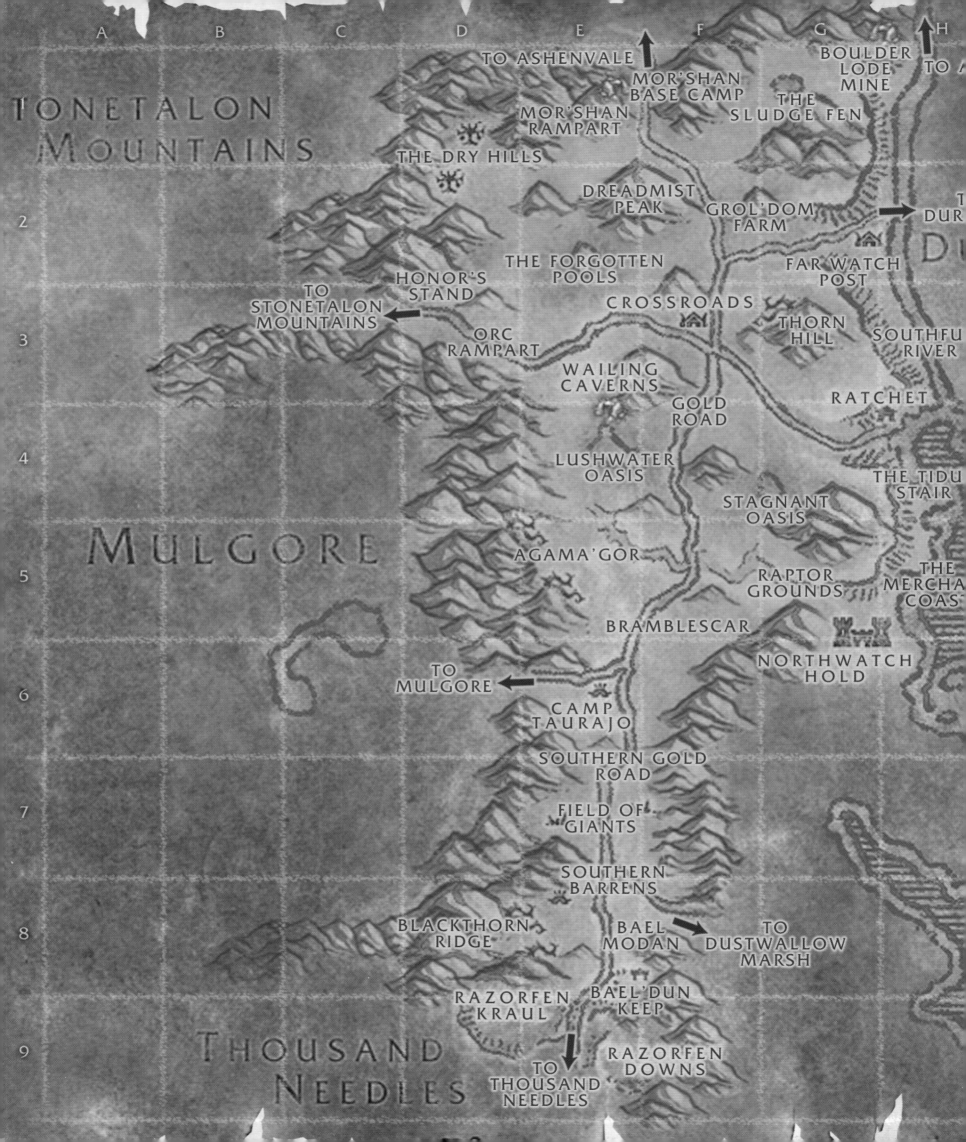

HENVALE

BARRENS

FLIGHT MASTER
Wind Rider Master...F:(3, 6)

TRAINERS
Cook...G-3
Expert Blacksmith..F-3
Expert Leatherworker...F-6
Expert Tailor..F-6
Fisherman..H-4
Journeyman Engineer..H-4
Journeyman Leatherworker.......................................E-4
Journeyman Tailor..F-3
Master Goblin Engineer...H-4
Skinner..F-6

VENDORS
Armorer & Shieldcrafter..H-4
Bael'dun Morale Officer..F-8
Bags & Sacks...F-3
Baker...F-3, G-3
Beverage Merchant..F-3
Blacksmithing Supplier...F-3
Bowyer & Gunsmith..F-3
Butcher...F:(3, 6)
Cloth & Leather Armor Merchant.................................H-4
Clothier...F-3
Engineering Goods..H-4
General Supplies..F-3, H-4
Innkeeper...F:(3, 6), H-4
Leather & Mail Armor Merchant..................................F-3
Leather Armor Merchant....................................E-4, F-6
Reagents and Herbs...F-3
Smokywood Pastures...E-1
Specialist Leatherworking Supplies.............................E-4
Stable Master..F:(3, 6), H-4
Stylish Clothier...E-4
Tailoring & Leatherworking Supplies............................F-6
Tailoring Supplies...F-3
Trade Supplies..F-3, H-4
Warsong Supply Officer...E-1
Weapon Dealer..G-4
Weaponsmith...F-3, H-4
Weaponsmith & Armorcrafter.....................................E-1

QUICK REFERENCE

CONNECTING REGIONS
ASHENVALE 12
DUROTAR 34
DUSTWALLOW MARSH 38
MULGORE 58
STONETALON MOUNTAINS.............................70
THOUSAND NEEDLES.................................82

TOWNS & CAMPS
CAMP TAURAJO 106
THE CROSSROADS 107
RATCHET 121

BLASTED LANDS

DEADWIND PASS

STRANGLETHORN VALE

THE
SEARING GORGE

ALTAR
OF STORMS

FLAME

BLACKROCK
MOUNTAIN

RUIN
THAUR

BLACKROCK
STRONGHOLD

PILLAR OF ASH

DRACODAR

YNN FOREST

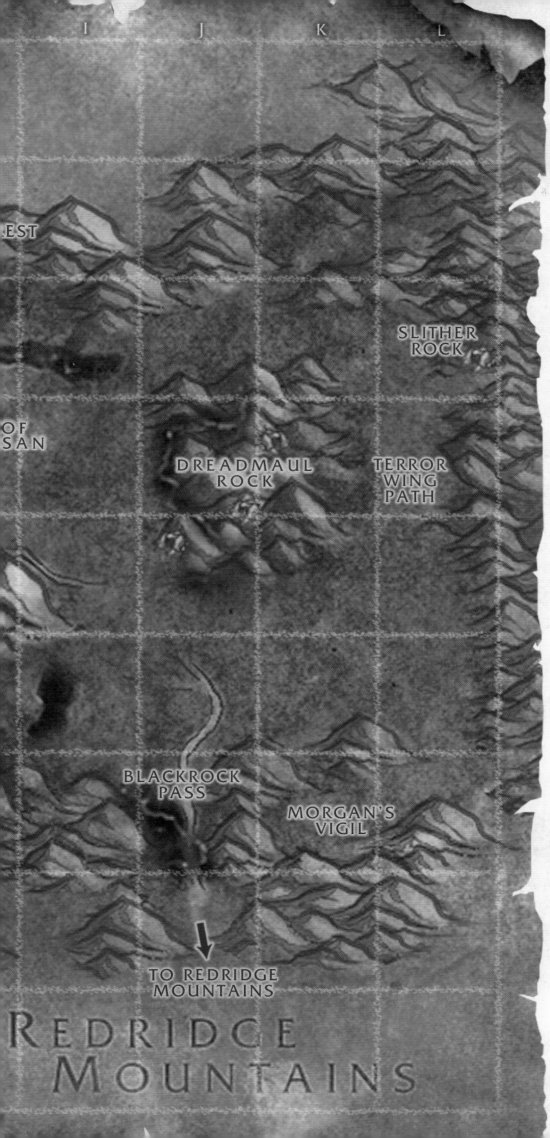

EST

OF
SAN

SLITHER
ROCK

DREADMAUL
ROCK

TERROR
WING
PATH

BLACKROCK
PASS

MORGAN'S
VIGIL

TO REDRIDGE
MOUNTAINS

REDRIDGE
MOUNTAINS

BURNING
S T E P P E S

FLIGHT MASTERS

Gryphon Master..K-7
Wind Rider Master H-2

VENDORS

Food & Drink ....°H-2, K-7
Weaponsmith K-7

QUICK REFERENCE

CONNECTING REGIONS

REDRIDGE MOUNTAINS...62

TOWNS & CAMPS

MORGAN'S VIGIL 118

DARKSHORE

THE
VEILED
SEA

TH

TWILIC
SHOI

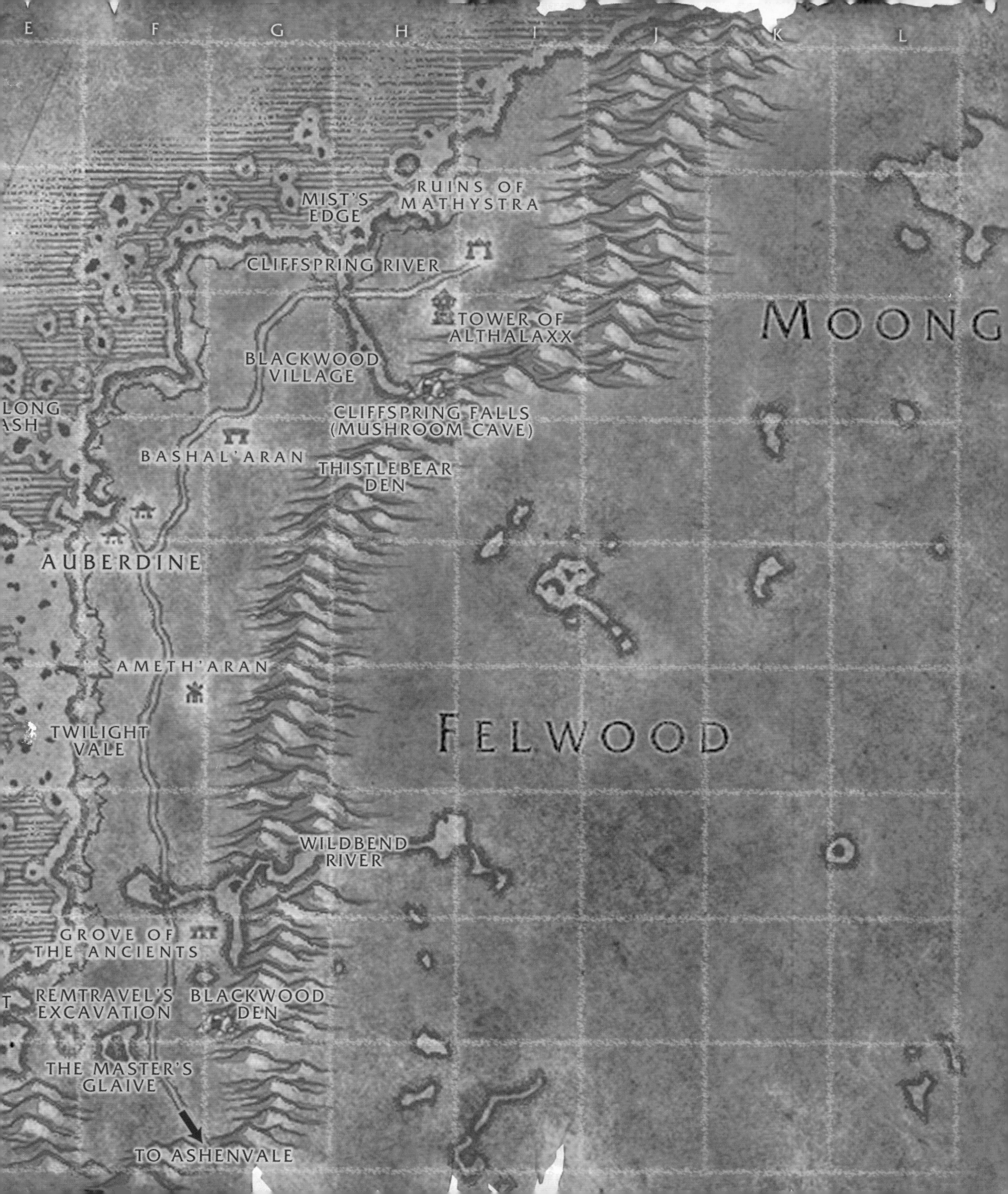
E
F
G
H
I
J
K
L
MIST'S EDGE
RUINS OF MATHYSTRA
CLIFFSPRING RIVER
TOWER OF ALTHALAXX
MOONG
BLACKWOOD VILLAGE
LONG
ASH
CLIFFSPRING FALLS (MUSHROOM CAVE)
BASHAL'ARAN
THISTLEBEAR DEN
AUBERDINE
AMETH'ARAN
TWILIGHT VALE
FELWOOD
WILDBEND RIVER
GROVE OF THE ANCIENTS
REMTRAVEL'S EXCAVATION
BLACKWOOD DEN
THE MASTER'S GLAIVE
TO ASHENVALE

DARNASSUS

CITY OFFICIALS

Alliance Cloth
   Quartermaster............. I-2
Alterac Valley
   Battlemaster...............H-4

Guild Master.................. I-2
Warsong Gulch
   Battlemaster................H-3

TRAINERS

Artisan Alchemist G-2
Artisan Leatherworker.... I-2
Cooking Trainer..............F-2
Druid Trainer D-1
Expert Enchanter H-1
Expert Leatherworker I-2
Expert Tailor H-2
First Aid Trainer.............G-1
Fishing Trainer...............F-5
Herbalism Trainer...........F-7
Hunter Trainer............... E-1
Journeyman Alchemist...G-2
Journeyman Enchanter..H-1

Journeyman
   Leatherworker.............. I-2
Journeyman Tailor I-2
Nightsaber Riding
   Instructor.................... E-1
Pet Trainer E-1
Portal Trainer................. E-8
Priest Trainer .... E:(8, 9)
Rogue Trainer.........D-2, E-2
Skinning Trainer I-2
Warrior Trainer ....H:(3, 4)
Weapon Master H-5

VENDORS

Alchemy Supplies.........G-2
Axe Merchant................ I-6
Bag Merchant I-5
Blade Merchant I-6
Bow Merchant H-6
Cloth Armor Merchant..H-7
Cooking Supplier F-2
Enchanting Supplies......H-1
Fish Vendor....................F-5
Fishing Supplier F-5
Food & Drink . D-1, F-2, K-4
General Goods
   Vendor I-5, K-5
General Trade Supplier..H-2
Herbalism Supplier F-7
Innkeeper .... I:(1, 2)
Leather Armor
   Merchant G-8
Leatherworking
   Supplies I-2

Mace & Staff Merchant.. I-6
Mail Armor Merchant ...H-7
Meat Vendor.................H-5
Night Elf Armorer H-4
Owl Trainer K-4
Poison Vendor D-2
Reagent Vendor D-1, F-7
Robe Vendor.................G-9
Saber Handler............... E-1
Shield Merchant H-7
Stable Master................ E-1
Staff Merchant G-9
Tabard Vendor I-2
Tailoring Supplies........... I-2
Thrown Weapons
   Merchant H-6
Two Handed
   Weapon Merchant......H-7
Weapon
   Merchant H-4, I-6

QUICK REFERENCE

CONNECTING REGIONS

TELDRASSIL 80

DEADWIND PASS

SWAMP
OF
SORROWS

THE
BLASTED LANDS

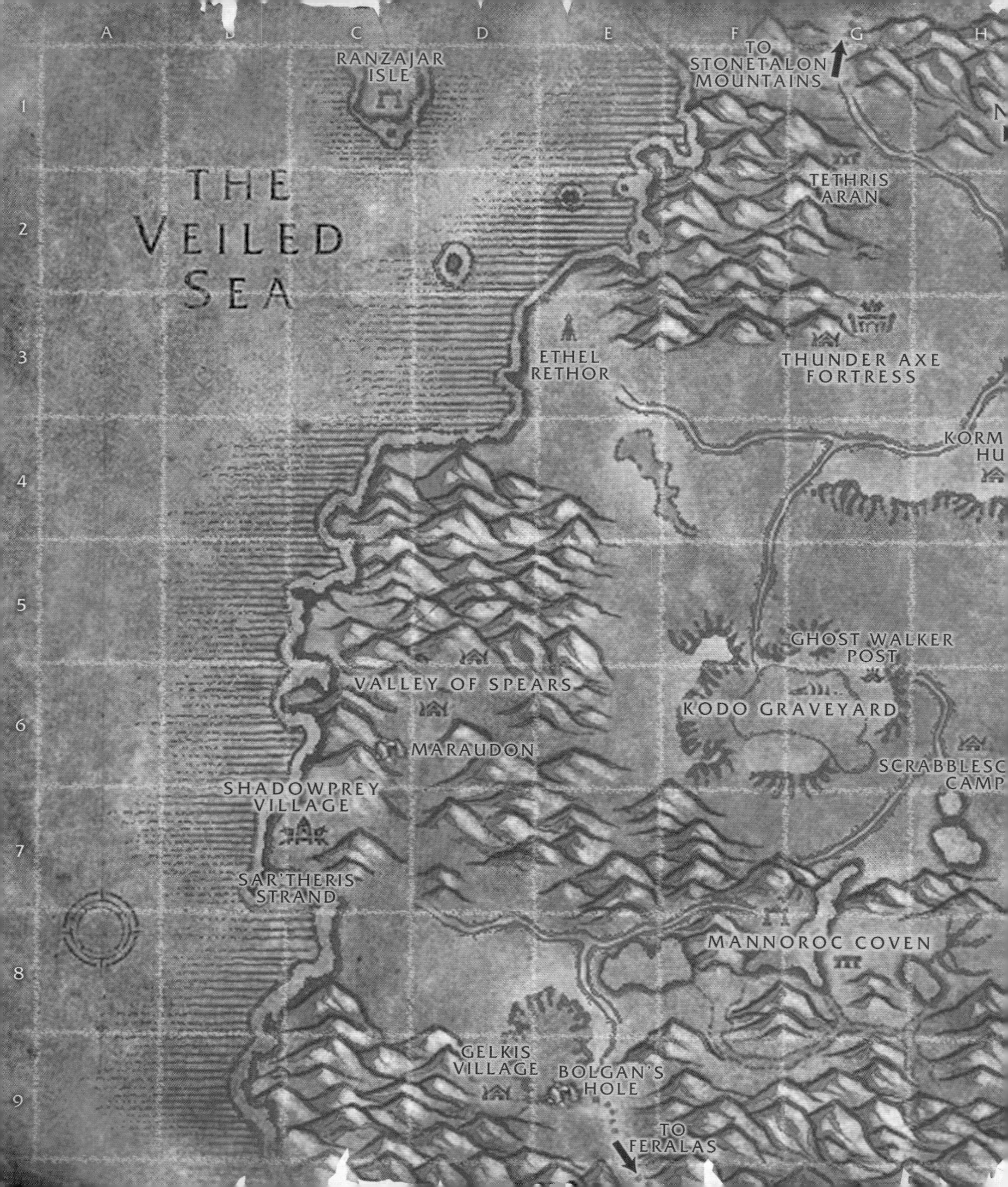
A
B
C
D
E
F
G
H
1
2
3
4
5
6
7
8
9
RANZAJAR ISLE
TO STONETALON MOUNTAINS
THE VEILED SEA
TETHRIS ARAN
ETHEL RETHOR
THUNDER AXE FORTRESS
KORM HU
GHOST WALKER POST
VALLEY OF SPEARS
KODO GRAVEYARD
MARAUDON
SCRABBLESC CAMP
SHADOWPREY VILLAGE
SAR'THERIS STRAND
MANNOROC COVEN
GELKIS VILLAGE
BOLGAN'S HOLE
TO FERALAS

DESOLACE

FLIGHT MASTERS

Hippogryph Master H-1
Wind Rider Master B-7

TRAINERS

Expert Leathercrafter G-6
Fisherman B-7
Skinning Trainer B-7

VENDORS

Cooking Supplies... C-7
Fishing Supplies B-7
Food & Drink G-5, I-1
General Goods C-7, I-1
Innkeeper C-7, I-1
Mail Armor Merchant I-1
Stable Master C-7, I-1
Superior Macecrafter...G-6
Trade Goods G-5
Trade Supplies B-7
Weapons Vendor C-7

QUICK REFERENCE

CONNECTING REGIONS

FERALAS 46
STONETALON MOUNTAINS....................................70

CAMPS & TOWNS

GHOST WALKER POST 111
NIJEL'S POINT 119
SHADOWPREY VILLAGE 125

DUN MOROGH

TRAINERS

Cooking Trainer..F-5, I-5
Demon Trainer...D-7, F-5
Fisherman...E-4
Hunter Trainer...D-7, F-5
Journeyman Blacksmith.....................................F-5
Journeyman Engineer...G-5
Mage Trainer..D-7, F-5
Mechanostrider Pilot..G-5
Mining Trainer.......................................G-5, J-6
Paladin Trainer...D-7, F-5
Pet Trainer...F-5
Physician...F-5
Priest Trainer...D-7, F-5
Ram Riding Instructor.......................................I-5
Rogue Trainer...D-7, F-5
Warlock Trainer...D-7, F-5
Warrior Trainer..D-7, F-5

VENDORS

Ale & Wine...D-5
Apprentice Weaponsmith..................................I-6
Armorer..D-7, F-5
Blacksmithing Supplies.....................................F-5
Cloth & Leather Armor Merchant..............D-7, F-5
Dwarven Weaponsmith.....................................I-5
Engineering Supplies..G-5
Fisherman Supplies..D-4
Food & Drink Merchant.....................................I-5
General Supplies..D-7, F-5
Gunsmith..E-6
Innkeeper...F-5
Leather Armor Merchant..................................D-4
Mechanostrider Merchant.................................G-5
Pet Vendor..I-5
Ram Breeder..I-5
Stable Master..F-5
Tradesman..F-5
Weaponsmith...D-7, F-5

QUICK REFERENCE

CONNECTING REGIONS

IRONFORGE..52
LOCH MODAN...54

TOWNS & CAMPS

COLDRIDGE VALLEY...106
KHARANOS..114

WETLANDS

E F G H I J K L

IRONFORGE

AIRSTRIP

NORTH GATE
PASS

TO LOCH
MODAN

NORTH GATE
OUTPOST

SHIMMER
RIDGE

MISTY PINE
REFUGE

LL BREEZE
VALLEY

STEELGRILL'S
DEPOT

SOUTH GATE
OUTPOST

KHARANOS

AMBERSTILL
RANCH

SOUTH GATE
PASS

HELM'S
BED LAKE

TO LOCH
MODAN

THE
GRIZZLED
DEN

GOL'BOLAR
QUARRY
AND MINE

DGE

IRONBAND'S
COMPOUND

THE
SEARING GORGE

DUROTAR

TRAINERS

Demon Trainer F-7, H-4
First Aid Trainer H-4
Fisherman H-8
Herbalist H-7
Hunter Trainer F-7, H-4
Journeyman Alchemist H-7
Journeyman Blacksmith H-4
Journeyman Engineer H-4
Mage Trainer F-7, H-7
Miner H-4
Pet Trainer H-4
Priest Trainer F-7, H-4
Raptor Riding Trainer H-7
Rogue Trainer F-7, H-4
Shaman Trainer F-7, H-4
Warlock Trainer F-7, H-4
Warrior Trainer F-7, H-4

VENDORS

Armorer & Shieldcrafter F-7, H-4
Bowyer H-4
Butcher .... F-7, H:(4, 7)
Cloth & Leather Armor Merchant F-7, H-4
Fishing Supplies H-7
General Goods .... F-7, H:(4, 7)
Innkeeper H-4
Raptor Handler H-7
Stable Master H-4
Trade Supplies .... H:(4, 7)
Weapon Merchant H-7
Weaponsmith F-7, H-4

QUICK REFERENCE

CONNECTING REGIONS

ASHENVALE 14
BARRENS 18
ORGRIMMAR 60

TOWNS & CAMPS

RAZOR HILL 122
SEN'JIN VILLAGE 123
VALLEY OF TRIALS 131

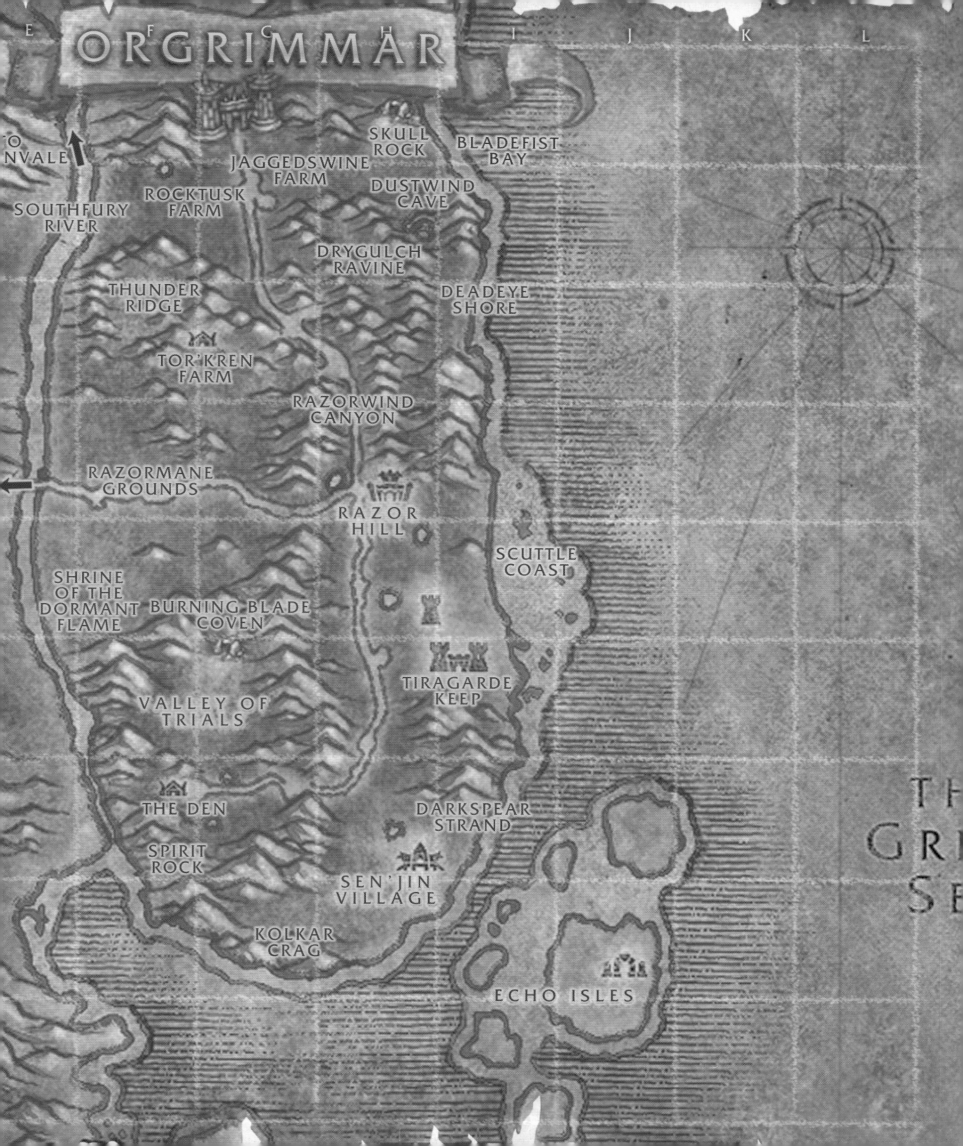

ORGRIMMAR

E   F   G   H   I   J   K   L

NVALE

SOUTHFURY
RIVER

ROCKTUSK
FARM

JAGGEDSWINE
FARM

SKULL
ROCK

BLADEFIST
BAY

DUSTWIND
CAVE

DRYGULCH
RAVINE

DEADEYE
SHORE

THUNDER
RIDGE

TOR'KREN
FARM

RAZORWIND
CANYON

RAZORMANE
GROUNDS

RAZOR
HILL

SCUTTLE
COAST

SHRINE
OF THE
DORMANT
FLAME

BURNING BLADE
COVEN

VALLEY OF
TRIALS

TIRAGARDE
KEEP

THE DEN

DARKSPEAR
STRAND

SPIRIT
ROCK

SEN'JIN
VILLAGE

KOLKAR
CRAG

ECHO ISLES

TH

GR

SE

DUSKWOOD

FLIGHT MASTER
Gryphon Master..K-4

TRAINERS
Expert Blacksmith...J-5
Expert Engineer..K-5
Mining Trainer...J-5

VENDORS
Alchemy Supplies Vendor....................................B-5
Armorer..J-5
Bartender..J-4
Bowyer...J-4
Engineering and Mining Supplies.........................K-5
General Goods Vendor...J-4
Innkeeper..J-4
Mushroom Seller..K-5
Poison Supplier..K-4
Rare Goods..K-2
Reagent Vendor..K-4
Stable Master...J-5
Tailoring Supplies..K:(4, 5)
Tradesman...J-4
Weaponsmith...J-5

QUICK REFERENCE
CONNECTING REGIONS
DEADWIND PASS 28
ELWYNN FOREST 42
REDRIDGE MOUNTAINS..62
STRANGLETHORN VALE 74
WESTFALL..94
TOWNS & CAMPS
DARKSHIRE 108
RAVEN HILL 121
RAVEN HILL CEMETERY 122

DUSTWALLOW
M A R S H

THE BARRENS

TO
THE BARRENS

BLUE

DARKMIST
CAVERN

BRACKENW
VILLAGE

LOST
POINT

BLOODFEN
BURROW

THE

FLA

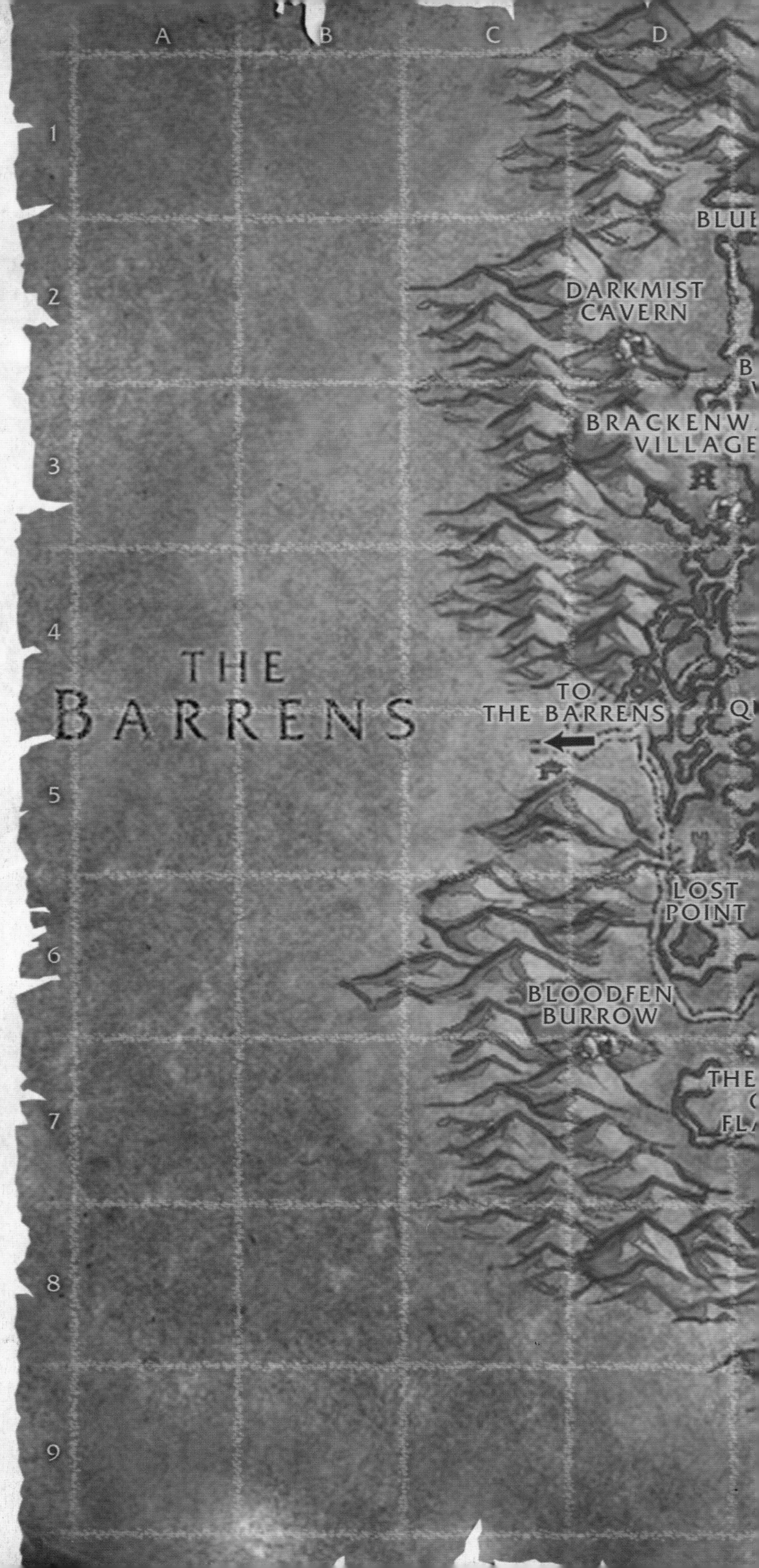

EASTERN PLAGUELANDS

FLIGHT MASTERS

Bat Handler K-5
Gryphon Master.. K-6

VENDORS

The Argent Dawn K-6
Trade Supplies K-6

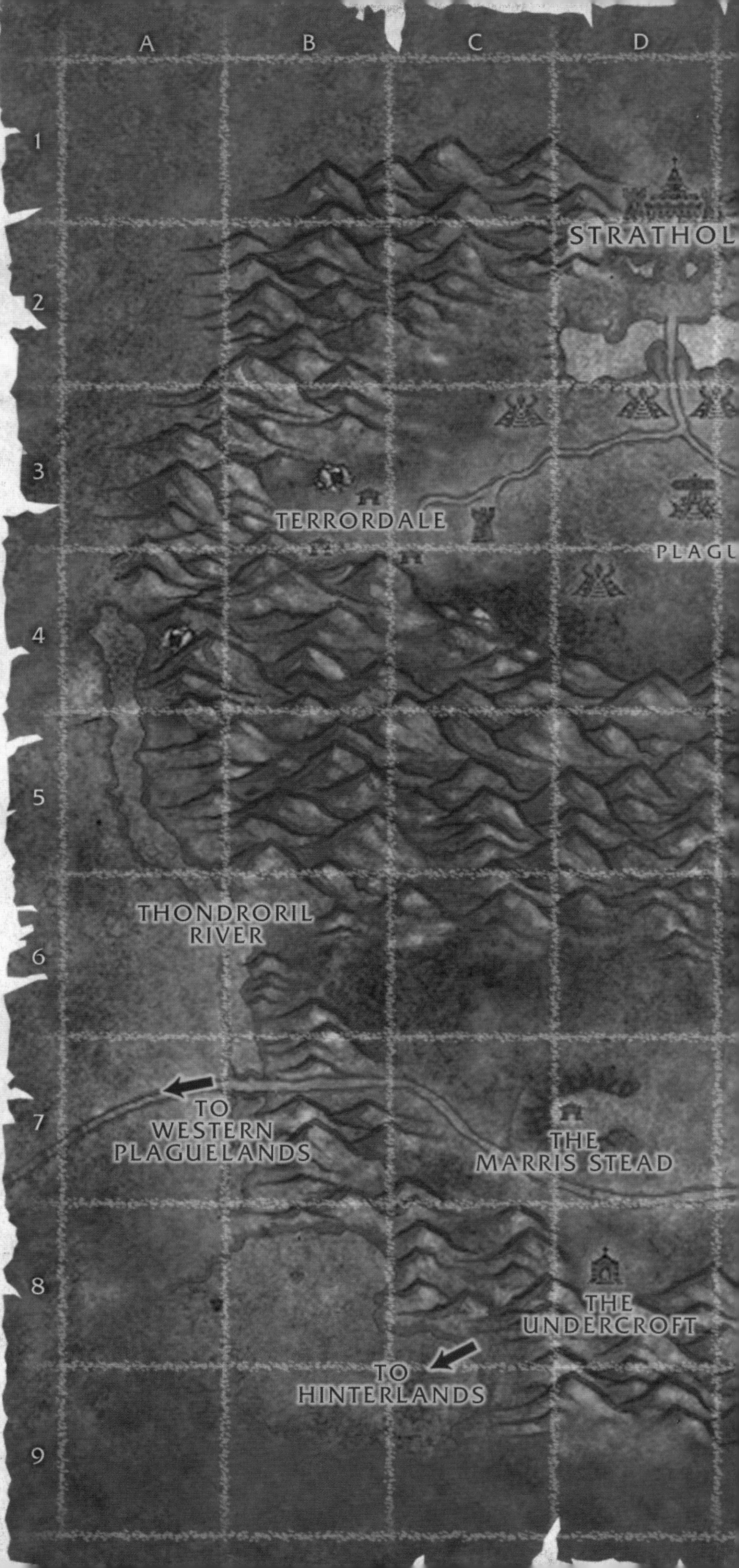

A
B
C
D
1
2
3
4
5
6
7
8
9
STRATHOL
TERRORDALE
PLAGU
THONDRORIL RIVER
TO WESTERN PLAGUELANDS
THE MARRIS STEAD
THE UNDERCROFT
TO HINTERLANDS

QUICK REFERENCE

CONNECTING REGIONS

TOWNS & CAMPS

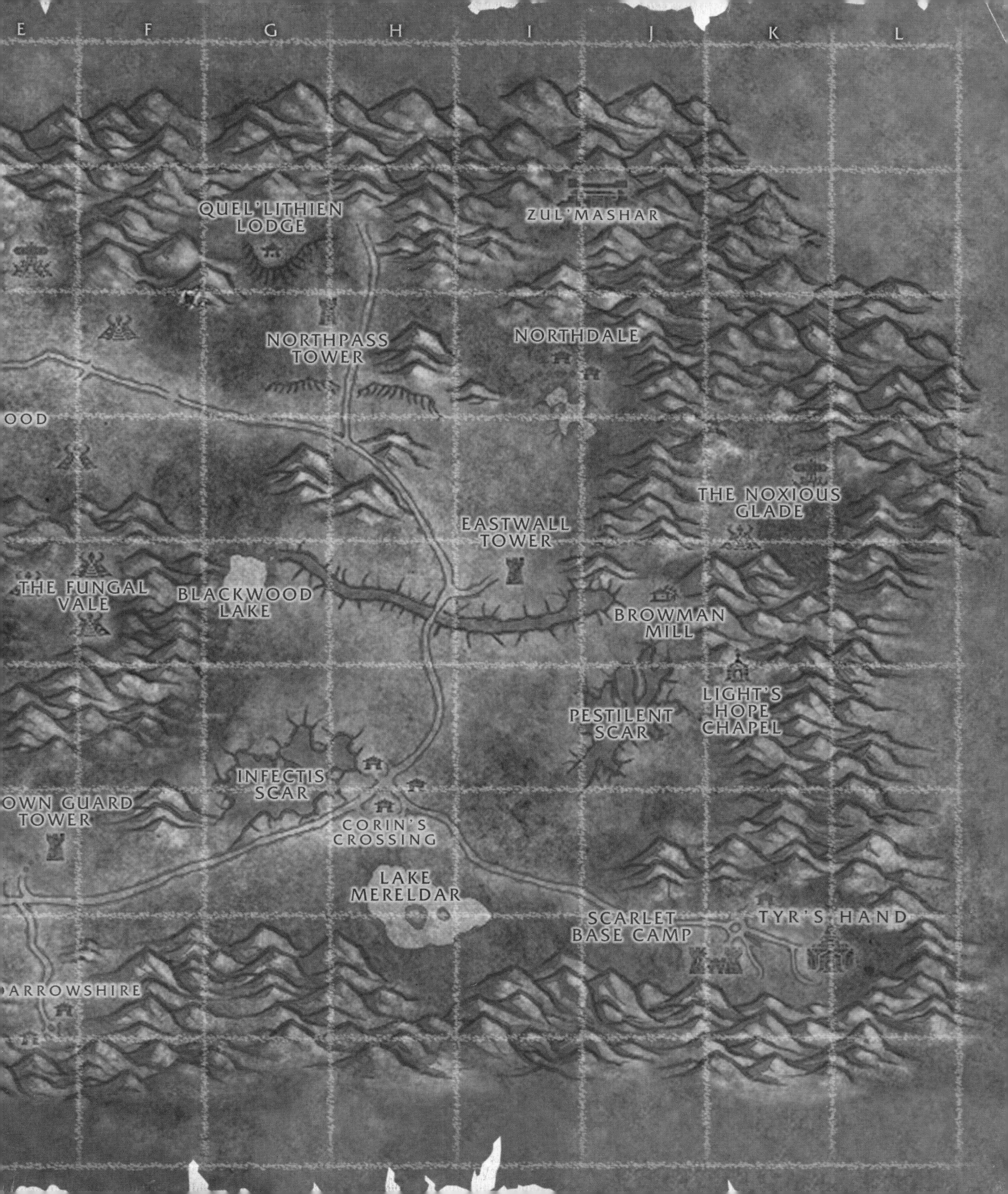
E
F
G
H
I
J
K
L
QUEL'LITHIEN LODGE
ZUL'MASHAR
NORTHPASS TOWER
NORTHDALE
OOD
THE NOXIOUS GLADE
EASTWALL TOWER
THE FUNGAL VALE
BLACKWOOD LAKE
BROWMAN MILL
LIGHT'S HOPE CHAPEL
PESTILENT SCAR
INFECTIS SCAR
OWN GUARD TOWER
CORIN'S CROSSING
LAKE MERELDAR
SCARLET BASE CAMP
TYR'S HAND
ARROWSHIRE

ELWYNN FOREST

TRAINERS

Artisan Enchanter	I-7
Cook	F-7
Demon Trainer	F-7, G-4
Fisherman	F-6
Herbalist Trainer	E-5
Horse Riding Instructor	L-6
Journeyman Alchemist	E-5
Journeyman Blacksmith	E-6
Journeyman Leatherworker	F-6
Journeyman Tailor	K-7
Mage Trainer	F-7, G-4
Paladin Trainer	E-7, G-4
Physician	F-7
Priest Trainer	F-7, G-4
Rogue Trainer	F-7, G-4
Skinner	F-6
Warlock Trainer	F-7, G-4
Warrior Trainer	E-7, G-4

VENDORS

Arcane Goods	I-7
Armorer & Shieldcrafter	C-7, E-7, F-4
Bartender	F-7
Bowyer	L-7
Butcher	F-7
Cloth & Leather Armor Merchant	E-6, F-4
Clothier	I-7
Crazy Cat Lady	F-5
Fishmonger	F-6
Fruit Seller	D-8
General & Trade Supplies	K-7
General Supplies	F:(4, 7)
Horse Breeder	L-6
Innkeeper	F-7
Leather Armor Merchant	C-7
Lumberjack	L-6
Master Weaponsmith	C-7
Stable Master	F-7
Trade Supplies	E-7
Traveling Baker	F-7
Vinter	F-9
Weaponsmith	E-7, F-4

QUICK REFERENCE

CONNECTING REGIONS

DUSKWOOD	36
REDRIDGE MOUNTAINS	62
STORMWIND	72
WESTFALL	94

TOWNS & CAMPS

GOLDSHIRE	112
NORTHSHIRE VALLEY	120

E F G H I J K L

BURNING STEPP

ECHO RIDGE
MINE

NORTHSHIRE
ABBEY

NORTHSHIRE
VALLEY

STONE CAIRN LAKE

NORTHSHIRE
VINEYARDS

HEROES'
VIGIL

JASPERLODE
MINE

EASTVALE
LOGGING CAMP

TOWER OF
AZORA

GOLDSHIRE   CRYSTAL LAKE

TO
REDRIDGE
MOUNTAINS

RGODEEP
MINE

RIDGEPOINT
TOWER

JEROD'S
LANDING

BRACKWELL
PUMPKIN PATCH

TO
DUSKWOOD

MACLURE
VINEYARDS

DUSKWOOD

FELWOOD

FLIGHT MASTERS

Hippogryph Master	H-3
Wind Rider Master	E-5

TRAINERS

Druid Trainer	H-3
Hunter Trainer	H-3
Pet Trainer	H-3

VENDORS

General Goods	E-5
General Goods	H-3
Weapon Merchant	E-5

QUICK REFERENCE

CONNECTING REGIONS

ASHENVALE	12
MOONGLADE	56
WINTERSPRING	98

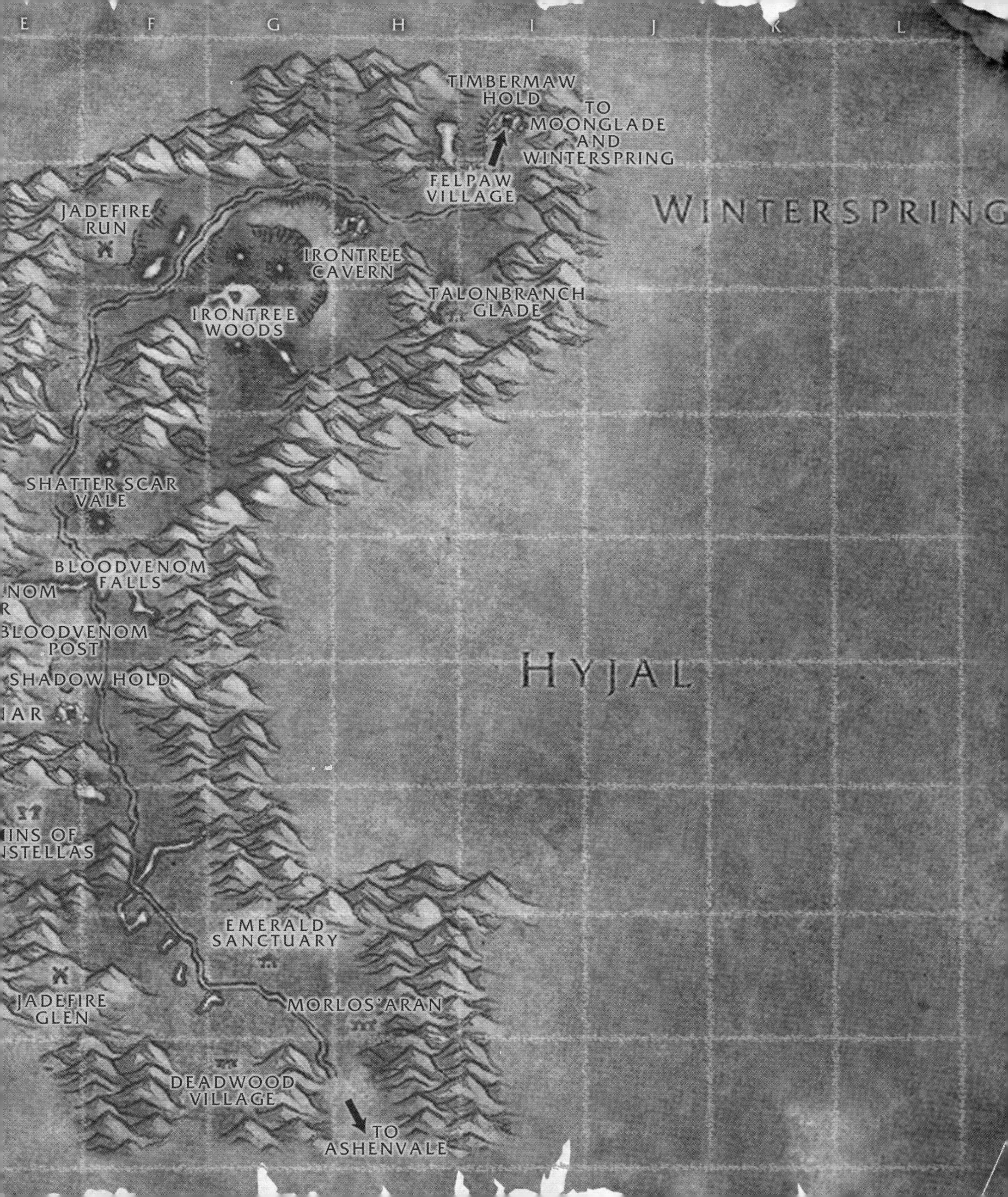

E F G H I J K L

TIMBERMAW
HOLD
TO
MOONGLADE
AND
WINTERSPRING

FELPAW
VILLAGE

WINTERSPRING

JADEFIRE
RUN

IRONTREE
CAVERN

IRONTREE
WOODS

TALONBRANCH
GLADE

SHATTER SCAR
VALE

BLOODVENOM
FALLS

NOM
R

BLOODVENOM
POST

SHADOW HOLD

HYJAL

IAR

INS OF
STELLAS

EMERALD
SANCTUARY

JADEFIRE
GLEN

MORLOS'ARAN

DEADWOOD
VILLAGE

TO
ASHENVALE

A B C D E F G H

THE
LED
EA

1

2

3

4

5

6

7

8

9

S

TO
DESOLACE

DREAM
BOUGH

JADEMIR
LAKE

THE RUINS
OF RAVENWIND

ONEIROS

THE
TWIN COLOSSALS

RAGE SCAR
HOLD

GRIMTO
COMPOU

DIRE MAUL

SARDOR
ISLE

THE
FORGOTTEN
COAST

FEATHERMOON
STRONGHOLD

FERAL
SCAR VALE

THE
HIGH WILDERNESS

RUINS OF
SOLARSAL

RUINS OF
ISILDIEN

FRAYFEATHER
HIGHLANDS

ISLE OF DREAD

MULGORE

GORDUNNI
OUTPOST

LARISS
PAVILION

CAMP
MOJACHE

WILDWING
LAKE

THE
LOWER WILDS

TO
THOUSAND
NEEDLES

WOODPAW
HILLS

THE WRITHING
DEEP

LITHUS

FLIGHT MASTERS

Hippogryph Master	C-4
Hippogryph Master	K-5
Wind Rider Master	I-4

TRAINERS

Druid Trainer	I-4
Expert Enchanter	C-4
Fisherman	C-4
Herbalism Trainer	I-4
Master Alchemist	C-4
Master Leatherworker	I-4
Skinning Trainer	I-4
Tribal Leatherworking Trainer	K-5

VENDORS

Alchemy Supplies	C-4
Alchemy Supplies	I-4
Cloth Armor Merchant	C-4
Fish Vendor	C-5
Fishing Supplies	C-5
Food & Drink	C-4
Food & Drink	I-4
General Supplies	C-4
Gunsmith & Bowyer	I-4
Innkeeper	C-4
Innkeeper	I-4
Leatherworking Supplies	C-4
Leatherworking Supplies	I-4
Light Armor Merchant	I-4
Reagent Vendor	C-4
Reagent Vendor	I-4
Stable Master	C-4
Stable Master	I-4
Tailoring Supplies	K-5
Trade Supplies	C-4
Trade Supplies	I-4

QUICK REFERENCE

CONNECTING REGIONS

DESOLACE	30
THOUSAND NEEDLES	82

TOWNS & CAMPS

CAMP MOJACHE	105
FEATHERMOON STRONGHOLD	110

47

TO WESTERN
PLAGUELANDS

RAVENHOLDT
MANOR

TO THE
HINTERLANDS

DURNHOLDE KEEP

THORADIN'S
WALL

TO
ARATHI
HIGHLANDS

ARATHI
HIGHLANDS

N GAROK

FLIGHT MASTERS

Bat Handler	G-2
Gryphon Master	F-5

TRAINERS

Expert Alchemist	G-2
Fisherman	F-6
Grand Master Rogue	K-2
Herbalist	G-2
Master Tailor	H-2

VENDORS

Alchemy Supplies	F-6
Bartender	F-6
Butcher	F-6
Cook	H-2
Fish Merchant	F-6
Freewheeling Tradeswoman	J-4
General Goods	F-5, H-2
Hillsbrad Tailor	D-4
Horse Breeder	F-6
Innkeeper	F-6, H-2
Leatherworking Supplies	L-4
Merchant Supreme	G-3
Mushroom Seller	G-2
Poison Vendor	K-2
Poisons and Reagents	F-6
Speciality Engineer	K-2
Stable Master	F-6, H-2
Superior Armorsmith	F-5
Tackle and Bait	F-6
Tailoring Supplies	G-2
Trade Goods	F-5
Tradesman	H-2
Waitress	F-6
Weaponsmith	G-3

QUICK REFERENCE

CONNECTING REGIONS

ALTERAC MOUNTAINS	8
ARATHI HIGHLANDS	10
HINTERLANDS	50
SILVERPINE FOREST	68
WESTERN PLAGUELANDS	92

TOWNS & CAMPS

HILLSBRAD FIELDS	113
SOUTHSHORE	125
TARREN MILL	128

HINTERLANDS

FLIGHT MASTERS

Gryphon Master...B-5
Wind Rider Master L-8

TRAINERS

Fishing Trainer and Supplies L-8
Master Leatherworking Trainer B-4

VENDORS

Bartender.. B-4
Blacksmithing Supplies B-4, L-8
Cooking Supplier L-8
Engineering Supplies E-4
Innkeeper B-4, L-8
Leatherworking Supplies.............................. B-4
Reagent Vendor L-8
Stable Master B-5, L-8
Trade Supplies E-4

QUICK REFERENCE

CONNECTING REGIONS

EASTERN PLAGUELANDS 40
HILLSBRAD FOOTHILLS 48
WESTERN PLAGUELANDS............................92

TOWNS & CAMPS

AERIE PEAK 100

IRONFORGE

CITY OFFICIALS

Alliance Cloth Quartermaster	F-3, J-5
Alterac Valley Battlemaster	J-9
Guild Master	D-8
Warsong Gulch Battlemaster	J-9

FLIGHT MASTER

Gryphon Master	G-5

TRAINERS

Artisan Blacksmith	G-4
Artisan Engineer	I-4
Cooking Trainer	H-4
Demon Trainer	G-1
Expert Alchemist	I-5
Expert Blacksmith	G-4
Expert Enchanter	H-4
Expert Engineer	I-4
Expert Leatherworker	E-3
Expert Tailor	F-3
First Aid Trainer	G-6
Fishing Trainer	F-1
Herbalism Trainer	G-6
Hunter Trainer	I-8, J:(8, 9)
Journeyman Alchemist	I-5
Journeyman Blacksmith	G-4
Journeyman Enchanter	H-4
Journeyman Engineer	I-4
Journeyman Leatherworker	E-3
Journeyman Tailor	F-3
Mage Trainer	C-1
Master Gnome Engineer	J-5
Mining Trainer	G-3
Paladin Trainer	C-1
Pet Trainer	J-8
Portal Trainer	C-1
Priest Trainer	C-1
Rogue Trainer	G-1
Skinning Trainer	E-3
Warlock Trainer	G-1
Warrior Trainer	I-9, J-9
Weapon Master	H-9

VENDORS

Alchemy Supplies	I-5
Armor Crafter	F-4, G-4
Axe Merchant	H-9
Bag Vendor	E-7
Blacksmithing Supplies	G-4
Blade Merchant	F-1, H-9
Bow Merchant	J-6
Bread Vendor	C-6, D-8
Cloth Armor Merchant	E-1
Cooking Supplier	H-4
Enchanting Supplies	H-4
Engineering Supplies	I-4
Fireworks Vendor	J-5
Fishing Supplier	F-1
Fruit Vendor	E-1, C-3
General Good Vendor	E-7
Guild Tabard Vendor	D-8
Gun Merchant	J-6
Heavy Armor Merchant	D-6, G-9
Herbalism Supplier	G-6
Innkeeper	B-5
Leatherworking Supplies	E-3
Light Armor Merchant	D-5, G-9
Maces & Staves	H-9
Mail Armor Merchant	G-9
Meat Vendor	H-8, I-7
Mining Supplier	G-3
Pie Vendor	E-4
Reagent Vendor	B-6, D-3
Robe Merchant	E-1
Shady Dealer	G-1
Special Weapon Crafter	G-5, H-5
Speciality Tailoring Supplies	F-3
Stable Master	I-8
Tailoring Supplies	F-3
Trade Supplier	E-7, F-3
Wands Merchant	C-2
Weapon Merchant	C-2, E:(6, 7), H-9

QUICK REFERENCE

CONNECTING REGIONS

DUN MOROGH	32
STORMWIND	72

THE MYSTIC WARD

THE COMMONS

THE GATES OF IRONFORGE

E   F   G   H   I   J   K   L

THE
FORLORN CAVERN

HALL of EXPLORERS

THE
GREAT FORGE

TINKER TOWN

THE
DEEPRUN TRAM

THE
MILITARY WARD

IRONFORGE

L O C H
M O D A N

MO'GROSH
CAVERN

MO'GROSH
STRONGHOLD

HUNTING
GROUNDS

'S

IRONBAND'S
EXCAVATION SITE

THE
FARSTRIDER
LODGE

FLIGHT MASTER
Gryphon Master	D-5

TRAINERS
Fisherman	E-4
Herbalist	D-5
Hunter Trainer	K-6
Journeyman Alchemist	E-5
Journeyman Engineer	F-1
Mining Trainer	E-5
Pet Trainer	K-6

VENDORS
Armorer	C-2
Baker	D-5
Bowyer	K-6
Clothier	I-7
Fishing Supplies	E-4
General Supplies	D-5, K-6
Gunsmith	D-4, K-6
Innkeeper	D-5
Leather Armor Merchant	K-6
Macecrafter	E-1
Metalsmith	D-5
Mining Supplies	E-5
Stable Master	D-5
Tailoring Supplies	D-5
Tradesman	D-5
Traveling Merchant	C-1

QUICK REFERENCE
CONNECTING REGIONS
BADLANDS	16
DUN MOROGH	32
SEARING GORGE	64
WETLANDS	96

TOWNS & MAPS
THELSAMAR	129

MOONGLADE

A   B   C   D

1

2

3

SH
RE

4

5

6

FELW
A
WINTE

7

8

9

MULGORE

TRAINERS

Cook E-6
Druid Trainer E-8, F-6
First Aid Trainer E-6
Fisherman E-6
Hunter Trainer .... E:(6, 8)
Journeyman Engineer H-3
Journeyman Leatherworker E-6
Kodo Riding Instructor E-6
Pet Trainer E-6
Shaman Trainer E-8, F-6
Skinner E-6
Warrior Trainer E-8, F-6

VENDORS

Armor Merchant E-8
Armorer & Shieldcrafter .... E:(6, 8)
Baker .... E:(6, 8)
Fishing Supplies E-6
General Goods .... E:(6, 8)
Gunsmith E-6
Innkeeper E-6
Kodo Mounts E-6
Leather Armor Merchant E-6
Stable Master E-6
Trade Goods E-6
Weaponsmith .... E:(6, 8)

TO THE
BARRENS

THE BARRENS

QUICK REFERENCE

CONNECTING REGIONS

BARRENS 18
THUNDER BLUFF 84

TOWNS & CAMPS

BLOODHOOF VILLAGE 102
CAMP NARACHE 105

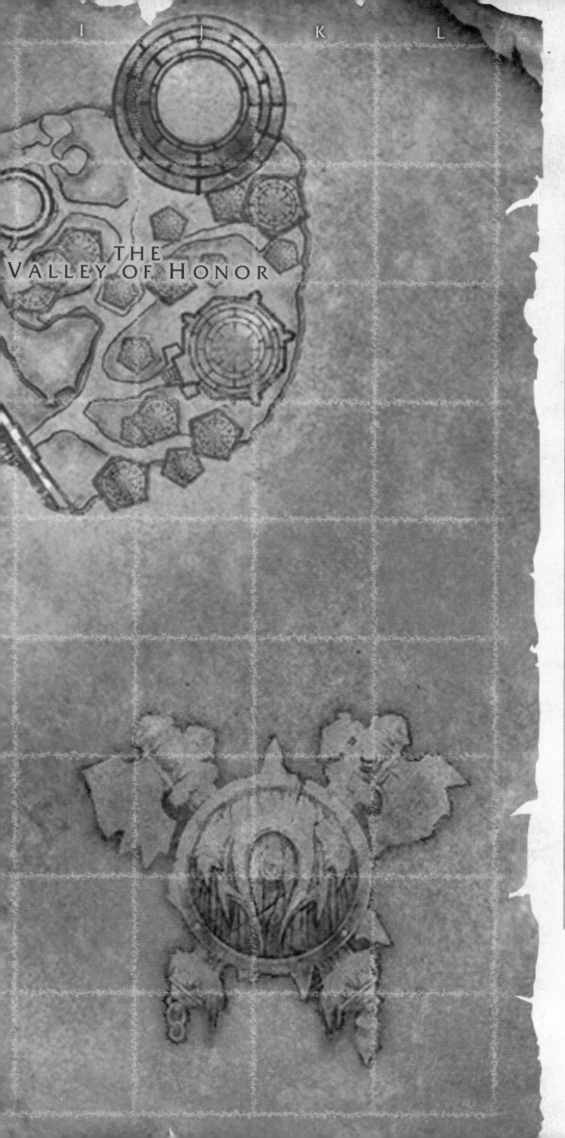

THE
VALLEY OF HONOR

ORGRIMMAR

CITY OFFICIALS

Alterac Valley Battlemaster J-3	Horde Cloth Quartermaster .... D:(8, 9), H-4
Guild Master E-7	Warsong Gulch Battlemaster I-2, J-2

FLIGHT MASTER

Wind Rider Master E-6

TRAINERS

Armorsmith J-2	Journeyman Engineer I-3, J-3
Artisan Blacksmith ..J-2, K-2	Journeyman Leatherworker H-4
Artisan Engineer I-3, J-3	
Cooking Trainer G-5	Journeyman Tailor H-5
Demon Trainer E-5, F-5	Mage Trainer .... D:(8, 9)
Expert Alchemist G-3	Mining Trainer I-3
Expert Blacksmith J-2	Pet Trainer .... H:(1, 2)
Expert Enchanter F-4	Portal Trainer .... D:(8, 9)
Expert Engineer I-3, J-3	Priest Trainer D-9
Expert Leatherworker ...H-4	Rogue Trainer E-5
Expert Tailor H-5	Shaman Trainer D-4
First Aid Trainer C-8	Skinning Trainer H-4
Fishing Trainer I-3	Warlock Trainer E-5, F-5
Herbalism Trainer ...F-4, G-4	Warrior Trainer J-3
Hunter Trainer............... H-2	Weapon Master J-2
Journeyman Alchemist..G-3	Weaponsmith J-2
Journeyman Blacksmith.. J-2	Wolf Riding Instructor I-1
Journeyman Enchanter ...F-4	

VENDORS

Accessories Quartermaster E-7	Innkeeper G-7
Alchemy Supplier G-3	Leather Armor Merchant G-8
Armor Crafter J-2	Leatherworking Supplies H-4
Bag Vendor................... G-5	
Barkeep G-7	Light Armor Merchant ..G-8
Blacksmithing Supplier J-2, K-2	Mace and Staff Vendor .. J-2
	Mail Armor Merchant ...G-8
Blade Merchant E-5	Meat Vendor.......... E-7, G-5
Bow Merchant J-4	Mining Supplier I-3
Cloth & Leather Armor Merchant ....H:(4, 5)	Mushroom Vendor E-5
	Poison Vendor E-5
Cooking Supplier G-5	Reagents Vendor...... E:(4-6)
Enchanting Supplier F-4	Riding Wolf (Kennel Master) I-1
Engineering Supplies I-3, J-3	
	Snake Vendor A-6, C-8
Fishing Supplier I-3	Stable Master............ I:(1-2)
Fruit Vendor D-5	Staff Merchant C-7, E-5
General Goods ....E:(4, 8), F-8	Sweet Treats E-7
	Tabard Vendor E-7
General Trade.............E-8, F-8, G-5	Tailoring Supplies..........H-5
	Two-Handed Weapons Merchant J-2
Guns and Ammo Merchant F-7, G-7	
	Wand Merchant............ E-5
Heavy Armor Merchant J-2, K-2	War Harness Maker I-4
	Weapon Crafter.............. J-2
Herbalism Supplier F-4, G-4	Weapon Merchant E-7
	Weapon Vendor............. J-2

QUICK REFERENCE

CONNECTING REGIONS

DUROTAR 34

REDRIDGE
MOUNTAINS

FLIGHT MASTER

Gryphon Master..D-6

TRAINERS

Butcher...C-4
Cooking Trainer..B-4
Fishing Trainer...C-5
Herbalism Trainer...B-4
Skinning Trainer...L-7

VENDORS

Armorer...D-5
Bait and Tackle Supplier.....................................C-5
Cooking Supplies..C-4
Fletcher...C-4
Food and Drinks...C-4
Fruit Seller..B-5
General Supplies...C-5
Gunsmith...C-4
Innkeeper..C-4
Leather Armor Merchant......................................L-7
Leatherworking Supplies......................................L-7
Mining and Smithing Supplies..............................D-5
Poison Supplier..C-4
Shield Crafter..D-5
Specialist Tailoring Supplies.................................J-8
Stable Master...C-5
Tailoring Supplies...C-4
Tradeswoman...C-5
Waitress..B-4

QUICK REFERENCE

CONNECTING REGIONS

BURNING STEPPES 22

DUSKWOOD..36

ELWYNN FOREST 42

TOWNS & CAMPS

LAKESHIRE 115

BURNING STEPPES

ENDER'S
AMP

TO
BURNING STEPPES

ALTHER'S
MILL

STONEWATCH
TOWER

GALARDELL
VALLEY

TOWER OF
ILGALAR

LAKE
EVERSTILL

STONEWATCH
KEEP

STONEWATCH
FALLS

LAKERIDGE
HIGHWAY

RENDER'S
VALLEY

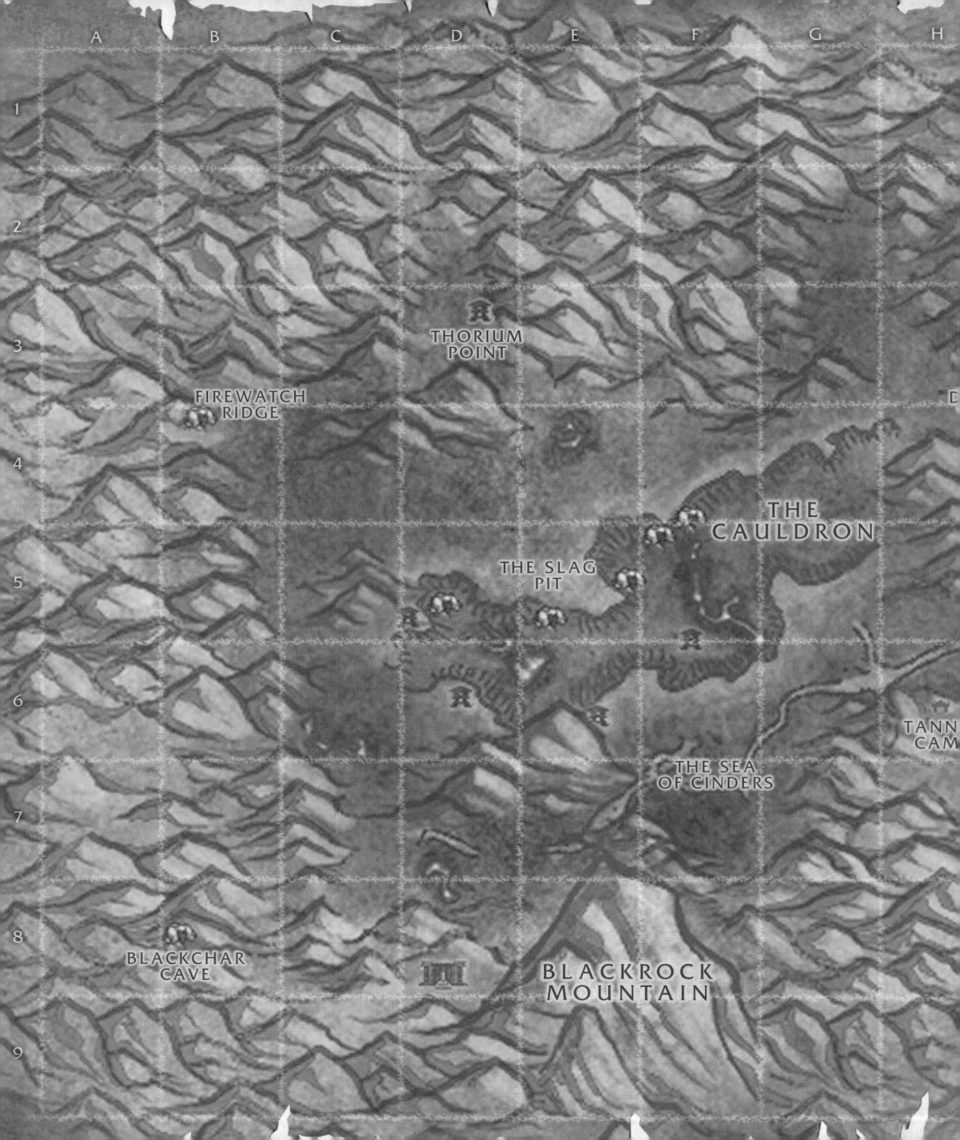

THORIUM
POINT

FIREWATCH
RIDGE

THE
CAULDRON

THE SLAG
PIT

TANN
CAM

THE SEA
OF CINDERS

BLACKCHAR
CAVE

BLACKROCK
MOUNTAIN

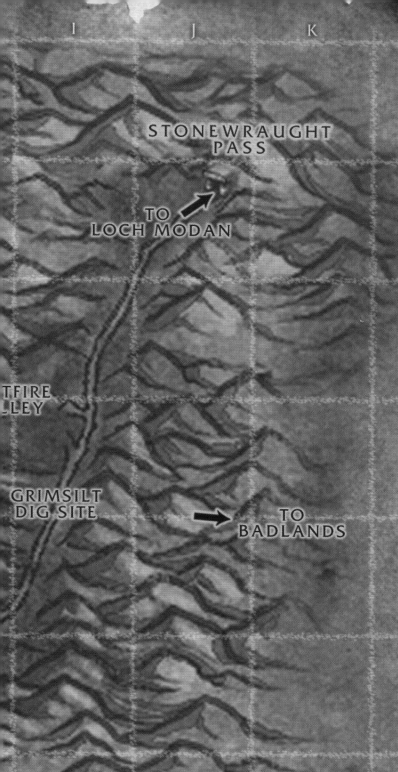

I J K L

STONEWRAUGHT
PASS

TO
LOCH MODAN

TFIRE
LEY

GRIMSILT
DIG SITE

TO
BADLANDS

FLIGHT MASTERS
Gryphon Master...D-3
Wind Rider Master D-3
TRAINER
Master Elemental Leatherworker........................H-7
VENDOR
Mail Armor Merchant E-7

QUICK REFERENCE
CONNECTING REGIONS

RAVAGED
TWILIGHT
CAMP

THE CRYSTAL
VALE

HIVE'ASHI

VALOR
REST

TWILIGHT
POST

THE SWARMING
PILLAR

TWILIGHT
BASE CAMP

SOUTHW
VILLAGE

HIVE'ZORA

BONES OF
GRAKKAROND

TWILIGHT
OUTPOST

HIVE'REGAL

THE SCARAB DAIS

THE SCARAB WALL

AHN'QUIRAJ

TO
UN'GORO
CRATER

UN'GORO CRATER

SILITHUS

QUICK REFERENCE

SILVERPINE
FOREST

FLIGHT MASTER

Bat Handler G-4

TRAINERS

Journeyman Blacksmith.......................................F-4
Miner   F-4

VENDORS

Armorer F-4
Bowyer..G-4
Clothier...G-4
Dalaran Brewmaster..I-6
Dalaran Miner I-6
Enchanting Supplies..F-5
Enchanting Supplies..H-8
Fisherman..E-2
General Supplies...G-4
Innkeeper F-4
Leather Armor Merchant G-4
Mushroom Merchant G-4
Poison Supplies F-4
Pyrewood Armorer..G-7
Pyrewood Leatherworker....................................G-7
Pyrewood Tailor G-7
Stable Master...F-4
Trade Goods F-4
Weaponsmith G-8

QUICK REFERENCE

CONNECTING REGIONS

ALTERAC MOUNTAINS 8
HILLSBRAD FOOTHILLS 48
TIRISFAL GLADES 86

TOWNS & CAMPS

THE SEPULCHER..124

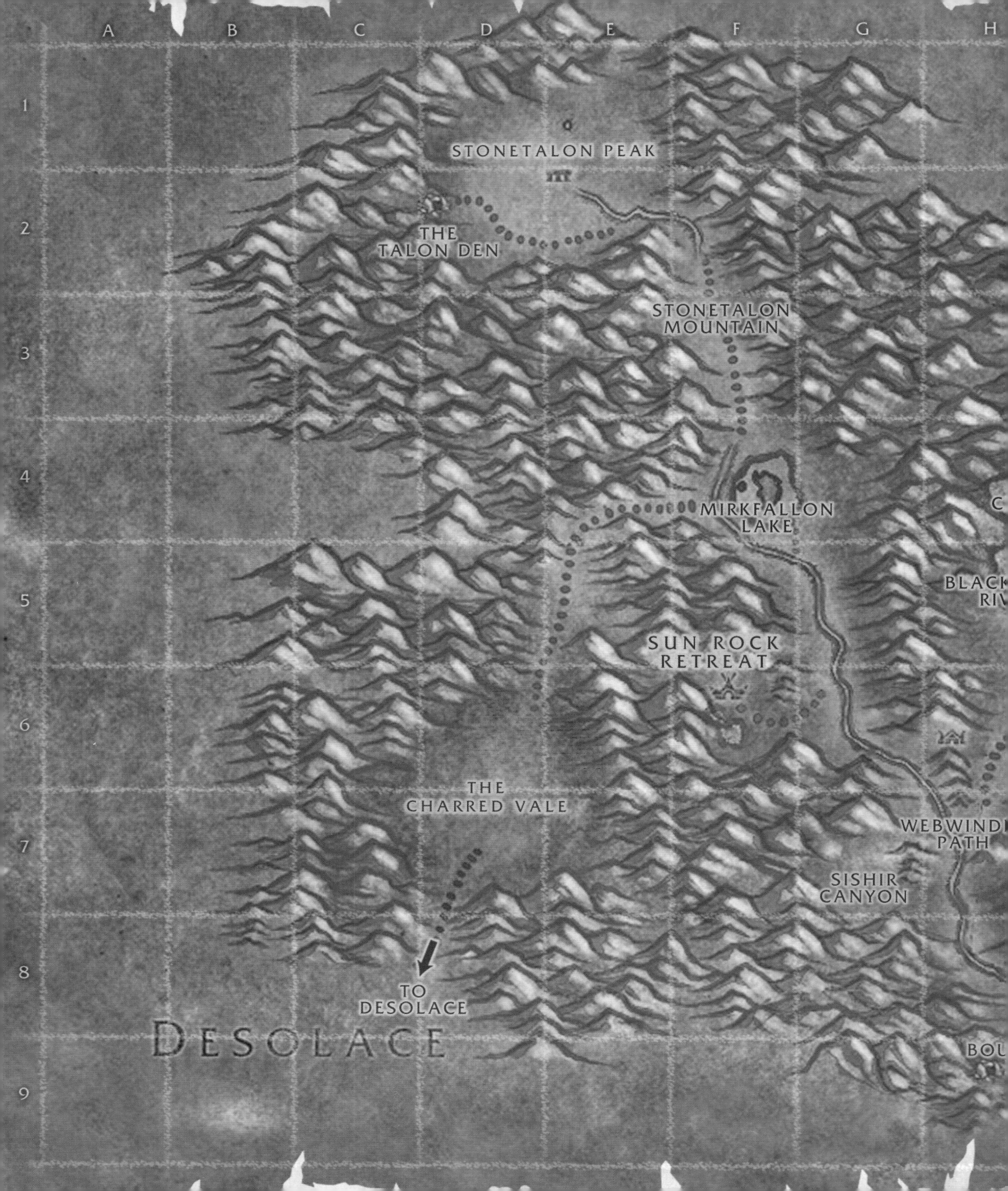

A
B
C
D
E
F
G
H
1
2
3
4
5
6
7
8
9
STONETALON PEAK
THE TALON DEN
STONETALON MOUNTAIN
MIRKFALLON LAKE
SUN ROCK RETREAT
THE CHARRED VALE
WEBWIND
PATH
SISHIR CANYON
TO DESOLACE
DESOLACE
BLACK
RIV
C
BOU

STONETALON
MOUNTAINS

FLIGHT MASTERS

Hippogryph Master	D-1
Wind Rider Master	E-6

TRAINER

Artisan Enchanter	F-6

VENDORS

Apprentice Witch Doctor	F-6
Bowyer	E-6
Butcher	E-6, I-9
Cloth Armor Merchant	D-1
General Goods	E-6
General Supplies	D-1
Innkeeper	F-6
Stable Master	F-6
Trade Supplies	E-6
Venture Armor Salesman	H-4
Venture Co. Merchant	G-5

QUICK REFERENCE

CONNECTING REGIONS

ASHENVALE	12
BARRENS	18
DESOLACE	30

TOWNS & CAMPS

SUN ROCK RETREAT	127

STORMWIND

CITY OFFICIALS

Alliance Cloth Quartermaster............G-7	Guild Master..........H-7, I-7
Alterac Valley Battlemaster..............L-2	Warsong Gulch Battlemaster..............L-2

FLIGHT MASTER

Gryphon Master...J-6

TRAINERS

Artisan Tailor.................G-7	Journeyman Enchanter...F-6
Cooking Trainer.............K-4	Journeyman Engineer....H-1
Demon Trainer..............D-8	Journeyman Leatherworker.............J-5
Druid Trainer...........C:(5, 6)	Journeyman Leatherworker.............J-5
Expert Alchemist..........G-8	Journeyman Tailor.........G-7
Expert Blacksmith.........H-2	Mage Trainer.................F-8
Expert Enchanter...........F-6	Master Shadoweave Tailor.....................D-8
Expert Engineer............H-1	Master Shadoweave Tailor.....................D-8
Expert Leatherworker....J-5	Mining Trainer..............H-2
Expert Tailor.................F-8	Paladin Trainer..............F-3
First Aid Trainer.............F-3	Pet Trainer.....................I-2
Fishing Trainer..............G-6	Portal Trainer.................F-8
Herbalism Trainer..........B-5, F-8, G-8	Priest Trainer..........C-5, F-3
Herbalism Trainer..........B-5, F-8, G-8	Rogue Trainer............K-5, L-6
Hunter Trainer.....I:(1-3), J-2	Skinning Trainer.............J-5
Journeyman Alchemist..G-8	Warlock Trainer.............D-8
Journeyman Blacksmith..............I-2, J-2	Warrior Trainer........L:(4, 5)
Journeyman Blacksmith..............I-2, J-2	Weapon Master.............H-6

VENDORS

Accessories Quartermaster............K-5	Innkeeper...............H:(6, 7)
Alchemy Supplies.........G-8	Leather Armor Merchant......H:(5, 6), J-5
Arcane Goods Vendor...H-6	Leather Armor Merchant......H:(5, 6), J-5
Arcane Trinkets Vendor.......................E-8	Leatherworking Supplies......................J-5
Axe Merchant...............H-1	Light Armor Merchant..G-7
Bag Vendor....................J-5	Mail Armor Merchant...F-4, H:(5, 6), K-5
Baker............................I-6	Mail Armor Merchant...F-4, H:(5, 6), K-5
Blacksmithing Supplies.....................H-2	Master of Cooking Recipes........................J-5
Blacksmithing Supplies.....................H-2	Master of Cooking Recipes........................J-5
Blade Merchant............K-4	Merlot Connoisseur.......H-7
Bow & Arrow Merchant....................H-6	Mining Supplier............H-2
Bow & Arrow Merchant....................H-6	Poison Supplier.............K-6
Bow & Gun Merchant...H-6	Reagent Vendor.........E-7, F-3, H-6
Cloth Armor Merchant.............H:(5, 6)	Reagent Vendor.........E-7, F-3, H-6
Cloth Armor Merchant.............H:(5, 6)	Robe Merchant..............F-8
Clothier....................G:(5, 6)	Robe Vendor..................F-4
Cobbler.........................J-4	Shady Dealer................L-6
Cooking Supplier..........K-4	Shield Merchant......I-4, J-4
Enchanting Supplies.......F-6	Stable Master...D-5, I-2, J-2
Engineering Supplier....H-1	Staff & Mace Merchant..F-3
Fireworks Vendor..........D-7	Staves Merchant......F:(6, 7)
Fishing Supplier............G-6	Tabard Vendor........H-7, I-7
Florist...........................J-6	Tailoring Supplies..........G-7
General Goods Vendor...I-6	Trade Supplier...............I-6
Guns Vendor..........H:(1, 2)	Two Handed Weapon Merchant.....................J-4
Hatter...........................F-8	Two Handed Weapon Merchant.....................J-4
Heavy Armor Merchant.....................K-5	Wand Merchant.......F:(6, 7)
Heavy Armor Merchant.....................K-5	Weapon Crafter............H-1
Herbalism Supplier..............G-8, J-6	Weapons Merchant......H-6
Herbalism Supplier..............G-8, J-6	Wine Vendor.................H-7

QUICK REFERENCE

CONNECTING REGIONS

ELWYNN FOREST..42

IRONFORGE...52

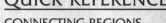

THE
DEEPRUN TRAM

STORMWIND
KEEP

THE
DWARVEN DISTRICT

CATHEDRAL
SQUARE

OLD TOWN

THE
STOCKADE

THE
TRADE DISTRICT

THE
GE QUARTER

THE
VALLEY OF HEROES

STORMWIND

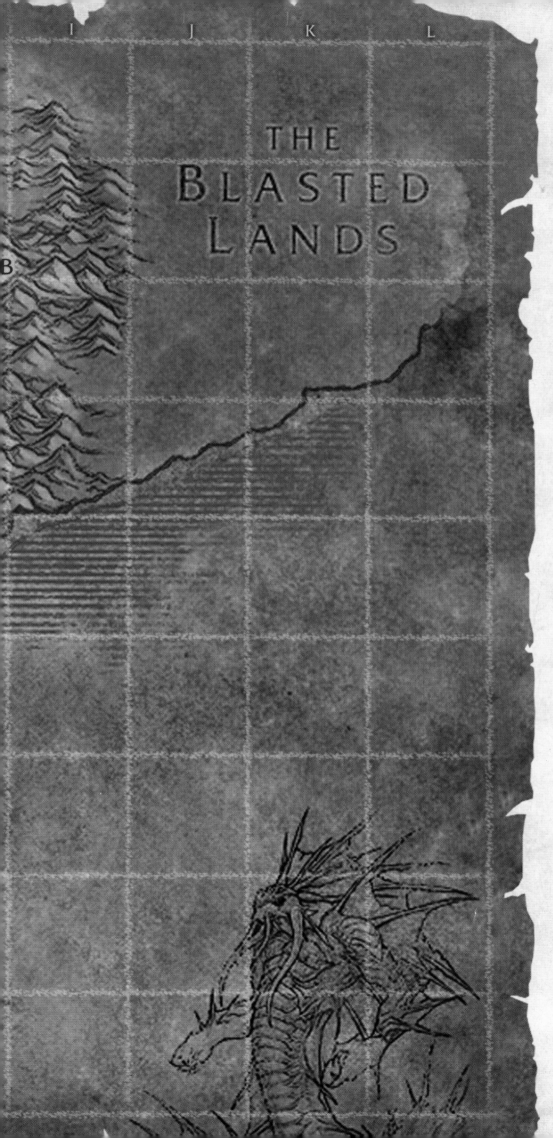

STRANGLETHORN VALE

FLIGHT MASTERS

Gryphon Master	B-8
Wind Rider Master	B-8
Wind Rider Master	C-3

TRAINERS

Artisan Blacksmith of the Mithril Order (Quest)	F-2
Expert Alchemist	B-8
Expert Leatherworker	C-3
Expert Tailor	B-8
Hunter Trainer	C-3
Master Blacksmith	C-8
Master Gnome Engineer	B-8
Master Tribal Leatherworker	D-4
Pet Trainer	C-3
Rogue Trainer	B-8
Superior Fisherman	B-8
Superior Herbalist	B-8, C-3

VENDORS

Alchemy Supplies	B-8
Blacksmithing Supplies	B-8, C-8
Blade Trader	B-8
Camp Trader	D-1
Cloth and Leather Armor Merchant	C-3
Cloth Armor and Accessories	B-8
Cook	B-8
Engineering Supplies	B-8, F-4
Fireworks Merchant	B-8
Fisherman	B-8
Food & Drink	B-8, C-3
General Supplies	C-3
Innkeeper	B-8
Leatherworking Supplies	B-8
Macecrafter	B-8
Pirate Supples	B-8
Shady Goods	B-8
Stable Master	B-8
Superior Armorer	B-8, C-3
Superior Axecrafter	C-1
Superior Bowyer	B-8
Superior Cook	C-3
Superior Fisherman	B-8
Superior Weaponsmith	B-8, C-3
Tailoring Supplies	B:(8, 9)
Tailoring Supplies	B-9
Trade Goods	C-3

QUICK REFERENCE

CONNECTING REGIONS

DUSKWOOD	36
WESTFALL	94

TOWNS & CAMPS

BOOTY BAY	103
GROM'GOL BASE CAMP	112

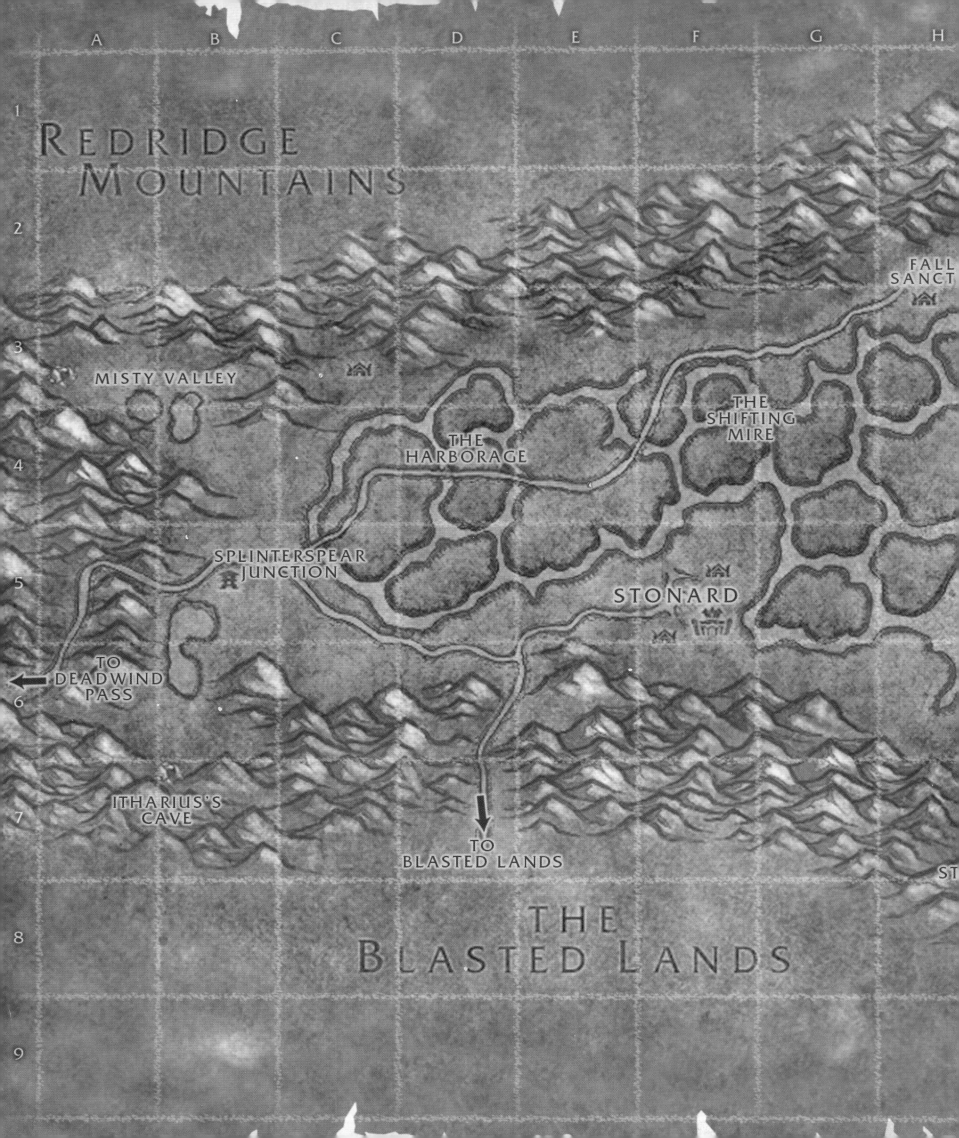

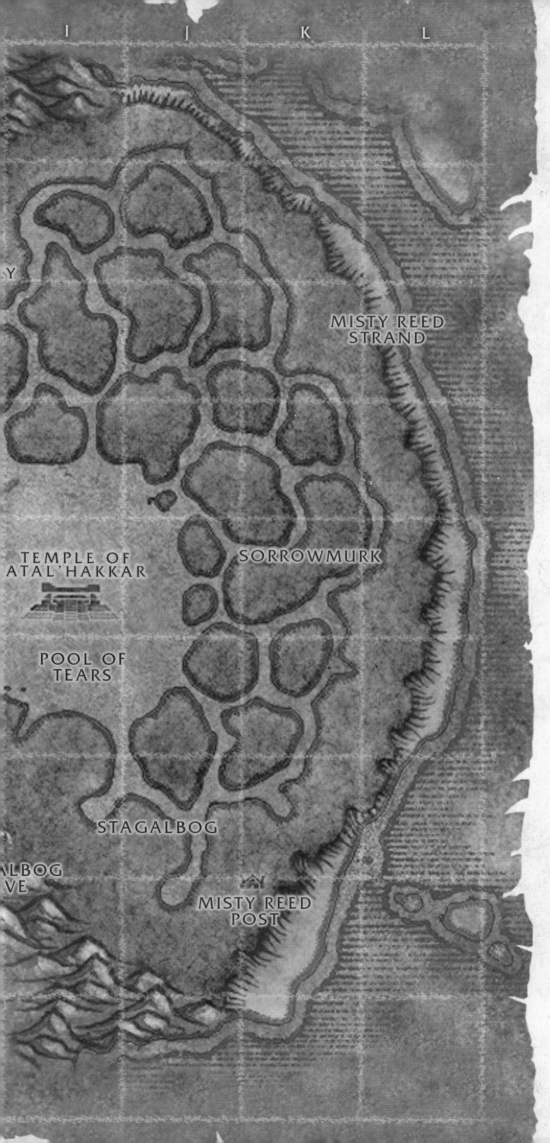

SWAMP OF
SORROWS

I J K L

MISTY REED
STRAND

TEMPLE OF
ATAL'HAKKAR

SORROWMURK

POOL OF
TEARS

STAGALBOG

ALBOG
VE

MISTY REED
POST

FLIGHT MASTER

Wind Rider Master	F-5

TRAINERS

Demon Master	F-5
Hunter Trainer	F-5
Master Alchemist	F-5
Pet Trainer	F-5
Shaman Trainer	F-6
Warlock Trainer	F-5
Warrior Trainer	F-5

VENDORS

Alchemy Supplies	F-5
Arcane Goods Vendor	F-5
Blacksmithing Supplies	F-5
Cloth & Leather Armor Merchant	F-5
Food & Drink Vendor	F-5
Innkeeper	F-5
Mail and Plate Merchant	F-5
Stable Master	F-5
Superior Leatherworker	C-3
Trade Goods	F-5
Weapon Merchant	F-5

QUICK REFERENCE

CONNECTING REGIONS

BLASTED LANDS	20
DEADWIND PASS	28

TOWNS & CAMPS

STONARD	126

TANARIS

FLIGHT MASTERS
Gryphon Master...H-3
Wind Rider Master..H-3

TRAINERS
Master Engineer H-3
Master Goblin Engineer H-3
Miner..G-3

VENDORS
Alchemy Supplies..G-3
Blacksmithing Supplies H-3
Butcher (Cooking)...H-3
Fisherman J-2
General Goods...J-2
Gunsmith...G-3
Innkeeper...H-3
Stable Master...H-3
Superior Armor Crafter G-3
Tailoring Supplies...G-3

QUICK REFERENCE

CONNECTING REGIONS
THOUSAND NEEDLES 82
UN'GORO CRATER....................................90

TOWNS & CAMPS
GADGETZAN 111

TELDRASSIL

FLIGHT MASTER

Hippogryph Master G-9

TRAINERS

Cook... G-6
Druid Trainer .... G:(4, 6)
First Aid Trainer... G-6
Fisherman.. G-9
Herbalist.. G-6
Hunter Trainer .... G:(4, 6)
Journeyman Alchemist... G-6
Journeyman Enchanter... D-3
Journeyman Leatherworker...................................... E-5
Pet Trainer G-6
Priest Trainer G-6, H-4
Rogue Trainer.. G-6, H-4
Skinner E-5
Warrior Trainer G-6, H-4

VENDORS

Armorer & Shieldcrafter .... G:(4, 6), H-4
Bowyer... G-6, H-4
Clothier.. G-6, H-4
Cooking Supplies... G-6
Fishing Supplies.. G-9
Food & Drink Vendor G-6, H-4
General Supplies... G-6, H-4
Innkeeper.. G-6
Leather Armor Merchant G-6, H-4
Stable Master.. G-6
Trades Supplies... G-6
Weaponsmith .... G:(4, 6), H-4

QUICK REFERENCE

CONNECTING REGIONS
    DARNASSUS..26
TOWNS & CAMPS
    DOLANAAR..109
    SHADOWGLEN...124

E   F   G   H   I   J   K   L

SHADOWTHREAD
CAVE

LLSPRING
RIVER

ALDRASSIL

LLSPRING
LAKE

THE CLEFT

SHADOWGLEN

FEL ROCK

BAN'ETHIL

ETHIL BARROW

AN'ETHIL
DEN

DOLANAAR

STARBREEZE
VILLAGE

S OF
RIEN

LAKE AL'AMETH

GNARLPINE
HOLD

THE
VEILED
SEA

RUT'THERAN
VILLAGE

THOUSAND
N E E D L E S

FLIGHT MASTER
Wind Rider Master F-5

VENDORS
Butcher F-5
Drink Vendor .... K:(7-8)
Engineering Supplies K-8
Food & Drink B-3
General Goods F-5
Gun Merchant K-8
Gunsmith & Bowyer F-5
Ice Cream Vendor J-8
Innkeeper F-5
Stable Master F-5
Trade Supplies F-5

QUICK REFERENCE
CONNECTING REGIONS
BARRENS 18
FERALAS 46
TANARIS 78
TOWNS & CAMPS
MIRAGE RACEWAY 118

THE
BARREN

TO
THE BARR

TO FERALAS

THE
GREAT LIFT

CAMP
E'THOK

WHITEREACH
POST

HIGHPERCH

THE
SCREECHING
CANYON

DARKCLOUD
PINNACLE

ROGUEFEATHER
DEN

UN'GORO
CRATER

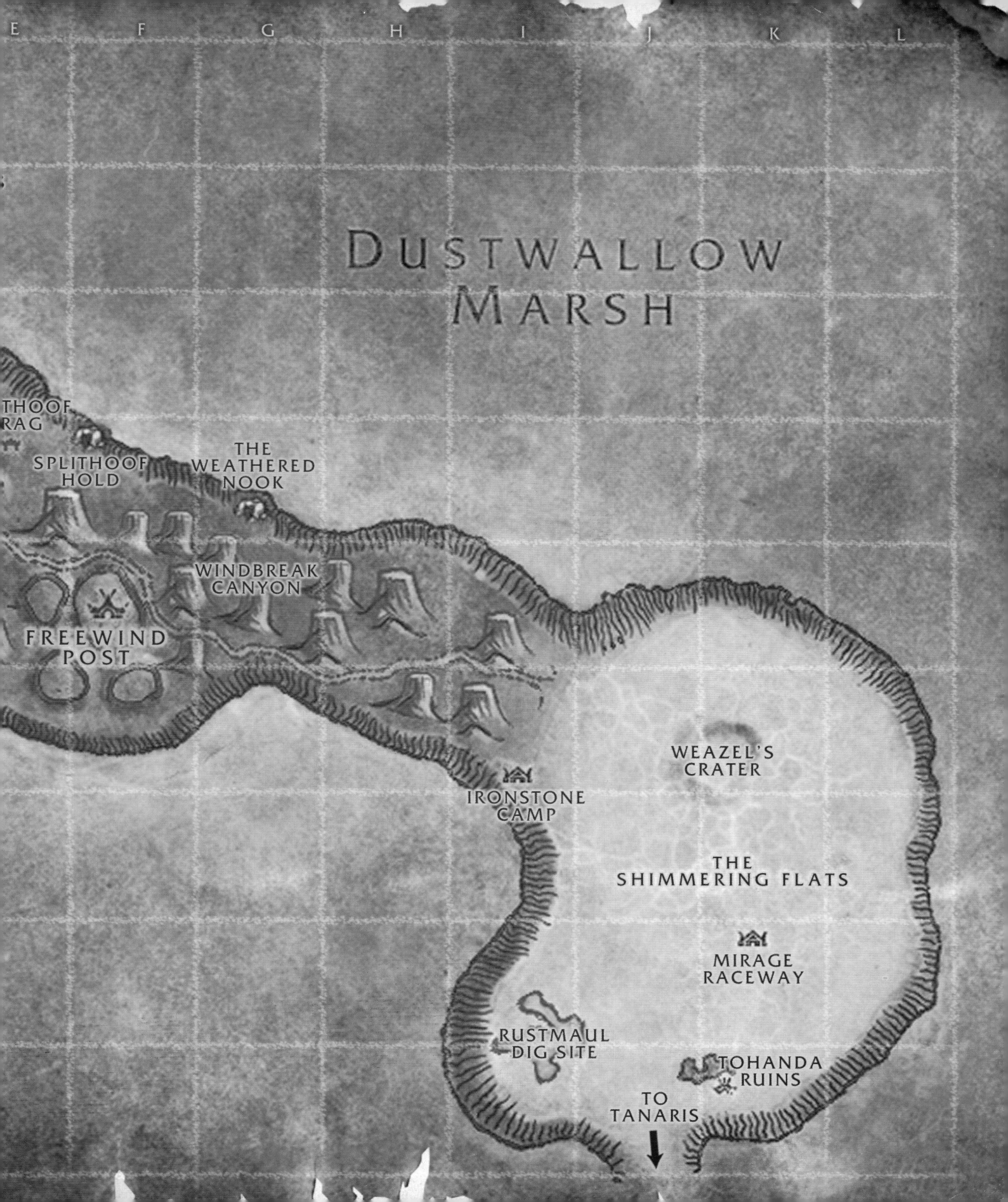
E F G H I J K L
DUSTWALLOW MARSH
THOOF
RAG
SPLITHOOF HOLD
THE WEATHERED NOOK
WINDBREAK CANYON
FREEWIND POST
WEAZEL'S CRATER
IRONSTONE CAMP
THE SHIMMERING FLATS
MIRAGE RACEWAY
RUSTMAUL DIG SITE
TOHANDA RUINS
TO TANARIS

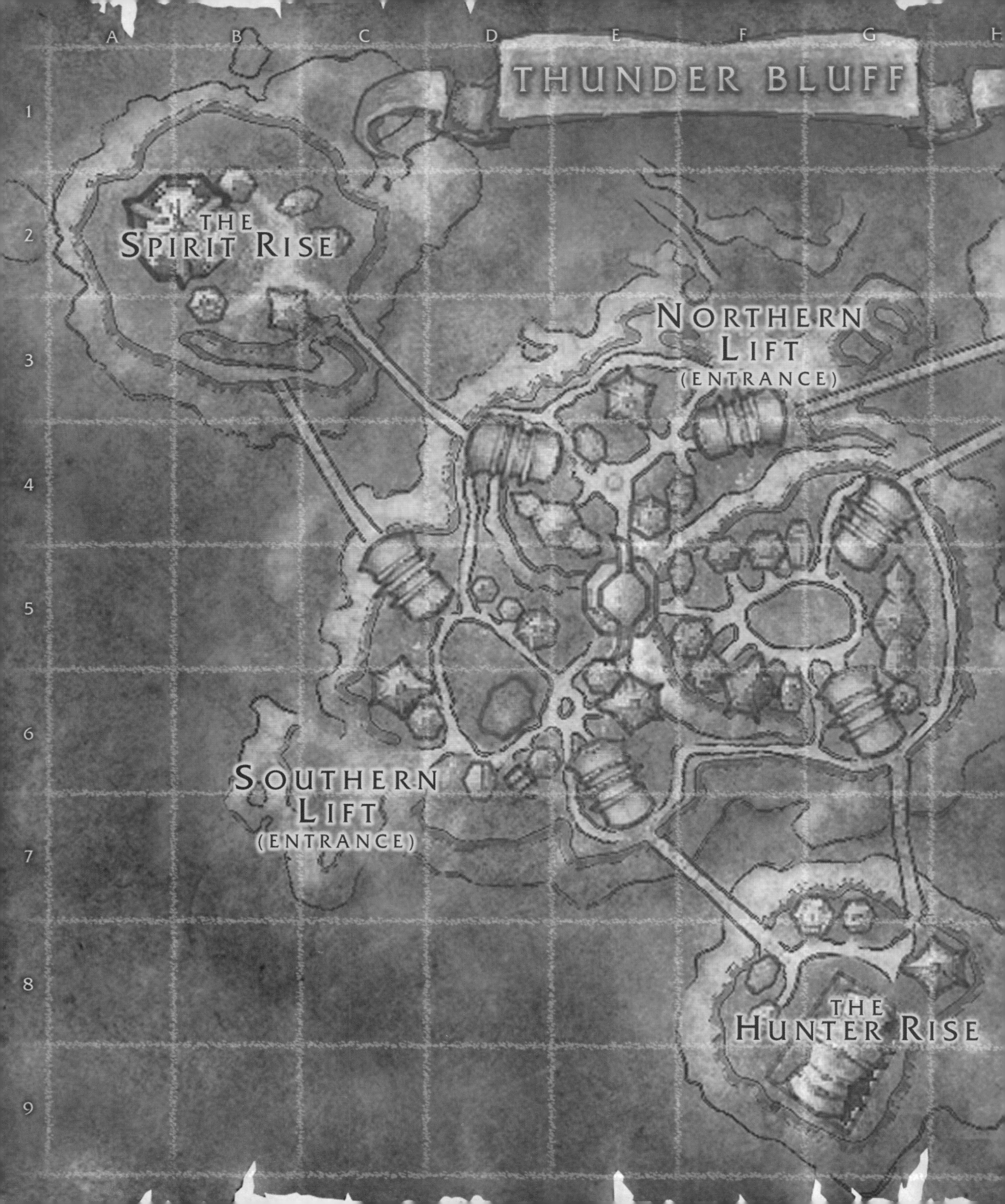

THUNDER BLUFF
A B C D E F G H
1 2 3 4 5 6 7 8 9
THE SPIRIT RISE
NORTHERN LIFT (ENTRANCE)
SOUTHERN LIFT (ENTRANCE)
THE HUNTER RISE

THE
ELDER·RISE

CITY OFFICIALS

Alterac Valley
  Battlemaster G-8
Guild Master.................D-6

Horde Cloth
  Quartermaster............ E-4
Warsong Gulch
  Battlemaster..............G-8

FLIGHT MASTER

Wind Rider Master E-5

TRAINERS

Artisan Leatherworker...D-4
Cooking Trainer..............F-5
Druid Trainer............I-3, J-3
Expert Alchemist E-3
Expert Blacksmith D-6
Expert Enchanter E-4
Expert Leatherworker ... E-4
Expert Tailor E-4
First Aid Trainer.............C-2
Fishing Trainer................F-5
Herbalism Trainer...........F-4
Hunter Trainer................G-9
Journeyman Alchemist.. E-3
Journeyman
  Blacksmith..................D-6

Journeyman Enchanter .. E-4
Journeyman
  Leatherworker D-4
Journeyman Tailor E-4
Mage Trainer C-3
Mining Trainer C-6
Pet Trainer F-8
Portal Trainer.................C-3
Priest Trainer C-3
Shaman Trainer B-2
Skinning Trainer E-4
Warrior Trainer ....G:(8, 9)
Weapon Master D-6

VENDORS

Alchemy Supplies E-3
Axe Merchant................F-6
Bag Vendor....................D-6
Basket Weaver.............. E-3
Blacksmithing
  Supplies D-6
Bowyer & Fletching
  Goods E-4
Bread..........................D-5
Cloth Armor
  Merchant .... E:(4, 6)
Cooking Supplier F-5
Enchanting Supplies...... E-4
Fishing Supplier F-5
Fruit Vendor E-4
General Goods..............D-6
Guns Merchant F-6
Heavy Armor
  Merchant D-4
Herbalism Supplier F-4

Innkeeper E-6
Leather Armor
  Merchant .... E:(4, 6)
Leatherworking &
  Tailoring Supplies E-4
Mace & Staff Merchant..F-6
Mail Armor Merchant ... E-6
Meat Vendor..................F-5
Mining Supplier C-6
Reagent Vendor D-6
Stable Master................ E-6
Staff Merchant E-5, F-5
Sword and Dagger
  Merchant F-6
Tabard Vendor D-6
Trade Goods Supplier....D-6
Two Handed Weapon
  Merchant F-6
War Harness Vendor F-5
Weapon's Merchant D-6

QUICK REFERENCE

CONNECTING REGIONS

MULGORE 58

TIRISFAL GLADES

TRAINERS

Apprentice Herbalist	H-5
Demon Trainer	C-7, H-5
First Aid Trainer	H-5
Fisherman	I-5
Journeyman Alchemist	H-5
Journeyman Enchanter	H-5
Journeyman Leatherworker	I-6
Journeyman Tailor	G-5
Mage Trainer	C-7, H-5
Priest Trainer	C-7, H-5
Rogue Trainer	D-6, H-5
Skinner	I-6
Undead Horse Riding Instructor	H-5
Warlock Trainer	D-6, H-5
Warrior Trainer	D-6, H-5

VENDORS

Alchemy & Herbalism Supplies	H-5
Apprentice Armorer	D-7, H-5
Apprentice Clothier	G-6
Apprentice Weaponsmith	D-7, H-5
Cloth and Leather Armor Merchant	D-6
Fishing Supplies	I-6
General Supplies	D-6, H-5
Innkeeper	H-5
Leather Armor Merchant	H-5
Leatherworking Supplies	K-7
Mushroom Farmer	H-5
Stable Master	H-5
Trade Supplies	H-5
Undead Horse Merchant	H-5

QUICK REFERENCE

CONNECTING REGIONS

ALTERAC MOUNTAINS	8
SILVERPINE FOREST	68
UNDERCITY	88
WESTERN PLAGUELANDS	92

TOWNS & CAMPS

AGAMAND MILLS	100
BRILL	104
DEATHKNELL	109

E
F
G
H
I
J
K
L
THE GREAT SEA
SCARLET WATCH POST
NORTH COAST
AGAMAND FAMILY CRYPT
GARREN'S HAUNT
AGAMAND MILLS
SCARLET MONASTERY
GUNTHER'S RETREAT
WHISPERING GARDENS
BRIGHTWATER LAKE
FAOL'S REST
CRUSADER OUTPOST
VENOMWEB VALE
STILLWATER POND
BRILL
BALNIR FARMSTEAD
COLD HEARTH MANOR
RUINS OF LORDAERON
NIGHTMARE VALE
THE BULWARK
TO WESTERN PLAGUELANDS
UNDERCITY
TO SILVERPINE FOREST
NE
TO ALTERAC MOUNTAINS
ALTERAC

UNDERCITY

CITY OFFICIALS

Alterac Valley	Horde Cloth	
Battlemaster.......G-9, H-9	Quartermaster.............J-3	
Guild Master..................J-4	Warsong Gulch	
	Battlemaster..............H-9	

FLIGHT MASTER

Bat Handler I-5

TRAINERS

Artisan Alchemist F-7	Journeyman Enchanter... I-6
Artisan Tailor..................J-3	Journeyman Engineer....K-7
Cooking Trainer...... H-4, I-4	Journeyman
Demon Trainer .... L:(1, 2)	Leatherworker J-6
Expert Alchemist G-7	Journeyman Tailor J-3
Expert Blacksmith I-3	Mage Trainer L-1
Expert Enchanter I-6	Master Shadowweave
Expert Engineer K-7	Tailor L-2
Expert Leatherworker I-6	Mining Trainer H-4
Expert Tailor J-3	Portal Trainer L-1
First Aid Trainer.............J-5	Priest Trainer F-2, G-2
Fishing Trainer...............K-3	Rogue Trainer................L-7
Herbalism Trainer..........H-5	Skinning Trainer J-6
Journeyman Alchemist...F-7	Warlock Trainer .... L:(1, 2)
Journeyman	Warrior Trainer F-2, G-1
Blacksmith..................H-3	Weapon Master H-3

VENDOR

Alchemy Supplies..........G-7	Innkeeper I-4, J-4
Bag Vendor.....................J-6	Leather Armor
Blacksmith Supplier I-3	Merchant J-6
Blade Merchant K-5	Leatherworking
Blue Moon Odds	Supplies J-6
and Ends, Quest.........H-5	Light Armor Merchant... I-4
Bow Merchant H-4	Mining Supplier H-4
Cloth Armor Merchant... J-3	Mushroom Vendor.........I-5
Cockroach Vendor.... I:(4, 5)	Poison Vendor K-5
Cooking Supplier I-4	Reagent Supplier L-2
Enchanting Supplies.......I-6	Reagent Vendor J-4
Engineer Supplier K-7	Robe Vendor..................J-3
Fishing Supplier K-3	Stable Master................I-4
Fungus Vendor..............K-2	Staff Merchant J-3
General Goods Vendor... J-5	Tabard Vendor J-4
General Trade Goods	Tailoring Supplies J-3
Vendor I-5	Thrown Weapons
General Trade Supplier... I-4	Merchant K-5
Gun Merchant...............I-3	Wand Vendor.................J-3
Heavy Armor	Weapon Merchant H-3
Merchant .... I:(3, 4)	Weapons
Herbalism Supplier H-5	Merchant H-4, I-4

QUICK REFERENCE

CONNECTING REGIONS

TIRISFAL GLADES..86

E F G H I J K L

THE
RUINS OF LORDAERON

THE
WAR QUARTER

THE
MAGIC QUARTER

THE
APOTHECARIUM

THE
ROGUES' QUARTER

UNDERCITY

UN'GORO
CRATER

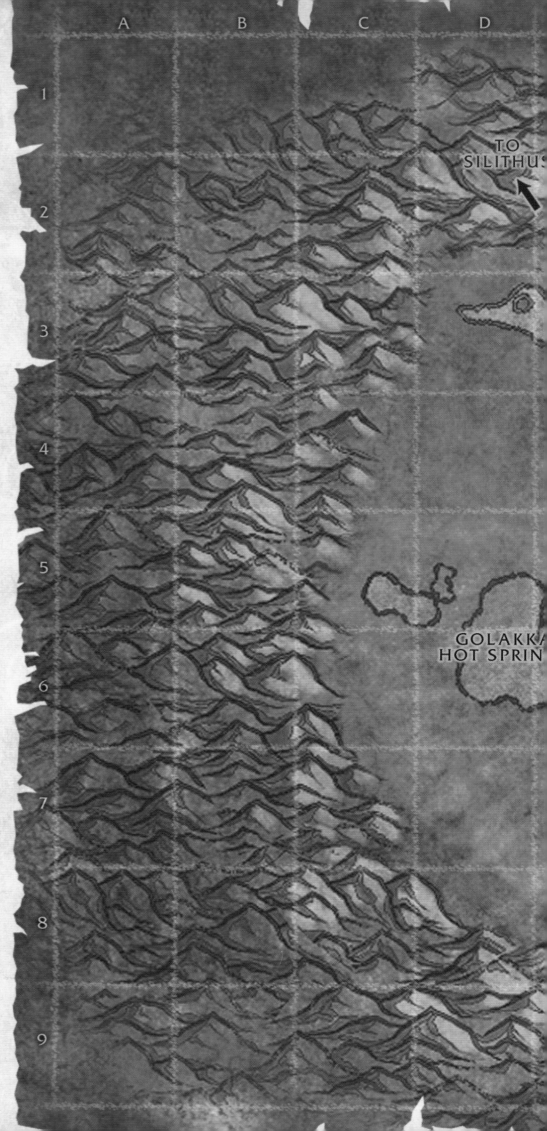

TO
SILITHUS

GOLAKKA
HOT SPRIN

A   B   C   D

1
2
3
4
5
6
7
8
9

FLIGHT MASTER

Gryphon Master..F-8

VENDORS

Baker Masterson I-8
Leatherworking Supplies.....................................F-8
Magnus Frostwake...I-8

THE
WEEPING
CAVE

TO
EASTERN
PLAGUELANDS

RON'S
ERING

DARROWMERE
LAKE

SCHOLOMANCE

CAER DARROW

QUICK REFERENCE

CONNECTING REGIONS

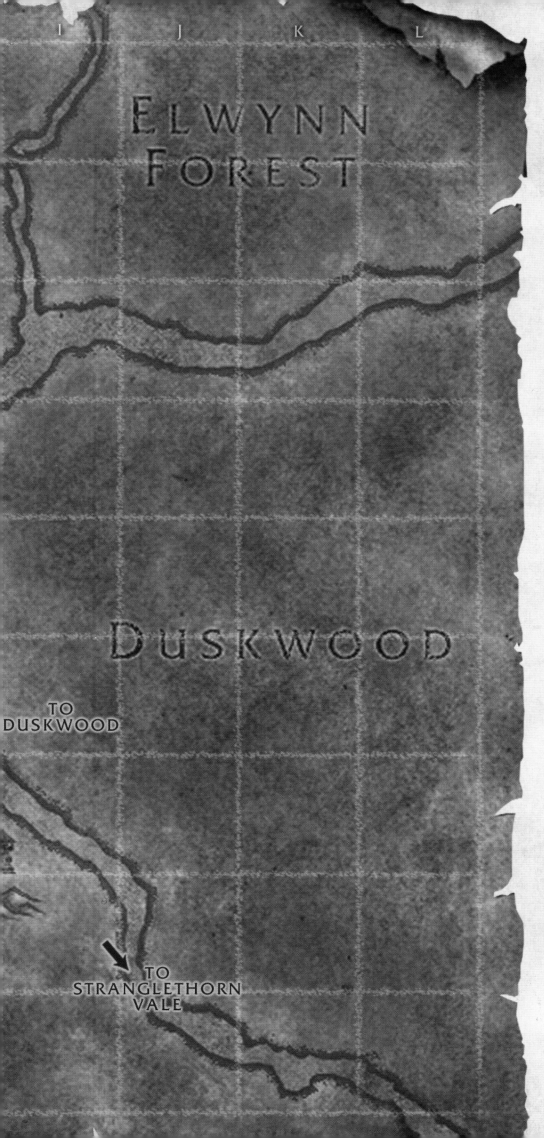

WESTFALL

WETLANDS

SALTSPRAY GLEN

THE LOST FLEET

SUNDOWN MARSH

BLUEGILL MARSH

BARADIN BAY

BLACK CHANNEL MARSH

WHE EXCAVA

MENETHIL BAY

MENETHIL HARBOR

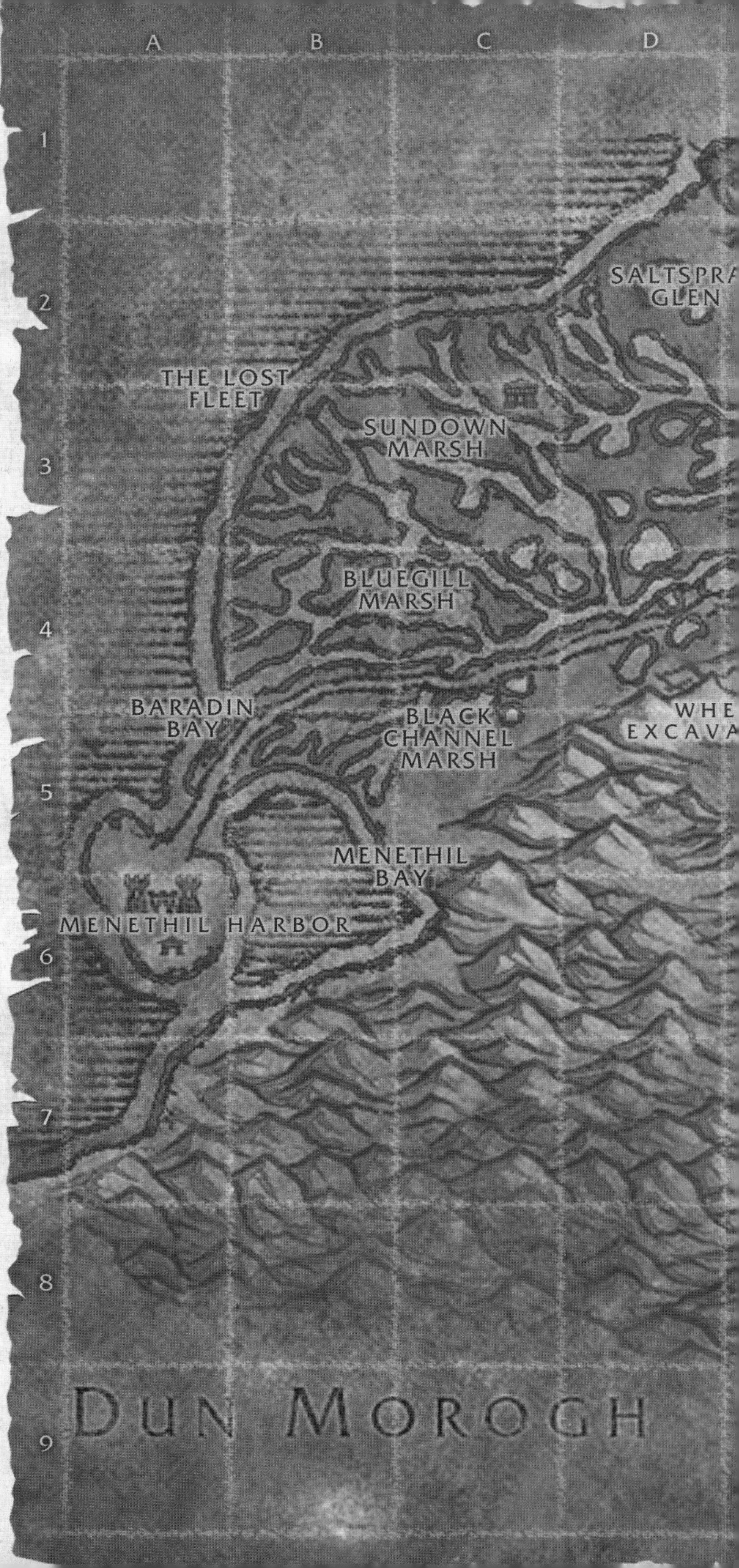

DUN MOROGH

E F G H I J K L

THANDOL SPAN

TO
ARATHI HIGHLANDS

DUN MODR

DIREFORGE
HILL

IRONBEARD'S
TOMB

THE
GREEN BELT

RAPTOR
RIDGE

DRAGONMAW
GATES

R'S
N SITE

ANGERFANG
ENCAMPMENT

THELGEN
ROCK

MOSSHIDE
FEN

GRIM BATOL

TO
LOCH MODAN

DUN ALGAZ

WINTERSPRING

FLIGHT MASTERS

Hippogryph Master I-4
Wind Rider Master I-4

TRAINER

Wintersaber Trainers G-1, J-3

VENDOR

Alchemy Supplies... I-4
Engineering Supplies I-4
Food & Drink H-3, I-4
General Goods... H-3
Heavy Armor Merchant I-4
Innkeeper I-4
Light Armor Merchant I-4
Mining Supplies... I-4
Stable Master I-4
Trade Goods H-3, I-4
Weaponsmith & Gunsmith............................... I-4

QUICK REFERENCE

CONNECTING REGIONS

FELWOOD...44
MOONGLADE 56

TOWNS & CAMPS

EVERLOOK..110

FELWOOD

TO
FELWOOD
AND
MOONGLADE

E F G H I J K L

FROSTSABER
ROCK

THE HIDDEN
GROVE

MOON HORROR
DEN

STARFALL
VILLAGE

WINTERFALL
VILLAGE

FROSTFIRE
HOT SPRINGS

EVERLOOK

TIMBERMAW
POST

LAKE
KEL'THERIL

ICE THISTLE
HILLS

THE RUINS OF
KEL'THERIL

MAZTHORIL

DUN
MANDARR

OWL WING
THICKET

YJAL

FROSTWHISPER
GORGE

DARKWHISPER
GORGE

AERIE PEAK

1   Gryphon Master Talonaxe

2   Guthrum Thunderfist, Gryphon Master

3   Falstad Wildhammer

4   Forge
     Anvil

5   WILDHAMMER KEEP
     Mailbox
     Killium Bouldertoe, Stable Master

5a Dorian Steelwing
     Drakk Stonehand, Master
       Leatherworking Trainer (Downstairs)
     Nioma, Leatherworking Supplies
       (Downstairs)

5b Agnar Beastamer (Downstairs)
     Dwarven Fire
     Innkeeper Thulfram,
       Innkeeper (Upstairs)

5c Truk Wildbeard, Bartender

5d Fraggar Thundermantle

5e Harggan, Blacksmithing
     Supplies (Upstairs)

6   Howin Kindfeather
     Claira Kindfeather

7   Kerr Ironsight

8   FEATHERBEARD'S HOVEL
     Dwarven Fire

9   Trained Razorbeak
     Mangy Silvermane

HINTERLANDS page 50

AERIE PEAK

AGAMAND MILLS

AGAMAND MILLS

1   Nissa Agamand

2   Darkeye Bonecaster
      Rattlecage Soldier

3   Lost Soul

4   Cracked Skull Soldier
      Darkeye Bonecaster

5   Tormented Spirit

6   Cracked Skull Soldier
      Rattlecage Soldier

7   Gregor Agamand

8   Rotting Ancestor

9   Wailing Ancestor

10   AGAMAND FAMILY CRYPT
      Wailing Ancestor
      Rotting Ancestor
      Captain Dargol

11   Wailing Ancestor
      Rotting Ancestor

TIRISFAL GLADES page 86

ASTRANAAR

ASTRANAAR

1 Daelyshia, Hippogryph Master

2 Llana, Reagent Supplies

3 Faldreas Goeth'Shael

4 Fahran Silentblade, Tools & Supplies
   Raene Wolfrunner

5 Maliynn, Food & Drink Vendor

6 Nantar, Baker

7 Innkeeper Kimlya, Innkeeper

8 Mailbox

9 Maluressian, Stable Master

10 Pelturas Whitemoon
   Relara Whitemoon

11 Campfire

12 Aayndia Floralwind, Expert
      Leatherworker
   Xai'ander, Weaponsmith

13 Dalria, Trade Goods

14 Haljan Oakheart, General Goods

15 Sentinel Thenysil

16 Aeolynn, Clothier

17 Tandaan Lightmane, Leather Armor
      Merchant

18 Lardan, Leatherworking Supplies

ASHENVALE page 12

AUBERDINE

1 Caylais Moonfeather,
      Hippogryph Master

2 Gwennyth Bly'Leggonde

3 Kyndri, Baker

4 Laird, Fish Vendor

5 Innkeeper Shaussiy,
      Innkeeper

6 Taldan, Drink Vendor

7 Allyndia, Food & Drink
      Vendor

8 Wizbang Cranktoggle
      (Upstairs)

9 Cerellean Whiteclaw

10 Wanted Poster: Murkdeep!

11 Jaelysia, Stable Master

12 Yalda

13 Barithras Moonshade
   Mailbox

14 Archaeologist Hollee
   Campfire

15 Harlon Thornguard,
      Armorer & Shieldsmith
   Mavralyn, Leather Armor &
      Leatherworking Supplies

16 Thundris Windweaver
   Dalmond, General Goods
   Naram Longclaw,
      Weaponsmith

17 Allandarian Nightsong

18 Shaldyn, Clothier
   Grondal Moonbreeze,
      Journeyman Tailor
   Valdaron, Tailoring Supplies

19 Gorbold Steelhand, General
      Trade Supplier
   Elisa Steelhand,
      Blacksmithing Supplies
   Delfrum Flintbeard,
      Journeyman Blacksmith
   Kurdram Stonehammer,
      Mining Trainer
   Jenna Lemkenilli,
      Journeyman Engineer
   Thelgrum Stonehammer,
      Mining Supplier
   Forge
   Anvil

20 Thanarian Treetender

21 Gershala Nightwhisper

22 Terenthis

23 Sentinel Elissa Starbreeze

24 Gubber Blump

25 Buzzbox 827

26 Moonwell

DARKSHORE page 24

AUBERDINE

BLOODHOOF VILLAGE

1 Harant Ironbrace, Armorer and Shieldcrafter
　Varg Wind Whisper, Leather Armor
　　Merchant
　Mahnott Roughwound, Weaponsmith
　Kennah Hawkseye, Gunsmith
2 Pyall Silentstride, Cook
　Chaw Stronghide, Journeyman
　　Leatherworker
　Yonn Deepcut, Skinner
3 Moorat Longstride, General Goods
　Brave Cloudmane
　Wunna Darkmane, Trade Goods
4 Brave Ironhorn
5 Brave Wildrunner
6 Baine Bloodhoof
7 Mailbox
8 Skorn Whitecloud
　Seikwa, Stable Master
9 Vira Younghoof, First Aid Trainer
10 Magrin Rivermane
11 Innkeeper Kauth, Innkeeper
12 Var'jun
13 Jhawna Oatwind, Baker
14 Ruul Eagletalon

MULGORE page 58

15 Brave Rainchaser
16 Mull Thunderhorn
17 Krang Stonehoof, Warrior Trainer
　Novice Warrior
　Hulfnar Stonetotem
　Thontek Rumblehoof
18 Gennia Runetotem, Druid Trainer
19 Harken Windtotem
20 Narm Skychaser, Shaman Trainer
21 Karm Stormsinger, Kodo Riding Instructor
　Harb Clawhoof, Kodo Mounts

22 Zarlman Two-Moons
　Tribal Fire
23 Maur Raincaller
24 Harn Longcast, Fishing Supplies
25 Reban Freerunner, Pet Trainer
　Yaw Sharpmane, Hunter Trainer
26 Brave Darksky
27 Brave Strongbash
28 Brave Swiftwind
29 Morin Cloudstalker
30 Brave Dawneagle
31 Uthan Stillwater, Fisherman

BOOTY BAY

1   Grizzlowe, Shipmaster

2   Wharfmaster Lozgil

3   Sprogger
     Captain Hecklebury Smotts
     "Shaky" Phillipe

4   PLATE-N-CHAIN
     Hurklor, Blacksmithing Supplies
     Fargon Mortalak, Superior Armorer

5   BOOTY BAY BLACKSMITH
     McGavan
     Jansen Underwood, Blacksmithing Supplies
     Brikk Keencraft, Master Blacksmith
     Anvil
     Forge

6   Dizzy One-Eye

7   Rikqiz, Leatherworking Supplies
     Stove, Cooking Fire

8   Oglethorpe Obnoticus, Master Gnome
     Engineer
     Stove, Cooking Fire

9   A TAILOR TO CITIES
     Xizk Goodstitch, Tailoring Supplies
     Grarnik Goodstitch, Expert Tailor
     Stove, Cooking Fire

10   DEEP SOUTH TANNERY
     Stove, Cooking Fire

11   TAN-YOUR-HIDE-LEATHERWORKS
     Drizzlik
     Blixrez Goodstitch, Leatherworking Supplies
     Qixdi Goodstitch, Cloth and Armor
     Accessories

12   OLD PORT AUTHORITY
     Markel Smythe

12a   CUTS-N-BRUISES INCORPORATED
     Zarena Cromwind, Superior Weaponsmith
     Kizz Bluntstrike, Macecrafter

12b   BOOMSTICK IMPORTS EAST
     Mazk Snipeshot, Engineering Supplies

12c   SWIFT FLIGHTS
     Haren Kanmae, Superior Bowyer

12d   NAUTICAL NEEDS
     Narkk, Pirate Supplies

12e   GOOD FOOD
     Kelsey Yance, Cook

13   Wigcik (Low Level), Superior Fisherman
     Stove, Cooking Fire

13a   Sly Garrett, Shady Goods
     Crazk Sparks, Fireworks Merchant

14   "Sea Wolf" MacKinley
     Book: The Sentinels and the Long Vigil
     (Top Level)

15   BOUCHER'S CAULDRON
     Jaxin Chong, Expert Alchemist
     Glyx Brewright, Alchemy Supplies
     Stove, Cooking Fire

16   ALL THINGS FLORA
     Flora Silverwind, Superior Herbalist

17   Scooty, Chief Engineer
     Jutak, Blade Trader
     Teleporter to Gnomeregan

18   SOUTHERN SKIES PLATFORM
     Gyll, Gryphon Master

19a   THE SALTY SAILOR, LOW LEVEL
     Whiskey Slim
     Crank Fizzlebub
     Innkeeper Skindle, Innkeeper
     Nixxrax Fillamug, Food and Drink

19b   THE SALTY SAILOR, MID LEVEL
     Catelyn the Blade
     Ian Strom, Rogue Trainer

19c   THE SALTY SAILOR, TOP LEVEL
     Deeg
     Krazek
     Kebok
     Book: Beyond the Dark Portal
     Mailbox

20   Fin Fizracket
     Old Man Heming (Low Level) Fisherman

21   Fleet Master Seahorn
     Baron Revilgaz

22   Gringer, Wind Rider Master

23   BOOTY BAY BANK
     Privateer Bloads
     Viznik Goldgrubber, Banker
     Rickle Goldgrubber, Banker
     Mailbox

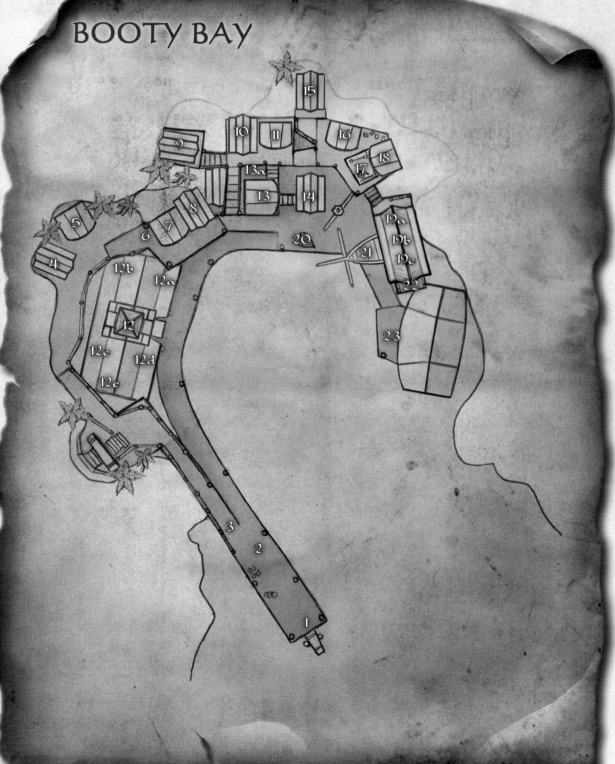

BOOTY BAY

STRANGLETHORN VALE page 74

103

BRACKENWALL VILLAGE

1 Tharg
2 Ogg'marr, Butcher
3 Do'gol
4 Krak, Armorer
5 Overlord Mok'Morokk
   Bonfire
6 Draz'Zilb
7 Krog
8 Zulrg, Weaponsmith
9 Shardi, Wind Rider Master
10 Ghok'kah, Tailoring Supplies
11 Nazeer Bloodpike
12 Zanara, Bowyer
13 Balai Lok'Wein, Potions, Scrolls &
    Reagents

DUSTWALLOW MARSH page 38

BRILL

1 Deathguard Terrence
2 Deathguard Mort
   Mailbox

3 GALLOW'S END TAVERN
   Nurse Nelia, First Aid Trainer
   Cain Firesong, Mage Trainer (Upstairs)
   Gretchen Dedmar

3a Yvette Farthing
   Ageron Kargal (Upstairs)
   Gina Lang, Demon Trainer (Upstairs)
   Rupert Boch, Warlock Trainer (Upstairs)

3b Austil De Mon, Warrior Trainer
   Coleman Farthing
   Ratslin Maime
   Innkeeper Renee, Innkeeper
   Dark Cleric Beryl, Priest Trainer (Upstairs)
   Marion Call, Rogue Trainer (Upstairs)

3c Captured Scarlet Zealot (Downstairs)
   Captured Mountaineer (Downstairs)
   Deathguard Royann (Downstairs)
   Deathguard Gavin (Downstairs)
   Vance Undergloom, Journeyman Enchanter
    (Upstairs)

4 Mrs. Winters, General Supplies
5 Abigail Shiel, Trade Supplies
6 Deathguard Burgess
7 Deathguard Cyrus
   Executor Zygand
   Wanted Poster: Maggot Eye

8 BRILL TOWN HALL
   Jamie Nore

8a Magistrate Sevren

9 Junior Apothecary Holland, Royal
   Apothecary Society

10 Deathguard Kel

11 Deathguard Barthomew
   Deathguard Lawrence
   Deathguard Dillinger

12 Hamlin Atkins, Mushroom Farmer
13 Deathguard Lundmark
14 Sawvan Bloodshadow
15 Carolai Anise, Journeyman Alchemist
   Apothecary Johaan, Royal Apothecary
    Society

16 Faruza, Apprentice Herbalist

17 Morganus, Stable Master
   Thomas Arlento
   Zachariah Post, Undead Horse Merchant
   Velma Warnam,
    Undead Horse Riding Instructor
   Deathguard Morris
   Doreen Beltis

18 Eliza Callen, Leather Armor Merchant

19 Abe Winters, Apprentice Armorer
   Oliver Dwor, Apprentice Weaponsmith
   Forge
   Anvil

TIRISFAL GLADES page 86

CAMP MOJACHE

CAMP MOJACHE

1 Shyn, Wind Rider Master
2 Loorana, Food & Drink Vendor
3 Sage Korolusk
4 Blaise Montgomery
  Mailbox
5 Tarhus, Reagent Vendor
  Innkeeper Greul
6 Cawind Trueaim, Gunsmith & Bowyer
7 Rok Orhan
8 Witch Doctor Uzer'i
  Shyrka Wolfrunner
9 Kulleg Stonehorn, Skinning Trainer
  Hahrana Ironhide, Master
    Leatherworker
  Jangdor Swiftstrider, Leatherworking
    Supplies
  Sheendra Tallgrass, Trade Supplies
  Worb Strongstitch, Light Armor
    Merchant
10 Hadoken Swiftstrider
11 Sage Palerunner
12 Ruw, Herbalism Trainer
  Bronk, Alchemy Supplies
13 Talo Thornhoof
14 Krueg Skullsplitter
15 Jannos Lighthoof, Druid Trainer
16 Orik'ando

FERALAS page 46

CAMP NARACHE

1 Brave Greathoof
2 Brave Proudsnout
3 Moodan Sungrain, Baker
4 Grull Hawkwind
  Brave Windfeather
5 Vorn Skyseer
6 Bronk Steelrage, Armorer and
    Shieldcrafter
  Marjak Keenblade, Weaponsmith
  Varia Hardhide, Leather Armor
    Merchant
7 Brave Running Wolf
8 Harutt Thunderhorn, Warrior Trainer
  Chief Hawkwind
  Lanka Farshot, Hunter Trainer
  Burning Embers
9 Seer Ravenfeather
10 Meela Dawnstrider, Shaman Trainer
  Gart Mistrunner, Druid Trainer
11 Kawnie Softbreeze, General Goods
12 Brave Lightninghorn

MULGORE page 58

CAMP NARACHE

CAMP TAURAJO

1　Kelsuwa, Stable Master
　　Innkeeper Byula, Innkeeper

2　Sanuye Runetotem, Leather Armor
　　　Merchant
　　Dranh, Skinner

3　Jorn Skyseer
　　Grunt Logmar
　　Mangletooth
　　Krulmoo Fullmoon, Expert
　　　Leatherworker
　　Gahroot, Butcher
　　Ruga Ragetotem
　　Mahani, Expert Tailor
　　Yonada, Tailoring and Leatherworking
　　　Supplies
　　Burning Embers, Cooking Fire

4　Mailbox

5　Kirge Strenhorn

6　Burning Embers, Cooking Fire
　　Barrel of Milk, Spawn Point

7　Tatternack Steelforge
　　Anvil
　　Forge

BARRENS page 18

CAMP TAURAJO

COLDRIDGE VALLEY

COLDRIDGE VALLEY

1　ANVILMAR
　　Solm Hargrin, Rogue Trainer
　　Felix Whindlebolt
　　Rybrad Coldbank, Weaponsmith
　　Grundel Harkin, Armorsmith
　　Bromos Grummner, Paladin Trainer
　　Thorgas Grimson, Hunter Trainer
　　Thran Khorman, Warrior Trainer
　　Branstock Khalder, Priest Trainer
　　Marryk Nurribit, Mage Trainer
　　Durnan Furcutter, Cloth & Leather
　　　Armor Merchant
　　Wren Darkspring, Demon Trainer
　　Alamar Grimm, Warlock Trainer

2　Balir Frosthammer
　　Sten Stoutarm
　　Adlin Pridedrift, General Supplies
　　Yori Crackhelm

3　Talin Keeneye

4　Grelin Whitebeard
　　Apprentice Soren
　　Nori Pridedrift

5　Mountaineer Thalos

6　Hands Springsprocket

DUN MOROGH page 32

THE CROSSROADS

1   Hraq Blacksmithing, Supplier
    Jahan Hawkwing, Leather and Mail
      Merchant
    Nargal Deatheye, Weaponsmith
    Traugh, Expert Blacksmith

2   Korran

3   Devrak, Wind Rider Master
    Apothecary Helbrim
    Hula'mahi, Reagents and Herbs

4   Sikwa, Stable Master
    Grenthar

5   Barg, General Supplies
    Tarl'qa, Trade Supplies

6   Gazrog
    Mailbox

7   Boorand Plainswind, Innkeeper
    Larhka, Beverage Merchant

8   Zargh, Butcher

9   Moorane Hearthgrain, Baker

10 Sergra Darkthorn

11 Thork
    Darsok Swiftdagger

12 Mankrik

13 Kil'hala, Journeyman Tailor
    Wrahk, Tailoring Supplies

14 Halija Whitestrider, Clothier
    Tonga Runetotem

15 Kalyimah Stormcloud, Bags and Sacks

BARRENS page 18

THE CROSSROADS

DARKSHIRE

1   SCARLET RAVEN TAVERN
    Mabel Solaj, General Goods Vendor

2   Tavernkeep Smitts
    Innkeeper Trelayne, Innkeeper
    Barkeep Han, Bartender

3   Chef Grual

4   Gunder Thornbush, Tradesman

5   Farrin Daris

6   Mailbox

7   Steven Black, Stable Master

8   Watcher Bukouris, The Night Watch

9   Commander Althea Ebonlocke, Leader of
    The Night Watch

10 DARKSHIRE TOWN HALL, FOYER
    Clerk Daltry

11 DARKSHIRE TOWN HALL, ANTEROOM
    Sirra Von'Indi, Historian of Darkshire

12 DARKSHIRE TOWN HALL, MAIN HALL
    Hogan Ference
    Councilman Millstripe, Council of Darkshire
    Ambassador Berrybuck, Council of Darkshire
    Role Dreuger, Deputy Mayor of Darkshire
    Lord Ello Ebonlocke, Mayor of Darkshire

13 Clarise Gnarltree, Expert Blacksmith
    Morg Gnarltree, Armorer
    Gavin Gnarltree, Weaponsmith
    Forge
    Anvil

14 Matt Johnson, Mining Trainer

15 Watcher Mokarski, The Night Watch

16 Watcher Frazier, The Night Watch

17 Watcher Keefer, The Night Watch

18 Watcher Ladimore, The Night Watch
    Town Crier

19 Calor

20 Elaine Carevin
    Jonathan Carevin

21 Scott Carevin, Mushroom Seller

22 Watchmaster Sorigal

23 Watcher Hartin, The Night Watch

24 Madame Eva
    Alyssa Eva, Reagent Vendor

25 Lohgan Eva, Tailoring Supplies

26 Danielle Zipstitch, Tailoring Supplies
    Sheri Zipstitch, Tailoring Supplies

27 Watcher Brownell, The Night Watch

28 Watcher Jan, The Night Watch

29 Finbus Geargrind, Expert Engineer
    Cog Glitzspinner

30 Herble Baubbletump, Engineering & Mining
    Supplies

31 Watcher Wollpert, The Night Watch

32 Watcher Royce, The Night Watch

33 Watcher Keller, The Night Watch

34 Whit Wantmal

35 Vitori Prism'Antras

36 Felicia Melline, Gryphon Master

DUSKWOOD page 36

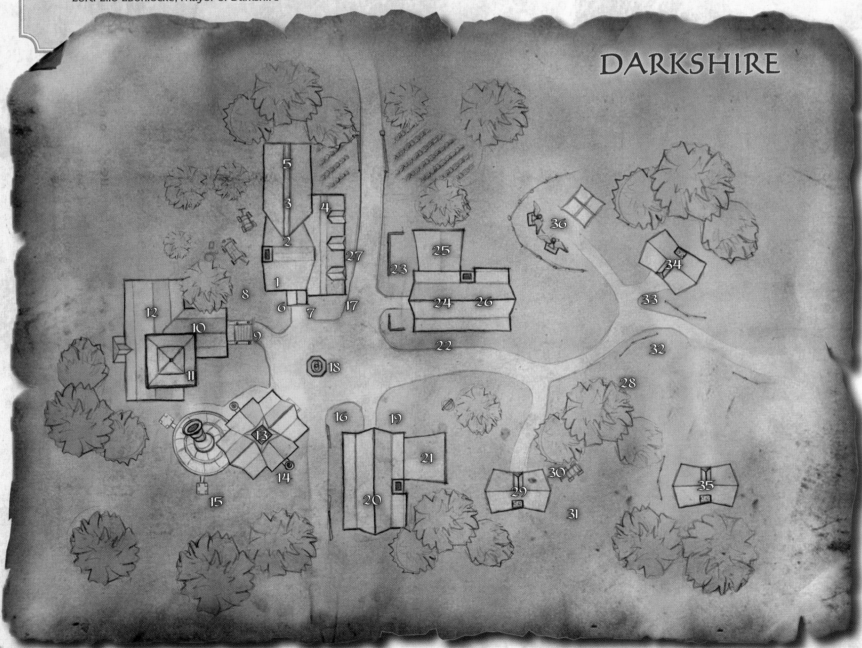

DARKSHIRE

DEATH KNELL

DEATH KNELL

1	Deathguard Oliver
2	Claire Willower
3	Executor Arren
4	Harold Raims, Apprentice Weaponsmith
	Blacksmith Rand, Apprentice Armorer
	Cozy Fire
5	Maquell Ebonwood
	Dark Cleric Duesten, Priest Trainer
	Isabella, Mage Trainer
	Novice Elreth
	Shadow Priest Sarvis
	Kayla Smithe, Demon Trainer
	Maximillion, Warlock Trainer
	Venya Marthand
6	Deathguard Saltain

7	Deathguard Randolph
8	Deathguard Bartrand
9	Deathguard Phillip
10	Joshua Kien, General Supplies
	Archibald Kava, Cloth & Leather Armor Merchant
11	David Trias, Rogue Trainer
	Dannal Stern, Warrior Trainer
12	Young Scavenger
	Duskbat
13	Mindless Zombie
	Wretched Zombie
14	Rattlecage Skeleton
	Wretched Zombie
15	Mangy Duskbat
	Ragged Scavenger

TIRISFAL GLADES page 86

DOLANAAR

1	Zenn Foulhoof
2	Ancient Protector
3	Malorne Bladeleaf, Herbalist
	Cyndra Kindwhisper, Journeyman Alchemist
4	Nyoma, Cooking Supplies
	Zarrin, Cook
	Cauldron
5	Sentinel Shaya
6	Corithras Moonrage
	Kal, Druid Trainer
	Moonwell
7	Keldas, Pet Trainer
	Dazalar, Hunter Trainer
	Seriadne, Stable Master
8	Jannok Breezesong, Rogue Trainer
9	Brannol Eaglemoon, Clothier
10	Sinda, Leather Armor Merchant
	Shaloman, Weaponsmith
	Meri Ironweave, Armorer & Shieldcrafter
11	Sentinel Kyra Starsong
12	Kyra Windblade, Warrior Trainer
13	Jeena Featherbow, Bowyer
14	Mailbox
15	Innkeeper Keldamyr, Innkeeper
	Melarith

16	Syral Bladeleaf
17	Athridas Bearmantle
18	Danlyia, Food & Drink Vendor (Bottom Floor)
	Byancie, First Aid Trainer (Bottom Floor)
	Laurna Morninglight, Priest Trainer (Bottom Floor)
	Narret Shadowgrove, Trade Supplies (Middle Floor)
	Aldia, General Supplies (Middle Floor)
	Tallonkai Swiftroot (Top Floor)
19	Moon Priestess Amara
	Huntress Yaeliura
	Huntress Nhemai

TELDRASSIL page 80

DOLANAAR

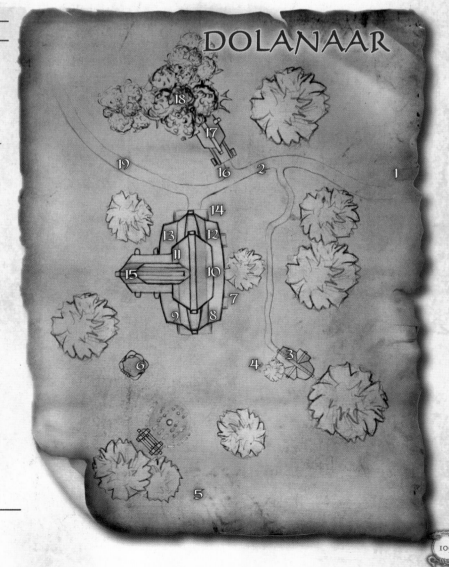

EVERLOOK

1   Yugrek, Wind Rider Master
2   Azzleby, Stable Master
3   Evie Whirlbrew, Alchemy
    Supplies
4   Umi Rumplesnicker
5   Zap Farflinger, Unbalanced
    Engineer
6   Qia, Trade Goods Supplies
    Seril Scourgebane
    Lilith the Lithe
    Kilram
    Izzy Coppergrab, Banker
7   Nixxrak, Heavy Armor
    Merchant
    Blixxrak, Light Armor Merchant
    Wixxrak, Weaponsmith &
    Gunsmith
8   Jack Sterling

9   Umaron Stragarelm
10 Lunnix Sprocketslip, Mining
    Supplies
11 Felnok Steelspring
    Legacki
12 Gogo
    Harlo Wigglesworth
    Mailbox
13 Innkeeper Vizzie
    Jessica Redpath
    Gregor Greystone
    Himmik, Food & Drink Vendor
14 Malyfous Darkhammer
    Forge
15 Xizzer Fizzbolt, Engineering
    Supplies
16 Meggi Peppinrocker
17 Maethrya, Hippogryph Master

WINTERSPRING page 98

EVERLOOK

FEATHERMOON STRONGHOLD

1   Fyldren Moonfeather, Hippogryph Master
2   Patt McGrubben, Leatherworking Supplies
3   Faralorn, General Supplies
4   Dulciea Frostmoon, Cloth Armor Merchant
5   Innkeeper Shyria, Innkeeper
6   Mardrack Greenwell, Food & Drink
7   Vivianna, Trade Supplies
8   Jadenvis Seawatcher, Reagent Vendor
9   Brannock, Fisherman
10   Antarius, Stable Master
11   Scholar Runethorn
     Mailbox
12   Xylinnia Starshine, Expert Enchanter
13   Vestia Moonspear
14   Shandris Feathermoon, General of the Sentinel
        Army
     Latronicus Moonspear
15   Savanne, Fishing Supplies
     Harklane, Fish Vendor
16   Kylanna Windwhisper, Master Alchemist
     Logannas, Alchemy Supplies
17   Bethan Bluewater
     Quintis Jonespyre
18   Troyas Moonbreeze
     Angelas Moonbreeze
19   Ginro Hearthkindle
20   Erik Felixe
     Paige Felixe

FERALAS page 46

FEATHERMOON STRONGHOLD

GADGETZAN

1 Bulkrek Ragefist, Wind Rider Master
2 Tran'rek
3 Jhordy Lapforge, Engineer
  Curgle Cranklehop
4 Nixx Sprocketspring, Master Goblin
  Engineer

5 Buzzek Bracketswing, Master Engineer
  Mailbox
6 Innkeeper Fizzgrimble
  Dirge Quikcleave, Butcher
7 Laziphus, Stable Master
8 Spigot Operator Luglunket
  Chief Engineer Bilgewhizzle

9 Qizzik, Banker
  Gimblethorn, Banker
10 Auctioneer Beardo
11 Marin Noggenfogger
12 Forge
   Krinkle Goodsteel, Blacksmithing Supplies
   Trenton Lighthammer
   Derotain Mudsipper
13 Pikkle, Miner
14 Quinn
15 Wrinkle Goodsteel, Superior Armor Crafter
   Blizrik Buckshot, Gunsmith
16 Vizzklick, Tailoring Supplies
   Shreev
17 Alchemist Pestlezugg, Alchemy Supplies
18 Sprinkle
19 Senior Surveyor Fizzledowser
20 Bera Stonehammer, Gryphon Master

TANARIS page 78

GHOST WALKER POST

1 Gurda Wildmane
  Felgur Twocuts
2 Muuran, Superior Macecrafter
  Nataka Longhorn
  Narv Hidecrafter, Expert
    Leathercrafter
3 Takata Steelblade
4 Maurin Bonesplitter
5 Harnor, Food and Drink
  Kireena, Trade Goods
6 KODO GRAVEYARD
  Dying Kodos
  Ancient Kodos
  Aged Kodos
  Carrion Horrors

DESOLACE page 30

GHOST WALKER POST

GOLDSHIRE

1 Graveyard

2 Bo
 Joshua
 Mark

3 Lyria Du Lac, Warrior Trainer
 Brother Wilhelm, Paladin Trainer
 Corina Steele, Weaponsmith
 Andrew Krighton, Armorer and
  Shieldcrafter

Smith Argus, Journeyman Blacksmith
Kurran Steele, Cloth and Leather Armor
 Merchant
Anvil
Forge

4 Marshal Dughan

5 Remy "Two Times"
 Tharynn Bouden, Trade Supplies
 Food Crate Spawn Point

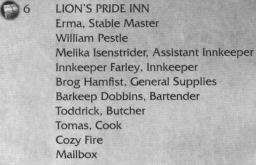 6 LION'S PRIDE INN
 Erma, Stable Master
 William Pestle
 Melika Isenstrider, Assistant Innkeeper
 Innkeeper Farley, Innkeeper
 Brog Hamfist, General Supplies
 Barkeep Dobbins, Bartender
 Toddrick, Butcher
 Tomas, Cook
 Cozy Fire
 Mailbox

6a LION'S PRIDE, BASEMENT
 Cylina Darkheart, Demon Trainer
 Maximillian Crowe, Warlock Trainer
 Remen Marcot

6b LION'S PRIDE, TOP LEVEL
 Zaldimar Wefhellt, Mage Trainer
 Priestess Josetta, Priest Trainer
 Michelle Belle, Physician
 Keryn Sylvius, Rogue Trainer
 Chest: Stalvan's Quest

7 Adele Fielder, Journeyman Leatherworker
 Helene Peltskinner, Skinner
 Dana
 Lisa
 Aaron
 John
 Cameron
 Jose
 Cozy Fire

8 CRYSTAL LAKE
 Jason Mathers, Fishmonger
 Lee Brown, Fisherman
 Matt

ELWYNN FOREST page 42

GROM'GOL BASE CAMP

1 Nez'raz, Zeppelin Master
 Squibby Overspeck, Zeppelin
  Master

2 Zudd, Pet Trainer

3 Kragg, Hunter Trainer

4 Hragran, Cloth & Leather Armor
  Merchant

5 Brawn, Expert Leatherworker

6 Mudduk, Superior Cook

7 Uthok, General Supplies

8 Nimboya
 Angrun, Superior Herbalist
 Kin'weelay

9 Vharr, Superior Weaponsmith
 Krakk, Superior Armorer
 Forge

10 Mailbox

11 Nerrist, Trade Goods

12 Thysta, Wind Rider Master

13 Commander Aggro'gosh

14 Nargatt, Food & Drink Vendor
 Far Seer Mok'thardin

STRANGLETHORN VALE page 74

GROM'GOL BASE CAMP

HAMMERFALL

1	Urda, Wind Rider Master	8	Mu'uta, Bowyer
2	Tharlidun, Stable Master		Forge
	Korin Fel		Anvil
	Mailbox	9	Gor'mul
3	Zengu	10	Jun'ha, Tailoring Supplies
4	Slagg, Superior Butcher	11	Doctor Gregory Victor, Trauma Surgeon
	Uttnar, Butcher	12	Tor'gan
	Drum Fel	13	Zaruk
5	Innkeeper Adegwa, Innkeeper	14	Tunkk, Leatherworking Supplies
6	Graud, General Goods		
7	Keena, Trade Goods		

ARATHI HIGHLANDS page 10

HILLSBRAD FIELDS

1 Hillsbrad Farmer
   Hillsbrad Peasant

2 Farmer Kalaba

3 Hillsbrad Footman

4 Hillsbrad Tailor

5 Hillsbrad Farmer
   Hillsbrad Farmhand

6 Hillsbrad Farmer
   Hillsbrad Farmhand
   Farmer Getz

7 Stanley

8 Hillsbrad Farmer
   Hillsbrad Farmhand
   Farmer Ray (Upstairs)

9 Hillsbrad Footman
   Hillsbrad Councilman

10 Hillsbrad Footman
    Hillsbrad Councilman
    Hillsbrad Peasant

11 HILLSBRAD
    Hillsbrad Footman
    Hillsbrad Councilman
    Clerk Horrace Whitesteed
    Magistrate Burnside
    Hillsbrad Peasant

12 Citizen Wilkes

13 Blacksmith Verringtan
    Hillsbrad Apprentice Blacksmith
    Hillsbrad Councilman
    Hillsbrad Footman

14 Hillsbrad Apprentice Blacksmith
    Shipment of Iron
    Forge
    Anvil

HILLSBRAD FOOTHILLS page 48

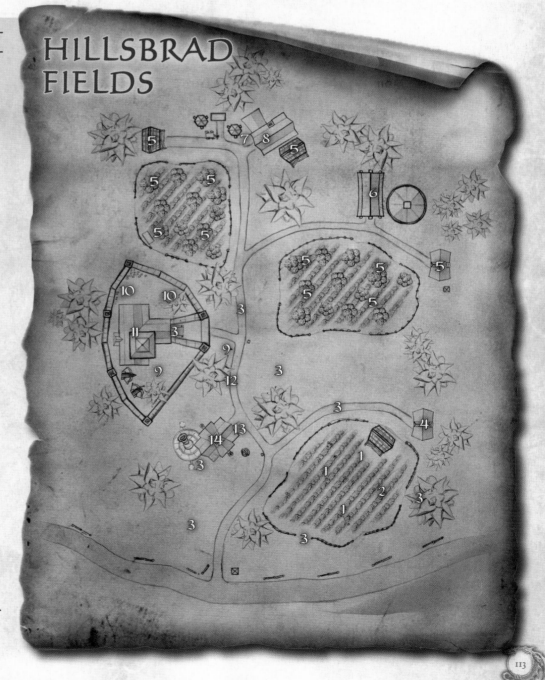

KARGATH

1 Gorrik, Wind Rider Master

2 Greth, Stable Master
Mailbox
Kill on Sight Poster: Dark Iron
Dwarves
Kill on Sight Poster: High Ranking
Dark Iron Officials

3 Grunt Gargal, Kargath Expeditionary
Force
Thunderheart, Kargath Expeditionary
Force
Initiate Amakkar, Kargath
Expeditionary Force
Thal'trak Proudtusk, Kargath
Expeditionary Force
Razal'blade, Kargath Expeditionary
Force

4 Hierophant Theodora Mulvadania,
Kargath Expeditionary Force
Shadowmage Vivian Lagrave,
Kargath Expeditionary Force
Bonfire

5 Sranda, Light Armor & Weapons
Merchant
Forge

6 Jarkol Mossmeld

7 Innkeeper Shul'kar, Innkeeper
Gorn
Grawl, General Goods
Burning Embers

8 Warlord Goretooth, Kargath
Expeditionary Force
Lexlort, Kargath Expeditionary Force
Galamav the Marksman, Kargath
Expeditionary Force

BADLANDS page 16

KARGATH

KHARANOS

KHARANOS

1 Peria Lamenur, Pet Trainer

2 Senir Whitebeard

3 Golorn Frostbeard, Tradesman

4 Shelby Stoneflint, Stable Master
Mailbox

5 Ragnar Thunderbrew

6 Dannie Fizzwizzle, Demon Trainer
Gimrizz Shadowcog, Warlock Trainer
Tog Rustsprocket

7 THUNDERBREW DISTILLERY

Azar Stronghammer, Paladin Trainer
Magis Sparkmantle, Mage Trainer
Maxan Anvol, Priest Trainer
Tannok Frosthammer, Innkeeper Assistant
Kreg Bilmn, General Supplies
Thamner Pol, Physician
Granis Swiftaxe, Warrior Trainer
Innkeeper Belm, Innkeeper
Gremlock Pilsnor, Cooking Trainer
Hogral Bokkan, Rogue Trainer
Jarven Thunderbrew

8 Mountaineer Dolf

9 Grif Wildheart, Hunter Trainer

10 Tharek Blackstone

11 Grawn Thromwyn, Weaponsmith
Tognus Flintfire, Journeyman Blacksmith
Gamili Frosthide, Cloth & Leather Armor Merchant
Boran Ironclink, Armorer
Kogan Forgestone
Thrawn Boltar, Blacksmithing Supplies

12 Ozzie Togglevolt
Razzle Sprysprocket

DUN MOROGH page 32

LAKESHIRE

LAKESHIRE

1   Deputy Feldon
     Ariena Stormfeather, Gryphon Master

2   Guard Howe

3   Guard Ashlock

4   Guard Pearce
     Guard Hiett

5   Marshal Marris

6   Foreman Oslow

7   Verner Osgood

8   Kara Adams, Shieldcrafter
     Dorin Songblade, Armorer

9   Karen Taylor, Mining and Smithing Supplies
     Forge

10   Wanted Poster: Gath'Ilzogg

11   LAKESHIRE TOWN HALL
     Baliff Conacher
     Magistrate Solomon

12   Amy Davenport, Tradeswoman
     Lindsay Ashlock, General Supplies

13   Dockmaster Baren

14   Penny, Stable Master
     Wanted Poster: Lieutenant Fangore
     Missing Poster: Corporal Keeshan
     Guard Berton
     Mailbox

15   LAKESHIRE INN
     Kimberly Hiett, Fletcher
     Darcy, Waitress
     Innkeeper Brianna
     Yorus Barleybrew
     Barkeep Daniels
     Bartender Wental, Food & Drinks
     Gloria Femmel, Cooking Supplies
     Sherman Femmel, Butcher

15a   LAKESHIRE INN, UPPER LEVEL
     Franklin Hamar, Tailoring Supplies
     Wiley the Black

16   Gerald Crawley, Poison Supplier

17   Erin
     Madison
     Guard Adams

18   Henry Chapal, Gunsmith

19   Chef Breanna
     Crystal Boughman, Cooking Trainer

19a   UPPER LEVEL
     Gretchen Vogel, Waitress

20   Alma Jainrose, Herbalism Trainer
     Hannah

21   Martie Jainrose

22   Bellygrub

23   Vernon Hale, Bait and Tackle Supplier

24   Matthew Hooper, Fishing Trainer
     Zem Leeward

25   Shawn
     Hilary

26   Jamin
     Roger

27   Arantir
     Lucius

28   Rachel
     Nathan

29   Submerged Tool Box

REDRIDGE MOUNTAINS page 62

LIGHT'S HOPE CHAPEL

LIGHT'S HOPE CHAPEL

1 Georgia, Bat Handler

2 Jase Farlane, Trade Supplies

3 Smokie LaRue
Campfire

4 Leonid Barthomew the Revered, The
Argent Dawn

5 Lord Maxwell Tyrosus, The Argent
Dawn

6 Khaelyn Steelwing, Grpyhon Master

7 Betina Bigglezink, The Argent Dawn
Duke Nicholas Zverenhoff, The
Argent Dawn
Carlin Redpath, The Argent Dawn

8 Quartermaster Miranda Breechlock,
The Argent Dawn

EASTERN PLAGUELANDS page 40

MARSHAL'S REFUGE

1 Karna Remtravel

2 Shizzle

3 Quixxil

4 Muigin

5 Spraggle Frock

6 Nurgle, General Goods Vendor

7 Dadanga
Petra Grossen

8 Williden Marshal
Gibbert, Weapon Merchant

9 Linken

10 Larion

11 Spark Nilminer

12 J.D. Collie

UN'GORO CRATER page 90

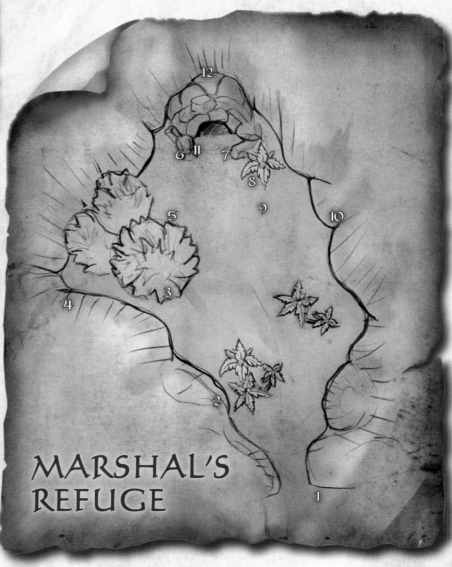

MARSHAL'S REFUGE

MENETHIL HARBOR

1 Shellei Brondir, Grpyhon Master
2 Adam Lind
3 Bart Tidewater
4 Karl Boran
   Harold Riggs, Fishing Trainer
   Stuart Fleming, Fisherman
5 Don Pompa
6 Falkan Armonis, Reagent Vendor
7 Telurinon Moonshadow, Herbalism Trainer

8 Dewin Shimmerdawn, Alchemy Supplies
9 Jennabink Powerseam, Tailoring Supplies &
   Specialty Goods (Upstairs)
10 James Halloran
11 Andrea Halloran
   Regina Halloran
   Jesse Halloran
12 Thomas Booker
   Unger Statford, Horse Breeder

13 MENETHIL KEEP
   Valstag Ironjaw
13a Neal Allen, Engineering & General Goods
   Supplier
13b Red Jack Flint
   Murphy West
   Timothy Clark (Upstairs)
   Captain Stoutfist (Upstairs)
14 Harlo Barnaby
15 Tarrel Rockweaver
16 Naela Trance, Bowyer
   Edwina Monzor, Fletcher
17 Gruham Rumdnul, General Supplies
   Derina Rumdnul
   Gimlok Rumdnul
18 Sida
19 Caitlin Grassman
20 Brahnmar, Armorer
   Brak Durnad, Weaponsmith
   Murndan Derth, Gunsmith
   Forge
   Anvil
21 First Mate Fitzsimmons
   Mailbox
22 Bethaine Flinthammer, Stable Master
23 DEEPWATER TAVERN
   Tapoke "Slim" Jahn
   Junder Brokk
   Vincent Hyal
   Glorin Steelbrow
   Hargin Mundar
   Kersok Prond, Tradesman
   Mikhail, Bartender
   Innkeeper Helbrek, Innkeeper
   Cozy Fire
   Samor Festivus, Shady Dealer (Upstairs)
   Archaeologist Flagongut, Explorer's League
     (Upstairs)
   Fremal Doohickey, First Aid Trainer
     (Upstairs)

WETLANDS page 96

MENETHIL HARBOR

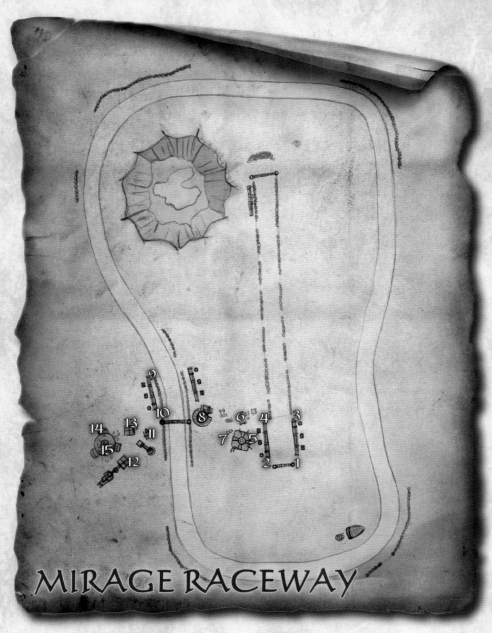

MIRAGE RACEWAY

1. Trackmaster Zherin
2. Zuzebee, Race Announcer
3. Drag Master Miglen
4. Riznek, Drink Vendor
5. Synge, Gun Merchant
6. Razzeric
   Pozzic
7. Zamek
   Dixie, Race Starter Girl
8. Fobeed, Race Announcer
   Race Master Kronkrider
9. Quentin
10. Magus Tirth
11. Wizzle Brassbolts
    Fizzle Brassbolts
12. Jinky Twizzlefixxit, Engineering
    Supplies
13. Kravel Koalbeard
14. Brivelthwerp, Ice Cream Vendor
15. Rizzle Brassbolts

THOUSAND NEEDLES page 82

MIRAGE RACEWAY

MORGAN'S VIGIL

1. Gabrielle Chase, Food & Drink
2. Borgus Stoutarm, Gryphon Master
3. Campfire
4. Felder Stover, Weaponsmith
5. Oralius
6. Marshal Maxwell
   Mayara Brightwing
7. Helendis Riverhorn
8. Jalinda Sprig

BURNING STEPPES page 22

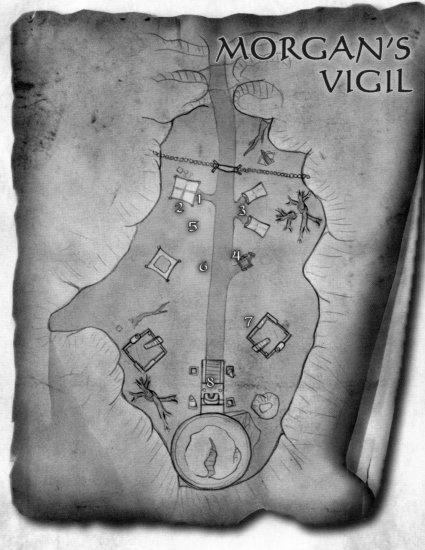

MORGAN'S VIGIL

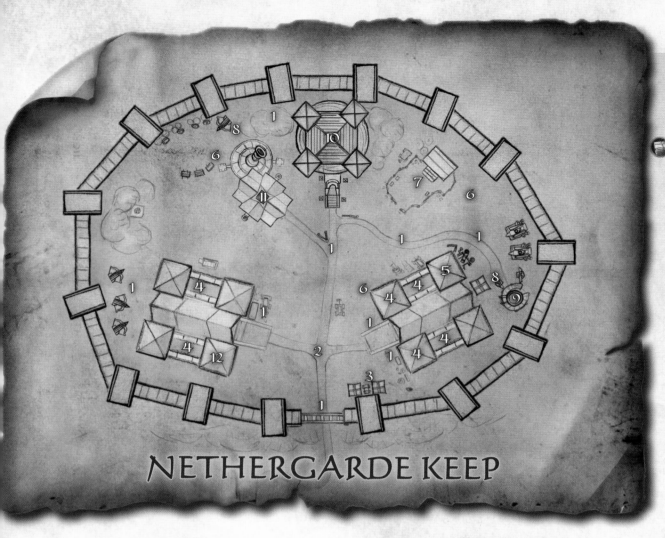

NETHERGARDE KEEP

1   Nethergarde Soldier
      Nethergarde Cleric
      Nethergarde Riftwatcher

2   Mailbox

3   Enohar Thunderbrew

4   Nethergarde Elite

5   Potbelly Stove

6   Nethergarde Officer

7   Quartermaster Lungertz

8   Nethergarde Analyst

9   Alexandra Constantine, Gryphon
      Master

10   Nethergarde Elite
      Watcher Mahar Ba (Upstairs)
      Ambassador Ardalan (Upstairs)
      Thadius Grimshade (Upstairs)
      Nina Lightbrew, Alchemy Supplies
       (Upstairs)

11   Strumner Flintheel, Armor Crafter
      Forge
      Anvil

12   Bernie Heisten, Food & Drink

BLASTED LANDS page 20

NIJEL'S POINT

1   Mailbox

2   Shelgrayn, Stable Master

3   Janet Hommers, Food & Drink
      Innkeeper Lishaerya, Innkeeper

4   Christi Galvanis, General Goods

5   Brother Anton, Scarlet Crusade
      Emissary

6   Keeper Marandis

7   Baritanas Skyriver, Hippogryph
      Master

8   Kreldig Ungor, Reclaimers Inc.

9   Maxton Strang, Mail Armor Merchant
      Forge
      Anvil

10   Talendria
      Cooking Brazier

11   Moonwell

12   Captain Pentigast
      Corporal Melkins

13   Vahlarriel Demonslayer

DESOLACE page 30

NIGHTHAVEN

NIGHTHAVEN

1   SHRINE OF REMULOS
    Keeper Remulos

2   My'lanna, Food and Drink Merchant
    Daeolyn Summerleaf, General Goods
    Umber

3   Bessany Plainswind

4   Darnall, Tailoring Supplies
    Geenia Sunshadow, Specialty Dress
      Maker
    Mylentha Riverbend

5   Celes Earthborne

6   Kharedon, Light Armor Merchant
    Dendrite Starblaze

7   Dargon, Food and Drink Merchant
    Lorelae Wintersong, Trade Supplies

8   Loganaar, Druid Trainer

9   Meliri, Weaponsmith
    Narianna, Bowyer
    Moren Riverbend
    Rabine Saturna

10 Malvor, Herbalist

11 Bunthen Plainswind, Thunder Bluff
      Flight Master
    Silva Fil'naveth, Darnassus Flight
      Master

MOONGLADE page 56

NORTHSHIRE VALLEY

NORTHSHIRE VALLEY

1   Deputy Willem

2   Janos Hammerknuckle,
      Weaponsmith
    Merissa Stilwell

3   Brother Danil, General Supplies
    Dermot Johns, Cloth & Leather
      Armor Merchant
    Godric Rothgar, Armorer &
      Shieldcrafter

4   NORTHSHIRE ABBEY
    Marshall McBride

4a HALL OF ARMS
    Llane Bashere, Warrior Trainer
    Brother Sammuel, Paladin Trainer

4b LIBRARY WING
    Brother Paxton, Librarian
    Priestess Anetta, Priest Trainer
    Khelden Bremen, Mage Trainer
      (Upstairs)

4c MAIN HALL
    Brother Neals (Upstairs)

5   Young Wolf

6   Eagan Peltskinner

7   ECHO RIDGE MINE
    Kobold Worker
    Kobold Laborer

8   Kobold Worker

9   Kobold Worker
    Kobold Vermin
    Timber Wolf
    Campfire

10 Milly Osworth

11 Timber Wolf

12 Falkhaan Isenstrider

13 Defias Thug

14 NORTHSHIRE VINYARDS
    Defias Thug
    Milly's Harvest

14a Defias Thug
    Garrick Padfoot

ELWYNN FOREST page 42

RATCHET

1 Graveyard

2 Anvil and Forge

3 Jorb, Lizzarik's Bodyguard
Lizzarik, Weapon Dealer

4 JAZZIK'S GENERAL GOODS
Ranik, Trade Supplies
Jazzik, General Supplies

5 BROKEN KEEL INN
Reggifuz, Stable Master
Zizzek, Fisherman
Innkeeper Wiley, Innkeeper
Stoves, Cooking Fire
Mailbox

6 Captain Thalo'thas Brightsun

7 PLATE-N-CHAIN
Brewmaster Drohn
Grazlix, Armorer and Shieldcrafter
Vexspindle, Cloth and Leather
Merchant

8 Liv Rizzlefix, Workshop Assistant
Archimonde's Return and the
Flight to Kalimdor, Book

9 Klixx, Fisherman

10 Wharfmaster Dizzywig
Grimble, Shipmaster

11 Crane Operator Bigglefuzz

12 IRONZAR'S IMPORTED
WEAPONRY
Ironzar
Mebok Mizzyrix
Anvil
Forge

13 BANK
Fuzruckle, Banker
Zikkel, Banker
Wanted Poster: Baron Longshore

14 Sputtervalve

15 Wrenix the Wretched
Wrenix's Gizmotronic Apparatus

16 Vazario Linkgrease, Master Goblin
Engineer
Tinkerwiz, Journeyman Engineer
Gagsprocket, Engineering Goods
Gazlowe
Charge of the Dragonflights, Book

17 Strahad Farsan
Manara Voidrender
Acolyte Fenrick
Acolyte Wytula
Acolyte Magaz

BARRENS page 18

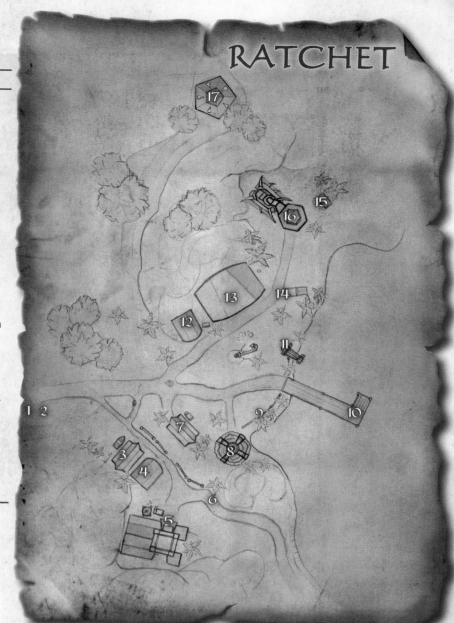

RATCHET

RAVEN HILL

RAVEN HILL

1 Jitters

2 Bliztik, Alchemy Supplies

3 Destroyed Inn

4 Food Crate Spawn Point

5 Empty Household

DUSKWOOD page 36

RAVEN HILL CEMETERY

1   Skeletal Horrors
2   Carrion Recluses
3   Grave Robbers
4   DAWNING WOODS CATACOMBS, WESTERN
    Skeletal Raiders
    Skeletal Healers
    Skeletal Warriors
    Skeletal Warders
5   FORLORN ROWE
    Morbent Fel
    Plague Spreaders
    Skeletal Raiders
    Skeletal Waders
    Brain Eaters
    Anvil
6   Gravesite, Mor'Ladim
7   Rotten Ones
    Flesh Eaters
8   DAWNING WOODS CATACOMBS, EASTERN
    Plague Spreaders
    Brain Eaters
    Bone Chewers
9   Abercrombie, The Hermit
10 Gravesite, Embalmer's Wife
11 Mor'Ladim Patrol Area

DUSKWOOD page 36

RAVEN HILL CEMETERY

RAZOR HILL

1   Takrin Pathseeker
2   Furl Scornbrow
3   Grimtak, Butcher
    Cook Torka
4   Shola'my, Stable Master
    Innkeeper Grosk, Innkeeper
    Yelnagi Blackarm
    Blazing Fire
5   Orgnil Soulscar
    Kaplak, Rogue Trainer
    Harruk, Pet Trainer
    Thotar, Hunter Trainer
    Gar'Throk
6   Wuark, Armorer and Shieldcrafter
    Krunn, Miner
    Dwukk, Journeyman Blacksmith
    Mukdrak, Journeyman Engineer
    Uhgar, Weaponsmith
    Anvil
    Forge

7   Ghrawt, Bowyer
    Cutac, Cloth and Leather Armor Merchant
8   Dhugru Gorelust, Warlock Trainer
    Ophek
    Kitha, Demon Trainer
9   RAZOR HILL BARRACKS
    Rawrk, First Aid Trainer
    Jark, General Goods
    Swart, Shaman Trainer
    Tai'jin, Priest Trainer
    Tarshaw Jaggedscar, Warrior Trainer
    Fierce Blaze

DUROTAR page 34

RAZOR HILL

SEN'JIN VILLAGE

1   Miao'zan, Journeyman Alchemist

2   Hai'zan, Butcher
     Smoking Rack

3   Vel'rin Fang

4   Master Vornal
     Master Gadrin

5   Ula'elek
     Kali Remik
     Forge

6   Tal'tasi, Trade Supplies
     K'wail, General Goods
     Trayexir, Weapon Merchant
     Zansoa, Fishing Supplies

7   Un'Thuwa, Mage Trainer

8   Bom'bay, Witch Doctor in Training

9   Mishiki, Herbalist

10   Zjolnir, Raptor Handler
     Xar'Ti, Raptor Riding Trainer

11   Lar Prowltusk, Patroller

DUROTAR page 34

SEN'JIN VILLAGE

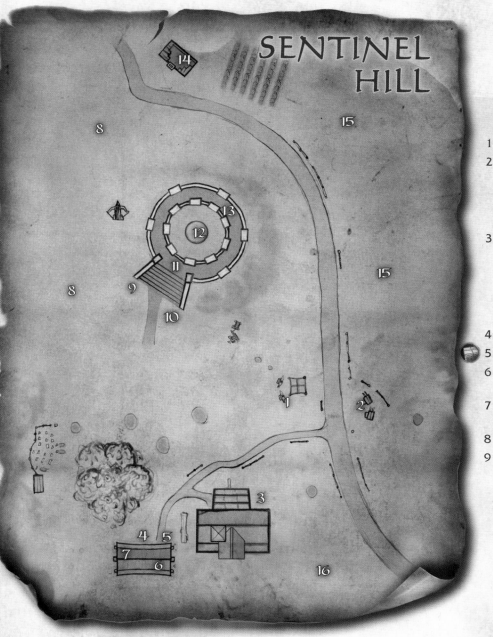

SENTINEL HILL

SENTINEL HILL

1   Thor, Gryphon Master

2   Mike Miller, Bread Merchant
     William MacGregor, Bowyer
     Gina MacGregor, Trade
       Supplies
     Campfire

3   Protector Deni, The People's
       Militia
     Protector Leick, The People's
       Militia
     Forge
     Anvil

4   Kirk Maxwell, Stable Master

5   Mailbox

6   Innkeeper Heather,
       Innkeeper

7   Christopher Hewen, General
       Trade Goods Vendor

8   Young Goretusk

9   Protector Bialon, The
       People's Militia
     The Defias Traitor

10   Protector Gariel, The
       People's Militia

11   Gryan Stoutmantle, The
       People's Militia
     Captain Danuvin, The
       People's Militia

12   SENTINEL TOWER
     Quartermaster Lewis,
       Quartermaster
     Scout Riell, The People's
       Milita (Upstairs)
     Protector Weaver, The
       People's Militia (Upstairs)

13   Protector Dutfield, The
       People's Militia

14   Fleshripper

15   Great Goretusk
     Greater Fleshripper

16   Goretusk

WESTFALL page 94

123

THE SEPULCHER

1. Karos Razok, Bat Handler
2. Nadia Vernon, Bowyer
3. Andrea Boynton, Clothier
   Alexandre Lefevre, Leather Armor
     Merchant
4. Dalar Dawnweaver
   Gwyn Farrow, Mushroom Merchant
   Edwin Harly, General Supplies
5. Shadow Priest Allister
6. Apothecary Renferrel
7. Sarah Goode, Stable Master
   Innkeeper Bates
   Deathguard Podrig
   Mailbox
8. Andrew Hilbert, Trade Goods
   Johan Focht, Miner
   High Executor Hadrec
   Sebastian Meloche, Armorer
   Guillaume Sorouy, Journeyman
     Blacksmith
9. Mura Runetotem
   Patrice Dwyer, Poison Supplies
10. Yuriv's Tombstone

SILVERPINE FOREST page 68

THE SEPULCHER

SHADOWGLEN

1. Conservator Ilthalaine
   Orenthil Whisperwind
2. Tarindrella
3. Young Nightsabre
   Young Thistle Boar
4. ALDRASSIL
   Melithar Staghelm
4a. Keina, Bowyer
4b. Dellylah, Food & Drink Vendor
4c. Andiss, Armorer & Shieldcrafter
     (Bottom Floor)
   Khardan Proudblade, Weaponsmith
     (Bottom Floor)
   Freja Nightwing, Leather Armor Merchant
     (Bottom Floor)
   Mardant Strongoak, Druid Trainer
     (Middle Floor)
   Ayanna Everstride, Hunter Trainer
     (Middle Floor)
   Tenaron Stormgrip (Top Floor)
4d. Alyissia, Warrior Trainer
   Frahun Shadewhisper, Rogue Trainer
4e. Gilshalan Windwalker
5. Thistle Boar
   Mangy Nightsabre
6. Dirania Silvershine
   Cauldron
7. Moonwell
8. Webwood Spider
9. Iverron
10. Githyiss the Vile
   Webwood Spider
11. Thistle Boar
   Grellkin
12. Grell
13. Porthannius

TELDRASSIL page 80

SHADOWGLEN

SHADOWPREY VILLAGE

SHADOWPREY VILLAGE

1   Thalon, Wind Rider Master
2   Jinar'Zillen
3   Lui'Mala, Fisherman
    Mai'Lahii, Fishing Supplies
4   Lah'Mawhani, Trade Supplies
5   Drulzegar Skraghook
    Meat Smoker
6   Malux, Skinning Trainer
    Vark Battlescar (Top Level)
7   Roon Wildmane
    Tukk, General Goods Vendor
8   Anvil
    Forge
9   Hae'Wilani, Axecrafter
10   Wulan, Cooking Supplies
11   Aboda, Stable Master
    Mailbox
12   Innkeeper Sikewa, Innkeeper
13   Taiga Wiseman

DESOLACE page 30

SOUTHSHORE

1   Darla Harris, Gryphon Master
2   Caretaker Smithers
3   Hecular's Grave
4   Darren Malvew, Stablehand
5   Merideth Carlson, Horse Breeder
6   Farmer Kent
7   Robert Aebischer, Superior
    Armorsmith
    Forge
    Anvil
8   Nandar Branson, Alchemy Supplies
    Apprentice Honeywell
9   Loremaster Dibbs
10   Phin Odelic
    Wesley, Stable Master
    Mailbox
11   Neema, Waitress
    Innkeeper Anderson
    Jaysen Lanyda (Upstairs)
12   Lieutenant Farren Orinelle
    Barkeep Kelly, Bartender
    Hemmit Armstrong (Upstairs)
    Tamara Armstrong (Upstairs)

13   Chef Jessen
    Brewmeister Bilger (Basement)
    Raleigh the Devout (Upstairs)
14   Donald Rabonne, Fisherman
    Lindea Rabonne, Tackle and Bait
15   Hal McAllister, Fish Merchant
16   Torn Fin Tidehunter
    Torn Fin Oracle
17   Daggerspine Siren
    Daggerspine Shorehunter
18   Marshal Redpath
19   SOUTHSHORE TOWN HALL
    Kundric Zanden, Town Historian
19a   Magistrate Henry Maleb
20   Bront Coldcleave, Butcher
21   Bartollo Ginsetti
22   Micha Yance, Trade Goods
    Cozy Fire
23   Sarah Raycroft, General Goods
    (Upstairs)

HILLSBRAD FOOTHILLS page 48

SOUTHSHORE

SPLINTERTREE POST

SPLINTERTREE POST

1 Ertog Ragetusk
2 Framnali
3 Vhulgra, Wind Rider Master
4 Pixel
5 Fahrak
6 Har'alen
7 Loruk Foreststrider
8 Mastok Wrilehiss
9 Burkrum, Heavy Armor Merchant
10 Innkeeper Kaylisk
11 Vera Nightshade
12 Yama Snowhoof
13 Mailbox
14 Senani Thunderheart

ASHENVALE page 12

STONARD

1 Breyk, Wind Rider Master
2 Hekkru, Stable Master
  Mailbox
3 Innkeeper Karakul
  Bengor
  Malosh, Warrior Trainer
  Dar
  Rartar, Alchemy Supplies
  Banalash, Trade Goods
4 Zun'dartha
5 Grunt Zuul
  Grunt Tharlak
  Infiltrator Marksen
6 Thultazor, Arcane Goods Vendor
7 Thralosh, Cloth & Leather Armor
    Merchant
  Gharash, Blacksmithing Supplies
  Grimnal, Mail & Plate Merchant
  Hartash, Weapon Merchant
  Forge

SWAMP OF SORROWS page 76

8 Ogromm, Hunter Trainer
  Grokor, Pet Trainer
9 Greshka, Demon Master
  Kartosh, Warlock Trainer
  Rogvar, Master Alchemist

9a UPPER LEVEL
   Helgrum the Swift
   Dispatch Commander Ruag
   Fel'zerul
10 Haromm, Shaman Trainer
11 Thultash, Food & Drink Vendor

STONARD

STROMGARDE KEEP

STROMGARDE KEEP

1. Syndicate Conjuror
   Voidwalker Minion
   Syndicate Prowler
   Syndicate Magus

2. Marez Cowl

3. Stromgarde Defender

4. Boulderfist Mauler

5. Stromgarde Troll Hunter
   Stromgarde Vindicator

6. Stromgarde Vindicator

7. Deneb Walker, Scrolls & Potions

8. CRYPT
   Caretaker Nevlin
   Caretaker Alaric
   Caretaker Weston

9. Witherbark Berserker

10. Boulderfist Shaman
    Boulderfist Mauler
    Boulderfist Lord

11. Or'Kalar
    Boulderfist Shaman

12. TOWER OF ARATHOR
    Boulderfist Shaman
    Boulderfist Lord

13. Syndicate Prowler
    Syndicate Conjuror
    Voidwalker Minion

14. Syndicate Prowler
    Syndicate Conjuror
    Voidwalker Minion
    Otto (Upstairs)
    Lord Falconcrest (Upstairs)

ARATHI HIGHLANDS page 10

SUN ROCK RETREAT

SUN ROCK RETREAT

1. Tharm, Wind Rider Master

2. Borand, Bowyer
   Kulwia, Trade Supplies

3. Grawnal, General Goods
   Krond, Butcher
   Forge

4. Tammra Windfield

5. Hgarth, Artisan Enchanter

6. Braelyn Firehand

7. Maggran Earthbinder

8. Gereck, Stable Master
   Mailbox

9. Innkeeper Jayka
   Jeeda, Apprentice Witch Doctor

STONETALON MOUNTAINS page 70

TARREN MILL

HILLSBRAD FOOTHILLS PG 48

TARREN MILL

THELSAMAR

1   Thorgrum Borrelson, Gryphon Master
2   Mountaineer Roghan
3   Mountaineer Stenn
4   Mountaineer Kadrell
5   Lina Hearthstove, Stable Master
    Mailbox
6   STOUTLAGER INN
    Innkeeper Hearthstove, Innkeeper
    Drac Roughcut, Tradesman
    Yanni Stoutheart, General Supplies
    Vidra Hearthstove
    Dwarven Fire
    Honni Goldenoat, Baker

7   Mountaineer Ozmok
8   Morhan Coppertongue, Metalsmith
9   Forge
    Anvil
10 Mountaineer Langarr
11 Magistrate Bluntnose
12 Mountaineer Kamdar
13 Mountaineer Gwarth
14 Vrok Blunderblast, Gunsmith
15 Dakk Blunderblast
16 Mountaineer Modax

17 Wanted Poster: Chok'sul
18 Karm Ironquill, Mining Supplies
    Jern Ironhelm, Explorer's League
    Brock Stoneseeker, Mining Trainer
    Torren Squarejaw, Explorer's League
19 Rann Flamespinner, Tailoring Supplies
20 Bailor Stonehand
21 Kali Healtouch, Herbalist
22 Ghak Healtouch, Journeyman Alchemist

LOCH MODAN page 54

THELSAMAR

THERAMORE

1   Decedra Willham
2   Privateer Groy
3   Theramore Lieutenant
4   Charity Mipsy, General Goods
5   Baldruc, Gryphon Master
6   Jensen Farran, Bowyer
7   Guard Lasiter
8   Helenia Olden, Trade Supplies
9   Timothy Worthington, Master Tailor
10   Gregor MacVince, Horse Breeder
11   Caz Twosprocket
     Hans Weston, Armorer & Shieldsmith
     Marie Holdston, Weaponsmith
12   Alchemist Narett, Expert Alchemist
     Brant Jasperbloom, Herbalist
     Uma Bartulm, Herbalism & Alchemy
        Supplies
13   Pained
     Lady Jaina Proudmoore, Ruler of Theramore
     Archmage Tervosh

14   Michael, Stable Master
     Mailbox
15   Guard Byron
     Smiling Jim
16   Feora Longears
     Morgan Stern
     Innkeeper Janene, Innkeeper
     Bartender Lillian, Bartender
     Craig Nollword, Cook
     Cozy Fire
17   Ingo Woolybush, Explorers' League
     Sara Pierce
     Amie Pierce
     Dahne Pierce
     Mikal Pierce
18   Brother Karman, Paladin Trainer
19   Spot
20   FOOTHOLD CITADEL
     Dwane Wertle, Chef
21   FOOTHOLD CITADEL
     Potbelly Stove

22   FOOTHOLD CITADEL
     Doctor Gustaf VanHowzen, Trauma Surgeon
23   FOOTHOLD CITADEL
     Piter Verance, Weaponsmith & Armorer
     Torq Ironblast, Gunsmith
24   FOOTHOLD CITADEL
     Theramore Lieutenant
     Adjutant Tesoran
     Captain Garran Vimes
     Commander Samaul
     Captain Evencane, Warrior Trainer
     Clerk Lendry

DUSTWALLOW MARSH page 38

THERAMORE

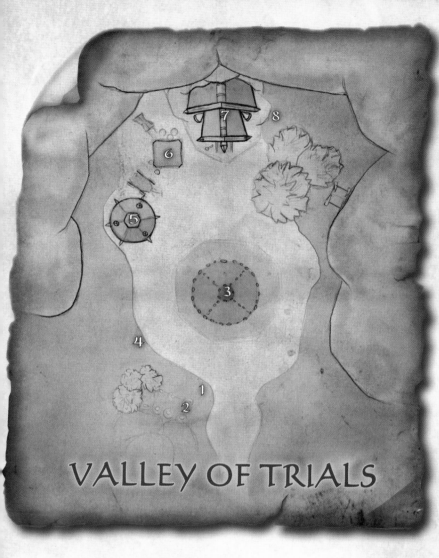

VALLEY OF TRIALS

1   Foreman Thazz'nil
2   Lazy Peon
3   Kaltunk
    Fire
4   Graveyard
5   Magga
    Frang, Warrior Trainer
    Jen'shan, Hunter Trainer
    Zureetha Fargaze
6   Ruzan
    Mai'ah, Mage Trainer
    Shikrik, Shaman Trainer
    Ken'jai, Priest Trainer
    Canaga Earthcaller

7   THE DEN
    Gornek
    Rwag, Rogue Trainer
    Huklah, Cloth and Leather Armor
        Merchant
    Rarc, Armorer and Shieldcrafter
    Kzan Thornslash, Weaponsmith
    Hraug, Demon Trainer
    Nartok, Warlock Trainer
    Crude Brazier
8   Duokna, General Goods
    Ziagk, Butcher
    Galgar
    Cooking Table

DUROTAR page 34

ZORAM'GAR OUTPOST

1   Talen
2   Andruk, Wind Rider Master
3   Warsong Rider
4   Muglash
5   Karang Amakkar
6   Marukai
    Mitsuwa
7   Je'neu Sancrea
8   Wik'Tar, Fish Merchant and
        Supplies
9   Kil'Hiwana, Fisherman

ASHENVALE page 12

ZORAM STRAND

1   Blackfathom Deeps Entrance
2   Hydra Island
3   Statue (Near Boat)
4   Talen
5   Zoram'gar Outpost
    Andruk, Wind Rider Master
    Muglash
    Karang Amakkar
    Marukai
    Mitsuwa
    Je'neu Sancrea
    Wik'Tar, Fish Merchant and Supplies
    Kil'Hiwana, Fisherman

ASHENVALE page 12

#

7:XT
Rare Spawn, Badlands (16), A-8, B-7, C-8, D:(5, 7), H-8, I-7, Camp Boff, Camp Cagg, The Dustbowl, Mirage Flats, Lvl 41 Very Rare; Roams small area around spawn point

A

A TORMENTED VOICE
Burning Steppes (22), H-2, On top of hill along northern border

AAYNDIA FLORALWIND
Expert Leatherworker, Ashenvale (12), E-5, Astranaar (101), Left as you enter southwest building

ABE WINTERS
Apprentice Armorer, Tirisfal Glades (86), H-5, Brill (104), Smithy

ABERCROMBIE
Duskwood (36), C-3, Raven Hill Cemetery (122), Shed northeast of Cemetery

ABIGAIL SAWYER
Bow Merchant, Undercity (88), H-4, The War Quarter

ABIGAIL SHIEL
Trade Supplies, Tirisfal Glades (86), H-5, Brill (104), Caravan between inn and town hall

ABODA
Stable Master, Desolace (30), C-7, Shadowprey Village (125), Front of inn

ABOMINATION
Eastern Plaguelands (40), D-6, E:(5, 6), F-5, K-4, The Fungal Vale

ACCURSED SLITHERBLADE
Rare Spawn, Desolace (30), C-2, D:(1-2), E-1, Sar'theris Strand, Lvl 35 Average Rare; Swims area between Ranzajar Isle and shore

ACHELLIOS THE BANISHED
Rare Spawn, Thousand Needles (82), B:(3-4), C-4, Whitereach Post, Lvl 31 Uncommon; Circles a couple plateaus in southwestern region

ACIDIC SWAMP OOZE
Dustwallow Marsh (38), F:(4-6), G:(5, 6), Beezil's Wreck, The Quagmire

ACOLYTE DELLIS
Stormwind (72), F-6, The Canals, Building South of Stockade

ACOLYTE FENRICK
Barrens (18), H-3, Ratchet (121), Tower in eastern hills

ACOLYTE MAGAZ
Barrens (18), H-3, Ratchet (121), Tower in eastern hills

ACOLYTE PORENA
Stormwind (72), D-8, Mage Quarter, The Slaughtered Lamb

ACOLYTE WYTULA
Barrens (18), H-3, Ratchet (121), Tower in eastern hills

ADAIR GILROY
Librarian, Stormwind (72), F-6, The Canals, Building South of Stockade

ADAM
Stormwind (72), Roams city

ADAM LIND
Wetlands (96), A-6, Baradin Bay, Southern dock

ADDLED LEPER
Dun Morogh (32), C-4, Gnomeregan

ADELE FIELDER
Journeyman Leatherworker, Elwynn Forest (42), F-6, Goldshire (112), House facing Crystal Lake

ADJUTANT TESORAN
Dustwallow Marsh (38), I-5, Theramore Isle (130), 2nd floor of Foothold Citadel

ADLIN PRIDEDRIFT
General Supplies, Dun Morogh (32), D-7, Coldridge Valley (106), By caravan

ADOLESCENT WHELP
Swamp of Sorrows (76), A:(5, 6), B:(5, 6), Itharius's Cave, Southwest lake

ADON
Eastern Plaguelands (40), H-2, At roadblock

ADRIAN BARTLETT
Undercity (88), K-1, The Magic Quarter, Green circle west of Skull Building

ADULT PLAINSTRIDER
Mulgore (58), C-3, D:(3-8), E:(3-7), F:(3-7), G:(4-7), H:(5, 6)

ADVISOR BELGRUM
Ironforge (52), K-1, Hall of Explorers, Library

AEAN SWIFTRIVER
Alliance Outrunner, Barrens (18), F-8, Southern Barrens, Spawns at border to Dustwallow Marsh and travels north to Lushwater Oasis

AEDIS BROM
Stormwind (72), K-4, Old Town, Roamer - Stops at Pig and Whistle Tavern

AELTHALYSTE
Priest Trainer, Undercity (88), G-2, The War Quarter, Outside Skull Building

AEOLYNN
Clothier, Ashenvale (12), E-5, Astranaar (101), Building to northwest of town

AETHALAS
Warsong Gulch Battlemaster, Darnassus (26), H-3, Warrior's Terrace, Lower northwest platform

AFFRAY CHALLENGER
Barrens (18), H-5, I-5, Fray Island

AFFRAY SPECTATOR
Barrens (18), H-5, I-5, Fray Island

AGAL
Teldrassil (80), F-5, Ban'ethil Hollow, Den south of the road

AGAM'AR
Barrens (18), E-9, Razorfen Kraul

AGATHELOS THE RAGING
Barrens (18), E-9, Razorfen Kraul

AGED KODO
Desolace (30), F:(1, 2, 5, 6), G:(1, 6, 9), H-9, J-6

AGENT KEARNEN
Westfall (94), H-7, The Dust Plains, Stealthed in the shade

AGERON KARGAL
Tirisfal Glades (86), H-5, Brill (104), Second floor of Gallows' End Tavern

AGGEM THORNCURSE
Barrens (18), E-9, Razorfen Kraul

AGNAR BEASTAMER
The Hinterlands (50), B-4, Aerie Peak (100), Wildhammer Keep

AG'TOR BLOODFIST
Azshara (14), B-5, Valormok

AGUSTUS MOULAINE
Mail Armor Merchant, Stormwind (72), F-4, Cathedral Square, Righteous Plates

AHANU
Leather Armor Merchant, Thunder Bluff (84), E-6, Lower rise, in Hewa's Armory

AINETHIL
Artisan Alchemist, Darnassus (26), G-2, Craftsmen's Terrace, Alchemy shop

AIR SPIRIT
Thousand Needles (82), H-5, Windbreak Canyon

AJECK ROUACK
Stranglethorn Vale (74), C-1, Nesingwary's Expedition, Camp

AKKRILUS
Rare Spawn, Ashenvale (12), C-6, D-6, Fire Scar Shrine, Lvl 26 Average Rare; Close to northern entrance to Fire Scar Shrine

AKUBAR THE SEER
Rare Spawn, Blasted Lands (20), G-5, H-5, I-5, Dark Portal, Lvl 54 Uncommon; Roams small area around spawn point

AKU'MAI
Ashenvale (12), B-2, Blackfathom Deeps

AKU'MAI FISHER
Ashenvale (12), B-2, Blackfathom Deeps

AKU'MAI SERVANT
Ashenvale (12), B-2, Blackfathom Deeps

AKU'MAI SNAPJAW
Ashenvale (12), B-2, Blackfathom Deeps

AK'ZELOTH
Barrens (18), H-2, Far Watch Post, Foot of Tower

ALAINDIA
Reagent Vendor, Darnassus (26), F-7, The Temple Gardens, Moves between front of temple to small building to the northwest

ALAMAR GRIMM
Warlock Trainer, Dun Morogh (32), D-7, Coldridge Valley (106), Anvilmar

ALANNA RAVENEYE
Journeyman Enchanter, Teldrassil (80), D-3, The Oracle Glade, Hill at end of road

ALANNDARIAN NIGHTSONG
Darkshore (24), F-4, Auberdine (101), Center of northern building

ALARM-A-BOMB 2600
Dun Morogh (32), C-4, Gnomeregan

ALASSIN
Stable Master, Darnassus (26), E-1, Cenarion Enclave, Northeast structure

ALCHEMIST ARBINGTON
Western Plaguelands (92), E-8, Chillwind Camp, In front of crate in camp

ALCHEMIST MALLORY
Journeyman Alchemist, Elwynn Forest (42), E-5, Secluded house on hill

ALCHEMIST NARETT
Expert Alchemist, Dustwallow Marsh (38), H-5, Theramore Isle (130), Hut in west corner

ALCHEMIST PESTLEZUGG
Alchemy Supplies, Tanaris (78), G-3, Gadgetzan (111), Northwestern hut

ALDIA
General Supplies, Teldrassil (80), G-6, Dolanaar (109), Middle floor inside building north of road

ALDREN CORDON
Clothier, Loch Modan (54), I-7, Ironband's Excavation Site, Camp outside of excavation site

ALDRIC MOORE
Mail Armor Merchant, Stormwind (72), H:(5, 6), Trade District, Lionheart Armory

ALDWIN LAUGHLIN
Guild Master, Stormwind (72), H-7, I-7, Trade District, Stormwind Visitor's Center

ALEGORN
Cooking Trainer, Darnassus (26), F-2, Craftsmen's Terrace, Cooking shop

ALENNDAAR LAPIDAAR
Hunter Trainer, Ashenvale (12), C-6, Shrine of Aessina, Hidden in a camp near mountains in far southwest of region

ALEXANDER CALDER
Warlock Trainer, Ironforge (52), G-1, The Forlorn Cavern, Building to the right of Traveling Fisherman

ALEXANDRA BLAZEN
Azshara (14), H-9, The Ruined Reaches, Inlet

ALEXANDRA BOLERO
Tailoring Supplies, Stormwind (72), G-7, Mage Quarter, Duncan's Textiles

ALEXANDRA CONSTANTINE
Gryphon Master, Blasted Lands (20), J-2, Nethergarde Keep (119), Rear right of keep

ALEXANDRE LEFEVRE
Leather Armor Merchant, Silverpine Forest (68), G-4, The Sepulcher (124), House on right side of sepulcher

ALEXI BAROV
House of Barov, Tirisfal Glades (86), K-7, The Bulwark, Camp on right side of road

ALEXIA IRONKNIFE
Western Plaguelands (92), E-8, Chillwind Camp, By fire in camp

ALGERNON
Alchemy Supplies, Undercity (88), G-7, The Apothecarium, Near Royal Quarter entry

ALIGAR THE TORMENTOR
Ashenvale (12), D-2, Spawns on road near Darkshore border

ALINA
Alterac Mountains (8), B-8, Lordamere Internment Camp, Building inside camp walls

ALLAN HAFGAN
Staves Merchant, Stormwind (72), F:(6, 7), Mage Quarter, Stormwind Staves

ALLESANDRO LUCA
Blue Moon Odds and Ends, Undercity (88), H-5, The Apothecarium

ALLYNDIA
Food & Drink Vendor, Darkshore (24), F-4, Auberdine (101), First floor of inn

ALMA JAINROSE
Herbalism Trainer, Redridge Mountains (62), B-4, Lakeshire (115), Roams inside small house on southwestern side of town

ALOWICIOUS CZERVIK
Sweet Treats, Orgrimmar (60), E-7, Valley of Strength

ALSHIRR BANEBREATH
Rare Spawn, Felwood (44), F-8, Jadefire Glen, Lvl 54 Uncommon; Roams Jadefire Glen

AL'TABIM THE ALL-SEEING
Stranglethorn Vale (74), A-2, Yojamba Isle

ALTAR OF SUNTARA
Searing Gorge (64), E-3, The Slag Pit, Lower level of the northernmost region of pit

ALTSOBA RAGETOTEM
Weapon Merchant, Felwood (44), E-5, Bloodvenom Post, Tent

ALYISSIA
Warrior Trainer, Teldrassil (80), H-4, Shadowglen (124), In northeast room inside main building

ALYSSA BLAYE
Undercity (88), F-3, The War Quarter, Platform in front of Skull Building

ALYSSA EVA
Reagent Vendor, Duskwood (36), K-4, Darkshire (108), First floor of house

ALYSSA GRIFFITH
Bag Vendor, Stormwind (72), J-5, Old Town, The Protective Hide

ALZZIN THE WILDSHAPER
Feralas (46), G-4, Dire Maul

ALZZIN'S MINION
Feralas (46), G-4, Dire Maul

AMAN
Wetlands (96), A-6, Deepwater Tavern, (Summon) Spawns second floor of inn

AMBASSADOR ARDALAN
Blasted Lands (20), J-2, Nethergarde Keep (119), Top floor of tower facing entrance of keep

AMBASSADOR BERRYBUCK
Council of Darkshire, Duskwood (36), J-5, Darkshire (108), Darkshire Town Hall

AMBASSADOR BLOODRAGE
Rare Spawn, Barrens (18), F-9, Razorfen Downs, Lvl 36 Semi-Rare; Spawns in/near huts

AMBASSADOR FLAMELASH
Burning Steppes (22), Searing Gorge (64), C-4/D-8, Blackrock Depths

AMBASSADOR INFERNUS
Badlands (16), F-3, Angor Fortress, Basement of fortress

AMBASSADOR MALCIN
Barrens (18), F-9, Razorfen Downs, Huts in hills

AMBEREYE BASILISK
Desolace (30), D-5, Mauradon

AMBEREYE REAVER
Desolace (30), D-5, Mauradon

AMBERSHARD CRUSHER
Desolace (30), D-5, Mauradon

AMBERSHARD DESTROYER
Desolace (30), D-5, Mauradon

A-ME 01
Un'Goro Crater (90), I-2, Fungal Rock, Southern section of the cave

AMIE PIERCE
Dustwallow Marsh (38), I-5, Theramore Isle (130), 2nd floor of inn

AMNENNAR THE COLDBRINGER
Barrens (18), F-9, Razorfen Downs

AMY DAVENPORT
Tradeswoman, Redridge Mountains (62), C-5, Lakeshire (115), Roams around of caravan in front of Lakeshire Town Hall

ANA'THEK THE CRUEL
Skullsplitter Chief, Stranglethorn Vale (74), E-5, Ruins of Zul'Mamwe, Patrols with a Skullsplitter Berserker and Skullsplitter Spiritchaser between cave and ruins

ANADYIA
Robe Vendor, Darnassus (26), G-9, Tradesmen's Terrace, Robe shop

ANASTASIA HARTWELL
Mage Trainer, Undercity (88), L-1, The Magic Quarter, Northwest corner of Skull Building

ANATHEMUS
Rare Spawn, Badlands (16), C-7, Lvl 45 Uncommon; Patrols large radius around entire region

ANAYA DAWNRUNNER
Darkshore (24), F-6, G-6, Ameth'Aran, Roams southern part of Ameth'Aran

ANCESTRAL SPIRIT
Mulgore (58), H-2, Red Rocks, On hill within burial ground

ANCIENT CORE HOUND
Burning Steppes (22), Searing Gorge (64), C-4/D-8, The Molten Core

ANCIENT EQUINE SPIRIT
Feralas (46), G-4, Dire Maul

ANCIENT KODO
Desolace (30), F:(5, 6), G-6, Ghost Walker Post (111), Kodo Graveyard

ANCIENT OF LORE
Darnassus (26), F-1, G-1, Craftsmen's Terrace, Northwest of First Aid

ANCIENT OF WAR
Darnassus (26), L:(3, 4), I-4, Warrior's Terrace, South of path

ANCIENT STONE KEEPER
Badlands (16), G-1, Uldaman

ANDER GERMAINE
Warrior Trainer, Stormwind (72), L-5, Old Town, Command Center

ANDI
Stormwind (72), Roams city with Miss Danna

ANDI LYNN
Tanaris (78), H-3, Gadgetzan (111), Northeast corner of town near fire

ANDISS
Armorer & Shieldcrafter, Teldrassil (80), G-4, H-4, Shadowglen (124), Inside main building

ANDORHAL TOWER FOUR
Western Plaguelands (92), F-7, Ruins of Andorhal, Southeastern tower ruins

ANDORHAL TOWER ONE
Western Plaguelands (92), E-7, Ruins of Andorhal, Southwestern tower ruins

ANDORHAL TOWER THREE
Western Plaguelands (92), F-6, Ruins of Andorhal, Central northern tower ruins

ANDORHAL TOWER TWO
Western Plaguelands (92), E-6, Ruins of Andorhal, Northwestern tower ruins

ANDRE FIREBEARD
Tanaris (78), K-5, Lost Rigger Cove, Center of fort

ANDREA BOYNTON
Clothier, Silverpine Forest (68), G-4, The Sepulcher (124), House on right side of sepulcher

ANDREA HALLORAN
Wetlands (96), A-5, Menethil Harbor (117), Roams in and out of house west of keep

ANDREW BROWNELL
Undercity (88), J-3, The Magic Quarter, Stall next to Tailors

ANDREW HARTWELL
Undercity (88), G-2, The War Quarter, Watches fights in War Quarter

ANDREW HILBERT
Trade Goods, Silverpine Forest (68), F-4, The Sepulcher (124), Basement of inn

ANDREW KRIGHTON
Armorer & Shieldcrafter, Elwynn Forest (42), E-7, Goldshire (112), Smithy

ANDROD FADRAN
Leatherworking Supplies, Arathi Highlands (10), F-5, Refuge Point, Roams camp south of Gryphon Master

ANDROL OAKHAND
Fisherman, Teldrassil (80), G-9, Rut'theran Village, By dock

ANDRON GANT
Undercity (88), H:(7, 8), The Apothecarium

ANDRUK
Wind Rider Master, Ashenvale (12), B-4, Zoram'gar Outpost (131)

ANDRUS
Staff Merchant, Darnassus (26), G-9, Tradesmen's Terrace, Staff shop

ANDUIN WRYNN
King of Stormwind, Stormwind (72), L-2, Stormwind Keep, Center of east wing

ANGELA CURTHAS
Warrior Trainer, Undercity (88), G-1, The War Quarter, In Skull Building

ANGELAS MOONBREEZE
Feralas (46), C-4, Feathermoon Stronghold (110), Southeast building

ANGER'REL
Burning Steppes (22), Searing Gorge (64), C-4/D-8, Blackrock Depths

ANGERCLAW BEAR
Felwood (44), E:(7, 8), F:(7, 8), G:(7-9), H:(8, 9)

ANGERCLAW GRIZZLY
Felwood (44), G:(2, 3), H:(1-3), I-2, Irontree Woods, Talonbranch Glade

ANGERCLAW MAULER
Felwood (44), E:(3-6), F:(2, 3, 6, 7), G:(2, 4)

ANGERED INFERNAL
Azshara (14), G-3, Thalassian Base Camp, Near Magus Rimtori

ANGRUN
Superior Herbalist, Stranglethorn Vale (74), C-3, Grom'gol Base Camp (112), Next to cauldron on the northern side of camp

ANGUISHED DEAD
Tirisfal Glades (86), K-3, L-3, Scarlet Monastery

ANGUISHED HIGHBORNE
Winterspring (98), H:(4, 5), Lake Kel'Theril

ANGUS STERN
Head Chef, Stormwind (72), F-9, Mage Quarter, The Blue Recluse

ANILIA
Ashenvale (12), J-4, Xavian, Dryad lying on ground in middle of camp

ANISHAR
Rogue Trainer, Darnassus (26), E-2, Cenarion Enclave, Den, bottom of ramp

ANNORA
Master Enchanter, Badlands (16), G-1, Uldaman

ANSEKHWA
Weapon Master, Thunder Bluff (84), D-6, Lower rise, Trains: 1H Mace, 2H Mace, Staves, & Guns

ANTARIUS
Stable Master, Feralas (46), C-4, Feathermoon Stronghold (110), East side of inn

ANTILOS
Rare Spawn, Azshara (14), A-5, I-2, Legashi Encampment, Lvl 50 Very Rare; Roams south from first spawnpoint and around second

ANTILUS THE SOARER
Feralas (46), C-4, Feathermoon Stronghold (110), Southwest building

ANTLERED COURSER
Stonetalon Mountains (70), D:(1, 2), E:(1, 2), F:(2-4), G:(3, 4), Mirkfallon Lake, Stonetalon Peak

ANTONIO PERELLI
Traveling Salesman, Westfall (94), G-6, Spawns at the intersection south of Sentinel Hill and travels along the road to Darkshire and on to Lakeshire

ANTUR FALLOW
Mulgore (58), D-8, Red Cloud Mesa, Along road leading from Camp Narache

ANTU'SUL
Tanaris (78), E-1, Zul'Farrak

ANUB'SHIAH
Burning Steppes (22), Searing Gorge (64), C-4/D-8, Blackrock Depths

ANUBISATH
Silithus (66), D-5, E-5

ANVILRAGE CAPTAIN
Burning Steppes (22), Searing Gorge (64), C-4/D-8, Blackrock Depths

ANVILRAGE FOOTMAN
Burning Steppes (22), Searing Gorge (64), C-4/D-8, Blackrock Depths

ANVILRAGE GUARDSMAN
Burning Steppes (22), Searing Gorge (64), C-4/D-8, Blackrock Depths

ANVILRAGE MARSHAL
Burning Steppes (22), Searing Gorge (64), C-4/D-8, Blackrock Depths

ANVILRAGE MEDIC
Burning Steppes (22), Searing Gorge (64), C-4/D-8, Blackrock Depths

ANVILRAGE OFFICER
Burning Steppes (22), Searing Gorge (64), C-4/D-8, Blackrock Depths

ANVILRAGE OVERSEER
Burning Steppes (22), Searing Gorge (64), C-4/D-8, Blackrock Depths

ANVILRAGE RESERVIST
Burning Steppes (22), Searing Gorge (64), C-4/D-8, Blackrock Depths

ANVILRAGE SOLDIER
Burning Steppes (22), Searing Gorge (64), C-4/D-8, Blackrock Depths

ANVILRAGE WARDEN
Burning Steppes (22), Searing Gorge (64), C-4/D-8, Blackrock Depths

ANYA MAULRAY
Stable Master, Undercity (88), I-4, The Trade Quarter, Upper Ring of Trade Quarter

APOTHECARY BERARD
Silverpine Forest (68), F-7, Pyrewood Village, Second floor of inn

APOTHECARY DITHERS
Tirisfal Glades (86), K-7, The Bulwark, Camp on left side of road

APOTHECARY DITHERS
Western Plaguelands (92), C-6, The Bulwark

APOTHECARY FALTHIS
Rare Spawn, Ashenvale (12), D-3, Bathran's Haunt, Lvl 22 Uncommon; Within haunt to the east

APOTHECARY FAUSTIN
Duskwood (36), L-3, Beggar's Haunt, Left side of tower by entrance

APOTHECARY HELBRIM
Barrens (18), F-3, The Crossroads (107), West of inn

APOTHECARY JOHAAN
Royal Apothecary Society, Tirisfal Glades (86), H-5, Brill (104), House on the right side of road

APOTHECARY JORELL
Arathi Highlands (10), H-6, Go'Shek Farm, First house on left side of farm

APOTHECARY KATRINA
Undercity (88), G-6, The Apothecarium, Roams Apothecarium and Canals

APOTHECARY KEEVER
Royal Apothecary Society, Undercity (88), G-7, The Apothecarium, In laboratory

APOTHECARY LYCANUS
Royal Apothecary Society, Undercity (88), G-6, The Apothecarium, Roams Apothecarium

APOTHECARY LYDON
Royal Apothecary Society, Hillsbrad Foothills (48), G-2, Tarren Mill (128), House on the left

APOTHECARY RENFERREL
Royal Apothecary Society, Silverpine Forest (68), F-4, The Sepulcher (124), Right side of inn under scaffolding

APOTHECARY VALLIA
Undercity (88), G-6, The Apothecarium, Roams Apothecarium, Trade Quarter

APOTHECARY ZAMAH
Thunder Bluff (84), C-3, Spirit Rise, The Pools of Vision

APOTHECARY ZINGE
Royal Apothecary Society, Undercity (88), G-7, The Apothecarium, In laboratory

APPRENTICE HONEYWELL
Hillsbrad Foothills (48), F:(5, 6), Southshore (125)

APPRENTICE KRYTEN
Arathi Highlands (10), F-5, Refuge Point, Camp

AQUEMENTAS
Tanaris (78), J-5, Lost Rigger Cove, (Summon) Near circle of stones southwest of fort

ARADOS THE DAMNED
Hillsbrad Foothills (48), A-8, Purgation Isle, In front of tower

ARAGA
Rare Spawn, Alterac Mountains (8), D:(7, 8), E-9, Dalaran, Sofera's Naze, The Headland, Lvl 35 Average Rare; Roams small area around spawn point

ARAJ THE SUMMONER
Western Plaguelands (92), F-7, Ruins of Andorhal, Idle with multiple mobs in the center of city

ARANAE VENOMBLOOD
Herbalist, Hillsbrad Foothills (48), G-2, Tarren Mill (128), Outside of the house on the left

ARANTIR
The Hand of Chaos, Redridge Mountains (62), C-5, Lakeshire (115), L shaped dock west of the bridge

ARASH-ETHIS
Rare Spawn, Feralas (46), D-2, E-2, The Twin Colossals, Lvl 49 Uncommon; Patrols area west of road near mountains

ARATHANDRIS SILVERSKY
Emerald Circle, Felwood (44), G-8, Morlos'Aran, North of road

ARCANE ABERRATION
Feralas (46), G-4, Dire Maul

ARCANE CHIMAEROK
Feralas (46), B:(7, 8), C:(7-9), Isle of Dread

ARCANE FEEDBACK
Feralas (46), G-4, Dire Maul

ARCANE NULLIFIER X-21
Dun Morogh (32), C-4, Gnomeregan

ARCANE TORRENT
Feralas (46), G-4, Dire Maul

ARCANIST DOAN
Tirisfal Glades (86), K-3, L-3, Scarlet Monastery

ARCH DRUID FANDRAL STAGHELM
Boss, Darnassus (26), D-1, Cenarion Enclave, Northwest structure, upper level

ARCH DRUID HAMUUL RUNETOTEM
Thunder Bluff (84), J-3, Elder Rise, Inside Hall of Elders

ARCHAEDAS
Badlands (16), G-1, Uldaman

ARCHAEOLOGIST FLAGONGUT
Explorers' League, Wetlands (96), A-6, Deepwater Tavern, Northeast, upstairs room

ARCHAEOLOGIST HOLLEE
Explorer's League, Darkshore (24), F-4, Auberdine (101), In front of northern building

ARCHBISHOP BENEDICTUS
Boss, Stormwind (72), F-3, Cathedral Square, Cathedral of Light

ARCHIBALD
Weapon Master, Undercity (88), H-3, The War Quarter, Trains: Crossbows, Daggers, 1H Sword, 2H Sword, & Polearms

ARCHIBALD KAVA
Cloth and Leather Armor Merchant, Tirisfal Glades (86), D-6, Deathknell (109), First floor of second house on right side of road

ARCHIVIST GALFORD
Eastern Plaguelands (40), D-2, Stratholme

ARCHMAGE ALLISTARJ
Blasted Lands (20), J-3, Serpent's Coil, Cave interior

ARCHMAGE ANSIREM RUNEWEAVER
Alterac Mountains (8), B-8, Dalaran, Road just north of Lordamere Internment Camp

ARCHMAGE ARUGAL
Silverpine Forest (68), F-7, Shadowfang Keep

ARCHMAGE ATAERIC
Silverpine Forest (68), I-6, Ambermill, Town hall

ARCHMAGE MALIN
Stormwind (72), F-8, Mage Quarter, Next to Tower

ARCHMAGE SHYMM
Mage Trainer, Thunder Bluff (84), C-3, Spirit Rise, The Pools of Vision

ARCHMAGE TEVROSH
Dustwallow Marsh (38), I-5, Theramore Isle (130), Top of central tower

ARCHMAGE XYLEM
Azshara (14), C-4, Bear's Head, Requires quest from Sanath Lim-yo to reach

ARDO DIRTPAW
Redridge Mountains (62), B-2, Rethban Cavern, Idle with several Redridge gnolls in cave

ARDWYN CAILEN
Wand Merchant, Stormwind (72), F:(6, 7), Mage Quarter, Stormwind Staves

AREI
Felwood (44), G-3, Irontree Woods, (Summon) Spawns in Irontree Woods and walks to Ashenvale

ARENA SPECTATOR
Burning Steppes (22), Searing Gorge (64), C-4/D-8, Blackrock Depths

ARGENT DEFENDER
Western Plaguelands (92), C-5, E-8, F-8, Chillwind Camp

ARGENT GUARD
Eastern Plaguelands (40), K-6, Light's Hope Chapel (116)

ARGENT GUARD MANADOS
The Argent Dawn, Darnassus (26), G-2, Craftsmen's Terrace, Argent Dawn

ARGENT GUARD THAELRID
Ashenvale (12), B-2, Blackfathom Deeps

ARGENT OFFICER GARUSH
The Argent Dawn, Tirisfal Glades (86), K-7, The Bulwark, Camp on left side of road

ARGENT OFFICER PUREHEART
The Argent Dawn, Western Plaguelands (92), F-8, Chillwind Camp, With two Argent Defenders in front of tent

ARGENT QUARTERMASTER HASANA
Western Plaguelands (92), C-5, The Bulwark

ARGENT QUARTERMASTER LIGHTSPARK
The Argent Dawn, Western Plaguelands (92), E-8, Chillwind Camp, By lumber pile

ARGENT RIDER
Eastern Plaguelands (40), K-6, Light's Hope Chapel (116)

ARGOS NIGHTWHISPER
Stormwind (72), C-6, The Park, By pool of water

ARIAS'TA BLADESINGER
Warrior Trainer, Darnassus (26), H-3, Warrior's Terrace, Lower northwest platform

ARIENA STORMFEATHER
Gryphon Master, Redridge Mountains (62), D-6, Left of bridge heading into Lakeshire

ARIKARA
Thousand Needles (82), E-4, Darkcloud Pinnacle, Atop small plateau east of water

ARIN'SOR
Ravasaur Trainers, Un'Goro Crater (90), D-2, Hill in far northwestern section of crater

ARIYELL SKYSHADOW
Weapon Merchant, Darnassus (26), H-4, Warrior's Terrace, Lower southwest platform

ARKKORAN CLACKER
Azshara (14), I-4, J:(3-5), K:(3, 4), Temple of Arkkoran

ARKKORAN MUCKDWELLER
Azshara (14), I-4, J:(3-5), K:(3, 4), Temple of Arkkoran

ARKKORAN ORACLE
Azshara (14), I-4, J:(3-5), K-4, Temple of Arkkoran

ARKKORAN PINCER
Azshara (14), I-4, J:(3-5), K-4, Temple of Arkkoran

ARMAND CROMWELL
Fishing Trainer, Undercity (88), K-3, The Magic Quarter, On Dock

ARMORED SCORPID
Durotar (34), E:(3, 4), F:(3-5), G:(2-5), H:(2-4), I:(2, 3)

ARNAK GRIMTOTEM
Thousand Needles (82), E-3, Darkcloud Pinnacle, On northern cliff, north of Darkcloud Pinnacle

ARNOK
First Aid Trainer, Orgrimmar (60), C-8, Valley of Spirit, Survival of the Fittest (near Spirit Lodge)

ARNOLD LELAND
Fishing Trainer, Stormwind (72), G-6, The Canals, Dock

ARRA'CHEA
Mulgore (58), F-2, The Golden Plains, Roams plains

ARTHUR MOORE
Expert Leatherworker, Undercity (88), I-6, The Rogues' Quarter

ARTHUR THE FAITHFUL
Paladin Trainer, Stormwind (72), F-3, Cathedral Square, Cathedral of Light

ARTILLERYMAN SHELDONORE
Ironforge (52), B-5, The Commons, The Stonefire Tavern

ARTIST RENFRAY
Western Plaguelands (92), I-7, Caer Darrow, Ghost In house by the docks

ARTORIUS THE AMIABLE
Winterspring (98), I-1, Roams northwest of grove

ARUGAL'S VOIDWALKER
Silverpine Forest (68), F-7, Shadowfang Keep

ASHENVALE BEAR
Ashenvale (12), D:(4, 5), E:(3-7), F:(4, 7), G:(4-6), H:(5, 7, 8), I:(7, 8)

ASHENVALE OUTRUNNER
Ashenvale (12), I-7, J:(6, 7), Nightsong Woods, Dor'Danil Barrow Den

ASHENVALE SENTINEL
Ashenvale (12), H-6, Nightsong Woods, Raynewood Retreat

ASHLAN STONESMIRK
Wetlands (96), G-2, Dun Modr, Next to wagons, west of road

ASKA MISTRUNNER
Cooking Trainer, Thunder Bluff (84), F-5, High rise, inside Aska's Kitchen tent

ASORAN
General Goods Vendor, Orgrimmar (60), E-4, Valley of Wisdom, Asoran's Market

ASPECT OF BANALITY
Western Plaguelands (92), I-7, Scholomance

ASPECT OF CORRUPTION
Western Plaguelands (92), I-7, Scholomance

ASPECT OF MALICE
Western Plaguelands (92), I-7, Scholomance

ASPECT OF SHADOW
Western Plaguelands (92), I-7, Scholomance

ASTAIA
Fishing Trainer, Darnassus (26), F-5, Tradesmen's Terrace, Dock

ASTARII STARSEEKER
Priest Trainer, Darnassus (26), E-8, The Temple Gardens, Balcony, north of fountain

ASTERION
Darkshore (24), G-4, Bashal'Aran, In blue-light lined structure

ASTOR HADREN
Silverpine Forest (68), G-4, Patrols between the road just east of The Sepulcher and the Gallows' End Tavern in Brill

ASTRANAAR SENTINEL
Ashenvale (12), D-5, E-5, F-6, Astranaar (101), Silverwind Refuge

ATAL'AI CORPSE EATER
Swamp of Sorrows (76), I-5, The Temple of Atal'Hakkar

ATAL'AI DEATHWALKER
Swamp of Sorrows (76), I-5, The Temple of Atal'Hakkar

ATAL'AI DEATHWALKER'S SPIRIT
Swamp of Sorrows (76), I-5, The Temple of Atal'Hakkar

ATAL'AI EXILE
The Hinterlands (50), E-7, Shadra'Alor, Lower left portion of temple

ATAL'AI HIGH PRIEST
Swamp of Sorrows (76), I-5, The Temple of Atal'Hakkar

ATAL'AI PRIEST
Swamp of Sorrows (76), I-5, The Temple of Atal'Hakkar

ATAL'AI SKELETON
Swamp of Sorrows (76), I-5, The Temple of Atal'Hakkar

ATAL'AI SLAVE
Swamp of Sorrows (76), I-5, The Temple of Atal'Hakkar

ATAL'AI WARRIOR
Swamp of Sorrows (76), I-5, The Temple of Atal'Hakkar

ATAL'AI WITCH DOCTOR
Swamp of Sorrows (76), I-5, The Temple of Atal'Hakkar

ATAL'ALARION
Swamp of Sorrows (76), I-5, The Temple of Atal'Hakkar

ATEPU
Banker, Thunder Bluff (84), E-6, Thunder Bluff Bank

ATHRIDAS BEARMANTLE
Teldrassil (80), G-6, Dolanaar (109), Outside building north of road

ATHRIKUS NARASSIN
Darkshore (24), H-3, Tower of Althalaxx, Top of tower

ATURK THE ANVIL
Orgrimmar (60), J-2, Valley of Honor, Next to the Burning Anvil

AUBERDINE SENTINEL
Darkshore (24), E:(4, 5), F:(4, 5), Auberdine (101), Mist's Edge, The Long Wash

AUCTIONEER BEARDO
Auctioneer, Tanaris (78), H-3, Gadgetzan (111), Auction House

AUCTIONEER BUCKLER
Auctioneer, Ironforge (52), C-7, The Commons, Auction House

AUCTIONEER GRIMFUL
Auctioneer, Orgrimmar (60), G-6, Valley of Strength, Auction House

AUCTIONEER GRIZZLIN
Auctioneer, Orgrimmar (60), G-6, Valley of Strength, Auction House

AUCTIONEER KRESKY
Auctioneer, Orgrimmar (60), G-6, Valley of Strength, Auction House

AUCTIONEER LYMPKIN
Auctioneer, Ironforge (52), C-7, The Commons, Auction House

AUCTIONEER REDMUSE
Auctioneer, Ironforge (52), C-7, The Commons, Auction House

AUCTIONEER THATHUNG
Auctioneer, Orgrimmar (60), G-6, Valley of Strength, Auction House

AUCTIONEER WABANG
Auctioneer, Orgrimmar (60), G-6, Valley of Strength, Auction House

AUGUSTUS THE TOUCHED
Eastern Plaguelands (40), B-3, Terrorweb Tunnel, Cave along western border

AULD STONESPIRE
Thunder Bluff (84), C-6, Lower rise, inside tent near elevators

"AUNTIE" BERNICE STONEFIELD
Elwynn Forest (42), D-8, The Stonefield Farm, Next to well

AURIUS
Eastern Plaguelands (40), D-2, Stratholme

AURORA SKYCALLER
Eastern Plaguelands (40), H-3, Northpass Tower, Tower

AUSTIL DE MON
Warrior Trainer, Tirisfal Glades (86), H-5, Brill (104), First floor of Gallows' End Tavern

AVALANCHION
World Boss, Azshara (14), J-2, Bitter Reaches, Roams northern peninsula

AVATAR OF HAKKAR
Swamp of Sorrows (76), I-5, The Temple of Atal'Hakkar

AVETTE FELLWOOD
Bowyer, Duskwood (36), J-4, Darkshire (108), Near carriages outside and left of the Scarlet Raven Inn

AWBIE
Burning Steppes (22), Searing Gorge (64), C-4/D-8, Blackrock Spire

AWENASA
Stable Master, Thousand Needles (82), F-5, Freewind Post, Outside Inn

AXTROZ
Wetlands (96), K-5, Dragonmaw Gates, Patrols path

AYANNA EVERSTRIDE
Hunter Trainer, Teldrassil (80), G-4, Shadowglen (124), First room off of ramp up tree

AZAR STRONGHAMMER
Paladin Trainer, Dun Morogh (32), F-5, Kharanos (114), Thunderbrew Distillery

AZJ'TORDIN
Feralas (46), J-4, Lariss Pavilion, In temple, northeast of Camp Mojache

AZORE ALDAMORT
The Argent Dawn, Desolace (30), E-3, Ethel Rethor, Temple ruins overlooking sea

AZSHARA SENTINEL
Azshara (14), A-8, Talrendis Point

AZSHIR THE SLEEPLESS
Tirisfal Glades (86), K-3, L-3, Scarlet Monastery

AZUREGOS
Azshara (14), H-9, Roams the central area of the southern landmass

AZUROUS
Rare Spawn, Winterspring (98), J-5, Ice Thistle Hills, Lvl 59 Average Rare; Wanders west of road

AZZERE THE SKYBLADE
Rare Spawn, Barrens (18), E-6, Southern Barrens, Lvl 25 Uncommon; Patrols area south of Camp Taurajo

AZZLEBY
Stable Master, Winterspring (98), I-4, Everlook (110), Outside of Everlook's entrance

B

BAEL'GAR
Burning Steppes (22), Searing Gorge (64), C-4/D-8, Blackrock Depths

BAEL'DUN APPRAISER
Mulgore (58), C-5, Bael'dun Digsite

BAEL'DUN DIGGER
Mulgore (58), C-5, D-5, Bael'dun Digsite

BAEL'DUN EXCAVATOR
Barrens (18), E-8, F:(8, 9), Bael Modan

BAEL'DUN FOREMAN
Barrens (18), E-8, Bael Modan

BAEL'DUN OFFICER
Barrens (18), F-8, Bael Modan

BAEL'DUN RIFLEMAN
Barrens (18), F-8, Bael Modan

BAEL'DUN SOLDIER
Barrens (18), F-8, Bael Modan

BAELOG
Badlands (16), G-1, Uldaman

BAILEY STONEMANTLE
Banker, Ironforge (52), E-6, The Commons, Vault of Ironforge

BAILIFF CONACHER
Redridge Mountains (62), C-4, Lakeshire (115), Lakeshire Town Hall

BAILOR STONEHAND
Loch Modan (54), D-4, Thelsamar (129), Third house left of the path

BAINE BLOODHOOF
Mulgore (58), E-6, Bloodhoof Village (102), Center of village

BAKER MASTERSON
Western Plaguelands (92), I-8, Caer Darrow, House inside city walls just right of entrance

BALAI LOK'WEIN
Potions, Scrolls and Reagents, Dustwallow Marsh (38), D-3, Brackenwall Village (104), Northern part of village

BALDRUC
Gryphon Master, Dustwallow Marsh (38), I-5, Theramore Isle (130), Southeast near docks

BALE
General Goods, Felwood (44), E-5, Bloodvenom Post, Tent

BALGARAS THE FOUL
Wetlands (96), F-2, H:(2, 3), I-3, Dun Modr, Direforge Hill, Spawns in a building at Dun Modr or in northwest camp in Direforge Hill

BALIR FROSTHAMMER
Dun Morogh (32), D-7, Coldridge Valley (106), By fence

BALIZAR THE UMBRAGE
Ashenvale (12), D-2, Spawns on road near Darkshore border

BALNAZZAR
Eastern Plaguelands (40), D-2, Stratholme

BALOS JACKEN
Dustwallow Marsh (38), D-5, Lost Point, Landing in tower

BALTHULE SHADOWSTRIKE
Darkshore (24), H-2, South of road, near a rock west of tower

BALTHUS STONEFLAYER
Skinning Trainer, Ironforge (52), E-3, The Great Forge, Finespindle's Leather Goods

BALTUS FOWLER
Warrior Trainer, Undercity (88), F-2, The War Quarter, In Skull Building

BANAL SPIRIT
Western Plaguelands (92), I-7, Scholomance

BANALASH
Trade Goods, Swamp of Sorrows (76), F-5, Stonard (126), Second floor of inn

BANNOK GRIMAXE
Burning Steppes (22), Searing Gorge (64), C-4/D-8, Blackrock Spire

BARAK KODOBANE
Barrens (18), E-2, The Forgotten Pools, Foot of structure on hill

BARBED CRUSTACEAN
Ashenvale (12), B-2, Blackfathom Deeps

BARBED LASHER
Desolace (30), D-5, Mauradon

BARDU SHARPEYE
Tirisfal Glades (86), K-7, The Bulwark, Camp on right side of road

BARDU SHARPEYE
Western Plaguelands (92), C-6, The Bulwark

BARG
General Supplies, Barrens (18), F-3, The Crossroads (107), Outside inn

BARIM JURGENSTAAD
Reagent Vendor, Ironforge (52), B-6, The Commons, Barim's Reagents

BARITANAS SKYRIVER
Cenarion Circle, Desolace (30), H-1, Nijel's Point (119), Up southwestern hill

BARITHRAS MOONSHADE
Darkshore (24), F-4, Auberdine (101), In front of inn

BARKEEP DANIELS
Redridge Mountains (62), C-4, Lakeshire (115), First floor of Lakeshire Inn

BARKEEP DOBBINS
Burning Steppes (22), Searing Gorge (64), C-4/D-8, The Molten Core

BARKEEP HANN
Bartender, Duskwood (36), J-4, Darkshire (108), Scarlet Raven Inn

BARKEEP KELLY
Bartender, Hillsbrad Foothills (48), F-6, Southshore (125), First floor of inn

BARKEEP MORAG
Orgrimmar (60), G-7, Valley of Strength, Inn

BARNABUS
Rare Spawn, Badlands (16), F-7, G-7, H:(6, 7), Agmond's End, Badlands, Mirage Flats, Lvl 38 Average Rare; Roams small area around spawn point

BARNIL STONEPOT
Stranglethorn Vale (74), C-1, Nesingwary's Expedition, Camp

BARNUM STONEMANTLE
Banker, Ironforge (52), E-6, The Commons, Vault of Ironforge

BARON AQUANIS
Ashenvale (12), B-2, Blackfathom Deeps, (Summon)

BARON CHARR
Un'Goro Crater (90), F:(4-6), G-4, G-6, H:(4-6), Fire Plume Ridge, Patrols around ridge

BARON GEDDON
Burning Steppes (22), Searing Gorge (64), C-4/D-8, The Molten Core

BARON LONGSHORE
Barrens (18), H-5, The Merchant Coast, Camps on coast

BARON REVILGAZ
Stranglethorn Vale (74), B-8, Booty Bay (103), Third floor balcony of The Salty Sailor Tavern

BARON RIVENDARE
Eastern Plaguelands (40), D-2, Stratholme

BARON SILVERLAINE
Silverpine Forest (68), F-7, Shadowfang Keep

BARON VARDUS
Alterac Mountains (8), H-4, Strahnbrad, Basement of inn

BARONESS ANASTARI
Eastern Plaguelands (40), D-2, Stratholme

BAROS ALEXSTON
City Architect, Stormwind (72), G-3, Cathedral Square, City Hall

BAROS ALEXSTON
Stormwind (72), F-6, The Stockade

BARRENS GIRAFFE
Barrens (18), D:(2, 3), E:(2-5), F:(1, 2, 4, 5), G:(1-5), H:(1-3)

BARRENS GUARD
Barrens (18), D-3, E-1, F-1, Gold Road, Honor's Stand, The Mor'shan Rampart

BARRENS KODO
Barrens (18), E:(5, 6, 8)

BART TIDEWATER
Captain of the Maiden's Virtue, Wetlands (96), A-6, Menethil Harbor (117), Roams path next to docks and along docks

BARTENDER LILLIAN
Barkeeper, Dustwallow Marsh (38), I-5, Theramore Isle (130), Inn

BARTENDER WENTAL
Food and Drinks, Redridge Mountains (62), C-4, Lakeshire (115), First floor of Lakeshire Inn

BARTLEBY
Drunk, Stormwind (72), K-4, Old Town, Roams Old Town to the Pig and Whistle Tavern

BARTOLO GINSETTI
Hillsbrad Foothills (48), F-5, Southshore (125), In front of house

BASHANA RUNETOTEM
Thunder Bluff (84), I-3, Elder Rise, Inside tent near bridge

BASIL FRYE
Journeyman Blacksmith, Undercity (88), H-3, The War Quarter

BATH'RAH THE WINDWATCHER
Alterac Mountains (8), K-7, Chillwind Point, Troll platform

BATTLE BOAR HORROR
Barrens (18), F-9, Razorfen Downs

BATTLEBOAR
Mulgore (58), F:(7, 8), G:(7-9), Brambleblade Ravine

BAYNE
Rare Spawn, Tirisfal Glades (86), E:(4, 5), F-5, G-4, Stillwater Pond, Lvl 10 Uncommon; Roams small area around spawn point

BAZIL THREDD
Stormwind (72), F-6, The Stockade

BAZZALAN
Orgrimmar (60), F-5, Ragefire Chasm

BEATEN CORPSE
Barrens (18), F-5, Southern Barrens, Hut south of ravine

BEFOULED WATER ELEMENTAL
Ashenvale (12), F:(6, 7), G:(6, 7), Mystral Lake, Silverwind Refuge

BELDIN STEELGRILL
Dun Morogh (32), G-5, Steelgrill's Depot, Outside of left building

BELDRUK DOOMBROW
Paladin Trainer, Ironforge (52), C-1, The Mystic Ward, Hall of Mysteries

BELFRY BAT
Tirisfal Glades (86), H-5, Brill (104)

BELGROM ROCKMAUL
Orgrimmar (60), I-3, J-3, Valley of Honor, Hall of the Brave

BELIA THUNDERGRANITE
Pet Trainer, Ironforge (52), J-8, The Military Ward, Hall of Arms

BELLYGRUB
Redridge Mountains (62), A-5, Roams on western side of Lake Everstill

BELNISTRASZ
Barrens (18), F-9, Razorfen Downs

BEN TRIAS
Apprentice of Cheese, Stormwind (72), I-6, Trade District, Trias' Cheese

BENA WINTERHOOF
Expert Alchemist, Thunder Bluff (84), E-3, Middle rise, inside Bena's Alchemy tent

BENGOR
Swamp of Sorrows (76), F-5, Stonard (126), First floor of inn

BENGUS DEEPFORGE
Artisan Blacksmith, Ironforge (52), G-4, The Great Forge, Next to anvils

BENIJAH FENNER
Weapon Merchant, Undercity (88), H-3, The War Quarter

BENJAMIN CAREVIN
Duskwood (36), J-5, Darkshire (108), Second floor of house

BENNY BLAANCO
Westfall (94), E-2, Furlbrow's Pumpkin Farm, In the house north of the pumpkin farm

BERA STONEHAMMER
Gryphon Master, Tanaris (78), H-3, Gadgetzan (111), South of town

BERAM SKYCHASER
Shaman Trainer, Thunder Bluff (84), B-2, Spirit Rise, Inside Hall of Spirits

BERNARD BRUBAKER
Leather Armor Merchant, Redridge Mountains (62), L-7, Camp

BERNARD GUMP
Florist, Stormwind (72), J-6, The Canals, Fragrant Flowers

BERNIE HEISTEN
Food & Drink, Blasted Lands (20), I-2, Nethergarde Keep (119), First floor of left castle

BERSERK OWLBEAST
Winterspring (98), I:(2, 6), J:(2, 6), The Hidden Grove, Owl Wing Thicket

BERSERK TROGG
Loch Modan (54), I:(6, 7), J:(6, 7), Ironband's Excavation Site

BESSANY PLAINSWIND
Moonglade (56), G-3, Nighthaven (120), North central side of town, north of moonwell

BESSELETH
Stonetalon Mountains (70), F-7, G-7, Sishir Canyon, Roams area west of path

BETHAINE FLINTHAMMER
Stable Master, Wetlands (96), A-6, Menethil Harbor (117), Outside tavern

BETHAN BLUEWATER
Feralas (46), C-4, Feathermoon Stronghold (110), Top floor of tree building in northeast

BETHOR ICESHARD
Undercity (88), L-2, The Magic Quarter, On Skull Building

BETINA BIGGLEZINK
The Argent Dawn, Eastern Plaguelands (40), K-6, Light's Hope Chapel (116), Roams camp on right side of chapel

BETTY QUIN
Journeyman Enchanter, Stormwind (72), F-6, The Canals, Shop south of stockade

BHAG'THERA
Stranglethorn Vale (74), E:(2, 3), F-2, Mosh'Ogg Ogre Mound, Roams small area around spawn point

BHALDARAN RAVENHADE
Bowyer, Ashenvale (12), G-6, Silverwind Refuge, Center of building

BIBBLY F'UTZBUCKLE
Desolace (30), H-4, Kormek's Hut, Fenced area left of hut

BIBILFAZ FEATHERWHISTLE
Gryphon Master, Western Plaguelands (92), F-8, Chillwind Camp, Just south of camp

BIG SAMRAS
Rare Spawn, Hillsbrad Foothills (48), I-3, K:(4, 5), Durnholde Keep, Lvl 27 Semi-Rare; Roams small area around spawn point

BIG WILL
Barrens (18), H-5, Fray Island, (Summon) Fighting pit

BIJOU
Burning Steppes (22), Searing Gorge (64), C-4/D-8, Blackrock Spire

BILBAN TOSSLESPANNER
Warrior Trainer, Ironforge (52), I-9, The Military Ward, Hall of Arms

BILE SLIME
Eastern Plaguelands (40), D-2, Stratholme

BILE SPEWER
Eastern Plaguelands (40), D-2, Stratholme

BILLIBUB COGSPINNER
Engineering Supplier, Stormwind (72), H-1, Dwarven District, North end of district, next to wagon

BILLY
Stormwind (72), Roams city

BILLY MACLURE
Elwynn Forest (42), F-8, The Maclure Vineyards, In front of barn

BIMBLE LONGBERRY
Fruit Vendor, Ironforge (52), E-1, C-3, The Mystic Ward, Roams the ward

BINGLES BLASTENHEIMER
Loch Modan (54), H-5, The Loch, Along the banks of the loch half way down the right side

BINGUS
Weapon Merchant, Ironforge (52), C-2, The Mystic Ward, The Fighting Wizard

BINJY FEATHERWHISTLE
Mechanostrider Pilot, Dun Morogh (32), G-5, Steelgrill's Depot, By mechanostrider's outside of depot

BINK
Mage Trainer, Ironforge (52), C-1, The Mystic Ward, Hall of Mysteries

BINNY SPRINGBLADE
Gnomeregan Exiles, Ironforge (52), F-1, The Forlorn Cavern, Stoneblade's

BISHOP DELAVEY
Stormwind (72), K-2, L-2, Stormwind Keep, East wing, in south room

BISHOP FARTHING
Stormwind (72), F-2, Cathedral Square, Cathedral of Light

BIXI WOBBLEBONK
Weapon Master, Ironforge (52), H-9, The Military Ward, Timberline Arms, Trains: Crossbows, Daggers, & Throwing Weapons

BJARN
Rare Spawn, Dun Morogh (32), G-6, H-6, I-6, The Tundrid Hills, Lvl 12 Uncommon; Roams small area around spawn point

BLACK BEAR PATRIARCH
Loch Modan (54), E-6, H-3, I:(3, 4), J-4, K-4, The Farstrider Lodge, Below Lodge

BLACK BROODLING
Burning Steppes (22), J:(3, 6), K:(2, 3, 5, 6), L:(3-6), Terror Wing Path

BLACK DRAGON WHELP
Redridge Mountains (62), B-7, C:(3, 6-8), D:(6, 7), E:(3, 7), F:(3, 4, 7, 8), G:(4, 7), H:(7, 8), I-7

BLACK DRAGONSPAWN
Burning Steppes (22), G-6, J-6, K:(3, 4), L:(4-6), The Pillar of Ash

BLACK DRAKE
Burning Steppes (22), K:(3, 6), L-4, Terror Wing Path

BLACK GUARD SENTRY
Eastern Plaguelands (40), D-2, Stratholme

BLACK GUARD SWORDSMITH
Eastern Plaguelands (40), D-2, Stratholme

BLACK OOZE
Wetlands (96), C:(5, 6), D-5, F:(2, 3), G-3, H:(3, 4), I:(4, 5)

BLACK RAVAGER
Duskwood (36), G:(5, 6), H-6, I-3, J-4, Brightwood Grove

BLACK RAVAGER MASTIFF
Duskwood (36), G:(5, 6), H-6, I:(3-4), Brightwood Grove

BLACK SLAYER
Blasted Lands (20), G-2, H-4, I:(3, 4), Dreadmaul Hold, Rise of the Defiler, Serpent's Coil

BLACK SLIME
Wetlands (96), G:(5-8), H:(6-8), I-6

BLACK WIDOW HATCHLING
Duskwood (36), C:(4, 5), D:(3-6), E:(3, 5, 6), K:(5, 6), L:(5, 6)

BLACK WYRMKIN
Burning Steppes (22), G-6, J-6, K:(3, 4), L:(4-6), Terror Wing Path

BLACKBREATH CRONY
Burning Steppes (22), Searing Gorge (64), C-4/D-8, Blackrock Depths

BLACKENED BASILISK
Stonetalon Mountains (70), D:(5, 6), E-5, F-4, The Charred Vale, Mirkfallon Lake

BLACKFATHOM MYRMIDON
Ashenvale (12), B-2, Blackfathom Deeps

BLACKFATHOM ORACLE
Ashenvale (12), B-2, Blackfathom Deeps

BLACKFATHOM SEA WITCH
Ashenvale (12), B-2, Blackfathom Deeps

BLACKFATHOM TIDE PRIESTESS
Ashenvale (12), B-2, Blackfathom Deeps

BLACKHAND ASSASSIN
Burning Steppes (22), Searing Gorge (64), C-4/D-8, Blackrock Spire

BLACKHAND DRAGON HANDLER
Burning Steppes (22), Searing Gorge (64), C-4/D-8, Blackrock Spire

BLACKHAND DREADWEAVER
Burning Steppes (22), Searing Gorge (64), C-4/D-8, Blackrock Spire

BLACKHAND ELITE
Burning Steppes (22), Searing Gorge (64), C-4/D-8, Blackrock Spire

BLACKHAND INCARCERATOR
Burning Steppes (22), Searing Gorge (64), C-4/D-8, Blackrock Spire

BLACKHAND IRON GUARD
Burning Steppes (22), Searing Gorge (64), C-4/D-8, Blackrock Spire

BLACKHAND SUMMONER
Burning Steppes (22), Searing Gorge (64), C-4/D-8, Blackrock Spire

BLACKHAND THUG
Burning Steppes (22), Searing Gorge (64), C-4/D-8, Blackrock Spire

BLACKHAND VETERAN
Burning Steppes (22), Searing Gorge (64), C-4/D-8, Blackrock Spire

BLACKLASH
Badlands (16), L-5, Lethlor Ravine, (Summon) Altar protected by Scorched Guardians

BLACKMOSS THE FETID
Rare Spawn, Teldrassil (80), E:(3-4), Wellspring River, Lvl 13 Uncommon; Patrols up and down river

BLACKROCK AMBUSHER
Burning Steppes (22), B:(2, 3), C-5, E-4, Blackrock Stronghold

BLACKROCK ASSASSIN
Redridge Mountains (62), F-4, G-4, Ilgalar

BLACKROCK BATTLEMASTER
Burning Steppes (22), D:(3, 4), E:(3, 4), Blackrock Stronghold

BLACKROCK CHAMPION
Redridge Mountains (62), D-1, Render's Rock, Cave

BLACKROCK CHAMPION
Burning Steppes (22), H:(8, 9), I:(8, 9), Blackrock Pass

BLACKROCK GLADIATOR
Redridge Mountains (62), I:(5, 6), Stonewatch Keep

BLACKROCK GRUNT
Redridge Mountains (62), E-4, F-4, H-4, I:(7, 8), J:(7, 8), Stonewatch Keep

BLACKROCK HUNTER
Redridge Mountains (62), I:(5, 6), Stonewatch Keep

BLACKROCK OUTRUNNER
Redridge Mountains (62), E:(1, 2, 4), F:(2, 4), H:(4, 7), I:(6-8), J:(6-8), K:(6, 7), Render's Rock

BLACKROCK OUTRUNNER
Burning Steppes (22), J-9

BLACKROCK RAIDER
Burning Steppes (22), B-3, E-4, Blackrock Stronghold

BLACKROCK RENEGADE
Redridge Mountains (62), E:(1, 2), F:(1, 2), H:(4, 7), I-6, J:(6, 7), K-7, Render's Camp

BLACKROCK RENEGADE
Burning Steppes (22), I-9, J-9

BLACKROCK SCOUT
Redridge Mountains (62), H:(5, 6), I:(5, 6), Stonewatch Keep

BLACKROCK SENTRY
Redridge Mountains (62), H:(5, 6), I:(5, 6), Stonewatch Keep

BLACKROCK SHADOWCASTER
Redridge Mountains (62), H-5, I:(5, 6), Stonewatch Keep

BLACKROCK SLAYER
Burning Steppes (22), B-3, D:(3-5), E:(3-6), F:(5, 6), G-5, The Pillar of Ash

BLACKROCK SOLDIER
Burning Steppes (22), B-3, D-5, E:(5, 6), F:(5, 6), G-5, The Pillar of Ash

BLACKROCK SORCERER
Burning Steppes (22), D:(3-5), E:(3-6), F:(5, 6), G-5, The Pillar of Ash

BLACKROCK SUMMONER
Redridge Mountains (62), D-1, E-1, F-1, H-4, J-8, Render's Rock, Cave

BLACKROCK SUMMONER
Burning Steppes (22), H:(8, 9), I:(8, 9), J-9, Blackrock Pass

BLACKROCK TRACKER
Redridge Mountains (62), D-1, E-1, Render's Rock, Cave

BLACKROCK TRACKER
Burning Steppes (22), H:(8, 9), I:(8, 9), J-9, Blackrock Pass

BLACKROCK WARLOCK
Burning Steppes (22), A-3, D:(3, 4), E:(3, 4), F:(5, 6), G-5, The Pillar of Ash

BLACKROCK WORG
Burning Steppes (22), B-3, D-5, E-6, F:(5, 6), G-5, The Pillar of Ash

BLACKSMITH RAND
Apprentice Armorer, Tirisfal Glades (86), D-7, Deathknell (109), First house on right side of road

BLACKSMITH VERRINGTAN
Hillsbrad Foothills (48), C-5, Hillsbrad Fields (113), Stands idle in or around smithy

BLACKWATER DECKHAND
Arathi Highlands (10), D-8, Faldir's Cove

BLACKWOOD PATHFINDER
Darkshore (24), F:(5, 6), The Long Wash, Twilight Shore, Twilight Vale

BLACKWOOD SHAMAN
Darkshore (24), F:(8, 9), G:(8, 9), Blackwood Den, The Master's Glaive, Twilight Vale

BLACKWOOD TOTEMIC
Darkshore (24), F:(8, 9), G-9, H-3

BLACKWOOD URSA
Darkshore (24), F:(8, 9), G:(8, 9), Blackwood Den, Grove of the Ancients, Twilight Vale

BLACKWOOD WARRIOR
Darkshore (24), F:(8, 9), G-3, H:(3, 4)

BLACKWOOD WINDTALKER
Darkshore (24), F:(5, 6), The Long Wash, Twilight Vale

BLAISE MONTGOMERY
Feralas (46), I-4, Camp Mojache (105), Northeast of inn

BLASTMASTER EMI SHORTFUSE
Dun Morogh (32), C-4, Gnomeregan

BLAZERUNNER
Un'Goro Crater (90), G-5, Fire Plume Ridge, West den on ridge

BLAZING ELEMENTAL
Searing Gorge (64), E:(3-5), F-5, G:(4, 5, 8), The Cauldron

BLAZING FIREGUARD
Burning Steppes (22), Searing Gorge (64), C-4/D-8, Blackrock Depths

BLAZING INVADER
Un'Goro Crater (90), F:(4-6), G:(4-6), Fire Plume Ridge

BLEAK WORG
Silverpine Forest (68), F-7, Shadowfang Keep

BLEAKHEART HELLCALLER
Ashenvale (12), J-5, K-5, Forest Song, Nightsong Woods, Satyrnaar

BLEAKHEART SATYR
Ashenvale (12), J-5, K-5, Forest Song, Nightsong Woods, Satyrnaar

BLEAKHEART SHADOWSTALKER
Ashenvale (12), J-5, Nightsong Woods, Satyrnaar, Xavian

BLEAKHEART TRICKSTER
Ashenvale (12), J-5, Nightsong Woods, Satyrnaar, Xavian

BLEEDING HORROR
Tirisfal Glades (86), J-6, K-6, Balnir Farmstead

BLIGHTED HORROR
Eastern Plaguelands (40), G-5, I:(3, 4), J-4, Blackwood Lake

BLIGHTED SURGE
Eastern Plaguelands (40), H:(7, 8), I:(7, 8), Lake Mereldar

BLIGHTED ZOMBIE
Western Plaguelands (92), F:(5, 6), Dalson's Tears

BLIGHTHOUND
Eastern Plaguelands (40), D-7, The Marris Stead

BLIMO GADGETSPRING
Trade Supplier, Azshara (14), E-9, The Ruined Reaches, Gnome tower

BLIND HUNTER
Rare Spawn, Barrens (18), E-9, Razorfen Kraul, Lvl 32 Rare

BLIND MARY
Duskwood (36), K-6, Inside house

BLINDLIGHT MUCKDWELLER
Ashenvale (12), B-2, Blackfathom Deeps

BLINDLIGHT MURLOC
Ashenvale (12), B-2, Blackfathom Deeps

BLINDLIGHT ORACLE
Ashenvale (12), B-2, Blackfathom Deeps

BLINK DRAGON
Ashenvale (12), G-5, H:(5, 7), Moonwell, Nightsong Woods, Raynewood Retreat

BLISTERPAW HYENA
Tanaris (78), E:(4, 5), F:(3-6), G:(3-6), H:(4-6), I:(4-6)

BLIXREZ GOODSTITCH
Leatherworking Supplies, Stranglethorn Vale (74), B-8, Booty Bay (103), Tan-Your-Hide Leatherworks (shop)

BLIXXRAK
Light Armor Merchant, Winterspring (98), I-4, Everlook (110), Inside northeast building

BLIZRIK BUCKSHOT
Gunsmith, Tanaris (78), G-3, Gadgetzan (111), Western structure

BLIZTIK
Alchemy Supplies Vendor, Duskwood (36), B-5, Raven Hill (121), Second floor of house

BLOOD ELF DEFENDER
Azshara (14), H-3, Thalassian Base Camp

BLOOD ELF RECLAIMER
Azshara (14), G-3, Thalassian Base Camp

BLOOD ELF SURVEYOR
Azshara (14), G-3, Thalassian Base Camp

BLOOD OF AGAMAGGAN
Barrens (18), E-9, Razorfen Kraul

B MAIN INDEX

BLOOD SEEKER
Silverpine Forest (68), F-7, Shadowfang Keep

BLOODAXE EVOKER
Burning Steppes (22), Searing Gorge (64), C-4/D-8, Blackrock Spire

BLOODAXE RAIDER
Burning Steppes (22), Searing Gorge (64), C-4/D-8, Blackrock Spire

BLOODAXE SUMMONER
Burning Steppes (22), Searing Gorge (64), C-4/D-8, Blackrock Spire

BLOODAXE VETERAN
Burning Steppes (22), Searing Gorge (64), C-4/D-8, Blackrock Spire

BLOODAXE WARMONGER
Burning Steppes (22), Searing Gorge (64), C-4/D-8, Blackrock Spire

BLOODAXE WORG
Burning Steppes (22), Searing Gorge (64), C-4/D-8, Blackrock Spire

BLOODAXE WORG PUP
Burning Steppes (22), Searing Gorge (64), C-4/D-8, Blackrock Spire

BLOODFEATHER FURY
Teldrassil (80), C-3, D-3, The Oracle Glade

BLOODFEATHER HARPY
Teldrassil (80), D:(3, 4), E-4, The Oracle Glade

BLOODFEATHER MATRIARCH
Teldrassil (80), C-3, D-3, The Oracle Glade

BLOODFEATHER ROGUE
Teldrassil (80), D:(3, 4), E-4, The Oracle Glade

BLOODFEATHER SORCERESS
Teldrassil (80), D:(3, 4), E-4, The Oracle Glade

BLOODFEATHER WIND WITCH
Teldrassil (80), C-3, D-3, The Oracle Glade

BLOODFEN LASHTAIL
Dustwallow Marsh (38), D:(6, 7), E-7, Bloodfen Burrow

BLOODFEN RAPTOR
Dustwallow Marsh (38), D:(1, 3), E:(1-3), F:(1-3), G:(1-4), H:(2-4)

BLOODFEN RAZORMAW
Dustwallow Marsh (38), D:(6, 7), E-7, Bloodfen Burrow

BLOODFEN SCREECHER
Dustwallow Marsh (38), F:(1, 2), Bluefen

BLOODFEN SCYTHECLAW
Dustwallow Marsh (38), D:(4-6), E:(3-6), F:(3-6), The Dragonmurk, Lost Point, The Quagmire

BLOODFURY AMBUSHER
Stonetalon Mountains (70), D-6, The Charred Vale

BLOODFURY HARPY
Stonetalon Mountains (70), D-6, E-5, The Charred Vale

BLOODFURY RIPPER
Stonetalon Mountains (70), C-6, The Charred Vale, Roams northwest area of Charred Vale

BLOODFURY ROGUEFEATHER
Stonetalon Mountains (70), C:(6, 7), D:(6, 7), E:(6, 7), The Charred Vale

BLOODFURY SLAYER
Stonetalon Mountains (70), C:(6, 7), D:(6, 7), E:(6, 7), The Charred Vale

BLOODFURY STORM WITCH
Stonetalon Mountains (70), C:(6, 7), D:(6, 7), E:(6, 7), The Charred Vale

BLOODFURY WINDCALLER
Stonetalon Mountains (70), D-6, The Charred Vale

BLOODHOUND
Burning Steppes (22), Searing Gorge (64), C-4/D-8, Blackrock Depths

BLOODHOUND MASTIFF
Burning Steppes (22), Searing Gorge (64), C-4/D-8, Blackrock Depths

BLOODLETTER
Eastern Plaguelands (40), E-8, Carrowshire

BLOODMAGE DRAZIAL
Blasted Lands (20), G-1, Dreadmaul Hold, Next to bonfire

BLOODMAGE LYNNORE
Blasted Lands (20), G-1, Dreadmaul Hold, Next to bonfire

BLOODMAGE THALNOS
Tirisfal Glades (86), K-3, L-3, Scarlet Monastery

BLOODPETAL FLAYER
Un'Goro Crater (90), F:(3, 4, 6, 7), G:(2-4, 6, 7), G:(2-4, 6-8), H:(2-8), I-4

BLOODPETAL LASHER
Un'Goro Crater (90), G-4, H:(3, 4), I:(2-4), J:(3-5, 7), Lakkari Tar Pits, The Marshlands

BLOODPETAL PEST
Un'Goro Crater (90), F-1, Marshal's Refuge (116)

BLOODPETAL THRESHER
Un'Goro Crater (90), G-4, H:(3, 4), I:(2-4), J:(3-5, 7), Lakkari Tar Pits, The Marshlands

BLOODPETAL TRAPPER
Un'Goro Crater (90), C:(4-7), D:(2-8), E:(2-8)

BLOODROAR THE STALKER
Feralas (46), F-6, Feral Scar Vale, In second set of caves

BLOODSAIL DECKHAND
Stranglethorn Vale (74), C-9, Wild Shore

BLOODSAIL ELDER MAGUS
Stranglethorn Vale (74), C-6, The Cape of Stranglethorn, Wild Shore

BLOODSAIL MAGE
Stranglethorn Vale (74), B-7, C:(7, 8)

BLOODSAIL RAIDER
Stranglethorn Vale (74), B-7, C:(7, 8)

BLOODSAIL SEA DOG
Stranglethorn Vale (74), C-6, The Cape of Stranglethorn, Wild Shore

BLOODSAIL SWABBY
Stranglethorn Vale (74), C-9, Wild Shore

BLOODSAIL SWASHBUCKLER
Stranglethorn Vale (74), B:(6, 8, 9), C:(8, 9)

BLOODSAIL WARLOCK
Stranglethorn Vale (74), B:(6, 8, 9), C:(8, 9)

BLOODSCALP AXE THROWER
Stranglethorn Vale (74), B-2, C-2, Bal'lal Ruins, The Savage Coast, Tkashi Ruins

BLOODSCALP BEASTMASTER
Stranglethorn Vale (74), B:(1, 2), Ruins of Zul'Kunda

BLOODSCALP BERSERKER
Stranglethorn Vale (74), A:(1, 2), B-1

BLOODSCALP HEADHUNTER
Stranglethorn Vale (74), A:(1, 2), B-1

BLOODSCALP HUNTER
Stranglethorn Vale (74), A-2, B:(1, 2), Ruins of Zul'Kunda

BLOODSCALP MYSTIC
Stranglethorn Vale (74), A-2, B:(1, 2), Ruins of Zul'Kunda

BLOODSCALP SCAVENGER
Stranglethorn Vale (74), C-2, Tkashi Ruins

BLOODSCALP SCOUT
Stranglethorn Vale (74), A-2, B:(1, 2), Ruins of Zul'Kunda

BLOODSCALP SHAMAN
Stranglethorn Vale (74), B-2, C-2, Bal'lal Ruins, The Savage Coast, Tkashi Ruins

BLOODSCALP WARRIOR
Stranglethorn Vale (74), B-2, C-2

BLOODSCALP WITCH DOCTOR
Stranglethorn Vale (74), A:(1, 2), B-1, Ruins of Zul'Kunda, Zuuldaia Ruins

BLOODSNOUT WORG
Silverpine Forest (68), G:(7, 8), H:(7, 8), The Greymane Wall

BLOODTALON SCYTHEMAW
Durotar (34), E:(2-5), F:(2-5), H:(1, 2)

BLOODTALON TAILLASHER
Durotar (34), F:(3-5), G:(2-5), H:(2-4), I:(2, 3, 7-9), J:(7-9)

BLOODTOOTH GUARD
Ashenvale (12), G-7, Bloodtooth Camp, Mystral Lake

BLOODVENOM POST BRAVE
Felwood (44), E-5, Bloodvenom Post

BLUE DRAGONSPAWN
Azshara (14), D:(7, 8), E-8, Forlorn Ridge, Lake Mennar

BLUE SCALEBANE
Azshara (14), E:(7, 8), Lake Mennar

BLUEGILL FORAGER
Wetlands (96), B:(3, 4), C-4, Bluegill Marsh

BLUEGILL MUCKDWELLER
Wetlands (96), A-3, B:(3, 4), C:(3, 4), Bluegill Marsh

BLUEGILL MURLOC
Wetlands (96), A-4, B-4, C-4, Bluegill Marsh

BLUEGILL ORACLE
Wetlands (96), B:(3, 4), Bluegill Marsh

BLUEGILL PUDDLEJUMPER
Wetlands (96), A-4, B:(3, 4), Bluegill Marsh

BLUEGILL RAIDER
Wetlands (96), A:(6, 7), B:(2, 6), C-2, D:(1, 2), Bluegill Marsh

BLUEGILL WARRIOR
Wetlands (96), A:(2, 3), B:(2-4), C-4, Bluegill Marsh

BLUFF RUNNER WINDSTRIDER
Thunder Bluff (84), D-6, Roams all around the rises

BLUFF WATCHERS
Thunder Bluff (84)

BOAHN
Barrens (18), E-4, Wailing Caverns

BOAR SPIRIT
Barrens (18), E-9, Razorfen Kraul

BOGLING
Teldrassil (80), H-7, Lake Al'Ameth, Spawns east of lake next to camp

BOILING ELEMENTAL
Thousand Needles (82), D:(3, 4), E-4, Darkcloud Pinnacle

BOLYUN
Pet Trainer, Ashenvale (12), C-6, Shrine of Aessina, Hidden in a camp near mountains in far southwest of region

BOM'BAY
Witch Doctor in Training, Durotar (34), H-8, Sen'jin Village (123), South side of pond

BOMBUS FINESPINDLE
Leatherworking Supplies, Ironforge (52), E-3, The Great Forge, Finespindle's Leather Goods

BONE CHEWER
Duskwood (36), B-3, C:(3, 4), Raven Hill Cemetery (122)

BONEFLAYER GHOUL
Barrens (18), F-9, Razorfen Downs

BONEPAW HYENA
Desolace (30), E-7, F-7, G-3, H-4, Ethel Rethor, Sar'theris Strand

BOOKIE HEROD
Stranglethorn Vale (74), E:(1, 2), Kurzen's Compound, Roams a small area around spawn point

BORAN IRONCLINK
Armorer, Dun Morogh (32), F-5, Kharanos (114), Smithy

BORAND
Bowyer, Stonetalon Mountains (70), E-6, Sun Rock Retreat (127), South of western structure

BORELGORE
Eastern Plaguelands (40), G-3, Patrols ravines by spawn point

BORER BEETLE
Burning Steppes (22), Searing Gorge (64), C-4/D-8, Blackrock Depths

BORGOSH COREBENDER
Weaponsmith, Orgrimmar (60), J-2, Valley of Honor, Across from Arms of Legend

BORGUS STEELHAND
Weapon Crafter, Stormwind (72), H-1, Dwarven District, Northwest building

BORGUS STOUTARM
Gryphon Master, Burning Steppes (22), K-7, Morgan's Vigil (118), Camp

BORSTAN
Meat Vendor, Orgrimmar (60), G-5, The Drag, Borstan's Firepit

BORYA
Tailoring Supplies, Orgrimmar (60), H-5, The Drag, Magar's Cloth Goods

BOR'ZEHN
Thousand Needles (82), I-6, Ironstone Camp, Camp just west of Shimmering Flats

BOSS COPPERPLUG
Barrens (18), G-1, H-1, Boulder Lode Mine, Southern cave in mine

BOSS GALGOSH
Rare Spawn, Loch Modan (54), I-6, Ironband's Excavation Site, Lvl 22 Uncommon; On excavation platform with a Stonesplitter Geomancer and Berserk Trogg

BOSS THO'GRUN
Badlands (16), I-7, Camp Boff, Patrols with entourage to Camp Wurg (D-6) and Camp Cagg (B-7)

BOULDERFIST BRUTE
Arathi Highlands (10), G:(7, 8), H-7, Boulderfist Hall

BOULDERFIST ENFORCER
Arathi Highlands (10), D:(4, 5), E-4, Boulderfist Outpost

BOULDERFIST LORD
Arathi Highlands (10), B:(6, 7), Boulderfist Hall

BOULDERFIST MAGUS
Arathi Highlands (10), G:(7, 8), Boulderfist Hall

BOULDERFIST MAULER
Arathi Highlands (10), B-7, C:(6, 7), Boulderfist Hall

BOULDERFIST OGRE
Arathi Highlands (10), D:(4, 5), E:(4, 5), Boulderfist Hall

BOULDERFIST SHAMAN
Arathi Highlands (10), B:(6, 7), C:(6, 7), Boulderfist Hall

BOULDERHEART
Rare Spawn, Redridge Mountains (62), L-6, Lvl 25 Semi-Rare; Roams small area around spawn point

BOUNTY HUNTER KOLARK
Orgrimmar (60), I-2, J-2, Valley of Honor, Roamer

BOWEN BRISBOISE
Journeyman Tailor, Tirisfal Glades (86), G-5, Cold Hearth Manor, House on northwestern edge of manor

BOYLE
Undercity (88), G-6, The Apothecarium, On dock near Royal Quarter

BRACK
Rare Spawn, Westfall (94), C-8, Longshore, Lvl 19 Uncommon; Runs entire Longshore coast

BRACKENWALL ENFORCER
Dustwallow Marsh (38), D-3, E-3, Brackenwall Village (104)

BRAELYN FIREHAND
Stonetalon Mountains (70), E-6, Sun Rock Retreat (127), Southeast of western structure, next to water

BRAENNA FLINTCRAG
Priest Trainer, Ironforge (52), C-1, The Mystic Ward, Hall of Mysteries

BRAHNMAR
Armorer, Wetlands (96), A-6, Menethil Harbor (117), Building northeast of tavern

BRAIN EATER
Duskwood (36), B-3, C:(3, 4), Raven Hill Cemetery (122)

BRAINWASHED NOBLE
Westfall (94), D-7, E-7, The Deadmines

BRAK DURNAD
Weaponsmith, Wetlands (96), A-6, Menethil Harbor (117), Building northeast of tavern

BRAKGUL DEATHBRINGER
Warsong Gulch Battlemaster, Orgrimmar (60), I-2, J-2, Valley of Honor

BRAKKAR
Wind Rider Master, Felwood (44), E-5, Bloodvenom Post, Up hill

BRANCH SNAPPER
Ashenvale (12), F:(4-5), Iris Lake, Circles Iris Lake

BRANDON
Stormwind (72), H-3, The Canals, Dock

BRANDUR IRONHAMMER
Paladin Trainer, Ironforge (52), C-1, The Mystic Ward, Hall of Mysteries

BRANNOCK
Fisherman, Feralas (46), C-4, Feathermoon Stronghold (110), Next to water, northeast of the inn

BRANNOL EAGLEMOON
Clothier, Teldrassil (80), G-6, Dolanaar (109), Inn

BRANSTOCK KHALDER
Priest Trainer, Dun Morogh (32), D-7, Coldridge Valley (106), Anvilmar

BRANT JASPERBLOOM
Herbalist, Dustwallow Marsh (38), H-5, Theramore Isle (130), Hut in west corner

BRAUG DIMSPIRIT
Stonetalon Mountains (70), E-7, Talondeep Path, Just south of the Talondeep Path entrance.

BRAVE CLOUDMANE
Mulgore (58), E-6, Bloodhoof Village (102), Patrols village

BRAVE DARKSKY
Mulgore (58), E-5, Patrols road north of village

BRAVE DAWNEAGLE
Mulgore (58), F-6, Patrols road east of village

BRAVE GREATHOOF
Mulgore (58), E-8, Camp Narache (105), Patrols camp

BRAVE IRONHORN
Mulgore (58), E-6, Bloodhoof Village (102), Patrols village

BRAVE LEAPING DEER
Mulgore (58), F-6, Patrols road east of village

BRAVE LIGHTNINGHORN
Mulgore (58), E-8, Red Cloud Mesa, Patrols east of camp

BRAVE MOONHORN
Thousand Needles (82), D-2, The Great Lift, Next to lift

BRAVE PROUDSNOUT
Mulgore (58), E-8, Camp Narache (105), Patrols camp

BRAVE RAINCHASER
Mulgore (58), E-6, Bloodhoof Village (102), Patrols village

BRAVE ROCKHORN
Mulgore (58), F-6, Patrols road east of village

BRAVE RUNNING WOLF
Mulgore (58), E-8, Camp Narache (105), Patrols camp

BRAVE STRONGBASH
Mulgore (58), E-6, Bloodhoof Village (102), Patrols village

BRAVE SWIFTWIND
Mulgore (58), F-6, Bloodhoof Village (102), Patrols village

BRAVE WILDRUNNER
Mulgore (58), E-6, Bloodhoof Village (102), Patrols village

BRAVE WINDFEATHER
Mulgore (58), E-8, Camp Narache (105), Patrols camp

BRAWLER
Loch Modan (54), D-9, Stonesplinter Valley, Stand with Grawmug and Gnasher in center of cave

BRAWN
Expert Leatherworker, Stranglethorn Vale (74), C-3, Grom'gol Base Camp (112), Next orcish carriage directly across from the eastern entrance into camp

BREK STONEHOOF
Mining Trainer, Thunder Bluff (84), C-6, Lower rise, inside Stonehoof Geology tent

BRENWYN WINTERSTEEL
Blade Merchant, Ironforge (52), H-9, The Military Ward, Timberline Arms

BRETTA GOLDFURY
Gun Merchant, Ironforge (52), J-6, The Military Ward, Goldfury's Hunting Supplies

BREWMASTER BILGER
Hillsbrad Foothills (48), F-6, Southshore (125), Basement of inn

BREWMASTER DROHN
Barrens (18), H-4, Ratchet (121), Outside Plate-n-Chain

BREYK
Wind Rider Master, Swamp of Sorrows (76), F-5, Stonard (126), Left of the inn

BRIARTHORN
Warlock Trainer, Ironforge (52), G-1, The Forlorn Cavern, Building to the right of Traveling Fisherman

BRIENNA STARGLOW
Tailoring Supplies, Feralas (46), K-5, Thalanaar, Hill northwest of well in stone structure

BRIGITTE CRANSTON
Portal Trainer, Thunder Bluff (84), C-3, Spirit Rise, The Pools of Vision

BRIKK KEENCRAFT
Master Blacksmith, Stranglethorn Vale (74), C-8, Booty Bay (103), Booty Bay Blacksmith (shop)

BRIMGORE
Dustwallow Marsh (38), F-8, Wyrmbog, Roams along the foothills northwest

BRINE
Barrens (18), E-8, Blackthorn Ridge, Hut on hill

BRINNA VALANAAR
Bowyer, Azshara (14), A-8, Talrendis Point

BRISTLEBACK BATTLEBOAR
Mulgore (58), G:(7-9), H-8, Brambleblade Ravine

BRISTLEBACK GEOMANCER
Barrens (18), D:(4, 5), E:(4, 5), F:(5, 6), Agama'gor, Bramblescar

BRISTLEBACK HUNTER
Barrens (18), D:(4, 5), E:(5, 6), F:(5, 6), Agama'gor, Bramblescar

BRISTLEBACK INTERLOPER
Mulgore (58), G-2, H-2, Red Rocks

BRISTLEBACK QUILBOAR
Mulgore (58), G:(7, 8), H-8, Brambleblade Ravine

BRISTLEBACK SHAMAN
Mulgore (58), G:(7, 8), H:(7, 8), Brambleblade Ravine

BRISTLEBACK THORNWEAVER
Barrens (18), E-5, F:(5, 6), Agama'gor, Bramblescar

BRISTLEBACK WATER SEEKER
Barrens (18), E-5, F:(5, 6), Agama'gor, Bramblescar

BRIVELTHWERP
Ice Cream Vendor, Thousand Needles (82), J-8, Mirage Raceway (118), Next to building west of racetrack

BROCK STONESEEKER
Mining Trainer, Loch Modan (54), E-5, Thelsamar (129), In second house on right of path

BROG HAMFIST
General Supplies, Elwynn Forest (42), F-7, Goldshire (112), First floor of Lion's Pride Inn

BROGUN STONESHIELD
Alterac Valley Battlemaster, Darnassus (26), H-4, Warrior's Terrace, Lower southwest platform

BROHANN CASKBELLY
Explorers' League, Stormwind (72), I-2, J-2, Dwarven District, Tavern

BROKEN CADAVER
Eastern Plaguelands (40), D-2, Stratholme

BROKEN TOOTH
Rare Spawn, Badlands (16), G-4, H-2, I-3, Angor Fortress, Dustwind Gulch, Lvl 37 Uncommon; Roams small area around spawn point

BROKESPEAR
Rare Spawn, Barrens (18), F:(4-5), G-4, The Stagnant Oasis, Lvl 17 Uncommon; Stays near spawn points

BRO'KIN
Alchemy Supplies, Alterac Mountains (8), E-4, Ruins of Alterac, Wall along northern side of ruins

BROM KILLIAN
Mining Trainer, Undercity (88), H-4, The War Quarter

BROMBAR HIGGLEBY
The Keymaster, Ironforge (52), G-4, The Great Forge, North of The Great Anvil

BROMIIR ORMSEN
Heavy Armor Merchant, Ironforge (52), D-6, The Commons, Ironforge Armory

BROMOS GRUMMNER
Paladin Trainer, Dun Morogh (32), D-7, Coldridge Valley (106), Anvilmar

BRONK
Alchemy Supplies, Feralas (46), I-4, Camp Mojache (105), East of bridge

BRONK GUZZLEGEAR
Journeyman Engineer, Dun Morogh (32), G-5, Steelgrill's Depot, Basement of right building

BRONK STEELRAGE
Armorer & Shieldcrafter, Mulgore (58), E-8, Camp Narache (105), Southwest tent

BRONT COLDCLEAVE
Butcher, Hillsbrad Foothills (48), F-6, Southshore (125), Small house right of path

BRONTUS
Rare Spawn, Barrens (18), E-8, Blackthorn Ridge, Lvl 27 Average Rare; Spawns near center hut and roams ridge

BROOKE STONEBRAID
Mining Supplier, Stormwind (72), H-2, Dwarven District, Building north of west entrance

BROTHER ANTON
Scarlet Crusade Emissary, Desolace (30), I-1, Nijel's Point (119), Second floor of inn

BROTHER BENJAMIN
Priest Trainer, Stormwind (72), F-3, Cathedral Square, Cathedral of Light

BROTHER CASSIUS
Reagent Vendor, Stormwind (72), F-3, Cathedral Square, Cathedral of Light

BROTHER CROWLEY
Scarlet Crusade Emissary, Stormwind (72), F-3, Cathedral Square, Cathedral of Light

BROTHER DANIL
General Supplies, Elwynn Forest (42), F-4, Northshire Valley (120), Caravan facing abbey

BROTHER JOSHUA
Priest Trainer, Stormwind (72), F-3, Cathedral Square, Cathedral of Light

BROTHER KARMAN
Paladin Trainer, Dustwallow Marsh (38), I-5, Theramore Isle (130), Outside Foothold Citadel

BROTHER KRISTOFF
Stormwind (72), G-4, Cathedral Square, By Fountain

BROTHER MALACH
Undercity (88), G-2, The War Quarter, Watches fights in War Quarter

BROTHER NEALS
Elwynn Forest (42), G-4, Northshire Valley (120), Top floor of abbey

BROTHER NIMETZ
Stranglethorn Vale (74), D-1, Rebel Camp, Camp

BROTHER PAXTON
Elwynn Forest (42), G-4, Northshire Valley (120), Library Wing of abbey

BROTHER SAMMUEL
Paladin Trainer, Elwynn Forest (42), G-4, Northshire Valley (120), Hall of Arms of abbey

BROTHER SARNO
Stormwind (72), F-3, Cathedral Square, Cathedral of Light

BROTHER WILHELM
Paladin Trainer, Elwynn Forest (42), E-7, Goldshire (112), Rear entrance of smith

BRUEGAL IRONKNUCKLE
Rare Spawn, Stormwind (72), F-6, The Stockade, Lvl 26 Rare

BRUMERAN
Winterspring (98), I-6, Dun Mandarr, Roams north to The Ruins of Kel'Theril

BRUMN WINTERHOOF
Arathi Highlands (10), D-4, Small camp on hill

BRUTUS
Stranglethorn Vale (74), C-9, Wild Shore

BRUUK BARLEYBEARD
Bartender, Ironforge (52), J:(7, 8), The Military Ward, Bruuk's Corner

BRYAN CROSS
Shield Merchant, Stormwind (72), I-4, J-4, Old Town, The Silver Sheild

BRYLLIA IRONBRAND
General Good Vendor, Ironforge (52), E-7, The Commons, Fizzlespinner's General Goods

BUBULO ACERBUS
Alliance Cloth Quartermaster, Ironforge (52), J-5, Tinker Town, North of the tram entrance

BULIWYF STONEHAND
Weapon Master, Ironforge (52), H-9, The Military Ward, Timberline Arms, Trains: 1H Axe, 2H Axe, Fist, Guns, 1H Mace, & 2H Mace

BULKREK RAGEFIST
Wind Rider Master, Tanaris (78), H-3, Gadgetzan (111), North of town

BULRUG
Stable Master, Thunder Bluff (84), E-6, On Thunder Bluff's lower rise; In Front of Thunder Bluff Bank & Next to Mail box

BUNTHEN PLAINSWIND
Thunder Bluff Flight Master, Moonglade (56), F-5, Nighthaven (120), Southwest side of town

BURBIK GEARSPANNER
Trade Supplier, Ironforge (52), F-3, The Great Forge, Burbik's Supplies

BURDRAK HARGLHELM
Leather Armor Merchant, Dun Morogh (32), D-4, Brewnall Village, In tent along northwest side of village

BURGLE EYE
Rare Spawn, Dustwallow Marsh (38), H:(1-3), Dreadmurk Shore, Lvl 38 Uncommon; Spawns on the five isles

BURKRUM
Heavy Armor Merchant, Ashenvale (12), I-6, Splintertree Post (126), Near some crates next to inn

BURLY ROCKJAW TROGG
Dun Morogh (32), B:(7, 8), C:(7, 8), D:(7, 8), Coldridge Pass, Coldridge Valley (106)

BURNING BLADE ACOLYTE
Barrens (18), E-2, F-2, Dreadmist Peak

BURNING BLADE ADEPT
Desolace (30), G:(2, 3), H-3, Thunder Axe Fortress

BURNING BLADE APPRENTICE
Durotar (34), F-3, H-1, Skull Rock, Thunder Ridge

BURNING BLADE AUGUR
Desolace (30), G:(2, 3), H-3, Thunder Axe Fortress

BURNING BLADE BRUISER
Barrens (18), E-2, F-2, Dreadmist Peak

BURNING BLADE CRUSHER
Barrens (18), E-2, F-2, Dreadmist Peak

BURNING BLADE CULTIST
Durotar (34), H:(2, 3), Dustwind Cave

BURNING BLADE FANATIC
Durotar (34), F-3, H-1, Skull Rock, Thunder Ridge

BURNING BLADE FELSWORN
Desolace (30), G:(2, 3), H-3, Thunder Axe Fortress

BURNING BLADE INVOKER
Desolace (30), K-8, Shadowbreak Ravine

BURNING BLADE NEOPHYTE
Durotar (34), H-3, Dustwind Cave

BURNING BLADE NIGHTMARE
Desolace (30), K-8, Shadowbreak Ravine

BURNING BLADE REAVER
Desolace (30), G:(2, 3), H-3, Thunder Axe Fortress

BURNING BLADE SEER
Desolace (30), G-3, Thunder Axe Fortress

BURNING BLADE SHADOWMAGE
Desolace (30), G-3, Thunder Axe Fortress

BURNING BLADE SUMMONER
Desolace (30), F:(7, 8), G:(7, 8), K-8, Mannoroc Coven, Shadowbreak Ravine

BURNING BLADE THUG
Durotar (34), H-3, Drygulch Ravine, Dustwind Cave

BURNING BLADE TOXICOLOGIST
Barrens (18), E-2, F-2, Dreadmist Peak

BURNING DESTROYER
Stonetalon Mountains (70), D-7, E-7, The Charred Vale

BURNING EXILE
Arathi Highlands (10), C-3, Circle of West Binding

BURNING FELGUARD
Burning Steppes (22), Searing Gorge (64), C-4/D-8, Blackrock Spire

BURNING FELHOUND
Burning Steppes (22), Searing Gorge (64), C-4/D-8, Blackrock Spire

BURNING IMP
Burning Steppes (22), Searing Gorge (64), C-4/D-8, Blackrock Spire

BURNING RAVAGER
Stonetalon Mountains (70), C-6, D-6, E-6, The Charred Vale

BURROWING THUNDERSNOUT
Burning Steppes (22), Searing Gorge (64), C-4/D-8, Blackrock Depths

BUZZARD
Badlands (16), G:(6, 8), H-6, I:(5-7), Agmond's End

BUZZEK BRACKETSWING
Master Engineer, Tanaris (78), H-3, Gadgetzan (111), Outside inn

BYANCIE
First Aid Trainer, Teldrassil (80), G-6, Dolanaar (109), Bottom floor inside building north of road

C

CADAVEROUS WORM
Feralas (46), G-4, Dire Maul, (Summon)

CAEDAKAR THE VICIOUS
Ashenvale (12), D-2, Spawns on road near Darkshore border

CAELYB
Pet Trainer, Ashenvale (12), F-6, Silverwind Refuge, Right wing of building

CAER DARROW CANNONEER
Western Plaguelands (92), I:(7, 8), Caer Darrow, Located throughout the city

CAER DARROW CITIZEN
Western Plaguelands (92), I-8, J:(7, 8), Caer Darrow, Located throughout the city

CAER DARROW GUARDSMAN
Western Plaguelands (92), I-8, J:(7, 8), Caer Darrow, Located throughout the city

CAER DARROW HORSEMAN
Western Plaguelands (92), I:(7, 8) J:(7, 8), Caer Darrow, Located throughout the city

CAIN FIRESONG
Mage Trainer, Tirisfal Glades (86), H-5, Brill (104), Second floor of Gallows' End Tavern

CAIRNE BLOODHOOF
High Chieftan, Thunder Bluff (84), G-5, High rise, next to bridge to Elder Rise

CAITLIN GRASSMAN
Wetlands (96), A-6, Menethil Harbor (117), Small house east of keep

CALEDRA DAWNBREEZE
Stormwind (72), K-3, Stormwind Keep, Petitioner's Chamber

CALIPH SCORPIDSTING
Tanaris (78), I-4, Waterspring Field, Near two tents between hills

CALOR
Duskwood (36), J-5, Darkshire (108), Outside of house

CALVIN MONTAGUE
Tirisfal Glades (86), E-6, Deathknell (109), Roaming just inside wall northeast of town

CAMERICK JONGLEUR
Wandering Minstrel, Wetlands (96), A-6, Menethil Harbor (117), Next to wagon, south of keep

CAMP MOJACHE BRAVE
Feralas (46), I:(4, 5), J-4, Lariss Pavilion, Lower Wilds, Wildwind Lake

CANAGA EARTHCALLER
Durotar (34), F-7, Valley of Trials (131)

CANNIBAL GHOUL
Eastern Plaguelands (40), B:(3, 4), C:(2-4), D:(3, 4), E:(2-4), F:(2-4), Plaguewood

CANNIBAL GHOUL
Eastern Plaguelands (40), D-2, Stratholme

CANNON MASTER WILLEY
Eastern Plaguelands (40), D-2, Stratholme

CANNONEER SMYTHE
Barrens (18), H-6, Northwatch Hold, Top of eastern tower

CANNONEER WHESSAN
Barrens (18), G-5, Northwatch Hold, Top of western tower

CAPTAIN ANDREWS
Red Team Captain, Dustwallow Marsh (38), I-5, Theramore Isle (130), Sparring grounds to northeast

CAPTAIN BELD
Rare Spawn, Dun Morogh (32), K-6, Ironband's Compound, Lvl 11 Common; Basement of compound

CAPTAIN DANUVIN
The People's Militia, Westfall (94), F-5, Sentinel Hill (123), Sentinel Tower

CAPTAIN DARGOL
Tirisfal Glades (86), G-3, Agamand Mills (100), Bottom floor of Agamand Family Crypt

CAPTAIN EVENCANE
Warrior Trainer, Dustwallow Marsh (38), I-5, Theramore Isle (130), 2nd floor of Foothold Citadel

CAPTAIN FAIRMOUNT
Barrens (18), H-5, Northwatch Hold, Top of main tower

CAPTAIN FLAT TUSK
Rare Spawn, Captain of the Battleguard, Durotar (34), F:(4, 5), G-5, Durotar, Razormane Grounds, Lvl 11 Uncommon; Near huts

CAPTAIN GARRAN VIMES
Dustwallow Marsh (38), I-5, Theramore Isle (130), 2nd floor of Foothold Citadel

CAPTAIN GEROGG HAMMERTOE
Rare Spawn, Bael'dun Captain of the Guard, Barrens (18), F-8, Bael'dun Keep, Lvl 27 Average Rare; Second floor of keep

CAPTAIN GRAYSON
Westfall (94), C-8, Westfall Lighthouse, Island near lighthouse

CAPTAIN GREENSKIN
Westfall (94), D-7, E-7, The Deadmines

CAPTAIN HALYNDOR
Wetlands (96), B-2, The Lost Fleet, Top of northern ship

CAPTAIN HECKLEBURY SMOTTS
Stranglethorn Vale (74), B-8, Booty Bay (103), On dock near ship launch on the northern side of bay

CAPTAIN IRONHILL
Hillsbrad Foothills (48), I-8, Dun Garok, Stands idle at spawn point

CAPTAIN KEELHAUL
Stranglethorn Vale (74), C-9, Wild Shore, Below deck to the stern of beached ship

CAPTAIN KROMCRUSH
Feralas (46), G-4, Dire Maul

CAPTAIN MELRACHE
Tirisfal Glades (86), K-3, Scarlet Watch Post, Idle with two Scarlet Bodyguards in tower ruins

CAPTAIN NIALS
Arathi Highlands (10), F-5, Refuge Point, Camp

CAPTAIN PENTIGAST
Desolace (30), I-1, Nijel's Point (119), Clearing near entrance

CAPTAIN PERRINE
Tirisfal Glades (86), F-7, Idle with a single Scarlet Zealot in tower ruins

CAPTAIN REDPATH
Eastern Plaguelands (40), E-8, Darrowshire, (Summon) Well in the center of town

CAPTAIN RUGELFUSS
Loch Modan (54), C-7, Valley of Kings, Third floor of tower

CAPTAIN SHATTERSKULL
Barrens (18), E-1, Mor'shan Base Camp, Outside entrance to Warsong Gulch

CAPTAIN STEELGUT
Arathi Highlands (10), D-8, Faldir's Cove, Seated by bonfire on hill

CAPTAIN STOUTFIST
Wetlands (96), A-6, Menethil Harbor (117), Second floor of keep

CAPTAIN THALO'THAS BRIGHTSUN
Barrens (18), H-4, Ratchet (121), Outside inn

CAPTAIN THOMAS
Blue Team Captain, Dustwallow Marsh (38), I-5, Theramore Isle (130), Sparring grounds to northeast

CAPTAIN VACHON
Tirisfal Glades (86), K-5, Crusader's Outpost, Idle with a single Scarlet Friar in tower ruins

CAPTAIN VANESSA BELTIS
Azshara (14), H-9, The Ruined Reaches, Inlet

CAPTURED ARKO'NARIN
Felwood (44), E-6, Shadow Hold, Cage at first landing

CAPTURED HAKKARI ZEALOT
Stranglethorn Vale (74), A-2, Yojamba Isle

CAPTURED LEPER GNOME
Dun Morogh (32), F-5, Kharanos (114), Cage in gnomish workshop

CAPTURED MOUNTAINEER
Tirisfal Glades (86), H-5, Brill (104), Basement of Gallows' End Tavern

CAPTURED SCARLET ZEALOT
Tirisfal Glades (86), H-5, Brill (104), Basement of Gallows' End Tavern

CAPTURED SERVANT OF AZORA
Specialist Tailoring Supplies, Redridge Mountains (62), J-8, Render's Valley, By cages in camp

CAPTURED SPRITE DARTER
Feralas (46), H-5, Lower Wilds

CARAVAN MASTER TSET
Azshara (14), E-6, Southridge Beach, Near cliff face and ruins

CARAVANEER RUZZGOT
Stranglethorn Vale (74), B-8, Booty Bay (103), On dock near ship launch on the northern side of bay

CARENDIN HALGAR
Undercity (88), L-2, The Magic Quarter, Geen circle east of Skull Building

CARETAKER ALARIC
Arathi Highlands (10), D-6, Crypt, Roams crypt

CARETAKER ALEN
The Argent Dawn, Eastern Plaguelands (40), K-6, Light's Hope Chapel (116), Next to caravan south of chapel

CARETAKER CAICE
Tirisfal Glades (86), C-7, D-7, Deathknell (109)

CARETAKER FOLSOM
Stormwind (72), D-6, The Canals, Far west end of canals

CARETAKER NEVLIN
Arathi Highlands (10), D-6, Crypt, Roams crypt

CARETAKER SMITHERS
Hillsbrad Foothills (48), F-5, Southshore (125), Graveyard

CARETAKER WESTON
Arathi Highlands (10), D-6, Crypt, Roams crypt

CARLA GRANGER
Cloth Armor Merchant, Stormwind (72), H:(5, 6), Trade District, Lionheart Armory

CARLIN REDPATH
The Argent Dawn, Eastern Plaguelands (40), K-6, Light's Hope Chapel (116), Camp on right side of chapel

CARLO AURELIUS
Assassin, Hillsbrad Foothills (48), J-2, K-2, In mountains

CARNIVOUS THE BREAKER
Rare Spawn, Darkshore (24), F-5, F-8, Twilight Vale, Lvl 16 Uncommon; Roams close to spawn point

CAROLAI ANISE
Journeyman Alchemist, Tirisfal Glades (86), H-5, Brill (104), House on the right side of road

CAROLYN WARD
Rogue Trainer, Undercity (88), L-7, The Rogues' Quarter, Inside Skull Building

CARRION DEVOURER
Eastern Plaguelands (40), B-3, C:(2-4), D-4, E-4, F:(3, 4), G:(3, 4), H:(2-5), I:(3-5), J:(3, 4), East Wall Tower

CARRION GRUB
Eastern Plaguelands (40), A:(4, 5), B:(5-7), C:(6-9), D:(6-8), E:(6-8), F:(6-8), G:(5-7), H:(5-8), I:(5-8), J:(5-7), K-6

CARRION HORROR
Desolace (30), F-6, G-6, Ghost Walker Post (111), Kodo Graveyard

CARRION LURKER
Western Plaguelands (92), E-5, F:(3-6), G:(3-7)

CARRION RECLUSE
Duskwood (36), B-4, C-4, Raven Hill Cemetery (122)

CARRION SWARMER
Feralas (46), G-4, Dire Maul

CARRION VULTURE
Western Plaguelands (92), D:(5, 6), The Bulwark

CARROSH
Teldrassil (80), F-4, Hills east of Wellspring Lake

CARYSSIA MOONHUNTER
Tribal Leatherworking Trainer, Feralas (46), K-5, Thalanaar, Next to well

CATELYN THE BLADE
Blackwater Raiders, Stranglethorn Vale (74), B-8, Booty Bay (103), Second floor of The Salty Sailor Tavern

CATHERINE LELAND
Fishing Supplier, Stormwind (72), G-6, The Canals, Dock

CAULDRON LORD BILEMAW
Western Plaguelands (92), E-6, Felstone Field, (Summon) Spawns at the base of the cauldron

CAULDRON LORD MALVINIOUS
Western Plaguelands (92), F-5, Dalson's Tears, (Summon) Spawns at the base of the cauldron

CAULDRON LORD RAZARCH
Western Plaguelands (92), G-6, The Writhing Haunt, (Summon) Spawns at the base of the cauldron

CAULDRON LORD SOULWRAITH
Western Plaguelands (92), H-6, Gahrron's Withering, (Summon) Spawns at the base of the cauldron

CAVALIER DURGEN
Western Plaguelands (92), G-2, Patrols up and down tower south of Hearthglen

CAVE CREEPER
Burning Steppes (22), Searing Gorge (64), C-4/D-8, Blackrock Depths

CAVE STALKER
Wetlands (96), F-6, G-6, Thelgen Rock

CAVE YETI
Hillsbrad Foothills (48), E-3, Darrow Hill, In and near cave

CAVERN LURKER
Desolace (30), D-5, Mauradon

CAVERN SHAMBLER
Desolace (30), D-5, Mauradon

CAVERNDEEP AMBUSHER
Dun Morogh (32), C-4, Gnomeregan

CAVERNDEEP BURROWER
Dun Morogh (32), C-4, Gnomeregan

CAVERNDEEP INVADER
Dun Morogh (32), C-4, Gnomeregan

CAVERNDEEP LOOTER
Dun Morogh (32), C-4, Gnomeregan

CAVERNDEEP PILLAGER
Dun Morogh (32), C-4, Gnomeregan

CAVERNDEEP REAVER
Dun Morogh (32), C-4, Gnomeregan

CAWIND TRUEAIM
Gunsmith & Bowyer, Feralas (46), I-4, Camp Mojache (105), Second floor balcony of inn

CAYLAIS MOONFEATHER
Hippogryph Master, Darkshore (24), F-4, Auberdine (101), Hippogryph platform

CAYNRUS
Shield Merchant, Darnassus (26), H-7, Tradesmen's Terrace, Shields shop

CAZ TWOSPROCKET
Gnomeregan Exiles, Dustwallow Marsh (38), I-5, Theramore Isle (130), Blacksmithing hut to west

CAZUL
Orgrimmar (60), F-5, The Cleft of Shadow, Next to Shadowdeep Reagents

CEDRIC STUMPEL
Undercity (88), K-6, The Rogues' Quarter, Roames Rogue Quarter

CEDRIK PROSE
Gryphon Master, Arathi Highlands (10), F-5, Refuge Point, Camp

CELEBRAS THE CURSED
Desolace (30), D-5, Mauradon

CELEBRAS THE REDEEMED
Desolace (30), D-5, Mauradon

CELEBRIAN DRYAD
Desolace (30), D-5, Mauradon

CELES EARTHBORNE
Moonglade (56), H-4, Nighthaven (120), On wood platform, north of lake, east of town

CENARION BOTANIST
Stonetalon Mountains (70), D:(1, 2), E:(1, 2), Stonetalon Peak

CENARION PROTECTOR
Ashenvale (12), H-5, Raynewood Retreat

CENARION VINDICATOR
Ashenvale (12), H-5, Raynewood Retreat

CENTAUR PARIAH
Desolace (30), F-9, Mannoroc Coven, Wanders hills and pauses at overlooks

CENTIPAAR SANDREAVER
Tanaris (78), E:(4, 5), The Noxious Lair

CENTIPAAR STINGER
Tanaris (78), E:(4, 5), The Noxious Lair

CENTIPAAR SWARMER
Tanaris (78), E:(4, 5), The Noxious Lair

CENTIPAAR TUNNELER
Tanaris (78), E:(4, 5), F-5, The Noxious Lair, Sandsorrow Watch

CENTIPAAR WASP
Tanaris (78), E:(4, 5), The Noxious Lair

CENTIPAAR WORKER
Tanaris (78), E:(4, 5), The Noxious Lair

CERELLEAN WHITECLAW
Darkshore (24), E-4, Auberdine (101), Dock

CHAL FAIRWIND
Wintersaber Trainers, Winterspring (98), J-3, Outside small shack in hills

CHAMBERMAID PILLACLENCHER
Searing Gorge (64), E-3, The Slag Pit, (Summon) Sleeping quarters

CHARDRYN
Herbalism Supplier, Darnassus (26), F-7, The Temple Gardens, Small building, northeast of temple

CHARITY MIPSY
General Goods, Dustwallow Marsh (38), I-5, Theramore Isle (130), Southeast near docks

CHARLES SEATON
Blade Merchant, Undercity (88), K-5, The Rogues' Quarter, Near Magic Quarter entry

CHARLGA RAZORFLANK
Barrens (18), E-9, Razorfen Kraul

CHARRED ANCIENT
Stonetalon Mountains (70), D:(6, 7), E:(6, 7), The Charred Vale

CHARYS YSERIAN
Arcane Trinkets Vendor, Stormwind (72), E-8, Mage Quarter, Ancient Curios

CHATTER
Rare Spawn, Redridge Mountains (62), G-4, H-5, Alther's Mill, Lvl 23 Uncommon; Roams small area around spawn point

CHAW STRONGHIDE
Journeyman Leatherworker, Mulgore (58), E-6, Bloodhoof Village (102), Northeast tent

CHEF BREANNA
Redridge Mountains (62), B-4, Lakeshire (115), First floor of large house on southwestern side of town

CHEF GRUAL
Duskwood (36), J-4, Darkshire (108), Scarlet Raven Inn

CHEF JESSEN
Hillsbrad Foothills (48), F-6, Southshore (125), First floor of inn

CHEMIST CUELY
Undercity (88), F-7, The Apothecarium, In laboratory

CHEMIST FUELY
Undercity (88), F-7, The Apothecarium, In laboratory

CHEPI
Reagent Vendor, Thunder Bluff (84), D-6, Roams around lower rise

CHESMU
Banker, Thunder Bluff (84), E-6, Thunder Bluff Bank

CHIEF ARCHAEOLOGIST GREYWHISKER
Explorers' League, Darnassus (26), D-8, The Temple of the Moon, Steps west of the temple

CHIEF ENGINEER BILGEWHIZZLE
Gadgetzan Water Co., Tanaris (78), H-3, Gadgetzan (111), Between bank and inn

CHIEF ENGINEER HINDERWEIR VII
Loch Modan (54), F-1, Stonewrought Dam, Under scaffolding on dam wall

CHIEF HAWKWIND
Mulgore (58), E-8, Camp Narache (105), Main tent (north)

CHIEF MURGUT
Ashenvale (12), G-6, Greenpaw Village

CHIEF SHARPTUSK THORNMANTLE
Mulgore (58), H-8, Brambleblade Ravine, Tent in north of ravine

CHIEF UKORZ SANDSCALP
Tanaris (78), E-1, Zul'Farrak

CHIEFTAIN BLOODMAW
Felwood (44), I-1, Felpaw Village, Camp at north side of pond

CHIEFTAIN NEK'ROSH
Wetlands (96), G-5, Angerfang Encampment, Southeast side of camp

CHILLWIND CHIMAERA
Winterspring (98), H:(4, 5), I:(4, 5), J:(2-5)

CHILLWIND RAVAGER
Winterspring (98), H:(2, 3), I:(1-3, 5, 6)

CHIMAERA MATRIARCH
Stonetalon Mountains (70), D-7, The Charred Vale, Roams southeastern section of Charred Vale

CHIMAEROK
Feralas (46), B:(7, 8), C:(7-9), Isle of Dread

CHIMAEROK DEVOURER
Feralas (46), B:(7, 8), C:(7-9), Isle of Dread

CHLOE CURTHAS
Undercity (88), G-2, The War Quarter, Watches fights in War Quarter

CHOK'SUL
Loch Modan (54), K-2, Mo'grosh Stronghold, Cave

CHOMPER
Dun Morogh (32), C-4, Gnomeregan

CHO'RUSH THE OBSERVER
Feralas (46), G-4, Dire Maul

CHRISTI GALVANIS
General Goods, Desolace (30), I-1, Nijel's Point (119), Inn

CHRISTOPH FARAL
Stormwind (72), K-4, Old Town, Roamer - Stops at Pig and Whistle Tavern

CHRISTOPH JEFFCOAT
Tradesman, Hillsbrad Foothills (48), H-2, Tarren Mill (128), First floor of inn

CHRISTOPH WALKER
Warrior Trainer, Undercity (88), F-2, The War Quarter, In Skull Building

CHRISTOPHER DRAKUL
Guild Master, Undercity (88), J-4, The Trade Quarter, East spoke from bank

CHRISTOPHER HEWEN
General Trade Goods Vendor, Westfall (94), F-5, Sentinel Hill (123), Inn

CHROMATIC DRAGONSPAWN
Burning Steppes (22), Searing Gorge (64), C-4/D-8, Blackrock Spire

CHROMATIC ELITE GUARD
Burning Steppes (22), Searing Gorge (64), C-4/D-8, Blackrock Spire

CHROMATIC WHELP
Burning Steppes (22), Searing Gorge (64), C-4/D-8, Blackrock Spire

CHROMIE
Western Plaguelands (92), E-7, Ruins of Andorhal, Second floor of inn

CHRONALIS
Tanaris (78), I-5, Caverns of Time, Near entrance to cavern

CHUCKY "TEN THUMBS"
Stranglethorn Vale (74), D-6, Ruins of Aboraz, Roaming around ruins

CHYLINA
General Supplies, Stonetalon Mountains (70), D-1, Stonetalon Peak, Building north of hipporgryphs

CITIZEN WILKES
Hillsbrad Foothills (48), C-4, Hillsbrad Fields (113), Patrols between the town hall, smithy and two houses in the eastern and northern parts of town

CIVILIAN GUARD PARKER
Redridge Mountains (62), A-7, Three Corners

CLACK THE REAVER
Rare Spawn, Blasted Lands (20), G-4, Dreadmaul Post, Lvl 53 Semi-Rare; Patrols to tower ruins at the edge of Serpent's Coil (I-3)

CLAIRA KINDFEATHER
The Hinterlands (50), C-5, Aerie Peak (100), Third floor of tower

CLAIRE WILLOWER
Tirisfal Glades (86), D-7, Deathknell (109), Outside of the first house on right side of road

CLARICE FOSTER
Thunder Bluff (84), C-3, Spirit Rise, The Pools of Vision

CLARISE GNARLTREE
Expert Blacksmith, Duskwood (36), J-5, Darkshire (108), Smithy

CLATTERING CRAWLER
Ashenvale (12), A:(2-4), B:(2-4), The Zoram Strand (131), Zoram'gar Outpost (131)

CLATTERING SCORPID
Durotar (34), G:(5, 7), H:(4-8), I:(4, 5, 7)

CLAUDE ERKSINE
Pet Trainer, Loch Modan (54), K-6, The Farstrider Lodge, In right hall of lodge

CLAVICUS KNAVINGHAM
Alliance Cloth Quartermaster, Stormwind (72), G-7, Mage Quarter, Duncan's Textiles

CLEFT SCORPID
Badlands (16), G-1, Uldaman

CLERK DALTRY
Duskwood (36), J-5, Darkshire (108), Darkshire Town Hall

CLERK HORACE WHITESTEED
Hillsbrad Foothills (48), C-4, Hillsbrad, Town hall

CLERK LENDRY
Dustwallow Marsh (38), I-5, Theramore Isle (130), 2nd floor of Foothold Citadel

CLIFF BREAKER
Azshara (14), E:(7-9), F:(7-9), G:(7-9), H:(1, 8, 9), I:(1, 2), J:(1-3), K-2, Bitter Reaches, Lake Mennar, Southridge Beach

CLIFF GIANT
Feralas (46), D:(2, 3), Ruins of Ravenwind, The Twin Colossals

CLIFF HADIN
Bowyer, Loch Modan (54), K-6, The Farstrider Lodge, On right side of lodge entrance

CLIFF LURKER
Loch Modan (54), F-7, G:(6-8), H:(5-8), I-5

CLIFF STORMER
Barrens (18), B:(2, 3), C:(2, 3) Stonetalon Mountains (70), G-7, H:(7, 9), J:(8, 9), K:(8, 9)

CLIFF THUNDERER
Azshara (14), E:(7-9), F:(7-9), G:(7-9), H:(1, 8, 9), I:(1, 2), J:(1-3), K-2, Bitter Reaches, Legash Encampment, Southridge Beach

CLIFF WALKER
Azshara (14), A-5, C-5, E:(7-9), F:(7-9), G:(7-9), H:(1, 8, 9), I:(1, 2), J:(1-3), K-2

CLIFFWATCHER LONGHORN
Thousand Needles (82), F-5, Freewind Post, Outside Inn, next to fire

CLOUD SERPENT
Thousand Needles (82), D:(3, 5), E:(4-6), F-6, G:(5, 6)

CLUNK
The Undermarket, Searing Gorge (64), D-5, The Cauldron, Next to Trade Master Kovic in cave

CLUTCHMOTHER ZAVAS
Rare Spawn, Un'Goro Crater (90), G-8, The Slithering Scar, Lvl 54 Semi-Rare; Inside The Slighering Scar

CLYDE KELLEN
Fisherman, Tirisfal Glades (86), I-5, Brightwater Lake, On the southwest bank of the lake

CLYDE RANTHAL
Leatherworking Supplies, Redridge Mountains (62), L-7, Camp

COAST CRAWL DEEPSEER
Feralas (46), A:(5, 6), B:(5, 6), C:(5, 6), D:(5, 6), Sardor Isle

COAST CRAWL SNAPCLAW
Feralas (46), A:(5, 6), B:(5, 6), C:(5, 6), D:(5, 6), Sardor Isle

COAST STRIDER
Tanaris (78), I:(6, 7), J-6, Southbreak Shore

COASTAL FRENZY
Darkshore (24), D-7, E:(6-8), F:(2, 3), G-2, Mist's Edge

COBALT BROODLING
Winterspring (98), H:(5-6), I-5, Mazthoril

COBALT MAGEWEAVER
Winterspring (98), H:(5, 6), I-5, Mazthoril

COBALT SCALEBANE
Winterspring (98), H:(5, 6), I-5, Mazthoril

COBALT WHELP
Winterspring (98), H:(5, 6), I-5, Mazthoril

COBALT WYRMKIN
Winterspring (98), H:(5, 6), I-5, Mazthoril

COG GLITZSPINNER
Duskwood (36), K-5, Darkshire (108), Second house on left side of road heading into Darkshire from the east

COLD EYE BASILISK
Stranglethorn Vale (74), B-4, C:(4, 5), D:(4, 5), Southern Savage Coast, The Cape of Stranglethorn, The Vile Reef

COLDRIDGE MOUNTAINEER
Dun Morogh (32), D-7, J-4, Coldridge Pass, Coldridge Valley (106)

COLEMAN FARTHING
Tirisfal Glades (86), H-5, Brill (104), First floor of Gallows' End Tavern

COLLIN MAUREN
Stormwind (72), F-8, Mage Quarter, East path leading into Mage Quarter

COLONEL KURZEN
Stranglethorn Vale (74), F-1, The Stockpile, By table to the rear of cave

COMAR VILLARD
Wetlands (96), G-1, Thandol Span, South of collapsed section of bridge

COMBAT MASTER CRITON
Dustwallow Marsh (38), I-5, Theramore Isle (130), Sparring grounds to northeast

COMBAT MASTER SZIGETI
Dustwallow Marsh (38), I-5, Theramore Isle (130), Sparring grounds to northeast

COMMANDER AGGRO'GOSH
Stranglethorn Vale (74), C-3, Grom'gol Base Camp (112), Roams near bonfire in center of camp

COMMANDER ALTHEA EBONLOCKE
Leader of the Night Watch, Duskwood (36), J-5, Darkshire (108), In front of the Darkshire Town Hall

COMMANDER AMAREN
Arathi Highlands (10), F-5, Refuge Point, Roams camp

COMMANDER ASHLAM VALORFIST
Western Plaguelands (92), E-8, Chillwind Camp, In front of tent

COMMANDER FELSTROM
Rare Spawn, Duskwood (36), A-3, B-4, Dawning Wood Catacombs, Lvl 32 Uncommon; Stands at spawn point

COMMANDER GOR'SHAK
Burning Steppes (22), Searing Gorge (64), C-4/D-8, Blackrock Depths

COMMANDER SAMAUL
Dustwallow Marsh (38), I-5, Theramore Isle (130), 2nd floor of Foothold Citadel

COMMANDER SPRINGVALE
Silverpine Forest (68), F-7, Shadowfang Keep

CONDEMNED ACOLYTE
Hillsbrad Foothills (48), A:(7, 8), Purgation Isle, Island

CONDEMNED CLERIC
Hillsbrad Foothills (48), A-8, Purgation Isle, Near top of island

CONDEMNED MONK
Hillsbrad Foothills (48), A-8, Purgation Isle, Island

CONNOR RIVERS
Apprentice Chef, Stormwind (72), F-9, Mage Quarter, The Blue Recluse

CONSERVATOR ILTHALAINE
Teldrassil (80), G-4, H-4, Shadowglen (124), Benches southwest of Aldrassil

CONSTANCE BRISBOISE
Apprentice Clothier, Tirisfal Glades (86), G-6, Cold Hearth Manor, House on northwestern edge of manor

CONSTRICTOR VINE
Desolace (30), D-5, Mauradon

COOK GHILM
Cooking Trainer, Dun Morogh (32), I-5, Gol'Bolar Quarry, Patrols kitchen area of camp

COOK TORKA
Durotar (34), H-4, Razor Hill (122), Western entrance on hill

COOKIE
Westfall (94), D-7, E-7, The Deadmines

COR GRIMTOTEM
Thunder Bluff (84), I-3, Elder Rise, In front of Magatha Grimtotem's tent

CORAL MOONGALE
Azshara (14), C-4, Bear's Head, Up hill to the right of tower

CORALSHELL LURKER
Azshara (14), E-9, F:(4, 7, 9), G:(4, 7, 9), H:(3, 4, 7-9), I:(3, 4, 7-9), J:(7-9), K:(3, 4, 8, 9), L:(2-4)

CORALSHELL TORTOISE
Azshara (14), E:(1, 2), F:(1, 2), G-1, H-1, I-1, J-1, K:(1, 2), L:(1, 2), Jagged Reef

CORAND
Darnassus (26), E-1, Cenarion Enclave, Tree stump, west of the northeast structure

CORBETT SCHNEIDER
Stormwind (72), Roams city

CORE HOUND
Burning Steppes (22), Searing Gorge (64), C-4/D-8, The Molten Core

CORE RAGER
Burning Steppes (22), Searing Gorge (64), C-4/D-8, The Molten Core

CORINA STEELE
Weaponsmith, Elwynn Forest (42), E-7, Goldshire (112), Smithy

CORITHRAS MOONRAGE
Teldrassil (80), G-6, Dolanaar (109), Moonwell south side of Dolanaar

CORK GIZELTON
Desolace (30), H-4, Spawns on road near Kormek's Hut, runs a loop along the roads, and pauses at the hut upon return

CORPORAL BLUTH
Camp Trader, Stranglethorn Vale (74), D-1, Rebel Camp, Camp

CORPORAL KALEB
Stranglethorn Vale (74), D-1, Rebel Camp, Camp

CORPORAL KEESHAN
Redridge Mountains (62), C-1, Render's Rock, Center of cave

CORPORAL MELKINS
Desolace (30), I-1, Nijel's Point (119), Clearing near entrance

CORPORAL SETHMAN
Stranglethorn Vale (74), D-1, Rebel Camp, Camp

CORPORAL TEEKA BLOODSNARL
Frostwolf Clan, Alterac Mountains (8), I-5, Alterac Valley, Cave

CORROSIVE LURKER
Dun Morogh (32), C-4, Gnomeregan

CORROSIVE SAP BEAST
Stonetalon Mountains (70), D:(1, 2), E:(1, 2), Stonetalon Peak, The Talon Den

CORROSIVE SWAMP OOZE
Dustwallow Marsh (38), F:(4-6), G:(5, 6), Beezil's Wreck, The Quagmire

CORRUPT FORCE OF NATURE
Desolace (30), D-5, Mauradon

CORRUPT MINOR MANIFESTATION OF WATER
Silverpine Forest (68), F-4, The Tides Run

CORRUPTED BLOODTALON SCYTHEMAW
Durotar (34), E-6, F:(2, 3), Rocktusk Farm, Thunder Ridge, Tor'kren Farm

CORRUPTED MOTTLED BOAR
Durotar (34), E-4, F-2, Thunder Ridge

CORRUPTED SCORPID
Durotar (34), E-3, F-5, H-1, Jaggedswine Farm, Thunder Ridge

CORRUPTED SPIRIT
Western Plaguelands (92), I-7, Scholomance

CORRUPTED SURF CRAWLER
Durotar (34), H-1, I-2, Bladefist Bay, Deadeye Shore, Skull Rock

CORRUPTOR
Desolace (30), D-5, Mauradon

COUNCILMAN BRUNSWICK
Pyrewood Council, Silverpine Forest (68), G-7, Pyrewood Village, (Summon) Spawns with Lord Mayor Morrison and Councilman Cooper in town hall

COUNCILMAN COOPER
Pyrewood Council, Silverpine Forest (68), G-7, Pyrewood Village, (Summon) Spawns with Lord Mayor Morrison and Councilman Brunswick in town hall

COUNCILMAN HARTIN
Pyrewood Council, Silverpine Forest (68), G-7, Pyrewood Village, (Summon) Spawns with Councilman Higarth and Councilman Wilhelm in town hall

COUNCILMAN HENDRICKS
Pyrewood Council, Silverpine Forest (68), G-7, Pyrewood Village, (Summon) Spawns with Councilman Thatcher in town hall

COUNCILMAN HIGARTH
Pyrewood Council, Silverpine Forest (68), G-7, Pyrewood Village, (Summon) Spawns with Councilman Hartin and Councilman Wilhelm in town hall

COUNCILMAN MILLSTIPE
Council of Darkshire, Duskwood (36), J-5, Darkshire (108), Darkshire Town Hall

COUNCILMAN SMITHERS
Pyrewood Council, Silverpine Forest (68), G-7, Pyrewood Village, (Summon) Spawns in town hall

COUNCILMAN THATCHER
Pyrewood Council, Silverpine Forest (68), G-7, Pyrewood Village, (Summon) Spawns with Councilman Hendricks in town hall

COUNCILMAN WILHELM
Pyrewood Council, Silverpine Forest (68), G-7, Pyrewood Village, (Summon) Spawns with Councilman Hartin and Councilman Higarth in town hall

COUNT REMINGTON RIDGEWELL
House of Nobles, Stormwind (72), K-3, Stormwind Keep, Petitioner's Chamber

COURIER HAMMERFALL
Ironforge (52), Roams entire city

COWARDLY CROSBY
Tailoring Supplies, Stranglethorn Vale (74), B-9, Wild Shore, Small camp on the southernmost tip of Stranglethorn Vale

COYOTE
Westfall (94), C:(3, 4), D:(2-4), E:(2, 3), F:(2-5), G:(1-4), Hills

COYOTE PACKLEADER
Westfall (94), C:(3, 4), D:(2-4), E:(2, 3), F:(3-5), G:(2-4), Gold Coast Quarry

CRACKED GOLEM
Darkshore (24), E:(8, 9), Remtravel's Excavation

CRACKED SKULL SOLDIER
Tirisfal Glades (86), E-3, F-3, Agamand Mills (100)

CRAG BOAR
Dun Morogh (32), D:(5, 6), E:(6, 7), F:(5-7), G:(5, 6)

CRAG COYOTE
Badlands (16), G:(3-5), H:(1-5), I-5, Hammertoe's Digsite, Digsite

CRAG STALKER
Thousand Needles (82), D:(2-4), E:(3, 5, 6), F:(5, 6), G-5, Darkcloud Pinnacle, Freewind Post, The Great Lift

CRAIG HEWITT
Hillsbrad Foothills (48), G-3, Tarren Mill (128)

CRAIG NOLLWARD
Cook, Dustwallow Marsh (38), I-5, Theramore Isle (130), Back of inn

CRANE OPERATOR BIGGLEFUZZ
Barrens (18), H-4, Ratchet (121), Tower near dock

CRANK FIZZLEBUB
Stranglethorn Vale (74), B-8, Booty Bay (103), First floor of The Salty Sailor Tavern

CRANKY BENJ
Rare Spawn, Alterac Mountains (8), A-5, Lordamere Lake, Lvl 32 Very Rare; Patrols eastern coast of lake

CRAVEN DROK
Orgrimmar (60), E-5, The Drag, Roams The Cleft of Shadow and The Drag

CRAZED ANCIENT
Ashenvale (12), G:(3, 4), H:(4, 5), Nightsong Woods, Raynewood Retreat

CRAZED OWLBEAST
Winterspring (98), I:(2, 6), J:(2, 6), The Hidden Grove, Owl Wing Thicket

CRAZK SPARKS
Fireworks Merchant, Stranglethorn Vale (74), B-8, Booty Bay (103), Shop on the back side of building near the overturned boat and hanging shark on the eastern side of bay

CREEPING SLUDGE
Desolace (30), D-5, Mauradon

CREEPTHESS
Rare Spawn, Hillsbrad Foothills (48), B-5, C-6, D:(5, 6), Azurelode Mine, Lvl 24 Semi-Rare; Roams small area around spawn point

CREST KILLER
Burning Steppes (22), Searing Gorge (64), C-4/D-8, Blackrock Depths

CRESTING EXILE
Arathi Highlands (10), I-3, Circle of East Binding

CRIER GOODMAN
Stormwind (72), Roams city

CRILDOR
Darnassus (26), C:(2, 3), F-5, The Temple Gardens, Strolls along path, pausing at dock and lake in Cenarion Enclave

CRIMSON BATTLE MAGE
Eastern Plaguelands (40), D-2, Stratholme

CRIMSON BODYGUARD
Eastern Plaguelands (40), D-2, Roams between Stratholme and Tyr's Hand

CRIMSON CONJUROR
Eastern Plaguelands (40), D-2, Stratholme

CRIMSON COURIER
Eastern Plaguelands (40), D-2, Stratholme, Patrols with four Crimson Bodyguards to Tyr's Hand (L-8)

CRIMSON DEFENDER
Eastern Plaguelands (40), D-2, Stratholme

CRIMSON ELITE
Western Plaguelands (92), G-2, (Summon) Both inside the tower and along the road west of the tower

CRIMSON GALLANT
Eastern Plaguelands (40), D-2, Stratholme

CRIMSON GUARDSMAN
Eastern Plaguelands (40), D-2, Stratholme

CRIMSON HAMMERSMITH
Eastern Plaguelands (40), D-2, Stratholme

CRIMSON INITIATE
Eastern Plaguelands (40), D-2, Stratholme

CRIMSON INQUISITOR
Eastern Plaguelands (40), D-2, Stratholme

CRIMSON MONK
Eastern Plaguelands (40), D-2, Stratholme

CRIMSON OOZE
Wetlands (96), F:(2, 3), Ironbeard's Tomb

CRIMSON PRIEST
Eastern Plaguelands (40), D-2, Stratholme

CRIMSON RIFLEMAN
Eastern Plaguelands (40), D-2, Stratholme

CRIMSON SORCERER
Eastern Plaguelands (40), D-2, Stratholme

CRIMSON WHELP
Wetlands (96), H:(3, 4), I:(3-5), J-5, The Green Belt

CROWD PUMMELLER 9-60
Dun Morogh (32), C-4, Gnomeregan

CRUSADER LORD VALDELMAR
Eastern Plaguelands (40), L-8, Tyr's Hand, Patrols in and out of The Scarlet Basilica

CRUSHRIDGE BRUTE
Alterac Mountains (8), F:(3, 4, 6), G:(4-6), Crushridge Hold, Slaughter Hollow

CRUSHRIDGE ENFORCER
Alterac Mountains (8), E:(5, 6), Ruins of Alterac, Ruins

CRUSHRIDGE MAGE
Alterac Mountains (8), E:(4, 5), F-5, Ruins of Alterac, Ruins

CRUSHRIDGE MAULER
Alterac Mountains (8), E:(4, 5), F-5, Ruins of Alterac, Ruins

CRUSHRIDGE OGRE
Alterac Mountains (8), E-3, F:(3-6), G:(3-6), Crushridge Hold, Slaughter Hollow

CRUSHRIDGE PLUNDERER
Alterac Mountains (8), E-5, Ruins of Alterac, Ruins

CRUSHRIDGE WARMONGER
Alterac Mountains (8), D-5, E:(5, 6), Ruins of Alterac, Ruins

CRYPT BEAST
Eastern Plaguelands (40), D-2, Stratholme

CRYPT CRAWLER
Eastern Plaguelands (40), D-2, Stratholme

CRYPT FIEND
Eastern Plaguelands (40), B-3, C:(2, 3), D:(3, 4), E:(3, 4), F-3, I-4, Terrordale

CRYPT HORROR
Eastern Plaguelands (40), I-4, Terrordale

CRYPT ROBBER
Eastern Plaguelands (40), D-8, Terrordale

CRYPT SLAYER
Eastern Plaguelands (40), E-5, F-5, K:(4, 5), The Noxious Glade

CRYPT WALKER
Eastern Plaguelands (40), B-3, C:(2, 3), D:(2-4), E:(3, 4), F-3, Terrordale

CRYSTAL BOUGHMAN
Cooking Trainer, Redridge Mountains (62), B-4, Lakeshire (115), First floor of large house on southwestern side of town

CRYSTAL FANG
Rare Spawn, Burning Steppes (22), Searing Gorge (64), C-4/D-8, Blackrock Spire, Lvl 60 Rare

CRYSTAL SPINE BASILISK
Stranglethorn Vale (74), B-2, E-1, Kurzen's Compound, The Savage Coast

CURATOR THORIUS
Ironforge (52), E-3, F-1, Hall of Explorers, Roams library

CURGLE CRANKLEHOP
Tanaris (78), H-3, Gadgetzan (111), Near Super Egg-O-Matic on north side of town

CURSED ATAL'AI
Swamp of Sorrows (76), I-5, The Temple of Atal'Hakkar

CURSED CENTAUR
Desolace (30), D-5, Mauradon

CURSED DARKHOUND
Tirisfal Glades (86), E:(4-7), F:(4-7), G:(6, 7), G:(3, 6), I:(3-6), J:(3-7), K:(6, 7)

CURSED HIGHBORNE
Darkshore (24), F-6, G-6, Ameth'Aran

CURSED JUSTICAR
Hillsbrad Foothills (48), A-8, Purgation Isle, Island

CURSED MAGE
Eastern Plaguelands (40), B:(3, 4), C:(2-4), D:(3, 4), E:(2-4), F:(2-4), Terrordale

CURSED MARINE
Wetlands (96), B:(2, 3), The Lost Fleet

CURSED OOZE
Felwood (44), E:(6, 7), F:(6, 7), Ruins of Constellas

CURSED PALADIN
Hillsbrad Foothills (48), A:(7, 8), Purgation Isle, Island

CURSED SAILOR
Wetlands (96), B:(2, 3), The Lost Fleet

CURSED SYCAMORE
Feralas (46), F-7, Ruins of Isildien, Roams as far north as the High Wilderness

CUTAC
Cloth & Leather Armor Merchant, Durotar (34), H-4, Razor Hill (122), Northern entrance

CYCLOK THE MAD
Rare Spawn, Tanaris (78), F:(5-7), G:(6, 7), Dunemaul Compound, Eastmoon Ruins, Southmoon Ruins, Lvl 48 Very Rare; Spawns in ruins or compound and sticks close to spawn point

CYCLONE WARRIOR
Silithus (66), D:(4, 5), E:(2, 3), F:(4, 5), G-3, Southwind Village

CYCLONIAN
Alterac Mountains (8), K-6, Chillwind Point, (Summon) Tiki Altar in front of ruins

CYLANIA
Night Elf Armorer, Darnassus (26), H-4, Warrior's Terrace, Lower southwest platform

CYLANIA ROOTSTALKER
Herbalist, Ashenvale (12), G-6, Silverwind Refuge, Left wing of building

CYLINA DARKHEART
Demon Trainer, Elwynn Forest (42), F-7, Goldshire (112), Basement of Lion's Pride Inn

CYNDRA KINDWHISPER
Journeyman Alchemist, Teldrassil (80), G-6, Dolanaar (109), Inside house east of inn

CYRIDAN
Leather Armor Merchant, Darnassus (26), G-8, Tradesmen's Terrace, Leather Armor shop

CYROEN
Reagent Vendor, Darnassus (26), D-1, Cenarion Enclave, Northwest structure

CYRUS THEREPENTOUS
Burning Steppes (22), L-3, Slither Rock, Cave

D

DABYRIE LABORER
Arathi Highlands (10), G-4, H-4, Dabyrie's Farmstead,

DABYRIE MILITIA
Arathi Highlands (10), G-4, H:(3, 4), Dabyrie's Farmstead

DADANGA
Un'Goro Crater (90), F-1, Marshal's Refuge (116), Entrance to cave

DAELYSHIA
Hippogryph Master, Ashenvale (12), E-5, Astranaar (101)

DAEOLYN SUMMERLEAF
General Goods, Moonglade (56), F-3, Nighthaven (120), Northwest building

DAERA BRIGHTSPEAR
Hunter Trainer, Ironforge (52), J-9, The Military Ward, Hall of Arms

DAGGERSPINE MARAUDER
Arathi Highlands (10), C:(8, 9), D-9, The Drowned Reef

DAGGERSPINE RAIDER
Arathi Highlands (10), B:(8, 9), C:(8, 9), The Drowned Reef

DAGGERSPINE SCREAMER
Hillsbrad Foothills (48), G:(7, 8), H:(8, 9), Eastern Strand

DAGGERSPINE SHOREHUNTER
Hillsbrad Foothills (48), F:(6, 7), G:(7, 8), Eastern Strand

DAGGERSPINE SHORESTALKER
Hillsbrad Foothills (48), G:(7, 8), H:(8, 9), Eastern Strand

DAGGERSPINE SIREN
Hillsbrad Foothills (48), F-6, G:(6-8), H-8, Eastern Strand

DAGGERSPINE SORCERESS
Arathi Highlands (10), B:(8, 9), C:(8, 9), The Drowned Reef

DAGRI
Raene's Pet, Ashenvale (12), E-5, Astranaar (101), First floor of inn near Raene

DAGUN THE RAVENOUS
Dustwallow Marsh (38), H-1, Dreadmurk Shore, (Summon) Spawns near largest of five isles after an herb is placed on the Seaworn Altar

DAHNE PIERCE
Dustwallow Marsh (38), I-5, Theramore Isle (130), 2nd floor of inn

DAIO THE DECREPIT
Blasted Lands (20), E-5, The Tainted Scar, Altar

DAISY
Race Starter Girl, Thousand Needles (82), K-8, Mirage Raceway (118), Inside racetrack

DAL BLOODCLAW
Ashenvale (12), E-4, Thistlefur Village, Roams between camps

DALAR DAWNWEAVER
Silverpine Forest (68), G-4, The Sepulcher (124), Roams on right side of sepulcher by crates

DALARAN APPRENTICE
Silverpine Forest (68), G:(6, 7), H:(6, 7)

DALARAN BREWMASTER
Silverpine Forest (68), I-6, Ambermill, Caravan right of entrance inside city walls

DALARAN CONJUROR
Silverpine Forest (68), I-6, Ambermill

DALARAN MAGE
Silverpine Forest (68), I:(6, 7), Ambermill

DALARAN MINER
Silverpine Forest (68), I-6, Ambermill, Shed left of entrance inside city walls

DALARAN PROTECTOR
Silverpine Forest (68), H:(5-7), I:(6, 7), Ambermill

DALARAN SHIELD GUARD
Alterac Mountains (8), B:(8, 9), Lordamere Internment Camp

DALARAN SPELLSCRIBE
Silverpine Forest (68), I-6, Ambermill

DALARAN SUMMONER
Alterac Mountains (8), A:(7, 8), B:(5-8), C-6, Dalaran

DALARAN THEURGIST
Alterac Mountains (8), B:(8, 9), Lordamere Internment Camp

DALARAN WARDER
Silverpine Forest (68), I-6, J-6, Ambermill, Keep

DALARAN WATCHER
Silverpine Forest (68), H-8, I:(6-8), J:(6, 8)

DALARAN WIZARD
Silverpine Forest (68), I:(6-8), J:(5-8)

DALARAN WORKER
Alterac Mountains (8), A:(7, 8), B:(6, 7), Dalaran

DALIN FORGEWRIGHT
Silverpine Forest (68), G-8, The Greymane Wall, Mounted on horse roaming along wall

DALINDA MALEM
Desolace (30), G-3, Thunder Axe Fortress, Kneeling near chest in center of fortress

DALMOND
General Goods, Darkshore (24), F-4, Auberdine (101), Back terrace of northern building

DALRIA
Trade Goods, Ashenvale (12), E-5, Astranaar (101), Back of building to the southwest

DAMNED SOUL
Deadwind Pass (28), C:(6-8), D:(7, 8), E:(7-9), F-8, Karazhan, Morgan's Plot

DAN GOLTHAS
Journeyman Leatherworker, Undercity (88), J-6, The Rogues' Quarter

DANE LINDGREN
Journeyman Blacksmith, Stormwind (72), I-2, J-2, Dwarven District, At the Forge

DANE WINSLOW
Demon Trainer, Elwynn Forest (42), G-4, Northshire Valley (120), Graveyard on right side of abbey

DANIEL BARTLETT
General Trade Supplier, Undercity (88), I-4, The Trade Quarter, Upper Ring of Trade Quarter

DANIEL ULFMAN
Tirisfal Glades (86), D-6, Deathknell (109)

DANIELLE ZIPSTITCH
Tailoring Supplies, Duskwood (36), K-5, Darkshire (108), Second floor of house

DANK DRIZZLECUT
Mining Trainer, Dun Morogh (32), J-6, Gol'Bolar Quarry, Far end of camp by machinery

DANLAAR NIGHTSHADE
Hunter Trainer, Ashenvale (12), F-6, G-6, Silverwind Refuge, Back of building

DANLYIA
Food & Drink Vendor, Teldrassil (80), G-6, Dolanaar (109), Bottom floor inside building north of road

DANNAL STERN
Warrior Trainer, Tirisfal Glades (86), D-6, Deathknell (109), First floor of second house on right side of road

DANNELOR
First Aid Trainer, Darnassus (26), G-1, Craftsmen's Terrace, First Aid shop

DANNIE FIZZWIZZLE
Demon Trainer, Dun Morogh (32), F-5, Kharanos (114), Gnomish camp on right of distillery

DAPHNE STILWELL
Westfall (94), D-9, The Dagger Hills, Roams the nearby orchard

DAR
Swamp of Sorrows (76), F-5, Stonard (126), First floor of inn

DARBEL MONTROSE
Rare Spawn, Arathi Highlands (10), C-7, D-6, Stromgarde Keep (127), Lvl 39 Semi-Rare; Roams with minion near spawn point

DARCY
Waitress, Redridge Mountains (62), C-4, Lakeshire (115), First floor of Lakeshire Inn

DARGH TRUEAIM
Hunter Trainer, Loch Modan (54), K-6, The Farstrider Lodge, In right hall of lodge

DARGON
Food & Drink Merchant, Moonglade (56), G-4, Nighthaven (120), At counter of central building

DARIAN SINGH
Fireworks Vendor, Stormwind (72), D-7, Mage Quarter, Pyrotechnics

DARIANNA
Journeyman Leatherworker, Darnassus (26), I-2, Craftsmen's Terrace, Leatherworking shop

DARK ADEPT
Eastern Plaguelands (40), E-5, F-5, I-4, K:(4, 5), The Fungal Vale

DARK CASTER
Eastern Plaguelands (40), H:(6, 7), Corin's Crossing

DARK CLERIC BERYL
Priest Trainer, Tirisfal Glades (86), H-5, Brill (104), Second floor of Gallows' End Tavern

DARK CLERIC DUESTEN
Priest Trainer, Tirisfal Glades (86), C-7, Deathknell (109), Church

DARK GUARD
Burning Steppes (22), Searing Gorge (64), C-4/D-8, Blackrock Depths

DARK IRON AGENT
Dun Morogh (32), C-4, Gnomeregan

DARK IRON AMBASSADOR
Dun Morogh (32), C-4, Gnomeregan

DARK IRON AMBUSHER
Loch Modan (54), G-7, Spawns at Caravan

DARK IRON BOMBARDIER
Wetlands (96), G-1, Dun Modr

DARK IRON DEMOLITIONIST
Wetlands (96), F-2, H-3, I-3, Dun Modr

DARK IRON DWARF
Wetlands (96), F-2, G-2, H:(2, 3), I-3, Dun Modr

DARK IRON ENTREPRENEUR
Specialty Goods, Wetlands (96), F-2, Dun Modr, Behind bar in southern building

DARK IRON GEOLOGIST
Searing Gorge (64), H-6, I-3, Dustfire Valley

DARK IRON INSURGENT
Loch Modan (54), H:(1, 2), Stonewrought Dam, Eastern side of dam

DARK IRON LOOKOUT
Searing Gorge (64), C-5, D:(5, 6), E-6, F-6

DARK IRON MARKSMAN
Searing Gorge (64), J-2, Dustfire Valley

DARK IRON RAIDER
Loch Modan (54), H:(6, 7), Spawns at Caravan

DARK IRON RIFLEMAN
Wetlands (96), G-2, Dun Modr

DARK IRON SABOTEUR
Wetlands (96), F-2, G:(1, 2), H:(2, 3), I-3, Dun Modr

DARK IRON SAPPER
Loch Modan (54), G-1, Stonewrought Dam

DARK IRON SENTRY
Searing Gorge (64), D:(5, 6), E:(4, 6), F-6, The Slag Pit, Throughout pit

DARK IRON SLAVER
Searing Gorge (64), D:(3-6), E:(2-6), F-4, G-4, The Cauldron

DARK IRON SPY
Dun Morogh (32), K-6, Ironband's Compound

DARK IRON STEAMSMITH
Searing Gorge (64), D-5, E-5, The Cauldron

DARK IRON TASKMASTER
Searing Gorge (64), D:(3-5), E:(2-5), F-4, G-4, The Cauldron

DARK IRON TUNNELER
Wetlands (96), F-2, G-2, H:(2, 3), I-3, Dun Modr

DARK IRON WATCHMAN
Searing Gorge (64), H-6, I-3, Dustfire Valley

DARK KEEPER BETHEK
Burning Steppes (22), Searing Gorge (64), C-4/D-8, Blackrock Depths

DARK KEEPER OFGUT
Burning Steppes (22), Searing Gorge (64), C-4/D-8, Blackrock Depths

DARK KEEPER PELVER
Burning Steppes (22), Searing Gorge (64), C-4/D-8, Blackrock Depths

DARK KEEPER UGGEL
Burning Steppes (22), Searing Gorge (64), C-4/D-8, Blackrock Depths

DARK KEEPER VORFALK
Burning Steppes (22), Searing Gorge (64), C-4/D-8, Blackrock Depths

DARK KEEPER ZIMREL
Burning Steppes (22), Searing Gorge (64), C-4/D-8, Blackrock Depths

DARK SCREECHER
Burning Steppes (22), Searing Gorge (64), C-4/D-8, Blackrock Depths

DARK SHADE
Western Plaguelands (92), I-7, Scholomance

DARK SPRITE
Teldrassil (80), F-5, G-5, Fel Rock

DARK STRAND ADEPT
Ashenvale (12), C-3, D-3, Ruins of Ordil'Aran

DARK STRAND ASSASSIN
Ashenvale (12), C-3, Ruins of Ordil'Aran

DARK STRAND CULTIST
Ashenvale (12), C-3, D-3, Ruins of Ordil'Aran

DARK STRAND ENFORCER
Ashenvale (12), C-3, D-3, Ruins of Ordil'Aran

DARK STRAND EXCAVATOR
Ashenvale (12), C-3, D-3, Ruins of Ordil'Aran

DARK STRAND FANATIC
Darkshore (24), H-3, I-3, Ruins of Mathystra, Tower of Althalaxx

DARK STRAND VOIDCALLER
Darkshore (24), H-3, Tower of Althalaxx

DARK SUMMONER
Cult of the Damned, Eastern Plaguelands (40), D:(2, 3), H:(6, 7), Corin's Crossing

DARKEYE BONECASTER
Tirisfal Glades (86), E:(3, 4), F:(3, 4), Agamand Mills (100)

DARKFANG CREEPER
Dustwallow Marsh (38), D:(5, 6), E:(5, 6), F:(5, 6), Stonemaul Ruins

DARKFANG LURKER
Dustwallow Marsh (38), D:(1, 3-5), E:(1-4), F:(1-4), G:(1-4), H:(2-4)

DARKFANG SPIDER
Dustwallow Marsh (38), D:(1, 3), E:(1-3), F:(1-3), G:(1-4), H:(2-4)

DARKFANG VENOMSPITTER
Dustwallow Marsh (38), D:(4-6), E:(3-6), F:(3-6)

DARKMASTER GANDLING
Western Plaguelands (92), I-7, Scholomance

DARKMIST LURKER
Dustwallow Marsh (38), C-2, D-2, Darkmist Cavern

DARKMIST RECLUSE
Dustwallow Marsh (38), D:(2, 3), Darkmist Cavern

DARKMIST SILKSPINNER
Dustwallow Marsh (38), C-2, D-2, Darkmist Cavern

DARKMIST SPIDER
Dustwallow Marsh (38), D:(2, 3), Darkmist Cavern

DARKMIST WIDOW
Rare Spawn, Dustwallow Marsh (38), D-2, Darkmist Cavern, Lvl 40 Uncommon; Back of cavern

DARKREAVER'S FALLEN CHARGER
Western Plaguelands (92), I-7, Scholomance

DARKSHORE THRESHER
Darkshore (24), D-5, E:(2-6), F-3, Mist's Edge, The Long Wash, Twilight Shore

DARKSLAYER MORDENTHAL
Ashenvale (12), J-7, Dor'Danil Barrow Den, Northwest of barrow den

DARLA HARRIS
Gryphon Master, Hillsbrad Foothills (48), F-5, Southshore (125), Northwest of town near tower

DARN TALONGRIP
Stonetalon Mountains (70), I-9, Malaka'jin, Next to shack

DARNALL
Tailoring Supplies, Moonglade (56), G-3, Nighthaven (120), First floor of northeast building

DARNASSIAN PROTECTOR
Teldrassil (80), B-5, C-5, Rut'theran Village

DARNASSUS SENTINEL
Teldrassil (80), B:(5, 6), C:(5, 6), D-5, G-9, Rut'theran Village

DARNATH BLADESINGER
Warrior Trainer, Darnassus (26), H-3, Warrior's Terrace, Lower northwest platform

DARREN MALVEW
Stablehand, Hillsbrad Foothills (48), F-6, Southshore (125), Right of stable

DARROWSHIRE BETRAYER
Eastern Plaguelands (40), E-8, Darrowshire

DARROWSHIRE DEFENDER
Eastern Plaguelands (40), E-8, Darrowshire

DARSOK SWIFTDAGGER
Barrens (18), F-3, The Crossroads (107), Top of tower south of inn

DART
Rare Spawn, Dustwallow Marsh (38), F-2, Lvl 38 Uncommon; Runs in a circle near spawn point

DARYL RIKNUSSUN
Cooking Trainer, Ironforge (52), H-4, The Great Forge, The Bronze Kettle

DARYL STACK
Master Tailor, Hillsbrad Foothills (48), H-2, Tarren Mill (128), Church

DARYL THE YOUNGLING
Loch Modan (54), K-6, The Farstrider Lodge, In left hall of lodge

DARYN LIGHTWIND
Cenarion Lore Keeper, Teldrassil (80), G-9, Rut'theran Village, Second floor of building

DASHEL STONEFIST
Stormwind (72), J-4, Old Town, By The Five Deadly Venoms

DAUGHTER OF CENARIUS
Stonetalon Mountains (70), D:(1, 2), E:(1, 2), Stonetalon Peak

DAVID LANGSTON
Stormwind (72), J-5, Old Town, Pig and Whistle Tavern

DAVID TRIAS
Rogue Trainer, Tirisfal Glades (86), D-6, Deathknell (109), First floor of second house on right side of road

DAVIL CROKFORD
Eastern Plaguelands (40), E-8, Darrowshire, (Summon) Town entrance along path

DAVIL LIGHTFIRE
Eastern Plaguelands (40), E-8, Darrowshire, (Summon) Town entrance along path

DAVITT HICKSON
Undercity (88), The Magic Quarter, Wanders Magic Quarter

DAWN BRIGHTSTAR
Arcane Goods, Elwynn Forest (42), I-7, Tower of Azora, Top floor of tower

DAWNWATCHER SELGORM
The Argent Dawn, Darnassus (26), G-2, Craftsmen's Terrace, Argent Dawn

DAWNWATCHER SHAEDLASS
The Argent Dawn, Darnassus (26), G-2, Craftsmen's Terrace, Argent Dawn

DAZALAR
Hunter Trainer, Teldrassil (80), G-6, Dolanaar (109), East of inn

DEADLY CLEFT SCORPID
Badlands (16), G-1, Uldaman

DEADMIRE
Dustwallow Marsh (38), F-5, The Quagmire, Follows the stream southwest and turns around

DEAD-TOOTH JACK
Elwynn Forest (42), L-8, Camp west of bridge heading into Duskwood

DEADWIND BRUTE
Deadwind Pass (28), E-6, F:(6-8), The Vice

DEADWIND MAULER
Deadwind Pass (28), E-6, F:(6-8), G:(7, 8), The Vice

DEADWIND OGRE MAGE
Deadwind Pass (28), E-6, F:(6-8), The Vice

DEADWIND WARLOCK
Deadwind Pass (28), E-6, F:(6-8), G:(7, 8), The Vice

DEADWOOD AVENGER
Felwood (44), H:(1, 2), I:(1, 2), Felpaw Village

DEADWOOD DEN WATCHER
Felwood (44), H:(1, 2), I:(1, 2), Felpaw Village

DEADWOOD GARDENER
Felwood (44), F:(8, 9), G:(8, 9), Deadwood Village

DEADWOOD PATHFINDER
Felwood (44), F-9, G-9, Deadwood Village

DEADWOOD SHAMAN
Felwood (44), H:(1, 2), I:(1, 2), Felpaw Village

DEADWOOD WARRIOR
Felwood (44), F:(8, 9), G:(8, 9), Deadwood Village

DEATH CULTIST
Eastern Plaguelands (40), C-2, D:(3, 4), E:(3, 4), F-3, Plaguewood

DEATH FLAYER
Rare Spawn, Durotar (34), E-5, F-5, Lvl 11 Uncommon; Roams clearing south of road

DEATH HOWL
Rare Spawn, Felwood (44), G:(7-8), H-9, Felwood, Morlos'Aran, Lvl 49 Average Rare; Roams near spawn points

DEATH KNIGHT DARKREAVER
Western Plaguelands (92), I-7, Scholomance

DEATH LASH
Feralas (46), G-4, Dire Maul

DEATH SINGER
Eastern Plaguelands (40), D-6, E:(5, 6), F-5, I-3, J:(3-5), K-4, Browman Mill

DEATH SPEAKER JARGBA
Barrens (18), E-9, Razorfen Kraul

DEATHEYE
Rare Spawn, Blasted Lands (20), G:(2, 3), Dreadmaul Hold, Lvl 49 Average Rare; Roams small area around spawn point

DEATHGUARD ABRAHAM
Tirisfal Glades (86), G-5, Bridge

DEATHGUARD BARTHOLOMEW
Tirisfal Glades (86), H-5, Brill (104)

DEATHGUARD BARTRAND
Tirisfal Glades (86), D-6, Deathknell (109)

DEATHGUARD BURGESS
Tirisfal Glades (86), H-5, Brill (104), Outside of the Brill Town Hall

DEATHGUARD CYRUS
Tirisfal Glades (86), H-5, Brill (104)

DEATHGUARD DILLINGER
Tirisfal Glades (86), H-5, Brill (104), Along road near graveyard

DEATHGUARD ELITE
Tirisfal Glades (86), E-5, H-6, Brill (104)

DEATHGUARD GARVIN
Tirisfal Glades (86), H-5, Brill (104)

DEATHGUARD HUMBERT
Hillsbrad Foothills (48), H-2, Tarren Mill (128), Left of church

DEATHGUARD KEL
Tirisfal Glades (86), H-5, Kneeling in front of northeastern entrance to graveyard

DEATHGUARD LAWRENCE
Tirisfal Glades (86), G-5, Brill (104)

DEATHGUARD LINNEA
Tirisfal Glades (86), I-6, In camp outside of Undercity

DEATHGUARD LUNDMARK
Tirisfal Glades (86), E-5, H-6, Roams Road

DEATHGUARD MORRIS
Tirisfal Glades (86), H-5, Brill (104)

DEATHGUARD MORT
Tirisfal Glades (86), H-5, Brill (104)

DEATHGUARD OLIVAR
Tirisfal Glades (86), D-6, Deathknell (109)

DEATHGUARD PHILLIP
Tirisfal Glades (86), D-6, Deathknell (109)

DEATHGUARD PODRIG
Silverpine Forest (68), F-4, The Sepulcher (124), Outside of inn entrance on left

DEATHGUARD RANDOLPH
Tirisfal Glades (86), D-6, Deathknell (109)

DEATHGUARD ROYANN
Tirisfal Glades (86), D-5, Deathknell (109)

DEATHGUARD SALTAIN
Tirisfal Glades (86), D-7, Deathknell (109), Roaming near the church

DEATHGUARD SAMSA
Hillsbrad Foothills (48), H-2, Tarren Mill (128), Roams outside of inn

DEATHGUARD SIMMER
Tirisfal Glades (86), E-5, At the fork in the road outside of Deathknell

DEATHGUARD TERRENCE
Tirisfal Glades (86), D-5, Deathknell (109)

DEATHLASH SCORPID
Burning Steppes (22), D:(5, 6), E-3, F:(3, 7), G:(2, 3, 6), H:(5, 6), I:(3-6), J-3

DEATHLY USHER
Blasted Lands (20), G-2, Rise of the Defiler, Summoned on activation of quest

DEATHMAW
Rare Spawn, Burning Steppes (22), I-3, J-6, K:(3, 5), Dreadmaul Rock, Terror Wing Path, Lvl 53 Uncommon; Roams small area around spawn point

DEATH'S HEAD ACOLYTE
Barrens (18), E-9, Razorfen Kraul

DEATH'S HEAD ADEPT
Barrens (18), E-9, Razorfen Kraul

DEATH'S HEAD CULTIST
Barrens (18), F-9, Razorfen Downs

DEATH'S HEAD GEOMANCER
Barrens (18), F-9, Razorfen Downs

DEATH'S HEAD NECROMANCER
Barrens (18), F-9, Razorfen Downs

DEATH'S HEAD PRIEST
Barrens (18), E-9, Razorfen Kraul

DEATH'S HEAD SAGE
Barrens (18), E-9, Razorfen Kraul

DEATH'S HEAD SEER
Barrens (18), E-9, Razorfen Kraul

DEATH'S HEAD WARD KEEPER
Barrens (18), E-9, Razorfen Kraul

DEATHSPEAKER SELENDRE
Rare Spawn, Cult of the Damned, Eastern Plaguelands (40), E-5, K:(4, 5), The Fungal Vale, The Noxious Glade, Lvl 56 Uncommon; In camp

DEATHSTALKER ADAMANT
Silverpine Forest (68), F-7, Shadowfang Keep

DEATHSTALKER ERLAND
Silverpine Forest (68), H-1, Malden's Orchard, House northeast of orchard

DEATHSTALKER FAERLEIA
Silverpine Forest (68), G-7, Pyrewood Village, Town hall

DEATHSTALKER LESH
Hillsbrad Foothills (48), A-5, Southpoint Tower, At base of tower

DEATHSTALKER VINCENT
Silverpine Forest (68), F-7, Shadowfang Keep

DEATHSTALKER ZRAEDUS
Duskwood (36), L-3, Beggar's Haunt, Tower entrance

DEATHSTRIKE TARANTULA
Swamp of Sorrows (76), G-6, H:(6, 7), I:(6-8), J:(7, 8)

DEATHSWORN CAPTAIN
Rare Spawn, Silverpine Forest (68), F-7, Shadowfang Keep, Lvl 25 Rare

DECAYING HORROR
Western Plaguelands (92), H:(3, 4), I:(3, 4), The Weeping Cave

DECEDRA WILLHAM
Dustwallow Marsh (38), J-6, Theramore Isle (130), Docks

DECKHAND MOISHE
Arathi Highlands (10), D-8, Faldir's Cove, Bow of ship

DECREPIT DARKHOUND
Tirisfal Glades (86), D-5, E:(4-6), F:(5, 6), G-5, H:(4-6), I:(4-6)

DEEB
Rare Spawn, Tirisfal Glades (86), G-3, H-3, The North Coast, Lvl 12 Uncommon; Stands idle at spawn point

DEEG
Blackwater Raiders, Stranglethorn Vale (74), B-8, Booty Bay (103), Third floor of The Salty Sailor Tavern

DEEK FIZZLEBIZZ
Journeyman Engineer, Loch Modan (54), F-1, Stonewrought Dam, Under scaffolding on dam wall

DEEP BORER
Desolace (30), D-5, Maraudon

DEEP DWELLER
Tanaris (78), I:(6, 7), J:(6, 7), K-6, Southbreak Shore

DEEP LURKER
Swamp of Sorrows (76), I-5, The Temple of Atal'Hakkar

DEEP POOL THRESHFIN
Ashenvale (12), B-2, Blackfathom Deeps

DEEP SEA THRESHADON
Darkshore (24), H-1, I-1, Mist's Edge

DEEP STINGER
Burning Steppes (22), Searing Gorge (64), C-4/D-8, Blackrock Depths

DEEP STRIDER
Feralas (46), C-3, D:(3-5), E:(5-7), The Forgotten Coast

DEEPMOSS CREEPER
Stonetalon Mountains (70), G-7, H:(7, 9), I:(8, 9)

DEEPMOSS VENOMSPITTER
Stonetalon Mountains (70), F:(4, 5), G:(4-7), H-6

DEEPMOSS WEBSPINNER
Stonetalon Mountains (70), G-7, H-5, I-4, J:(4, 5)

DEEPROT STOMPER
Desolace (30), D-5, Mauradon

DEEPROT TANGLER
Desolace (30), D-5, Mauradon

DEEPSTRIDER GIANT
Desolace (30), B-9, C-6, F-1, Ethel Rethor, Sar'theris Strand

DEEPSTRIDER SEARCHER
Desolace (30), B-9, C-6, F-1, Mannoroc Coven, Sar'theris Strand

DEFIAS AMBUSHER
Elwynn Forest (42), D-6

DEFIAS BANDIT
Elwynn Forest (42), C-6, D-6, F:(7, 8), G:(6, 8), I-8, J-8, L-8

DEFIAS BLACKGUARD
Westfall (94), D-7, E-7, The Deadmines

DEFIAS BODYGUARD
Elwynn Forest (42), F-9, Jerod's Landing

DEFIAS CAPTIVE
Stormwind (72), F-6, The Stockade

DEFIAS COMPANION
Westfall (94), D-7, E-7, The Deadmines

DEFIAS CONJURER
Westfall (94), D-7, E-7, The Deadmines

DEFIAS CONVICT
Stormwind (72), F-6, The Stockade

DEFIAS CUTPURSE
Elwynn Forest (42), D:(6, 7), E:(5-7), F:(5, 6), Mirror Lake, Mirror Lake Orchard

DEFIAS DIGGER
Westfall (94), D-7, E-7, The Deadmines

DEFIAS DOCKMASTER
Elwynn Forest (42), F-9, Jerod's Landing, House on riverbank

DEFIAS DRONE
Westfall (94), H-7, Tower

DEFIAS ENCHANTER
Duskwood (36), B-7, C-7, G-8, The Yorgen Farmstead

DEFIAS EVOKER
Westfall (94), D-7, E-7, The Deadmines

DEFIAS FOOTPAD
Westfall (94), F-2, G-2, The Jansen Stead

DEFIAS HENCHMAN
Westfall (94), D-7, E-7, The Deadmines

DEFIAS HIGHWAYMAN
Westfall (94), D-8, E-8, F:(7, 8), The Dagger Hills

DEFIAS INMATE
Stormwind (72), F-6, The Stockade

DEFIAS INSURGENT
Stormwind (72), F-6, The Stockade

DEFIAS KNUCKLEDUSTER
Westfall (94), C:(7, 8), D:(7-8), E-8, F:(7, 8), G-6, The Dagger Hills

DEFIAS LOOTER
Westfall (94), B-5, C:(3-6), D:(5-7), E:(2, 6, 7), Gold Coast Quarry

DEFIAS MAGICIAN
Westfall (94), D-7, E-7, The Deadmines

DEFIAS MESSENGER
Westfall (94), E-7, Moonbrook, Roams along the road from Moonbrook to the back of the Jangolode Mine

DEFIAS MINER
Westfall (94), D-7, E-7, The Deadmines

DEFIAS NIGHT BLADE
Duskwood (36), B-7, C-7, F:(7, 8), G-8, The Yorgen Farmstead

DEFIAS NIGHT RUNNER
Duskwood (36), B:(6, 7), C:(6, 7), F-7, G:(7, 8), H-7, The Yorgen Farmstead

DEFIAS OVERSEER
Westfall (94), D-7, E-7, The Deadmines

DEFIAS PATHSTALKER
Westfall (94), C:(7, 8), D:(6, 7), E-8, F:(7, 8), The Dagger Hills

DEFIAS PILLAGER
Westfall (94), B-5, C:(4-6), D:(5-7), E:(6, 7), Gold Coast Quarry

DEFIAS PIRATE
Westfall (94), D-7, E-7, The Deadmines

DEFIAS PRISONER
Stormwind (72), F-6, The Stockade

DEFIAS PROFITEER
Freewheeling Merchant, Westfall (94), E-7, Moonbrook, Top floor of Moonbrook inn

DEFIAS RAIDER
Westfall (94), D-8, Moonbrook

DEFIAS RENEGADE MAGE
Elwynn Forest (42), C-6, D-6, G:(6, 8), J:(5, 6), K-5

DEFIAS ROGUE WIZARD
Elwynn Forest (42), C-6, D-6, G:(6, 8), J:(5, 6), K-5

DEFIAS SMUGGLER
Westfall (94), D-4, E:(2-5), F:(2, 4, 5), Jangolode Mine

DEFIAS SQUALLSHAPER
Westfall (94), D-7, E-7, The Deadmines

DEFIAS STRIP MINER
Westfall (94), D-7, E-7, The Deadmines

DEFIAS TASKMASTER
Westfall (94), D-7, E-7, The Deadmines

DEFIAS THUG
Elwynn Forest (42), G:(4, 5), H:(4, 5), Northshire Valley (120)

DEFIAS TOWER PATROLLER
Westfall (94), I-7, Tower

DEFIAS TOWER SENTRY
Westfall (94), I-7, Tower

DEFIAS TRAITOR
Westfall (94), F-5, Sentinel Hill (123), Sentinel Tower

DEFIAS TRAPPER
Westfall (94), C-3, D-4, E:(2-5), F:(2, 4, 5)

DEFIAS WATCHMAN
Westfall (94), D-7, E-7, The Deadmines

DEFIAS WIZARD
Westfall (94), D-7, E-7, The Deadmines

DEFIAS WORKER
Westfall (94), D-7, E-7, The Deadmines

DEILIA VERANA
Hillsbrad Foothills (48), H-2, Tarren Mill (128)

DEINO
Mage Trainer, Orgrimmar (60), D-8, Valley of Spirit, Darkbriar Lodge

DELFRUM FLINTBEARD
Journeyman Blacksmith, Darkshore (24), F-4, Auberdine (101), In front of northern building

DELGO RAGETOTEM
Axe Merchant, Thunder Bluff (84), F-6, High rise, inside Ragetotem Arms tent

DELGREN THE PURIFIER
Ashenvale (12), D-4, Maestra's Post, Near Stones south of outpost

DELLA
Jessir's Pet, Felwood (44), G-8, Emerald Sanctuary, Near Pool

DELLYLAH
Food & Drink Vendor, Teldrassil (80), H-4, Shadowglen (124), Open room in front of main building

DELMANIS THE HATED
Darkshore (24), H-3, Tower of Althalaxx, Roams hills east of tower to bonfire

DEMETRIA
The Scarlet Oracle, Eastern Plaguelands (40), K-8, Tyr's Hand, (Summon) Patrols with nine Scarlet troopers to Stratholme (D-2)

DEMISETTE CLOYCE
Warlock Trainer, Stormwind (72), D-8, Mage Quarter, The Slaughtered Lamb

DEMNUL FARMOUNTAIN
Ironforge (52), J-9, The Military Ward, Hall of Arms

DEMON PORTAL GUARDIAN
Desolace (30), F:(7, 8), G:(7, 8), Mannoroc Coven

DEMON SPIRIT
Desolace (30), G-3, Thunder Axe Fortress

DEN GRUNT
Durotar (34), F-7, G-7, Valley of Trials (131)

DEN MOTHER
Darkshore (24), H-4, Mist's Edge

DENALAN
Teldrassil (80), H-7, Lake Al'Ameth, Camp east of lake

DENATHARION
Druid Trainer, Darnassus (26), D-1, Cenarion Enclave, Northwest structure

DENDRITE STARBLAZE
Moonglade (56), H-3, Nighthaven (120), Second floor of far northeast building on hill

DENDRYTHIS
Food & Drink Vendor, Darnassus (26), D-1, F-2, Cenarion Enclave, Roams path between enclave & Craftsmen's Terrace

DENEB WALKER
Scrolls and Potions, Arathi Highlands (10), C-6, Stromgarde Keep (127), Well near church

DENNI'KA
Butcher, Stonetalon Mountains (70), I-9, Malaka'jin, Next to wagon, north of den

DEPUTY FELDON
Redridge Mountains (62), D-6, Next to Gryphon Master outside of Lakeshire

DEPUTY RAINER
Elwynn Forest (42), C-7, Westbrook Garrison, Right of garrison entrance

DEPUTY WILLEM
Elwynn Forest (42), F-4, Northshire Valley (120), Outside to the right of abbey

DERAK NIGHTFALL
Cook, Hillsbrad Foothills (48), H-2, Tarren Mill (128), Between the inn and graveyard

DERINA RUMDNUL
Wetlands (96), A-6, Menethil Harbor (117), In and out of small house east of keep

DERMOT
Alterac Mountains (8), B-8, Lordamere Internment Camp, Building within camp walls

DERMOT JOHNS
Cloth & Leather Armor Merchant, Elwynn Forest (42), F-4, Northshire Valley (120), Caravan facing abbey

DEROTAIN MUDSIPPER
The Thorium Brotherhood, Tanaris (78), H-3, Gadgetzan (111), Near southern entrance

DESERT RAGER
Silithus (66), D:(4, 5), F:(4, 5)

DESERT RUMBLER
Silithus (66), D-1, E:(1-3), F:(3, 4), G-3, Ravaged Twilight Camp

DESSECUS
Rare Spawn, Felwood (44), H-2, Irontree Cavern, Lvl 56 Semi-Rare; Bottom cave

DETH'RYLL SATYR
Darkshore (24), G-4, Bashal'Aran

DEVIATE ADDER
Barrens (18), E-4, Wailing Caverns

DEVIATE COILER
Barrens (18), E-4, Wailing Caverns

DEVIATE CREEPER
Barrens (18), E-4, Wailing Caverns

DEVIATE CROCOLISK
Barrens (18), E-4, Wailing Caverns

DEVIATE DREADFANG
Barrens (18), E-4, Wailing Caverns

DEVIATE GUARDIAN
Barrens (18), E-4, Wailing Caverns

DEVIATE LASHER
Barrens (18), E-4, Wailing Caverns

DEVIATE MOCASSIN
Barrens (18), E-4, Wailing Caverns

DEVIATE PYTHON
Barrens (18), E-4, Wailing Caverns

DEVIATE RAVAGER
Barrens (18), E-4, Wailing Caverns

DEVIATE SHAMBLER
Barrens (18), E-4, Wailing Caverns

DEVIATE SLAYER
Barrens (18), E-4, Wailing Caverns

DEVIATE STALKER
Barrens (18), E-4, Wailing Caverns

DEVIATE STINGLASH
Barrens (18), E-4, Wailing Caverns

DEVIATE VENOMWING
Barrens (18), E-4, Wailing Caverns

DEVIATE VIPER
Barrens (18), E-4, Wailing Caverns

DEVILSAUR
Un'Goro Crater (90), D:(3, 4), F-8, H:(3, 8), J-4

DEVLIN AGAMAND
Tirisfal Glades (86), F-4, Agamand Mills (100), Roams small area around spawn point

DEVOURING ECTOPLASM
Barrens (18), E-4, Wailing Caverns

DEVOURING OOZE
Western Plaguelands (92), H:(3, 4), I:(3, 4), The Weeping Cave

DEVRAK
Wind Rider Master, Barrens (18), F-3, The Crossroads (107), West of inn

DEWIN SHIMMERDAWN
Alchemy Supplies, Wetlands (96), A-6, Menethil Harbor (117), Building west of keep

DEXTREN WARD
Stormwind (72), F-6, The Stockade

DHUGRU GORELUST
Warlock Trainer, Durotar (34), H-4, Razor Hill (122), Behind barracks

DIAMOND HEAD
Rare Spawn, Feralas (46), A:(5-6), C:(5-6), Sardor Isle, Lvl 45 Semi-Rare; Seabed off coast of isle

DIATHORUS THE SEEKER
Ashenvale (12), J-7, Demon Fall Ridge, Overlooking central intersection at bottom of dungeon

DIEMETRADON
Un'Goro Crater (90), E-2, F:(3, 6, 7), G:(2-4, 6, 7), H:(2, 5-8)

DIGGER FLAMEFORGE
Rare Spawn, Excavation Specialist, Barrens (18), E-8, Bael Modan, Lvl 24 Uncommon; In excavation site tent

DIGGERSPINE SHORESTALKER
Hillsbrad Foothills (48), H-8, Eastern Strand

DIGMASTER SHOVELPHLANGE
Rare Spawn, Badlands (16), G-1, Uldaman, Lvl 38 Semi-Rare

DINITA STONEMANTLE
Vault Administrator, Ironforge (52), D-6, The Commons, Vault of Ironforge

DINK
Mage Trainer, Ironforge (52), C-1, The Mystic Ward, Hall of Mysteries

DIRANIA SILVERSHINE
Teldrassil (80), H-4, Shadowglen (124), Cauldron southeast of Aldrassil

DIRE CONDOR
Redridge Mountains (62), C-3, D-7, F:(3, 4, 7, 8), G:(4, 5, 7), H:(5, 7, 8), I-7

DIRE MOTTLED BOAR
Durotar (34), F:(3-5), G:(3-5, 7), H:(3-8), H-8, I:(4, 5)

DIRGE QUIKCLEAVE
Trainer/Butcher (Cooking), Tanaris (78), H-3, Gadgetzan (111), Inn

DISCIPLE OF NARALEX
Barrens (18), E-4, Wailing Caverns

DISEASED BLACK BEAR
Western Plaguelands (92), C-6, D:(5-7), E:(6, 7), The Bulwark

DISEASED FLAYER
Eastern Plaguelands (40), D-6, E:(5, 6), F-5, I-4, J:(4, 5), K-4, The Noxious Glade

DISEASED GHOUL
Western Plaguelands (92), I-7, Scholomance

DISEASED GRIZZLY
Western Plaguelands (92), G:(5, 6), H:(4-6), I:(4-6)

DISEASED WOLF
Western Plaguelands (92), E-5, F:(3-6), G:(3-7)

DISHU
Rare Spawn, Barrens (18), F:(2-3), Lvl 13 Uncommon; Patrols close to spawn points

DISPATCH COMMANDER RUAG
Swamp of Sorrows (76), F-5, Stonard (126), Third floor of main hall

DIZZY ONE-EYE
Blackwater Raiders, Stranglethorn Vale (74), B-8, Booty Bay (103), Outside near waterfall on the third level along the eastern side of bay

DOAN KARHAN
Barrens (18), F-6, Southern Barrens, Northeast of Camp Taurajo

DOC MIXILPIXIL
Gnomeregan Exiles, Stormwind (72), L-6, Old Town, SI:7

DOCKMASTER BAREN
Redridge Mountains (62), C-5, Lakeshire (115), In front of shed near docks west of the bridge

DOCTOR DRAXLEGAUGE
Arathi Highlands (10), D-8, Faldir's Cove, Bonfire on hill

DOCTOR GREGORY VICTOR
Trauma Surgeon (First Aid), Arathi Highlands (10), J-4, Hammerfall (113), Inside west building

DOCTOR GUSTAF VANHOWZEN
Trauma Surgeon (First Aid), Dustwallow Marsh (38), I-5, Theramore Isle (130), First floor of Foothold Citadel

DOCTOR HERBERT HALSEY
Artisan Alchemist, Undercity (88), F-7, The Apothecarium, In laboratory

DOCTOR MARSH
Expert Alchemist, Undercity (88), G-7, The Apothecarium, Near Royal Quarter entry

DOCTOR MARTIN FELBEN
Journeyman Alchemist, Undercity (88), F-7, The Apothecarium, In laboratory

DOCTOR THEOLEN KRASTINOV
Western Plaguelands (92), I-7, Scholomance

DOG
Sire, Thousand Needles (82), F-5, Freewind Post, Roaming near hut, west of inn

DO'GOL
Dustwallow Marsh (38), D-3, Brackenwall Village (104), Northern part of village

DOLKIN CRAGHELM
Mail Armor Merchant, Ironforge (52), G-9, The Military Ward, Craghelm's Plate and Chain

DOLMAN STEELFURY
Weapon Merchant, Ironforge (52), E:(6, 7), The Commons, Steelfury's Weapon Emporium

DOLORAN SHIELD GUARD
Alterac Mountains (8), B-8, Lordamere Internment Camp

DON GAROK PRIEST
Hillsbrad Foothills (48), I-8, Dun Garok

DON POMPA
Wetlands (96), A-6, Baradin Bay, Northern dock

DONALD RABONNE
Fisherman, Hillsbrad Foothills (48), F-6, Southshore (125), On docks in front of shed

DONNI ANTHANIA
Crazy Cat Lady, Elwynn Forest (42), F-5, House southwest of Northshire Valley

DONOVA SNOWDEN
Winterspring (98), E-5, Frostfire Hot Springs, Tent in valley

DONYAL TOVALD
Librarian, Stormwind (72), K-1, Stormwind Keep, Royal Library

DOOM'REL
Burning Steppes (22), Searing Gorge (64), C-4/D-8, Blackrock Depths

DOOMFORGE ARCANASMITH
Burning Steppes (22), Searing Gorge (64), C-4/D-8, Blackrock Depths

DOOMFORGE CRAFTSMAN
Burning Steppes (22), Searing Gorge (64), C-4/D-8, Blackrock Depths

DOOMFORGE DRAGOON
Burning Steppes (22), Searing Gorge (64), C-4/D-8, Blackrock Depths

DOOMGUARD COMMANDER
Blasted Lands (20), E-6, F:(6-8), G-7, H-6, I-6, Dark Portal, The Tainted Scar

DOOMGUARD MINION
Feralas (46), G-4, Dire Maul

DOOMWARDER
Desolace (30), F:(7, 8), G:(7, 8), Mannoroc Coven

DOOMWARDER CAPTAIN
Desolace (30), G-8, Mannoroc Coven

DOPE'REL
Burning Steppes (22), Searing Gorge (64), C-4/D-8, Blackrock Depths

DORAN STEELWING
The Hinterlands (50), B-4, Aerie Peak (100), Wildhammer Keep

DORAS
Wind Rider Master, Orgrimmar (60), E-6, Valley of Strength, The Skytower, top floor

DOREEN BELTIS
Tirisfal Glades (86), H-5, Brill (104)

DORIN SONGBLADE
Armorer, Redridge Mountains (62), D-5, Lakeshire (115), Stable

DORION
Hunter Trainer, Darnassus (26), E-1, Cenarion Enclave, Northeast structure, upper level

DORIUS STONETENDER
Searing Gorge (64), H-6, Grimesilt Dig Site, Lying injured in dig site

DORN PLAINSTALKER
Thousand Needles (82), G-4, The Weathered Nook, Den

DOYO'DA
Orgrimmar (60), F-7 , Valley of Strength, Inn

DRAC ROUGHCUT
Tradesman, Loch Modan (54), D-5, Thelsamar (129), Stoutlager Inn

DRACONIC MAGELORD
Azshara (14), E:(7, 8), Lake Mennar

DRACONIC MAGEWEAVER
Azshara (14), D:(7, 8), E:(7, 8), Lake Mennar

DRAENEI EXILE
Swamp of Sorrows (76), C-3, The Harborage

DRAENEI REFUGEE
Blasted Lands (20), G-3, H-3, Rise of the Defiler

DRAG MASTER MIGLEN
Thousand Needles (82), K-8, Mirage Raceway (118), Grandstands at drag strip

DRAGONMAW BATTLEMASTER
Wetlands (96), G-5, Angerfang Encampment

DRAGONMAW BONEWARDER
Wetlands (96), F:(4, 5), G:(4, 5), Angerfang Encampment

DRAGONMAW CENTURION
Wetlands (96), G-5, Angerfang Encampment

DRAGONMAW GRUNT
Wetlands (96), F:(7, 8), G:(6-8), Dun Algaz, Thelgen Rock

DRAGONMAW RAIDER
Wetlands (96), E:(4, 5), F:(4, 5), G:(4, 5), Angerfang Encampment, The Green Belt

DRAGONMAW SCOUT
Wetlands (96), F:(7, 8), G:(7, 8), Dun Algaz

DRAGONMAW SHADOWWARDER
Wetlands (96), G-5, Angerfang Encampment

DRAGONMAW SWAMPRUNNER
Wetlands (96), E-5, F:(4, 5), G:(4, 5), Angerfang Encampment, Whelgar's Excavation Site

DRAKE LINDGREN
General & Trade Supplies, Elwynn Forest (42), K-7, Eastvale Logging Camp, House

DRAKK STONEHAND
Master Leatherworking Trainer, The Hinterlands (50), B-4, Aerie Peak (100), Wildhammer Keep

DRAN DROFFERS
Droffers and Son Salvage, Orgrimmar (60), G-4, The Drag, Droffer and Sons Salvage

DRANH
Skinner, Barrens (18), F-6, Camp Taurajo (106), Near hides

DRAYL
Thunder Bluff (84), G-8, Hunter Rise, On Hunter's Rise in Thunder Bluff

DRAZ'ZILB
Dustwallow Marsh (38), D-3, Brackenwall Village (104), In cave to southeast

DREAD FLYER
Desolace (30), D-4, E:(4-6), F:(4-6), G:(4, 5), H:(4-6), J:(1, 4, 5), K:(2, 4, 5)

DREAD GUARD
Feralas (46), G-4, Dire Maul

DREAD RIPPER
Desolace (30), C-8, D-8, G-8, H:(7, 8), Mannoroc Coven, Sar'theris Strand

DREAD SWOOP
Desolace (30), D-7, E:(2-4, 6-8), F:(1-4, 7), G:(1-4, 6, 7), H:(1-4), I:(2-7), J:(3-6), K-4

DREAD WEAVER
Eastern Plaguelands (40), J:(4, 5), K-4, The Noxious Glade

DREADLORD
Blasted Lands (20), E:(6, 7), F:(7, 8), G-7, The Tainted Scar

DREADMAUL BRUTE
Blasted Lands (20), F:(1, 2), G-1, Dreadmaul Hold

DREADMAUL MAULER
Blasted Lands (20), G:(4, 5), Dreadmaul Post

DREADMAUL OGRE
Blasted Lands (20), F:(1, 2), G-1, Dreadmaul Hold

DREADMAUL OGRE MAGE
Blasted Lands (20), F:(1, 2), G-1, Dreadmaul Hold

DREADMAUL WARLOCK
Blasted Lands (20), G:(4, 5), Dreadmaul Post

DREADSCORN
Rare Spawn, Blasted Lands (20), F-3, Altar of Storms, Lvl 57 Uncommon; Patrols to foot of hill in Blasted Lands (F-4)

DREADSTEED SPIRIT
Feralas (46), G-4, Dire Maul

DREADWHISPER
Rare Spawn, Western Plaguelands (92), H-6, Gahrron's Withering, Lvl 58 Semi-Rare; Roams small area around spawn point

DREAMING WHELP
Swamp of Sorrows (76), A:(5, 6), B:(5, 6), Itharius's Cave

DREAMROARER
Feralas (46), F-1, Dream Bough, Roams small land mass

DREAMSCYTHE
Swamp of Sorrows (76), I-5, The Temple of Atal'Hakkar

DREAMSTALKER
Ashenvale (12), L-4, Bough Shadow, Hovers on dais in front of portal

DREAMTRACKER
The Hinterlands (50), I-2, Seradane, Idles at spawn point

DREDGE CRUSHER
Silithus (66), D:(2, 3), E:(2-4), F:(3, 4), G:(3, 4)

DREDGE STRIKER
Silithus (66), E:(1, 2), F:(1, 2), G:(1-3), H:(1-3), Hive'Ashi, Southwind Village

DREDGE WORM
Burning Steppes (22), Searing Gorge (64), C-4/D-8, Blackrock Depths

DREKA'SUR
Felwood (44), E-5, Bloodvenom Post, Campfire

DRIZZLIK
Stranglethorn Vale (74), B-8, Booty Bay (103), Tan-Your-Hide Leatherworks (shop)

DROGOTH THE ROAMER
Rare Spawn, Dustwallow Marsh (38), D-1, Bluefen, Lvl 37 Uncommon; Roams throughout Bluefen

DROVNAR STRONGBREW
Alchemy Supplies, Arathi Highlands (10), F-5, Refuge Point, Roams camp

DRUID OF THE FANG
Barrens (18), E-4, Wailing Caverns

DRULL
Hillsbrad Foothills (48), J-4, Durnholde Keep, Building in lower level of keep

DRULZEGAR SKRAGHOOK
Desolace (30), B-7, Shadowprey Village (125), Down by dock

DRUM FEL
Arathi Highlands (10), J-3, Hammerfall (113), Platform of north building

DRUNKEN FOOTPAD
Alterac Mountains (8), H:(6, 7), Sofera's Naze

DRUSILLA LA SALLE
Warlock Trainer, Elwynn Forest (42), G-4, Northshire Valley (120), Graveyard on right side of abbey

DRYSNAP CRAWLER
Desolace (30), B:(5-9), C:(3-5, 8), D:(3, 4), Ethel Rethor, Sar'theris Strand

DRYWALLOW CROCOLISK
Dustwallow Marsh (38), D:(2, 3), E:(1-3, F:(2, 3), G:(2-4), H-3, Bluefen, Brackenwall Village (104)

DRYWALLOW DAGGERMAW
Dustwallow Marsh (38), E:(6-8), F:(7, 8), F:(7, 8), The Dragonmurk

DRYWALLOW SNAPPER
Dustwallow Marsh (38), D:(3-6), E:(3-6), F:(4-6), G:(5, 6), The Dragonmurk, The Quagmire

DRYWALLOW VICEJAW
Dustwallow Marsh (38), D:(2-4), E:(1-4), F:(2-4), G:(2-4), H-3, Bluefen, The Quagmire

DRYWHISKER DIGGER
Arathi Highlands (10), L:(3, 4), Drywhisker Gorge

DRYWHISKER KOBOLD
Arathi Highlands (10), K:(3, 4), L-4, Drywhisker Gorge

DRYWHISKER SURVEYOR
Arathi Highlands (10), L-3, Drywhisker Gorge

DUGGAN WILDHAMMER
Rare Spawn, Eastern Plaguelands (40), B-7, C-6, D-8, E-7, The Undercroft, Lvl 55 Semi-Rare; Roams small area around spawn point

DUGHAL STORMWING
Burning Steppes (22), Searing Gorge (64), C-4/D-8, Blackrock Depths

DUHNG
Cook, Barrens (18), G-3, Inside hut east of Crossroads

DUKE HYDRAXIS
Azshara (14), J-7, Bay of Storms, Island off the coast

DUKE NICHOLAS ZVERENHOFF
The Argent Dawn, Eastern Plaguelands (40), K-6, Light's Hope Chapel (116), Camp on right side of chapel

DULCIEA FROSTMOON
Cloth Armor Merchant, Feralas (46), C-4, Feathermoon Stronghold (110), Inn

DUN GAROK MOUNTAINEER
Hillsbrad Foothills (48), I-8, Dun Garok

DUN GAROK RIFLEMAN
Hillsbrad Foothills (48), I-8, Dun Garok

DUN MOROGH MOUNTAINEER
Dun Morogh (32), D:(4, 5), I:(5, 6), L:(3-5)

DUNCAN CULLEN
Light Armor Merchant, Stormwind (72), G-7, Mage Quarter, Duncan's Textiles

DUNE SMASHER
Tanaris (78), E-8, F-8, Uldum, Valley of the Watchers

DUNEMAUL BRUTE
Tanaris (78), F:(5-7), G:(6, 7), Dunemaul Compound, Eastmoon Ruins, Southmoon Ruins

DUNEMAUL ENFORCER
Tanaris (78), F:(5-7), G:(6, 7), Dunemaul Compound, Eastmoon Ruins, Southmoon Ruins

DUNEMAUL OGRE
Tanaris (78), F:(5-7), G:(6, 7), Dunemaul Compound, Eastmoon Ruins, Southmoon Ruins

DUNEMAUL OGRE MAGE
Tanaris (78), F:(5-7), G:(6, 7), Dunemaul Compound, Eastmoon Ruins, Southmoon Ruins

DUNEMAUL WARLOCK
Tanaris (78), F:(5-7), G:(6, 7), Dunemaul Compound, Eastmoon Ruins, Southmoon Ruins

DUNGAR LONGDRINK
Gryphon Master, Stormwind (72), J-6, Trade District, Next to gryphons

DUOKNA
General Goods, Durotar (34), F-7, Valley of Trials (131), Northwest structure

DURIEL MOONFIRE
Ashenvale (12), H-7, Silverwing Outpost

DURNAN FURCUTTER
Cloth & Leather Armor Merchant, Dun Morogh (32), D-7, Coldridge Valley (106), Anvilmar

DUROTAR TIGER
Durotar (34), I:(8, 9), J:(7-9), Echo Isles

DURTHAM GRELDON
Ironforge (52), G-1, The Forlorn Cavern, South building, inside east entrance

DUSKBAT
Tirisfal Glades (86), C:(6, 7), D:(6, 7), Deathknell (109)

DUSKSTALKER
Rare Spawn, Teldrassil (80), F-8, G-8, Lvl 9 Uncommon; Patrols south of Lake Al'Ameth

DUSKWING
Eastern Plaguelands (40), D-6, Patrols large portion of Eastern Plaguelands

DUST DEVIL
Westfall (94), C:(3, 5, 7), D:(2, 4, 6), E-5, F-4, G:(3, 5), H-7, Gold Coast Quarry, Thoughout Westfall

DUST STORMER
Silithus (66), D:(1, 2), E:(1, 2), F-2, G:(1, 2), H:(1, 2), Hive'Ashi, The Crystal Vale

DUSTBELCHER BRUTE
Badlands (16), D-6, I-7, Camp Wurg, Rock and Fire

DUSTBELCHER LORD
Badlands (16), A-9, B-9, Dustbelcher Grotto

DUSTBELCHER MAULER
Badlands (16), A:(7, 8), B:(7, 8), I-7, Dustbelcher Grotto

DUSTBELCHER MYSTIC
Badlands (16), I-7, J:(2, 3), Camp Kosh

DUSTBELCHER OGRE
Badlands (16), D-6, I-7, Dustbelcher Grotto

DUSTBELCHER OGRE MAGE
Badlands (16), A-9, B-9, Dustbelcher Grotto

DUSTBELCHER SHAMAN
Badlands (16), A:(8, 9), B:(7, 8), I-7, Dustbelcher Grotto

DUSTBELCHER WARRIOR
Badlands (16), J-2, Camp Kosh

DUSTBELCHER WYRMHUNTER
Badlands (16), A:(7, 8), B:(7, 8), I-7, Dustbelcher Grotto

DUSTWIND HARPY
Durotar (34), G:(2, 3), H-3, Drygulch Ravine, Razorwind Canyon, Tor'kren Farm

DUSTWIND PILLAGER
Durotar (34), G:(2, 3), H-3, Drygulch Ravine, Jaggedswine Farm, Razorwind Canyon

DUSTWIND SAVAGE
Durotar (34), H:(2, 3), Drygulch Ravine

DUSTWIND STORM WITCH
Durotar (34), H-2, Drygulch Ravine

DUTHORIAN RALL
Stormwind (72), F-2, Cathedral Square, Cathedral of Light

DWANE WERTLE
Chef, Dustwallow Marsh (38), I-5, Theramore Isle (130), First floor of Foothold Citadel

DWUKK
Journeyman Blacksmith, Durotar (34), H-4, Razor Hill (122), Northeast of inn

DYING ARCHAEOLOGIST
Searing Gorge (64), E-3, The Slag Pit, Lying next to the Altar of Suntara

DYING KODO
Desolace (30), F:(1, 2, 5, 6), G:(1, 6, 9), H-9, J-6, Ghost Walker Post (111), Kodo Graveyard

E

EAGAN PELTSKINNER
Elwynn Forest (42), F-4, Northshire Valley (120), Camp on left side of abbey

EALYSHIA DEWWHISPER
Two Handed Weapon Merchant, Darnassus (26), H-7, Tradesmen's Terrace, Two Handed Weapons shop

EARTHBORER
Orgrimmar (60), F-5, Ragefire Chasm

EARTHCALLER HALMGAR
Barrens (18), E-9, Razorfen Kraul

EARTHEN CUSTODIAN
Badlands (16), G-1, Uldaman

EARTHEN GUARDIAN
Badlands (16), G-1, Uldaman

EARTHEN HALLSHAPER
Badlands (16), G-1, Uldaman

EARTHEN ROCKSMASHER
Badlands (16), G-1, Uldaman

EARTHEN SCULPTOR
Badlands (16), G-1, Uldaman

EARTHEN STONEBREAKER
Badlands (16), G-1, Uldaman

EARTHEN STONECARVER
Badlands (16), G-1, Uldaman

EASTVALE LUMBERJACK
Elwynn Forest (42), K-6, Eastvale Logging Camp

EASTVALE PEASANT
Elwynn Forest (42), K-7, Eastvale Logging Camp

EBRU
Disciple of Naralex, Barrens (18), E-4, The Wailing Caverns, Right eye of cave above entrance

ECHEYAKEE
Barrens (18), G-2, (Summon) Bones northeast of Grol'dom Farm

ECK'ALOM
Rare Spawn, Ashenvale (12), F-7, G-7, Mystral Lake, Lvl 27 Average Rare; Spawns in areas around lake

EDAN THE HOWLER
Rare Spawn, Dun Morogh (32), E-5, F-5, The Grizzled Den, Lvl 9 Uncommon; In cave

EDANA HATETALON
Feralas (46), D-1, Ruins of Ravenwind, (Summon) Use the horn to call her

EDNA MULLBY
Trade Supplier, Stormwind (72), I-6, Trade District, Everyday Merchandise

EDRICK KILLIAN
Undercity (88), The War Quarter, Wanders Canals and War Quarter

EDRIS BARLEYBEARD
Barmaid, Ironforge (52), J:(7, 8), The Military Ward, Bruuk's Corner

EDWARD
Undercity (88), G-2, The War Quarter, Fights Captives in War Quarter

EDWARD REMINGTON
Guild Tabard Designer, Undercity (88), J-4, The Trade Quarter, East spoke from bank

EDWIN HARLY
General Supplies, Silverpine Forest (68), G-4, The Sepulcher (124), In front of crates on right side of sepulcher

EDWIN VANCLEEF
Westfall (94), D-7, E-7, The Deadmines

EDWINA MONZOR
Fletcher, Wetlands (96), A-6, Menethil Harbor (117), Next to wagon, east of keep

EFFSEE
Pet, Redridge Mountains (62), C-5, Lakeshire (115), L-shaped dock west of the bridge

EGAN
Eastern Plaguelands (40), B-3, Terrordale, House

EINAR STONEGRIP
Wetlands (96), G-4, Intersection of road to Menethil Harbor and road to Dun Modr

EINRIS BRIGHTSPEAR
Hunter Trainer, Stormwind (72), I-2, J-2, Dwarven District, Building south of tram entrance

EITRIGG
Orgrimmar (60), C-4, Valley of Wisdom, Grommash Hold

ELADRIEL
Skinning Trainer, Darnassus (26), I-2 , Craftsmen's Terrace, Leatherworking shop

ELAINE CAREVIN
Duskwood (36), J-5, Darkshire (108), First floor of house

ELAINE TRIAS
Mistress of Cheese, Stormwind (72), I-6, Trade District, Trias' Cheese

ELANARIA
Darnassus (26), H-3 , Warrior's Terrace, Lower northwest platform

ELDER ASHENVALE BEAR
Ashenvale (12), H:(5, 6), I:(5, 6)

ELDER BLACK BEAR
Loch Modan (54), B:(7, 8), C:(1-6), D:(2-4, 6, 7), E:(3, 5-7), Dun Algaz

ELDER CLOUD SERPENT
Thousand Needles (82), A-3, B:(3, 4), G:(4, 5), H-5, Highperch, Whitereach Post, Windbreak Canyon

ELDER CRAG BOAR
Dun Morogh (32), C:(4, 5), D:(3-5), E:(3-5), F:(3, 4), G:(5, 6), H:(5, 6), I:(5, 6), J:(5, 6), K:(4-6)

ELDER CRAG COYOTE
Badlands (16), A-6, B:(6-8), C:(5, 6, 8), D:(5-7), E:(6, 7), F:(6, 7), Apocryphan's Rest

ELDER DARKSHORE THRESHER
Darkshore (24), D:(6, 7, 9), E:(7-9), G:(1, 2), H:(1. 2), I-1, Twilight Shore

ELDER DIEMETRADON
Un'Goro Crater (90), C:(3-7), D:(3-8), E:(2-8), F:(3, 5)

ELDER DRAGONKIN
Swamp of Sorrows (76), J:(4, 5), K:(4, 5), Sorrowmurk

ELDER GRAY BEAR
Hillsbrad Foothills (48), B:(1-6), C:(1-3, 5-7), D:(3, 5, 6), E:(5, 6), G-5, H:(4-6), I:(2, 3), J:(3-7), K:(3-5), L-4, Throughout Hillsbrad

ELDER LAKE CREEPER
Silverpine Forest (68), K:(2-4), The Dawning Isles

ELDER LAKE SKULKER
Silverpine Forest (68), K-4, Fenris Isle

ELDER MESA BUZZARD
Arathi Highlands (10), B:(6, 7), C-7, D-7, G-8

ELDER MISTVALE GORILLA
Stranglethorn Vale (74), C:(6, 7)

ELDER MOSS CREEPER
Hillsbrad Foothills (48), G:(5-7), H:(7, 8), I:(6, 7), J-7

ELDER MOTTLED BOAR
Durotar (34), E:(2-5), F:(1-6), G:(1-3), H:(1-3), I:(2, 3)

ELDER MOUNTAIN BOAR
Loch Modan (54), H:(3, 4), I:(3, 4), J:(4, 5), K-5, The Farstrider Lodge

ELDER MYSTIC RAZORSNOUT
Rare Spawn, Barrens (18), G:(2, 3), Thorn Hill, Lvl 15 Uncommon; Eastern Razormane camp

ELDER NIGHTSABER
Teldrassil (80), D-3, E:(3, 4), F:(3, 4), The Oracle Glade, Wellspring Lake

ELDER PLAINSTRIDER
Mulgore (58), C:(2, 3), D:(1-5), E:(1-5), F:(1-5), G:(2-7), H:(3, 5, 6)

ELDER RAGE SCAR
Feralas (46), F-3, Rage Scar Hold

ELDER RAZORMAW
Wetlands (96), D:(1, 2), E-2, I-3, J-3, Raptor Ridge

ELDER SALTWATER CROCOLISK
Stranglethorn Vale (74), A-2, B-2, C:(3, 4)

ELDER SHADOWHORN STAG
Ashenvale (12), G:(3, 4), H:(3-7), I:(5-7), J:(5, 6)

ELDER SHADOWMAW PANTHER
Stranglethorn Vale (74), C-6, D-6

ELDER SHARDTOOTH
Winterspring (98), H-2, I:(1-3, 5, 6)

ELDER STRANGLETHORN TIGER
Stranglethorn Vale (74), C-2, D-2

ELDER THUNDER LIZARD
Desolace (30), C:(7, 8), D:(7, 8), E:(4-6, 8), F:(5, 6, 9), G:(5, 8, 9), H:(5-9), J:(1, 4, 5), K-2

ELDER TIMBERLING
Teldrassil (80), E-3, The Oracle Glade, Wellspring River

ELDER TORNTUSK
The Hinterlands (50), I-8, Jintha'Alor, Chained to altar

ELDIN PARTRIDGE
Undercity (88), F-3, The War Quarter, Platform in front of Skull Building

ELDRAEITH
Herbalism Supplier, Stormwind (72), G-8, Mage Quarter, Alchemy Need

ELDRETH APPARITION
Feralas (46), G-4, Dire Maul

ELDRETH DARTER
Feralas (46), G-4, Dire Maul

ELDRETH PHANTASM
Feralas (46), G-4, Dire Maul

ELDRETH SEETHER
Feralas (46), G-4, Dire Maul

ELDRETH SORCERER
Feralas (46), G-4, Dire Maul

ELDRETH SPECTRE
Feralas (46), G-4, Dire Maul

ELDRETH SPIRIT
Feralas (46), G-4, Dire Maul

ELDRIN
Journeyman Tailor, Elwynn Forest (42), K-7, Eastvale Logging Camp, House

ELEANOR RUSK
General Goods Vendor, Undercity (88), J-5, The Trade Quarter, Upper Ring of Trade Quarter

ELECTROCUTIONER 6000
Dun Morogh (32), C-4, Gnomeregan

ELEMENTAL SLAVE
Alterac Mountains (8), A:(7, 8), B:(5-8), C-6, Dalaran

ELFARRAN
Warsong Gulch Battlemaster, Stormwind (72), L-2, Stormwind Keep, East Wing

ELISA STEELHAND
Blacksmithing Supplies, Darkshore (24), F-4, Auberdine (101), In front of northern building

ELISSA DUMAS
Portal Trainer, Darnassus (26), E-8, The Temple of the Moon, Northeast of fountain

ELIZA
Bride of the Embalmer, Duskwood (36), D-3, Raven Hill Cemetery (122), (Summon) Fresh grave

ELIZA CALLEN
Leather Armor Merchant, Tirisfal Glades (86), H-5, Brill (104), Outside of smithy

ELIZABETH VAN TALEN
Engineer Supplier, Undercity (88), K-7, The Rogues' Quarter

ELKI
Mail Armor Merchant, Thunder Bluff (84), E-6, Lower rise, in Hewa's Armory

ELLANDRIETH
General Goods Vendor, Darnassus (26), I-5, Tradesmen's Terrace, General Goods shop

ELLING TRIAS
Master of Cheese, Stormwind (72), I-6, Trade District, Trias' Cheese

ELLY LANGSTON
Barmaid, Stormwind (72), J-5, Old Town, Pig and Whistle Tavern

ELSHARIN
Mage Trainer, Stormwind (72), F-8, Mage Quarter, Wizard's Sanctum

ELU
Wind Rider Apprentice, Thousand Needles (82), F-5, Freewind Post, North side of plateau, opposite inn

ELYNNA
Tailoring Supplies, Darnassus (26), I-2 , Craftsmen's Terrace, Tailoring shop

ELYSA
Alterac Mountains (8), E-2, Dandred's Fold, Second floor of house

EMBER WORG
Burning Steppes (22), J-3, K:(2, 3, 5, 6), L:(3-6), Terror Wing Path

EMBERSTRIFE
Dustwallow Marsh (38), G-8, Emberstrife's Den, Southern part of cave on landing

EMERALD OOZE
The Hinterlands (50), J:(6, 7), Jintha'Alor

EMERALDON BOUGHGUARD
Ashenvale (12), K-4, L-4

EMERALDON ORACLE
Ashenvale (12), K-4, L-4, Bough Shadow, Forest Song

EMERALDON TREE WARDER
Ashenvale (12), K-4, L-4, Bough Shadow, Forest Song

EMOGG THE CRUSHER
Loch Modan (54), J-2, Mo'grosh Stronghold, Patrols a path in front of the three caves

EMPEROR DAGRAN THAURISSAN
Burning Steppes (22), Searing Gorge (64), C-4/D-8, Blackrock Depths

EMRUL RIKNUSSUN
Cooking Supplier, Ironforge (52), H-4, The Great Forge, The Bronze Kettle

ENCRUSTED SURF CRAWLER
Durotar (34), H-1, I:(1, 2), Bladefist Bay, Skull Rock

ENCRUSTED TIDE CRAWLER
Darkshore (24), E-8, H-2, Cliffspring River, Mist's Edge, Twilight Shore

ENFORCER EMILGUND
Rare Spawn, Mulgore (58), D-2, Lvl 11 Uncommon; Venture Co. camp

ENGINEER WHIRLEYGIG
Rare Spawn, Barrens (18), G-1, The Sludge Fen, Lvl 19 Uncommon; Control room

ENOHAR THUNDERBREW
Blasted Lands (20), I-2, Nethergarde Keep (119), Just right of entrance inside keep

ENRAGED FERAL SCAR
Feralas (46), F:(5, 6), Feral Scar Vale

ENRAGED FOULWEALD
Ashenvale (12), G-6, Greenpaw Village

ENRAGED PANTHER
Thousand Needles (82), B-2, Locked in cage, next to destroyed wagons

ENRAGED REEF CRAWLER
Desolace (30), C:(3-5), D:(2-4), Ethel Rethor, Sar'theris Strand

ENRAGED ROCK ELEMENTAL
Badlands (16), H:(8, 9), In hills behind Theldurin the Lost

ENRAGED SILVERBACK GORILLA
Stranglethorn Vale (74), C-7, Mistvale Valley, Spirit Den

ENRAGED STONE SPIRIT
Stonetalon Mountains (70), D-6, E-6, The Charred Vale

ENSLAVED ARCHAEOLOGIST
Searing Gorge (64), D-2, E:(2, 3), The Slag Pit

ENSLAVED DRUID OF THE TALON
Teldrassil (80), E-8, Gnarlpine Hold, Southwest camp

ENTHRALLED ATAL'AI
Swamp of Sorrows (76), I-5, The Temple of Atal'Hakkar

ENTROPIC BEAST
Felwood (44), E-4, F-4, Shatter Scar Vale

ENTROPIC HORROR
Felwood (44), E-4, F-4, Shatter Scar Vale

ENYO
Mage Trainer, Orgrimmar (60), D:(8, 9), Valley of Spirit, Darkbriar Lodge

ERELAS AMBERSKY
Teldrassil (80), G-9, Rut'theran Village, First floor of building

ERIC "THE SWIFT"
Badlands (16), G-1, Uldaman

ERICH LOHAN
Stormwind (72), F-8, G-7, Mage Quarter, Roams around district

ERIDAN BLUEWIND
Emerald Circle, Felwood (44), G-8, Emerald Sanctuary, Building

ERIK FELIXE
Feralas (46), B-4, Feathermoon Stronghold (110), Next to log west of inn

ERIKA TATE
Cooking Supplier, Stormwind (72), K-4, Old Town, Pig and Whistle Tavern

ERIN
Redridge Mountains (62), C-4, Lakeshire (115)

ERION SHADEWHISPER
Rogue Trainer, Darnassus (26), D-2, Cenarion Enclave, Den, small room on lower level

ERIS HAVENFIRE
Eastern Plaguelands (40), B-2, Plaguewood, On hill (note that the NPC is only visible to Lvl 60 priests that have the Eye of Divinity equipped!)

ERLAN DRUDGEMOOR
Elwynn Forest (42), J-8, Brackwell Pumpkin Patch, In house with Morgan the Collector and Surena Caledon

ERMA
Stable Master, Elwynn Forest (42), F-7, Goldshire (112), Outside the Lion's Pride Inn

ERTOG RAGETUSK
Ashenvale (12), I-6, Splintertree Post (126), Up hill to left as you enter main outpost (near watch tower)

ESTELLE GENDRY
Undercity (88), K-7, The Rogues' Quarter, Southwest of Skull Building

ETU RAGETOTEM
Mace & Staff Merchant, Thunder Bluff (84), F-6, High rise, inside Ragetotem Arms tent

EUNICE BURCH
Cooking Trainer, Undercity (88), H-4, I-4, The Trade Quarter, West spoke from bank

EVA SARKHOFF
Western Plaguelands (92), J-7, Caer Darrow, Just outside of entrance to Scholomance

EVAN LARSON
Hatter, Stormwind (72), F-8, Mage Quarter, Larson Clothiers

EVERLOOK BRUISER
Winterspring (98), I-4, Everlook (110)

EVIE WHIRLBREW
Alchemy Supplies, Winterspring (98), I-4, Everlook (110), Hut north of entrance

EVISCERATOR
Burning Steppes (22), Searing Gorge (64), C-4/D-8, Blackrock Depths

EVOLVING ECTOPLASM
Barrens (18), E-4, Wailing Caverns

EVONICE SOOTSMOKER
The Thorium Brotherhood, Searing Gorge (64), D-3, Thorium Point, Right of tower ramp

EXECUTOR ARREN
Tirisfal Glades (86), D-7, Deathknell (109), Between both houses on right side of road

EXECUTOR ZYGAND
Tirisfal Glades (86), H-5, Brill (104), Mounted outside of the Brill Town Hall

EXPEDITIONARY MOUNTAINEER
Burning Steppes (22), A-6

EXPEDITIONARY PRIEST
Burning Steppes (22), A-6

EXZHAL
Stranglethorn Vale (74), A-2, Yojamba Isle

EYAHN EAGLETALON
Thunder Bluff (84), D-6, Lower rise, near elevator

EYE OF IMMOL'THAR
Feralas (46), G-4, Dire Maul

EYE OF NAXXRAMAS
Eastern Plaguelands (40), D-2, Stratholme

EYELESS WATCHER
Eastern Plaguelands (40), E-5, I-3, J-3, K-5, The Noxious Glade

EZEKIEL GRAVES
Poison Vendor, Undercity (88), K-5, The Rogues' Quarter

F

FAELYSSA
Darnassus (26), D-2, Cenarion Enclave, Southwest structure

FAHRAD
Grand Master Rogue, Hillsbrad Foothills (48), K-2, Balcony of Chateau Ravenholdt

FAHRAK
Ashenvale (12), I-6, Splintertree Post (126), Right of flightpoint

FAHRAN SILENTBLADE
Tools & Supplies, Ashenvale (12), E-5, Astranaar (101), Left as you enter inn from west

FALDREAS GOETH'SHAEL
Ashenvale (12), E-5, Astranaar (101), Outside inn to west

FALDRON
Expert Leatherworker, Darnassus (26), I-2, Craftsmen's Terrace, Leatherworking shop

FALFINDEL WAYWARDER
Feralas (46), K-5, Thalanaar, Next to well

FALGRAN HASTIL
Dustwallow Marsh (38), I-5, Theramore Isle (130), East side of town

FALKAN ARMONIS
Reagent Vendor, Wetlands (96), A-6, Menethil Harbor (117), Outside building, west of keep

FALKHAAN ISENSTRIDER
Elwynn Forest (42), F-5, Northshire Valley (120), In front of fountain at Northshire Valley entrance

FALLA SAGEWIND
Barrens (18), E-3, F-3, Atop mountain

FALLEN CHAMPION
Tirisfal Glades (86), K-3, L-3, Scarlet Monastery

FALLENROOT HELLCALLER
Ashenvale (12), B-2, Blackfathom Deeps

FALLENROOT ROGUE
Ashenvale (12), B-2, Blackfathom Deeps

FALLENROOT SATYR
Ashenvale (12), B-2, Blackfathom Deeps

FALLENROOT SHADOWSTALKER
Ashenvale (12), B-2, Blackfathom Deeps

FALSTAD WILDHAMMER
The Hinterlands (50), B-5, Aerie Peak (100), Base of Peak fortification

FALTHIR THE SIGHTLESS
Stranglethorn Vale (74), A-2, Yojamba Isle

FAM'RETOR GUARDIAN
Badlands (16), D-5, The Dustbowl, (Summon) Circular seal on ground

FAR SEER MOK'THARDIN
Stranglethorn Vale (74), C-3, Grom'gol Base Camp (112), Scaffolding just left of zepplin tower

FARALORN
General Supplies, Feralas (46), C-4, Feathermoon Stronghold (110), Inn

FARDEL DABYRIE
Arathi Highlands (10), H-4, Dabyrie's Farmstead, Roams in front of shed right of barn

FARGON MORTALAK
Superior Armorer, Stranglethorn Vale (74), B-8, Booty Bay (103), Plate-n-Chain (shop)

FARMER DALSON
Western Plaguelands (92), F-5, Dalson's Tears, (Summon) Spawns at the outhouse

FARMER FURLBROW
Westfall (94), G-2, The Jansen Stead, Cart near Old Blanchy

FARMER GETZ
Hillsbrad Foothills (48), D-4, Hillsbrad Fields (113), Barn on the eastern side of town

FARMER KALABA
Hillsbrad Foothills (48), D-5, Hillsbrad Fields (113), Roams in southernmost farm

FARMER KENT
Hillsbrad Foothills (48), F-6, Southshore (125), Patrols between crop field and docks

FARMER RAY
Hillsbrad Foothills (48), C-3, Hillsbrad Fields (113), First floor of house at northern end of town

FARMER SALDEAN
Westfall (94), F-3, Saldean's Farm, Farmhouse

FARMER SOLLIDEN
Rare Spawn, Tirisfal Glades (86), D-5, E-5, Solliden Farmstead, Lvl 8 Uncommon; Stands idle at spawn point

FARRIN DARIS
Duskwood (36), J-4, Darkshire (108), Inn

FARUZA
Apprentice Herbalist, Tirisfal Glades (86), H-5, Brill (104), Between the stable and house on right side of road

FATHER COBB
Priest Trainer, Thunder Bluff (84), C-3, Spirit Rise, The Pools of Vision

FATHER GAVIN
Dun Morogh (32), H-4, Misty Pine Refuge, Altar outside of house

FATHER LANKESTER
Priest Trainer, Undercity (88), G-2, The War Quarter, Outside Skull Building

FATHER LAZARUS
Priest Trainer, Undercity (88), F-2, The War Quarter, Outside Skull Building

FAULTY WAR GOLEM
Rare Spawn, Searing Gorge (64), C-6, D-5, E-4, F-7, G-6, The Sea of Cinders, Lvl 46 Semi-Rare; Roams small area around spawn point

FAUSTRON
Wind Rider Master, Moonglade (56), D-7, At end of beaten path, west of road

FEATHERMOON SENTINEL
Feralas (46), C:(4, 5), Feathermoon Stronghold (110), Sardor Isle

FEDFENNEL
Rare Spawn, Elwynn Forest (42), I-4, Stone Cairn Lake, Lvl 12 Uncommon; Stands idle at spawn point

FEEBOZ
Arathi Highlands (10), I-3, Circle of East Binding, Patrols with Fozruck to each of the four Circles of Binding

FEEGLY THE EXILED
Barrens (18), F-9, Bael Modan, Camp overlooking excavation

FEERO IRONHAND
Ashenvale (12), D-4, Maestra's Post, Near Stones south of outpost

FEL LASH
Feralas (46), G-4, Dire Maul

FEL STEED
Silverpine Forest (68), F-7, Shadowfang Keep

FEL'ZERUL
Swamp of Sorrows (76), F-5, Stonard (126), Third floor of main hall

FELA
Heavy Armor Merchant, Thunder Bluff (84), D-4, Middle rise, inside Thunder Bluff Armorers tent

FELBEAST
Blasted Lands (20), G:(3, 5), H:(4-6), I:(3, 4)

FELCULAR
Blasted Lands (20), G-3, Rise of the Defiler, (Summon) Summoned by Razelikh the Defiler at 25% health

FELDER STOVER
Weaponsmith, Burning Steppes (22), K-7, Morgan's Vigil (118), Caravan, left side of camp

FELGUARD
Ashenvale (12), J:(6-8), K:(6, 7), Demon Fall Canyon, Felfire Hill, Nightsong Woods

FELGUARD ELITE
Blasted Lands (20), E:(5, 6), F:(5-7), G:(6, 7), H:(5, 6), I:(5, 6), The Tainted Scar

FELGUARD SENTRY
Blasted Lands (20), H:(5, 6), I:(5, 6), Dark Portal

FELGUR TWOCUTS
Desolace (30), G-6, Ghost Walker Post (111), Southern hut

FELHOUND
Blasted Lands (20), H:(5, 6), I:(5, 6), Dark Portal

FELICIA DOAN
General Trade Goods Vendor, Undercity (88), I-5, The Trade Quarter, Upper Ring of Trade Quarter

FELICIA GUMP
Herbalism Supplier, Stormwind (72), J-6, The Canals, Fragrant Flowers

FELICIA MALINE
Gryphon Master, Duskwood (36), K-4, Darkshire (108), Right side of road heading into Darkshire from the east

FELIKA
General Trade Good Merchant, Orgrimmar (60), G-5, The Drag, Roams The Drag

FELIX WHINDLEBOLT
Dun Morogh (32), D-7, Coldridge Valley (106), Anvilmar

FELLICENT'S SHADE
Rare Spawn, Tirisfal Glades (86), J-6, Balnir Farmstead, Lvl 12 Uncommon; Patrols a circular path around crop field

FELMUSK FELSWORN
Ashenvale (12), H-5, I-5, Night Run

FELMUSK ROGUE
Ashenvale (12), H:(5, 6), I:(5, 6), Night Run

FELMUSK SATYR
Ashenvale (12), H-5, I-5, Night Run

FELMUSK SHADOWSTALKER
Ashenvale (12), H:(5, 6), I:(5, 6), Night Run

FELNOK STEELSPRING
Winterspring (98), I-4, Everlook (110), East of inn

FELPAW RAVAGER
Felwood (44), G:(2, 3), H:(1-3), I-2, Irontree Woods, Talonbranch Glade

FELPAW SCAVENGER
Felwood (44), E:(3-6), F:(2-4, 6, 7), G:(2-4)

FELPAW WOLF
Felwood (44), E:(7, 8), F:(7, 8), G:(7-9), H-9, Deadwood Village, Emerald Sanctuary, Morlos'Aran

FELSLAYER
Ashenvale (12), C-6, D-6, Fire Scar Shrine

FELSTALKER
Durotar (34), F-5, G-5, Burning Blade Coven, Valley of Trials (131)

FELWEAVER SCORNN
Durotar (34), H-1, Skull Rock, Cave (north side or deep in cave)

FEN CREEPER
Wetlands (96), B:(2, 3), C:(2-4), D:(2-4), E-3, F:(3, 4), G:(3-5), H-5

FEN DWELLER
Wetlands (96), B:(4, 5), C:(4, 5), H:(5-7), I:(6, 7)

FENROS
Rare Spawn, Duskwood (36), H-4, Brightwood Grove, Lvl 32 Uncommon; Patrols to two additional worgen camps (I-6, H-3)

FENRUS THE DEVOURER
Silverpine Forest (68), F-7, Shadowfang Keep

FENTHWICK
Rogue Trainer, Ironforge (52), G-1, The Forlorn Cavern, South building, inside east entrance

FENWICK THATROS
Silverpine Forest (68), I-3, Lordamere Lake, Roams at the edge of dock

FERAL CRAG COYOTE
Badlands (16), G:(7, 8), H:(5-7), I:(5-7), Agmond's End

FERAL MOUNTAIN LION
Hillsbrad Foothills (48), G:(5-7), H:(6-8), I-7

FERAL NIGHTSABER
Teldrassil (80), D:(2, 3), E:(2, 3), F:(2, 3), The Oracle Glade

FERAL SCAR YETI
Feralas (46), F:(5, 6), G-6, Feral Scar Vale, High Wilderness

FERAN STRONGWIND
Ashenvale (12), I-7, Nightsong Woods, Camp southwest of Splintertree Post (126)

FEROCIOUS GRIZZLED BEAR
Silverpine Forest (68), G:(2-5), H:(2, 4, 5), Thoughout Silverpine

FEROCIOUS RAGE SCAR
Feralas (46), F-3, Rage Scar Hold, The Twin Colossals

FEROCIOUS YETI
Hillsbrad Foothills (48), E-3, Darrow Hill, In and near cave

FEROCITAS THE DREAM EATER
Teldrassil (80), I-5, Gnarlpine camp northeast of Starbreeze Village

FERRA
Feralas (46), G-4, Dire Maul

FETID CORPSE
Duskwood (36), J-4, K:(3, 4), Manor Mistmantle

FETID ZOMBIE
Western Plaguelands (92), G:(6, 7), The Writhing Haunt

FIELD MARSHAL AFRASIABI
Stormwind (72), J-7, Stormwind City, Northeast of statue at entrance

FILLIUS FIZZLESPINNER
Trade Supplier, Ironforge (52), E-7, The Commons, Fizzlespinner's General Goods

FIMBLE FINESPINDLE
Expert Leatherworker, Ironforge (52), E-3, The Great Forge, Finespindle's Leather Goods

FIN FIZRACKET
Blackwater Raiders, Stranglethorn Vale (74), B-8, Booty Bay (103), Lying under overturned boat on the eastern side of bay

FINBUS GEARGRIND
Expert Engineer, Duskwood (36), K-5, Darkshire (108), Second house on left side of road heading into Darkshire from the east

FINEOUS DARKVIRE
Burning Steppes (22), Searing Gorge (64), C-4/D-8, Blackrock Depths

FINGAT
Rare Spawn, Swamp of Sorrows (76), H-8, Stagalbog Cave, Lvl 43 Semi-Rare; Patrols cave

FINKLE EINHORN
Burning Steppes (22), Searing Gorge (64), C-4/D-8, Blackrock Spire

FIORA LONGEARS
Dustwallow Marsh (38), I-5, Theramore Isle (130), Inn

FIRE BEETLE
Burning Steppes (22), A:(5, 6), B:(6, 7), C-6, D-5, E:(4-6), F-5, G-6, H:(4-6), I-5, J:(3, 4), K:(3, 5, 6), L:(4, 5) Searing Gorge (64), B:(4, 7), C:(5-7), D:(3, 4, 6), E:(4, 5, 7), F:(4, 6, 7), G:(3, 4, 6-8), H-7, I:(3-5), J-2

FIRE ROC
Tanaris (78), E:(4, 5), F-4, G:(4, 5), H:(4, 5), I-4

FIRE SPIRIT
Durotar (34), F-5, Shrine of the Dormant Flame, (Summon) Atop hill near altar

FIREBRAND DARKWEAVER
Burning Steppes (22), Searing Gorge (64), C-4/D-8, Blackrock Spire

FIREBRAND DREADWEAVER
Burning Steppes (22), Searing Gorge (64), C-4/D-8, Blackrock Spire

FIREBRAND GRUNT
Burning Steppes (22), Searing Gorge (64), C-4/D-8, Blackrock Spire

FIREBRAND INVOKER
Burning Steppes (22), Searing Gorge (64), C-4/D-8, Blackrock Spire

FIREBRAND LEGIONNAIRE
Burning Steppes (22), Searing Gorge (64), C-4/D-8, Blackrock Spire

FIREBRAND PYROMANCER
Burning Steppes (22), Searing Gorge (64), C-4/D-8, Blackrock Spire

FIRECALLER RADISON
Rare Spawn, Darkshore (24), F-9, The Master's Glaive, Lvl 19 Semi-Rare; Wanders center isle

FIREGUARD
Burning Steppes (22), Searing Gorge (64), C-4/D-8, Blackrock Depths

FIREGUARD DESTROYER
Burning Steppes (22), Searing Gorge (64), C-4/D-8, Blackrock Depths

FIREGUT BRUTE
Burning Steppes (22), J:(4, 5), K:(4, 5), Dreadmaul Rock

FIREGUT CAPTAIN
Burning Steppes (22), B-3, Dreadmaul Rock

FIREGUT OGRE
Burning Steppes (22), I:(4, 5), J:(3-6), K:(3-5), Dreadmaul Rock

FIREGUT OGRE MAGE
Burning Steppes (22), I:(4, 5), J:(3-5), K:(3-5), Dreadmaul Rock

FIRELORD
Burning Steppes (22), Searing Gorge (64), C-4/D-8, The Molten Core

FIREMANE ASH TAIL
Dustwallow Marsh (38), D-7, E:(6-8), F:(6, 7), The Dragonmurk

FIREMANE FLAMECALLER
Dustwallow Marsh (38), F:(7, 8), G:(7, 8), H-8, The Dragonmurk

FIREMANE SCALEBANE
Dustwallow Marsh (38), D-7, E-7, F:(7, 8), G:(7, 8), H-8, The Dragonmurk

FIREMANE SCOUT
Dustwallow Marsh (38), D-7, E:(6-8), F:(6, 7), The Dragonmurk

FIRESWORN
Burning Steppes (22), Searing Gorge (64), C-4/D-8, The Molten Core

FIRETAIL SCORPID
Burning Steppes (22), A-5, B:(4-7), C:(5, 6), Dreadmaul Rock

FIREWALKER
Burning Steppes (22), Searing Gorge (64), C-4/D-8, The Molten Core

FIRODREN MOONCALLER
Herbalism Trainer, Darnassus (26), F-7, The Temple Gardens, Small building, northeast of temple

FIRST MATE CRAZZ
Blackwater Raiders, Stranglethorn Vale (74), B-8, Booty Bay (103), On the dock just past The Old Port Authority on the eastern side of bay

FIRST MATE FITZSIMMONS
Wetlands (96), A-6, Menethil Harbor (117), Outside tavern

FIRST MATE NILZLIX
Arathi Highlands (10), D-8, Faldir's Cove, Roams around dock

FIRST MATE SNELLIG
Wetlands (96), B-3, The Lost Fleet, Bottom of southern ship

FIZZLE BRASSBOLTS
Thousand Needles (82), K-8, Mirage Raceway (118), West of racetrack

FIZZLE DARKSTORM
Durotar (34), F-3, Thunder Ridge, Eastern part of ridge in clearing

FIZZLEBANG BOOMS
Fireworks Vendor, Ironforge (52), J-5, Tinker Town, Things That Go Boom

FLAGGLEMURK THE CRUEL
Rare Spawn, Darkshore (24), E:(6-7), G-2, Mist's Edge, Twilight Shore, Lvl 16 Uncommon; Roams the shore close to spawn point

FLAKK
Trade Supplies, Durotar (34), H-4, Razor Hill (122), Outside barracks

FLAME IMP
Burning Steppes (22), Searing Gorge (64), C-4/D-8, The Molten Core

FLAMEGUARD
Burning Steppes (22), Searing Gorge (64), C-4/D-8, The Molten Core

FLAMEKIN RAGER
Burning Steppes (22), C-6, D-6, E-4, F:(3, 6), G:(5, 6), H-3, I-3, Ruins of Thourissan

FLAMEKIN SPITTER
Burning Steppes (22), G-6, I-6, J:(3-5, 7), Dreadmaul Rock

FLAMEKIN SPRITE
Burning Steppes (22), G-6, I-6, J:(3-5, 7), Dreadmaul Rock

FLAMEKIN TORCHER
Burning Steppes (22), C-6, D-6, E-4, F:(3, 6), G:(5, 6), H-3, I-3, Ruins of Thourissan

FLAMESCALE BROODLING
Burning Steppes (22), A-5, B:(4-7), C:(5, 6), Draco'dar

FLAMESCALE DRAGONSPAWN
Burning Steppes (22), A:(4, 5), B:(4, 5), C:(5-7), D:(5, 7), Blackrock Mountain

FLAMESCALE WYRMKIN
Burning Steppes (22), A:(4, 5), B:(4, 5), C:(6, 7), D:(5, 7), Blackrock Mountain, Road

FLAMESNORTING WHELP
Wetlands (96), I:(3, 4), J:(4, 5), The Green Belt

FLAMEWAKER
Burning Steppes (22), Searing Gorge (64), C-4/D-8, The Molten Core

FLAMEWAKER ELITE
Burning Steppes (22), Searing Gorge (64), C-4/D-8, The Molten Core

FLAMEWAKER HEALER
Burning Steppes (22), Searing Gorge (64), C-4/D-8, The Molten Core

FLAMEWAKER PRIEST
Burning Steppes (22), Searing Gorge (64), C-4/D-8, The Molten Core

FLAMEWAKER PROTECTOR
Burning Steppes (22), Searing Gorge (64), C-4/D-8, The Molten Core

FLATLAND COUGAR
Mulgore (58), C:(3, 4), D:(2-5), E:(3-5), F:(3-5), G:(3-7), H:(5-7)

FLATLAND PROWLER
Mulgore (58), C-2, D:(1, 2), E:(1-3), F:(1-3), G:(2, 3), H:(2, 3, 6, 7)

FLAWLESS DRAENETHYST FRAGMENT
Blasted Lands (20), H-4

FLAWLESS DRAENETHYST SPHERE
Blasted Lands (20), H-4

FLEDGLING CHILLWIND
Winterspring (98), D-5, E:(4, 5), F-4, G:(3-5), H-4

FLEDGLING CHIMAERA
Stonetalon Mountains (70), D-7, E-7, The Charred Vale

FLEDGLING PTERRORDAX
Un'Goro Crater (90), H-4, I:(2, 4), J:(4, 6), K:(4, 6), Ironstone Plateau, Lakkari Tar Pits, The Marshlands

FLEET MASTER FIRALLON
Stranglethorn Vale (74), C-9, Wild Shore

FLEET MASTER SEAHORN
Blackwater Raiders, Stranglethorn Vale (74), B-8, Booty Bay (103), Third floor balcony of The Salty Sailor Tavern

FLEETING PLAINSTRIDER
Barrens (18), E:(2-4), F:(1-4), G:(2-4), H:(2-4)

FLESH EATER
Duskwood (36), C:(3, 4), Raven Hill Cemetery (122)

FLESH GOLEM
Western Plaguelands (92), E-7, F-7, Ruins of Andorhal

FLESHFLAYER GHOUL
Eastern Plaguelands (40), D-2, Stratholme

FLESHRIPPER
Westfall (94), C:(4, 6), D:(2-7), E:(2, 4-6), F:(2, 6), G:(4, 5), Alexston Farmstead

FLINT SHADOWMORE
SI:7, Western Plaguelands (92), F-8, Chillwind Camp, In front of ruined building

FLORA SILVERWIND
Superior Herbalist, Stranglethorn Vale (74), B-8, Booty Bay (103), All Things Flora (shop)

FOBEED
Race Announcer, Thousand Needles (82), K-8, Mirage Raceway (118), Atop Starters tower inside track

FOE REAPER 4000
Rare Spawn, Westfall (94), D-5, E-4, F-2, F-7, G-6, Alexston Farmstead, The Dead Acre, Fulbrow's Pumpkin Farm, The Molsen Farm, Moonbrook, Lvl 20 Semi-Rare; Roams around spawn points

FOGGY MACKREEL
Arathi Highlands (10), F-9, Thandol Span, Ruins near bridge connecting Arathi Highlands and Wetlands

FOREMAN BONDS
Hillsbrad Foothills (48), C-6, Azurelode Mine, Raised wooden platform in mine

FOREMAN COZZLE
Stranglethorn Vale (74), E-2, Venture Co. Operations Center, Second floor control room of structure

FOREMAN GRILLS
Rare Spawn, Barrens (18), G-1, The Sludge Fen, Lvl 19 Semi-Rare; Patrols derrick

FOREMAN JERRIS
Rare Spawn, Western Plaguelands (92), F:(1, 2), Hearthglen, Lvl 62 Uncommon; Roams small area around spawn point

FOREMAN MARCRID
Rare Spawn, Western Plaguelands (92), F-3, Northridge Lumber Camp, Lvl 58 Average Rare; Roams small area around spawn point

FOREMAN OSLOW
Redridge Mountains (62), D-5, Lakeshire (115), In Lakeshire just left of bridge

FOREMAN RIGGER
Rare Spawn, Stonetalon Mountains (70), H-5, I-5, Blackwolf River, Windshear Crag, Lvl 24 Uncommon; West end of the crag

FOREMAN SILIXIZ
Barrens (18), F-1, Outside tower northwest of Sludge Fen

FOREMAN STONEBROW
Miners' League, Dun Morogh (32), I-6, Gol'Bolar Quarry, Hill overlooking quarry

FOREMAN THAZZ'RIL
Durotar (34), G-7, Valley of Trials (131), Road heading east

FOREMAN THISTLENETTLE
Westfall (94), D-7, E-7, The Deadmines

FOREST LURKER
Loch Modan (54), B:(7, 8), C:(2-6), D:(2-7), E:(3, 7), Silver Stream Mine

FOREST MOSS CREEPER
Hillsbrad Foothills (48), A:(4, 5), B:(4, 5), C-5, F-1, G:(1-4), H:(1-4), I:(1, 3, 4), J-5, Throughout Hillsbrad

FOREST OOZE
Azshara (14), D-7, E-7, H:(2, 3), I:(2, 3), J:(1-3), K:(2, 3)

FOREST SPIDER
Elwynn Forest (42), C-7, D:(6, 7), E:(6-8), F:(6-8), Goldshire (112), Mirror Lake, Mirror Lake Orchard

FORESTSTRIDER
Darkshore (24), F:(7, 8), G:(3, 4, 7), H-3, Bashal'Aran, Cliffspring River, Twilight Shore

FORESTSTRIDER FLEDGLING
Darkshore (24), E-9, F:(2-7, 9), G:(2-7)

FORLORN SPIRIT
Westfall (94), D-7, Moonbrook, (Summon) Town hall dais

FORSAKEN ASSASSIN
Ashenvale (12), J-7, Dor'Danil Barrow Den

FORSAKEN BODYGUARD
Arathi Highlands (10), H-6, Patrols the road from Thoradin's Wall to the Go'Shek Farm

FORSAKEN COURIER
, Arathi Highlands (10), H-6, Go'Shek Farm, Patrols with guards along road to Tarren Mill (see Hillsbrad Foothills)

FORSAKEN DARK STALKER
Ashenvale (12), J-7, Dor'Danil Barrow Den

FORSAKEN HERBALIST
Ashenvale (12), D-3, Bathran's Haunt, Ruins of Ordil'Aran

FORSAKEN INFILTRATOR
Ashenvale (12), J-7, Dor'Danil Barrow Den

FORSAKEN INTRUDER
Ashenvale (12), J-7, Dor'Danil Barrow Den

FORSAKEN SCOUT
Ashenvale (12), C-3

FORSAKEN SEEKER
Ashenvale (12), D-3, Bathran's Haunt, Ruins of Ordil'Aran

FORSAKEN THUG
Ashenvale (12), D-3, Bathran's Haunt, Ruins of Ordil'Aran

FOULBELLY
Rare Spawn, Arathi Highlands (10), B-6, Stromgarde Keep (127), Lvl 42 Very Rare; Stands to the right of tower in ogre quarter of keep

FOULMANE
Rare Spawn, Western Plaguelands (92), F-5, Dalson's Tears, Lvl 52 Semi-Rare; Patrols around cauldron

FOULWEALD DEN WATCHER
Ashenvale (12), F-6, G-6, Greenpaw Village

FOULWEALD PATHFINDER
Ashenvale (12), G-6, Greenpaw Village

FOULWEALD SHAMAN
Ashenvale (12), F-6, G-6, Greenpaw Village

FOULWEALD TOTEMIC
Ashenvale (12), F-6, G-6, Greenpaw Village

FOULWEALD URSA
Ashenvale (12), F-6, G-6, Greenpaw Village

FOULWEALD WARRIOR
Ashenvale (12), F-6, G-6, Greenpaw Village, Silverwind Refuge

FOZRUK
Arathi Highlands (10), I-3, Circle of East Binding, Patrols to each of the four Circles of Binding

FRADD SWIFTGEAR
Engineering Supplies, Wetlands (96), C-3, Sundown Marsh, Outside building next to windmill

FRAGGAR THUNDERMANTLE
The Hinterlands (50), B-4, Aerie Peak (100), Wildhammer Keep

FRAHUN SHADEWHISPER
Rogue Trainer, Teldrassil (80), H-4, Shadowglen (124), In northeast room inside main building

FRAMNALI
Ashenvale (12), I-6, Splintertree Post (126), Atop western watch tower

FRANCIS ELIOT
Weapon Merchant, Undercity (88), H-3, The War Quarter

FRANG
Warrior Trainer, Durotar (34), F-7, Valley of Trials (131), Structure to south

FRANKLIN HAMAR
Tailoring Supplies, Redridge Mountains (62), C-4, Lakeshire (115), Second floor of Lakeshire Inn

FRANKLIN LLOYD
Expert Engineer, Undercity (88), K-7, The Rogues' Quarter

FRANKLIN THE FRIENDLY
Burning Steppes (22), B-7, Draco'dar, Patrols circular path through southwestern portion of Burning Steppes

FRAS SIABI
Eastern Plaguelands (40), D-2, Stratholme

FRAST DOKNER
Apprentice Weaponsmith, Dun Morogh (32), I-6, Gol'Bolar Quarry, Patrols in and out of camp tent

FRAYFEATHER HIPPOGRYPH
Feralas (46), F-6, G-6

FRAYFEATHER PATRIARCH
Feralas (46), F-7, G-7, Frayfeather Highlands, Ruins of Isildien

FRAYFEATHER SKYSTORMER
Feralas (46), F:(6, 7), G-7, Frayfeather Highlands, High Wilderness, Ruins of Isildien

FRAYFEATHER STAGWING
Feralas (46), F:(6, 7), G-6, Frayfeather Highlands, Ruins of Isildien

FREDERICK STOVER
Bow & Arrow Merchant, Stormwind (72), H-6, Trade District, The Empty Quiver

FREEWIND BRAVE
Thousand Needles (82), E-5, F-5, Freewind Post

FREEZING GHOUL
Western Plaguelands (92), G:(6, 7), The Writhing Haunt

FREEZING SPIRIT
Barrens (18), F-9, Razorfen Downs

FREJA NIGHTWING
Leather Armor Merchant, Teldrassil (80), H-4, Shadowglen (124), Inside main building

FREMAL DOOHICKEY
First Aid Trainer, Wetlands (96), A-6, Deepwater Tavern, Southeast, upstairs room

FRENZIED BLACK DRAKE
Burning Steppes (22), L-3, Slither Rock, (Summon) Summoned by Cyrus Therepentous

FRENZIED BLACK DRAKE
Burning Steppes (22), L-3, Slither Rock

FRENZIED PLAGUEHOUND
Eastern Plaguelands (40), B-3, C:(2-4), D-4, E-4, F:(3, 4), G:(2-4), H:(2-5), I:(3-5), J:(3, 4), East Wall Tower

FRENZIED PTERRORDAX
Un'Goro Crater (90), B:(4, 6), C:(2-7), D:(3-5, 7, 8), E:(2-8)

FREZZA
Zeppelin Master, Durotar (34), H-1, Atop tower

FROST SPECTRE
Barrens (18), F-9, Razorfen Downs

FROSTMANE HEADHUNTER
Dun Morogh (32), B-5, C-5, E-4, G-2, I-4, J-4, Frostmane Hold, Shimmer Ridge

FROSTMANE HIDESKINNER
Dun Morogh (32), B-5, C-5, I-4, J-4, Frostmane Hold

FROSTMANE NOVICE
Dun Morogh (32), D-8, I-4, J-4, Coldridge Valley (106)

FROSTMANE SEER
Dun Morogh (32), E:(3-5), F:(3-5), I-4, J-4, Shimmer Ridge

FROSTMANE SHADOWCASTER
Dun Morogh (32), B-5, C-5, G-2, I-4, J-4, Frostmane Hold

FROSTMANE SNOWSTRIDER
Dun Morogh (32), C-5, E:(3, 4), F-4, G-2, I-4, J-4, Frostmane Hold, Iceflow Lake, Shimmer Ridge

FROSTMANE TROLL
Dun Morogh (32), C-5, E-4, I-4, J-4, Frostmane Hold, Shimmer Ridge

FROSTMANE TROLL WHELP
Dun Morogh (32), B:(7, 8), C-8, D-8, Coldridge Valley (106)

FROSTMAUL GIANT
Winterspring (98), I:(6, 7), J-7, Frostwhisper Gorge

FROSTMAUL PRESERVER
Winterspring (98), I:(6, 7), J-7, Frostwhisper Gorge

FROSTMAW
Alterac Mountains (8), E-7, Growless Cave, (Summon) Cave south of Ruins of Alterac

FROSTSABER
Winterspring (98), G-2, H:(1, 2), Frostsaber Rock

FROSTSABER COMPANION
Teldrassil (80), B:(5, 6), C:(4, 5), Cenarion Enclave

FROSTSABER CUB
Winterspring (98), G:(1, 2), H:(1, 2), Frostsaber Rock

FROSTSABER HUNTRESS
Winterspring (98), G:(1, 2), H:(1, 2), Frostsaber Rock

FROSTSABER PRIDE WATCHER
Winterspring (98), G-1, H-1, Frostsaber Rock

FROSTSABER STALKER
Winterspring (98), G:(1, 2), H:(1, 2), Frostsaber Rock

FROSTWOLF AMBASSADOR ROKHSTROM
Orgrimmar (60), F-7, Valley of Strength, Alterac Valley Battlemaster

FROSTWOLF BATTLEGUARD
Alterac Mountains (8), I:(5, 6), Alterac Valley

FROZEN SOUL
Barrens (18), F-9, Razorfen Downs

FUNGAL OOZE
Swamp of Sorrows (76), I-5, The Temple of Atal'Hakkar

FUREN LONGBEARD
Stormwind (72), I-2, J-2, Dwarven District, At the forge

FURIOUS STONE SPIRIT
Stonetalon Mountains (70), D-7, E-7, The Charred Vale

FURL SCORNBROW
Durotar (34), G-4, Atop watchtower

FURY SHELDA
Rare Spawn, Teldrassil (80), D:(3-4), The Oracle Glade, Lvl 8 Uncommon; Patrols near harpy camps west of road

FUZRUCKLE
Banker, Barrens (18), H-4, Ratchet (121), Bank

FYLDAN
Cooking Supplier, Darnassus (26), F-2, Craftsmen's Terrace, Cooking shop

FYLDREN MOONFEATHER
Hippogryph Master, Feralas (46), C-4, Feathermoon Stronghold (110), West of inn

FYLERIAN NIGHTWING
Druid Trainer, Darnassus (26), D-1, Cenarion Enclave, Northwest structure

FYR MISTRUNNER
Bread, Thunder Bluff (84), D-5, Lower rise, inside Breads and Grains tent

FYRENNA
Food & Drink, Darnassus (26), K-4, Craftsmen's Terrace, South of path just after entrance to city

G

GABRIELLE CHASE
Food & Drink, Burning Steppes (22), K-7, Morgan's Vigil (118), Scaffolding, right side of camp

GADGETZAN BRUISER
Tanaris (78), G-3, H-3, Gadgetzan (111)

GAERIYAN
Tanaris (78), H-2, Gadgetzan (111), Only visible when dead; Northeast of town in hills

GAEROLAS TALVETHREN
Teldrassil (80), I-6, Starbreeze Village, Second floor of southwest building

GAGSPROCKET
Engineering Goods, Barrens (18), H-4, Ratchet (121), Building northeast of town

GAHROOT
Butcher, Barrens (18), F-6, Camp Taurajo (106), Southern building

GAHZ'RILLA
Tanaris (78), E-1, Zul'Farrak

GAKIN THE DARKBINDER
Stormwind (72), D-8, Mage Quarter, The Slaughtered Lamb

GALAK ASSASSIN
Thousand Needles (82), B-3, Whitereach Post

GALAK CENTAUR
Mulgore (58), H-6, I-6, The Rolling Plains

GALAK MARAUDER
Thousand Needles (82), B:(2, 3), E-3, F-3, Camp E'thok, Splithoof Crag, Splithoof Hold

GALAK MAULER
Thousand Needles (82), B:(2, 3), E-3, F-3, Camp E'thok, Splithoof Crag, Splithoof Hold

GALAK MESSENGER
Thousand Needles (82), E-3, Splithoof Crag, Runs between Camp E'thok and Splithoof Crag

GALAK OUTRUNNER
Mulgore (58), H-6, I-6, The Rolling Plains

GALAK PACKHOUND
Thousand Needles (82), B-4, Whitereach Post

GALAK SCOUT
Thousand Needles (82), E:(3, 4), F-4

GALAK STORMER
Thousand Needles (82), B:(2, 3), E-3, F-3, Camp E'thok, Splithoof Hold

GALAK WINDCHASER
Thousand Needles (82), E:(3, 4), F-4

GALAK WRANGLER
Thousand Needles (82), E:(3, 4), F-4

GALAMAV THE MARKSMAN
Badlands (16), A-5, Kargath (114), Tower platform

GALEN GOODWARD
Swamp of Sorrows (76), H-2, Caged next to hut

GALGANN FIREHAMMER
Badlands (16), G-1, Uldaman

GALGAR
Durotar (34), F-7, Valley of Trials (131), Northwest structure

GALTHUK
Two-Handed Weapons Merchant, Orgrimmar (60), J-2, Valley of Honor, Arms of Legend

GALVAN THE ANCIENT
Artisan Blacksmith of the Mithril Order, Stranglethorn Vale (74), F-2, By anvil in camp

GAMILI FROSTHIDE
Cloth & Leather Armor Merchant, Dun Morogh (32), F-5, Kharanos (114), Smithy

GAMMERITA
The Hinterlands (50), L-5, The Overlook Cliffs, Patrols the coastline

GAMON
Orgrimmar (60), G-7, Valley of Strength, Inn

GAN'RUL BLOODEYE
Orgrimmar (60), F-4, The Cleft of Shadow, Darkfire Enclave

GANGLED GOLEM
Eastern Plaguelands (40), K-4, The Noxious Glade

GANN STONESPIRE
Barrens (18), E-7, Southern Gold Road, Spawns on Southern Gold Road and pauses at road to Dustwallow Marsh

GANOOSH
Undercity (88), F-6, The Apothecarium, On wooden pathway leading to back of Apothecarium

GAN'ZULAH
Bloodscalp Chief, Stranglethorn Vale (74), B-1, Ruins of Zul'Kunda, Idle with several trolls in the northwestern corner of ruins

GAREK
Badlands (16), I-5, Left of bone pile

GARNEG CHARSKULL
Rare Spawn, Wetlands (96), E-5, F:(4, 5), Angerfang Encampment, Lvl 29 Uncommon; Spawns in a few different camps

GARR
Burning Steppes (22), Searing Gorge (64), C-4/D-8, The Molten Core

GARR SALTHOOF
Stranglethorn Vale (74), C-9, Wild Shore, Roams below deck of beached ship

GARRICK PADFOOT
Elwynn Forest (42), H-5, Northshire Vineyards, In front of shed

GARRYETH
Banker, Darnassus (26), D-4, Bank

GART MISTRUNNER
Druid Trainer, Mulgore (58), E-8, Camp Narache (105), North tent

GAR'THOK
Durotar (34), H-4, Razor Hill (122), Bunker

GARYL
Tabard Vendor, Orgrimmar (60), E-7, Valley of Strength, Horde Embassy

GASHER
Swamp of Sorrows (76), I-5, The Temple of Atal'Hakkar

GATEKEEPER RAGEROAR
Rare Spawn, Azshara (14), D-3, Timbermaw Hold, Lvl 49 Semi-Rare; Guards gate

GATH'ILZOGG
Warlord of the Blackrock Clan, Redridge Mountains (62), I-5, Stonewatch, Second floor of Stonewatch Keep

GAVIN GNARLTREE
Weaponsmith, Duskwood (36), J-5, Darkshire (108), Roams in and out of smithy

GAXIM RUSTFIZZLE
Stonetalon Mountains (70), G-7, Webwinder Path, Camp east of road

GAZBAN
Stranglethorn Vale (74), A-3, The Savage Coast, Roams around island

GAZIN TENORM
Stormwind (72), F-3, Cathedral Square, Cathedral of Light

GAZLOWE
Barrens (18), H-4, Ratchet (121), Building northeast of town

GAZROG
Barrens (18), F-3, The Crossroads (107), Front of inn

GAZZ'UZ
Durotar (34), H-1, Skull Rock, Deep in cave

GEARCUTTER COGSPINNER
Engineering Supplies, Ironforge (52), I-4, Tinker Town, Springspindle's Gadgets

GEENIA SUNSHADOW
Speciality Dress Maker, Moonglade (56), G-3, Nighthaven (120), First floor of northeast building

GEHENNAS
Burning Steppes (22), Searing Gorge (64), C-4/D-8, The Molten Core

GELIHAST
Ashenvale (12), B-2, Blackfathom Deeps

GELKAK GYROMAST
Darkshore (24), H-2, Mist's Edge, Rocky outcropping off shore

GELKIS EARTHCALLER
Desolace (30), D:(8, 9), E:(8, 9), Bolgan's Hole, Gelkis Village

GELKIS MARAUDER
Desolace (30), D-9, E-9, Bolgan's Hole, Gelkis Village

GELKIS MAULER
Desolace (30), D-9, E-9, Bolgan's Hole, Gelkis Village

GELKIS OUTRUNNER
Desolace (30), D:(8, 9), E:(8, 9), Bolgan's Hole, Gelkis Village

GELKIS SCOUT
Desolace (30), D:(8, 9), E:(8, 9), Bolgan's Hole, Gelkis Village

GELKIS STAMPER
Desolace (30), D:(8, 9), E:(8, 9), Bolgan's Hole, Gelkis Village

GELKIS WINDCHASER
Desolace (30), D:(8, 9), E:(8, 9), Bolgan's Hole, Gelkis Village

GELMAN STONEHAND
Mining Trainer, Stormwind (72), H-2, Dwarven District, Building north of west entrance

GELTHARIS
Ashenvale (12), J-4, Xavian, Far north within Xavian in a small gully

GENAVIE GALLOW
Undercity (88), I-5, The Trade Quarter, Upper Ring of Trade Quarter

GENERAL ANGERFORGE
Burning Steppes (22), Searing Gorge (64), C-4/D-8, Blackrock Depths

GENERAL COLBATANN
Rare Spawn, Winterspring (98), H-5, Mazthoril, Lvl 57 Semi-Rare; Central cavern

GENERAL DRAKKISATH
Burning Steppes (22), Searing Gorge (64), C-4/D-8, Blackrock Spire

GENERAL FANGFERROR
Rare Spawn, Azshara (14), E-5, Temple of Zin-Malor, Lvl 50 Semi-Rare; Top of main temple

GENERAL MARCUS JONATHEN
High Commander of Stormwind Defense, Stormwind (72), I-7, Stormwind City, Next to statue at entrance

GENNIA RUNETOTEM
Druid Trainer, Mulgore (58), F-6, Bloodhoof Village (102), East tent

GEOFF
Stormwind (72), Roams city with Miss Danna

GEOFFREY HARTWELL
Weapon Merchant, Undercity (88), H-3, The War Quarter

GEOFRAM BOULDERTOE
Mining Trainer, Ironforge (52), G-3, The Great Forge, Deep Mountain Mining Guild

GEOLORD MOTTLE
Rare Spawn, Durotar (34), F-4, G-5, Razormane Grounds, Lvl 9 Uncommon; Found near huts

GEOPRIEST GUKK'ROK
Rare Spawn, Barrens (18), E:(4-5), Agama'gor, Lvl 19 Uncommon; Guards Bristleback den

GEORGE CANDARTE
Leatherworking Supplies, Hillsbrad Foothills (48), L-4, Thoradin's Wall, Behind two trees at the far left corner of the wall

GEORGIA
Bat Handler, Eastern Plaguelands (40), K-5, Light's Hope Chapel (116), Camp on left side of chapel

GEORGIO BOLERO
Artisan Tailor, Stormwind (72), G-7, Mage Quarter, Duncan's Textiles

GERALD CRAWLEY
Poison Supplier, Redridge Mountains (62), C-4, Lakeshire (115), Small house on a hill on northwestern side of town

GERARD ABERNATHY
Undercity (88), G-3, The War Quarter, By Mining Trainer, Close to Canal

GERARD TILLER
Elwynn Forest (42), F-8, The Maclure Vineyards, In front of barn

GERECK
Stable Master, Stonetalon Mountains (70), F-6, Sun Rock Retreat (127), Front of inn

GERENZO WRENCHWHISTLE
Stonetalon Mountains (70), H-4, Cragpool Lake, Wood platform above lake

GERIK KOEN
Two Handed Weapon Merchant, Stormwind (72), J-4, Old Town, Heavy Handed Weapons

GERRIG BONEGRIP
Ironforge (52), G-1, The Forlorn Cavern, Building to the right of Traveling Fisherman

GERSHALA NIGHTWHISPER
Darkshore (24), F-4, Auberdine (101), Pavillion east of inn across bridge

GESHARAHAN
Rare Spawn, Barrens (18), E-4, Lushwater Oasis, Lvl 20 Average Rare; Swims in the oasis

GEST
Rogue Trainer, Orgrimmar (60), E-5, The Cleft of Shadow, Shadowswift Brotherhood

GHAK HEALTOUCH
Journeyman Alchemist, Loch Modan (54), E-5, Thelsamar (129), In first house on right of path

GHAMOO-RA
Ashenvale (12), B-2, Blackfathom Deeps

GHARASH
Blacksmithing Supplies, Swamp of Sorrows (76), F-5, Stonard (126), Smithy

GHEDE
Thunder Bluff (84), J-2, Elder Rise, Behind Hall of Elders

GHOK BASHGUUD
Rare Spawn, Burning Steppes (22), Searing Gorge (64), C-4/D-8, Blackrock Spire, Lvl 59 Uncommon

GHOK'KAH
Tailoring Supplies, Dustwallow Marsh (38), D-3, Brackenwall Village (104), West entrance

GHOST HOWL
Rare Spawn, Mulgore (58), C-2, D:(1, 4), F-1, Lvl 12 Uncommon; Roams plains in multiple areas

GHOST OF THE PROTECTOR
Eastern Plaguelands (40), E-8, Darrowshire

GHOST WALKER BRAVE
Desolace (30), G:(5, 6), Ghost Walker Post (111), Kodo Graveyard

GHOSTLY CITIZEN
Eastern Plaguelands (40), D-2, Stratholme

GHOSTLY MARAUDER
Desolace (30), D-5, Mauradon

GHOSTLY RAIDER
Desolace (30), D-5, Mauradon

GHOSTPAW ALPHA
Ashenvale (12), G:(3, 4), H:(3-7), I:(5-7), J:(5, 6), Falfarren River, Nightsong Woods, Splintertree Post (126)

GHOSTPAW HOWLER
Ashenvale (12), G:(6, 7), H:(6, 7)

GHOSTPAW RUNNER
Ashenvale (12), B:(2-5), C:(2-6), D:(2-6), E:(5, 6), H:(7, 8), I:(7, 8), J:(6, 7)

GHOUL
Westfall (94), D:(3, 7), G-8

GHOUL RAVENER
Eastern Plaguelands (40), D-2, Stratholme

GHRAWT
Bowyer, Durotar (34), H-4, Razor Hill (122), Northern entrance

GIANT ASHENVALE BEAR
Ashenvale (12), J:(5, 6), K:(4-6), L:(5, 6)

GIANT BUZZARD
Badlands (16), A-7, B:(5, 6), C:(6-8), D:(6-8), E-8, Apocryphan's Rest

GIANT DARKFANG SPIDER
Dustwallow Marsh (38), F:(4, 5), G:(5-7)

GIANT EMBER WORG
Burning Steppes (22), A-5, B:(4-7), C:(5, 6), Blackrock Mountain

GIANT FORESTSTRIDER
Darkshore (24), E:(8, 9), F:(8, 9), G-9, I:(1, 2)

GIANT GRIZZLED BEAR
Silverpine Forest (68), E-2, F:(1, 2), G:(2, 7), H:(5-7)

GIANT MOSS CREEPER
Hillsbrad Foothills (48), B:(2-7), C:(1-3, 5-7), D:(3, 5, 6), E:(5, 6), G-5, H:(4-6), I:(2, 3, 5, 6), J:(3, 5, 6), K:(3-5), L-4

GIANT PLAINS CREEPER
Arathi Highlands (10), E-3, F:(3, 4, 7, 8), G:(5, 6), H:(5-7), Northfold Manor

GIANT SURF GLIDER
Tanaris (78), G:(8, 9), H-9, I:(8, 9), Land's End Beach

GIANT WEBWOOD SPIDER
Teldrassil (80), D:(2, 3), E:(2, 3), F:(2, 3), The Oracle Glade

GIANT WETLANDS CROCOLISK
Wetlands (96), B:(2, 3, 6), C-2, D-2

GIANT YETI
Alterac Mountains (8), D:(4-7), E:(3, 4, 6, 7), F:(6, 7), Growless Cave

GIBBERING GHOUL
Eastern Plaguelands (40), H:(6, 7), Corin's Crossing

GIBBERT
Weapon Merchant, Un'Goro Crater (90), F-1, Marshal's Refuge (116), Near entrance to cave

GIBBLESNIK
Rare Spawn, Thousand Needles (82), G:(4-5), H:(5-6), Windbreak Canyon, Lvl 28 Semi-Rare; Several spawn points around Windbreak Canyons

GIBBLEWILT
Rare Spawn, Dun Morogh (32), C-4, Gnomeregan, Lvl 11 Uncommon; Roams small area around spawn point

GIGGET ZIPCOIL
Trade Supplies, The Hinterlands (50), E-4, The Hinterlands, Gnomish camp on recessed hill east of Quel'Danil Lodge

GIGGLER
Rare Spawn, Desolace (30), F-1, G-1, H:(2-3), I:(2-3), Tethris Aran, Lvl 34 Semi-Rare; Roams near spawn points

GIKKIX
Fisherman, Tanaris (78), J-2, Steamwheedle Port, Small northern hut

GIL
Stormwind (72), Roams city with Karlee

GILLIAN MOORE
Leather Armor Merchant, Undercity (88), J-6, The Rogues' Quarter

GILMORIAN
Rare Spawn, Swamp of Sorrows (76), J-9, The Forbidding Sea, Lvl 43 Average Rare; Patrols up and down the eastern coastline

GILNID
Westfall (94), D-7, E-7, The Deadmines

GILSHALAN WINDWALKER
Teldrassil (80), G-4, Shadowglen (124), By ramp leading up tree

GILTHARES FIREBOUGH
Barrens (18), H-5, Northwatch Hold, First floor of main tower

GILVERADIN SUNCHASER
The Hinterlands (50), D-5, Shindigger's Camp, Camp

GIMBLE THISTLEFUZZ
Expert Enchanter, Ironforge (52), H-4, The Great Forge, Thistlefuzz Arcanery

GIMBLETHORN
Banker, Tanaris (78), H-3, Gadgetzan (111), Bank

GIMLOK RUMDNUL
Wetlands (96), A-6, Menethil Harbor (117), Roaming eastern side of town

GIMRIZZ SHADOWCOG
Warlock Trainer, Dun Morogh (32), F-5, Kharanos (114), Gnomish camp on right of distillery

GINA LANG
Demon Trainer, Tirisfal Glades (86), H-5, Brill (104), Second floor of Gallows' End Tavern

GINA MACGREGOR
Trade Supplies, Westfall (94), G-5, Sentinel Hill (123), At intersection east of the Sentinel Tower

GINNY LONGBERRY
Reagent Vendor, Ironforge (52), D-3, The Mystic Ward, Longberry's Reagents

GINRO HEARTHKINDLE
Feralas (46), C-4, Feathermoon Stronghold (110), Second floor of southeastern building

GISH THE UNMOVING
Rare Spawn, Eastern Plaguelands (40), F-4, I-6, Pestilent Scar, Lvl 56 Average Rare; Patrols between its two spawn points

GITHYISS THE VILE
Teldrassil (80), G-3, Shadowthread Cave, On ledge in back of cave

GIZELTON CARAVAN KODO
Desolace (30), H:(4, 6), Kormek's Hut, Scrabblescrew's Camp

GIZRUL THE SLAVENER
Burning Steppes (22), Searing Gorge (64), C-4/D-8, Blackrock Spire

GLACIER
Rivern's Guardian, Winterspring (98), G-1, Frostsaber Rock, Atop Frostsaber Rock

GLASSHIDE BASILISK
Tanaris (78), E:(2, 3), F:(2-4), G:(2-4), H:(2-4), I:(2, 3), J-3

GLASSHIDE GAZER
Tanaris (78), E:(4-7), F:(4-7), G:(4-7), H:(4-6), I:(4-6)

GLASSHIDE PETRIFIER
Tanaris (78), D:(5-8), E:(5-8), F:(7, 8), G:(7, 8)

GLASSWEB SPIDER
Searing Gorge (64), G:(5, 7), H:(3-5, 7), I:(2, 5), J-2, Tanner Camp

GLOMMUS
Alterac Mountains (8), E-4, Ruins of Alterac, Small house

GLOOM'REL
Burning Steppes (22), Searing Gorge (64), C-4/D-8, Blackrock Depths

GLORANDIIR
Axe Merchant, Darnassus (26), I-6, Tradesmen's Terrace, Weapons shop

GLORDRUM STEELBEARD
Alterac Valley Battlemaster, Ironforge (52), J-9, The Military Ward, Hall of Arms

GLORIA FEMMEL
Cooking Supplies, Redridge Mountains (62), C-4, Lakeshire (115), First floor of Lakeshire Inn

GLORIN STEELBROW
Wetlands (96), A-6, Deepwater Tavern, First floor

GLUGGLE
Rare Spawn, Stranglethorn Vale (74), C-3, Kal'ai Ruins, Lvl 37 Semi-Rare; Patrols between ruins and path heading north

GLUTINOUS OOZE
Un'Goro Crater (90), C:(3-7), D:(3-8), E:(2-8), F:(5, 6), Fire Plume Ridge, Golakka Hot Springs, Terror Run

GLUTTON
Barrens (18), F-9, Razorfen Downs

GLYX BREWRIGHT
Alchemy Supplies, Stranglethorn Vale (74), B-8, Booty Bay (103), Boucher's Cauldron (shop)

GNARL LEAFBROTHER
Rare Spawn, Feralas (46), I-6, The Writhing Deep, Lvl 44 Very Rare; Roams west to the Woodpaw Hills

GNARLED THISTLESHRUB
Tanaris (78), D:(6, 7), E:(6, 7), Thistleshrub Valley

GNARLPINE AMBUSHER
Teldrassil (80), E-5, F-5, Ban'ethil Hollow

GNARLPINE AUGUR
Teldrassil (80), E:(6, 7), F:(6, 8), G-7, Ban'ethil Barrow Den

GNARLPINE AVENGER
Teldrassil (80), D-8, E-8, Gnarlpine Hold

GNARLPINE DEFENDER
Teldrassil (80), D:(6, 7), E:(6, 7), F:(6-8), G:(7, 8), Ban'ethil Barrow Den, Ban'ethil Hollow, Gnarlpine Hold

GNARLPINE GARDENER
Teldrassil (80), H-6, I:(5, 6), Starbreeze Village

GNARLPINE INSTIGATOR
Teldrassil (80), F-6

GNARLPINE MYSTIC
Teldrassil (80), I-5, Ban'ethil Barrow Den

GNARLPINE PATHFINDER
Teldrassil (80), D-8, E-8, Gnarlpine Hold

GNARLPINE SHAMAN
Teldrassil (80), D:(6, 7), E:(6, 7), F:(6-8), G:(7, 8), Ban'ethil Barrow Den, Ban'ethil Hollow, Gnarlpine Hold

GNARLPINE TOTEMIC
Teldrassil (80), D-8, E-8, Gnarlpine Hold

GNARLPINE URSA
Teldrassil (80), H-6, I:(5, 6), Starbreeze Village

GNARLPINE WARRIOR
Teldrassil (80), F:(6, 7), H-6, I:(5, 6), Lake Al'Ameth, Starbreeze Village

GNASHER
Loch Modan (54), D-9, Stonesplinter Valley, With Grawmug and Brawler in center of cave

GNAWBONE
Rare Spawn, Wetlands (96), D-3, E-3, Sundown Marsh, Lvl 24 Average Rare; Patrols mosshide camps north of road across from excavation site

GNAZ BLUNDERFLAME
Engineering Supplies, Stranglethorn Vale (74), F-4, Outside of gnomish workshop

GNOARN
Ironforge (52), I-5, Tinker Town, Outside tram entrance

GNOME ENGINEER
Dun Morogh (32), J-3

GNOMEREGAN EVACUEE
Dun Morogh (32), C-4, Gnomeregan

GOBBLER
Wetlands (96), B-4, Bluegill Marsh, South central section of marsh

GOBLIN CRAFTSMAN
Westfall (94), D-7, E-7, The Deadmines

GOBLIN ENGINEER
Westfall (94), D-7, E-7, The Deadmines

GOBLIN SHIPBUILDER
Westfall (94), D-7, E-7, The Deadmines

GOBLIN WOODCARVER
Westfall (94), D-7, E-7, The Deadmines

GODAN
Expert Enchanter, Orgrimmar (60), F-4, The Drag, Godan's Runeworks

GODRIC ROTHGAR
Armorer & Shieldcrafter, Elwynn Forest (42), F-4, Northshire Valley (120), Caravan facing abbey

GODRICK FARSAN
Undercity (88), L-1, The Magic Quarter, Inside Skull Building

GOGGEROC
Stonetalon Mountains (70), H-9, Boulderslide Cavern, South of water deep in cave

GOGO
Winterspring (98), I-4, Everlook (110), Outside inn

GOL'DIR
Alterac Mountains (8), H-4, Strahnbrad, Second floor of inn

GOLDTOOTH
Elwynn Forest (42), E-8, Fargodeep Mine, Rear of mine

GOLEM LORD ARGELMACH
Burning Steppes (22), Searing Gorge (64), C-4/D-8, Blackrock Depths

GOLEMAGG THE INCINERATOR
Burning Steppes (22), Searing Gorge (64), C-4/D-8, The Molten Core

GOLHINE THE HOODED
Druid Trainer, Felwood (44), H-3, Talonbranch Glade, Front of building

GOLNIR BOULDERTOE
Mining Supplier, Ironforge (52), G-3, The Great Forge, Deep Mountain Mining Guild

GOLORN FROSTBEARD
Tradesman, Dun Morogh (32), F-5, Kharanos (114), By caravan

GOMA
Orgrimmar (60), G-7, Valley of Strength, Inn

GOR'TESH
Burning Steppes (22), D-5, Entrance of orc burrow

GORALUK ANVILCRACK
Burning Steppes (22), Searing Gorge (64), C-4/D-8, Blackrock Spire

GORBOLD STEELHAND
General Trade Supplier, Darkshore (24), F-4, Auberdine (101), In front of northern building

GORDO
Tirisfal Glades (86), E-5, Patrols along road between the fork near Deathknell and the bridge near Cold Hearth Manor

GORDOK BRUTE
Feralas (46), G-4, Dire Maul

GORDOK BUSHWACKER
Feralas (46), G-4, Dire Maul

GORDOK CAPTAIN
Feralas (46), G-4, Dire Maul

GORDOK ENFORCER
Feralas (46), F:(4, 5), G:(4, 5), H:(3, 5), Dire Maul, High Wilderness

GORDOK HYENA
Feralas (46), F:(4, 5), G:(3, 4), H-4, Dire Maul, High Wilderness

GORDOK MAGE-LORD
Feralas (46), G-4, Dire Maul

GORDOK MASTIFF
Feralas (46), G-4, Dire Maul

GORDOK MAULER
Feralas (46), G:(3, 4), H:(3, 4), Dire Maul

GORDOK OGRE-MAGE
Feralas (46), F-4, G:(3-5), H:(3-5), Dire Maul, High Wilderness

GORDOK REAVER
Feralas (46), G-4, Dire Maul

GORDOK SPIRIT
Feralas (46), G-4, Dire Maul

GORDOK WARLOCK
Feralas (46), G-4, Dire Maul

GORDON WENDHAM
Weapons Merchant, Undercity (88), H-4, The Trade Quarter, Upper Ring of Trade Quarter

GORDUNNI BATTLEMASTER
Feralas (46), G-7, H-7, High Wilderness, Ruins of Isildien

GORDUNNI BRUTE
Feralas (46), G:(5, 6), I:(2, 3), J:(3, 4)

GORDUNNI MAGE-LORD
Feralas (46), G-7, H-7, High Wilderness, Ruins of Isildien

GORDUNNI MAULER
Feralas (46), G:(5-7), High Wilderness, Ruins of Isildien

GORDUNNI OGRE
Feralas (46), I:(2, 3), J:(3, 4), Gordunni Outpost, Lariss Pavilion

GORDUNNI OGRE MAGE
Feralas (46), I:(2, 3), J:(3, 4), Gordunni Outpost, Lariss Pavilion

GORDUNNI SHAMAN
Feralas (46), G:(6, 7), H-7, High Wilderness, Ruins of Isildien

GORDUNNI WARLOCK
Feralas (46), G:(5-7), High Wilderness, Ruins of Isildien

GORDUNNI WARLORD
Feralas (46), G:(6, 7), H-7, High Wilderness, Ruins of Isildien

GOREFANG
Rare Spawn, Silverpine Forest (68), G:(2, 3), H-2, I-1, Malden's Orchard, Silverpine Forest, Lvl 13 Uncommon; Roams small area around spawn point

GOREHOOF THE BLACK
Stonetalon Mountains (70), J-8, Grimtotem Post, Inside eastern hut

GORETUSK
Westfall (94), C:(3, 4, 6-8), D:(2-7), E:(4-6), F-6, G:(4, 5)

GORGON'OCH
Rare Spawn, Burning Steppes (22), J-4, Dreadmaul Rock, Lvl 54 Average Rare

GORINA
Mining Supplier, Orgrimmar (60), I-3, Valley of Honor, Red Canyon Mining

GORISHI HIVE GUARD
Un'Goro Crater (90), F-8, The Slithering Scar

GORISHI HIVE QUEEN
Un'Goro Crater (90), G-8, The Slithering Scar, Northwest chamber

GORISHI REAVER
Un'Goro Crater (90), F:(7-9), G:(7-9), The Slithering Scar

GORISHI STINGER
Un'Goro Crater (90), F:(8, 9), G-8, The Slithering Scar

GORISHI TUNNELER
Un'Goro Crater (90), F:(8, 9), G-8, The Slithering Scar

GORISHI WASP
Un'Goro Crater (90), F:(7-9), G:(7-9), The Slithering Scar

GORISHI WORKER
Un'Goro Crater (90), F:(7-9), G:(7-9), The Slithering Scar

GORKAS
Wind Rider Master, The Hinterlands (50), L-8, Revantusk Village, End of dock

GORLASH
Stranglethorn Vale (74), D-7, The Crystal Shore, Roams small area around spawn point

GORM GRIMTOTEM
Thunder Bluff (84), I-3, Elder Rise, In front of Magatha Grimtotem's tent

GOR'MAROK THE RAVAGER
Tanaris (78), F-6, Dunemaul Compound, Cave

GOR'MUL
Arathi Highlands (10), J-3, Hammerfall (113), Gallows

GORN
Badlands (16), A-5, Kargath (114), First floor orc burrow

GORNEK
Durotar (34), F-7, Valley of Trials (131), Entrance of cave

GOROSH THE DERVISH
Burning Steppes (22), Searing Gorge (64), C-4/D-8, Blackrock Depths

GORRIK
Wind Rider Master, Badlands (16), A-5, Kargath (114), Camp

GORZEEKI WILDEYES
Burning Steppes (22), A-3, Altar of Storms, In graveyard above and left of the Altar of Storms

GOTHARD WINSLOW
Undercity (88), L-6, The Rogues' Quarter

GOTHOR BRUMN
Armorer, Loch Modan (54), C-2, Dun Algaz, Algaz Station

GOTRI
Bag Vendor, Orgrimmar (60), G-5, The Drag, Gotri's Traveling Gear

GRACINA SPIRITMIGHT
Darnassus (26), E-8, The Temple of the Moon, Balcony, east of fountain

GRADOK
Loch Modan (54), H-7, Patrols large circular paths with Haren Swifthoof and Thragomm along the eastern side of the loch

GRAHAM VAN TALEN
Journeyman Engineer, Undercity (88), K-7, The Rogues' Quarter

GRAMMA STONEFIELD
Elwynn Forest (42), D-8, The Stonefield Farm, House

GRAND ADMIRAL JES-TERETH
Stormwind (72), L-1, Stormwind Keep, War Room

GRAND CRUSADER DATHROHAN
Eastern Plaguelands (40), D-2, Stratholme

GRAND FOREMAN PUZIK GALLYWIX
Barrens (18), F-1, Top of tower northwest of Sludge Fen

GRAND INQUISITOR ISILLIEN
Western Plaguelands (92), G-2 (Summon) Spawns in the tower south of Hearthglen

GRAND MASON MARBLESTEN
Royal Stonecutters Union, Ironforge (52), C-7, F-5, The Commons, Building next to visitor's center

GRANDPA VISHAS
Rare Spawn, Alterac Mountains (8), D-3, The Uplands, Lvl 34 Common; Inside house

GRANIS SWIFTAXE
Warrior Trainer, Dun Morogh (32), F-5, Kharanos (114), Thunderbrew Distillery

GRANISTAD
Hillsbrad Foothills (48), K-3, Durnholde Keep, Roams a small area northeast of keep

GRARK LORKRUB
Burning Steppes (22), D-3, Blackrock Stronghold, Center of stronghold

GRARNIK GOODSTITCH
Expert Tailor, Stranglethorn Vale (74), B-8, Booty Bay (103), A Tailor to Cities (shop)

GRAUD
General Goods, Arathi Highlands (10), J-3, Hammerfall (113), First floor north building

GRAVE ROBBER
Duskwood (36), B:(4, 5), Raven Hill Cemetery (122)

GRAVELFLINT BONESNAPPER
Darkshore (24), E-9, Remtravel's Excavation

GRAVELFLINT GEOMANCER
Darkshore (24), E-8, Remtravel's Excavation

GRAVELFLINT SCOUT
Darkshore (24), E-8, Remtravel's Excavation

GRAVELSNOUT DIGGER
Thousand Needles (82), A:(1, 2), G:(4, 5), H:(5, 6), I-5, Windbreak Canyon

GRAVELSNOUT FORAGER
Thousand Needles (82), B:(2, 4), C:(3-5), D-5, E-5, G:(4, 5), H-6, The Screeching Canyon, Windbreak Canyon

GRAVELSNOUT KOBOLD
Thousand Needles (82), B:(2, 4), C:(3-5), D:(3, 5), E:(3, 5), F-6, Darkcloud Pinnacle, The Screeching Canyon

GRAVELSNOUT SURVEYOR
Thousand Needles (82), A:(1, 2), H:(5, 6), I-5, Ironstone Camp

GRAVELSNOUT VERMIN
Thousand Needles (82), D-3, E:(3, 5), F-6, Darkcloud Pinnacle

GRAVIS SLIPKNOT
Rare Spawn, Alterac Mountains (8), H-4, Strahnbrad, Lvl 36 Uncommon; Windmill on western side of town

GRAW CORNERSTONE
Mail Armor Merchant, Searing Gorge (64), E-7, Left side of camp

GRAWL
General Goods, Badlands (16), A-5, Kargath (114), First floor orc burrow

GRAWMUG
Loch Modan (54), D-9, Stonesplinter Valley, With Brawler and Gnasher in center of cave

GRAWN THROMWYN
Weaponsmith, Dun Morogh (32), F-5, Kharanos (114), Smithy

GRAWNAL
General Goods, Stonetalon Mountains (70), E-6, Sun Rock Retreat (127), Western building

GRAY BEAR
Hillsbrad Foothills (48), A:(4, 5), B:(4, 5), C-5, F:(1, 2), G:(1-4), H:(1-4), I-1, Tarren Mill (128), Throughout Hillsbrad

GRAY FOREST WOLF
Elwynn Forest (42), H:(6, 7), I:(6, 7), J:(6, 7)

GRAZLE
Felwood (44), I-1, Timbermaw Hold, Near entrance to the hold

GRAZLIX
Armorer & Shieldcrafter, Barrens (18), H-4, Ratchet (121), Plate-n-Chain

GREAT BEAR SPIRIT
Moonglade (56), E-3, Uphill of northwest corner of town

GREAT CAT SPIRIT
Moonglade (56), H-7, South of east side of lake

GREAT COURSER
Stonetalon Mountains (70), D:(1, 2), E:(1, 2), Stonetalon Peak

GREAT FATHER ARCTIKUS
Rare Spawn, Dun Morogh (32), B-5, C-5, Frostmane Hold, Lvl 11 Uncommon; Cave at Frostmane Hold

GREAT GORETUSK
Redridge Mountains (62), A:(5, 7, 8), B:(4, 5, 7), C:(6-8), D:(6-8), E:(1, 2, 7), F:(1-3), G-4, Westfall (94), E-7, F-7, G:(5-7), H:(5, 7)

GREAT WAVETHRASHER
Azshara (14), E-9, F:(7, 9), G:(7, 9), H:(7-9), I:(7-9), J:(7-9), K:(8, 9)

GREATER BARRENS KODO
Barrens (18), E:(6, 8)

GREATER DUSKBAT
Tirisfal Glades (86), D:(4, 5), E:(4-6), F:(4-6), G:(5, 6), H:(4-6), I:(4-6)

GREATER FIREBIRD
Rare Spawn, Tanaris (78), F-4, Abyssal Sands, Lvl 46 Average Rare; Flies throughout northern sands

GREATER FLESHRIPPER
Westfall (94), B-4, G:(5, 6), H-6, The Dead Acre

GREATER KRAUL BAT
Barrens (18), E-9, Razorfen Kraul

GREATER LAVA SPIDER
Searing Gorge (64), B:(7, 8), C:(4-8), D-3, E-7

GREATER OBSIDIAN ELEMENTAL
Burning Steppes (22), C-6, D-6, E-4, F:(3, 6), G:(5, 6), H-3, I-3

GREATER PLAINSTRIDER
Barrens (18), E:(1-4), F:(1-3), G:(2, 3), Grol'dom Farm, The Mor'shan Rampart, Thorn Hill

GREATER ROCK ELEMENTAL
Badlands (16), A:(7, 8), B:(8, 9), C-8, Camp Cagg

GREATER TARANTULA
Redridge Mountains (62), F-4, G-4, I-7, Alther's Mill

GREATER THUNDERHAWK
Barrens (18), E:(7, 8), F:(7, 8), Blackthorn Ridge, Southern Barrens

GREATMOTHER HAWKWIND
Mulgore (58), F-8, Red Cloud Mesa, Water mill southeast of camp

GREEN RECLUSE
Duskwood (36), A:(4-6), B-7, G-2, H-2, I-2, J:(2, 3), Brightwood Grove

GREEN SCALEBANE
Swamp of Sorrows (76), H-4, I-4, J:(4, 6, 7)

GREEN SLUDGE
The Hinterlands (50), G:(4, 5), H-4, I:(4, 5), Skull Rock, Cave

GREEN WYRMKIN
Swamp of Sorrows (76), H:(5, 6), I:(6, 7), K:(5-7), L:(5, 6)

GREENPAW
Teldrassil (80), E-6, Ban'ethil Barrow Den, Lower level of den

GREGAN BREWSPEWER
Feralas (46), E-3, The Twin Colossals, Camp on hill

GREGOR AGAMAND
Tirisfal Glades (100), F-3, Agamand Mills (100), Roams around the windmills to the rear of mill

GREGOR GREYSTONE
The Argent Dawn, Winterspring (98), I-4, Everlook (110), Inside inn

GREGOR MACVINCE
Horse Breeder, Dustwallow Marsh (38), I-5, Theramore Isle (130), Stables to southwest

GREGORY ARDUS
Staff & Mace Merchant, Stormwind (72), F-3, Cathedral Square, Just Maces

GREGORY CHARLES
Rogue Trainer, Undercity (88), L-7, The Rogues' Quarter, Inside Skull Building

GREISHAN IRONSTOVE
Traveling Merchant, Loch Modan (54), C-1, Dun Algaz, Patrols between Dun Algaz, Thelsamar, and the Valley of Kings

GREL'BORG THE MISER
Alterac Mountains (8), E-5, Ruins of Alterac, Patrols between castle basement and Ruins of Alterac (E-4)

GRELIN WHITEBEARD
Dun Morogh (32), C-7, Coldridge Valley (106), Camp

GRELL
Teldrassil (80), G:(4, 5), H-4, Shadowglen (124)

GRELLKIN
Teldrassil (80), G:(3, 4), H:(3, 4), Shadowglen (124)

GREMLOCK PILSNOR
Cooking Trainer, Dun Morogh (32), F-5, Kharanos (114), Thunderbrew Distillery

GRENIL STEELFURY
Weapon Merchant, Ironforge (52), E-6, The Commons, Steelfury's Weapon Emporium

GRENKA BLOODSCREECH
Thousand Needles (82), C-5, Roguefeather Den, Deep inside den

GRENTHAR
Barrens (18), F-3, The Crossroads (107), Outside inn

GRESHKA
Demon Master, Swamp of Sorrows (76), F-5, Stonard (126), Second floor of main hall

GRETA MOSSHOOF
Emerald Circle, Felwood (44), G-8, Emerald Sanctuary, Roams entry path

GRETCHEN DEDMAR
Tirisfal Glades (86), H-5, Brill (104), Second floor of Gallows' End Tavern

GRETCHEN VOGEL
Waitress, Redridge Mountains (62), B-4, Lakeshire (115), Second floor of large house on southwestern side of town

GRETH
Stable Master, Badlands (16), A-5, Kargath (114), Outside orc burrow

GRETHEER
Rare Spawn, Silithus (66), E-2, F-3, G-4, Hive'Regal, Lvl 57 Very Rare; Roams close to spawn points

GRETTA FINESPINDLE
Journeyman Leatherworker, Ironforge (52), E-3, The Great Forge, Finespindle's Leather Goods

GRETTA GANTER
Fisherman Supplies, Dun Morogh (32), D-4, Iceflow Lake, Dock at southwest corner of lake

GREYMIST COASTRUNNER
Darkshore (24), E:(5, 6, 8), F:(2, 3, 6), Mist's Edge, The Long Wash, Twilight Shore

GREYMIST HUNTER
Darkshore (24), E-8, Twilight Shore

GREYMIST NETTER
Darkshore (24), E-7, G-2, Mist's Edge, Twilight Shore

GREYMIST ORACLE
Darkshore (24), E:(8, 9), H-1, Twilight Shore

GREYMIST RAIDER
Darkshore (24), E-5, The Long Wash

GREYMIST SEER
Darkshore (24), E:(6, 7), F:(2, 3, 6), Mist's Edge, The Long Wash, Twilight Shore

GREYMIST TIDEHUNTER
Darkshore (24), E:(8, 9), H-1, Mist's Edge, Twilight Shore

GREYMIST WARRIOR
Darkshore (24), E-8, G-2, Mist's Edge, Twilight Shore

GREZZ RAZORFIST
Warrior Trainer, Orgrimmar (60), J-3, Valley of Honor, Hall of the Brave

GRIF WILDHEART
Hunter Trainer, Dun Morogh (32), F-5, Kharanos (114), On hill at southwest end of town

GRIK'NIR THE COLD
Dun Morogh (32), D-8, Coldridge Valley (106), Cave

GRIM PATRON
Burning Steppes (22), Searing Gorge (64), C-4/D-8, Blackrock Depths

GRIMAND ELMORE
Stormwind (72), H-1, Dwarven District, Northwest Building

GRIMBLE
Shipmaster, Barrens (18), H-4, Ratchet (121), Dock

GRIMBOOZE THUNDERBREW
Westfall (94), E-8, The Dagger Hills, Camp in the Dagger Hills south of Moonbrook

GRIMCLAW
Darkshore (24), F-8, Twilight Vale, Just off road to the east

GRIMESTACK
Stable Master, Stranglethorn Vale (74), B-8, Booty Bay (103), Outside of The Salty Sailor Tavern

GRIMLOK
Badlands (16), G-1, Uldaman

GRIMMAW
Rare Spawn, Teldrassil (80), E-8, Gnarlpine Hold, Lvl 11 Uncommon; Patrols Gnarlpine camps

GRIMNAL
Mail and Plate Merchant, Swamp of Sorrows (76), F-5, Stonard (126), Smithy

GRIMNUR STONEBRAND
Fishing Trainer, Ironforge (52), F-1, The Forlorn Cavern, Traveling Fisherman

GRIMSON THE PALE
Silverpine Forest (68), I-4, Deep Elem Mine, Back on mine

GRIMTAK
Butcher, Durotar (34), H-4, Razor Hill (122), Western entrance on hill

GRIMTOTEM BANDIT
Thousand Needles (82), D:(3, 4), E:(3-4), Darkcloud Pinnacle, The Great Lift

GRIMTOTEM BRUTE
Stonetalon Mountains (70), I-8, J:(8, 9), K:(8, 9), Camp Aparaje, Greatwood Vale, Grimtotem Post

GRIMTOTEM GEOMANCER
Thousand Needles (82), D:(3, 4), E:(3-4), Darkcloud Pinnacle, The Great Lift

GRIMTOTEM MERCENARY
Stonetalon Mountains (70), J:(8, 9), K:(8, 9), Camp Aparaje, Greatwood Vale, Grimtotem Post

GRIMTOTEM NATURALIST
Feralas (46), H:(4, 5), Grimtotem Compound, Lower Wilds

GRIMTOTEM RAIDER
Feralas (46), H:(4, 5), Grimtotem Compound, Lower Wilds

GRIMTOTEM REAVER
Thousand Needles (82), D-4, E:(3, 4), Darkcloud Pinnacle

GRIMTOTEM RUFFIAN
Stonetalon Mountains (70), J:(8, 9), K:(8, 9), Camp Aparaje, Greatwood Vale, Grimtotem Post

GRIMTOTEM SHAMAN
Feralas (46), H:(4, 5), Grimtotem Compound, Lower Wilds

GRIMTOTEM SORCERER
Stonetalon Mountains (70), I-8, J:(8, 9), K-8, Camp Aparaje, Greatwood Vale, Grimtotem Post

GRIMTOTEM STOMPER
Thousand Needles (82), D:(3, 4), E:(3-4), Darkcloud Pinnacle

GRIMUNGOUS
Rare Spawn, The Hinterlands (50), K-5, The Overlook Cliffs, Lvl 50 Very Rare; Patrols the southeastern ridgeline

GRINGER
Wind Rider Master, Stranglethorn Vale (74), B-8, Booty Bay (103), Kalimdor Airlines

GRINIBLIX THE SPECTATOR
Feralas (46), G-4, Dire Maul, On ledge of The Maul

GRINIBLIX THE SPECTATOR
Feralas (46), G-4, Dire Maul

GRINNING DOG
Orgrimmar (60), K-2, Valley of Honor, Arms of Legend

GRISH LONGRUNNER
Thousand Needles (82), D-2, The Great Lift, Next to lift

GRISHA
Wind Rider Master, Searing Gorge (64), D-3, Thorium Point, Ridgeline outcropping southwest of camp

GRITJAW BASILISK
Desolace (30), E-3, F:(1-4), G:(1, 2, 4, 6, 7), H:(1-4, 6), I:(2-4), J:(2-4), K:(3, 4)

GRIZLAK
Rare Spawn, Loch Modan (54), D-3, Silver Stream Mine, Lvl 15 Uncommon; Roams small area around spawn point

GRIZLOWE
Shipmaster, Stranglethorn Vale (74), B-8, Booty Bay (103)

GRIZZLE
Burning Steppes (22), Searing Gorge (64), C-4/D-8, Blackrock Depths

GRIZZLE HALFMANE
Alterac Valley Battlemaster, Undercity (88), G-9, H-9, Royal Quarter, In Throne room

GRIZZLE SNOWPAW
Rare Spawn, Winterspring (98), J-4, Winterfall Village, Lvl 59 Uncommon; Patrols village

GRIZZLED BLACK BEAR
Loch Modan (54), E:(5-7), F-6, H:(4, 7, 8), I:(4, 5, 7), J:(5, 6), K-7

GRIZZLED IRONFUR BEAR
Feralas (46), F-5, G-5, H-6, I-6

GRIZZLED THISTLE BEAR
Darkshore (24), F:(7-9), G-8

GROD
Leather Armor Merchant, Thunder Bluff (84), E-4, Middle rise, inside Thunder Bluff Armorers tent

GRODDOC APE
Feralas (46), E-5, F-5, G:(5, 6), H-5, I-5

GRODDOC THUNDERER
Feralas (46), D:(1, 2), E:(1-4), F-3, Ruins of Ravenwind, The Twin Colossals

GROKOR
Pet Trainer, Swamp of Sorrows (76), F-5, Stonard (126), Behind orcish carriage left of entrance to main hall

GROL THE DESTROYER
Blasted Lands (20), F-1, Dreadmaul Hold, In center of hold

GROL'DAR
Warlock Trainer, Orgrimmar (60), E-5, F-5, The Cleft of Shadow, Darkfire Enclave

GROM'GOL GRUNT
Stranglethorn Vale (74), C-3

GRONDAL MOONBREEZE
Journeyman Tailor, Darkshore (24), F-4, Auberdine (101), Right wing of northern building

GROUM STONEBEARD
Journeyman Blacksmith, Ironforge (52), G-4, The Great Forge, Next to anvils

GROUND POUNDER
Tanaris (78), E-3, F-3, G:(3, 4), H:(3, 4), Noonshade Ruins, Sandsorrow Watch, Waterspring Field

GRUB
Barrens (18), G-3, Inside hut east of Crossroads

GRUBBIS
Dun Morogh (32), C-4, Gnomeregan

GRUBTHOR
Rare Spawn, Silithus (66), E-4, Lvl 58 Semi-Rare; Roams close to spawn points

GRUFF
Un'Goro Crater (90), D:(7-8), E:(7-8), Terror Run, Roams around Terror Run

GRUFF SWIFTBITE
Rare Spawn, Elwynn Forest (42), C-9, Forest's Edge, Lvl 12 Uncommon; Patrols small area around spawn point

GRUHAM RUMDNUL
General Supplies, Wetlands (96), A-6, Menethil Harbor (117), Small house east of keep

GRUK
Barrens (18), G-3, Inside hut east of Crossroads

GRUKLASH
Rare Spawn, Burning Steppes (22), A-3, D-3, E-5, Altar of Storms, Blackrock Stronghold, Lvl 59 Uncommon

GRULL HAWKWIND
Mulgore (58), E-8, Camp Narache (105), Center of camp

GRUM REDBEARD
Winterspring (98), G-3, Starfall Village, Caverns in hills behind village

GRUMNUS STEELSHAPER
Armor Crafter, Ironforge (52), F-4, G-4, The Great Forge, The Great Anvil

GRUNA
Food & Drink, Burning Steppes (22), H-2, Flame Crest, Next to Wind Rider Master

GRUNDEL HARKIN
Armorer, Dun Morogh (32), D-7, Coldridge Valley (106), Anvilmar

GRUNDIG DARKCLOUD
Stonetalon Mountains (70), J-8, Grimtotem Post, Western hut

GRUNT DOGRAN
Barrens (18), E-5, Agama'gor, Eastern hut

GRUNT GARGAL
Badlands (16), A-5, Kargath (114), Group left of orc burrow

GRUNT KOMACK
Orgrimmar (60), Valley of Strength

GRUNT KOR'JA
Durotar (34), H-5, Along southern road leading out from Razor Hill

GRUNT LOGMAR
Barrens (18), F-6, Camp Taurajo (106), Western entrance

GRUNT THARLAK
Swamp of Sorrows (76), F-5, Stonard (126), Guarding holding pen in northwest corner of camp

GRUNT ZUUL
Swamp of Sorrows (76), F-5, Stonard (126), Guarding holding pen in northwest corner of camp

GRUNTER
Rare Spawn, Blasted Lands (20), H-3, I-3, Serpent's Coil, Lvl 50 Very Rare; Roams small area around spawn point

GRUUL DARKBLADE
Weaponsmith, Azshara (14), B-5, Valormok

GRYAN STOUTMANTLE
The People's Militia, Westfall (94), G-5, Sentinel Hill (123), Sentinel Tower

GRYPHON MASTER TALONAXE
The Hinterlands (50), B-4, Aerie Peak (100), Inside of Peak fortification

GRYTH THURDEN
Gryphon Master, Ironforge (52), G-5, The Great Forge, Next to Gryphons

GUARD ADAMS
Redridge Mountains (62), C-5, Lakeshire (115), Patrols around Lakeshire

GUARD ASHLOCK
Redridge Mountains (62), D-6, Patrols back and forth over the bridge heading into Lakeshire

GUARD BERTON
Redridge Mountains (62), C-5, Lakeshire (115), Next to mailbox outside of Lakeshire Inn

GUARD BYRON
Dustwallow Marsh (38), I-5, Theramore Isle (130), Outside inn to north

GUARD CLARKE
Redridge Mountains (62), C-5, Lakeshire (115), Patrols around Lakeshire

GUARD EDWARD
Dustwallow Marsh (38), I-5, Theramore Isle (130), Sparring grounds to northeast

GUARD FENGUS
Feralas (46), G-4, Dire Maul

GUARD HIETT
Redridge Mountains (62), D-6, Roams right of bridge heading into Lakeshire

GUARD HOWE
Redridge Mountains (62), D-6, Left of bridge heading into Lakeshire

GUARD JARAD
Dustwallow Marsh (38), I-5, Theramore Isle (130), Sparring grounds to northeast

GUARD KAHIL
Dustwallow Marsh (38), I-5, Theramore Isle (130), Sparring grounds to northeast

GUARD LANA
Dustwallow Marsh (38), I-5, Theramore Isle (130), Sparring grounds to northeast

GUARD LASITER
Dustwallow Marsh (38), I-5, Theramore Isle (130), East archery range

GUARD MOL'DAR
Feralas (46), G-4, Dire Maul

GUARD NARRISHA
Dustwallow Marsh (38), I-5, Theramore Isle (130), Sparring grounds to northeast

GUARD PARKER
Redridge Mountains (62), A-7, Three Corners, Patrols a circular path around the area

GUARD PEARCE
Redridge Mountains (62), D-6, Right of bridge heading into Lakeshire

GUARD ROBERTS
Elwynn Forest (42), F-7, Crystal Lake, Kneeling by a tree at the edge of the lake

GUARD SLIP'KIK
Feralas (46), G-4, Dire Maul

GUARD TARK
Dustwallow Marsh (38), I-5, Theramore Isle (130), Sparring grounds to northeast

GUARD TARUC
Barrens (18), G-3, Inside hut east of Crossroads

GUARD THOMAS
Elwynn Forest (42), J-7, Left of bridge

GUARD WACHABE
Thousand Needles (82), F-5, Freewind Post, Northwest of inn, next to pole

GUARDIAN OF ELUNE
Winterspring (98), J-6, Owl Wing Thicket, (Summon) Behind altar

GUBBER BLUMP
Darkshore (24), E-4, Auberdine (101), On beach near hippogryph platform

GUILLAUME SOROUY
Journeyman Blacksmith, Silverpine Forest (68), F-4, The Sepulcher (124), Basement of inn

GUNDER THORNBUSH
Tradesman, Duskwood (36), J-4, Darkshire (108), Scarlet Raven Inn

GUNTHER ARCANUS
Tirisfal Glades (86), I-4, Gunther's Retreat, Large island in the center of Brightwater Lake

GUNTHER WELLER
Weapons Merchant, Stormwind (72), H-6, Trade District, Weller's Arsenal

GURDA RAGESCAR
Ashenvale (12), I-7, Nightsong Woods, Camp to southwest of Splintertree Post (126)

GURDA WILDMANE
Desolace (30), G-6, Ghost Walker Post (111), Southern hut

GURUBASHI WARRIOR
Stranglethorn Vale (74), E-2, F-2, Zul'Gurub

GUSTING VORTEX
Tanaris (78), E:(4-6), F:(4-7), G:(4, 5), H:(4, 5), I:(4-6)

GUTHRUM THUNDERFIST
Gryphon Master, The Hinterlands (50), B-5, Aerie Peak (100), Left of Peak fortification entrance

GUTSPILL
Duskwood (36), J-8, Roland's Doom, Patrols the length of the mine

GUZZLING PATRON
Burning Steppes (22), Searing Gorge (64), C-4/D-8, Blackrock Depths

GWENNA FIREBREW
Barmaid, Ironforge (52), B-5, The Commons, The Stonefire Tavern

GWENNYTH BLY'LEGGONDE
Darkshore (24), F-4, Auberdine (101), Hippogryph platform

GWINA STONEBRANCH
Herbalism Supplier, Ironforge (52), G-6, The Great Forge, Ironforge Physician

GWYN FARROW
Mushroom Merchant, Silverpine Forest (68), G-4, The Sepulcher (124), In front of crates on right side of sepulcher

GYLL
Gryphon Master, Stranglethorn Vale (74), B-8, Booty Bay (103), Southern Skies Platform

GYTH
Burning Steppes (22), Searing Gorge (64), C-4/D-8, Blackrock Spire

H

HAARKA THE RAVENOUS
Rare Spawn, Tanaris (78), H-7, The Gaping Chasm, Lvl 50 Average Rare; Spawns in one of the chambers and sticks close to spawn point

HADOKEN SWIFTSTRIDER
Feralas (46), I-4, Camp Mojache (105), Between tents, near waterfall

HAE'WILANI
Weapons Vendor, Desolace (30), C-7, Shadowprey Village (125), Small eastern structure

HAGAR LIGHTNINGHOOF
Thousand Needles (82), F-5, Freewind Post, Next to western bridge

HAGG TAURENBANE
Rare Spawn, Razormane Champion, Barrens (18), D-8, E-8, Blackthorn Ridge, Lvl 26 Uncommon

HAGGARD REFUGEE
Silverpine Forest (68), G:(8, 9), The Greymane Wall

HAGGLE
Ironforge (52), L-5, The Deeprun Tram, Roams around Deeprun Tram

HAGGRUM BLOODFIST
Azshara (14), B-5, Valormok

HAGRUS
Reagents Vendor, Orgrimmar (60), E-5, The Cleft of Shadow, Shadowdeep Reagents

HAHK'ZOR
Rare Spawn, Burning Steppes (22), J:(4, 5), K-4, Dreadmaul Rock, Lvl 54 Semi-Rare: Roams small area around spawn point

HAHRANA IRONHIDE
Master Leatherworker, Feralas (46), I-4, Camp Mojache (105), Big western tent

HAI'ZAN
Butcher, Durotar (34), H-7, Sen'jin Village (123), Northern part of village

HAKKAR'I BLOODKEEPER
Swamp of Sorrows (76), I-5, The Temple of Atal'Hakkar

HAKKAR'I FROST WING
Swamp of Sorrows (76), I-5, The Temple of Atal'Hakkar

HAKKARI PRIEST
Stranglethorn Vale (74), E-2, F-2, Zul'Gurub

HAKKAR'I SAPPER
Swamp of Sorrows (76), I-5, The Temple of Atal'Hakkar

HAL MCALLISTER
Fish Merchant, Hillsbrad Foothills (48), F-6, Southshore (125), Edge of docks

HALDARR FELSWORN
Azshara (14), B-6, Haldarr Encampment

HALDARR SATYR
Azshara (14), B-6, Haldarr Encampment

HALDARR TRICKSTER
Azshara (14), B-6, Haldarr Encampment

HALEH
Winterspring (98), H-5, Mazthoril, Atop mountain, reachable by portal deep in Mazthoril

HALIJA WHITESTRIDER
Clothier, Barrens (18), F-3, The Crossroads (107), Southern entrance

HALJAN OAKHEART
General Goods, Ashenvale (12), E-5, Astranaar (101), Right as you enter building to the southwest

HALYCON
Burning Steppes (22), Searing Gorge (64), C-4/D-8, Blackrock Spire

HAMHOCK
Stormwind (72), F-6, The Stockade

HAMLIN ATKINS
Mushroom Farmer, Tirisfal Glades (86), H-5, Brill (104), Patrols along road between the mausoleum in the graveyard and the eastern and western city limits of Brill

HAMMERED PATRON
Burning Steppes (22), Searing Gorge (64), C-4/D-8, Blackrock Depths

HAMMERFALL GRUNT
Arathi Highlands (10), H:(5, 6), I:(5, 6), Hammerfall (113)

HAMMERFALL GUARDIAN
Arathi Highlands (10), J:(3, 4), K-4, Hammerfall (113)

HAMMERFALL PEON
Arathi Highlands (10), H:(5, 6), I:(5, 6), Hammerfall (113)

HAMMERSPINE
Rare Spawn, Dun Morogh (32), J-5, Gol'Bolar Quarry, Lvl 12 Uncommon; Roams small area around spawn point

HAMMERTOE GREZ
Badlands (16), G-1, Uldaman

HAMMON KARWN
Superior Tradesman, Arathi Highlands (10), F-5, Refuge Point, Camp

HANASHI
Weapon Master, Orgrimmar (60), J-2, Valley of Honor, Arms of Legend, Trains: Bows, 1H Axe, 2H Axe, Staves, & Thrown

HANA'ZUA
Durotar (34), F-6, Valley of Trials (131), Laying in the shade of a tree to the west

HAND OF RAVENCLAW
Silverpine Forest (68), H-3, I:(3, 4), The Decrepit Ferry, East of road near lake

HANDOR
Cloth & Leather Armor Merchant, Orgrimmar (60), H-4, The Drag, Kodohide Leatherworkers

HANDS SPRINGSPROCKET
Dun Morogh (32), D-7, Coldridge Pass, Outside of pass entrance

HANK THE HAMMER
The Mithril Order, Stormwind (72), H-2, Dwarven District, By Forge

HANNAH
Redridge Mountains (62), B-4, Lakeshire (115), Western point of Lake Everstill

HANNAH AKELEY
Reagent Supplier, Undercity (88), L-2, The Magic Quarter, Outside Skull Building

HANNAH BLADELEAF
Alliance Outrunner, Barrens (18), F-8, Southern Barrens, Spawns at border to Dustwallow Marsh and travels north to Lushwater Oasis

HANS WESTON
Armorer & Shieldsmith, Dustwallow Marsh (38), I-5, Theramore Isle (130), Blacksmithing hut to west

HANS ZANDIN
Hillsbrad Foothills (48), G-2 , Tarren Mill (128), Orchard

HANSEL HEAVYHANDS
The Thorium Brotherhood, Searing Gorge (64), D-3, Thorium Point, Right side of tower

HAR'ALEN
Ashenvale (12), I-6, Splintertree Post (126), Building just north of flightpoint

HARANT IRONBRACE
Armorer & Shieldcrafter, Mulgore (58), E-6, Bloodhoof Village (102), Northeast tent

HARB CLAWHOOF
Kodo Mounts, Mulgore (58), E-6, Bloodhoof Village (102), Northern clearing

HARB FOULMOUNTAIN
Rare Spawn, Thousand Needles (82), D-3, E-3, Darkcloud Pinnacle, Lvl 27 Uncommon; Patrols across three small plateaus, north of pinnacle

HARBINGER BALTHAZAD
Undercity (88), Canals, Roams inner circle

HAREN KANMAE
Superior Bowyer, Stranglethorn Vale (74), B-8, Booty Bay (103), Swift Flights (shop) on the northern side of The Old Port Authority

HAREN SWIFTHOOF
Loch Modan (54), H-7, Patrols large circular paths with Gradok and Thragomm along the eastern side of the loch

HARGGAN
Blacksmithing Supplies, The Hinterlands (50), B-4, Aerie Peak (100), Wildhammer Keep

HARGIN MUNDAR
Wetlands (96), A-6, Menethil Harbor (117), Deepwater Tavern, Roams in and out of tavern

HARICK BOULDERDRUM
Wands Merchant, Ironforge (52), C-2, The Mystic Ward, The Fighting Wizard

HARKEN WINDTOTEM
Mulgore (58), F-6, Bloodhoof Village (102), East tent

HARKLAN MOONGROVE
Alchemy Supplies, Ashenvale (12), G-6, Silverwind Refuge, Left wing of building

HARKLANE
Fish Vendor, Feralas (46), C-5, Feathermoon Stronghold (110), Southwest building

HARLAN BAGLEY
Stormwind (72), H:(5, 6), Trade District, Lionheart Armory

HARLO BARNABY
Wetlands (96), A-5, Menethil Harbor (117), Front of keep

HARLO WIGGLESWORTH
Winterspring (98), I-4, Everlook (110), Outside inn

HARLON THORNGUARD
Armorer & Shieldsmith, Darkshore (24), F-4, Auberdine (101), Left wing of northern building

HARLOWN DARKWEAVE
Leatherworking Supplies, Ashenvale (12), C-6, Shrine of Aessina, Hidden in a camp near mountains in far southwest of region

HARN LONGCAST
Fishing Supplies, Mulgore (58), E-6, Bloodhoof Village (102), North tents

HARNOR
Food & Drink, Desolace (30), G-5, Ghost Walker Post (111), Western hut

HAROLD RAIMS
Apprentice Weaponsmith, Tirisfal Glades (86), D-7, Deathknell (109), First house on right side of road

HAROLD RIGGS
Fishing Trainer, Wetlands (96), A-6, Menethil Harbor (117), Dock

HAROMM
Shaman Trainer, Swamp of Sorrows (76), F-6, Stonard (126), Scaffolding just inside camp walls left of southern entrance

HARROC
Durotar (34), H-3, Garden next to house

HARRUK
Pet Trainer, Durotar (34), H-4, Razor Hill (122), Bunker

HARRY BURLGUARD
Stormwind (72), J-5, Old Town, Pig and Whistle Tavern

HARTASH
Weapon Merchant, Swamp of Sorrows (76), F-5, Stonard (126), Smithy

HARUTT THUNDERHORN
Warrior Trainer, Mulgore (58), E-8, Camp Narache (105), Main tent (north)

HARVEST GOLEM
Westfall (94), C:(4, 5), D-5, E:(3, 6, 7), F:(3, 4), G:(3, 4), Saldean's Farm

HARVEST REAPER
Westfall (94), G-6, H-6, The Dead Acre

HARVEST WATCHER
Westfall (94), D-5, E:(3, 4), F:(2, 3), Saldean's Farm

HASTAT THE ANCIENT
Felwood (44), G-3, Irontree Woods, (Summon) Talk to the ancients on the island

HATE SHRIEKER
Eastern Plaguelands (40), C-3, D-3, E:(2, 3), H:(6, 7), Corin's Crossing

HATE'REL
Burning Steppes (22), Searing Gorge (64), C-4/D-8, Blackrock Depths

HATECREST MYRMIDON
Feralas (46), B:(6, 7), Isle of Dread

HATECREST SCREAMER
Feralas (46), B:(5, 6), C:(5, 6), Ruins of Solarsal, Sardor Isle

HATECREST SERPENT GUARD
Feralas (46), E:(4-6), Isle of Dread, Shalzaru's Lair

HATECREST SIREN
Feralas (46), B:(5, 6), C:(5, 6), Ruins of Solarsal, Sardor Isle

HATECREST SORCERESS
Feralas (46), B:(6, 7), Isle of Dread, Shalzaru's Lair

HATECREST WARRIOR
Feralas (46), B:(5, 6), C:(5, 6), Ruins of Solarsal, Sardor Isle

HATECREST WAVE RIDER
Feralas (46), B:(5, 6), C:(5, 6), Ruins of Solarsal, Sardor Isle

HATEFURY BETRAYER
Desolace (30), I:(1, 2), J:(1-3), K:(1-3), Sargeron

HATEFURY FELSWORN
Desolace (30), I:(1, 2), J:(1-3), K:(1-3), Sargeron

HATEFURY HELLCALLER
Desolace (30), I:(1, 2), J:(1-3), K:(1-3), Sargeron

HATEFURY ROGUE
Desolace (30), I:(1, 2), J:(1-3), K:(1-3), Sargeron

HATEFURY SHADOWSTALKER
Desolace (30), I:(1, 2), J:(1-3), K:(1-3), Sargeron

HATEFURY TRICKSTER
Desolace (30), I:(1, 2), J:(1-3), K:(1-3), Sargeron

HAUNTED SERVITOR
Silverpine Forest (68), F-7, Shadowfang Keep

HAUNTING PHANTASM
Tirisfal Glades (86), K-3, L-3, Scarlet Monastery

HAUNTING SPIRIT
Curse spell effect, Silverpine Forest (68), F-7, Shadowfang Keep

HAUNTING VISION
Western Plaguelands (92), H:(5, 6), I:(5, 6), Gahrron's Withering

HAYOC
Dustwallow Marsh (38), D-3, Brackenwall Village (104), West entrance

HAZZALI SANDREAVER
Tanaris (78), G-7, H:(6-8), The Gaping Chasm

HAZZALI STINGER
Tanaris (78), G:(7, 8), H:(6-8), I:(6, 7), The Gaping Chasm

HAZZALI SWARMER
Tanaris (78), G:(7, 8), H:(6-8), I:(6, 7), The Gaping Chasm

HAZZALI TUNNELER
Tanaris (78), G:(7, 8), H:(6-8), The Gaping Chasm

HAZZALI WASP
Tanaris (78), G:(7, 8), H:(6-8), I:(6, 7), The Gaping Chasm

HAZZALI WORKER
Tanaris (78), G-7, H:(6-8), The Gaping Chasm

HAZZAS
Swamp of Sorrows (76), I-5, The Temple of Atal'Hakkar

HEARTHSINGER FORRESTEN
Rare Spawn, Eastern Plaguelands (40), D-2, Stratholme, Lvl 57 Rare

HEARTRAZOR
Thousand Needles (82), A-4, B-4, Highperch, Patrols entrance to Highperch

HEAVY WAR GOLEM
Searing Gorge (64), C-5, D:(5, 6), E:(4-6), F:(4, 6), The Cauldron

HECHT COPPERPINCH
Smokywood Pastures, Barrens (18), E-1, Mor'shan Base Camp, Outside entrance to Warsong Gulch

HECKLEFANG HYENA
Barrens (18), D:(2, 3), E:(2-4), F:(1, 2, 4, 5), G:(1-5), H:(1-4)

HECKLEFANG HYENA
Durotar (34), D:(2, 5), E:(1, 2, 5, 6)

HECKLEFANG SNARLER
Barrens (18), E:(4-6), F:(5, 6), Agama'gor, Bramblescar, Southern Barrens

HECKLEFANG STALKER
Barrens (18), E:(7, 8), F:(7, 8), Blackthorn Ridge, Southern Barrens

HEDERINE INITIATE
Winterspring (98), H:(8, 9), I:(7-9), J-8, Darkwhisper Gorge

HEDERINE MANASTALKER
Winterspring (98), H:(8, 9), I:(8, 9), J-8, Darkwhisper Gorge

HEDERINE SLAYER
Winterspring (98), H:(8, 9), I:(8, 9), J-8, Darkwhisper Gorge

HED'MUSH THE ROTTING
Rare Spawn, Eastern Plaguelands (40), E-7, G-3, I-5, Crown Guard Tower, Eastwall Tower, Northpass Tower, Lvl 57 Very Rare; Roams small area around spawn point

HEDRUM THE CREEPER
Burning Steppes (22), Searing Gorge (64), C-4/D-8, Blackrock Depths

HEGGIN STONEWHISKER
Rare Spawn, Bael'dun Chief Engineer, Barrens (18), E-8, Bael Modan, Lvl 24 Uncommon; Crane

HEGNAR RUMBLESHOT
Gunsmith, Dun Morogh (32), E-6, Camp

HEGNAR SWIFTAXE
Axe Merchant, Ironforge (52), H-9, The Military Ward, Timberline Arms

HEINRICH STONE
Blade Merchant, Stormwind (72), K-4, Old Town, Honest Blades

HEKKRU
Stable Master, Swamp of Sorrows (76), F-5, Stonard (126), Next to mailbox out side of inn

HELCULAR'S REMAINS
Hillsbrad Foothills (48), F-5, Southshore (125), Graveyard

HELDAN GALESONG
Fisherman, Darkshore (24), E-6, Twilight Shore, Grassy outcropping near shore

HELENA ATWOOD
Undercity (88), H-2, The War Quarter, Shooting at target

HELENDIS RIVERHORN
Burning Steppes (22), K-7, Morgan's Vigil (118), House ruins, left side of camp

HELENE PELTSKINNER
Skinner, Elwynn Forest (42), F-6, Goldshire (112), House facing Crystal Lake

HELENIA OLDEN
Trade Supplies, Dustwallow Marsh (38), I-5, Theramore Isle (130), Southern house

HELGRUM THE SWIFT
Swamp of Sorrows (76), F-5, Stonard (126), Third floor of main hall

HEMATOS
Rare Spawn, Burning Steppes (22), D-3, Blackrock Mountain, Lvl 60 Very Rare; Patrols circular path around Draco'dar

HEMATUS
Badlands (16), L-5, Lethlor Ravine, (Summon) Altar protected by Scorched Guardians

HEMET NESINGWARY
Stranglethorn Vale (74), C-1, Nesingwary's Expedition, Camp

HEMMIT ARMSTRONG
Hillsbrad Foothills (48), E-6, Southshore (125), Inn

HENCHMAN VALIK
Alterac Mountains (8), H-7, Sofera's Naze, Right of camp on hill

HENEN RAGETOTEM
Thunder Bluff (84), G-8, Hunter Rise, In front of Hunter's Hall on Hunter Rise in Thunder Bluff

HENRY CHAPAL
Gunsmith, Redridge Mountains (62), C-4, Lakeshire (115), Small house on a hill on northwestern side of town

HENRY STERN
Recipe Trainer (Cooking), Barrens (18), F-9, Razorfen Downs

HENZE FAULK
Elwynn Forest (42), J-5, Heroes' Vigil, Lying on hill facing megalith formation

HEPZIBAH SEDGEWICK
Undercity (88), K-6, The Rogues' Quarter, Wanders Rogues' Quarter and Canals

HERALATH FALLOWBROOK
Barrens (18), E-9, Razorfen Kraul

HERALD MOONSTALKER
Darnassus (26), D-4, The Temple Gardens, Roams path throughout city

HERBALIST POMEROY
Herbalism Trainer, Elwynn Forest (42), E-5, Secluded house on hill

HERBLE BAUBBLETUMP
Engineering and Mining Supplies, Duskwood (36), K-5, Darkshire (108), Outside the second house on left side of road heading into Darkshire from the east

HEROD
Tirisfal Glades (86), K-3, L-3, Scarlet Monastery

HESUWA THUNDERHORN
Pet Trainer, Thunder Bluff (84), F-8, Hunter Rise, In building west of Hunter's Hall

HETAERA
Azshara (14), H-5, Hetaera's Clutch, Roams underwater and among the outer islands

HEWA
Cloth Armor Merchant, Thunder Bluff (84), E-6, Lower rise, in Hewa's Armory

HEXED TROLL
Durotar (34), J:(8, 9), Echo Isles

HEZRUL BLOODMARK
Barrens (18), E-4, Lushwater Oasis, Circles the oasis, pausing at camps

HGARTH
Artisan Enchanter, Stonetalon Mountains (70), F-6, Sun Rock Retreat (127), Alone on a cliff northeast of inn

HIEROPHANT THEODORA MULVADANIA
Badlands (16), A-5, Kargath (114), Bonfire left of orc burrow

HIGH CHIEF WINTERFALL
Winterspring (98), J-4, Winterfall Village, Spawns in upper cave

HIGH EXECUTOR DARTHALIA
Hillsbrad Foothills (48), H-2, Tarren Mill (128), Roams in front of church

HIGH EXECUTOR DERRINGTON
Tirisfal Glades (86), K-7, The Bulwark, Camp on left side of road

HIGH EXECUTOR DERRINGTON
Western Plaguelands (92), C-5, The Bulwark

HIGH EXECUTOR HADREC
Silverpine Forest (68), F-4, The Sepulcher (124), Basement of inn

HIGH EXPLORER MAGELLAS
Explorers' League, Ironforge (52), I-2, Hall of Explorers, Out front of library

HIGH GENERAL ABBENDIS
Rare Spawn, Eastern Plaguelands (40), K-8, L-8, Tyr's Hand, Lvl 59 Uncommon; Second floor of castle or in The Scarlet Basilica

HIGH INQUISITOR FAIRBANKS
Tirisfal Glades (86), K-3, L-3, Scarlet Monastery

HIGH INQUISITOR WHITEMANE
Tirisfal Glades (86), K-3, L-3, Scarlet Monastery

HIGH INTERROGATOR GERSTAHN
Burning Steppes (22), Searing Gorge (64), C-4/D-8, Blackrock Depths

HIGH JUSTICE GRIMSTONE
Burning Steppes (22), Searing Gorge (64), C-4/D-8, Blackrock Depths

HIGH OVERLORD SAURFANG
Orgrimmar (60), F:(7, 8), Valley of Strength, Near main entrance

HIGH PRIEST ROHAN
Priest Trainer, Ironforge (52), C-1, The Mystic Ward, Hall of Mysteries

HIGH PRIEST THEL'DANIS
Western Plaguelands (92), G-8, Uther's Tomb, Patrols in and out of tomb

HIGH PRIESTESS HAI'WATNA
Rare Spawn, Stranglethorn Vale (74), F-2, Zul'Gurub, Lvl 57 Semi-Rare; Ruins just before the entrance to Zul'Gurub

HIGH PRIESTESS LAURENA
Priest Trainer, Stormwind (72), F-3, Cathedral Square, Cathedral of Light

HIGH PRIESTESS MACDONNELL
Western Plaguelands (92), F-8, Chillwind Camp, In front of carriage

HIGH PRIESTESS OF THAURISSAN
Burning Steppes (22), Searing Gorge (64), C-4/D-8, Blackrock Depths

HIGH PROTECTOR LORIK
Western Plaguelands (92), F-2, Hearthglen, Patrols path around city

HIGH PROTECTOR TARSEN
Western Plaguelands (92), F-3, Northridge Lumber Camp, Patrols around lumber mill

HIGH SORCERER ANDROMATH
Stormwind (72), F-8, Mage Quarter, Wizard's Sanctum

HIGH TINKER MEKKATORQUE
King of Gnomes, Ironforge (52), I-5, Tinker Town, Out front of tram entrance

HIGHBORNE APPARITION
Azshara (14), A-7, Shadowsong Shrine

HIGHBORNE LICHLING
Azshara (14), A-7, Haldarr Encampment, Shadowsong Shrine

HIGHBORNE SUMMONER
Feralas (46), G-4, Dire Maul

HIGHLAND FLESHSTALKER
Arathi Highlands (10), F:(7, 8), G:(6-8), H-6, River

HIGHLAND LASHTAIL
Wetlands (96), D-2, E-2, H:(2-4), Direforge Hill

HIGHLAND RAPTOR
Wetlands (96), E-2, F-2, G:(2, 3), H:(2-4), Direforge Hill, Ironbeard's Tomb

HIGHLAND RAZORMAW
Wetlands (96), D-2, E-2, I:(3, 4), J:(3, 4), Direforge Hill, Raptor Ridge

HIGHLAND SCYTHECLAW
Wetlands (96), D-2, E-2, H:(2-4), Direforge Hill, The Green Belt

HIGHLAND STRIDER
Arathi Highlands (10), B:(3, 4), C:(2-4), D:(2-4), E:(4-7), F:(3-6, 8), G:(3-5), H:(4, 5), I:(3-5), J:(3-5), K-3

HIGHLAND THRASHER
Arathi Highlands (10), B:(4-6), C-5, D:(5, 6), E:(3, 4, 6, 7), F:(3, 4, 6), G-6, H-7, I-6, Northfold Manor

HIGHLORD BOLVAR FORDRAGON
Boss, Stormwind (72), L-2, Stormwind Keep, Center of east wing

HIGHLORD DEMITRIAN
Silithus (66), D-1, Ravaged Twilight Camp, Far northwest of camp on hill

HIGHLORD MASTROGONDE
Rare Spawn, Searing Gorge (64), A-4, C-3, Firewatch Ridge, Lvl 51 Uncommon; Roams small area around spawn point

HIGHLORD OMOKK
Burning Steppes (22), Searing Gorge (64), C-4/D-8, Blackrock Spire

HIGHLORD TAELAN FORDRING
Highlord of the Scarlet Crusade, Western Plaguelands (92), E-1, Mardenholde Keep, Second floor of keep

HIGHPERCH CONSORT
Thousand Needles (82), A:(3, 4), G-4, Highperch

HIGHPERCH SOARER
Thousand Needles (82), A-4, B-4, Highperch, Flies around Highperch

HIGHPERCH WYVERN
Thousand Needles (82), A:(3, 4), G-4, Highperch

HIGHVALE MARKSMAN
The Hinterlands (50), D-5, E:(4, 5), Quel'Danil Lodge

HIGHVALE OUTRUNNER
The Hinterlands (50), D-5, E:(4, 5), Quel'Danil Lodge

HIGHVALE RANGER
The Hinterlands (50), D:(4, 5), E:(4, 5), Quel'Danil Lodge

HIGHVALE SCOUT
The Hinterlands (50), D-5, E:(4, 5), Quel'Danil Lodge

HILARY
Redridge Mountains (62), C-5, Lakeshire (115), L-shaped dock west of the bridge

HILLSBRAD APPRENTICE BLACKSMITH
Hillsbrad Foothills (48), C:(4, 5), Hillsbrad Fields (113), Forge

HILLSBRAD COUNCILMAN
Hillsbrad Foothills (48), C:(4, 5), Hillsbrad Fields (113)

HILLSBRAD FARMER
Hillsbrad Foothills (48), C:(3-5), D:(4, 5), Hillsbrad Fields (113), Orchard

HILLSBRAD FARMHAND
Hillsbrad Foothills (48), C:(3, 4), D-4, Hillsbrad Fields (113)

HILLSBRAD FOOTMAN
Hillsbrad Foothills (48), C:(4, 5), D-5, Hillsbrad Fields (113)

HILLSBRAD FOREMAN
Hillsbrad Foothills (48), B:(5, 6), C:(5, 6), Azurelode Mine, Mine

HILLSBRAD MINER
Hillsbrad Foothills (48), B:(5, 6), C:(5, 6), Azureload Mine, Mine

HILLSBRAD PEASANT
Hillsbrad Foothills (48), C:(4, 5), D:(4, 5), Hillsbrad Fields (113)

HILLSBRAD SENTRY
Hillsbrad Foothills (48), B-6, C-6, Azureload Mine, Mine

HILLSBRAD TAILOR
Hillsbrad Foothills (48), D-4, Hillsbrad Fields (113), House northeast of southernmost crop field

HIMMIK
Food & Drink, Winterspring (98), I-4, Everlook (110), Inside inn

HIN DENBURG
Zeppelin Master, Tirisfal Glades (86), H-6, Zepplin tower just north of Undercity

HISSPERAK
Rare Spawn, Desolace (30), E:(4-6), F-5, G-5, Kodo Graveyard, Lvl 37 Semi-Rare; Roams area northwest of the Kodo Graveyard

HISTORIAN KARNIK
Ironforge (52), K-1, Hall of Explorers, The Library

HITAH'YA THE KEEPER
The Hinterlands (50), I-9, Jintha'Alor, Patrols with two Vilebranch Aman'zasi Guards around glowing rock

HIVE'ASHI AMBUSHER
Silithus (66), G-3, Southwind Village

HIVE'ASHI DEFENDER
Silithus (66), E-1, F:(1, 2), Hive'Ashi

HIVE'ASHI DRONE
Silithus (66), G-3, Southwind Village

HIVE'ASHI SANDSTALKER
Silithus (66), E-1, F:(1, 2), Hive'Ashi

HIVE'ASHI STINGER
Silithus (66), E-1, F:(1-3), G:(2, 3), Hive'Ashi

HIVE'ASHI SWARMER
Silithus (66), E-1, F:(1-3), G:(2, 3), Hive'Ashi

HIVE'ASHI WORKER
Silithus (66), F:(1, 2), Hive'Ashi

HIVE'REGAL AMBUSHER
Silithus (66), F:(4, 5), G:(4, 5), H-4, Hive'Regal

HIVE'REGAL BURROWER
Silithus (66), F-4, G:(4, 5), Hive'Regal

HIVE'REGAL HIVE LORD
Silithus (66), F:(4, 5), G:(4, 5), H-4, Hive'Regal

HIVE'REGAL SLAVEMAKER
Silithus (66), F:(4, 5), G:(4, 5), H-4, Hive'Regal

HIVE'REGAL SPITFIRE
Silithus (66), F:(4, 5), G:(4, 5), H-4, Hive'Regal

HIVE'ZORA HIVE SISTER
Silithus (66), D:(3, 4), E:(3, 4), Hive'Zora

HIVE'ZORA REAVER
Silithus (66), D:(3, 4), E:(3, 4), Hive'Zora

HIVE'ZORA TUNNELER
Silithus (66), D:(3, 4), E:(3, 4), Hive'Zora

HIVE'ZORA WASP
Silithus (66), D:(3, 4), E:(3, 4), Hive'Zora

HIVE'ZORA WAYWATCHER
Silithus (66), D:(3, 4), E:(3, 4), Hive'Zora

HJOLDIR STONEBLADE
Blade Merchant, Ironforge (52), F-1, The Forlorn Cavern, Stoneblade's

HOGAN FERENCE
Duskwood (36), J-5, Darkshire Town Hall

HOGGER
Elwynn Forest (42), C-9, Forest's Edge, Roams small area around spawn point

HOGOR THUNDERHOOF
Guns Merchant, Thunder Bluff (84), F-6, High rise, inside Thunderhoof's Firearms

HOGRAL BAKKAN
Rogue Trainer, Dun Morogh (32), F-5, Kharanos (114), Thunderbrew Distillery

HOL'ANYEE MARSHAL
Un'Goro Crater (90), F-1, Marshal's Refuge (116), Entrance to cave

HOLDOUT MEDIC
Dun Morogh (32), C-4, Gnomeregan

HOLDOUT TECHNICIAN
Dun Morogh (32), C-4, Gnomeregan

HOLDOUT WARRIOR
Dun Morogh (32), J-4

HOLT THUNDERHORN
Hunter Trainer, Thunder Bluff (84), G-9, Hunter Rise, Inside Hunter's Hall

HOMER STONEFIELD
Fruit Seller, Elwynn Forest (42), D-8, The Stonefield Farm, In front of barn

HOMING ROBOT OOX-09/HL
The Hinterlands (50), G-4, The Hinterlands, Lying on rock at the southern end of cove

HOMING ROBOT OOX-17/TN
Tanaris (78), I-6, In hills

HOMING ROBOT OOX-22/FE
Feralas (46), F-6, Feral Scar Vale, Laying in clearing

HONNI GOLDENOAT
Baker, Loch Modan (54), D-5, Thelsamar (129), Stoutlager Inn

HORATIO MONTOGOMERY, M.D. STATUE
Stormwind (72), L-6, Old Town, SI:7

HORDE AXE THROWER
Barrens (18), E-3

HORDE DEFENDER
Barrens (18), E-3, The Forgotten Pools

HORDE DEFORESTER
Ashenvale (12), I:(7, 8), K:(5, 6)

HORDE ELITE
Barrens (18), E-1, Mor'shan Base Camp

HORDE GRUNT
Ashenvale (12), I:(7, 8), K:(5, 6)

HORDE GUARD
Barrens (18), E-6, F-3, G-2, H-2

HORDE LABORER
Barrens (18), E-1, Mor'shan Base Camp

HORDE PEON
Ashenvale (12), I:(7, 8), K:(5, 6)

HORDE SCOUT
Ashenvale (12), I:(7, 8), K:(5, 6)

HORDE SHAMAN
Ashenvale (12), I:(7, 8), K:(5, 6), L-6

HORDE SUPPLY CRATE (5)
The Hinterlands (50), H-5, I:(4, 5), Skulk Rock, Five crates are placed randomly within cave

HORGUS THE RAVAGER
Eastern Plaguelands (40), E-8, Darrowshire, (Summon) Downed tree right side of path heading into town

HORIZON SCOUT COOK
Azshara (14), F-9, The Ruined Reaches, South of camp on border of Great Sea in back cabin of ship beneath debris

HORIZON SCOUT CREWMAN
Azshara (14), F-9, G-9, The Ruined Reaches, At beach and inlet

HORIZON SCOUT ENGINEER
Azshara (14), F-9, The Ruined Reaches, South of camp on border of Great Sea in back cabin of ship beneath debris

HORIZON SCOUT FIRST MATE
Azshara (14), F-9, The Ruined Reaches, South of camp on border of Great Sea in back cabin of ship beneath debris

HORNIZZ BRIMBUZZLE
Desolace (30), F-6, Kodo Graveyard, Camp on hills to east

HORTHUS
Reagents Vendor, Orgrimmar (60), E-6 , Valley of Strength, Spitfire Reagents

HOUNDMASTER GREBMAR
Raid Sub-Boss, Burning Steppes (22), Searing Gorge (64), C-4/D-8, Blackrock Depths

HOUNDMASTER LOKSEY
Tirisfal Glades (86), K-3, L-3, Scarlet Monastery

HOWIN KINDFEATHER
The Hinterlands (50), C-5, Aerie Peak (100), Third floor of tower

HRAGRAN
Cloth and Leather Armor Merchant, Stranglethorn Vale (74), C-3, Grom'gol Base Camp (112), Under tent in front of zepplin tower

HRAQ
Blacksmithing Supplier, Barrens (18), F-3, The Crossroads (107), Western entrance

HRAUG
Demon Trainer, Durotar (34), F-7, Valley of Trials (131), Back of cave

HUKKU
Swamp of Sorrows (76), I-5, The Temple of Atal'Hakkar

HUKLAH
Cloth & Leather Armor Merchant, Durotar (34), F-7, Valley of Trials (131)

HULA'MAHI
Reagents and Herbs, Barrens (18), F-3, The Crossroads (107), West of inn

HULDAR
Loch Modan (54), G-7, The Loch, Next to dynamite filled carriage on the southern end of loch

HULFDAN BLACKBEARD
Rogue Trainer, Ironforge (52), G-1, The Forlorn Cavern, South building, inside east entrance

HULFNAR STONETOTEM
Mulgore (58), F-6, Bloodhoof Village (102), Combat ground east of village

HULKING FERAL SCAR
Feralas (46), F-6, Feral Scar Vale

HULKING GRITJAW BASILISK
Desolace (30), D-4, E:(4-6), F:(4-6), G:(4, 5), H:(4-6), J:(1, 4, 5), K:(2, 4, 5), Ghost Walker Post (111), Kodo Graveyard, Sargeron

HULKING MOUNTAIN LION
Alterac Mountains (8), D:(8, 9), E:(3, 8, 9), F:(2, 7-9), G:(2, 3, 8), H-3, I-5, J:(5, 6), K:(5, 6)

HUMAN SKULL
Eastern Plaguelands (40), D-7, The Marris Stead

HUMAR THE PRIDELORD
Barrens (18), H-3, North of Ratchet

HUNGERING DEAD
Tirisfal Glades (86), I-4, Brightwater Lake

HUNGERING WRAITH
Western Plaguelands (92), H:(5, 6), I:(5, 6), Gahrron's Withering

HUNTRESS NHEMAI
Teldrassil (80), F:(5-6), G-6, Dolanaar (109), Patrols road between Dolanaar and east of Ban'ethil Hollow

HUNTRESS YAELIURA
Teldrassil (80), F:(5-6), G-6, Dolanaar (109), Patrols road between Dolanaar and east of Ban'ethil Hollow

HUNTSMAN MARKHOR
Stable Master, The Hinterlands (50), L-8, Revantusk Village, To the right of hut on southeast side of village

HUNTSMAN RADLEY
Western Plaguelands (92), H-4, Stand idle with wolf in small camp to the right of path heading towards Hearthglen

HURICANIAN
Rare Spawn, Silithus (66), D-1, The Crystal Vale, Lvl 58 Uncommon; Roams vale

HURKLOR
Blacksmithing Supplies, Stranglethorn Vale (74), B-8, Booty Bay (103), Plate-n-Chain (shop)

HURLEY BLACKBREATH
Burning Steppes (22), Searing Gorge (64), C-4/D-8, Blackrock Depths

HYDRAXIAN HONOR GUARD
Azshara (14), J:(7, 8), K-7, Bay of Storms

HYDROLING
Feralas (46), G-4, Dire Maul

HYDROMANCER VELRATHA
Tanaris (78), E-1, Zul'Farrak

HYDROSPAWN
Feralas (46), G-4, Dire Maul

I

IAN STROM
Rogue Trainer, Stranglethorn Vale (74), B-8, Booty Bay (103), Second floor of The Salty Sailor Tavern

ICE CLAW BEAR
Dun Morogh (32), C:(4-6), D:(3-6), E:(3-5), F:(3, 6), G:(4-6), H:(4-6), I:(5, 6), J-5, K-5

ICE THISTLE MATRIARCH
Winterspring (98), J:(4, 5), K-4, Ice Thistle Hills

ICE THISTLE PATRIARCH
Winterspring (98), J:(4, 5), K-4, Ice Thistle Hills

ICE THISTLE YETI
Winterspring (98), H-3, I:(3, 4), J:(4, 5), K-4, Starfall Village, Ice Thistle Hills

IDRIANA
Banker, Darnassus (26), D-4, Bank

ILIFAR
Blasted Lands (20), G-3, Rise of the Defiler, (Summon) Summoned by Razelikh the Defiler at 75% health

ILKRUD MAGTHRULL
Ashenvale (12), C-6, Fire Scar Shrine, Near the altar to the north

ILLIYANA
Ashenvale (12), C-5, Shrine of Aessina, Center of Shrine

ILLIYANA MOONBLAZE
Silverwing Supply Officer, Ashenvale (12), H-8, Silverwing Grove, In tent to the right of ramp

ILLUSION OF JANDICE BAROV
Western Plaguelands (92), I-7, Scholomance

ILLUSIONARY PHANTASM
Tirisfal Glades (86), K-3, L-3, Scarlet Monastery

ILLYANIE
Cloth Armor Merchant, Stonetalon Mountains (70), D-1, Stonetalon Peak, House west of hippocryphs

ILLYANNA RAVENOAK
Feralas (46), G-4, Dire Maul

ILSA CORBIN
Warrior Trainer, Stormwind (72), L:(4, 5), Old Town, Command Center

ILYENIA MOONFIRE
Weapon Master, Darnassus (26), H-5, Warrior's Terrace, Lower southwest platform, Trains: Bows, Daggers, Fist, Thrown, & Staves

IMELDA
Stormwind (72), C-5, The Park, Northwest section

IMMOLATUS
Rare Spawn, Felwood (44), F-4, Shatter Scar Vale, Lvl 56 Semi-Rare; Roams eastern craters

IMMOL'THAR
Feralas (46), G-4, Dire Maul

IMPSY
Niby's Minion, Felwood (44), F-5, Bloodvenom Falls, North of pond near dock

INCENDOSAUR
Searing Gorge (64), D-5, E:(2-5), F:(2-4), The Slag Pit, Northern area of the pit

INFERNAL BODYGUARD
Felwood (44), F-4, Shatter Scar Vale

INFERNAL SENTRY
Felwood (44), F-4

INFERNO ELEMENTAL
Searing Gorge (64), B-5, C:(4, 6-8), D:(4, 6, 8), E-6, F-6, Firewatch Ridge, Lava

INFILTRATOR HAMEYA
Eastern Plaguelands (40), I-2, Zul'Mashar, Patrols circular path around graves

INFILTRATOR MARKSEN
Swamp of Sorrows (76), F-5, Stonard (126), Holding pen in northwest corner of camp

INGO WOOLYBUSH
Explorers' League, Dustwallow Marsh (38), I-5, Theramore Isle (130), 2nd floor of inn

INGRYS STONEBROW
Cloth Armor Merchant, Ironforge (52), E-1, The Mystic Ward, Maeva's Mystical Apparel

INITIATE AMAKKAR
Badlands (16), A-5, Kargath (114), Group left of orc burrow

INJURED PEASANT
Eastern Plaguelands (40), C-2

INNKEEPER ABEQWA
Innkeeper, Thousand Needles (82), F-5, Freewind Post, Inn

INNKEEPER ADEGWA
Innkeeper, Arathi Highlands (10), J-3, Hammerfall (113), First floor north building

INNKEEPER ALLISON
Innkeeper, Stormwind (72), H:(6, 7), Trade District, The Gilded Rose

INNKEEPER ANDERSON
Innkeeper, Hillsbrad Foothills (48), F-6, Southshore (125), First floor of inn

INNKEEPER BATES
Innkeeper, Silverpine Forest (68), F-4, The Sepulcher (124), Right side of entrance to inn

INNKEEPER BELM
Innkeeper, Dun Morogh (32), F-5, Kharanos (114), Thunderbrew Distillery

INNKEEPER BOORAND PLAINSWIND
Innkeeper, Barrens (18), F-3, The Crossroads (107), Inn

INNKEEPER BRIANNA
Innkeeper, Redridge Mountains (62), C-4, Lakeshire (115), First floor of Lakeshire Inn

INNKEEPER BYULA
Innkeeper, Barrens (18), F-6, Camp Taurajo (106), Inn

INNKEEPER FARLEY
Innkeeper, Elwynn Forest (42), F-7, Goldshire (112), First floor of Lion's Pride Inn

INNKEEPER FIREBREW
Innkeeper, Ironforge (52), B-5, The Commons, The Stonefire Tavern

INNKEEPER FIZZGRIMBLE
Innkeeper, Tanaris (78), H-3, Gadgetzan (111), Inn

INNKEEPER GREUL
Innkeeper, Feralas (46), I-4, Camp Mojache (105), Inn

INNKEEPER GROSK
Innkeeper, Durotar (34), H-4, Razor Hill (122), Inn

INNKEEPER GRYSHKA
Innkeeper, Orgrimmar (60), G-7, Valley of Strength, Inn

INNKEEPER HEARTHSTOVE
Innkeeper, Loch Modan (54), D-5, Thelsamar (129), Stoutlager Inn

INNKEEPER HEATHER
Innkeeper, Westfall (94), F-5, Sentinel Hill (123), Inn

INNKEEPER HELBREK
Innkeeper, Wetlands (96), A-6, Deepwater Tavern, By bar

INNKEEPER JANENE
Innkeeper, Dustwallow Marsh (38), I-5, Theramore Isle (130), Inn

INNKEEPER JAYKA
Innkeeper, Stonetalon Mountains (70), F-6, Sun Rock Retreat (127), Inn

INNKEEPER KARAKUL
Innkeeper, Swamp of Sorrows (76), F-5, Stonard (126), First floor of inn

INNKEEPER KAUTH
Innkeeper, Mulgore (58), E-6, Bloodhoof Village (102), Inn

INNKEEPER KAYLISK
Innkeeper, Ashenvale (12), I-6, Splintertree Post (126), Center of inn

INNKEEPER KELDAMYR
Innkeeper, Teldrassil (80), G-6, Dolanaar (109), Inn

INNKEEPER KIMLYA
Innkeeper, Ashenvale (12), E-5, Astranaar (101), Second floor of inn

INNKEEPER LYSHAERYA
Innkeeper, Desolace (30), I-1, Nijel's Point (119), Inn

INNKEEPER NORMAN
Innkeeper, Undercity (88), I-4, J-4, The Trade Quarter, Upper Ring of Trade Quarter

INNKEEPER PALA
Innkeeper, Thunder Bluff (84), E-6, Building near bridges to Hunter's Rise

INNKEEPER RENEE
Innkeeper, Tirisfal Glades (86), H-5, Brill (104), First floor of Gallows' End Tavern

INNKEEPER SAELIENNE
Innkeeper, Darnassus (26), I:(1, 2), Craftsmen's Terrace, Inn

INNKEEPER SHAUSSIY
Innkeeper, Darkshore (24), F-4, Auberdine (101), First floor of inn

INNKEEPER SHAY
Innkeeper, Hillsbrad Foothills (48), H-2, Tarren Mill (128), First floor of inn

INNKEEPER SHUL'KAR
Innkeeper, Badlands (16), A-5, Kargath (114), First floor orc burrow

INNKEEPER SHYRIA
Innkeeper, Feralas (46), C-4, Feathermoon Stronghold (110), Inn

INNKEEPER SIKEWA
Innkeeper, Desolace (30), C-7, Shadowprey Village (125), Inn

INNKEEPER SKINDLE
Innkeeper, Stranglethorn Vale (74), B-8, Booty Bay (103), First floor of The Salty Sailor Tavern

INNKEEPER THULFRAM
Innkeeper, The Hinterlands (50), B-4, Aerie Peak (100), Wildhammer Keep

INNKEEPER TRELAYNE
Innkeeper, Duskwood (36), J-4, Darkshire (108), Scarlet Raven Inn

INNKEEPER VIZZIE
Innkeeper, Winterspring (98), I-4, Everlook (110), Inside inn

INNKEEPER WILEY
Innkeeper, Barrens (18), H-4, Ratchet (121), Inn

INSANE GHOUL
Duskwood (36), K-7, Tranquil Gardens Cemetery, Roams in church

INSTRUCTOR MALICIA
Western Plaguelands (92), I-7, Scholomance

INTERROGATOR VISHAS
Tirisfal Glades (86), K-3, L-3, Scarlet Monastery

IRENE SURESHOT
Gunsmith, Loch Modan (54), K-6, The Farstrider Lodge, On left side of lodge entrance

IRONAYA
Badlands (16), G-1, Uldaman

IRONBACK
Rare Spawn, The Hinterlands (50), L:(5, 6), The Overlook Cliffs, Lvl 51 Semi-Rare; Roams small area around spawn point

IRONBARK PROTECTOR
Feralas (46), G-4, Dire Maul

IRONBEAK HUNTER
Felwood (44), E-4:(4-6), F:(2, 4-7), G:(2-4)

IRONBEAK OWL
Felwood (44), E-7, F:(7, 8), G:(7, 8), H:(8, 9), Deadwood Village, Emerald Sanctuary, Morlos'Aran

IRONBEAK SCREECHER
Felwood (44), G:(2, 3), H:(1-3), I-2, Felpaw Village, Irontree Woods, Talonbranch Glade

IRONEYE THE INVINCIBLE
Thousand Needles (82), L:(7-8), Mirage Raceway (118), The Shimmering Flats, Far east near cliffs

IRONFORGE GUARD
Dun Morogh (32), F-4, G:(2-4), H:(2, 3), I:(2, 3), J:(2-4), Gates of Ironforge, Kharanos (114), Steelgrill's Depot

IRONFORGE MOUNTAINEER
Dun Morogh (32), E-6, F:(4-6), G-5, H-5, I:(2, 5), J:(2-4)

IRONFUR BEAR
Feralas (46), F-5, G:(5, 6), H:(4, 5), I:(3-5), J:(4, 5), K:(4, 5)

IRONFUR PATRIARCH
Feralas (46), D:(1, 2), E:(1-4), F-3, Rage Scar Hold, Ruins of Ravenwind, The Twin Colossals

IRONHIDE DEVILSAUR
Un'Goro Crater (90), D:(3, 4), F-8, H:(3, 8), J-4

IRONJAW BASILISK
Stranglethorn Vale (74), D-5, Crystalvein Mine

IRONPATCH
Stranglethorn Vale (74), C-9, Wild Shore, On Boat

IRONSPINE
Tirisfal Glades (86), K-3, L-3, Scarlet Monastery

IRONTREE STOMPER
Felwood (44), F-3, G:(2, 3), Irontree Woods

IRONTREE WANDERER
Felwood (44), F-3, G:(2, 3), Irontree Woods

IRONUS COLDSTEEL
Special Weapon Crafter, Ironforge (52), G-5, H-5, The Great Forge, The Great Anvil

IRONZAR
Weaponsmith, Barrens (18), H-4, Ratchet (121), Ironzar's Imported Weaponry

IRRADIATED HORROR
Dun Morogh (32), C-4, Gnomeregan

IRRADIATED INVADER
Dun Morogh (32), C-4, Gnomeregan

IRRADIATED PILLAGER
Dun Morogh (32), C-4, Gnomeregan

IRRADIATED SLIME
Dun Morogh (32), C-4, Gnomeregan

ISABELLA
Mage Trainer, Tirisfal Glades (86), C-7, Deathknell (109), Church

ISHA AWAK
Barrens (18), H-5, The Merchant Coast, Northwatch Hold, Swims off the shore

ISHAMUHALE
Barrens (18), G-3, Thorn Hill, (Summon) Spawns on southeast side of Thorn Hill

ISLEN WATERSEER
Barrens (18), H-4, The Tidus Stair, Outside hut

ITHARIUS
Swamp of Sorrows (76), B-7, Itharius's Cave, Cave

IVAR THE FOUL
Silverpine Forest (68), H-1, The Ivar Patch, Barn

IVERRON
Teldrassil (80), G-3, Shadowglen (124), Up hill west of entrance to Shadowthread Cave

IVY LEAFRUNNER
Emerald Circle, Felwood (44), G-8, Emerald Sanctuary, Tent

IZZY COPPERGRAB
Banker, Winterspring (98), I-4, Everlook (110), Inside building directly north of inn

J

J.D. COLLIE
Un'Goro Crater (90), F-1, Marshal's Refuge (116), Northwest chamber of cave

JABBERING GHOUL
Western Plaguelands (92), E-6, Felstone Field, Roams near cauldron

JABBEY
General Goods, Tanaris (78), J-2, Steamwheedle Port, Big northern building

JACK STERLING
Winterspring (98), I-4, Everlook (110), Outside northeast building

JACOB
Angelas' Pet, Feralas (46), C-4, Feathermoon Stronghold (110), Southeastern building

JADE
Rare Spawn, Swamp of Sorrows (76), I-5, Temple of Atal'Hakkar, Lvl 47 Very Rare; Entrance to the Temple of Atal'Hakkar

JADE OOZE
The Hinterlands (50), G:(4, 5), H:(4, 5), I:(4, 5), Skull Rock, Cave

JADE SLUDGE
The Hinterlands (50), I:(7, 8), Jintha'Alor

JADEFIRE BETRAYER
Felwood (44), E-2, F:(2, 6, 7), Jadefire Run

JADEFIRE FELSWORN
Felwood (44), D:(6, 7), E:(6-8), F:(8, 9), Jadefire Run, Ruins of Constellas

JADEFIRE HELLCALLER
Felwood (44), E:(2, 6), F:(2, 6, 7), Jadefire Run, Shadow Hold

JADEFIRE ROGUE
Felwood (44), D:(6, 7), E:(6, 7), Ruins of Constellas

JADEFIRE SATYR
Felwood (44), E-8, F:(8, 9), Jadefire Run

JADEFIRE SHADOWSTALKER
Felwood (44), D:(6, 7), E:(6, 7), Ruins of Constellas

JADEFIRE TRICKSTER
Felwood (44), E:(2, 6), F:(2, 6, 7), Jadefire Run, Shadow Hold

JADEMIR BOUGHGUARD
Feralas (46), E:(1, 2), F:(1, 2), Jademir Lake, Oneiros, Ruins of Ravenwind

JADEMIR ORACLE
Feralas (46), E:(1, 2), F:(1, 2), Jademir Lake, Oneiros, Ruins of Ravenwind

JADEMIR TREE WARDER
Feralas (46), E:(1, 2), F:(1, 2), Jademir Lake, Oneiros, Ruins of Ravenwind

JADENVIS SEAWATCHER
Reagent Vendor, Feralas (46), C-4, Feathermoon Stronghold (110), North of inn on dock

JADESPINE BASILISK
Badlands (16), G-1, Uldaman

JAEANA
Meat Vendor, Darnassus (26), H-5, Tradesmen's Terrace, Roams around Fletcher & Weapons shops

JAEDENAR ADEPT
Felwood (44), E-6, Barrow Dens, Jaedenar, Shrine of the Deceiver

JAEDENAR CULTIST
Felwood (44), E-6, Barrow Dens, Jaedenar, Shrine of the Deceiver

JAEDENAR DARKWEAVER
Felwood (44), E:(5, 6), F-5, Jadefire Run, Shadow Hold

JAEDENAR ENFORCER
Felwood (44), E:(5, 6), F-5, Jadefire Run, Shadow Hold

JAEDENAR GUARDIAN
Felwood (44), E-6, Barrow Dens, Jaedenar, Shadow Hold, Shrine of the Deceiver

JAEDENAR HOUND
Felwood (44), E-6, Barrow Dens, Jaedenar, Shrine of the Deceiver

JAEDENAR HUNTER
Felwood (44), E:(5, 6), Jadefire Run, Shadow Hold

JAEDENAR LEGIONNAIRE
Felwood (44), E:(5, 6), Shadow Hold

JAEDENAR WARLOCK
Felwood (44), E:(5, 6), Shadow Hold

JAELYSIA
Stable Master, Darkshore (24), F-4, Auberdine (101), In front of inn

JAGGED ROCK ELEMENTAL
Alterac Mountains (8), B-7, Dalaran

JAGUERO STALKER
Stranglethorn Vale (74), D:(8, 9), Jaguero Isle, Wild Shore

JAHAN HAWKWING
Leather & Mail Armor Merchant, Barrens (18), F-3, The Crossroads (107), Western entrance

JAILOR BORHUIN
Alterac Mountains (8), I-4, Strahnbrad, First floor of house

JAILOR ESTON
Hillsbrad Foothills (48), J-4, Durnholde Keep, Roams small area around spawn point

JAILOR MARLGEN
Hillsbrad Foothills (48), J-4, Durnholde Keep, Roams small area around spawn point

JALANE AYROLE
Master Shadoweave Tailor, Stormwind (72), D-8, Mage Quarter, The Slaughtered Lamb

JALINDA SPRIG
Burning Steppes (22), K-7, Morgan's Vigil (118), Tower ruins, center of camp

JALINDE SUMMERDRAKE
Rare Spawn, The Hinterlands (50), D-5, E:(4, 5), Quel'Danil Lodge, Lvl 49 Uncommon; Roams small area around spawn point

JAMES CLARK
Elwynn Forest (42), K-7, Eastvale Logging Camp, House in front of crop field

JAMES HALLORAN
Wetlands (96), A-5, Menethil Harbor (117), Roaming outside house to the west of keep

JAMES VAN BRUNT
Expert Blacksmith, Undercity (88), I-3, The War Quarter

JAMIE NOR
Tirisfal Glades (86), H-5, Brill (104)

JAMIN
Redridge Mountains (62), C-5, Lake Everstill, Dock

JAMMAL'AN THE PROPHET
Swamp of Sorrows (76), I-5, The Temple of Atal'Hakkar

JANDI
Herbalism Trainer, Orgrimmar (60), F-4, G-4, The Drag, Jandi's Arboretum

JANDIA
Trade Supplies, Thousand Needles (82), F-5, Freewind Post, Inn

JANDICE BAROV
Western Plaguelands (92), I-7, Scholomance

JANDRIA
Priest Trainer, Darnassus (26), E-8, Temple of the Moon, Just inside temple, north of fountain

JANET HOMMERS
Food & Drink, Desolace (30), I-1, Nijel's Point (119), Inn

JANEY ANSHIP
Stormwind (72), F-8, Mage Quarter, Roamer - sits by tower

JANGDOR SWIFTSTRIDER
Leatherworking Supplies, Feralas (46), I-4, Camp Mojache (105), Big western tent

JANICE FELSTONE
Western Plaguelands (92), E-5, Felstone Field, Second floor of house

JANNA BRIGHTMOON
Clothier, Teldrassil (80), H-4, Shadowglen (124), Second level of main building

JANNOK BREEZESONG
Rogue Trainer, Teldrassil (80), G-6, Dolanaar (109), Inn

JANNOS IRONWILL
Superior Macecrafter, Arathi Highlands (10), F-5, Refuge Point, Camp

JANNOS LIGHTHOOF
Druid Trainer, Feralas (46), I-4, Camp Mojache (105), In tent, east of water

JANOS HAMMERKNUCKLE
Weaponsmith, Elwynn Forest (42), F-4, Northshire Valley (120), Caravan facing abbey

JANSEN UNDERWOOD
Blacksmithing Supplies, Stranglethorn Vale (74), C-8, Booty Bay (103), Booty Bay Blacksmith (shop)

JAQUILINA DRAMET
Superior Axecrafter, Stranglethorn Vale (74), C-1, Nesingwary's Expedition, Camp

JAREL MOOR
Bartender, Stormwind (72), D-7, Mage Quarter, The Slaughtered Lamb

JARETH WILDWOODS
Darnassus (26), I-6, Tradesmen's Terrace, East of General Goods

JARK
General Goods, Durotar (34), H-4, Razor Hill (122), Barracks

JARKAL MOSSMELD
Badlands (16), A-5, Kargath (114), Second floor orc burrow

JARON STONESHAPER
Explorers' League, Winterspring (98), H-3, Starfall Village, Terrace of main building

JARQUIA
Swamp of Sorrows (76), L:(5, 6), Misty Reed Strand, Roams small area around spawn point

JARRODENUS
Hippogryph Master, Azshara (14), A-8, Talrendis Point

JARTSAM
Nightsaber Riding Instructor, Darnassus (26), E-1, Cenarion Enclave, Intersection of paths

JARUND STOUTSTRIDER
The Cenarion Circle, Silithus (66), I-1, Valor's Rest, Hut south of road

JARVEN THUNDERBREW
Dun Morogh (32), F-5, Kharanos (114), Thunderbrew Distillery

JASE FARLANE
Trade Supplies, Eastern Plaguelands (40), K-6, Light's Hope Chapel (116), Camp on left side of chapel

JASON LEMIEUX
Mushroom Seller, Hillsbrad Foothills (48), G-2, Tarren Mill (128), Patrols "figure eight" path around town

JASON MATHERS
Fishmonger, Elwynn Forest (42), F-6, Crystal Lake, Dock

JASPER FEL
Shady Dealer, Stormwind (72), L-6, Old Town, SI:7

JAWN HIGHMESA
General Goods, Thousand Needles (82), F-5, Freewind Post, Inn

JAXIN CHONG
Expert Alchemist, Stranglethorn Vale (74), B-8, Booty Bay (103), Boucher's Cauldron (shop)

JAYLA
Skinner, Ashenvale (12), F-6, Silverwind Refuge, Center of building

JAYSIN LANYDA
Poisons and Reagents, Hillsbrad Foothills (48), F-6, Southshore (125), Second floor of inn

JAZ
Burning Steppes (22), Searing Gorge (64), C-4/D-8, Blackrock Depths

JAZZIK
General Supplies, Barrens (18), H-4, Ratchet (121), Jazzik's General Goods

JAZZRIK
Blacksmithing Supplies, Badlands (16), F-5, Valley of Fangs, Camp

JED RUNEWATCHER
Rare Spawn, Burning Steppes (22), Searing Gorge (64), C-4/D-8, Blackrock Spire, Lvl 59 Uncommon

JEDIGA
Azshara (14), B-5, Valormok

JEEDA
Apprentice Witch Doctor, Stonetalon Mountains (70), F-6, Sun Rock Retreat (127), Second floor of inn

JEEN'RA NIGHTRUNNER
Hunter Trainer, Darnassus (26), E-1, Cenarion Enclave, Top of structure, connected to the northeast structure

JEENA FEATHERBOW
Bowyer, Teldrassil (80), G-6, Dolanaar (109), Inn

J'EEVEE
Western Plaguelands (92), I-7, Scholomance

JEKYLL FLANDRING
Rewards Vendor, Alterac Mountains (8), I-6, Left camp outside Alterac Valley (Horde)

JEMMA QUIKSWITCH
Journeyman Engineer, Ironforge (52), I-4, Tinker Town, Springspindle's Gadgets

JE'NEU SANCREA
The Earthen Ring, Ashenvale (12), B-4, Zoram'gar Outpost (131), Northern Structure

JENN LANGSTON
Stormwind (72), Old Town, Roams Old Town

JENNA LEMKENILLI
Journeyman Engineer, Darkshore (24), F-4, Auberdine (101), In front of northern building

JENNABINK POWERSEAM
Tailoring Supplies & Specialty Goods, Wetlands (96), A-6, Menethil Harbor (117), Second floor of building west of keep

JENNEA CANNON
Mage Trainer, Stormwind (72), F-8, Mage Quarter, Wizard's Sanctum

JENOVA STONESHIELD
Stable Master, Stormwind (72), I-2, J-2, Dwarven District, South of tram entrance

JENSEN FARRAN
Bowyer, Dustwallow Marsh (38), I-5, Theramore Isle (130), East archery range

JEN'SHAN
Hunter Trainer, Durotar (34), F-7, Valley of Trials (131), Structure to south

JEREMIAH PAYSON
Cockroach Vendor, Undercity (88), I:(4, 5), The Trade Quarter, Under Bridge in Trade Quarter

JERGOSH THE INVOKER
Orgrimmar (60), F-5, Ragefire Chasm

JER'KAI MOONWEAVER
Feralas (46), H-4, Lower Wilds, In hills overlooking Grimtotem Compound

JERN HORNHELM
Loch Modan (54), E-5, Thelsamar (129), In second house on right of path

JES'RIMON
Orgrimmar (60), G-3, The Drag, Yelmak's Alchemy and Potions, top floor

JESSARA CORDELL
Enchanting Supplies, Stormwind (72), F-6, The Canals, Shop south of stockade

JESSE HALLORAN
Wetlands (96), A-5, Menethil Harbor (117), Roams in and out of house west of keep

JESSICA REDPATH
Winterspring (98), I-4, Everlook (110), Inside inn

JESSIR MOONBOW
Felwood (44), G-8, Emerald Sanctuary, Near pool

JEWEL
Troyas' Pet, Feralas (46), C-4, Feathermoon Stronghold (110), Southeastern building

JEZELLE PRUITT
Undercity (88), K-1, The Magic Quarter, Green circle west of Skull Building

JEZIBA
Western Plaguelands (92), E-7, Ruins of Andorhal, Second floor of inn

JHAG
Journeyman Enchanter, Orgrimmar (60), F-4, The Drag, Godan's Runeworks

JHAWNA OATWIND
Baker, Mulgore (58), E-6, Bloodhoof Village (102), Mill

JHORDY LAPFORGE
Engineer, Tanaris (78), H-3, Gadgetzan (111), Transporter northeast of cage

JILLIAN TANNER
Leatherworking Supplies, Stormwind (72), J-5, Old Town, The Protective Hide

JIMMY
Stormwind (72), Roams city with Miss Danna

JIMMY THE BLEEDER
Rare Spawn, Alterac Mountains (8), F-8, H-7, Corrahn's Dagger, Sofera's Naze, Lvl 27 Average Rare; Roams around camp

JIN'SORA
Bow Merchant, Orgrimmar (60), J-4, Valley of Honor, Orgrimmar Bowyer

JINAR'ZILLEN
Desolace (30), B-7, Shadowprey Village (125), Dock

JINKY TWIZZLEFIXXIT
Engineering Supplies, Thousand Needles (82), K-8, Mirage Raceway (118), Tent west of racetrack

JIN'ROKH THE BREAKER
Stranglethorn Vale (74), A-2, Yojamba Isle

JIN'ZALLAH THE SANDBRINGER
Tanaris (78), F-3, Sandsorrow Watch, In hut near east watchtower

JITTERS
Duskwood (36), B-6, Raven Hill (121), Circling well in town

JOACHIM BRENLOW
Bartender, Stormwind (72), F-9, Mage Quarter, The Blue Recluse

JOANNA WHITEHALL
Undercity (88), G-3, The War Quarter, By Mining Trainer, Close to Canal

JOCASTE
Hunter Trainer, Darnassus (26), E-1, Cenarion Enclave, Northeast structure

JOHAN FOCHT
Miner, Silverpine Forest (68), F-4, The Sepulcher (124), Basement of inn

JOHN BURNSIDE
Banker, Stormwind (72), H-7, Trade District, Stormwind Counting House

JOHN TURNER
Ironforge (52), C-5, E-8, The Commons, Roams The Commons

JONATHAN CAREVIN
Duskwood (36), J-5, Darkshire (108), First floor of house

JONATHAN CHAMBERS
Bag Vendor, Undercity (88), J-6, The Rogues' Quarter, Near Apothecarium entry

JONDOR STEELBROW
Guild Master, Ironforge (52), D-8, The Commons, Ironforge Visitor's Center

JON-JON THE CROW
Stranglethorn Vale (74), C-5, Ruins of Jubuwal, Camp

JORAH ANNISTON
Undercity (88), K-4, The Magic Quarter, Near Rogues' Quarter entry

JORB
Lizzarik's Bodyguard, Barrens (18), G-4, Ratchet (121)

JORDAN STILWELL
Dun Morogh (32), G-4, Gates of Ironforge, Next to anvil outside of Ironforge

JORGEN
Stormwind (72), K-8, Valley of Heroes, Northeast of entrance

JORIK KERRIDAN
Rogue Trainer, Elwynn Forest (42), G-4, Northshire Valley (120), Abbey stable

JORMUND STONEBROW
Expert Tailor, Ironforge (52), F-3, The Great Forge, Stonebrow's Clothier

JORN SKYSEER
Barrens (18), F-6, Camp Taurajo (106), Outside southern building

JORY ZAGA
Darkshore (24), J-2, Hut, northeast of lake

JOSEF GREGORIAN
Artisan Tailor, Undercity (88), J-3, The Magic Quarter

JOSEPH DIRTE
Waste Management, Western Plaguelands (92), I-7, Caer Darrow, In front of shed left of entrance to Scholomance

JOSEPH MOORE
Leatherworking Supplies, Undercity (88), J-6, The Rogues' Quarter

JOSEPH REDPATH
Western Plaguelands (92), G-7, Sorrow Hill, (Summon) Spawns at gravestone Eastern Plaguelands (40), E-8, Darrowshire, (Summon) Well in the center of town

JOSEPHINE LISTER
Master Shadoweave Tailor, Undercity (88), L-2, The Magic Quarter, Outside Skull Building

JOSHUA KIEN
General Supplies, Tirisfal Glades (86), D-6, Deathknell (109), First floor of second house on right side of road

JOSHUA MACLURE
Vintner, Elwynn Forest (42), F-9, The Maclure Vineyards, Next to well on the south side of farm

JOY AR'NARETH
Azshara (14), C-4, Bear's Head, Requires quest from Sanath Lim-yo to reach

JUBAHL CORPSESEEKER
Demon Trainer, Ironforge (52), G-1, The Forlorn Cavern, First building on north from east entrance

JUBIE GADGETSPRING
Engineering Supplier, Azshara (14), E-9, The Ruined Reaches, Gnome tower

JUDGE THELGRAM
Hillsbrad Foothills (48), A-8, Purgation Isle, To the right of tower

JUGKAR GRIM'ROD
Desolace (30), G-8, Mannoroc Coven, Northeast of ruins

JULI STORMKETTLE
Mage Trainer, Ironforge (52), C-1, The Mystic Ward, Hall of Mysteries

JULIA GALLINA
Wine Vendor, Stormwind (72), H-7, The Canals, Gallina Winery

JUNGLE STALKER
Stranglethorn Vale (74), B-5, C:(4, 5)

JUNGLE THUNDERER
Stranglethorn Vale (74), D:(3, 4), E:(3, 4)

JUN'HA
Tailoring Supplies, Arathi Highlands (10), J-4, Hammerfall (113), Inside west building

JUNIOR APOTHECARY HOLLAND
Royal Apothecary Society, Tirisfal Glades (86), G-5, Brill (104), Patrols back and forth in graveyard between the gazeebo and northeastern entrance

JUSTIN
Stormwind (72), H-3, The Canals, Dock

JUSTINE DEMALIER
Stormwind Recruiter, Stormwind (72), H-6, Trade District, Next to tree

JUTAK
Blade Trader, Stranglethorn Vale (74), B-8, Booty Bay (103)

JUVENILE SNOW LEOPARD
Dun Morogh (32), E-6, F-6, Coldridge Pass, The Grizzled Den

JYN STONEHOOF
Weapon's Merchant, Thunder Bluff (84), D-6, Lower rise, in Thunder Bluff Weapons tent

K

KAAL SOULREAPER
Warlock Trainer, Undercity (88), L-2, The Magic Quarter, Inside Skull Building

KADRAK
Barrens (18), F-1, The Mor'shan Rampart, Top of eastern tower

KAELA SHADOWSPEAR
Stonetalon Mountains (70), G-7, Webwinder Path, Hill between road and Windshear Crag

KAELYSTIA HATEBRINGER
Mage Trainer, Undercity (88), L-1, The Magic Quarter, Inside Skull Building

KAERBRUS
Hunter Trainer, Felwood (44), H-3, Talonbranch Glade, Near pond

KAGA MISTRUNNER
Meat Vendor, Thunder Bluff (84), F-5, High rise, in Kodo Steak and Ribs tent

KAGORO
Dustwallow Marsh (38), D-3, Brackenwall Village (104)

KAH MISTRUNNER
Fishing Trainer, Thunder Bluff (84), F-5, High rise, in Mountaintop Bait & Tackle tent

KAITA DEEPFORGE
Blacksmithing Supplies, Stormwind (72), H-2, Dwarven District, At the Forge

KAJA
Guns and Ammo Merchant, Orgrimmar (60), F-7, G-7, Valley of Strength, Boomstick Imports

KAL
Druid Trainer, Teldrassil (80), G-6, Dolanaar (109), Moonwell south side of Dolanaar

KALARAN WINDBLADE
Searing Gorge (64), D-4, Amongst Mutilated Dark Iron Remains

KALDAN FELMOON
Specialist Leatherworking Supplies, Barrens (18), E-4, Wailing Caverns

KALI HEALTOUCH
Herbalist, Loch Modan (54), D-5, Thelsamar (129), On porch of first house on right of path

KALI REMIK
Durotar (34), H-7, Sen'jin Village (123), Atop northern structure

KALIN WINDFLIGHT
Feralas (46), E-2, The Twin Colossals, Atop eastern colossal

KALLDAN FELMOON
Specialist Leatherworking Supplies, Barrens (18), E-4, The Wailing Caverns, Right eye of cave above entrance

KALTUNK
Durotar (34), F-7, Valley of Trials (131), Center fire

KALYIMAH STORMCLOUD
Bags & Sacks, Barrens (18), F-3, The Crossroads (107), Southern entrance

KAM DEEPFURY
Stormwind (72), F-6, The Stockade

KAMARI
Journeyman Leatherworker, Orgrimmar (60), H-4, The Drag, Kodohide Leatherworkers

KANATI GREYCLOUD
Thousand Needles (82), B-3, Whitereach Post, Front of hut

KANDRIS DREAMSEEKER
Shaman Trainer, Orgrimmar (60), D-4, Valley of Wisdom, Grommash Hold

KAPLAK
Rogue Trainer, Durotar (34), H-4, Razor Hill (122), Bunker

KAR STORMSINGER
Kodo Riding Instructor, Mulgore (58), E-6, Bloodhoof Village (102), Northern clearing

KARA ADAMS
Shield Crafter, Redridge Mountains (62), D-5, Lakeshire (115), Stable

KARANG AMAKKAR
Ashenvale (12), B-4, Zoram'gar Outpost (131), Center of outpost

KARD RAGETOTEM
Sword and Dagger Merchant, Thunder Bluff (84), F-6, High rise, inside Ragetotem Arms tent

KAREN TAYLOR
Mining and Smithing Supplies, Redridge Mountains (62), D-5, Lakeshire (115), By carriage in front of Lakeshire Town Hall

KARETH
Blade Merchant, Orgrimmar (60), E-5, The Cleft of Shadow, The Slow Blade

KARGAL BATTLESCAR
Barrens (18), H-2, Far Watch Post, Southside of road

KARL BORAN
Wetlands (96), A-6, Menethil Harbor (117), Dock

KARLEE CHADDIS
Stormwind (72), Roams city

KARM IRONQUILL
Mining Supplies, Loch Modan (54), E-5, Thelsamar (129), In second house on right of path

KARN STONEHOOF
Expert Blacksmith, Thunder Bluff (84), D-6, Lower rise, next to pond

KARNA REMTRAVEL
Un'Goro Crater (90), F-1, G-1, Lakkari Tar Pits, Next to northeast tar pit

KAROLEK
Expert Leatherworker, Orgrimmar (60), H-4, The Drag, Kodohide Leatherworkers

KAROS RAZOK
Bat Handler, Silverpine Forest (68), G-4, The Sepulcher (124), Left of road heading into sepulcher

KARREL GRAYVES
Tirisfal Glades (86), D-6, Deathknell (109)

KARRINA MEKENDA
Pet Trainer, Stormwind (72), I-2, Dwarven District, Building south of tram entrance

KARTOSH
Warlock Trainer, Swamp of Sorrows (76), F-5, Stonard (126), Second floor of main hall

KARTRA BLOODSNARL
Alterac Valley Battlemaster, Orgrimmar (60), J-3, Valley of Honor

KARUS
Banker, Orgrimmar (60), F-7, Valley of Strength

KARY THUNDERHORN
Hunter Trainer, Thunder Bluff (84), G-9, Hunter Rise, Inside Hunter's Hall

KASHOCH THE REAVER
Rare Spawn, Winterspring (98), I-7, Frostwhisper Gorge, Lvl 60 Average Rare; Guards tower in gorge

KASKK
Rare Spawn, Desolace (30), F-7, G:(7-8), Mannoroc Coven, Lvl 40 Very Rare; Patrols spawn points

KAT SAMPSON
Leather Armor Merchant, Loch Modan (54), K-6, The Farstrider Lodge, In left center of lodge

KATAR
Swamp of Sorrows (76), K-7, Misty Reed Strand, Just above banks near Misty Reed Post

KATHERINE THE PURE
Paladin Trainer, Stormwind (72), F-3, Cathedral Square, Cathedral of Light

KATHRUM AXEHAND
Axe Merchant, Stormwind (72), H-1, Dwarven District, Northwest Building

KATIE HUNTER
Horse Breeder, Elwynn Forest (42), L-6, Eastvale Logging Camp, Corale

KATIS
Wand Merchant, Orgrimmar (60), E-5, The Cleft of Shadow, Ironwood Staves and Wands

KATOOM THE ANGLER
Trainer/Fishing Trainer and Supplies, The Hinterlands (50), L-8, Revantusk Village, On crate on docka

KATRINA ALLIESTAR
Herbalism Supplier, Undercity (88), H-5, The Apothecarium, Near War Quarter entry

KAWNIE SOFTBREEZE
General Goods, Mulgore (58), E-8, Camp Narache (105), North tent

KAYA FLATHOOF
Stonetalon Mountains (70), J-8, Grimtotem Post, Western hut

KAYLA SMITHE
Demon Trainer, Tirisfal Glades (86), C-7, Deathknell (109), Church

KAYNETH STILLWIND
Ashenvale (12), K-4, Forest Song, Northwest of Forest Song

KAYREN SOOTHALLOW
General Goods, Hillsbrad Foothills (48), H-2, Tarren Mill (128), Outside of inn

KAZAN MOGOSH
Food & Drink Merchant, Dun Morogh (32), I-5, Gol'Bolar Quarry, Patrols kitchen area of camp

KAZKAZ THE UNHOLY
Swamp of Sorrows (76), I-5, The Temple of Atal'Hakkar

KAZON
Rare Spawn, Redridge Mountains (62), D-1, Render's Camp, Lvl 27 Uncommon; Idle by hut

KEBOK
Stranglethorn Vale (74), B-8, Booty Bay (103), Third floor of The Salty Sailor Tavern

KEEG GIBN
Ale & Wine, Dun Morogh (32), D-5, Brewnall Village, By caravan

KEENA
Trade Goods, Arathi Highlands (10), J-3, Hammerfall (113), First floor north building

KEEPER ALBAGORM
Stonetalon Mountains (70), D-1, Stonetalon Peak, Next to moonwell

KEEPER BEL'DUGUR
Undercity (88), G-5, The Apothecarium, In front of bridge

KEEPER BEL'VARIL
Hillsbrad Foothills (48), G-2, Tarren Mill (128), House on the right side

KEEPER MARANDIS
Hippogryph Master, Desolace (30), H-1, Nijel's Point (119), Building on southwestern hill

KEEPER ORDANUS
Ashenvale (12), H-5, Raynewood Retreat, Top floor of building

KEEPER REMULOS
Moonglade (56), E-4, Shrine of Remulos, Next to tree

KEGAN DARKMAR
Alterac Mountains (8), B-8, Lordamere Internment Camp, Third floor of building west of camp

KEINA
Bowyer, Teldrassil (80), H-4, Shadowglen (124), Open room in front of main building

KELDAS
Pet Trainer, Teldrassil (80), G-6, Dolanaar (109), East of inn

KELDRAN
Orgrimmar (60), D-6, Talon Gate, Near South Fury River entrance

KELDRIC BOUCHER
Arcane Goods Vendor, Stormwind (72), H-6, Trade District, Pestle's Apothecary

KELEK SKYKEEPER
Emerald Circle, Felwood (44), G-8, Emerald Sanctuary, Between tent and building

KELGRUK BLOODAXE
Weapon Crafter, Orgrimmar (60), J-2, Valley of Honor, Arms of Legend

KELLY GRANT
Stormwind (72), C-5, The Park, Roams park

KELM HARGUNTH
Warsong Supply Officer, Barrens (18), E-1, Mor'shan Base Camp, Outside entrance to Warsong Gulch

KELOMIR IRONHAND
Maces & Staves, Ironforge (52), H-9, The Military Ward, Timberline Arms

KELSEY YANCE
Cook, Stranglethorn Vale (74), B-8, Booty Bay (103), Good Food (shop) on the northern side of The Old Port Authority

KELSTRUM STONEBREAKER
Warrior Trainer, Ironforge (52), I-9, The Military Ward, Hall of Arms

KELSUWA
Stable Master, Barrens (18), F-6, Camp Taurajo (106), Outside inn

KELT THOMASIN
Loch Modan (54), K-6, The Farstrider Lodge, In left rear of lodge

KELV STERNHAMMER
Warrior Trainer, Ironforge (52), J-9, The Military Ward, Hall of Arms

KENATA DABYRIE
Arathi Highlands (10), H-4, Dabyrie's Farmstead, House on hill

KENDOR KABONKA
Master of Cooking Recipes, Stormwind (72), J-5, Old Town, Pig and Whistle Tavern

KEN'JAI
Priest Trainer, Durotar (34), F-7, Valley of Trials (131)

KENNAH HAWKSEYE
Gunsmith, Mulgore (58), E-6, Bloodhoof Village (102), Northeast tent

KEN'ZIGLA
Stonetalon Mountains (70), I-9, Malaka'jin, Next to shack

KER RAGETOTEM
Warrior Trainer, Thunder Bluff (84), G-8, Hunter Rise, Inside Hunter's Hall

KERGUL BLOODAXE
Warsong Gulch Battlemaster, Thunder Bluff (84), G-8, Hunter Rise, Between bridges in a tent

KERLONIAN EVERSHADE
Druid of the Claw, Darkshore (24), G-8, Grove of the Ancients, Sleeping in clearing near the water

KERNOBEE
Dun Morogh (32), C-4, Gnomeregan

KERR IRONSIGHT
The Hinterlands (50), C-5, Aerie Peak (100), First floor of tower

KERSOK PROND
Tradesman, Wetlands (96), A-6, Deepwater Tavern, Next to stairs

KERYN SYLVIUS
Rogue Trainer, Elwynn Forest (42), F-7, Goldshire (112), Second floor of Lion's Pride Inn

KHAELYN STEELWING
Gryphon Master, Eastern Plaguelands (40), K-6, Light's Hope Chapel (116), Camp on right side of chapel

KHAN DEZ'HEPAH
Desolace (30), J:(4-5), Kolkar Village, Big hut or landing

KHAN HRATHA
Desolace (30), C-5, Valley of Spears, (Summon) Under stone bridge

KHAN JEHN
Desolace (30), I-8, Magram Village, Big hut

KHAN SHAKA
Desolace (30), E-9, Bolgan's Hole, Deep in caverns

KHARA DEEPWATER
Fishing Supplies, Loch Modan (54), E-4, The Loch, On porch of house on the western shore of loch

KHARAN MIGHTHAMMER
Burning Steppes (22), Searing Gorge (64), C-4/D-8, Blackrock Depths

KHARDAN PROUDBLADE
Weaponsmith, Teldrassil (80), G-4, H-4, Shadowglen (124), Inside main building

KHAREDON
Light Armor Merchant, Moonglade (56), H-3, Nighthaven (120), First floor of far northeast building on hill

KHELDEN BREMEN
Mage Trainer, Elwynn Forest (42), G-4, Northshire Valley (120), Second floor of abbey

KIBLER
Burning Steppes (22), H-2, Flame Crest, Cave

KIERAN
Weapon Merchant, Darnassus (26), I-6, Tradesmen's Terrace, Weapons shop, second floor

KIKNIKLE
Stylish Clothier, Barrens (18), E-4, Near mountains west of oasis

KILDAR
Wolf Riding Instructor, Orgrimmar (60), I-1, Valley of Honor, Outside of Hunter's Hall

KIL'HALA
Journeyman Tailor, Barrens (18), F-3, The Crossroads (107), Southern entrance

KIL'HIWANA
Fisherman, Ashenvale (12), B-4, Zoram'gar Outpost (131), Near coast

KILLIAN HAGEY
Skinning Trainer, Undercity (88), J-6, The Rogues' Quarter

KILLIAN SANATHA
Fisherman, Silverpine Forest (68), E-2, North Tide's Run, Camp along shoreline

KILLIUM BOULDERTOE
Stable Master, The Hinterlands (50), B-5, Aerie Peak (100), Wildhammer Keep

KILRAM
Winterspring (98), I-4, Everlook (110), North building

KILXX
Fisherman, Barrens (18), H-4, Ratchet (121), Near dock

KIMBERLY GRANT
Stormwind (72), C-5, The Park, Roams park

KIMBERLY HIETT
Fletcher, Redridge Mountains (62), C-4, Lakeshire (115), First floor of Lakeshire Inn

KIM'JAEL
Azshara (14), G-2, Legash Encampment, Camp atop tor

KINDAL MOONWEAVER
Feralas (46), H-4, Lower Wilds, In hills overlooking Grimtotem Compound

KINELORY
Arathi Highlands (10), H-5, Go'Shek Farm, Hill northwest of farm

KING BANGALASH
Stranglethorn Vale (74), D-4, Roams small area around spawn point

KING GORDOK
Feralas (46), G-4, Dire Maul

KING MAGNI BRONZEBEARD
Lord of Ironforge, Ironforge (52), E-5, The Great Forge, The High Seat

KING MOSH
Un'Goro Crater (90), D:(3-5), E:(3-4), Golakka Hot Springs, Spawns in different spots north of springs

KING MUKLA
Stranglethorn Vale (74), D-9, Jaguero Isle, Roams small area around spawn point

KING TERENAS MENETHRILL II
King's Tomb, Undercity (88), I-4, Ruins of Lordaeron

KIN'WEELAY
Stranglethorn Vale (74), C-3, Grom'gol Base Camp (112), To the left of forge

KIRA SONGSHINE
Traveling Baker, Elwynn Forest (42), F-7, Goldshire (112), Patrols between the Gates of Stormwind and the two roads in southern Goldshire

KIREENA
Trade Goods, Desolace (30), G-5, Ghost Walker Post (111), Western hut

KIRGE STERNHORN
Barrens (18), E-6, Camp Taurajo (106), North of road

KIRITH THE DAMNED
Blasted Lands (20), J-3, Serpent's Coil, Cave interior

KIRK MAXWELL
Stable Master, Westfall (94), F-5, Sentinel Hill (123), Outside Inn

KIRO
War Harness Maker, Orgrimmar (60), I-4, Valley of Honor, Kiro's Harnesses

KIRSTA DEEPSHADOW
Western Plaguelands (92), G-3, Northridge Lumber Camp, Kneeling by carriage along path to the northeast of camp

KIRTONOS THE HERALD
Western Plaguelands (92), I-7, Scholomance

KITHA
Demon Trainer, Durotar (34), H-4, Razor Hill (122), Behind barracks

KITHAS
Enchanting Supplier, Orgrimmar (60), F-4, The Drag, Godan's Runeworks

KITTA FIREWIND
Artisan Enchanter, Elwynn Forest (42), I-7, Tower of Azora, Top floor of tower

KIXXLE
Potions & Herbs, Wetlands (96), G-4, Next to road to Dun Modr, by bridge

KIZZ BLUNTSTRIKE
Macecrafter, Stranglethorn Vale (74), B-8, Booty Bay (103), Cuts-n-Bruises Incorporated (shop) on the southern side of The Old Port Authority

KLANNOC MACLEOD
Barrens (18), H-5, Fray Island, Outside southern building

KLAVEN MORTWAKE
Westfall (94), I-7, The Dust Plains, Top of tower

KLOCKMORT SPANNERSPAN
Ironforge (52), I-5, Tinker Town, Outside Springspindle's Gadgets

KNAZ BLUNDERFLAME
Engineering Supplies, Stranglethorn Vale (74), F-4, Outside of gnomish workshop

KNOT THIMBLEJACK
Feralas (46), G-4, Dire Maul

KOBOLD DIGGER
Westfall (94), E-2, Gold Coast Quarry

KOBOLD GEOMANCER
Elwynn Forest (42), H-6, I-6, Jasperlode Mine

KOBOLD MINER
Elwynn Forest (42), H:(5, 6), I:(5, 6), Fargodeep Mine, Jasperlode Mine

KOBOLD TUNNELER
Elwynn Forest (42), E:(8, 9), Fargodeep Mine, The Maclure Vineyards, The Stonefield Farm

KOBOLD VERMIN
Elwynn Forest (42), F:(3, 4), G-4, Echo Ridge Mine, Northshire Valley (120)

KOBOLD WORKER
Elwynn Forest (42), F:(3, 4), G:(3, 4), Echo Ridge Mine, Northshire Valley (120)

KODO BULL
Mulgore (58), C:(2, 3), D:(4, 7), E-2, G-2

KODO CALF
Mulgore (58), C:(2, 3), D:(4, 7), E-2, G-2

KODO MATRIARCH
Mulgore (58), C:(2, 3), D:(4, 7), E-2, G-2

KODO SPIRIT
Desolace (30), F-6, G-6, Kodo Graveyard, Southwest in graveyard

KOITER
Fallen Hero, Twincruiser, Barrens (18), E-3, Shrine of the Fallen Warrior, North of Wailing Caverns, south of road

KOLKAR AMBUSHER
Desolace (30), I:(4, 5), Kolkar Village

KOLKAR BATTLE LORD
Desolace (30), I:(4, 5), J:(4, 5), Kolkar Village

KOLKAR BLOODCHARGER
Barrens (18), E-4, F-4, G:(4, 5), Lushwater Oasis, The Stagnant Oasis, The Wailing Caverns

KOLKAR CENTAUR
Desolace (30), I:(4, 5), J:(4, 5), Kolkar Village

KOLKAR DESTROYER
Desolace (30), I:(4, 5), J:(4, 5), Kolkar Village

KOLKAR DRUDGE
Durotar (34), G-8, H-8, Darkspear Strand, Kolkar Crag

KOLKAR INVADER
Barrens (18), E-3, The Crossroads (107), The Forgotten Pools

KOLKAR MARAUDER
Barrens (18), F:(4, 5), G:(4, 5), Lushwater Oasis, The Stagnant Oasis

KOLKAR MAULER
Desolace (30), I:(4, 5), J:(4, 5), Kolkar Village

KOLKAR OUTRUNNER
Durotar (34), G-8, Kolkar Crag

KOLKAR PACK RUNNER
Barrens (18), E-4, F-4, G:(4, 5), Lushwater Oasis, The Stagnant Oasis

KOLKAR PACKHOUND
Barrens (18), E-4, F-4, G:(4, 5), Lushwater Oasis, The Stagnant Oasis

KOLKAR SCOUT
Desolace (30), I:(4, 5), J:(4, 5), Kolkar Village

KOLKAR STORMER
Barrens (18), E:(2-4), F-4, G-4, The Forgotten Pools, Lushwater Oasis, The Stagnant Oasis

KOLKAR STORMSEER
Barrens (18), E-3, The Forgotten Pools

KOLKAR WAYLAYER
Desolace (30), I:(4, 5), Kolkar Village

KOLKAR WINDCHASER
Desolace (30), I:(4, 5), J:(4, 5), Kolkar Village

KOLKAR WRANGLER
Barrens (18), E:(2-4), F-4, The Forgotten Pools, Lushwater Oasis

KOMA
Banker, Orgrimmar (60), F-7, Valley of Strength

KOMIN WINTERHOOF
Herbalism Trainer, Thunder Bluff (84), F-4, Middle rise, in Holistic Herbalism tent

KON YELLOWEYES
Thunder Bluff (84), G-8, Hunter Rise, In front of Hunter's Hall

KONDA
Stranglethorn Vale (74), C-7, Mistvale Valley, (Summon) Spawns in with several gorillas

KOR'GELD
Alchemy Supplier, Orgrimmar (60), G-3, The Drag, Yelmak's Alchemy and Potions

KOR'GRESH COLDRAGE
Arathi Highlands (10), G-8, Boulderfist Hall, Inside lower of two caves at Boulderfist Hall

KOR'JUS
Mushroom Vendor, Orgrimmar (60), E-5, The Cleft of Shadow, Darkearth Fungus and Mushrooms

KOR'GHAN
Orgrimmar (60), F-5, The Drag, In building above Dark Earth Fungus and Mushrooms

KORIN FEL
Arathi Highlands (10), J-3, Hammerfall (113), Platform of north building

KORRA
Ashenvale (12), E-5, Astranaar (101), First floor of inn near Raene

KORRAN
Barrens (18), F-3, The Crossroads (107), Western entrance

KORU
Mace and Staff Vendor, Orgrimmar (60), J-2, Valley of Honor, Arms of Legend, second floor

KOVORK
Rare Spawn, Arathi Highlands (10), D-5, Boulderfist Outpost, Lvl 36 Uncommon; Inside cave at Boulder'gor

KOZISH
Orgrimmar (60), G-7, Valley of Strength, Inn

KRAGG
Hunter Trainer, Stranglethorn Vale (74), C-3, Grom'gol Base Camp (112), Just inside camp walls to the left of western entrance

KRAH'RANIK
Darkshore (24), J-2, Hut, northeast of lake

KRAK
Armorer, Dustwallow Marsh (38), D-3, Brackenwall Village (104), Northern part of village

KRAKK
Superior Armorer, Stranglethorn Vale (74), C-3, Grom'gol Base Camp (112), Next to anvil by forge

KRAKLE
Un'Goro Crater (90), D-5, Golakka Hot Springs, West of big spring, next to big rock

KRAKLE'S THERMOMETER
Un'Goro Crater (90), F-5, G:(4-5), H-5, Fire Plume Ridge, Found in a few spots on ridge

KRANAL FISS
Barrens (18), G-2, Grol'dom Farm, Roams outside tower east of farm

KRANG STONEHOOF
Warrior Trainer, Mulgore (58), F-6, Bloodhoof Village (102), Combat ground east of village

KRATHOK MOLTENFIST
Orgrimmar (60), J-2, Valley of Honor, Across from Arms of Legend

KRAUL BAT
Barrens (18), E-9, Razorfen Kraul

KRAVEL KOALBEARD
Thousand Needles (82), K-8, Mirage Raceway (118), West of racetrack

KRAY
Journeyman Alchemist, Thunder Bluff (84), E-3, Middle rise, inside Bena's Alchemy tent

KRAZEK
Stranglethorn Vale (74), B-8, Booty Bay (103), Third floor of The Salty Sailor Tavern

KREENIG SNARLSNOUT
Barrens (18), G-3, Thorn Hill, Roams northeast side of hill

KREG BILMN
General Supplies, Dun Morogh (32), F-5, Kharanos (114), Thunderbrew Distillery

KREGG KEELHAUL
Rare Spawn, Tanaris (78), J-5, K-5, Lost Rigger Cove, Lvl 47 Uncommon; In west building, ship being built, or far ship at dock

KRELDIG UNGOR
Reclaimers Inc., Desolace (30), I-1, Nijel's Point (119), Between paths leading to flight point and inn

KRELLACK
Rare Spawn, Silithus (66), G-2, Southwind Village, Lvl 56 Semi-Rare; Roams close to spawn points

KRESH
Barrens (18), E-4, Wailing Caverns

KRETHIS SHADOWSPINNER
Rare Spawn, Silverpine Forest (68), E-1, The Skittering Dark, Lvl 15 Uncommon; Roaming in or around cave

KRIGGON TALSONE
Fisherman, Westfall (94), D-9, Longshore, Dock on southern tip of jutty

KRINKLE GOODSTEEL
Blacksmithing Supplies, Tanaris (78), H-3, Gadgetzan (111), Near southern entrance

KRIS LEGACE
Freewheeling Tradeswoman, Hillsbrad Foothills (48), J-4, Durnholde Keep, Just below rear of ruins in the upper level of keep

KRISS GOLDENLIGHT
Eastern Plaguelands (40), G-3, Northpass Tower, Tower

KRISTY GRANT
Feralas (46), K-5, Thalanaar, Roaming northwest of well

KROG
Dustwallow Marsh (38), D-3, Brackenwall Village (104), Center of village

KROLG
Ashenvale (12), G-7, Mystral Lake, South near mountain inlet

KROM STOUTARM
Ironforge (52), J-1, Hall of Explorers, The Library

KROM'GRUL
Rare Spawn, Burning Steppes (22), J:(4, 5), K:(4, 5), Dreadmaul Rock, Lvl 54 Common; Roams small area around spawn point

KROND
Butcher, Stonetalon Mountains (70), E-6, Sun Rock Retreat (127), Western building

KROSHIUS
Felwood (44), F-4, Shatter Scar Vale, North of the eastern crater

KROUM
Wind Rider Master, Azshara (14), B-5, Valormok, North of camp

KRUEG SKULLSPLITTER
Feralas (46), I-4, Camp Mojache (105), Next to tent, east of water

KRULMOO FULLMOON
Expert Leatherworker, Barrens (18), F-6, Camp Taurajo (106), Southern building

KRUMN
Guild Master, Thunder Bluff (84), D-6, Lower rise, in Thunder Bluff Civic Information tent

KRUNN
Miner, Durotar (34), H-4, Razor Hill (122), Northeast of inn

KRUSK
Hillsbrad Foothills (48), H-2, Tarren Mill (128), Church

KUL TIRAS MARINE
Durotar (34), H:(5, 6), I:(5, 6), Scuttle Coast, Tiragarde Keep

KUL TIRAS SAILOR
Durotar (34), H:(5, 6), I:(5, 6), Scuttle Coast, Tiragarde Keep

KULLEG STONEHORN
Skinning Trainer, Feralas (46), I-4, Camp Mojache (105), Big western tent

KULWIA
Trade Supplies, Stonetalon Mountains (70), E-6, Sun Rock Retreat (127), South of western structure

KUM'ISHA THE COLLECTOR
Blasted Lands (20), H-4, Rise of the Defiler, Behind ruins wall

KUNA THUNDERHORN
Bowyer & Fletching Goods, Thunder Bluff (84), E-4, Middle rise, inside Thunderhorn's Archery tent

KUNDRIC ZANDEN
Hillsbrad Foothills (48), E-5, Southshore (125), Church

KURAY'BIN
Ashenvale (12), I-6, Splintertree Post (126), Foot of outlying watch tower near road

KURDEN BLOODCLAW
Warsong Gulch Battlemaster, Undercity (88), H-9, Royal Quarter

KURDRAM STONEHAMMER
Mining Trainer, Darkshore (24), F-4, Auberdine (101), In front of northern building

KURDROS
Hillsbrad Foothills (48), K-3, Durnholde Keep, Roams a small area northeast of keep

KURGUL
Demon Trainer, Orgrimmar (60), E-5, F-5, The Cleft of Shadow, Darkfire Enclave

KURLL
Food & Drink, Azshara (14), B-5, Valormok, Bivouac

KURM STONEHOOF
Mining Supplier, Thunder Bluff (84), C-6, Lower rise, inside Stonehoof Geology tent

KURMOKK
Rare Spawn, Stranglethorn Vale (74), D-6, Ruins of Aboraz, Lvl 42 Very Rare; Patrols through Mistvale Valley toward the road heading into Booty Bay

KURRAN STEELE
Cloth & Leather Armor Merchant, Elwynn Forest (42), E-6, Goldshire (112), Smithy

KURUK
General Goods, Thunder Bluff (84), D-6, Lower rise, inside Kuruk's Goods tent

KURZEN COMMANDO
Stranglethorn Vale (74), E-1, Kurzen's Compound

KURZEN HEADSHRINKER
Stranglethorn Vale (74), E-1, Kurzen's Compound

KURZEN JUNGLE FIGHTER
Stranglethorn Vale (74), E:(1, 2), Kurzen's Compound

KURZEN MEDICINE MAN
Stranglethorn Vale (74), E:(1, 2), Kurzen's Compound

KURZEN MINDSLAVE
Mogh the Undying's Minion, Stranglethorn Vale (74), E-5, Ruins of Zul'Mamwe, (Summon) By campfire

KURZEN WAR PANTHER
Stranglethorn Vale (74), E-1, The Stockpile

KURZEN WAR TIGER
Stranglethorn Vale (74), E-1, The Stockpile

KURZEN WITCH DOCTOR
Stranglethorn Vale (74), E-1, The Stockpile

KURZEN WRANGLER
Stranglethorn Vale (74), E-1, The Stockpile

KURZEN'S AGENT
Stranglethorn Vale (74), D-1, (Summon) Two agents spawn in near the path leading to the Rebel Camp

KUZ
Barrens (18), E-8, Blackthorn Ridge, Roams the ridge

K'WAII
General Goods, Durotar (34), H-7, Sen'jin Village (123), Main floor of big hut

KYLANNA
Expert Alchemist, Ashenvale (12), G-6, Silverwind Refuge, Left wing of building

KYLANNA WINDWHISPER
Master Alchemist, Feralas (46), C-4, Feathermoon Stronghold (110), Bottom floor of tree building in northeast

KYM WILDMANE
Druid Trainer, Thunder Bluff (84), I-3, Elder Rise, Inside Hall of Elders

KYNDRI
Baker, Darkshore (24), F-4, Auberdine (101), First floor of inn

KYRA BOUCHER
Reagent Vendor, Stormwind (72), H-6, Trade District, Pestle's Apothecary

KYRA WINDBLADE
Warrior Trainer, Teldrassil (80), G-6, Dolanaar (109), Inn

KYRAI
Poison Vendor, Darnassus (26), D-2, Cenarion Enclave, Southwest structure

KZAN THORNSLASH
Weaponsmith, Durotar (34), F-7, Valley of Trials (131)

KZIXX
Rare Goods, Duskwood (36), K-2, By carriage

L

LADY ANACONDRA
Barrens (18), E-4, Wailing Caverns

LADY HEDERINE
Rare Spawn, Winterspring (98), H-8, Darkwhisper Gorge, Lvl 61 Very Rare; Deep within the gorge

LADY ILLUCIA BAROV
Western Plaguelands (92), I-7, Scholomance

LADY JAINA PROUDMOORE
Ruler of Theramore, Dustwallow Marsh (38), I-5, Theramore Isle (130), Top of central tower

LADY KATRANA PRESTOR
Stormwind (72), L-2, Stormwind Keep, Center of east wing

LADY MOONGAZER
Darkshore (24), F-6, G-6, Ameth'Aran, Roams southern part of Ameth'Aran

LADY SAREVESS
Ashenvale (12), B-2, Blackfathom Deeps

LADY SATHRAH
Teldrassil (80), E-3, F-3, The Oracle Glade, Patrols north of The Oracle Glade east towards the hills

LADY SESSPIRA
Rare Spawn, Azshara (14), D-5, Ruins of Eldarath, Lvl 51 Uncommon; Patrols the ruins

LADY SEVINE
Blasted Lands (20), F-3, Altar of Storms, Rear of altar on right side

LADY SYLVANUS WINDRUNNER
Boss, Banshee Queen, Undercity (88), H-9, Royal Quarter, In Throne room

LADY SZALLAH
Rare Spawn, Feralas (46), B-7, Isle of Dread, Lvl 46 Uncommon; Roams various areas outside of Shalzaru's Lair

LADY VESPIA
Rare Spawn, Ashenvale (12), B:(2-3), The Zoram Strand (131), Lvl 22 Uncommon; Roams coastline

LADY VESPIRA
Rare Spawn, Darkshore (24), I-2, Ruins of Mathystra, Lvl 22 Semi-Rare; Roams throughout ruins

LADY ZEPHRIS
Rare Spawn, Hillsbrad Foothills (48), H-9, Eastern Strand, Lvl 33 Uncommon; Patrols southeastern coastline

LAER STEPPERUNNER
Food & Drink, Thousand Needles (82), B-3, Whitereach Post, Next to hut

LAGO BLACKWRENCH
Ironforge (52), F-1, The Forlorn Cavern, Outside Traveling Fisherman

LAH'MAWHANI
Trade Supplies, Desolace (30), B-7, Shadowprey Village (125), Down by dock

LAIRD
Fish Vendor, Darkshore (24), F-4, Auberdine (101), First floor of inn

LAIRN
Banker, Darnassus (26), D-4, Bank

LAKE CREEPER
Silverpine Forest (68), K-3, L:(2, 3), The Dawning Isles

LAKE FRENZY
Silverpine Forest (68), I:(2-4), J:(2, 4), K:(1, 4), L:(1-3), Lordamere Lake

LAKE SKULKER
Silverpine Forest (68), J:(3, 4), K:(3, 4), Fenris Isle

LAKOTA WINDSONG
Thousand Needles (82), E-3, Darkcloud Pinnacle, On northern cliff, north of Darkcloud Pinnacle

LAKOTA'MANI
Barrens (18), E-5, F-5, Agama'gor, Bramblescar, Patrols across Southern Gold Road

LALINA SUMMERMOON
Journeyman Enchanter, Darnassus (26), H-1, Craftsmen's Terrace, Enchanting shop

LAMAR VEISILLI
Fruit Seller, Redridge Mountains (62), B-5, Lakeshire (115), Behind small house on southwestern side of town

LAND RAGER
Tanaris (78), E:(5, 6), F:(5-7), G:(4, 5), I:(5, 6)

LAND WALKER
Feralas (46), D:(2, 3), Ruins of Ravenwind, The Twin Colossals

LANDRIA
Bow Merchant, Darnassus (26), H-6, Tradesmen's Terrace, Fletcher

LANDSLIDE
Desolace (30), D-5, Mauradon

LANIE REED
Gryphon Master, Searing Gorge (64), D-3, Thorium Point, Ridgeline outcropping southeast of camp

LANKA FARSHOT
Hunter Trainer, Mulgore (58), E-8, Camp Narache (105), Main tent (north)

LANTI'GAH
Barrens (18), E-3, Roams road west of Crossroads

LAPRESS
Rare Spawn, Silithus (66), G-5, Hive'Regal, Lvl 60 Very Rare; Spawns in far southeast of hive and roams hive

LAR PROWLTUSK
Durotar (34), H-7, Sen'jin Village (123), Between two rocks west of the village

LARA MOORE
Leather Armor Merchant, Stormwind (72), H:(5, 6), Trade District, Lionheart Armory

LARD
Innkeeper, The Hinterlands (50), L-8, Revantusk Village, First floor of inn on eastern side of village

LARDAN
Leatherworking Supplies, Ashenvale (12), E-5, Astranaar (101), Second floor library of northwest building (south of road)

LARGE CRAG BOAR
Dun Morogh (32), D-5, E:(3, 5), F:(3-6), G:(4-6), H-5, I-5

LARGE VILE SLIME
Western Plaguelands (92), H:(3, 4), I:(3, 4), The Weeping Cave

LARHKA
Beverage Merchant, Barrens (18), F-3, The Crossroads (107), Inn

LARIIA
Priest Trainer, Darnassus (26), E-9, The Temple of the Moon, South of fountain

LARIMAINE PURDUE
Portal Trainer, Stormwind (72), F-8, Mage Quarter, Wizard's Sanctum

LARION
Un'Goro Crater (90), F-1, Marshal's Refuge (116), South of cave

LARIS GEARDAWDLE
Ironforge (52), K-2, Hall of Explorers, The Library

LAR'KORWI
Un'Goro Crater (90), K-5, The Marshlands, (Summon) Attacks uphill into clearing

LAR'KORWI MATE
Un'Goro Crater (90), H:(5-8), I:(5-8), J:(5, 6), The Marshlands

LARS
Duskwood (36), A-3, The Hushed Bank, Camp

LASHTAIL RAPTOR
Stranglethorn Vale (74), C:(2, 3), D:(2, 3)

LATHERION
Barrens (18), F-6, Southern Barrens

LATHORIC THE BLACK
Searing Gorge (64), E-3, The Slag Pit, (Summon) Spawns next to Obsidion

LATRONICUS MOONSPEAR
Feralas (46), C-5, Feathermoon Stronghold (110), Southwest building

LAUGHING SISTER
Ashenvale (12), G:(5, 6), H:(5, 6), Nightsong Woods, Raynewood Retreat

LAUREN NEWCOMB
Light Armor Merchant, Undercity (88), I-4, The Trade Quarter, Upper Ring of Trade Quarter

LAURNA MORNINGLIGHT
Priest Trainer, Teldrassil (80), G-6, Dolanaar (109), Bottom floor inside building north of road

LAU'TIKI
Fisherman, Durotar (34), H-8, Darkspear Strand, Structure on coast

LAVA ANNIHILATOR
Burning Steppes (22), Searing Gorge (64), C-4/D-8, The Molten Core

LAVA CRAB
Burning Steppes (22), A-3, B-4, C:(5, 6), D:(3, 5-7), E:(4, 5), F:(5, 6), G:(5, 6), H:(3, 4), I:(3, 4), J:(3-5, 7), Found near lava pools and streams Searing Gorge (64), C:(3, 4, 6, 7), D:(4, 7, 8), E:(3-6), F:(5, 6), G:(4, 5, 7, 8), Near lava pools

LAVA ELEMENTAL
Burning Steppes (22), Searing Gorge (64), C-4/D-8, The Molten Core

LAVA REAVER
Burning Steppes (22), Searing Gorge (64), C-4/D-8, The Molten Core

LAVA SPAWN
Burning Steppes (22), Searing Gorge (64), C-4/D-8, The Molten Core

LAVA SURGER
Burning Steppes (22), Searing Gorge (64), C-4/D-8, The Molten Core

LAVINIA CROWE
Expert Enchanter, Undercity (88), I-6, The Apothecarium, Near Rogues' Quarter entry

LAWRENCE SCHNEIDER
Journeyman Tailor, Stormwind (72), G-7, Mage Quarter, Duncan's Textiles

LAYO STARSTRIKE
The Cenarion Circle, Silithus (66), I-1, Valor's Rest, Hut south of road

LAZIPHUS
Stable Master, Tanaris (78), H-3, Gadgetzan (111), Outside inn

LAZY PEON
Durotar (34), F-6, G:(6, 7), Valley of Trials (131), Sleeping or working around trees

LEE BROWN
Fisherman, Elwynn Forest (42), F-6, Crystal Lake, Dock

LEECH STALKER
Wetlands (96), F-6, G:(6, 7), H:(6, 7), Dun Algaz, Mosshide Fen

LEECH WIDOW
Rare Spawn, Wetlands (96), G-6, Thelgen Rock, Lvl 24 Uncommon; Patrols southwest area of cave

LEGACKI
Winterspring (98), I-4, Everlook (110), East of inn

LEGASHI HELLCALLER
Azshara (14), F-2, G-2, H:(2, 3), I-2, Bitter Reaches, Legash Encampment, Thalassian Base Camp

LEGASHI ROGUE
Azshara (14), F-2, G-2, H:(2, 3), I-2, Legash Encampment, Thalassian Base Camp, The Shattered Strand

LEGASHI SATYR
Azshara (14), F-2, G-2, H:(2, 3), I-2, Legash Encampment, Thalassian Base

LEGION HOUND
Ashenvale (12), J:(7, 8), K-7, Demon Fall Canyon

LELANAI
Saber Handler, Darnassus (26), E-1, Cenarion Enclave, Intersection of paths

LENNY "FINGERS" MCCOY
Stormwind (72), J-4, Old Town, Across from the Five Deadly Venoms

LEO SARN
Enchanting Supplies, Silverpine Forest (68), H-8, Camp

LEONA THARPE
Undercity (88), G-3, The War Quarter, By Mining Trainer, Close to Canal

LEONARD PORTER
Leatherworking Supplies, Western Plaguelands (92), F-8, Chillwind Camp, Behind ruined house

LEONID BARTHALOMEW THE REVERED
The Argent Dawn, Eastern Plaguelands (40), K-6, Light's Hope Chapel (116), Patrols in and out of chapel

LEPER GNOME
Dun Morogh (32), C-4, Frostmane Hold, Gnomeregan

LEPRITHUS
Rare Spawn, Westfall (94), D-3, G-8, The Dust Plains, Lvl 19 Uncommon; Appears near coffin/tombstones under tree

LEPROUS ASSISTANT
Dun Morogh (32), C-4, Gnomeregan

LEPROUS DEFENDER
Dun Morogh (32), C-4, Gnomeregan

LEPROUS MACHINESMITH
Dun Morogh (32), C-4, Gnomeregan

LEPROUS TECHNICIAN
Dun Morogh (32), C-4, Gnomeregan

LESSER FELGUARD
Ashenvale (12), C-6, D-6, Fire Scar Shrine

LESSER INFERNAL
Desolace (30), F:(7, 8), G:(7, 8), Mannoroc Coven

LESSER ROCK ELEMENTAL
Badlands (16), B-4, C:(4, 5), D-5, The Dustbowl, Hill Side

LESSER WATER ELEMENTAL
Stranglethorn Vale (74), A:(2, 3), B-3, The Savage Coast, The Vile Reef

LETHLAS
Feralas (46), F-1, Dream Bough, Roams small land mass

LETHTENDRIS
Feralas (46), G-4, Dire Maul

LEXINGTON MORTAIM
Portal Trainer, Undercity (88), L-1, The Magic Quarter, On Skull Building

LEXLORT
Badlands (16), A-5, Kargath (114), Tower platform

LEY HUNTER
Desolace (30), F-8, G-8, J-7, K-8, Mannoroc Coven, Shadowbreak Ravine

LEY SPRITE
Deadwind Pass (28), D:(6-8), E:(6, 8), Karazhan, Sleeping Gorge

LIBRARIAN MAE PALEDUST
Explorers' League, Ironforge (52), J-1, Hall of Explorers, The Library

LICILLIN
Rare Spawn, Darkshore (24), G-4, Bashal'Aran, Lvl 14 Uncommon; Wanders through ruins

LIEUTENANT BENEDICT
Durotar (34), I-6, Tiragarde Keep, Receiving room of castle

LIEUTENANT DOREN
Stranglethorn Vale (74), D-1, Rebel Camp, Camp

LIEUTENANT FANGORE
Redridge Mountains (62), K-4, Galardell Valley, Roams small area around spawn point

LIEUTENANT FARREN ORINELLE
Hillsbrad Foothills (48), F-6, Southshore (125), First floor of inn

LIEUTENANT HAGGERDIN
Alterac Mountains (8), E-8, The Headland, Left camp outside Alterac Valley

LIEUTENANT ROTIMER
Stormpike Guard Recruitment Officer, Ironforge (52), E-6, The Commons, Outside Bank

LIEUTENANT SANDERS
Tirisfal Glades (86), L-4, Venomweb Vale, Patrols an arc around camp

LIEUTENANT VALORCALL
Arathi Highlands (10), G-4, Dabyrie's Farmstead, Patrols along road to Stromgarde Keep

LIGHTNING HIDE
Durotar (34), F:(2, 3), Thunder Ridge

LIL TIMMY
Boy with kittens, Stormwind (72), Cathedral Square, The Canals, Roams Cathedral Square and The Canals

LILADRIS MOONRIVER
Ashenvale (12), D-4, Maestra's Post, Back porch of outpost

LILITH THE LITHE
Winterspring (98), I-4, Everlook (110), Inside building directly north of inn

LILLIAM SPARKSPINDLE
Expert Engineer, Stormwind (72), H-1, Dwarven District, North end of district, by tent

LILLITH NEFARA
Tirisfal Glades (86), I-4, Brightwater Lake, (Summon) Spawns on small island in the center of Brightwater Lake

LILLY
Enchanting Supplies, Silverpine Forest (68), F-5, Camp

LILYN DARKRIVER
Ashenvale (12), C-5, Shrine of Aessina, Roams north side of Shrine

LILYSSIA NIGHTBREEZE
Expert Alchemist, Stormwind (72), G-8, Mage Quarter, Alchemy Needs

LINA HEARTHSTOVE
Stable Master, Loch Modan (54), D-5, Thelsamar (129), Outside of inn to the left of entrance

LINA STOVER
Bow & Gun Merchant, Stormwind (72), H-6, Trade District, The Empty Quiver

LINDEA RABONNE
Tackle and Bait, Hillsbrad Foothills (48), F-6, Southshore (125), On docks in front of shed

LINDROS
Azshara (14), H-9, The Ruined Reaches, Inlet

LINDSAY ASHLOCK
General Supplies, Redridge Mountains (62), C-5, Lakeshire (115), Next to caravan in front of Lakeshire Town Hall

LINGERING HIGHBORNE
Azshara (14), D:(4-6), E-5, Ruins of Eldarath, Temple of Zin-Malor

LINKEN
Un'Goro Crater (90), F-1, Marshal's Refuge (116), South of cave, next to hollowed out stump

LISAN PIERCE
Stormwind (72), F-8, Mage Quarter, Roams and sits by tower

LISBETH SCHNEIDER
Clothier, Stormwind (72), G:(5, 6), The Canals, Canal Tailor and Fit Shop

LISSYPHUS FINESPINDLE
Light Armor Merchant, Ironforge (52), G-9, The Military Ward, Craghelm's Plate and Chain

LIV RIZZLEFIX
Workshop Assistant, Barrens (18), H-4, Ratchet (121), Building near dock

LIVING BLAZE
Un'Goro Crater (90), F:(5, 6), G:(4-6), Fire Plume Ridge

LIVING DECAY
Eastern Plaguelands (40), G:(6, 7), H-6, I-6, J-6, Pestilent Scar

LIVING STORM
Tanaris (78), E:(6, 8), F-7

LIZBETH CROMWELL
Fishing Supplier, Undercity (88), K-3, The Magic Quarter, On Dock

LIZZARIK
Weapon Dealer, Barrens (18), G-4, Ratchet (121), South of road

LLANA
Reagent Supplies, Ashenvale (12), E-5, Astranaar (101), Northwest building (north of road)

LLANE BESHERE
Warrior Trainer, Elwynn Forest (42), G-4, Northshire Valley (120), Hall of Arms of abbey

LO'GROSH
Rare Spawn, Alterac Mountains (8), F-3, G-5, Crushridge Hold, Slaughter Hollow, Lvl 39 Average Rare; Roams small area around spawn point

LOCH CROCOLISK
Loch Modan (54), G:(2-6), H:(2-6), The Loch

LOCH FRENZY
Loch Modan (54), E:(2, 3), F:(1-3), G:(1-3), The Loch, In lake

LOCHEED
Searing Gorge (64), H-6, Grimesilt Dig Site, Wooden outhouse

LOCKE OKARR
Ashenvale (12), I-6, Splintertree Post (126), North of outlying watch tower near road

LOGANAAR
Druid Trainer, Moonglade (56), G-4, Nighthaven (120), Next to moonwell, by northern section of lake

LOGANNAS
Alchemy Supplies, Feralas (46), C-4, Feathermoon Stronghold (110), Bottom floor of tree building in northeast

LOH'ATU
Azshara (14), A-8, Talrendis Point, Tent

LOHGAN EVA
Tailoring Supplies, Duskwood (36), K-4, Darkshire (108), First floor of house

LOHGAN EVA *(corrected)*

LOK ORCBANE
Barrens (18), D-8, Blackthorn Ridge, Westernmost hut on ridges

LOKHTOS DARKBARGAINER
Burning Steppes (22), Searing Gorge (64), C-4/D-8, Blackrock Depths

LOLO THE LOOKOUT
Arathi Highlands (10), D-8, Faldir's Cove, Roams on hill opposite dock

LOMAC GEARSTRIP
Ironforge (52), J-5, Tinker Town, Outside tram entrance

LONGBRAID THE GRIM
Wetlands (96), G-2, Dun Modr, Next to wagons, west of road

LONGTOOTH HOWLER
Feralas (46), F-5, G-5, H:(5, 6), I:(5, 6)

LONGTOOTH RUNNER
Feralas (46), B:(4, 5), C-5, H:(4, 5), I:(3-5), J:(4, 5), K:(4, 5)

LOOKOUT CAPTAIN LOLO LONGSTRIKER
The Thorium Brotherhood, Searing Gorge (64), D-3, Thorium Point, Left of tower ramp

LOORANA
Food & Drink, Feralas (46), I-4, Camp Mojache (105), East of inn

LORAMUS THALIPEDES
Azshara (14), H-7, Bay of Storms, Southern end of island, near cave

LORAX
Winterspring (98), I-7, Frostwhisper Gorge, Southeast of gorge

LORD ALEXEI BAROV
Western Plaguelands (92), I-7, Scholomance

LORD ALIDEN PERENOLDE
Alterac Mountains (8), E-2, Dandred's Fold, Second floor of house

LORD ANGLER
Rare Spawn, Dustwallow Marsh (38), G-6, Tidefury Cove, Lvl 44 Average Rare; Roams the cove

LORD ARKKOROC
Azshara (14), J-4, Temple of Arkkoran, Top floor of temple above entrance

LORD AZRETHOC
Desolace (30), G-8, Mannoroc Coven, Roams eastern clearing

LORD BANEHOLLOW
Felwood (44), E-6, Shadow Hold, Top floor of the final area

LORD BAURLES K. WISHOCK
House of Nobles, Stormwind (72), K-3, Stormwind Keep, Petitioner's Chamber

LORD CAPTAIN WYRMAK
Rare Spawn, Swamp of Sorrows (76), H-4, Lvl 45 Uncommon; Patrols the upper right portion of swampland surrounding the Temple of Atal'Hakkar

LORD COBRAHN
Barrens (18), E-4, Wailing Caverns

LORD CONDAR
Rare Spawn, Loch Modan (54), H-8, J-7, K-7, Ironband's Excavation Site, The Farstrider Lodge, Lvl 15 Semi-Rare; Roams small area around spawn point

LORD CYRIK BLACKFORGE
Barrens (18), E-8, Bael Modan, Landing pad

LORD DARKSCYTHE
Rare Spawn, Eastern Plaguelands (40), D-3, E:(3, 4), F-3, Plaguewood, Lvl 57 Average Rare; Roams small area around spawn point

LORD ELLO EBONLOCKE
Mayor of Darkshire, Duskwood (36), J-5, Darkshire (108), Darkshire Town Hall

LORD FALCONCREST
Arathi Highlands (10), C-6, Stromgarde Keep (127), Third floor castle

LORD GRAYSON SHADOWBREAKER
Paladin Trainer, Stormwind (72), F-3, Cathedral Square, Cathedral of Light

LORD GREGOR LESCOVAR
Stormwind (72), K-1, Stormwind Keep, Royal Library

LORD HEL'NURATH
Feralas (46), G-4, Dire Maul

LORD INCENDIUS
Burning Steppes (22), Searing Gorge (64), C-4/D-8, Blackrock Depths

LORD JORACH RAVENHOLDT
Hillsbrad Foothills (48), K-2, Second floor of Chateau Ravenholdt

LORD KAZZAK
Raid Boss, Blasted Lands (20), E-8, The Tainted Scar, Roams medium area around spawn point

LORD KRAGARU
Desolace (30), C-1, Ranzajar Isle, Serpent Statue

LORD LAKMAERAN
Feralas (46), C-7, Isle of Dread, Roams hill near Chimaeroks

LORD MALATHROM
Rare Spawn, Duskwood (36), C:(2, 3), Dawning Wood Catacombs, Lvl 31 Uncommon; Roams small area around spawn point

LORD MALDAZZAR
Rare Spawn, Western Plaguelands (92), F-8, G:(7, 8), Sorrow Hill, Lvl 56 Uncommon; Roams small area around spawn point

LORD MAXWELL TYROSUS
The Argent Dawn, Eastern Plaguelands (40), K-6, Light's Hope Chapel (116), Chapel

LORD MAYOR MORRISON
Pyrewood Council, Silverpine Forest (68), G-7, Pyrewood Village, (Summon) Spawns with Councilman Brunswick and Councilman Cooper in town hall

LORD MELENAS
Teldrassil (80), G-5, Fel Rock, Ledge in middle of cave

LORD PYTHAS
Barrens (18), E-4, Wailing Caverns

LORD ROCCOR
Rare Spawn, Burning Steppes (22), Searing Gorge (64), C-4/D-8, Blackrock Depths, Lvl 51 Rare

LORD SAKRASIS
Rare Spawn, Stranglethorn Vale (74), B-6, Nek'Mani Wellspring, Lvl 45 Uncommon; Far end of bridge in front of altar

LORD SERPENTIS
Barrens (18), E-4, Wailing Caverns

LORD SINSLAYER
Rare Spawn, Darkshore (24), H-3, Cliffspring Falls, Lvl 15 Uncommon; In caves

LORD TIRION FORDRING
Order of the Silver Hand, Western Plaguelands (92), G-3, (Summon) Rides in along path and fights elites

LORD TONY ROMANO
Rogue Trainer, Stormwind (72), L-6, Old Town, SI:7

LORD VICTOR NEFARIUS
Burning Steppes (22), Searing Gorge (64), C-4/D-8, Blackrock Spire

LORD VYLETONGUE
Desolace (30), D-5, Mauradon

LOREKEEPER JAVON
Feralas (46), G-4, Dire Maul

LOREKEEPER KILDRATH
Feralas (46), G-4, Dire Maul

LOREKEEPER LYDROS
Feralas (46), G-4, Dire Maul

LOREKEEPER MYKOS
Feralas (46), G-4, Dire Maul

LOREKEEPER POLKELT
Western Plaguelands (92), I-7, Scholomance

LOREKEEPER RAINTOTEM
Mulgore (58), G-3, Red Rocks, Small camp near tree

LORELAE WINTERSONG
Trade Supplies, Moonglade (56), G-4, Nighthaven (120), Central building

LOREMASTER DIBBS
Hillsbrad Foothills (48), F-6, Southshore (125), In front of small house

LORGUS JETT
Ashenvale (12), B-2, Blackfathom Deeps

LORO
Swamp of Sorrows (76), I-5, The Temple of Atal'Hakkar

LORUK FORESTSTRIDER
Ashenvale (12), I-6, Splintertree Post (126), In entrance of northern caves

LOSLOR RUDGE
Engineering Supplies, Dun Morogh (32), G-5, Steelgrill's Depot, In front of barrels outside of right building

LOST BARRENS KODO
Barrens (18), D-2, E:(2-4), F:(1, 4, 5), G:(2, 4)

LOST ONE CHIEFTAIN
Rare Spawn, Swamp of Sorrows (76), H-2, Fallow Sanctuary, Lvl 39 Semi-Rare; Idle near huts in the northwest corner of camp

LOST ONE COOK
Rare Spawn, Swamp of Sorrows (76), H-2, Fallow Sanctuary, Lvl 37 Uncommon; Idle by one of the two cauldrons in camp

LOST ONE FISHERMAN
Swamp of Sorrows (76), F:(3, 4), G-3, H-3, Fallow Sanctuary

LOST ONE HUNTER
Swamp of Sorrows (76), G-3, H:(2, 3), Fallow Sanctuary

LOST ONE MUCKDWELLER
Swamp of Sorrows (76), G-3, H:(2, 3), I-2, Fallow Sanctuary

LOST ONE MUDLURKER
Swamp of Sorrows (76), F:(3, 4), G-3, The Shifting Mire

LOST ONE RIFTSEEKER
Swamp of Sorrows (76), H:(2, 3), Fallow Sanctuary

LOST ONE SEER
Swamp of Sorrows (76), H:(2, 3), Fallow Sanctuary

LOST SOUL
Rare Spawn, Tirisfal Glades (86), F-4, G-5, Agamand Mills (100), Lvl 6 Uncommon; Roams small area around spawn point

LOST WHELP
Wetlands (96), H:(3-5), I:(4, 5), Mosshide Fen, The Green Belt

LOTHERIAS
Darnassus (26), I-2, Craftsmen's Terrace, Leatherworking shop

LOTHOS RIFTWAKER
Burning Steppes (22), Searing Gorge (64), C-4/D-8, The Molten Core

LOTWIL VERIATUS
Badlands (16), H-4, The Dustbowl, Camp

LOUIS WARREN
Weapons Merchant, Undercity (88), H-4, I-4, The Trade Quarter, Upper Ring of Trade Quarter

LOUIS WARREN *(corrected)*

LUCAN CORDELL
Expert Enchanter, Stormwind (72), F-6, The Canals, Shop south of stockade

LUCIAN FENNER
Undercity (88), K-7, The Rogues' Quarter, Near anvil and forge

LUCIEN SARKHOFF
Western Plaguelands (92), J-7, Caer Darrow, Just outside of entrance to Scholomance

LUCIEN TOSSELWRENCH
Badlands (16), H-4, The Dustbowl, Camp

LUCIFRON
Burning Steppes (22), Searing Gorge (64), C-4/D-8, The Molten Core

LUCILLE CASTLETON
Robe Vendor, Undercity (88), J-3, The Magic Quarter

LUCIUS
Redridge Mountains (62), C-5, Lakeshire (115), L-shaped dock west of the bridge

LUI'MALA
Fisherman, Desolace (30), B-7, Shadowprey Village (125), Dock

LUMAK
Fishing Trainer, Orgrimmar (60), I-3, Valley of Honor, Lumak's Fishing

LUMBERJACK
Westfall (94), F-5, Sentinel Hill (123)

LUNACLAW
Darkshore (24), F-4

LUNNIX SPROCKETSLIP
Mining Supplies, Winterspring (98), I-4, Everlook (110), Inside building east of inn

LUPINE DELUSION
Silverpine Forest (68), F-7, Shadowfang Keep

LUPINE HORROR
Silverpine Forest (68), F-7, Shadowfang Keep

LUPOS
Rare Spawn, Duskwood (36), C-3, D-3, E-3, H-3, I-3, J-3, Brightwood Grove, The Darkened Bank, Lvl 23 Uncommon; Roams small area around spawn point

LURKING FERAL SCAR
Feralas (46), F-5, (Summon) Appears in ambush

LUTHER PICKMAN
Warlock Trainer, Undercity (88), L-2, The Magic Quarter, Inside Skull Building

LYESA STEELBROW
Guild Tabard Vendor, Ironforge (52), D-8, The Commons, Ironforge Visitor's Center

157

LYLANDRIS
Warsong Gulch Battlemaster, Ironforge (52), J-9, The Military Ward, Hall of Arms

LYON MOUNTAINHEART
Ironforge (52), I-1, Hall of Explorers, The Library

LYRAI
General Supplies, Teldrassil (80), H-4, Shadowglen (124), Second level of main building

LYRANNE FEATHERSONG
Food & Drink, Winterspring (98), H-3, Starfall Village, North end of main building

LYRIA DU LAC
Warrior Trainer, Elwynn Forest (42), E-7, Goldshire (112), Rear entrance of smith

LYSHEANA
Guild Master, Darnassus (26), I-2 , Craftsmen's Terrace, Southeast building, second floor

LYSTA BANCROFT
Undercity (88), G-2, The War Quarter, Watches fights in War Quarter

M

MA STONEFIELD
Elwynn Forest (42), D-8, The Stonefield Farm, In front of house

MABEL SOLAJ
General Goods Vendor, Duskwood (36), J-4, Darkshire (108), Scarlet Raven Tavern

MAD MAGGLISH
Barrens (18), E-4, The Wailing Caverns

MADAME EVA
Duskwood (36), K-4, Darkshire (108), First floor of house

MADISON
Redridge Mountains (62), C-5, Lake Everstill, Dock

MAETHRYA
Hippogryph Master, Winterspring (98), I-4, Everlook (110), Northeast of town

MAEVA SNOWBRAID
Robe Merchant, Ironforge (52), E-1, The Mystic Ward, Maeva's Mystical Apparel

MAGAR
Expert Tailor, Orgrimmar (60), H-5, The Drag, Magar's Cloth Goods

MAGATHA GRIMTOTEM
Thunder Bluff (84), I-3, Elder Rise, Inside tent on Elder Rise, guarded by Cor and Gorm Grimtotem

MAGE HUNTER
Desolace (30), G:(7, 8), H-7, Mannoroc Coven

MAGENIUS
Reagents Vendor, Orgrimmar (60), E-4, Valley of Wisdom, Asoran's Market

MAGGA
Durotar (34), F-7, Valley of Trials (131), Structure to south

MAGGOT EYE
Tirisfal Glades (86), H-3, Garren's Haunt, Shed at northern end of crop field

MAGGRAN EARTHBINDER
Stonetalon Mountains (70), F-6, Sun Rock Retreat (127), Outside inn

MAGINOR DUMAS
Master Mage, Stormwind (72), F-8, Mage Quarter, Wizard's Sanctum

MAGIS SPARKMANTLE
Mage Trainer, Dun Morogh (32), F-5, Kharanos (114), Thunderbrew Distillery

MAGISTER HAWKHELM
Rare Spawn, Azshara (14), G-3, Thalassian Base Camp, Lvl 52 Average Rare; Roams close to spawn points

MAGISTER KALENDRIS
Feralas (46), G-4, Dire Maul

MAGISTRATE BARTHILAS
Eastern Plaguelands (40), D-2, Stratholme

MAGISTRATE BLUNTNOSE
Loch Modan (54), D-4, Thelsamar (129), Outside of second house on left of path

MAGISTRATE BURNSIDE
Hillsbrad Foothills (48), C-4, Hillsbrad, Town hall

MAGISTRATE HENRY MALEB
Hillsbrad Foothills (48), E-6, Southshore (125), Southshore Town Hall

MAGISTRATE MARDUKE
Western Plaguelands (92), I-7, Scholomance, Ghost in throne room of pre-instance portion of Scholomance

MAGISTRATE SEVREN
Tirisfal Glades (86), H-5, Brill (104), Brill Town Hall

MAGISTRATE SOLOMON
Redridge Mountains (62), C-4, Lakeshire (115), Lakeshire Town Hall

MAGMA ELEMENTAL
Searing Gorge (64), B-5, C:(6, 7), D:(4, 6-8), E:(3-6), F:(5, 6), G:(4, 5, 7, 8), The Cauldron

MAGMADAR
Burning Steppes (22), Searing Gorge (64), C-4/D-8, The Molten Core

MAGMAKIN
Burning Steppes (22), Searing Gorge (64), C-4/D-8, The Molten Core

MAGMAR FELLHEW
Loch Modan (54), I-7, Ironband's Excavation Site, Camp outside of excavation site

MAGMUS
Burning Steppes (22), Searing Gorge (64), C-4/D-8, Blackrock Depths

MAGNUS FROSTWAKE
Western Plaguelands (92), I-8, Caer Darrow, Ghost in smithy

MAGOSH
Rare Spawn, Loch Modan (54), I-7, Ironband's Excavation Site, Lvl 21 Uncommon; With two Stonesplitter Diggers on hilltop on center excavation site

MAGRAM BONEPAW
Desolace (30), I:(7, 8), J-8, Magram Village

MAGRAM MARAUDER
Desolace (30), I:(7, 8), J:(7, 8), Magram Village

MAGRAM OUTRUNNER
Desolace (30), I:(7, 8), J:(6, 7), Magram Village

MAGRAM PACK RUNNER
Desolace (30), I:(7, 8), J-8, Magram Village

MAGRAM SCOUT
Desolace (30), I:(7, 8), J:(6, 7), Magram Village

MAGRAM STORMER
Desolace (30), I:(7, 8), J:(7, 8), Magram Village

MAGRAM WINDCHASER
Desolace (30), I:(7, 8), J:(6-8), Magram Village

MAGRAM WRANGLER
Desolace (30), I:(7, 8), J:(6-8), Magram Village

MAGRAMI SPECTRE
Desolace (30), H-9, I-9, Valley of Bones

MAGREGAN DEEPSHADOW
Badlands (16), G-1, Uldaman

MAGRIN RIVERMANE
Mulgore (58), E-6, Bloodhoof Village (102), Inn

MAGRONOS THE UNYIELDING
Rare Spawn, Blasted Lands (20), G-4, Dreadmaul Post, Lvl 56 Average Rare; Roams small area around spawn point

MAGTOOR
Swamp of Sorrows (76), C-3, The Harborage, Idle in draenei camp

MAGUS RIMTORI
Azshara (14), G-3, Thalassian Base Camp, East of the base camp

MAGUS TIRTH
Thousand Needles (82), K-8, Mirage Raceway (118), West grandstands

MAGUS WORDEEN VOIDGLARE
Hillsbrad Foothills (48), G-2, Tarren Mill (128), House on the right

MAHANI
Expert Tailor, Barrens (18), F-6, Camp Taurajo (106), Southern building

MAHNOTT ROUGHWOUND
Weaponsmith, Mulgore (58), E-6, Bloodhoof Village (102), Northeast tent

MAHREN SKYSEER
Barrens (18), H-4, The Tidus Stair, Outside hut

MAHU
Leatherworking & Tailoring Supplies, Thunder Bluff (84), E-4, Middle rise, inside Thunder Bluff Armorers tent

MAI'AH
Mage Trainer, Durotar (34), F-7, Valley of Trials (131), Structure to south

MAIDEN'S VIRTUE CREWMAN
Wetlands (96), A-6, Baradin Bay, Menethil Harbor (117)

MAI'LAHII
Fishing Supplies, Desolace (30), B-7, Shadowprey Village (125), Down by dock

MAI'ZOTH
Stranglethorn Vale (74), F-3, Mosh'Ogg Ogre Mound, Idle with several ogres in the rear of cave

MAJOR MATTINGLY
Stormwind (72), J-8, Stormwind City, Southwest of statue at entrance

MAJOR SAMUELSON
Stormwind City Guard, Stormwind (72), K-2, Stormwind Keep, East wing, north room

MAJORDOMO EXECUTUS
Burning Steppes (22), Searing Gorge (64), C-4/D-8, The Molten Core

MAK
Journeyman Leatherworker, Thunder Bluff (84), D-4, Middle rise, inside Thunder Bluff Armorers tent

MAKABA FLATHOOF
Barrens (18), D-3, Camp at Stonetalon border

MAKARU
Mining Trainer, Orgrimmar (60), I-3, Valley of Honor, Red Canyon Mining

MAKASGAR
Durotar (34), I-7, Darkspear Strand, Coast of northernmost edge of strand

MAKRINNI RAZORCLAW
Azshara (14), E-9, F:(7, 9), G:(7, 9), H:(7-9), I:(7-9), J:(7-9), K:(8, 9)

MAKRINNI SCRABBLER
Azshara (14), G-4, H:(3, 4), I-4, J-5, K:(3, 4), L:(2-4)

MAKRINNI SNAPCLAW
Azshara (14), E:(1, 2), F:(1, 2), G-1, H-1, I-1, J-1, K:(1, 2), L:(1, 2), Jagged Reef

MAKRURA CLACKER
Durotar (34), H-8, I:(4-9), J:(5-9), K-7, Darkspear Strand, Echo Isles, Scuttle Coast

MAKRURA ELDER
Durotar (34), I:(1-4), Bladefist Bay

MAKRURA SHELLHIDE
Durotar (34), H-8, I:(4-9), J:(5-9), K-7, Darkspear Strand, Echo Isles, Scuttle Coast

MAKRURA SNAPCLAW
Durotar (34), I:(1-4), Bladefist Bay, Deadeye Shore, Scuttle Coast

MALAKAI CROSS
Priest Trainer, Thunder Bluff (84), C-3, Spirit Rise, The Pools of Vision

MALCOMB WYNN
Journeyman Enchanter, Undercity (88), I-6, The Apothecarium, Near Rogues' Quarter entry

MALDRYN
Druid Trainer, Stormwind (72), C-5, The Park, By pool of water

MALEKI THE PALLID
Eastern Plaguelands (40), D-2, Stratholme

MALFORMED DEFIAS DRONE
Westfall (94), H-7, Circles tower

MALFUNCTIONING REAVER
Rare Spawn, Burning Steppes (22), J-3, K:(3, 6), L-5, Dreadmaul Rock, Terror Wing Path, Lvl 56 Semi-Rare; Roams small area around spawn point

MALGIN BARLEYBREW
Bael'dun Morale Officer, Barrens (18), F-8, Bael'dun Keep, Back of right wing

MALICIOUS SPIRIT
Western Plaguelands (92), I-7, Scholomance

MALISSA
Poison Supplier, Duskwood (36), K-4, Darkshire (108), Outside the first house on right side of road heading into Darkshire from the east

MALIYNN
Food & Drink Vendor, Ashenvale (12), E-5, Astranaar (101), First floor of inn

MALLEN SWAIN
Tailoring Supplies, Hillsbrad Foothills (48), G-2, Tarren Mill (128), Roams near well

MALOR THE ZEALOUS
Eastern Plaguelands (40), D-2, Stratholme

MALORNE BLADELEAF
Herbalist, Teldrassil (80), G-6, Dolanaar (109), Inside house east of inn

MALOSH
Warrior Trainer, Swamp of Sorrows (76), F-5, Stonard (126), First floor of inn

MALTON DROFFERS
Droffer and Sons Salvage, Orgrimmar (60), G-4, The Drag, Droffer and Sons Salvage

MALURESSIAN
Stable Master, Ashenvale (12), E-5, Astranaar (101), Entrance of inn across from mailbox

MALUX
Skinning Trainer, Desolace (30), B-7, Shadowprey Village (125), Landing of western structure

MALVOR
Herbalist, Moonglade (56), F-5, Nighthaven (120), Small house next to a moonwell, north of western section of lake

MALYFOUS DARKHAMMER
The Thorium Brotherhood, Winterspring (98), I-4, Everlook (110), West of inn, near south wall

MALYGEN
General Goods, Felwood (44), H-3, Talonbranch Glade, Behind building near gazebo

MANA BURST
Feralas (46), G-4, Dire Maul

MANA EATER
Desolace (30), G-7, Mannoroc Coven

MANA REMNANT
Feralas (46), G-4, Dire Maul

MANA SPRITE
Deadwind Pass (28), D:(6-8), E:(6, 8), Karazhan, Sleeping Gorge

MANA SURGE
Dustwallow Marsh (38), F-6, The Quagmire

MANACLAW
Winterspring (98), H-5, Mazthoril, Deep in caverns

MANAHOUND
Blasted Lands (20), E:(5, 6), F:(6-8), G-7, H-6, I-6, Dark Portal, The Tainted Scar

MANGECLAW
Dun Morogh (32), K-4, North Gate Outpost, Top of a deadend hill on the left side of the outpost

MANGLED CADAVER
Eastern Plaguelands (40), D-2, Stratholme

MANGLETOOTH
Barrens (18), F-6, Camp Taurajo (106), Cage near west entrance

MANGORN FLINTHAMMER
Heavy Armor Merchant, Ironforge (52), D-6, The Commons, Ironforge Armory

MANGY DUSKBAT
Tirisfal Glades (86), D:(6, 7), Deathknell (109)

MANGY MOUNTAIN BOAR
Loch Modan (54), D-6, E:(5, 6), F:(6, 7), G:(6, 7), H:(5, 6), I:(5-7), J:(5, 7), K-7, Ironband's Excavation Site

MANGY NIGHTSABER
Teldrassil (80), H:(3, 4), Shadowglen (124)

MANGY SILVERMANE
The Hinterlands (50), B-5, C:(5, 6), D-5, The Hinterlands

MANGY WOLF
Elwynn Forest (42), B:(7, 8), C:(7, 8), D:(6-8), E:(6, 7), F:(5-7), G:(6, 7), H:(6, 7)

MANI WINTERHOOF
Alchemy Supplies, Thunder Bluff (84), E-3, Middle rise, inside Bena's Alchemy tent

MANIFESTATION OF WATER
Barrens (18), H-4, The Tidus Stair, (Summon)

MANKRIK
Barrens (18), F-3, The Crossroads (107), Southern entrance

MANNOROC LASHER
Ashenvale (12), J:(6-8), K:(6, 7), Demon Fall Canyon, Felfire Hill, Nightsong Woods

MAQUELL EBONWOOD
Tirisfal Glades (86), D-6, Deathknell (109), Roams from Church to Inn

MARANDIS' SISTER
Desolace (30), C-8, H-1, Nijel's Point (119), Sar'theris Strand

MARAUDINE BONEPAW
Desolace (30), E-6, Valley of Spears

MARAUDINE KHAN ADVISOR
Desolace (30), C-5, Valley of Spears

MARAUDINE MARAUDER
Desolace (30), C:(5, 6), D:(5, 6), Maraudon, Valley of Spears

MARAUDINE MAULER
Desolace (30), C:(5, 6), D:(5, 6), Maraudon, Valley of Spears

MARAUDINE PRIEST
Desolace (30), D-5, Maraudon

MARAUDINE SCOUT
Desolace (30), C:(6, 7), D:(5-7), E-6, Maraudon, Valley of Spears

MARAUDINE STORMER
Desolace (30), C:(5, 6), D-5, Maraudon, Valley of Spears

MARAUDINE WINDCHASER
Desolace (30), C:(5, 6), D:(5, 6), Maraudon, Valley of Spears

MARAUDINE WRANGLER
Desolace (30), C:(6, 7), D:(5-7), E-6, Maraudon, Valley of Spears

MARAUDING CORPSE
Eastern Plaguelands (40), E-8, Darrowshire

MARAUDING OWLBEAST
The Hinterlands (50), I-5, The Hinterlands

MARAUDING SKELETON
Eastern Plaguelands (40), E-8, Darrowshire

MARCEL DABYRIE
Arathi Highlands (10), G-4, Dabyrie's Farmstead, Roams in stable

MARCUS BEL
Alliance Outrunner, Barrens (18), F-8, Southern Barrens, Spawns at border to Dustwallow Marsh and travels north to Lushwater Oasis

MARDA WELLER
Weapons Merchant, Stormwind (72), H-6, Trade District, Weller's Arsenal

MARDANT STRONGOAK
Druid Trainer, Teldrassil (80), G-4, Shadowglen (124), First room off of ramp up tree

MARDRACK GREENWELL
Food & Drink, Feralas (46), C-4, Feathermoon Stronghold (110), Inn

MARDUK BLACKPOOL
Western Plaguelands (92), I-7, Scholomance

MAREK IRONHEART
Loch Modan (54), K-6, The Farstrider Lodge, In right hall of lodge

MAREZ COWL
Arathi Highlands (10), D:(5, 6), Stromgarde Keep (127), Roams in Stromgarde Keep

MARGOL THE RAGER
Searing Gorge (64), I-8, Patrols the canyons around cave

MARGOZ
Durotar (34), H-2, Tent

MARIA LUMERE
Alchemy Supplies, Stormwind (72), G-8, Mage Quarter, Alchemy Need

MARIE HOLDSTON
Weaponsmith, Dustwallow Marsh (38), I-5, Theramore Isle (130), Blacksmithing hut to west

MARIN NOGGENFOGGER
Tanaris (78), H-3, Gadgetzan (111), Outside entrance to Auction House

MARION CALL
Rogue Trainer, Tirisfal Glades (86), H-5, Brill (104), Second floor of Gallows' End Tavern

MARIS GRANGER
Skinning Trainer, Stormwind (72), J-5, Old Town, The Protective Hide

MARISA DU'PAIGE
Westfall (94), D-7, E-7, The Deadmines

MARJAK KEENBLADE
Weaponsmith, Mulgore (58), E-8, Camp Narache (105), Southwest tent

MARK OF DETONATION
Eastern Plaguelands (40), C-2, D:(3, 4), E:(2, 4), F-3, Plaguewood

MARKEL SMYTHE
Stranglethorn Vale (74), B-8, Booty Bay (103)

MARLA FOWLER
Undercity (88), G-2, The War Quarter, Watches fights in War Quarter

MARLENE REDPATH
Western Plaguelands (92), F-8, Sorrow Hill, Roams inside house on western side of graveyard

MARLETH BARLEYBREW
Dun Morogh (32), D-4, Brewnall Village, Under scaffolding

MARLI WISHRUNNER
Feralas (46), C-2, The Twin Colossals, Off road near western colossal

MARRYK NURRIBIT
Mage Trainer, Dun Morogh (32), D-7, Coldridge Valley (106), Back room of Anvilmar (first floor)

MARSH FLESHEATER
Swamp of Sorrows (76), H:(7, 8), I:(7-9), K:(7, 8), L:(2, 3, 5-7), Misty Reed Strand

MARSH INKSPEWER
Swamp of Sorrows (76), H:(7, 8), I:(7-9), K:(7-9), L:(5-7), Misty Reed Strand

MARSH MURLOC
Swamp of Sorrows (76), K:(8, 9), Misty Reed Strand

MARSH ORACLE
Swamp of Sorrows (76), H-8, L:(2, 3, 5-7), Misty Reed Strand

MARSHAL DUGHAN
Elwynn Forest (42), E-7, Goldshire (112), In front of smithy

MARSHAL HAGGARD
Elwynn Forest (42), L-7, Eastvale Logging Camp, Under lantern post in front of house

MARSHAL MARRIS
Redridge Mountains (62), D-5, Lakeshire (115), In Lakeshire just right of bridge

MARSHAL MAXWELL
Burning Steppes (22), K-7, Morgan's Vigil (118), Adjacent to camp entrance

MARSHAL MCBRIDE
Elwynn Forest (42), F-4, Northshire Valley (120), In hallway just inside abbey

MARSHAL REDPATH
Hillsbrad Foothills (48), F-6, Southshore (125), Right of Southshore Town Hall

MARSHAL REGINALD WINDSOR
Burning Steppes (22), Searing Gorge (64), C-4/D-8, Blackrock Depths

MARTEK THE EXILED
Badlands (16), F-5, Valley of Fangs, Camp

MARTHA ALLIESTAR
Herbalism Trainer, Undercity (88), H-5, The Apothecarium, Near War Quarter entry

MARTHA STRAIN
Demon Trainer, Undercity (88), L:(1, 2), The Magic Quarter, Inside Skull Building

MARTHA STRAIN
Tirisfal Glades (86), D-6, Deathknell (109)

MARTIE JAINROSE
Redridge Mountains (62), B-4, Lakeshire (115), Outside small house on southwestern side of town

MARTINE TRAMBLAY
Fishing Supplies, Tirisfal Glades (86), I-6, By wagon at fork in road

MA'RUK WYRMSCALE
Rare Spawn, Wetlands (96), G-7, Dun Algaz, Lvl 25 Uncommon; Patrols water south of windmill

MARUKAI
Ashenvale (12), B-4, Zoram'gar Outpost (131), Southern structure

MARVON RIVETSEEKER
Tanaris (78), H-5, Broken Pillar, In west corner

MARY EDRAS
First Aid Trainer, Undercity (88), J-5, The Rogues' Quarter, Directly across from Skull Building

MASAT T'ANDR
Superior Leatherworker, Swamp of Sorrows (76), C-3, The Harborage, Idle in draenei camp

MASTER APOTHECARY FARANELL
Undercity (88), G-7, The Apothecarium, In laboratory

MASTER DIGGER
Rare Spawn, Westfall (94), E-2, Jangolode Mine, Lvl 15 Uncommon; In back of mine

MASTER FEARDRED
Rare Spawn, Azshara (14), H:(2-3), Legash Encampment, Lvl 51 Average Rare

MASTER GADRIN
Durotar (34), H-7, Sen'jin Village (123), Center pond

MASTER KANG
Hillsbrad Foothills (48), J-2, Next to sparing ring right of Chateau Ravenholdt

MASTER MATHIAS SHAW
Leader of SI:7, Stormwind (72), K-6, Old Town, SI:7

MASTER MECHANIC CASTPIPE
Ironforge (52), J-5, Tinker Town, Outside tram entrance

MASTER SMITH BURNINATE
The Thorium Brotherhood, Searing Gorge (64), D-3, Thorium Point, Right side of camp next to the forge

MASTER VORNAL
Durotar (34), H-7, Sen'jin Village (123), Center pond

MASTER WOOD
Stormwind (72), I-5, Old Town, Command Center

MASTOK WRILEHISS
Ashenvale (12), I-6, Splintertree Post (126), Between cave entrance and inn

MATHIEL
Darnassus (26), H-4, Warrior's Terrace, Lower southwest platform

MATHREDIS FIRESTAR
Burning Steppes (22), H-2, Flame Crest, Right of scaffolding

MATHRENGYL BEARWALKER
Druid Trainer, Darnassus (26), D-1, Cenarion Enclave, Northwest structure, on balcony

MATT JOHNSON
Mining Trainer, Duskwood (36), J-5, Darkshire (108), Outside to the rear of smithy

MATTHEW HOOPER
Fishing Trainer, Redridge Mountains (62), C-5, Lakeshire (115), Straight dock west of the bridge

MATTIE ALRED
Undercity (88), G-3, The War Quarter, Wanders Canals and War Quarter

MAUR GRIMTOTEM
Orgrimmar (60), F-5, Ragefire Chasm

MAUR RAINCALLER
Mulgore (58), E-6, Bloodhoof Village (102), North part of camp

MAURIN BONESPLITTER
Desolace (30), G-5, Ghost Walker Post (111), Northern plateau

MAURY "CLUB FOOT" WILKINS
Stranglethorn Vale (74), C-5, Ruins of Jubuwal, Ruins near camp

MAVORIS CLOUDSBREAK
Ashenvale (12), J-7, Dor'Danil Barrow Den, Deep within den in a side passage

MAVRALYN
Leather Armor & Leatherworking Supplies, Darkshore (24), F-4, Auberdine (101), Left wing of northern building

MAXAN ANVOL
Priest Trainer, Dun Morogh (32), F-5, Kharanos (114), Thunderbrew Distillery

MAXIMILLIAN CROWE
Warlock Trainer, Elwynn Forest (42), F-7, Goldshire (112), Basement of Lion's Pride Inn

MAXIMILLION
Warlock Trainer, Tirisfal Glades (86), D-6, Deathknell (109), Church

MAXTON STRANG
Mail Armor Merchant, Desolace (30), I-1, Nijel's Point (119), Northwestern ruins

MAXWORT UBERGLINT
Burning Steppes (22), H-2, Flame Crest, Under scaffolding

MAYARA BRIGHTWING
Burning Steppes (22), K-7, Morgan's Vigil (118), Adjacent to camp entrance

MAYBELL MACLURE
Elwynn Forest (42), F-9, The Maclure Vineyards, House

MAYBESS RIVERBREEZE
Emerald Circle, Felwood (44), F-8, Near a pool west of the road

MAYDA THANE
Cobbler, Stormwind (72), J-4, Old Town, Thane's Boots

MAYWIKI OF ZULDAZAR
Stranglethorn Vale (74), A-2, Yojamba Isle

MAZEN MAC'NADIR
Academy of Arcane Arts and Sciences, Stormwind (72), F-6, The Canals, Building South of Stockade

MAZK SNIPESHOT
Engineering Supplies, Stranglethorn Vale (74), B-8, Booty Bay (103), Boomstick Imports East (shop) on the southern side of The Old Port Authority

MAZZRANACHE
Mulgore (58), C-4, Roams across Mulgore to the eastern hills and back

MCGAVAN
The Mithril Order, Stranglethorn Vale (74), C-8, Booty Bay (103), In front of forge outside of Booty Bay Blacksmith

ME'LYNN
Expert Tailor, Darnassus (26), H-2, Craftsmen's Terrace, Tailoring shop

MEBOK MIZZYRIX
Barrens (18), H-4, Ratchet (121), Outside Ironzar's Imported Weaponry

MECHANIZED GUARDIAN
Dun Morogh (32), C-4, Gnomeregan

MECHANIZED SENTRY
Dun Morogh (32), C-4, Gnomeregan

MECHANO-FLAMEWALKER
Dun Morogh (32), C-4, Gnomeregan

MECHANO-FROSTWALKER
Dun Morogh (32), C-4, Gnomeregan

MECHANO-TANK
Dun Morogh (32), C-4, Gnomeregan

MEDIC HELAINA
Dustwallow Marsh (38), I-5, Theramore Isle (130), Sparring grounds to northeast

MEDIC TAMBERLYN
Dustwallow Marsh (38), I-5, Theramore Isle (130), Sparring grounds to northeast

MEELA DAWNSTRIDER
Shaman Trainer, Mulgore (58), E-8, Camp Narache (105), North tent

MEGGI PEPPINROCKER
Winterspring (98), I-4, Everlook (110), Roams town

MEILOSH
Felwood (44), I-1, Timbermaw Hold, Central intersection

MEKGINEER THERMAPLUGG
Dun Morogh (32), C-4, Gnomeregan

MELARITH
Teldrassil (80), G-6, Dolanaar (109), Inn

MELEA
Mail Armor Merchant, Darnassus (26), H-7, Tradesmen's Terrace, Mail Armor shop

MELIA
Western Plaguelands (92), I-8, Caer Darrow, Ghost By fountain

MELIKA ISENSTRIDER
Assistant Innkeeper, Elwynn Forest (42), F-7, Goldshire (112), First floor of Lion's Pride Inn

MELIRI
Weaponsmith, Moonglade (56), G-4, Nighthaven (120), Just inside southeast building

MELISARA
Hillsbrad Foothills (48), H-2, Tarren Mill (128), Right of church

MELITHAR STAGHELM
Teldrassil (80), H-4, Shadowglen (124), On steps leading to main building

MELIZZA BRIMBUZZLE
Desolace (30), D-5, Valley of Spears, Caged outside of large hut

MELOR STONEHOOF
Thunder Bluff (84), G-8, Hunter Rise, In front of Hunter's Hall

MELRIS MALAGAN
Captain of the Guard, Stormwind (72), H-6, Trade District, Next to tree

MENARA VOIDRENDER
Barrens (18), H-3, Ratchet (121), Tower in eastern hills

MENETHIL SENTRY
Wetlands (96), A:(5, 6), Baradin Bay, Menethil Bay, Menethil Harbor (117)

MENNET CARKAD
Undercity (88), L-7, The Rogues' Quarter, In front of Skull Building

MERCUTIO FILTHGORGER
Eastern Plaguelands (40), D-8, The Undercroft, (Summon) Behind crypt by carriage

MERELYSSA
Blade Merchant, Darnassus (26), I-6, Tradesmen's Terrace, Weapons shop

MERI IRONWEAVE
Armorer & Shieldcrafter, Teldrassil (80), G-6, Dolanaar (109), Inn

MERIDETH CARLSON
Horse Breeder, Hillsbrad Foothills (48), F-6, Southshore (125), Stable

MERILL PLEASANCE
Tabard Vendor, Undercity (88), J-4, The Trade Quarter, East spoke from bank

MERISSA STILWELL
Elwynn Forest (42), F-4, Northshire Valley (120), Caravan facing abbey

MERRIN ROCKWEAVER
Wetlands (96), E-5, Whelgar's Excavation Site, Den across the bridge in east section of site

MESA BUZZARD
Arathi Highlands (10), B-5, D:(5, 6), E:(2-4, 6, 7), F-3, G-7, H:(6, 7)

MESA EARTH SPIRIT
Mulgore (58), F-8, Kodo Rock, (Summon) Earth side of rock

MESHLOK THE HARVESTER
Rare Spawn, Desolace (30), D-5, Mauradon, Lvl 48 Rare

MEVEN KORGAL
Tirisfal Glades (86), D-7, Deathknell (109), In front of tent

MEZZIR THE HOWLER
Rare Spawn, Winterspring (98), E-4, Frostfire Hot Springs, Lvl 55 Uncommon; Roams to the west

MIAO'ZAN
Journeyman Alchemist, Durotar (34), H-7, Sen'jin Village (123), Northwest structure

MIBLON SNARLTOOTH
Feralas (46), E-1, Ruins of Ravenwind, Steps of ruins

MICHA YANCE
Trade Goods, Hillsbrad Foothills (48), F-5, Southshore (125), First floor of house

MICHAEL
Stable Master, Dustwallow Marsh (38), I-5, Theramore Isle (130), Outside inn to north

MICHAEL GARRETT
Bat Handler, Undercity (88), I-5, The Trade Quarter, Upper Ring of Trade Quarter

MICHELLE BELLE
Physician, Elwynn Forest (42), F-7, Goldshire (112), Second floor of Lion's Pride Inn

MICKEY LEVINE
Tirisfal Glades (86), K-7, The Bulwark, Camp on right side of road

MICKEY LEVINE
Western Plaguelands (92), C-6, The Bulwark

MIJAN
Swamp of Sorrows (76), I-5, The Temple of Atal'Hakkar

MIKAL PIERCE
Dustwallow Marsh (38), I-5, Theramore Isle (130), 2nd floor of inn

MIKE MILLER
Bread Merchant, Westfall (94), G-5, Sentinel Hill (123), At intersection east of the Sentinel Tower

MIKEY
Stormwind (72), Roams city with Miss Danna

MIKHAIL
Bartender, Wetlands (96), A-6, Deepwater Tavern, Near bar

MILES DEXTER
Rogue Trainer, Undercity (88), L-7, The Rogues' Quarter, Inside Skull Building

MILES WELSH
Priest Trainer, Thunder Bluff (84), C-3, Spirit Rise, The Pools of Vision

MILLA FAIRANCORA
Journeyman Alchemist, Darnassus (26), G-2, Craftsmen's Terrace, Alchemy shop

MILLI FEATHERWHISTLE
Mechanostrider Merchant, Dun Morogh (32), G-5, Steelgrill's Depot, By mechanostrider's outside of depot

MILLIE GREGORIAN
Tailoring Supplies, Undercity (88), J-3, The Magic Quarter

MILLY OSWORTH
Elwynn Forest (42), G-4, Northshire Valley (120), Next to carriage near the abbey stable

MILSTAFF STORMEYE
Portal Trainer, Ironforge (52), C-1, The Mystic Ward, Hall of Mysteries

MILTON BEATS
Giver of the Beatings, Hillsbrad Foothills (48), J-2, (Summon) Cave leading to Chateau Ravenholdt

MILTON SHEAF
Librarian, Stormwind (72), K-1, Stormwind Keep, Royal Library

MINDLESS SKELETON
Eastern Plaguelands (40), D-2, Stratholme

MINDLESS UNDEAD
Eastern Plaguelands (40), D-2, Stratholme

MINDLESS ZOMBIE
Tirisfal Glades (86), C-6, D-6, Deathknell (109)

MINER HACKETT
Hillsbrad Foothills (48), C:(5, 6), Azurelode Mine, (Random spawn)

MINER JOHNSON
Westfall (94), D-7, E-7, The Deadmines

MINION OF MORGANTH
Morganth's Guardian, Redridge Mountains (62), K-5, Tower of Ilgalar, (Summon) Summoned by Morganth during boss encounter

MINION OF SETHIR
Teldrassil (80), D-2, The Oracle Glade, North of the glade on tree branches

MINOR MANIFESTATION OF AIR
Thousand Needles (82), H-5, Within rock pattern atop plateau

MINOR MANIFESTATION OF EARTH
Durotar (34), G-7, Spirit Rock

MINOR MANIFESTATION OF FIRE
Durotar (34), F-6, Shrine of the Dormant Flame

MINOR MANIFESTATION OF WATER
Silverpine Forest (68), F-4, The Tides Run, Coast of pond

MIRADOR
Eastern Plaguelands (40), A-4, Thondroril River, Roams by house on banks of Thondroril River

MIRAN
Loch Modan (54), G-7, The Loch, Next to dynamite filled carriage at the southern end of loch

MIRE LORD
Swamp of Sorrows (76), A-3, Misty Valley, Cave

MIREFIN COASTRUNNER
Dustwallow Marsh (38), G:(1, 2), H:(1-3), I-3, Dreadmurk Shore

MIREFIN MUCKDWELLER
Dustwallow Marsh (38), G:(1, 2), H:(1-3), I-3, Dreadmurk Shore

MIREFIN MURLOC
Dustwallow Marsh (38), G-2, H-2, Dreadmurk Shore

MIREFIN ORACLE
Dustwallow Marsh (38), G-1, H:(1-3), I-3, Dreadmurk Shore

MIREFIN PUDDLEJUMPER
Dustwallow Marsh (38), G-2, H-2, Dreadmurk Shore

MIREFIN WARRIOR
Dustwallow Marsh (38), G-1, H:(1-3), I-3, Dreadmurk Shore

MIRELLE TREMAYNE
Heavy Armor Merchant, Undercity (88), I-3, The War Quarter

MIRELOW
Rare Spawn, Wetlands (96), B:(3, 4), C:(2-4), Bluegill Marsh, Sundown Marsh, Lvl 25 Semi-Rare; Patrols water west and south of windmill and around bluegill camps

MIRKET
Warlock Trainer, Orgrimmar (60), F-5, The Cleft of Shadow, Darkfire Enclave

MISHA
Desolace (30), G-1, Spawns on road near Stonetalon border and patrols roads with Rexxar

MISHA TOR'KREN
Durotar (34), G-3, Tor'kren Farm, Farmhouse

MISHELLENA
Hippogryph Master, Felwood (44), H-3, Talonbranch Glade, North of building

MISHIKI
Herbalist, Durotar (34), H-7, Sen'jin Village (123), West structure

MISS DANNA
School Mistress, Stormwind (72), Roams city

MIST
Teldrassil (80), C-3, The Oracle Glade, West of glade

MIST CREEPER
Silverpine Forest (68), E-1, The Skittering Dark, Cave

MIST HOWLER
Rare Spawn, Ashenvale (12), C:(2-3), D-1, Lvl 22 Semi-Rare; Roams forest near spawn points

MISTINA STEELSHIELD
Alliance Cloth Quartermaster, Ironforge (52), F-3, The Great Forge, Outside Stonebrow's Clothier

MISTRESS NAGMARA
Burning Steppes (22), Searing Gorge (64), C-4/D-8, Blackrock Depths

MISTVALE GORILLA
Stranglethorn Vale (74), D-2, Lake Nazferiti

MISTWING RAVAGER
Azshara (14), H:(2, 3), I:(2, 3), J:(1-3), K:(2, 3), Bitter Reaches, Thalassian Base Camp, The Shattered Strand

MISTWING ROGUE
Azshara (14), A-8, B-8, C-8, D:(7, 8), E-7, Forlorn Ridge, Lake Mennar, Ruins of Eldarath

MITHRAS IRONHILL
Stormwind (72), K-1, Stormwind Keep, War Room

MITH'RETHIS THE ENCHANTER
Rare Spawn, The Hinterlands (50), I-8, J-8, Jintha'Alor, Lvl 52 Average Rare; Roams from camp to camp

MITSUWA
Ashenvale (12), B-4, Zoram'gar Outpost (131), Southern structure

MIZZLE THE CRAFTY
Feralas (46), G-4, Dire Maul

MOBILE ALERT SYSTEM
Dun Morogh (32), C-4, Gnomeregan

MOGG
Barrens (18), E-1, Roams in and out of building west of road

MOGH THE UNDYING
Skullsplitter Clan Witchdoctor, Stranglethorn Vale (74), E-5, Ruins of Zul'Mamwe, By campfire

MO'GROSH BRUTE
Loch Modan (54), I-2, J:(1-3), K:(1, 2), Mo'grosh Stronghold

MO'GROSH ENFORCER
Loch Modan (54), H:(2, 3), I:(2, 3), J:(2, 3), Mo'grosh Stronghold

MO'GROSH MYSTIC
Loch Modan (54), H:(2, 3), I:(1-3), K-2, Mo'grosh Stronghold

MO'GROSH OGRE
Loch Modan (54), H:(2, 3), I:(2, 3), J:(2, 3), Mo'grosh Stronghold

MO'GROSH SHAMAN
Loch Modan (54), H:(2, 3), I:(2, 3), J:(2, 3), Mo'grosh Stronghold

MOJO THE TWISTED
Rare Spawn, Blasted Lands (20), F-1, G-2, Dreadmaul Hold, Lvl 48 Uncommon; Roams small area around spawn point

MOKK THE SAVAGE
Stranglethorn Vale (74), C-7, Mistvale Valley, (Summon) Spawns in with several gorillas

MOK'RASH
Stranglethorn Vale (74), B-7, Janeiro's Point, Southern end of island

MOKTAR KRIN
Thousand Needles (82), I-6, Ironstone Camp, Camp just west of Shimmering Flats

MOLOK THE CRUSHER
Rare Spawn, Arathi Highlands (10), G-8, Boulderfist Hall, Lvl 39 Semi-Rare; Westernmost point in cave

MOLT THORN
Rare Spawn, Swamp of Sorrows (76), C-5, D-4, The Shifting Mire, Lvl 42 Average Rare; Patrols back and forth between connecting bridges along the western waterways

MOLTEN DESTROYER
Burning Steppes (22), Searing Gorge (64), C-4/D-8, The Molten Core

MOLTEN ELEMENTAL
Orgrimmar (60), F-5, Ragefire Chasm

MOLTEN GIANT
Burning Steppes (22), Searing Gorge (64), C-4/D-8, The Molten Core

MOLTEN WAR GOLEM
Burning Steppes (22), Searing Gorge (64), C-4/D-8, Blackrock Depths

MONGRESS
Rare Spawn, Felwood (44), F:(7-8), Lvl 50 Very Rare; Roams near spawn points

MONIKA SENGUTZ
Hillsbrad Foothills (48), H-2, Tarren Mill (128), First floor of inn

MONNOS THE ELDER
Rare Spawn, Azshara (14), H-9, K-2, Bitter Reaches, Lvl 54 Uber-Rare; Roams across northern and southern peninsulas

MONSTROUS CRAWLER
Swamp of Sorrows (76), I-9, J:(1, 9), K:(1, 9), L:(1-9), Misty Reed Strand

MONSTROUS OOZE
Wetlands (96), F:(2, 3), I:(4, 5), J:(4, 5), Direforge Hill, Ironbeard's Tomb

MONSTROUS PLAGUEBAT
Eastern Plaguelands (40), B-3, C:(2-4), D-4, E-4, F:(3-4), G:(2-4), H:(2-5), I:(3-5), J:(3, 4), Plaguewood

MONTARR
Lorekeeper, Thousand Needles (82), F-5, Freewind Post, Next to hut, west of inn

MONTY
Rat Extermination Specialist, Ironforge (52), L-5, The Deeprun Tram, Deeprun Tram

MOODAN SUNGRAIN
Baker, Mulgore (58), E-8, Camp Narache (105), Mill

MOON PRIESTESS AMARA
Teldrassil (80), F:(5-6), G-6, Dolanaar (109), Patrols road between Dolanaar and east of Ban'ethil Hollow

MOONGLADE WARDEN
Moonglade (56), E-4, F:(3-5), G:(3, 4), H-3, I-6, J:(5, 6), Nighthaven (120)

MOONKIN
Darkshore (24), F:(4, 5), G:(4, 5)

MOONKIN ORACLE
Darkshore (24), G-5

MOONRAGE ARMORER
Silverpine Forest (68), G-7, Preywood Village

MOONRAGE BLOODHOWLER
Silverpine Forest (68), G:(7, 8), H:(7, 8), I-4, In hills

MOONRAGE DARKRUNNER
Silverpine Forest (68), G:(2, 3), H:(2, 3), Valagan's Field, Farm

MOONRAGE DARKSOUL
Silverpine Forest (68), F:(2, 3), G-3, I-4, North Tide's Hollow

MOONRAGE ELDER
Silverpine Forest (68), F-7, G-7, Preywood Village

MOONRAGE GLUTTON
Silverpine Forest (68), F:(2, 3), G:(2, 3), H:(1, 2), North Tide's Hollow

MOONRAGE LEATHERWORKER
Silverpine Forest (68), G-7, Preywood Village

MOONRAGE SENTRY
Silverpine Forest (68), F-7, G-7, Preywood Village

MOONRAGE TAILOR
Silverpine Forest (68), G-7, Preywood Village

MOONRAGE WATCHER
Silverpine Forest (68), F-7, G-7, Preywood Village

MOONRAGE WHITESCALP
Silverpine Forest (68), G:(3, 4), H:(2-5), The Shining Strand

MOONSTALKER
Darkshore (24), F:(2, 5-8), G:(2-4, 6, 7), H:(2-4)

MOONSTALKER MATRIARCH
Darkshore (24), E:(8, 9), F-9, G-9, I-1, Mist's Edge, The Master's Glaive, Twilight Vale

MOONSTALKER RUNT
Darkshore (24), F:(2-6), G:(2-6), Ameth'Aran, Bashal'Aran, Mist's Edge

MOONSTALKER SIRE
Darkshore (24), E:(8, 9), F:(7-9), G:(8, 9), I-1

MOONTOUCHED OWLBEAST
Winterspring (98), I:(2, 6), J:(2, 6), The Hidden Grove, Owl Wing Thicket

MOORA
Felwood (44), E-6, Shadow Hold, Anteroom after spiral tunnel

MOORANE HEARTHGRAIN
Baker, Barrens (18), F-3, The Crossroads (107), Eastern entrance

MOORANTA
Skinning Trainer, Thunder Bluff (84), E-4, Middle rise, next to Thunder Bluff Armorers

MOORAT LONGSTRIDE
General Goods, Mulgore (58), E-6, Bloodhoof Village (102), Northeast tent

MORBENT FEL
Duskwood (36), B-3, Forlorn Rowe, Second floor of house

MORDRESH FIRE EYE
Barrens (18), F-9, Razorfen Downs

MOREN RIVERBEND
Moonglade (56), G-4, Nighthaven (120), West wing of southeast building

MORG GNARLTREE
Armorer, Duskwood (36), J-5, Darkshire (108), Smithy

MORGAINE THE SLY
Rare Spawn, Elwynn Forest (42), D-6, Mirror Lake Orchard, Lvl 10 Uncommon; House next to lake

MORGAN LADIMORE
Duskwood (36), B-3, Forlorn Rowe, (Summon) Fresh grave

MORGAN PESTLE
Stormwind (72), H-6, Trade District, Pestle's Apothecary

MORGAN STERN
Dustwallow Marsh (38), I-5, Theramore Isle (130), Inn

MORGAN THE COLLECTOR
Elwynn Forest (42), J-8, Brackwell Pumpkin Patch, In house with Erlan Drudgemoor and Surena Caledon

MORGANTH
Redridge Mountains (62), K-5, Tower of Ilgalar, Idle on top floor of tower

MORGANUS
Stable Master, Tirisfal Glades (86), H-5, Brill (104), In front of stable

MORGG STORMSHOT
Stormwind (72), I-2, Dwarven District, West of tavern

MORGUM
Leather Armor Merchant, Orgrimmar (60), G-8, Valley of Strength, Soran's Leather and Steel

MORHAN COPPERTONGUE
Metalsmith, Loch Modan (54), D-5, Thelsamar (129), On porch of first house on left of path

MORI HILDELVE
Dun Morogh (32), K-4, North Gate Outpost, Corpse at foot of a deadend hill on left side of the outpost

MORIN CLOUDSTALKER
Mulgore (58), F-6, Travels road east of village

MOR'LADIM
Duskwood (36), B-4, Forlorn Rowe, Patrols a circular path around Raven Hill Cemetery, Forlorn Rowe, and the entrance to the Dawning Wood Catacombs

MORLEY BATES
Fungus Vendor, Undercity (88), K-2, The Magic Quarter, Roams Magic Quarter

MORLEY EBERLEIN
Clothier, Elwynn Forest (42), I-7, Tower of Azora, Second floor of tower

MORPHAZ
Swamp of Sorrows (76), I-5, The Temple of Atal'Hakkar

MORRIDUNE
Ashenvale (12), B-2, Blackfathom Deeps

MORRIS LAWRY
Stormwind (72), F-5, G-5, The Canals, Just east of The Finest Thread

MOR'ROGAL
Stonetalon Mountains (70), F-6, Sun Rock Retreat (127), Hut on cliff south of inn

MORTA'GYA THE KEEPER
The Hinterlands (50), G-7, The Altar of Zul, Top of altar

MORTIMER MONTAGUE
Banker, Undercity (88), I-4, The Trade Quarter

MOR'VEK
Ravasaur Trainers, Un'Goro Crater (90), J-7, The Marshlands, East of far south tip of river

MOR'ZUL BLOODBRINGER
Burning Steppes (22), A-3, Altar of Storms, Graveyard above and left of the Altar of Storms

MOSARN
Thunder Bluff (84), F-8, Hunter Rise, In building west of Hunter's Hall

MOSH'OGG BRUTE
Stranglethorn Vale (74), C-3, D-3, Mizjah Ruins, The Savage Coast

MOSH'OGG BUTCHER
Stranglethorn Vale (74), F-3, Mosh'Ogg Ogre Mound

MOSH'OGG LORD
Stranglethorn Vale (74), F-3, Mosh'Ogg Ogre Mound

MOSH'OGG MAULER
Stranglethorn Vale (74), F-3, Mosh'Ogg Ogre Mound

MOSH'OGG SHAMAN
Stranglethorn Vale (74), F-3, Mosh'Ogg Ogre Mound

MOSH'OGG SPELLCRAFTER
Stranglethorn Vale (74), F-3, Mosh'Ogg Ogre Mound

MOSH'OGG WARMONGER
Stranglethorn Vale (74), E-3, F-3, Mosh'Ogg Ogre Mound

MOSH'OGG WITCH DOCTOR
Stranglethorn Vale (74), C-3, D-3, Mizjah Ruins, The Savage Coast

MOSS STALKER
Silverpine Forest (68), E:(1, 2), F-2, The Skittering Dark, Cave

MOSSFLAYER CANNIBAL
Eastern Plaguelands (40), H:(2, 3), I:(2, 3), J-2, Zul'Masha

MOSSFLAYER SCOUT
Eastern Plaguelands (40), H:(2, 3), I:(2, 3), J-2, Zul'Masha

MOSSFLAYER SHADOWHUNTER
Eastern Plaguelands (40), H:(2, 3), I:(2, 3), J-2, Zul'Masha

MOSSFLAYER ZOMBIE
Eastern Plaguelands (40), D-8, The Undercroft

MOSSHIDE ALPHA
Wetlands (96), D-3, E-3, Saltspray Glen, Sundown Marsh

MOSSHIDE BRUTE
Wetlands (96), D-3, E-3, F-3, Saltspray Glen, Sundown Marsh

MOSSHIDE FENRUNNER
Wetlands (96), C-4, D:(3, 4), E-3, F:(3, 4), G-3, H:(5, 6), I:(5, 6), Mosshide Fen, Sundown Marsh

MOSSHIDE GNOLL
Wetlands (96), G-7, H:(6-8), I:(6, 7), Dun Algaz, Mosshide Fen

MOSSHIDE MISTWEAVER
Wetlands (96), E-3, F-3, G-3, H-6, I-7, Ironbeard's Tomb, Mosshide Fen

MOSSHIDE MONGREL
Wetlands (96), H:(5-7), I:(5-7), Mosshide Fen

MOSSHIDE MYSTIC
Wetlands (96), D-3, E-3, Saltspray Glen, Sundown Marsh

MOSSHIDE TRAPPER
Wetlands (96), C-4, D:(3, 4), E-3, F-3, G-3, Bluegill Marsh, Saltspray Glen, Sundown Marsh

MOSSHOOF COURSER
Azshara (14), D-7, E:(7, 8), F:(1-4, 7, 8), G:(2-4, 8, 9), H:(1, 2, 8), I:(2, 3), J:(2, 3), K:(2, 3)

MOSSHOOF RUNNER
Azshara (14), A:(5-7), B:(5-7), Haldarr Encampment, Shadowsong Shrine, Valormok

MOSSHOOF STAG
Azshara (14), A-8, B:(7, 8), C-8, D-8, Lake Mennar

MOT DAWNSTRIDER
Journeyman Enchanter, Thunder Bluff (84), E-4, Middle rise, next to Dawnstrider Enchantments

MOTEGA FIREMANE
Thousand Needles (82), B-3, Whitereach Post, Next to hut

MOTHER FANG
Rare Spawn, Elwynn Forest (42), H-5, Jasperlode Mine, Lvl 10 Uncommon; Roams in mine

MOTHER SMOLDERWEB
Burning Steppes (22), Searing Gorge (64), C-4/D-8, Blackrock Spire

MOTLEY GARMASON
Wetlands (96), G-2, Dun Modr, Next to wagons, west of road

MOTTLED BOAR
Durotar (34), F:(6, 7), G:(6, 7), Hidden Path, Valley of Trials (131)

MOTTLED DRYWALLOW CROCOLISK
Dustwallow Marsh (38), D:(5, 6), E:(5, 6), F:(5, 6), G:(5, 6), Beezil's Wreck, The Dragonmurk, The Quagmire

MOTTLED RAPTOR
Wetlands (96), B-5, C:(4-6), D:(4, 5), E-4, Black Channel Marsh, Menethil Bay, Whelgar's Excavation Site

MOTTLED RAZORMAW
Wetlands (96), D-5, E-5, Whelgar's Excavation Site

MOTTLED SCREECHER
Wetlands (96), C:(5, 6), D:(4, 5), Black Channel Marsh, Menethil Bay

MOTTLED SCYTHECLAW
Wetlands (96), D:(4, 5), E:(4, 5), Whelgar's Excavation Site

MOTTLED WORG
Silverpine Forest (68), G:(1-3), H:(1, 2), I:(1, 2), Thoughout Silverpine

MOUNTAIN BOAR
Loch Modan (54), C:(1-5), D:(2-4), E:(3, 4)

MOUNTAIN BUZZARD
Loch Modan (54), I:(5, 7), J:(5-7), K:(6-8), The Farstrider Lodge

MOUNTAIN COUGAR
Mulgore (58), D:(8, 9), E:(8, 9), F-9, G-9, Red Cloud Mesa

MOUNTAIN LION
Alterac Mountains (8), D:(7-9), E:(8, 9), F:(7-9), G-8, I-5, J:(5, 6), K:(5, 6)

MOUNTAIN YETI
Alterac Mountains (8), D:(6, 7), E-7, Growless Cave

MOUNTAINEER ANGST
Loch Modan (54), F-1, Stonewrought Dam, Roams dam

MOUNTAINEER BARLEYBREW
Dun Morogh (32), L-5, South Gate Outpost, Next to tower

MOUNTAINEER BARN
Loch Modan (54), F-1, Stonewrought Dam, Roams dam

MOUNTAINEER BROKK
Loch Modan (54), C:(1, 2), Dun Algaz

MOUNTAINEER COBBLEFLINT
Loch Modan (54), B-7, Valley of Kings, In front of tower

MOUNTAINEER CRAGG
Loch Modan (54), D-4, Thelsamar (129)

MOUNTAINEER DALK
Loch Modan (54), D-4, E-4, Thelsamar (129)

MOUNTAINEER DOKKIN
Wetlands (96), G-8, H-8, Dun Algaz, Patrols tunnel

MOUNTAINEER DOLF
Dun Morogh (32), F-5, Kharanos (114), Kneeling on cliff edge left of the path leading to Kharanos

MOUNTAINEER DROKEN
Loch Modan (54), D-5, Thelsamar (129)

MOUNTAINEER FLINT
Loch Modan (54), C-2, D-4, Algaz Station, Roams road

MOUNTAINEER GANN
Loch Modan (54), B-2, North Gate Pass

MOUNTAINEER GRAVELGAW
Loch Modan (54), C-8, Valley of Kings, By tower entrance

MOUNTAINEER GRUGELM
Wetlands (96), G-8, H-8, Dun Algaz, Patrols tunnel

MOUNTAINEER GWARTH
Loch Modan (54), D-4, Thelsamar (129)

MOUNTAINEER HAGGIS
Loch Modan (54), E-1, Stonewrought Dam

MOUNTAINEER HAGIL
Loch Modan (54), G-1, Stonewrought Dam

MOUNTAINEER HAMMERFALL
Loch Modan (54), C-2, Algaz Station

MOUNTAINEER KADRELL
Loch Modan (54), D-5, Thelsamar (129), Patrols along path running through Thelsamar

MOUNTAINEER KALMIR
Loch Modan (54), Valley of Kings, Roams road

MOUNTAINEER KAMDAR
Loch Modan (54), D-4, Thelsamar (129)

MOUNTAINEER LANGARR
Loch Modan (54), D-5, Thelsamar (129)

MOUNTAINEER LUXST
Loch Modan (54), C-2, Algaz Station, Tower

MOUNTAINEER MODAX
Loch Modan (54), E-4, Thelsamar (129)

MOUNTAINEER MORLIC
Loch Modan (54), F-1, Stonewrought Dam, By engineer tent

MOUNTAINEER MORRAN
Loch Modan (54), C-2, Algaz Station, Roams from Algaz Station to road

MOUNTAINEER NAARTH
Loch Modan (54), B-7, Valley of Kings, Roams road

MOUNTAINEER OSMOK
Loch Modan (54), D-5, Thelsamar (129)

MOUNTAINEER PEBBLEBITTY
Loch Modan (54), B-8, Valley of Kings, Mounted by mountain pass heading into Searing Gorge

MOUNTAINEER RHAREN
Wetlands (96), H-8, Dun Algaz, Stands guard of tunnel

MOUNTAINEER ROCKGAR
Loch Modan (54), C-1, Dun Algaz, By mountain pass heading into Wetlands

MOUNTAINEER ROGHAN
Loch Modan (54), D-5, Thelsamar (129)

MOUNTAINEER STORMPIKE
Loch Modan (54), C-2, Dun Algaz, Algaz Station

MOUNTAINEER THALOS
Dun Morogh (32), C-7, Coldridge Pass, On road heading to pass entrance

MOUNTAINEER THAR
Wetlands (96), H-8, Dun Algaz, Stands guard of tunnel

MOUNTAINEER TYRAW
Loch Modan (54), B-7, Valley of Kings

MOUNTAINEER VEEK
Loch Modan (54), B-8, B-7, Valley of Kings

MOUNTAINEER WALLBANG
Loch Modan (54), C-7, Valley of Kings, First floor of tower

MOUNTAINEER WUAR
Loch Modan (54), D-4, Thelsamar (129)

MOUNTAINEER YUTTHA
Loch Modan (54), C-2, Algaz Station

MOUNTAINEER ZAREN
Loch Modan (54), B-7, C-6, Valley of Kings, Roams road

MOUNTAINEER ZWARN
Loch Modan (54), B-7, C-6, Algaz Station, Tent

MOUNTED IRONFORGE MOUNTAINEER
Dun Morogh (32), J:(2, 3)

MR. SMITE
Westfall (94), D-7, E-7, The Deadmines

MRS. WINTERS
General Supplies, Tirisfal Glades (86), H-5, Brill (104), Standing by carriage left of Gallows' End Tavern

MUAD
Rare Spawn, Tirisfal Glades (86), D-4, Whispering Shore, Lvl 10 Uncommon; Patrols in and along shoreline

MUCK FRENZY
Barrens (18), H-5, Fray Island

MUCK SPLASH
Searing Gorge (64), A:(3, 4), Firewatch Ridge, In the pools

MUCKRAKE
Alterac Mountains (8), E-5, Ruins of Alterac, Town Hall

MUCKSHELL CLACKER
Dustwallow Marsh (38), F:(3, 4), G:(4, 5), H:(4, 5), Dustwallow Bay

MUCKSHELL PINCER
Dustwallow Marsh (38), H:(6, 7), Tidefury Cove

MUCKSHELL RAZORCLAW
Dustwallow Marsh (38), G-6, Tidefury Cove

MUCKSHELL SCRABBLER
Dustwallow Marsh (38), G-6, H-7, Tidefury Cove

MUCKSHELL SNAPCLAW
Dustwallow Marsh (38), F:(3, 4), G:(4, 5), H:(4, 5), Dustwallow Bay

MUCULENT OOZE
Un'Goro Crater (90), H:(3, 4), I:(3, 4), J:(2-4, 6, 7), Lakkari Tar Pits, The Marshlands

MUDCRUSH DURTFEET
Dustwallow Marsh (38), D-4, Small camp south of Brackenwall Village

MUDDUK
Superior Cook, Stranglethorn Vale (74), C-3, Grom'gol Base Camp (112), Under scaffolding just inside camp walls to the right of western entrance

MUDROCK BORER
Dustwallow Marsh (38), G-6, H:(5, 6), Dustwallow Bay, Tidefury Cove

MUDROCK BURROWER
Dustwallow Marsh (38), F:(3, 4), G:(4, 5), H:(4, 5), Dustwallow Bay

MUDROCK SNAPJAW
Dustwallow Marsh (38), G-6, H:(5, 6), Dustwallow Bay, Tidefury Cove

MUDROCK SPIKESHELL
Dustwallow Marsh (38), G:(1, 2), H:(1-4), I:(1-4), Dreadmurk Shore, Theramore Isle, Witch Hill

MUDROCK TORTOISE
Dustwallow Marsh (38), G:(1, 2), H:(1-4), I:(1-4), Dreadmurk Shore, Theramore Isle

MUDSNOUT GNOLL
Hillsbrad Foothills (48), G-6, H-6, Nethander Stead

MUDSNOUT SHAMAN
Hillsbrad Foothills (48), H-6, Nethander Stead

MUG'THOL
Alterac Mountains (8), E-5, Ruins of Alterac, Second floor of castle

MUGGLEFIN
Rare Spawn, Ashenvale (12), C-4, Lake Falathim, Lvl 23 Semi-Rare; Roams near spawn points

MUGLASH
Ashenvale (12), B-4, Zoram'gar Outpost (131), Southeast structure

MUIGIN
Un'Goro Crater (90), F-1, Marshal's Refuge (116), Southeast of cave

MUIREDON BATTLEFORGE
Ironforge (52), C-1, The Mystic Ward, Hall of Mysteries

MUKDRAK
Journeyman Engineer, Durotar (34), H-4, Razor Hill (122), Northeast of inn

MULGORE PROTECTOR
Mulgore (58), D-8, Red Cloud Mesa

MULGRIS DEEPRIVER
Western Plaguelands (92), G-6, The Writhing Haunt, Lying in house on the nothern side of farm

MULL THUNDERHORN
Mulgore (58), E-6, Bloodhoof Village (102), Outside east tent

MUMMIFIED ATAL'AI
Swamp of Sorrows (76), I-5, The Temple of Atal'Hakkar

MURA RUNTETOTEM
Silverpine Forest (68), F-4, The Sepulcher (124), Left side of inn by fireplace

MURAGUS
Staff Merchant, Orgrimmar (60), E-5, The Cleft of Shadow, Ironwood Staves and Wands

MURDALOC
Badlands (16), G-7, Agmond's End, Roams camp

MURDEROUS BLISTERPAW
Rare Spawn, Tanaris (78), H-4, Lvl 43 Very Rare; Roams from one set of hills to the other

MUREN STORMPIKE
Ironforge (52), J-9, The Military Ward, Hall of Arms

MURK SLITHERER
Swamp of Sorrows (76), I-5, The Temple of Atal'Hakkar

MURK SPITTER
Swamp of Sorrows (76), I-5, The Temple of Atal'Hakkar

MURK THRESHER
Dustwallow Marsh (38), G-6, H:(5, 6), Dustwallow Bay, Tidefury Cove

MURK WORM
Swamp of Sorrows (76), I-5, The Temple of Atal'Hakkar

MURKDEEP
Darkshore (24), E-8, Twilight Shore, Spawns off shore

MURKGILL FORAGER
Stranglethorn Vale (74), C:(2, 3), Kal'ai Ruins

MURKGILL HUNTER
Stranglethorn Vale (74), C:(2, 3), Kal'ai Ruins

MURKGILL LORD
Stranglethorn Vale (74), C-3, Kal'ai Ruins

MURKGILL ORACLE
Stranglethorn Vale (74), C-3, Kal'ai Ruins

MURKGILL WARRIOR
Stranglethorn Vale (74), C:(2, 3), Kal'ai Ruins

MURKSHALLOW SNAPCLAW
Ashenvale (12), B-2, Blackfathom Deeps

MURLOC
Elwynn Forest (42), G:(6, 7), H:(6, 7), Crystal Lake

MURLOC COASTRUNNER
Westfall (94), D-1, E-1, F-1, Longshore

MURLOC FLESHEATER
Redridge Mountains (62), E:(4, 5), F:(5-7), G:(6, 7), H-6, Lake Everstill

MURLOC FORAGER
Elwynn Forest (42), G-9, H-8, I-8, J:(8, 9), K:(4-6, 8, 9)

MURLOC HUNTER
Westfall (94), B:(3-6), C-3, Longshore

MURLOC LURKER
Elwynn Forest (42), J-8, K:(4-6, 8, 9), L:(8, 9), Stone Cairn Lake

MURLOC MINOR ORACLE
Westfall (94), C-2, D:(1, 2), E-1, Longshore

MURLOC MINOR TIDECALLER
Redridge Mountains (62), F:(6, 7), G:(6, 7), H-6, Lake Everstill

MURLOC NETTER
Westfall (94), C:(2, 3), D:(1, 2), Longshore

MURLOC NIGHTCRAWLER
Redridge Mountains (62), K-6, Stonewatch Falls

MURLOC ORACLE
Westfall (94), B:(5-7), C-8, Longshore

MURLOC RAIDER
Westfall (94), E-1, F-1, Longshore

MURLOC SCOUT
Redridge Mountains (62), E:(4, 5), F-5, G-5, H-5, Lake Everstill

MURLOC SHORESTRIKER
Redridge Mountains (62), F:(6, 7), G-7, Lake Everstill

MURLOC STREAMRUNNER
Elwynn Forest (42), G:(6, 7), H:(6, 7), Crystal Lake

MURLOC TIDECALLER
Redridge Mountains (62), G-5, H-5, K-6, Lake Everstill

MURLOC TIDEHUNTER
Westfall (94), B-7, C-8, Longshore

MURLOC WARRIOR
Westfall (94), B:(3-5), C:(2, 3), Longshore

MURNDAN DERTH
Gunsmith, Wetlands (96), A-6, Menethil Harbor (117), Building northeast of tavern

MURPHY WEST
Wetlands (96), A-6, Menethil Harbor (117), First floor of keep, next to stairs

MUSHGOG
Rare Spawn, Feralas (46), G-4, Dire Maul, Lvl 60 Rare

MUSHGOG
Feralas (46), G-4, The Maul, In arena

MUTANUS THE DEVOURER
Barrens (18), E-4, Wailing Caverns

MUTATED VENTURE CO. DRONE
Barrens (18), F-1, First floor of tower northeast of Sludge Fen

MUURAN
Superior Macecrafter, Desolace (30), G-6, Ghost Walker Post (111), Outside center hut

MU'UTA
Bowyer, Arathi Highlands (10), J-3, Hammerfall (113), Next to forge

MYDRANNUL
General Goods Vendor, Darnassus (26), K-4, Warrior's Terrace, South of path just after entrance to city

MYIZZ LUCKYCATCH
Superior Fisherman, Stranglethorn Vale (74), B-8, Booty Bay (103), On the eastern side of the bay directly beneath hanging shark

MY'LANNA
Food & Drink Merchant, Moonglade (56), F-3, Nighthaven (120), Northwest building

MYLENTHA RIVERBEND
Moonglade (56), G-3, Nighthaven (120), Second floor of northeast building

MYOLOR SUNDERFURY
Ironforge (52), G-4, The Great Forge, North of The Great Anvil

MYRA TYRNGAARDE
Bread Vendor, Ironforge (52), C-6, D-8, The Commons, Roams in a circle

MYRANDA THE HAG
Western Plaguelands (92), G-8, Sorrow Hill, On tree stump where path forks

MYRIAM MOONSINGER
Barrens (18), F-9, Razorfen Downs, Atop large bramble in dark area

MYROKOS SILENTFORM
Hillsbrad Foothills (48), K-2, First floor of Chateau Ravenholdt

MYSTIC YAYO'JIN
Reagent Vendor, The Hinterlands (50), L-8, Revantusk Village, Roams hut on eastern side of village

MYSTLASH FLAYER
Ashenvale (12), A:(2-4), The Zoram Strand (131)

MYSTLASH HYDRA
Ashenvale (12), A:(2-4), B:(2, 3), The Zoram Strand (131), Zoram'gar Outpost (131)

MYTHIDAN
Mace & Staff Merchant, Darnassus (26), I-6, Tradesmen's Terrace, Weapons shop

MYTHRIN'DIR
General Trade Supplier, Darnassus (26), H-2, Craftsmen's Terrace, General Trade shop

MYZRAEL
Arathi Highlands (10), I-3, (Summon) Shard of Myzrael

N

NAAL MISTRUNNER
Cooking Supplier, Thunder Bluff (84), F-5, High rise, outside Aska's Kitchen tent

NADIA VERNON
Bowyer, Silverpine Forest (68), G-4, The Sepulcher (124), Next to house on the right side of sepulcher

NADYIA MANEWEAVER
Journeyman Leatherworker, Teldrassil (80), E-5, House at end of road

NAELA TRANCE
Bowyer, Wetlands (96), A-6, Menethil Harbor (117), Next to wagon, east of keep

NAGA EXPLORER
Stranglethorn Vale (74), B:(6, 7)

NAGAZ
Alterac Mountains (8), E-2, Dandred's Fold, First floor of house

NAG'ZEHN
Thousand Needles (82), I-6, Ironstone Camp, Camp just west of Shimmering Flats

NAK
Barrens (18), E-8, Blackthorn Ridge, Roams the ridge

NALESETTE WILDBRINGER
Pet Trainer, Felwood (44), H-3, Talonbranch Glade, Front of building

NALPAK
Disciple of Naralex, Barrens (18), E-4, The Wailing Caverns, Right eye of cave above entrance

NALPAK
Barrens (18), E-4, Wailing Caverns

NAMDO BIZZFIZZLE
Engineering Supplies, Dun Morogh (32), C-4, Gnomeregan

NAN MISTRUNNER
Fruit Vendor, Thunder Bluff (84), E-4, Middle rise, in Fruits and Vegetables tent

NANCY VISHAS
Alterac Mountains (8), D-3, The Uplands, Patrols between house and dock

NANDAR BRANSON
Alchemy Supplies, Hillsbrad Foothills (48), F-6, Southshore (125), Small house on left of path

NANTAR
Baker, Ashenvale (12), E-5, Astranaar (101), First floor of inn

NARA MEIDEROS
Priest Trainer, Stormwind (72), C-5, The Park, By pool of water

NARA WILDMANE
Thunder Bluff (84), I-3, Elder Rise, Inside Hall of Elders

NARAIN SOOTHFANCY
Tanaris (78), J-2, Steamwheedle Port, Engineer tower to the north of the port

NARAM LONGCLAW
Weaponsmith, Darkshore (24), F-4, Auberdine (101), Back terrace of northern building

NARAXIS
Rare Spawn, Duskwood (36), L-5, Lvl 27 Uncommon; Cave

NARG THE TASKMASTER
Rare Spawn, Elwynn Forest (42), E-8, Fargodeep Mine, Lvl 10 Uncommon; Roams in mine

NARGAL DEATHEYE
Weaponsmith, Barrens (18), F-3, The Crossroads (107), Western entrance

NARGATT
Food & Drink, Stranglethorn Vale (74), C-3, Grom'gol Base Camp (112), Scaffolding just left of zepplin tower

NARIANNA
Bowyer, Moonglade (56), G-4, Nighthaven (120), East wing of southeast building

NARILLASANZ
Rare Spawn, Alterac Mountains (8), J:(5, 6), K:(4-6), Chillwind Point, Lvl 44 Semi-Rare; Patrols area between lake and road

NARJ DEEPSLICE
Butcher, Arathi Highlands (10), F-4, Refuge Point, Roams in camp

NARKK
Pirate Supples, Stranglethorn Vale (74), B-8, Booty Bay (103), Nautical Needs (shop) on the northern side of The Old Port Authority

NARM FAULK
Dun Morogh (32), K-6, Ironband's Compound, Dead on hill at the southern end of Helm's Bed Lake

NARM SKYCHASER
Shaman Trainer, Mulgore (58), F-6, Bloodhoof Village (102), East tent

NARNIE
Pet, Redridge Mountains (62), C-4, Lakeshire (115), First floor of Lakeshire Inn

NARRET SHADOWGROVE
Trades Supplies, Teldrassil (80), G-6, Dolanaar (109), Middle floor inside building north of road

NARTOK
Warlock Trainer, Durotar (34), F-7, Valley of Trials (131), Back of cave

NARV HIDECRAFTER
Expert Leathercrafter, Desolace (30), G-6, Ghost Walker Post (111), Center hut

NAT PAGLE
Artisan Fisherman, Dustwallow Marsh (38), H-6, Tidefury Cove, On isle in the cove

NATA DAWNSTRIDER
Enchanting Supplies, Thunder Bluff (84), E-4, Middle rise, next to Dawnstrider Enchantments

NATAKA LONGHORN
Desolace (30), G-6, Ghost Walker Post (111), Center hut

NATHANIEL DUMAH
Western Plaguelands (92), F-8, Chillwind Camp, In front of shed by ruined building

NATHANIEL STEENWICK
Thrown Weapons Merchant, Undercity (88), K-5, The Rogues' Quarter, Near Magic Quarter entry

NATHANOS BLIGHTCALLER
Champion of the Banshee Queen, Eastern Plaguelands (40), D-7, The Marris Stead, In front of house with two Blighthounds

NATHERIL RAINCALLER
General Goods, Winterspring (98), H-3, Starfall Village, South end of main building

NAZEER BLOODPIKE
Dustwallow Marsh (38), D-3, Brackenwall Village (104), West entrance

NAZGREL
Advisor to Thrall, Orgrimmar (60), C:(3, 4), Valley of Wisdom, Grommash Hold

NAZGREL
Advisor to Thrall, Orgrimmar (60), C:(3, 4), Valley of Wisdom, Grommash Hold

NEAL ALLEN
Engineering & General Goods Supplier, Wetlands (96), A-6, Menethil Harbor (117), Northeast room on first floor of keep

NECROFIEND
Western Plaguelands (92), I-7, Scholomance

NECROMANCER
Cult of the Damned, Eastern Plaguelands (40), C-2, D:(2-4), E:(3, 4), F-3, Plaguewood, In structures

NEEDLES COUGAR
Thousand Needles (82), A:(1-3), B:(2-4), C:(2-5), D:(4, 5), E-5, F:(5, 6), G:(4, 5), H:(5, 6), I:(5, 6)

NEEKA BLOODSCAR
Badlands (16), A-5, Kargath (114), Tower platform

NEEMA
Waitress, Hillsbrad Foothills (48), F-6, Southshore (125), First floor of inn

NEERU FIREBLADE
Orgrimmar (60), E-5, The Cleft of Shadow, Building ouside Ragefire Chasm entry

NEFARU
Rare Spawn, Duskwood (36), I-8, J-8, Roland's Doom, Lvl 34 Uncommon; Roams small area around spawn point

NEGOLASH
Stranglethorn Vale (74), C-8, Wild Shore, (Summon) Patrols to the ruined lifeboat on shore

NEKRUM GUTCHEWER
Tanaris (78), E-1, Zul'Farrak

NELSON THE NICE
Silithus (66), E-4, Hive'Zora, Roams south to the Twilight Outpost, down to the wall and back

NERGAL
General Goods Vendor, Un'Goro Crater (90), F-1, Marshal's Refuge (116), Near entrance to cave

NERRIST
Trade Goods, Stranglethorn Vale (74), C-3, Grom'gol Base Camp (112), Just inside camp walls to the right of eastern entrance

NERUB'ENKAN
Eastern Plaguelands (40), D-2, Stratholme

NESSA SHADOWSONG
Fishing Supplies, Teldrassil (80), G-9, Rut'theran Village, At intersection

NETHER MAIDEN
Desolace (30), F:(7, 8), G-7, Mannoroc Coven

NETHER SISTER
Desolace (30), G-8, Mannoroc Coven

NETHER SORCERESS
Desolace (30), F:(7, 8), G:(7, 8), Mannoroc Coven

NETHERGARDE ANALYST
Blasted Lands (20), I-2, J:(1, 2), Nethergarde Keep (119)

NETHERGARDE CLERIC
Blasted Lands (20), I:(1, 2), Nethergarde Keep (119)

NETHERGARDE ELITE
Blasted Lands (20), I-2, J-2, Nethergarde Keep (119)

NETHERGARDE ENGINEER
Blasted Lands (20), H-1, I-1, J-1, K-1, Garrison Armory, Nethergarde Keep (119)

NETHERGARDE FOREMAN
Blasted Lands (20), H-1, I-1, J-1, K-1, Garrison Armory, Nethergarde Keep (119)

NETHERGARDE MINER
Blasted Lands (20), H-1, I-1, J-1, K-1, Garrison Armory, Nethergarde Keep (119)

NETHERGARDE OFFICER
Blasted Lands (20), I-2, J-2, Nethergarde Keep (119)

NETHERGARDE RIFTWATCHER
Blasted Lands (20), I-2, J-2, Nethergarde Keep (119)

NETHERGARDE SOLDIER
Blasted Lands (20), I:(1-3), J:(1-3), Garrison Armory, Nethergarde Keep (119), Serpent's Coil

NETHERWALKER
Feralas (46), G-4, Dire Maul

NEWTON BURNSIDE
Banker, Stormwind (72), H-7, Trade District, Stormwind Counting House

NEZ'RAZ
Zeppelin Master, Stranglethorn Vale (74), C-3, Grom'gol Base Camp (112), Atop tower

NEZZLIOK THE DIRE
Bloodscalp Clan Witchdoctor, Stranglethorn Vale (74), B-1, Ruins of Zul'Kunda, Idle with several trolls in the northwestern corner of ruins

NIBY THE ALMIGHTY
Felwood (44), F-5, Shatter Scar Vale, North of pond near dock

NICHOLAS ATWOOD
Gun Merchant, Undercity (88), I-3, The War Quarter

NIDA WINTERHOOF
Herbalism Supplier, Thunder Bluff (84), F-4, Middle rise, in front of Holistic Herbalism

NIGHT WEB MATRIARCH
Tirisfal Glades (86), C-6, Night Web's Hollow

NIGHT WEB SPIDER
Tirisfal Glades (86), C-6, Night Web's Hollow

NIGHTBANE DARK RUNNER
Duskwood (36), H:(4, 5, 7), I:(4-8), Brightwood Grove

NIGHTBANE SHADOW WEAVER
Duskwood (36), H:(3-5, 7), I:(4-8), Brightwood Grove

NIGHTBANE TAINTED ONE
Duskwood (36), H-8, I-8, J:(7, 8)

NIGHTBANE VILE FANG
Duskwood (36), H-8, I-8, J-7

NIGHTBANE WORGEN
Duskwood (36), H:(3-5, 7), I:(3, 4, 6, 7), Brightwood Grove

NIGHTLASH
Silverpine Forest (68), G-2, The Dead Field, Spawns (on timer) in the center of crop field

NIGHTMARE ECTOPLASM
Barrens (18), E-4, Wailing Caverns

NIGHTMARE SCALEBANE
Swamp of Sorrows (76), I-5, The Temple of Atal'Hakkar

NIGHTMARE SUPPRESSOR
Swamp of Sorrows (76), I-5, The Temple of Atal'Hakkar

NIGHTMARE WANDERER
Swamp of Sorrows (76), I-5, The Temple of Atal'Hakkar

NIGHTMARE WHELP
Swamp of Sorrows (76), I-5, The Temple of Atal'Hakkar

NIGHTMARE WYRMKIN
Swamp of Sorrows (76), I-5, The Temple of Atal'Hakkar

NIGHTSABER
Teldrassil (80), F:(5, 6), G:(5, 6), H:(5, 6), I-5

NIGHTSABER STALKER
Teldrassil (80), D-6, E:(5-7), F:(7, 8), G-7, H-7, Dolanaar (109), Lake Al'Ameth, Pools of Arlithrien

NIGHTSHADE
Jeen'ra's Pet, Darnassus (26), E-1, Cenarion Enclave, Top of structure, connected to the northeast structure

NIJEL'S POINT GUARD
Desolace (30), H-1, I:(1, 2), Nijel's Point (119)

NIKOVA RASKOL
Stormwind (72), J-4, Old Town, Hanging out in Old Town street

NILITH LOKRAV
Searing Gorge (64), E-7, Kneeling on right side of camp

NILLEN ANDEMAR
Macecrafter, Loch Modan (54), E-1, Stonewrought Dam, By keg on cart on dam wall

NIMAR THE SLAYER
Rare Spawn, Arathi Highlands (10), I:(6, 7), J-6, Witherbark Village, Lvl 37 Uncommon; Roams in village

NIMBOYA
Stranglethorn Vale (74), C-3, Grom'gol Base Camp (112), Just inside camp walls near cauldron by the northern entrance

NINA LIGHTBREW
Alchemy Supplies, Blasted Lands (20), J-2, Nethergarde Keep (119), Top floor of tower facing entrance of keep

NIOMA
Leatherworking Supplies, The Hinterlands (50), B-4, Aerie Peak (100), Wildhammer Keep

NIPSY
Stormwind (72), I-1, Dwarven District, Deeprun Tram

NISSA AGAMAND
Tirisfal Glades (86), F-4, Agamand Mills (100), Patrols two story house on right side of mill

NISSA FIRESTONE
First Aid Trainer, Ironforge (52), G-6, The Great Forge, Ironforge Physician

NITTLEBUR SPARKFIZZLE
Mage Trainer, Ironforge (52), C-1, The Mystic Ward, Hall of Mysteries

NIXX SPROCKETSPRING
Master Goblin Engineer, Tanaris (78), H-3, Gadgetzan (111), Northeast hut

NIXXRAK
Heavy Armor Merchant, Winterspring (98), I-4, Everlook (110), Inside northeast building

NIXXRAX FILLAMUG
Food & Drink, Stranglethorn Vale (74), B-8, Booty Bay (103), Behind the bar on the first floor of The Salty Sailor Tavern

NIZZIK
Venture Armor Salesman, Stonetalon Mountains (70), H-4, Cragpool Lake, Wood platform above lake, next to wheel

NOBORU THE CUDGEL
Swamp of Sorrows (76), G-3, Patrols with two Lost One Muckdwellers between spawn point and an area near the Harborage with two Lost One Muckdwellers

NOGG
Expert Engineer, Orgrimmar (60), I-3, J-3, Valley of Honor, Nogg's Machine Shop

NORI PRIDEDRIFT
Dun Morogh (32), C-7, Coldridge Valley (106), Camp

NORTHSHIRE GUARD
Elwynn Forest (42), F-5, Northshire Valley (120)

NORTHSPRING HARPY
Feralas (46), D:(1, 2), Ruins of Ravenwind

NORTHSPRING ROGUEFEATHER
Feralas (46), D:(1, 2), Ruins of Ravenwind

NORTHSPRING SLAYER
Feralas (46), D:(1, 2), Ruins of Ravenwind

NORTHSPRING WINDCALLER
Feralas (46), D:(1, 2), Ruins of Ravenwind

NOVICE ELRETH
Tirisfal Glades (86), C-7, Deathknell (109), Church

NOVICE THAIVAND
Hillsbrad Foothills (48), H-2, Tarren Mill (128), Graveyard

NOXIOUS PLAGUEBAT
Eastern Plaguelands (40), F-6, G:(5, 6), H:(5, 6), I:(6, 7), J:(6, 7), K-7

NOXIOUS SLIME
Desolace (30), D-5, Mauradon

NOXXION
Desolace (30), D-5, Mauradon

NOXXIOUS ESSENCE
Desolace (30), D-5, Mauradon

NOXXIOUS SCION
Desolace (30), D-5, Mauradon

NURSE LILLIAN
Stormwind (72), F-6, The Canals, Top of steps to stockade

NURSE NEELA
First Aid Trainer, Tirisfal Glades (86), H-5, Brill (104), First floor of Gallows' End Tavern

NYOMA
Cooking Supplies, Teldrassil (80), G-6, Dolanaar (109), Next to cauldron southeast of inn

NYRILL
Xylem's Apprentice, Azshara (14), C-5, Requires quest from Sanath Lim-yo to reach

NYSE
Wind Rider Master, Thousand Needles (82), F-5, Freewind Post, North side of plateau, opposite inn

O

OAKENSCOWL
Teldrassil (80), G-7, Lake Al'Ameth, In den south of lake

OAKPAW
Rare Spawn, Ashenvale (12), F-6, G-6, Greenpaw Village, Lvl 27 Semi-Rare; Roams throughout village

OASIS SNAPJAW
Barrens (18), E-4, F-4, G-4, Lushwater Oasis, The Stagnant Oasis

OBEN RAGECLAW
Teldrassil (80), E-6, Ban'ethil Barrow Den, Room in south section of den

OBI
Un'Goro Crater (90), D-2, Hill in far northwestern section of crater

OBSIDIAN ELEMENTAL
Burning Steppes (22), G-6, I-6, J:(3-5, 7), Blackrock Pass

OBSIDIAN GOLEM
Badlands (16), G-1, Uldaman

OBSIDIAN SENTINEL
Badlands (16), G-1, Uldaman

OBSIDIAN SHARD
Badlands (16), G-1, Uldaman

OBSIDION
Searing Gorge (64), E-2, The Slag Pit, (Summon) Animates when Lathoric the Black encounter is triggered

OCCULUS
Tanaris (78), I-5, Caverns of Time, Land bridge leading to cavern

ODO THE BLINDWATCHER
Silverpine Forest (68), F-7, Shadowfang Keep

OFFICER AREYN
Accessories Quartermaster, Stormwind (72), K-5, Old Town, Outside SI:7

OFFICER BRADY
Stormwind (72), Roams city

OFFICER JAXON
Stormwind (72), Roams city

OFFICER POMEROY
Stormwind (72), Roams city

OGG'MARR
Butcher, Dustwallow Marsh (38), D-3, Brackenwall Village (104), Northern part of village

OGGLEFLINT
Orgrimmar (60), F-5, Ragefire Chasm

OGLETHORPE OBNOTICUS
Master Gnome Engineer, Stranglethorn Vale (74), B-8, Booty Bay (103), Small house on third level along the eastern side of bay

OGOM THE WRETCHED
Swamp of Sorrows (76), I-5, The Temple of Atal'Hakkar

OGRABISI
Burning Steppes (22), Searing Gorge (64), C-4/D-8, Blackrock Depths

OGROMM
Hunter Trainer, Swamp of Sorrows (76), F-5, Stonard (126), Behind orcish carriage left of entrance to main hall

OGRON
Dustwallow Marsh (38), E-4, Just off road

OGTINC
Azshara (14), E-4, The Shattered Strand, Overlooking ruins atop cliff

OGUNARO WOLFRUNNER
Riding Wolf (Kennel Master), Orgrimmar (60), I-1, Valley of Honor, Outside of Hunter's Hall

OHANAKO
Two Handed Weapon Merchant, Thunder Bluff (84), F-6, High rise, inside Ragetotem Arms tent

OK'THOR THE BREAKER
Raid Sub-Boss, Burning Steppes (22), Searing Gorge (64), C-4/D-8, Blackrock Depths

OKLA
Barrens (18), G-2, Grol'dom Farm, Roams tower east of farm

OKOTHOS IRONRAGER
Armorsmith, Orgrimmar (60), J-2, Valley of Honor

OL' BEASLEY
Stormwind (72), J-4, Old Town, Across from The Five Deadly Venoms

OL' EMMA
Stormwind (72), H-4, The Canals, Roams around Cathedral Square and Canals

OL' SOOTY
Loch Modan (54), D-6, Grizzlepaw Ridge, Roams area along the southwestern end of the loch

OLAF
Badlands (16), G-1, Uldaman

OLD BLANCHY
Westfall (94), G-2, The Jansen Stead, Near Furlbrows

OLD CLIFF JUMPER
Rare Spawn, The Hinterlands (50), C:(5, 6), The Hinterlands, Lvl 42 Semi-Rare; Patrols small area around spawn point

OLD GRIZZLEGUT
Rare Spawn, Feralas (46), G-6, H-4, Lower Wilds, Ruins of Isildien, Lvl 43 Very Rare; Roams in a wide area

OLD ICEBEARD
Dun Morogh (32), E-5, Chill Breeze Valley, Roams small area around spawn point

OLD IRONBARK
Feralas (46), G-4, Dire Maul

OLD MAN HEMING
Fisherman, Stranglethorn Vale (74), B-8, Booty Bay (103), The Happy Bobber (shop)

OLD MURK-EYE
Westfall (94), C-8, Longshore, Roams southern part of Longshore

OLD SERRA'KIS
Ashenvale (12), B-2, Blackfathom Deeps

OLD VICEJAW
Rare Spawn, Silverpine Forest (68), H:(5, 6), Lvl 14 Uncommon; Roams small area around spawn point

OLIVER DWOR
Apprentice Weaponsmith, Tirisfal Glades (86), H-5, Brill (104), Smithy

OLIVIA BURNSIDE
Banker, Stormwind (72), H-7, Trade District, Stormwind Counting House

OLLANUS
Light Armor Merchant, Orgrimmar (60), G-8, Valley of Strength, Soran's Leather and Steel

OLM THE WISE
Rare Spawn, Cenarion Circle, Felwood (44), G:(2-3), H:(1-3), Irontree Woods, Lvl 52 Average Rare; Roams near spawn point

OLMIN BURNINGBEARD
Hunter Trainer, Ironforge (52), J-8, The Military Ward, Hall of Arms

OLTHRAN CRAGHELM
Heavy Armor Merchant, Ironforge (52), G-9, The Military Ward, Craghelm's Plate and Chain

OLVIA
Meat Vendor, Orgrimmar (60), E-7, Valley of Strength, Chop House

OMGORN THE LOST
Rare Spawn, Tanaris (78), F:(6, 7), G:(6, 7), Dunemaul Compound, Eastmoon Ruins, Southmoon Ruins, Lvl 50 Semi-Rare; Roams a wide path around spawn point

OMUSA THUNDERHORN
Wind Rider Master, Barrens (18), F-6, Camp Taurajo (106), Western entrance

ONGEKU
Swamp of Sorrows (76), H-2, Fallow Sanctuary, Roams small area around spawn point

ONIN MACHAMMAR
Dun Morogh (32), C-4, Gnomeregan, Stealthed on top of helipad

ONU
Darkshore (24), G-8, Grove of the Ancients, Center of temple

ONYXIA
Raid Boss, Dustwallow Marsh (38), G-8, Onyxia's Lair

ONYXIAN WARDER
Dustwallow Marsh (38), G-8, Onyxia's Lair

ONYXIAN WHELP
Dustwallow Marsh (38), G-8, Onyxia's Lair

OOZEWORM
Rare Spawn, Dustwallow Marsh (38), D:(6-7), E-6, The Den of Flame, The Dragonmurk, Lvl 42 Very Rare; Roams spawn points

OOZLINGS
Swamp of Sorrows (76), I-5, The Temple of Atal'Hakkar

OPHEK
Durotar (34), H-4, Razor Hill (122), Behind barracks

OPHELIA MONTAGUE
Banker, Undercity (88), I-4, The Trade Quarter

OPUS
Burning Steppes (22), I:(2, 3)

OR'KALAR
Arathi Highlands (10), B:(6, 7), C-6, Stromgarde Keep (127), Ogre quarter of Stromgarde Keep

ORALIUS
Burning Steppes (22), K-7, Morgan's Vigil (118), Next to Gryphon Master

ORAN SNAKEWRITHE
Undercity (88), J-3, The Magic Quarter, Stall next to Tailors

ORENDIL BROADLEAF
Ashenvale (12), D-4, Maestra's Post, Near Stones to the south of main outpost

ORENTHIL WHISPERWIND
Teldrassil (80), G-4, H-4, Shadowglen (124), Benches southwest of Aldrassil

ORGRIMMAR GRUNT
Durotar (34), E-1, F-1, G-1, H-1, Valley of Trials (131)

ORIK'ANDO
Feralas (46), I-4, Camp Mojache (105), Next to tent, east of water

ORM STONEHOOF
Thunder Bluff (84), D-6, Lower rise, next to pond

ORMAK GRIMSHOT
Hunter Trainer, Orgrimmar (60), H-2, Valley of Honor, Hunter's Hall

ORMER IRONBRAID
Wetlands (96), E-5, Whelgar's Excavation Site, Just across bridge in east section of site

ORMOK
Rogue Trainer, Orgrimmar (60), E-5, The Cleft of Shadow, Next to Shadowswift Brotherhood building

ORMYR FLINTEYE
Rogue Trainer, Ironforge (52), G-1, The Forlorn Cavern, South building, inside east entrance

ORNERY PLAINSTRIDER
Barrens (18), D:(2, 3), E:(1, 2, 4, 5), F-5, G:(1, 3-5), H-3

OROKK OMOSH
Orgrimmar (60), J-2, Valley of Honor, Across from Arms of Legend

ORPHAN MATRON BATTELWALL
Orgrimmar (60), I-2, Valley of Honor, Building near Lumak's Fishing

ORPHAN MATRON NIGHTINGALER
Stormwind (72), G-4, Cathedral Square, Outside Orphanage

ORWIN GIZZMICK
Feralas (46), I-4, Camp Mojache (105), East of inn, next to water

OSBORNE THE NIGHT MAN
Rogue Trainer, Stormwind (72), K-5, Old Town, Outside SI:7

OSRIC STRANG
Heavy Armor Merchant, Stormwind (72), K-5, Old Town, Limited Immunity

OTHO MOJI'KO
Cooking Supplier, The Hinterlands (50), L-8, Revantusk Village, Dancing in hut on southeast side of village

OTT
Weaponsmith, Hillsbrad Foothills (48), G-3, Tarren Mill (128), Caravan at southern end of town

OTTO
Arathi Highlands (10), C-6, Stromgarde Keep (127), Third floor of castle

OUTCAST NECROMANCER
Desolace (30), H-9, I-9, Valley of Bones

OUTFITTER ERIC
Speciality Tailoring Supplies, Ironforge (52), F-3, The Great Forge, Stonebrow's Clothier

OUTHOUSE
Western Plaguelands (92), F-5, Dalson's Tears, Located on the north end of the farm behind the house and barn

OVERLORD MOK'MOROKK
Dustwallow Marsh (38), D-3, Brackenwall Village (104), Center of village

OVERLORD RAMTUSK
Barrens (18), E-9, Razorfen Kraul

OVERLORD ROR
Felwood (44), G-9, Deadwood Village, Southern camp

OVERLORD RUNTHAK
Orgrimmar (60), F:(7, 8), Valley of Strength, Near main entrance

OVERLORD WYRMTHALAK
Burning Steppes (22), Searing Gorge (64), C-4/D-8, Blackrock Spire

OVERMASTER PYRON
Burning Steppes (22), Searing Gorge (64), C-4/D-8, Blackrock Depths

OVERSEER GLIBBY
Barrens (18), G-1, The Sludge Fen

OVERSEER MALTORIUS
Searing Gorge (64), E-4, The Slag Pit, Roams with two Dark Iron Sentry's around upper level platform

OVERSEER OILFIST
The Thorium Brotherhood, Searing Gorge (64), D-3, Thorium Point, Second floor of tower

OWATANKA
Barrens (18), E-6, F-6, Southern Barrens, Roams areas south and east of Camp Taurajo

OWEN VAUGHN
Reagent Vendor, Stormwind (72), E-7, Mage Quarter, Essential Components

OX
The Mithril Order, Orgrimmar (60), J-2, Valley of Honor, Across from Arms of Legend

OZZIE TOGGLEVOLT
Dun Morogh (32), F-5, Kharanos (114), In gnomish building

P

PA MACLURE
Elwynn Forest (42), F-9, The Maclure Vineyards, In front of house

PACK KODO
Thousand Needles (82), B-3, Whitereach Post, Next to hut

PAIGE CHADDIS
Stormwind (72), Roams city with Karlee

PAIGE FELIXE
Feralas (46), B-4, Feathermoon Stronghold (110), Next to log west of inn

PAINED
Dustwallow Marsh (38), I-5, Theramore Isle (130), Top of central tower

PAKWA
Bag Vendor, Thunder Bluff (84), D-6, Lower rise, in front of Kuruk's Goods tent

PALEMANE POACHER
Mulgore (58), C-6, F-7, G-7, Palemane Rock, Winterhoof Water Well

PALEMANE SKINNER
Mulgore (58), C-6, D-6, E-7, F-7, G-7, Palemane Rock, Red Cloud Mesa, Winterhoof Water Well

PALEMANE TANNER
Mulgore (58), C-6, D-6, E-7, F-7, G-7, Palemane Rock, Red Cloud Mesa

PAMELA REDPATH
Eastern Plaguelands (40), E-8, Darrowshire, Roams house ruins in northwestern part of town

PAND STONEBINDER
First Aid Trainer, Thunder Bluff (84), C-2, Spirit Rise, Inside Spiritual Healing tent

PANTHER
Stranglethorn Vale (74), B:(1, 2), C:(1, 2), E-1

PANZOR THE INVINCIBLE
Rare Spawn, Burning Steppes (22), Searing Gorge (64), C-4/D-8, Blackrock Depths, Lvl 57 Rare

PAO'KA SWIFTMOUNTAIN
Thousand Needles (82), B-4, Highperch, Entrance to Highperch

PARQUAL FINTALLAS
Undercity (88), F-7, The Apothecarium, On the bridge

PAT
Stormwind (72), Roams city with Miss Danna

PATCHWORK HORROR
Eastern Plaguelands (40), D-2, Stratholme

PATHSTRIDER
Eastern Plaguelands (40), G-2, Quel'Lithien Lodge

PATRICE DWYER
Poison Supplies, Silverpine Forest (68), F-4, The Sepulcher (124), Left side of inn by fireplace

PATRICK GARRETT
Undercity (88), I-5, The Trade Quarter, Upper Ring of Trade Quarter

PATRICK MILLS
Azshara (14), H-9, The Ruined Reaches, Inlet

PAVAL REETHE
Dustwallow Marsh (38), E-4, Camp on small island

PAWE MISTRUNNER
Thunder Bluff (84), B-3, Spirit Rise, Ouside of tents

PAXTON GANTER
Fisherman, Dun Morogh (32), E-4, Iceflow Lake, Fishing at a break in the ice on lake

PEACEKEEPER SECURITY SUIT
Dun Morogh (32), C-4, Gnomeregan

PELTURAS WHITEMOON
Ashenvale (12), E-5, Astranaar (101), Southeast building

PENNY
Stable Master, Redridge Mountains (62), C-5, Lakeshire (115), Next to stack of kegs outside of Lakeshire Inn

PEPHREDO
Mage Trainer, Orgrimmar (60), D:(8, 9), Valley of Spirit, Darkbriar Lodge

PERIA LAMENUR
Pet Trainer, Dun Morogh (32), F-5, Kharanos (114), In caravan

PESTERHIDE HYENA
Thousand Needles (82), B:(2, 4), C:(2-5), D:(2-5), E:(3, 5, 6), F:(5, 6), G-5

PESTERHIDE SNARLER
Thousand Needles (82), A:(1-3), B:(2-4), G:(4, 5), H:(5, 6), I:(5, 6)

PETER GALEN
Master Dragonscale Leatherworker, Azshara (14), D-6, Ruins of Eldarath, Camp in hills south of ruins

PETRA GROSSEN
Un'Goro Crater (90), F-1, Marshal's Refuge (116), Entrance to cave

PETRIFIED GUARDIAN
Feralas (46), G-4, Dire Maul

PETRIFIED TREANT
Feralas (46), G-4, Dire Maul

PHALANX
Burning Steppes (22), Searing Gorge (64), C-4/D-8, Blackrock Depths

PHANTIM
Ashenvale (12), L-4, Bough Shadow, Patrols area near portal

PHASE LASHER
Feralas (46), G-4, Dire Maul

PHIN ODELIC
Hillsbrad Foothills (48), F-6, Southshore (125), Right of inn by carriage

PIERCE SHACKLETON
Mage Trainer, Undercity (88), L-1, The Magic Quarter, Inside Skull Building

PIKKLE
Miner, Tanaris (78), G-3, Gadgetzan (111), Southwestern hut

PILLAR OF AMETHYST
Badlands (16), L-6, Lethlor Ravine, Pillar on hill

PILLAR OF DIAMOND
Badlands (16), L-3, Lethlor Ravine, Pillar on hill

PILLAR OF OPAL
Badlands (16), K-7, Lethlor Ravine, Pillar on hill

PILOT BELLOWFIZ
Dun Morogh (32), G-5, Steelgrill's Depot, By siege tank outside of depot

PILOT HAMMERFOOT
Dun Morogh (32), L-4, North Gate Outpost, By siege tank next to tower

PILOT LONGBEARD
Ironforge Siege Brigade, Ironforge (52), J-9, The Military Ward, Hall of Arms

PILOT STONEGEAR
Dun Morogh (32), G-5, Steelgrill's Depot, By siege tank outside of depot

PILOT WIZZLECRANK
Barrens (18), G-1, Hut

PILOT XIGGS FUSELIGHTER
Azshara (14), J-9, The Ruined Reaches, Landing pad on island

PIMGIB
Feralas (46), G-4, Dire Maul

PITER VERANCE
Weaponsmith & Armorer, Dustwallow Marsh (38), I-5, Theramore Isle (130), First floor of Foothold Citadel

PITHWICK
Bag Vendor, Ironforge (52), E-7, The Commons, Fizzlespinner's General Goods

PIXEL
Ashenvale (12), I-6, Splintertree Post (126), On crates to right of flightpoint

PIZNIK
Stonetalon Mountains (70), J-6, Windshear Mine, West deadend of mine

PIZZNUKLE
Leather Armor Merchant, Barrens (18), E-4, Near mountains west of oasis

PLAGUE GHOUL
Eastern Plaguelands (40), D-2, Stratholme

PLAGUE LURKER
Western Plaguelands (92), G:(5, 6), H:(4-6), I:(4-6)

PLAGUE MONSTROSITY
Eastern Plaguelands (40), G-5, I:(3, 4), J-4, Blackwood Lake

PLAGUE RAVAGER
Eastern Plaguelands (40), H:(7, 8), I:(7, 8), Lake Mereldar

PLAGUE SPREADER
Duskwood (36), B-3, C:(3, 4), Raven Hill Cemetery (122)

PLAGUEBAT
Eastern Plaguelands (40), A:(4, 5), B:(5-7), C:(6-8), D:(6-9), E:(6-8), F:(6-8), G:(7, 8), H:(7, 8), I:(7, 8), J-8

PLAGUED HATCHLING
Western Plaguelands (92), I-7, Scholomance

PLAGUED PEASANT
Eastern Plaguelands (40), C-2, Plaguewood

PLAGUED RAT
Eastern Plaguelands (40), D-2, Stratholme

PLAGUEHOUND
Eastern Plaguelands (40), F-6, G:(5, 6), H:(5, 6), I:(5-7), J:(6, 7), K-7

PLAGUEHOUND RUNT
Eastern Plaguelands (40), A:(4, 5), B:(5-7), C:(6-8), D:(6-9), E:(6-8), F:(6-8), G:(7, 8), H:(7, 8), I:(7, 8), J-8

PLAGUELAND TERMITE
Western Plaguelands (92), F-3

PLAGUEMAW THE ROTTING
Barrens (18), F-9, Razorfen Downs

PLAINS CREEPER
Arathi Highlands (10), B:(4, 5), C:(3-5), D:(2, 3, 5, 6), E:(3-7), F:(4, 6, 7), G:(3-6), H:(3-5), I:(3-6), J:(3-6), K-3, Refuge Point, Outside Refuge Point and throughout highlands

PLAINSTRIDER
Mulgore (58), E:(7-9), F:(7-9), Camp Narache (105), Kodo Rock

PLATED STEGODON
Un'Goro Crater (90), C:(5-7), D:(6-8), E:(6-8), Golakka Hot Springs, Terror Run

PLUGGER SPAZZRING
Burning Steppes (22), Searing Gorge (64), C-4/D-8, Blackrock Depths

POISON SPRITE
Desolace (30), D-5, Mauradon

POOKA
Barrens (18), E-1, Roams in and out of building west of road

PORANNA SNOWBRAID
Tailoring Supplies, Ironforge (52), F-3, The Great Forge, Stonebrow's Clothier

PORTHANNIUS
Teldrassil (80), H-5, Shadowglen (124), Side of road leading out of Shadowglen

POSTMASTER MALOWN
Eastern Plaguelands (40), D-2, Stratholme

POZZIK
Thousand Needles (82), K-8, Mirage Raceway (118), Inside racetrack

PRAIRIE STALKER
Mulgore (58), C:(3, 4), D:(2-5), E:(3-5), F:(3-5), G:(3-7), H:(5-7)

PRAIRIE WOLF
Mulgore (58), C-8, D:(5-8), E:(5-7), F:(6, 7), G:(6, 7)

PRAIRIE WOLF ALPHA
Mulgore (58), C-2, D:(1, 2), E:(1-3), F:(1-3), G:(2, 3), H:(2, 3, 6, 7)

PRATE CLOUDSEER
Thousand Needles (82), G-4, The Weathered Nook, Front of den

PRATT MCGRUBBEN
Leatherworking Supplies, Feralas (46), C-4, Feathermoon Stronghold (110), Behind Inn, next to water

PRECIOUS
Un'Goro Crater (90), E:(4-8), F-6, F-8, G:(6-8), Golakka Hot Springs, The Slithering Scar, Terror Run, Walks big area from The Slithering Scar to north of the springs

"PRETTY BOY" DUNCAN
Stranglethorn Vale (74), B-7, Southern Savage Coast, Roams around shoreline camp

PRIDEWING CONSORT
Stonetalon Mountains (70), E-4, F:(4, 5), G-4, Mirkfallon Lake

PRIDEWING PATRIARCH
Rare Spawn, Stonetalon Mountains (70), F:(4-5), G-4, Mirkfallon Lake, Lvl 25 Uncommon; Spawns in mountains east or south of Mirkfallon Lake

PRIDEWING SKYHUNTER
Stonetalon Mountains (70), F-5, G-4, Mirkfallon Lake

PRIDEWING SOARER
Stonetalon Mountains (70), E-4, F-4, Mirkfallon Lake, Soars between high ledges northwest of lake and in middle of lake

PRIDEWING WYVERN
Stonetalon Mountains (70), F:(4, 5), G-4, Mirkfallon Lake

PRIESTESS ALATHEA
Priest Trainer, Darnassus (26), E-8, Temple of the Moon, Balcony, north of fountain

PRIESTESS A'MOORA
Darnassus (26), D-9, Temple of the Moon, Balcony, west of fountain

PRIESTESS ANETTA
Priest Trainer, Elwynn Forest (42), G-4, Northshire Valley (120), Room behind the Library Wing of abbey

PRIESTESS JOSETTA
Priest Trainer, Elwynn Forest (42), F-7, Goldshire (112), Second floor of Lion's Pride Inn

PRIESTESS OF ELUNE
Winterspring (98), J-6, Owl Wing Thicket, (Summon) Near altar

PRIMAL OOZE
Un'Goro Crater (90), E-2, F:(3, 6, 7), G:(2-4, 6, 7), H:(2, 5-8), J-3

PRIMAL TORNTUSK
The Hinterlands (50), L-8, Revantusk Village, Second floor of inn on eastern side of village

PRIMITIVE OWLBEAST
The Hinterlands (50), E-6, F:(4-7), G:(4-6), H:(4-6), The Hinterlands

PRIMORDIAL BEHEMOTH
Desolace (30), D-5, Mauradon

PRINCE GALEN TROLLBANE
Arathi Highlands (10), D-6, Stromgarde Keep (127), Roams church near crypt

PRINCE KELLEN
Rare Spawn, Desolace (30), J-2, Sargeron, Lvl 33 Average Rare; Top of hill or east by hill

PRINCE NAZJAK
Rare Spawn, Arathi Highlands (10), C:(8, 9), The Drowned Reef, Lvl 41 Very Rare; Roams in the reef

PRINCE RAZE
Rare Spawn, Ashenvale (12), J:(4-5), Xavian, Lvl 32 Uncommon; Can be found near delta, next to a totem in middle of camp, or next to Geltharis

PRINCE THUNDERAAN
Silithus (66), D-1, Ravaged Twilight Camp, (Summon)

PRINCE TORTHELDRIN
Feralas (46), G-4, Dire Maul

PRINCE XAVALIS
Felwood (44), E-6, Shadow Hold, Small incline in first room

PRINCESS
Elwynn Forest (42), J-8, Brackwell Pumpkin Patch, Roams with two Porcine Entourage around pumpkin patch

PRINCESS MOIRA BRONZEBEARD
Burning Steppes (22), Searing Gorge (64), C-4/D-8, Blackrock Depths

PRINCESS POOBAH
Stranglethorn Vale (74), D-8, Jaguero Isle, Small camp on the northern side of island

PRINCESS TEMPESTRIA
World Boss, Winterspring (98), H-4, Lake Kel'Theril, Spawns on the lake

PRINCESS THERADRAS
Desolace (30), D-5, Mauradon

PRISONER OF JIN'ZIL
Stonetalon Mountains (70), J-9, Malaka'jin, Den, inside one of three cages

PRIVATE HENDEL
Dustwallow Marsh (38), F-2, Dock near small camp

PRIVATE MERLE
Stranglethorn Vale (74), D-1, Rebel Camp, Camp

PRIVATE THORSEN
Stranglethorn Vale (74), D-1, Rebel Camp, Patrols between camp and an area down the hill

PRIVATEER BLOADS
Stranglethorn Vale (74), B-8, Booty Bay (103), Idle in front of Stranglethorn Trust Bank

PRIVATEER GROY
Dustwallow Marsh (38), I-5, Theramore Isle (130), Southeast near docks

PROFESSOR PHIZZLETHORPE
Arathi Highlands (10), D-8, Faldir's Cove, By bonfire on hill

PROSPECTOR GEHN
Explorers' League, Dun Morogh (32), I-5, Gol'Bolar Quarry, By caravan along back wall of camp

PROSPECTOR GUNSTAN
Explorers' League, Tanaris (78), E-8, Valley of the Watchers, Camp near entrance to Uldum

PROSPECTOR IRONBAND
Loch Modan (54), I-7, Ironband's Excavation Site, Camp outside of excavation site

PROSPECTOR IRONBOOT
Tanaris (78), J-2, Steamwheedle Port, Outside southern building

PROSPECTOR KHAZGORM
Explorer's League, Barrens (18), F-9, Bael Modan, Roams southeast area in excavation

PROSPECTOR REMTRAVEL
Explorer's League, Darkshore (24), E-8, Remtravel's Excavation, Behind rock

PROSPECTOR RYEDOL
Badlands (16), H-4, Camp

PROSPECTOR STONEHEWER
Alterac Mountains (8), E-8, The Headland, Right camp outside Alterac Valley (Alliance)

PROSPECTOR STORMPIKE
Ironforge (52), J-1, Hall of Explorers, Library

PROSPECTOR WHELGAR
Wetlands (96), E-5, Whelgar's Excavation Site, Den across the bridge in east section of site

PROTECTOR BIALON
Westfall (94), F-5, Sentinel Hill (123), Outside Sentinel Tower

PROTECTOR DENI
Westfall (94), F-5, Sentinel Hill (123), Outside Saw Mill

PROTECTOR DORANA
Westfall (94), G-5, Sentinel Hill (123), Spawns near the merchants outside Sentinel Hill and roams south along the road

PROTECTOR DUTFIELD
Westfall (94), G-5, Sentinel Hill (123), Roams Sentinel Tower

PROTECTOR GARIEL
Westfall (94), F-5, Sentinel Hill (123), Outside Sentinel Tower

PROTECTOR KORELOR
Westfall (94), F-5, Sentinel Hill (123), Spawns near the Saw Mill and roams to the bridge leading to Duskwood

PROTECTOR LEICK
Westfall (94), F-5, Sentinel Hill (123), Outside Saw Mill

PROTECTOR WEAVER
Westfall (94), G-5, Sentinel Hill (123), Circles top of Sentinel Tower

PROWLER
Elwynn Forest (42), I-4, J:(4, 6-8), K:(4, 6-8), L:(6-8), Eastvale Logging Camp, Ridgepoint Tower, Stone Cairn Lake

PRYNNE
Gnomeregan Exiles, Ironforge (52), F-1, The Forlorn Cavern, Stoneblade's

PTERRORDAX
Un'Goro Crater (90), F:(7, 9), G:(1, 2, 7, 9), H:(1, 2, 5, 7, 9), J-5

PUSILLIN
Feralas (46), G-4, Dire Maul

PUTRID GARGOYLE
Eastern Plaguelands (40), B:(6, 7), C:(2, 7, 9), D:(3, 6, 7), E:(2, 4, 6-8), F:(3, 6-8), G:(5, 8), H:(5-8), I:(5, 7), J:(5, 7), Plaguewood

PUTRID SHRIEKER
Eastern Plaguelands (40), C-4, D-4, F-4, G:(3, 4), H:(3-5), I:(4, 5), J-3, Quel'Lithien Lodge

PUTRIDIUS
Rare Spawn, Western Plaguelands (92), F-7, Ruins of Andorhal, Lvl 58 Uber-Rare; Roamd around city

PUTRIDUS SATYR
Desolace (30), D-5, Mauradon

PUTRIDUS SHADOWSTALKER
Desolace (30), D-5, Mauradon

PUTRIDUS TRICKSTER
Desolace (30), D-5, Mauradon

PYALL SILENTSTRIDE
Cook, Mulgore (58), E-6, Bloodhoof Village (102), Northeast tent

PYGMY SURF CRAWLER
Durotar (34), H-8, I:(4-8), J:(5, 6)

PYGMY TIDE CRAWLER
Darkshore (24), E:(4, 5), F-4, Auberdine, The Long Wash, Mist's Edge

PYGMY VENOM WEB SPIDER
Duskwood (36), A:(3-7), B:(3, 7), C-3, D-3, E-2, F-2, G:(1, 2), H-2, I-2, J-2, K-2, L-2, The Darkened Bank

PYREWOOD ARMORER
Silverpine Forest (68), G-7, Pyrewood Village, Smithy

PYREWOOD ELDER
Silverpine Forest (68), F-7, G-7, Preywood Village

PYREWOOD LEATHERWORKER
Silverpine Forest (68), G-7, Pyrewood Village, House next to inn

PYREWOOD SENTRY
Silverpine Forest (68), F-7, G-7, Preywood Village

PYREWOOD TAILOR
Silverpine Forest (68), G-7, Pyrewood Village, Patrols between house and smithy

PYREWOOD WATCHER
Silverpine Forest (68), F-7, G-7, Preywood Village

PYROGUARD EMBERSEER
Burning Steppes (22), Searing Gorge (64), C-4/D-8, Blackrock Spire

PYROMANCER LOREGRAIN
Burning Steppes (22), Searing Gorge (64), C-4/D-8, Blackrock Depths

Q

QIA
Trade Goods Supplies, Winterspring (98), I-4, Everlook (110), Inside building directly north of inn

QIAGA THE KEEPER
The Hinterlands (50), G-7, The Altar of Zul, Top of altar

QIROT
Rare Spawn, Feralas (46), I-6, The Writhing Deep, Lvl 47 Uncommon; In hive

QIXDI GOODSTITCH
Cloth Armor and Accessories, Stranglethorn Vale (74), B-8, Booty Bay (103), Tan-Your-Hide Leatherworks (shop)

QIZZIK
Banker, Tanaris (78), H-3, Gadgetzan (111), Bank

QUAE
Arathi Highlands (10), H-5, Go'Shek Farm, Hill northwest of farm

QUARRY SLAVE
Burning Steppes (22), Searing Gorge (64), C-4/D-8, Blackrock Depths

QUARRYMASTER THESTEN
Miners' League, Dun Morogh (32), J-5, Gol'Bolar Quarry, Under tent along back wall of camp

QUARTERMASTER HICKS
Master Weaponsmith, Elwynn Forest (42), C-7, Westbrook Garrison, First floor armory in garrison

QUARTERMASTER HUDSON
Armorer & Shieldcrafter, Elwynn Forest (42), C-7, Westbrook Garrison, First floor armory in garrison

QUARTERMASTER LEWIS
Quartermaster, Westfall (94), G-5, Sentinel Tower, Sentinel Tower

QUARTERMASTER LUNGERTZ
Blasted Lands (20), J-2, Nethergarde Keep (119), Stable

QUARTERMASTER MIRANDA BREECHLOCK
The Argent Dawn, Eastern Plaguelands (40), K-6, Light's Hope Chapel (116), Camp on right side of chapel

QUARTERMASTER ZIGRIS
Rare Spawn, Burning Steppes (22), Searing Gorge (64), C-4/D-8, Blackrock Spire, Lvl 59 Uncommon

QUEL'LITHIEN PROTECTOR
Eastern Plaguelands (40), G-2, Quel'Lithien Lodge

QUENTIN
Thousand Needles (82), K-8, Mirage Raceway (118), West grandstands

QUILGUARD CHAMPION
Barrens (18), E-9, Razorfen Kraul

QUINN
Tanaris (78), G-3, Gadgetzan (111), Outside southwestern hut

QUINN YORICK
Silverpine Forest (68), H-1, The Ivar Patch, Second floor of house

QUINTIS JONESPYRE
Feralas (46), C-4, Feathermoon Stronghold (110), Top floor of tree building in northeast

QUIXXIL
Un'Goro Crater (90), F-1, Marshal's Refuge (116), South of cave

R

RABID BLISTERPAW
Tanaris (78), D:(5-8), E:(5-8), F:(4-8), G:(4, 5, 7, 8)

RABID BONEPAW
Desolace (30), E-4, G-4, Scrabblescrew's Camp

RABID CRAG COYOTE
Badlands (16), J:(3, 4), K:(3, 4), Dustwind Gulch

RABID DIRE WOLF
Duskwood (36), A:(3-7), B-3, C-3, D:(2, 3), E:(2, 3), F-2, G-2, H-2, I-2, J:(2, 3), K-2, Brightwood Grove

RABID LONGTOOTH
Feralas (46), D:(1, 2), E:(1-4), F-3, Ruins of Ravenwind, The Twin Colossals

RABID SHADOWHIDE GNOLL
Redridge Mountains (62), J:(4-6), Galardell Valley

RABID SHARDTOOTH
Winterspring (98), H-7, I-7, J-7, Frostwhisper Gorge

RABID THISTLE BEAR
Darkshore (24), F:(2, 5-8), G:(2-4, 6, 7), H:(2-4)

RABINE SATURNA
Moonglade (56), G-4, Nighthaven (120), South wing of southeast building

RACE MASTER KRONKRIDER
Thousand Needles (82), K-8, Mirage Raceway (118), Atop Starters tower inside track

RACHEL
Redridge Mountains (62), C-4, Lakeshire (115)

RADNAAL MANEWEAVER
Skinner, Teldrassil (80), E-5, Outside house

RAEDON DUSKSTRIKER
Alliance Cloth Quartermaster, Darnassus (26), I-2, Craftsmen's Terrace, Tailoring shop

RAENA FLINTHAMMER
Light Armor Merchant, Ironforge (52), D-5, The Commons, Ironforge Armory

RAENE WOLFRUNNER
Ashenvale (12), E-5, Astranaar (101), First floor of inn near Korra and Dagri

RAGE SCAR YETI
Feralas (46), F-3, Rage Scar Hold

RAGE TALON CAPTAIN
Burning Steppes (22), Searing Gorge (64), C-4/D-8, Blackrock Spire

RAGE TALON DRAGON GUARD
Burning Steppes (22), Searing Gorge (64), C-4/D-8, Blackrock Spire

RAGE TALON DRAGONSPAWN
Burning Steppes (22), Searing Gorge (64), C-4/D-8, Blackrock Spire

RAGE TALON FIRE TONGUE
Burning Steppes (22), Searing Gorge (64), C-4/D-8, Blackrock Spire

RAGE TALON FLAMESCALE
Burning Steppes (22), Searing Gorge (64), C-4/D-8, Blackrock Spire

RAGECLAW
Teldrassil (80), E-6, Ban'ethil Barrow Den, Roams circular path in northern section of den

RAGEFIRE SHAMAN
Orgrimmar (60), F-5, Ragefire Chasm

RAGEFIRE TROGG
Orgrimmar (60), F-5, Ragefire Chasm

RAGEPAW
Rare Spawn, Felwood (44), G-9, Deadwood Village, Lvl 51 Uncommon; Roams southern area of camp

RAGEREAVER GOLEM
Burning Steppes (22), Searing Gorge (64), C-4/D-8, Blackrock Depths

RAGGED GHOUL
Western Plaguelands (92), I-7, Scholomance

RAGGED JOHN
Burning Steppes (22), H-2, Flame Crest, Right of scaffolding

RAGGED OWLBEAST
Winterspring (98), D:(4, 5), E:(4, 5), F-4, G:(3-5), H-4, Frostfire Hot Springs, Timbermaw Post

RAGGED SCAVENGER
Tirisfal Glades (86), D-6, E-6, Deathknell (109)

RAGGED TIMBER WOLF
Dun Morogh (32), C:(7, 8), D:(7, 8), Coldridge Valley (106)

RAGGED YOUNG WOLF
Dun Morogh (32), C:(7, 8), D:(7, 8), Coldridge Valley (106)

RAGGLESNOUT
Boss, Barrens (18), F-9, Razorfen Downs

RAGING AGAM'AR
Barrens (18), E-9, Razorfen Kraul

RAGING CLIFF STORMER
Stonetalon Mountains (70), F:(3, 4), G:(3, 4), H:(4-7), I:(4, 6), J:(4, 5)

RAGING DUNE SMASHER
Tanaris (78), E-8, F-8, Uldum, Valley of the Watchers

RAGING MOONKIN
Darkshore (24), G:(4, 5)

RAGING OWLBEAST
Winterspring (98), H-3, I:(3, 4), Moon Horror Den, Everlook

RAGING REEF CRAWLER
Darkshore (24), D-9, E-9, H:(1, 2), I-1, Mist's Edge, Twilight Shore

RAGING ROT HIDE
Silverpine Forest (68), J:(2, 3), Fenris Isle

RAGING THUNDER LIZARD
Desolace (30), D-7, E:(2-4, 6-8), F:(1-4, 7), G:(2-4), H:(3, 4), I:(5-7), J:(5, 6)

RAGNAR THUNDERBREW
Dun Morogh (32), F-5, Kharanos (114), Outside of distillery

RAGNAROS
Burning Steppes (22), Searing Gorge (64), C-4/D-8, The Molten Core

RAHAURO
Thunder Bluff (84), I-3, Elder Rise, Outside of Magatha Grimtotem's tent

RAIDER JHASH
Durotar (34), H-4, Razor Hill (122), Spawns at trough in Razor Hill and patrols to the Den and back

RAIDER KERR
Durotar (34), H-4, Razor Hill (122), Spawns at trough in Razor Hill and patrols to the Den and back

RAKAIAH
Felwood (44), E-6, Shadow Hold, Altar room

RAK'SHIRI
Rare Spawn, Winterspring (98), G:(1, 2), H-1, Frostsaber Rock, Lvl 57 Semi-Rare; Roams base of rock

RALEIGH ANDREAN
Ex-Chef, Undercity (88), I-4, The Trade Quarter, West spoke from bank

RALEIGH THE DEVOUT
Hillsbrad Foothills (48), F-6, Southshore (125), Second floor of inn

RALLIC FINN
Bowyer, Elwynn Forest (42), L-7, Eastvale Logging Camp, Next to target

RALSTON FARNSLEY
Horde Cloth Quartermaster, Undercity (88), J-3, The Magic Quarter, Quest Giver

RAMSTEIN THE GORGER
Eastern Plaguelands (40), D-2, Stratholme

RAN BLOODTOOTH
Ashenvale (12), G-7, Bloodtooth Camp, Far south deep in camp

RAND RHOBART
Skinner, Tirisfal Glades (86), I-6, In camp outside of Undercity

RANDAL HUNTER
Horse Riding Instructor, Elwynn Forest (42), L-6, Eastvale Logging Camp, Corale

RANDAL WORTH
Journeyman Leatherworker, Stormwind (72), J-5, Old Town, The Protective Hide

RANDOLPH MONTAGUE
Banker, Undercity (88), I-4, The Trade Quarter

RANE YORICK
Deathstalker, Silverpine Forest (68), H-1, The Ivar Patch, In front of house

RANGER
Eastern Plaguelands (40), G-2, Quel'Lithien Lodge

RANGER LORD HAWKSPEAR
Rare Spawn, Eastern Plaguelands (40), G-2, Quel'Lithien Lodge, Lvl 60 Uncommon; Patrols lodge

RANIK
Trade Supplies, Barrens (18), H-4, Ratchet (121), Jazzik's General Goods

RANN FLAMESPINNER
Tailoring Supplies, Loch Modan (54), D-5, Thelsamar (129), Porch of third house north of path

RANSHALLA
Winterspring (98), I-6, Owl Wing Thicket, Off road to east by pillar

RARC
Armorer & Shieldcrafter, Durotar (34), F-7, Valley of Trials (131)

RARTAR
Alchemy Supplies, Swamp of Sorrows (76), F-5, Stonard (126), Second floor of inn

RAS FROSTWHISPER
Western Plaguelands (92), I-7, Scholomance

RASCAL SPRITE
Teldrassil (80), G-5, Fel Rock

RASCHAL THE COURIER
Feralas (46), I-6, The Writhing Deep, Cocoon in hive

RASHONA STRAGLASH
Horde Cloth Quartermaster, Orgrimmar (60), H-4, The Drag, Magar's Cloth Goods

RATCHET BRUISER
Barrens (18), G-4, H-4, Ratchet (121)

RATHORIAN
Rare Spawn, Barrens (18), E-2, F-2, Dreadmist Den, Lvl 15 Uncommon; In cave atop Dreadmist Peak

RATSLIN MAIME
Tirisfal Glades (86), H-5, Brill (104), First floor of Gallows' End Tavern

RATTLECAGE SKELETON
Tirisfal Glades (86), D-6, Agamand Mills (100)

RATTLECAGE SOLDIER
Tirisfal Glades (86), E-4, F:(3, 4), Agamand Mills (100)

RATTLEGORE
Western Plaguelands (92), I-7, Scholomance

RAU CLIFFRUNNER
Thousand Needles (82), F-5, Freewind Post, Inn

RAVAGE
Rare Spawn, Blasted Lands (20), G-4, I-4, Lvl 51 Semi-Rare; Roams small area around spawn point

RAVAGED CADAVER
Eastern Plaguelands (40), D-2, Stratholme

RAVAGED CORPSE
Tirisfal Glades (86), F-5, G:(4-6)

RAVASAUR
Un'Goro Crater (90), H:(6-8), I:(6-8), The Marshlands, The Slithering Scar

RAVASAUR HUNTER
Un'Goro Crater (90), H:(5, 6), I:(5, 6), J:(5, 6), The Marshlands

RAVASAUR MATRIARCH
Un'Goro Crater (90), H-7, I:(6, 7), The Marshlands

RAVASAUR RUNNER
Un'Goro Crater (90), H:(6-8), I:(6-8), The Marshlands

RAVENCLAW APPARITION
Silverpine Forest (68), G-2, The Dead Field

RAVENCLAW CHAMPION
Silverpine Forest (68), H:(3, 4), The Decrepit Ferry, East of road near lake

RAVENCLAW DRUDGER
Silverpine Forest (68), I-7, Beren's Peril, Cave

RAVENCLAW GUARDIAN
Silverpine Forest (68), I-7, Beren's Peril, Cave

RAVENCLAW RAIDER
Silverpine Forest (68), G:(5, 6), Olsen's Farthing, Farm

RAVENCLAW REGENT
Rare Spawn, Desolace (30), J-2, Sargeron, Lvl 22 Uncommon; Southwest of Nijel's Point

RAVENCLAW SERVANT
Silverpine Forest (68), H:(3, 4), The Decrepit Ferry, East of road near lake

RAVENCLAW SLAVE
Silverpine Forest (68), G-5, H:(1, 2), The Ivar Patch, Farm

RAVENHOLDT ASSASSIN
Assassin's League, Hillsbrad Foothills (48), K-2, Ravenholdt Manor, In and around the Ravenholdt Manor

RAVENHOLDT GUARD
Hillsbrad Foothills (48), J:(1, 2), K-2

RAVENOUS DARKHOUND
Tirisfal Glades (86), K:(4, 5), L:(4, 5), Venomweb Vale

RAWRK
First Aid Trainer, Durotar (34), H-4, Razor Hill (122), Barracks

RAYAN DAWNRISEN
Azshara (14), C-4, Bear's Head, Requires quest from Sanath Lim-yo to reach

RAYTAF
Loramus's Guardian, Azshara (14), H-7, Bay of Storms, Patrols near Loramus

RAZAL'BLADE
Badlands (16), A-5, Kargath (114), Group left of orc burrow

RAZE
Nilith's Guardian, Searing Gorge (64), E-7, Behind Nilith Lokrav on right side of camp

RAZELIKH THE DEFILER
Blasted Lands (20), G-3, Rise of the Defiler, (Summon) Summoned by player via Altar of the Defiler

RAZOR HILL GRUNT
Durotar (34), G-4, H-4, Razor Hill (122)

RAZORBEAK GRYPHON
The Hinterlands (50), D-7, E:(4, 5), F:(4, 6), G-5, H-6

RAZORBEAK SKYLORD
The Hinterlands (50), H-6, I:(4, 6)

RAZORCLAW THE BUTCHER
Silverpine Forest (68), F-7, Shadowfang Keep

RAZORFEN BATTLEGUARD
Barrens (18), E-9, F-9, Razorfen Downs, Southern Gold Road

RAZORFEN BEAST TRAINER
Barrens (18), E-9, Razorfen Kraul

RAZORFEN BEASTMASTER
Barrens (18), E-9, Razorfen Kraul

RAZORFEN DEFENDER
Barrens (18), E-9, Razorfen Kraul

RAZORFEN DUSTWEAVER
Barrens (18), E-9, Razorfen Kraul

RAZORFEN EARTHBREAKER
Barrens (18), E-9, Razorfen Kraul

RAZORFEN GEOMANCER
Barrens (18), E-9, Razorfen Kraul

RAZORFEN GROUNDSHAKER
Barrens (18), E-9, Razorfen Kraul

RAZORFEN HANDLER
Barrens (18), E-9, Razorfen Kraul

RAZORFEN QUILGUARD
Barrens (18), E-9, Razorfen Kraul

RAZORFEN SERVITOR
Barrens (18), F-9, Razorfen Downs, Razorfen Kraul, Southern Gold Road

RAZORFEN SPEARHIDE
Barrens (18), E-9, Razorfen Kraul

RAZORFEN STALKER
Barrens (18), E-9, Razorfen Kraul

RAZORFEN THORNWEAVER
Barrens (18), F-9, Razorfen Downs

RAZORFEN TOTEMIC
Barrens (18), E-9, Razorfen Kraul

RAZORFEN WARDEN
Barrens (18), E-9, Razorfen Kraul

RAZORFEN WARRIOR
Barrens (18), E-9, Razorfen Kraul

RAZORLASH
Desolace (30), D-5, Mauradon

RAZORMANE BATTLEGUARD
Durotar (34), F:(4, 5), G-4, Razormane Grounds

RAZORMANE DEFENDER
Barrens (18), G:(2, 3), Thorn Hill

RAZORMANE DUSTRUNNER
Durotar (34), F:(4, 5), G-4, Razormane Grounds

RAZORMANE GEOMANCER
Barrens (18), G:(2, 3), Thorn Hill

RAZORMANE HUNTER
Barrens (18), H:(2, 3), G:(2, 3), Thorn Hill

RAZORMANE MYSTIC
Barrens (18), G-3, Thorn Hill

RAZORMANE PATHFINDER
Barrens (18), E-8, Blackthorn Ridge, Southern Barrens

RAZORMANE QUILBOAR
Durotar (34), F-5, G-5, H-5, Razormane Grounds

RAZORMANE SCOUT
Durotar (34), F-5, G-5, H-5, Razormane Grounds

RAZORMANE SEER
Barrens (18), D-8, E-8, Blackthorn Ridge, Southern Gold Road

RAZORMANE STALKER
Barrens (18), E-8, Blackthorn Ridge, Southern Gold Road

RAZORMANE THORNWEAVER
Barrens (18), F:(2, 3), G-3, Gold Road, Thorn Hill

RAZORMANE WARFRENZY
Barrens (18), D-8, E-8, Blackthorn Ridge

RAZORMANE WATER SEEKER
Barrens (18), F:(2, 3), G-3, Gold Road, Thorn Hill

RAZORMAW MATRIARCH
Rare Spawn, Wetlands (96), I-3, J-3, Raptor Ridge, Lvl 31 Uncommon; Spawns in western or northeastern chamber of cave

RAZORTALON
Rare Spawn, The Hinterlands (50), D:(5, 7), E-5, F-5, Bogen's Ledge, Lvl 44 Average Rare; Roams small area around spawn point

RAZZERIC
Thousand Needles (82), K-8, Mirage Raceway (118), Inside racetrack

RAZZLE SPRYSPROCKET
Dun Morogh (32), F-5, Kharanos (114), In gnomish building

REANIMATED CORPSE
Western Plaguelands (92), I-7, Scholomance

REBAN FREERUNNER
Pet Trainer, Mulgore (58), E-6, Bloodhoof Village (102), North tents

REBECCA LAUGHLIN
Tabard Vendor, Stormwind (72), H-7, I-7, Trade District, Stormwind Visitor's Center

REBEL WATCHMAN
Stranglethorn Vale (74), D-1, Rebel Camp, Patrols back and forth in camp

RED DRAGONSPAWN
Wetlands (96), K:(4, 5), Dragonmaw Gates, Raptor Ridge

RED JACK FLINT
Wetlands (96), A-6, Menethil Harbor (117), First floor of keep, next to stairs

RED SCALEBANE
Wetlands (96), K-5, L-5, Dragonmaw Gates

RED WHELP
Wetlands (96), H:(4, 5), I-5, Mosshide Fen, The Green Belt

RED WYRMKIN
Wetlands (96), K:(4, 5), L-5, Dragonmaw Gates, Raptor Ridge

REDPATH MILITIA
Eastern Plaguelands (40), E-8, Darrowshire, (Summon) Path heading into town

REDPATH THE CORRUPTED
Eastern Plaguelands (40), E-8, Darrowshire, (Summon) Path heading into town

REDRIDGE ALPHA
Redridge Mountains (62), C-2, Redridge Canyons

REDRIDGE BASHER
Redridge Mountains (62), B-3, C:(2, 3), D:(2, 3), Redridge Canyons

REDRIDGE BRUTE
Redridge Mountains (62), B:(3, 4), C:(3, 4), D-2, E:(3, 4), Redridge Canyons

REDRIDGE DRUDGER
Redridge Mountains (62), B-3, Rethban Caverns

REDRIDGE MONGREL
Redridge Mountains (62), A-6, B-6, C-8, D-8, E-7, Lakeridge Highway

REDRIDGE MYSTIC
Redridge Mountains (62), B:(3, 4), C:(2-4), D:(2, 3), E:(3, 4), Redridge Canyons

REDRIDGE POACHER
Redridge Mountains (62), C-8, D-8, E-7, Lakeridge Highway

REDRIDGE THRASHER
Redridge Mountains (62), A-6, B-6, C-8, D-8, Three Corners

REDROCK EARTH SPIRIT
Durotar (34), G:(7, 8)

REDSTONE BASILISK
Blasted Lands (20), H-3, I-3, Serpent's Coil

REDSTONE CRYSTALHIDE
Blasted Lands (20), G:(3-5), H:(4-6), Dark Portal, Dreadmaul Post, Rise of the Defiler

REEF CRAWLER
Darkshore (24), E:(7, 8), G-2, H-2, Cliffspring River, Mist's Edge, Twilight Shore

REESE LANGSTON
Tavernkeeper, Stormwind (72), J-5, Old Town, Pig and Whistle Tavern

REFUGE POINTE DEFENDER
Arathi Highlands (10), F:(4, 5), G:(4, 5), Refuge Point

REGGIFUZ
Stable Master, Barrens (18), H-4, Ratchet (121), Front of inn

REGINA HALLORAN
Wetlands (96), A-5, Menethil Harbor (117), House, west of keep

REGINALD GRIMSFORD
Undercity (88), The Magic Quarter, Wanders Magic Quarter

REGNUS THUNDERGRANITE
Hunter Trainer, Ironforge (52), I-8, The Military Ward, Hall of Arms

REGTHAR DEATHGATE
Barrens (18), E-3, Bunker along road west of Crossroads

REJOLD BARLEYBREW
Dun Morogh (32), D-4, Brewnall Village, Under scaffolding

REKK'TILAC
Rare Spawn, Searing Gorge (64), C-7, D-3, F-7, G-3, H-7, I-7, Tanner Camp, The Sea of Cinders, Thorium Point, Lvl 48 Average Rare; Stands idle at spawn point

REKKUL
Poison Vendor, Orgrimmar (60), E-5, The Cleft of Shadow, Rekkul's Poisons

RELARA WHITEMOON
Ashenvale (12), E-5, Astranaar (101), On bed in southeast building

RELLIAN GREENSPYRE
Darnassus (26), E-2, Cenarion Enclave, Next to bridge

REMA SCHNEIDER
Stormwind (72), G:(5, 6), The Canals, Canal Tailor and Fit Shop

REMAINS OF TREY LIGHTFORGE
Felwood (44), E-6, Shadow Hold, On altar in altar room

REMEN MARCOT
Elwynn Forest (42), F-7, Goldshire (112), Basement of Lion's Pride Inn

REMORSEFUL HIGHBORNE
Winterspring (98), H-4, The Ruins of Kel'Theril, In ruins

REMY "TWO TIMES"
Elwynn Forest (42), F-7, Goldshire (112), Standing by the road at the far end of town

RENATO GALLINA
Stormwind (72), H-6, Trade District, Outside Pestle's Apothecary

RENDOW
Feralas (46), K-5, Thalanaar, Northwest of well

RENZIK "THE SHIV"
SI:7 Operative, Stormwind (72), K-6, Old Town, SI:7

RESIDUAL MONSTROSITY
Feralas (46), G-4, Dire Maul

RESSAN THE NEEDLER
Rare Spawn, Tirisfal Glades (86), E-7, F:(6, 7), G-6, Nightmare Vale, Lvl 11 Uncommon; Roams a small area around spawn point

RESTLESS SHADE
Deadwind Pass (28), C:(6-8), D:(7, 8), E:(7-9), F-8, Karazhan, Morgan's Plot

RETHEROKK THE BERSERKER
Rare Spawn, The Hinterlands (50), G:(6, 7), H-6, The Altar of Zul, Lvl 48 Uncommon; Roams around base of altar

RETHIEL THE GREENWARDEN
Wetlands (96), H-4, The Green Belt, In bare spot, east of road to Dun Modr

RETHILGORE
Silverpine Forest (68), F-7, Shadowfang Keep

REVANTUSK DRUMMER
The Hinterlands (50), L-8, Revantusk Village

REVANTUSK WATCHER
The Hinterlands (50), K-8, L-8, Revantusk Village

REVELOSH
Badlands (16), G-1, Uldaman

REX ASHIL
Rare Spawn, Silithus (66), F-2, Hive'Ashi, Lvl 57 Average Rare; Patrols above and within hive

REXXAR
Champion of the Horde, Desolace (30), G-1, Spawns on road near Stonetalon Mts. border and patrols roads with Misha

REYNA STONEBRANCH
Herbalism Trainer, Ironforge (52), G-6, The Great Forge, Ironforge Physician

REZLAK
Tinkers' Union, Durotar (34), G-2, Along road south of Orgrimmar entrance

RHAG GARMASON
Wetlands (96), G-2, Dun Modr, Next to wagons, west of road

RHAHK'ZOR
Westfall (94), D-7, E-7, The Deadmines

RHAPSODY SHINDIGGER
The Hinterlands (50), D-5, Shindigger's Camp, Camp

RHIANNON DAVIS
Expert Tailor, Undercity (88), J-3, The Magic Quarter

RHINAG
Durotar (34), F-2, Among boulders south of Rocktusk Farm

RIBBLY SCREWSPIGOT
Burning Steppes (22), Searing Gorge (64), C-4/D-8, Blackrock Depths

RIBBLY'S CRONY
Burning Steppes (22), Searing Gorge (64), C-4/D-8, Blackrock Depths

RIBCHASER
Rare Spawn, Redridge Mountains (62), A-6, D-8, Lakeridge Highway, Three Corners, Lvl 17 Uncommon; Patrols around gnoll camp

RICHARD KERWIN
Warlock Trainer, Undercity (88), L:(1, 2), The Magic Quarter, Northeast corner of Skull Building

RICHARD VAN BRUNT
Undercity (88), G-2, The War Quarter, Watches fights in War Quarter

RICKLE GOLDGRUBBER
Banker, Stranglethorn Vale (74), B-8, Booty Bay (103), Stranglethorn Trust Bank

RICTER
Alterac Mountains (8), B-8, Lordamere Internment Camp, Roams inside camp walls

RIDGE HUNTRESS
Badlands (16), D-5, E-5, F:(5-7), G:(5-8), H:(4-8), I:(5-7), J-7, The Dustbowl, Plains

RIDGE STALKER
Badlands (16), E-4, F:(4, 5), G-4, H:(1-3), I:(3-5), J:(3, 4), The Dustbowl

RIDGE STALKER PATRIARCH
Badlands (16), A:(6, 7), B:(5-8), C:(6-8), D:(6-8), Apocryphan's Rest

RIGGER GIZELTON
Desolace (30), H-4, Spawns on road near Kormek's Hut, runs a loop along the roads, and pauses at the hut upon return

RIGGLEFUZZ
Badlands (16), F-5, Valley of Fangs, Camp

RIKQIZ
Leatherworking Supplies, Stranglethorn Vale (74), B-8, Booty Bay (103), Two story house on third level along the eastern side of bay

RILAN HOWARD
Winterspring (98), I-1, Small camp near hills

RILEY WALKER
Undercity (88), G-2, The War Quarter, Watches fights in War Quarter

RILLI GREASYGOB
Orgrimmar (60), I-3, J-3, Valley of Honor, Nogg's Machine Shop

RINGO
Un'Goro Crater (90), G-5, Fire Plume Ridge, East den on ridge

RIN'JI
Witherbark Troll, The Hinterlands (50), E-5, Quel'Danil Lodge, Cage towards the rear of main lodge

RIPPA
Rare Spawn, Stranglethorn Vale (74), B-6, Southern Savage Coast, Lvl 44 Very Rare; Patrols the cove on the northern side of The Cape of Stranglethorn

RIPSCALE
Rare Spawn, Dustwallow Marsh (38), E-5. F:(5-6), The Quagmire, Lvl 39 Semi-Rare; Roams swamp

RISEN ABERRATION
Western Plaguelands (92), I-7, Scholomance

RISEN BONEWARDER
Western Plaguelands (92), I-7, Scholomance

RISEN CONSTRUCT
Western Plaguelands (92), I-7, Scholomance

RISEN GUARD
Western Plaguelands (92), I-7, Scholomance

RISEN GUARDIAN
Western Plaguelands (92), I-7, Scholomance

RISEN LACKEY
Western Plaguelands (92), I-7, Scholomance

RISEN PROTECTOR
Western Plaguelands (92), I-7, Scholomance

RISEN WARRIOR
Western Plaguelands (92), I-7, Scholomance

RIVER CROCOLISK
Stranglethorn Vale (74), C-1, D:(1, 2), Lake Nazferiti

RIVERN FROSTWIND
Wintersaber Trainers, Winterspring (98), G-1, Frostsaber Rock, Atop Frostsaber Rock

RIVERPAW BANDIT
Westfall (94), E-6, F:(6, 7), G-7, H-7, Stendel's Pond

RIVERPAW BRUTE
Westfall (94), B-5, C-7, E-6, F:(6, 7), G-7, H-1, The Dust Plains

RIVERPAW GNOLL
Westfall (94), D-2, E:(1, 2), F:(1, 2), G-1, The Jansen Stead

RIVERPAW HERBALIST
Westfall (94), B-6, C:(5-7), Alexston Farmstead

RIVERPAW MINER
Westfall (94), B-5, C:(4, 5), Gold Coast Quarry

RIVERPAW MONGREL
Westfall (94), B:(6, 7), C:(3, 5-7), D-3

RIVERPAW MYSTIC
Westfall (94), G:(7, 8), H:(7, 8), The Dust Plains

RIVERPAW OUTRUNNER
Elwynn Forest (42), C:(8, 9), I:(4, 5), J-4, K-4, Forest's Edge

RIVERPAW OVERSEER
Westfall (94), G-8, H-8, The Dust Plains

RIVERPAW RUNT
Elwynn Forest (42), C:(8, 9), D:(8, 9), I:(4, 5), J-4, Forest's Edge

RIVERPAW SCOUT
Westfall (94), C:(3, 5), D:(2, 3), E:(1, 2), F:(1, 2), G-1, The Jansen Stead

RIVERPAW SHAMAN
Westfall (94), D-2, Jangolode Mine

RIVERPAW TASKMASTER
Westfall (94), F-7, G:(7, 8), H:(7, 8), The Dust Plains

RIZNEK
Drink Vendor, Thousand Needles (82), K:(7-8), Mirage Raceway (118), Roams infield of racetrack from drag strip grandstands to starting tower

RIZZ LOOSEBOLT
Engineering Supplies, Alterac Mountains (8), F-4, Slaughter Hollow, Captive in cage on left of cave

RIZZLE BRASSBOLTS
Thousand Needles (82), J-8, Mirage Raceway (118), Building west of racetrack

RO'BARK
Rare Spawn, Hillsbrad Foothills (48), H-6, Nethander Stead, Lvl 28 Uncommon; Patrols crop field

ROBERT AEBISCHER
Superior Armorsmith, Hillsbrad Foothills (48), F-5, Southshore (125), Behind small house left of path

ROBERT GOSSOM
Undercity (88), G-2, The War Quarter, Watches fights in War Quarter

ROBERTO PUPELLYVERBOS
Merlot Connoisseur, Stormwind (72), H-7, The Canals, Gallina Winery

ROC
Tanaris (78), E-3, F-3, G:(3, 4), H:(3, 4)

ROCK BORER
Desolace (30), D-5, Mauradon

ROCK ELEMENTAL
Badlands (16), B:(3, 4), C-4, E:(7, 8), F:(7-9), G:(8, 9), Kargath

ROCK STALKER
Silithus (66), D:(4, 5), E:(4, 5), F:(4, 5), G:(4, 5), H-4, The Scarab Dais

ROCK WORM
Desolace (30), D-5, Mauradon

ROCKBITER
Feralas (46), D-2, The Twin Colossals, Camp southwest of western colossal

ROCKHIDE BOAR
Elwynn Forest (42), F:(7-9), G:(7, 8), H:(7, 8), I:(7, 8), J:(7, 8), Brackwell Pumpkin Patch, Jerod's Landing

ROCKJAW AMBUSHER
Dun Morogh (32), J:(5, 6), K-6, Gol'Bolar Quarry, Helm's Bed Lake, Ironband's Compound

ROCKJAW BACKBREAKER
Dun Morogh (32), J-6, K:(5, 6), Gol'Bolar Quarry, Helm's Bed Lake, Ironband's Compound

ROCKJAW BONESNAPPER
Dun Morogh (32), J:(5, 6), K:(5, 6), Gol'Bolar Quarry, Helm's Bed Lake, Ironband's Compound

ROCKJAW RAIDER
Dun Morogh (32), D-7, E:(6, 7), Coldridge Pass

ROCKJAW SKULLTHUMPER
Dun Morogh (32), I-6, J:(5, 6), Gol'Bolar Quarry

ROCKJAW TROGG
Dun Morogh (32), B:(7, 8), C:(7, 8), D:(7, 8), Coldridge Pass, Coldridge Valley (106)

ROCKLANCE
Barrens (18), G-4, The Stagnant Oasis, Patrols the oasis

ROCKWING GARGOYLE
Eastern Plaguelands (40), D-2, Stratholme

ROCKWING SCREECHER
Eastern Plaguelands (40), D-2, Stratholme

ROETTEN STONEHAMMER
Reclaimers Inc., Ironforge (52), I-2, Hall of Explorers, Out front of library

ROGER
Redridge Mountains (62), C-5, Lake Everstill

ROGGO HARLBARROW
Wetlands (96), G-2, Dun Modr, Next to wagons, west of road

ROGUE BLACK DRAKE
Burning Steppes (22), A-6

ROGUE FLAME SPIRIT
Stonetalon Mountains (70), D:(5, 6), E:(5, 6), F-4, The Charred Vale, Mirkfallon Lake

ROGUE ICE THISTLE
Winterspring (98), D-5, E:(4, 5), F:(3, 4), G:(3-5), H-4, Frostfire Hot Springs, Timbermaw Post

ROGUE VALE SCREECHER
Feralas (46), D-4, E:(4-6), F-5, G-5

ROGVAR
Master Alchemist, Swamp of Sorrows (76), F-5, Stonard (126), Second floor of main hall

ROHH THE SILENT
Rare Spawn, Redridge Mountains (62), J:(3, 4), K:(5, 6), Galardell Valley, Stonewatch Falls, Tower of Ilgalar, Lvl 26 Semi-Rare; Stands idle at spawn point

ROK ORHAN
Feralas (46), I-4, Camp Mojache (105), Spawns near western mill and walks to the eastern mill

ROK'ALIM THE POUNDER
Thousand Needles (82), A:(2-3), B-4, C-4, Spawns in a few different spots along southeastern plateaus

ROKAR BLADESHADOW
Durotar (34), H-3, Farmhouse

ROLAND GEARDABBLER
Azshara (14), F-9, The Ruined Reaches, South of camp on border of Great Sea in back cabin of ship beneath debris

ROLE DREUGER
Duskwood (36), J-5, Darkshire Town Hall

ROLOCH
Rare Spawn, Stranglethorn Vale (74), D-3, Mizjah Ruins, Lvl 38 Average Rare; Patrols between ruins and the path to the north

ROMAN
Stormwind (72), H-3, The Canals, Dock

RONALD BURCH
Cooking Supplier, Undercity (88), I-4, The Trade Quarter, West spoke from bank

ROOGUG
Barrens (18), E-9, Razorfen Kraul

ROOKERY GUARDIAN
Burning Steppes (22), Searing Gorge (64), C-4/D-8, Blackrock Spire

ROOKERY HATCHER
Burning Steppes (22), Searing Gorge (64), C-4/D-8, Blackrock Spire

ROOKERY WHELP
Burning Steppes (22), Searing Gorge (64), C-4/D-8, Blackrock Spire

ROON WILDMANE
Desolace (30), C-7, Shadowprey Village (125), Near entrance

RORGISH JOWL
Rare Spawn, Ashenvale (12), E-4, Thistlefur Village, Lvl 25 Uncommon; Roams camp near spawn locations

RORY
Western Plaguelands (92), I-7, Caer Darrow, Roams around the dock on the western side of city

ROT HIDE BRUISER
Silverpine Forest (68), J:(2, 3), Fenris Isle

ROT HIDE BRUTE
Silverpine Forest (68), J:(2-4), Fenris Isle

ROT HIDE GLADERUNNER
Silverpine Forest (68), G-2, The Dead Field

ROT HIDE GNOLL
Tirisfal Glades (86), G:(3, 4), H:(3, 4), Garren's Haunt

ROT HIDE GRAVEROBBER
Tirisfal Glades (86), G:(4, 5)

ROT HIDE MONGREL
Tirisfal Glades (86), G-3, H:(3, 4), Garren's Haunt

ROT HIDE MYSTIC
Silverpine Forest (68), G-2, The Dead Field

ROT HIDE PLAGUE WEAVER
Silverpine Forest (68), J:(2-4), Fenris Isle

ROT HIDE SAVAGE
Silverpine Forest (68), J:(2, 3), Fenris Isle

ROTGATH STONEBEARD
Expert Blacksmith, Ironforge (52), G-4, The Great Forge, Next to anvils

ROTGRIP
Desolace (30), D-5, Mauradon

ROTHOS
The Hinterlands (50), I-3, Seradane, Patrols around portal

ROTTED ONE
Duskwood (36), C:(3, 4), Raven Hill Cemetery (122)

ROTTING AGAM'AR
Barrens (18), E-9, Razorfen Kraul

ROTTING ANCESTOR
Tirisfal Glades (86), F-3, G-3, Agamand Mills (100)

ROTTING BEHEMOTH
Western Plaguelands (92), H:(3, 4), I:(3, 4), The Weeping Cave

ROTTING CADAVER
Western Plaguelands (92), F:(5, 6), Dalson's Tears

ROTTING DEAD
Tirisfal Glades (86), F:(5, 6), G:(5, 6)

ROTTING GHOUL
Western Plaguelands (92), G:(6, 7), The Writhing Haunt

ROTTING HIGHBORNE
Feralas (46), G-4, Dire Maul

ROTTING SLIME
Ashenvale (12), I:(7, 8), J:(6, 7), Felfire Hill, Nightsong Woods, Dor'Danil Barrow Den, Warsong Labor Camp

ROTTING SLIME
Barrens (18), E-OUT

ROTTING SLUDGE
Eastern Plaguelands (40), G:(6, 7), H-6, I-6, J:(5, 6), Pestilent Scar

ROXXIK
Artisan Engineer, Orgrimmar (60), I-3, J-3, Valley of Honor, Nogg's Machine Shop

ROYAL FACTOR BATHRILOR
Stormwind Census, Stormwind (72), G-3, Cathedral Square, City Hall

ROYAL HISTORIAN ARCHESONUS
Ironforge (52), E-5, The Great Forge, The High Seat

ROYAL OVERSEER BAUHAUS
Undercity Census, Undercity (88), J-4, The Trade Quarter, By Guild Master, East spoke from bank

RUDRA AMBERSTILL
Dun Morogh (32), I-5, Amberstill Ranch, By building

RUGA RAGETOTEM
Barrens (18), F-6, Camp Taurajo (106), Southern building

RUKLAR THE TRAPPER
Elwynn Forest (42), I-6, Jasperlode Mine, Small camp to the right of mine entrance

RUMBLER
Rare Spawn, Badlands (16), A-8, B-9, Camp Cagg, Lvl 45 Uncommon; Roams small area around spawn point

RUMBLING EXILE
Arathi Highlands (10), E:(5, 6), Circle of Inner Binding

RUMSTAG PROUDSTRIDER
Horde Cloth Quartermaster, Thunder Bluff (84), E-4, Middle rise, inside Thunder Bluff Armorers tent

RUPERT BOCH
Warlock Trainer, Tirisfal Glades (86), H-5, Brill (104), Second floor of Gallows' End Tavern

RUPPO ZIPCOIL
Engineering Supplies, The Hinterlands (50), E-4, The Hinterlands, Gnomish camp on recessed hill east of Quel'Danil Lodge

RUSTY HARVEST GOLEM
Westfall (94), F:(2, 3), G-2, Furlbrow's Pumpkin Patch

RUUL EAGLETALON
Mulgore (58), E-6, Bloodhoof Village (102), South tent

RUUL ONESTONE
Rare Spawn, Arathi Highlands (10), B-7, The Tower of Arathor, Lvl 39 Average Rare; Roams the top floor of tower

RUUL SNOWHOOF
Ashenvale (12), E-3, Thistlefur Hold, Cage in water in back of hold

RUUZEL
Ashenvale (12), A-2, The Zoram Strand (131), Patrols entire island

RUUZLU
Tanaris (78), E-1, Zul'Farrak

RUW
Herbalism Trainer, Feralas (46), I-4, Camp Mojache (105), East of bridge

RUZAN
Durotar (34), F-7, Valley of Trials (131)

RWAG
Rogue Trainer, Durotar (34), F-7, Valley of Trials (131)

RYBRAD CLODBANK
Weaponsmith, Dun Morogh (32), D-7, Coldridge Valley (106), Anvilmar

RYNTHARIEL THE KEYMASTER
Stonetalon Mountains (70), C-2, The Talon Den, Southern room of den

S

SAEAN
Loch Modan (54), G-7, The Loch, (Summon) Attacks player and NPC's during escort

SAENORION
Leatherworking Supplies, Darnassus (26), I-2, Craftsmen's Terrace, Leatherworking shop

SAERN PRIDERUNNER
Thunder Bluff (84), G-8, Hunter Rise, Inside Tent next to Hunter's Hall

SAGE KOROLUSK
Feralas (46), I-4, Camp Mojache (105), Patrols road north of inn

SAGE PALERUNNER
Feralas (46), I-4, Camp Mojache (105), Small tent near waterfall

SAGE TRUTHSEEKER
Thunder Bluff (84), C-5, Inside bridge to Spirit Rise

SAGORNE CRESTRIDER
Shaman Trainer, Orgrimmar (60), D-4, Valley of Wisdom, Grommash Hold

SAHRAN BLOODSHADOW
Tirisfal Glades (86), G-6, H-5, Brill (104)

SAH'RHEE
Barrens (18), F-9, Razorfen Downs

SALAZAR BLOCH
Book Dealer, Undercity (88), K-4, The Magic Quarter, Near Rogues' Quarter entry

SALFA
Winterspring (98), D4, Frostfire Hot Springs, West edge of Felwood entrance

SALIA
Felwood (44), E-6, Shadow Hold, Anteroom after spiral tunnel

SALMA SALDEAN
Westfall (94), F-3, Saldean's Farm, Farmhouse

SALT FLATS SCAVENGER
Thousand Needles (82), I:(5-7), J:(5-7), K:(6, 7), L-6, Ironstone Camp, The Shimmering Flats, Weazel's Crater

SALT FLATS VULTURE
Thousand Needles (82), I:(8, 9), J-9, K:(7, 8), L-8, Tahonda Ruins, The Rustmaul Dig Site, The Shimmering Flats

SALTSCALE FORAGER
Stranglethorn Vale (74), B-3, Bal'lal Ruins, The Savage Coast, The Vile Reef

SALTSCALE HUNTER
Stranglethorn Vale (74), B-3, The Savage Coast, The Vile Reef

SALTSCALE ORACLE
Stranglethorn Vale (74), B-3, The Vile Reef

SALTSCALE TIDE LORD
Stranglethorn Vale (74), B-3, The Vile Reef

SALTSCALE WARRIOR
Stranglethorn Vale (74), B-3, The Savage Coast, The Vile Reef

SALTSPITTLE MUCKDWELLER
Ashenvale (12), C-4, Lake Falathim

SALTSPITTLE ORACLE
Ashenvale (12), C-4, Lake Falathim

SALTSPITTLE PUDDLEJUMPER
Ashenvale (12), C:(4, 5), Lake Falathim

SALTSPITTLE WARRIOR
Ashenvale (12), C:(4, 5), Lake Falathim

SALTSTONE BASILISK
Thousand Needles (82), I:(5-6), J:(5-7), K-6, Ironstone Camp, The Shimmering Flats, Weazel's Crater

SALTSTONE CRYSTALHIDE
Thousand Needles (82), I-8, J:,(6-9), K:(5-9), L:(6-8), Tahonda Ruins, The Shimmering Flats, Weazel's Crater

SALTSTONE GAZER
Thousand Needles (82), J:(8, 9), K:(8, 9), Tahonda Ruins, The Shimmering Flats, Mirage Raceway

SALTWATER CROCOLISK
Stranglethorn Vale (74), A-2, B-2, C:(3, 4)

SALTWATER SNAPJAW
The Hinterlands (50), K:(6-9), L:(4-9), Overlook Cliffs, Coast

SAMANTHA SHACKELTON
Undercity (88), J-3, The Magic Quarter, Stall next to Tailors

SAMANTHA SWIFTHOOF
Stranglethorn Vale (74), D-1, Patrols between the bridge into Duskwood and the entrance to Booty Bay

SAMMY
Western Plaguelands (92), I-8, Caer Darrow, Ghost By fountain

SAMOR FESTIVUS
Shady Dealer, Wetlands (96), A-6, Deepwater Tavern, Northwest, upstairs room

SAMUEL FIPPS
Tirisfal Glades (86), D-6, Deathknell (109), Ruined camp on right side of road heading out of town

SAMUEL VAN BRUNT
Blacksmith Supplier, Undercity (88), I-3, The War Quarter

SANA
Mail Armor Merchant, Orgrimmar (60), G-8, Valley of Strength, Soran's Leather and Steel

SANATH LIM-YO
Azshara (14), C-5, Camp in foothills

SAND CRAWLER
Westfall (94), D-1, E-1, F-1, Longshore

SAND SKITTERER
Silithus (66), E:(1, 2), F:(1, 2), G:(1-3), H:(1-3), Southwind Village

SANDAHL
Warlock Trainer, Stormwind (72), D-8, Mage Quarter, The Slaughtered Lamb

SANDFURY AXE THROWER
Tanaris (78), E-3, F:(2, 3), Sandsorrow Watch, Zul'Farrak

SANDFURY BLOOD DRINKER
Tanaris (78), E-1, Zul'Farrak

SANDFURY CRETIN
Tanaris (78), E-1, Zul'Farrak

SANDFURY EXECUTIONER
Tanaris (78), E-1, Zul'Farrak

SANDFURY FIRECALLER
Tanaris (78), E-3, F:(2, 3), Sandsorrow Watch, Zul'Farrak

SANDFURY GUARDIAN
Tanaris (78), E-1, Zul'Farrak

SANDFURY HIDESKINNER
Tanaris (78), E-3, F:(2, 3), Sandsorrow Watch, Zul'Farrak

SANDFURY SHADOWCASTER
Tanaris (78), E-1, Zul'Farrak

SANDFURY SHADOWHUNTER
Tanaris (78), E-1, Zul'Farrak

SANDFURY SOUL EATER
Tanaris (78), E-1, Zul'Farrak

SANDFURY WITCH DOCTOR
Tanaris (78), E-1, Zul'Farrak

SANUYE RUNETOTEM
Leather Armor Merchant, Barrens (18), F-6, Camp Taurajo (106), Near hides

SAP BEAST
Stonetalon Mountains (70), D:(1, 2), E:(1, 2), F:(2-4), G:(3, 4), Mirkfallon Lake, Stonetalon Peak, The Talon Den

SAR BROWNEYE
Winterspring (98), I-1, Small camp near hills

SARA BALLOO
Ironforge (52), I-7, The Military Ward, North patio

SARA PIERCE
Dustwallow Marsh (38), I-5, Theramore Isle (130), 2nd floor of inn

SARA TIMBERLAIN
Elwynn Forest (42), K-7, Eastvale Logging Camp, Front steps of house

SARAH GOODE
Stable Master, Silverpine Forest (68), F-4, The Sepulcher (124), Outside of inn entrance on right

SARAH KILLIAN
Mining Supplier, Undercity (88), H-4, The War Quarter

SARAH RAYCROFT
General Goods, Hillsbrad Foothills (48), F-5, Southshore (125), Second floor of house

SARAH TANNER
Master Elemental Leatherworker, Searing Gorge (64), H-7, Tanner Camp, In front of tent

SARGATH
Ashenvale (12), D-4, Maestra's Post, Near Stones south of main outpost

SARILUS FOULBORNE
Barrens (18), E-2, Dreadmist Peak, Atop Dreadmist Peak

SARIN STARLIGHT
Darnassus (26), C-5, The Temple Gardens, South of teleporter

SARK RAGETOTEM
Warrior Trainer, Thunder Bluff (84), G-9, Hunter Rise, Inside Hunter's Hall

SARKOTH
Durotar (34), F-7, Valley of Trials (131), Roams western hills

SARLEK
Orgrimmar (60), G-5, The Drag, Building south of Jandi's Arboretum

SARLTOOTH
Wetlands (96), D-5, Whelgar's Excavation Site, On upper ledge, in southwestern section of site

SAROK
Orgrimmar (60), G-7, Valley of Strength, Inn

SARU STEELFURY
Artisan Blacksmith, Orgrimmar (60), J-2, K-2, Valley of Honor, The Bruning Anvil

SATURATED OOZE
Swamp of Sorrows (76), I-5, The Temple of Atal'Hakkar

SAVAGE OWLBEAST
The Hinterlands (50), H:(4-6), I:(4-6), J:(5, 6), The Hinterlands

SAVANNAH HIGHMANE
Barrens (18), F:(2, 3), G-3, Gold Road

SAVANNAH HUNTRESS
Barrens (18), F:(1-3), G:(2, 3), Gold Road, Thorn Hill

SAVANNAH MATRIARCH
Barrens (18), H-3, Thorn Hill

SAVANNAH PATRIARCH
Barrens (18), E:(1, 2), G-3, H-3, The Dry Hills

SAVANNAH PROWLER
Barrens (18), D:(2, 3), E:(2-4), F:(1, 2), G:(1-4), H:(1-3), Boulder Lode Mine, The Dry Hills

SAVANNE
Fishing Supplies, Feralas (46), C-5, Feathermoon Stronghold (110), Southwest building

SAWFIN FRENZY
Swamp of Sorrows (76), H-6, I:(4-6), J-5, Pool of Tears

SAWTOOTH CROCOLISK
Swamp of Sorrows (76), F-4, G:(3-5), H-3, I-2, The Shifting Mire

SAWTOOTH SNAPPER
Swamp of Sorrows (76), I-9, J:(1-3, 6, 9), K:(1-7, 9), L:(2, 3, 8, 9), Sorrowmurk

SAYOC
Weapon Master, Orgrimmar (60), J-2, Valley of Strength, Arms of Legend, Trains: Bows, Daggers, Fist Weapons, 1H Axe, 2H Axe, Thrown

SCALD
Rare Spawn, Searing Gorge (64), D-5, G-4, The Cauldron, Lvl 49 Average Rare; Patrols path near spawn point

SCALDING BROODLING
Burning Steppes (22), D:(5, 6), E-3, F:(3, 7), G:(2, 3, 6), H:(5, 6), I:(3-6), J-3

SCALDING DRAKE
Burning Steppes (22), D-6, F-7, I-6

SCALDING ELEMENTAL
Thousand Needles (82), D:(3, 4), E-4, Darkcloud Pinnacle, Splithoof Crag

SCALDING WHELP
Badlands (16), J-5, K:(3, 5-7), L:(3, 4, 6), Lethor Ravine

SCALE BELLY
Rare Spawn, Stranglethorn Vale (74), F-5, Crystalvein Mine, Lvl 45 Uncommon; Mine

SCALEBANE CAPTAIN
Swamp of Sorrows (76), H-4, I-4, J:(4-7), K:(4, 5)

SCALEBANE LIEUTENANT
Wetlands (96), L:(5, 6), Grim Batol

SCALEBANE ROYAL GUARD
Wetlands (96), K-7, L:(6, 7), Grim Batol

SCALEBEARD
Rare Spawn, Azshara (14), G-5, Bay of Storms, Lvl 52 Uncommon; Spawns in Scalebeard's Cave and roams

SCARAB
Tanaris (78), E-1, Zul'Farrak

SCARGIL
Rare Spawn, Hillsbrad Foothills (48), B-7, C-7, Western Strand, Lvl 30 Uncommon

SCARLET ABBOT
Tirisfal Glades (86), K-3, L-3, Scarlet Monastery

SCARLET ADEPT
Tirisfal Glades (86), K-3, L-3, Scarlet Monastery

SCARLET ARCHMAGE
Eastern Plaguelands (40), J-8, K:(7, 8), L:(7, 8), Tyr's Hand

SCARLET ASSASSIN
Western Plaguelands (92), I:(2, 3), Northridge Lumber Camp

SCARLET AUGUR
Tirisfal Glades (86), K-3, The Grand Vestibule, Scarlet Monastery

SCARLET AUGUR
Tirisfal Glades (86), K-3, L-3, Scarlet Monastery

SCARLET AVENGER
Western Plaguelands (92), G:(2, 4), H-4, Northridge Lumber Camp

SCARLET BEASTMASTER
Tirisfal Glades (86), K-3, L-3, Scarlet Monastery

SCARLET BODYGUARD
Tirisfal Glades (86), K:(2, 3), Scarlet Watch Post

SCARLET CAVALIER
Western Plaguelands (92), E-1, Mardenholde Keep

SCARLET CENTURIAN
Tirisfal Glades (86), K-3, L-3, Scarlet Monastery

SCARLET CHAMPION
Tirisfal Glades (86), K-3, L-3, Scarlet Monastery

SCARLET CHAPLAIN
Tirisfal Glades (86), K-3, L-3, Scarlet Monastery

SCARLET CLERIC
Eastern Plaguelands (40), I-8, J:(7, 8), K:(7, 8), Scarlet Base Camp

SCARLET COMMANDER MOGRAINE
Tirisfal Glades (86), K-3, L-3, Scarlet Monastery

SCARLET CONJURER
Tirisfal Glades (86), K-3, L-3, Scarlet Monastery

SCARLET CONVERT
Tirisfal Glades (86), D:(6, 7), E:(6, 7), Deathknell (109)

SCARLET CURATE
Eastern Plaguelands (40), K:(7, 8), L:(7, 8), Tyr's Hand

SCARLET DEFENDER
Tirisfal Glades (86), K-3, L-3, Scarlet Monastery

SCARLET DISCIPLE
Tirisfal Glades (86), K-3, The Grand Vestibule, Scarlet Monastery, Scarlet Monastery

SCARLET DIVINER
Tirisfal Glades (86), K-3, L-3, Scarlet Monastery

SCARLET ENCHANTER
Eastern Plaguelands (40), I-8, J:(7, 8), K:(7, 8), Scarlet Base Camp

SCARLET EVOKER
Tirisfal Glades (86), K-3, L-3, Scarlet Monastery

SCARLET EXECUTIONER
Rare Spawn, Western Plaguelands (92), F-2, Hearthglen, Lvl 60 Very Rare; Roams in tower on the southern end of city

SCARLET FRIAR
Tirisfal Glades (86), J:(5, 6), K:(2-6), L-4, Scarlet Watch Post

SCARLET GALLANT
Tirisfal Glades (86), K-3, L-3, Scarlet Monastery

SCARLET GUARDSMAN
Tirisfal Glades (86), K-3, L-3, Scarlet Monastery

SCARLET HIGH CLERIST
Rare Spawn, Western Plaguelands (92), G-2, Lvl 63 Average Rare; Spawns inside or on top of tower south of Hearthglen

SCARLET HUNTER
Western Plaguelands (92), E-5, G-4

SCARLET INITIATE
Tirisfal Glades (86), D-7, E:(6, 7), Deathknell (109)

SCARLET INTERROGATOR
Rare Spawn, Western Plaguelands (92), F-1, Hearthglen, Lvl 61 Uncommon; Spawns on the first or second floor of tower in the northeast corner of city

SCARLET INVOKER
Western Plaguelands (92), E-5, G-4

SCARLET JUDGE
Rare Spawn, Western Plaguelands (92), E-2, Hearthglen, Lvl 60 Semi-Rare; Roams in town hall

SCARLET KNIGHT
Western Plaguelands (92), F-3, G-4, H-4, Dalson's Tears, Northridge Lumber Camp

SCARLET LUMBERJACK
Western Plaguelands (92), F:(3, 4), Northridge Lumber Camp

SCARLET MAGE
Western Plaguelands (92), G-4, H-4, Northridge Lumber Camp

SCARLET MAGICIAN
Tirisfal Glades (86), K:(3, 4), Scarlet Monastery, Whispering Gardens

SCARLET MAGUS
Western Plaguelands (92), F:(1, 2), Hearthglen

SCARLET MEDIC
Western Plaguelands (92), E-5, G-4, Dalson's Tears, Felstone Field, Ruins of Andorhal

SCARLET MISSIONARY
Tirisfal Glades (86), E-6, F:(6, 7), G-7, Tower

SCARLET MONK
Tirisfal Glades (86), K-3, L-3, Scarlet Monastery

SCARLET MYRMIDON
Tirisfal Glades (86), K-3, L-3, Scarlet Monastery

SCARLET NEOPHYTE
Tirisfal Glades (86), J-3, K:(2, 3), Scarlet Watch Post

SCARLET PALADIN
Western Plaguelands (92), E:(1, 2), F:(1, 2), Hearthglen

SCARLET PRAETORIAN
Eastern Plaguelands (40), J-8, K:(7, 8), L:(7, 8), Tyr's Hand

SCARLET PRESERVER
Tirisfal Glades (86), K:(3, 4), Whispering Gardens

SCARLET PRIEST
Western Plaguelands (92), E-2, F:(1, 2), Hearthglen

SCARLET PROTECTOR
Tirisfal Glades (86), K-3, L-3, Scarlet Monastery

SCARLET SCOUT
Tirisfal Glades (86), K:(3, 4), L-3, Scarlet Monastery, Whispering Gardens

SCARLET SCRYER
Tirisfal Glades (86), K-3, L-3, Scarlet Monastery

SCARLET SENTINEL
Western Plaguelands (92), E:(1, 2), F:(1, 2), Hearthglen, Northridge Lumber Camp

SCARLET SENTRY
Tirisfal Glades (86), K-3, The Grand Vestibule, Scarlet Monastery, Scarlet Monastery

SCARLET SMITH
Rare Spawn, Western Plaguelands (92), F-1, Hearthglen, Lvl 58 Uncommon; Spawns in around to the right of smithy

SCARLET SOLDIER
Tirisfal Glades (86), K-3, L-3, Scarlet Monastery

SCARLET SORCERER
Tirisfal Glades (86), K-3, L-3, Scarlet Monastery

SCARLET SPELLBINDER
Western Plaguelands (92), G:(2, 4), H-4, Mardenholde Keep

SCARLET TORTURER
Tirisfal Glades (86), K-3, L-3, Scarlet Monastery

SCARLET TRACKING HOUND
Tirisfal Glades (86), K-3, L-3, Scarlet Monastery

SCARLET TRAINEE
Tirisfal Glades (86), K-3, L-3, Scarlet Monastery

SCARLET TROOPER
Eastern Plaguelands (40), K-8, Roams between Stratholme and Tyr's Hand

SCARLET VANGUARD
Tirisfal Glades (86), J:(3, 4), K:(2-4), Scarlet Watch Post

SCARLET WARDER
Eastern Plaguelands (40), I-8, J:(7, 8), K:(7, 8), Scarlet Base Camp

SCARLET WARRIOR
Tirisfal Glades (86), C-5, D:(4, 5), Crusader's Outpost, Tower

SCARLET WIZARD
Tirisfal Glades (86), K-3, L-3, Scarlet Monastery

SCARLET WORKER
Western Plaguelands (92), F:(1, 2), Mardenholde Keep

SCARLET ZEALOT
Tirisfal Glades (86), F:(6, 7), G-7, J:(5, 6), K:(5, 6), L-4, Venomweb Vale, Camp

SCARRED CRAG BOAR
Dun Morogh (32), J:(5, 6), K:(3-6), L:(3-5), Helm's Bed Lake, Ironband's Compound

SCARSHIELD ACOLYTE
Burning Steppes (22), Searing Gorge (64), C-4/D-8, Blackrock Spire

SCARSHIELD GRUNT
Burning Steppes (22), Searing Gorge (64), C-4/D-8, Blackrock Spire

SCARSHIELD LEGIONNAIRE
Burning Steppes (22), Searing Gorge (64), C-4/D-8, Blackrock Spire

SCARSHIELD RAIDER
Burning Steppes (22), Searing Gorge (64), C-4/D-8, Blackrock Spire

SCARSHIELD SENTRY
Burning Steppes (22), Searing Gorge (64), C-4/D-8, Blackrock Spire

SCARSHIELD SPELLBINDER
Burning Steppes (22), Searing Gorge (64), C-4/D-8, Blackrock Spire

SCARSHIELD WARLOCK
Burning Steppes (22), Searing Gorge (64), C-4/D-8, Blackrock Spire

SCARSHIELD WORG
Burning Steppes (22), Searing Gorge (64), C-4/D-8, Blackrock Spire

SCHOLAR RUNETHORN
Feralas (46), C-4, Feathermoon Stronghold (110), Circles path in front of inn

SCHOLOMANCE ACOLYTE
Western Plaguelands (92), I-7, Scholomance

SCHOLOMANCE ADEPT
Western Plaguelands (92), I-7, Scholomance

SCHOLOMANCE DARK SUMMONER
Western Plaguelands (92), I-7, Scholomance

SCHOLOMANCE HANDLER
Western Plaguelands (92), I-7, Scholomance

SCHOLOMANCE NECROLYTE
Western Plaguelands (92), I-7, Scholomance

SCHOLOMANCE NECROMANCER
Western Plaguelands (92), I-7, Scholomance

SCHOLOMANCE NEOPHYTE
Western Plaguelands (92), I-7, Scholomance

SCHOLOMANCE OCCULTIST
Western Plaguelands (92), I-7, Scholomance

SCHOLOMANCE STUDENT
Western Plaguelands (92), I-7, Scholomance

SCOOTY
Chief Engineer, Stranglethorn Vale (74), B-8, Booty Bay (103), By the Gnomeregan Polytransporter underneath the Southern Skies Platform

SCORCHED BASILISK
Stonetalon Mountains (70), D-7, E-7, The Charred Vale

SCORCHED GUARDIAN
Badlands (16), L:(5, 6), Lethor Ravine

SCORCHING ELEMENTAL
Un'Goro Crater (90), F:(5, 6), G:(4-6), Fire Plume Ridge

SCORPASHI LASHER
Desolace (30), D-7, E:(4-7), F:(5-7), G-5, H:(5, 6), I:(6, 7), J:(1, 4-6), K-2

SCORPASHI SNAPPER
Desolace (30), F-1, G:(1, 2, 6, 7), H:(1-4, 6), I:(2-4), J:(2-4), K:(3, 4)

SCORPASHI VENOMLASH
Desolace (30), C:(7, 8), D:(7, 8), E-8, F-9, G:(8, 9), H:(7-9)

SCORPID DUNEBURROWER
Tanaris (78), I-5, Caverns of Time

SCORPID DUNESTALKER
Tanaris (78), D:(5-8), E:(4-8), F:(4-8), G:(4-8), H:(5, 6), I:(5, 6)

SCORPID HUNTER
Tanaris (78), G:(3, 4), H:(2-4), I:(2, 3), J-3

SCORPID REAVER
Thousand Needles (82), I:(5-7), J:(5-7), K:(6, 7), L-6, Ironstone Camp, The Shimmering Flats, Weazel's Crater

SCORPID TAIL LASHER
Tanaris (78), E:(2, 3), F:(2-4), G:(2-4), H:(4, 5), I:(4, 5)

SCORPID TERROR
Thousand Needles (82), I:(7, 8), J:(7-9), K:(7-9), L:(7, 8), Tahonda Ruins, The Rustmaul Dig Site, The Shimmering Flats

SCORPID WORKER
Durotar (34), F:(6, 7), G:(6, 7), Valley of Trials (131)

SCORPOK STINGER
Blasted Lands (20), F-3, G:(2, 3), H-3, I:(3, 4), Dark Portal, Dreadmaul Hold, Rise of the Defiler

SCOTT CAREVIN
Mushroom Seller, Duskwood (36), K-5, Darkshire (108), First floor of house

SCOURGE ARCHER
Eastern Plaguelands (40), C-2

SCOURGE CHAMPION
Eastern Plaguelands (40), D-6, E:(5, 6), F-5, J:(4, 5), K-4, Browman Mill

SCOURGE GUARD
Eastern Plaguelands (40), I-4, Northdale

SCOURGE SOLDIER
Eastern Plaguelands (40), B:(3, 4), C:(2-4), D:(2-4), E:(2-4), F:(2-4), Plaguewood

SCOURGE SUMMONING CRYSTAL
Western Plaguelands (92), E:(6, 7), F:(6, 7), Ruins of Andorhal, The crystals spawn inside each of the four tower ruins within the city

SCOURGE WARDER
Eastern Plaguelands (40), C-3, D-3, E:(2, 3), H:(6, 7), Plaguewood

SCOUT GALIAAN
The People's Militia, Westfall (94), F-5, Sentinel Hill (123), Sawmill

SCOUT RIELL
The People's Militia, Westfall (94), G-5, Sentinel Tower, Top of Sentinel Tower

SCOUT THARR
Orgrimmar (60), Valley of Honor, Roams between Valleys of Strength and Honor

SCREECHING HARPY
Thousand Needles (82), C:(5, 6), Roguefeather Den, The Screeching Canyon

SCREECHING ROGUEFEATHER
Thousand Needles (82), C:(5, 6), Roguefeather Den, The Screeching Canyon

SCREECHING WINDCALLER
Thousand Needles (82), C:(5, 6), Roguefeather Den, The Screeching Canyon

SCRYER
Winterspring (98), H-5, Mazthoril, Deep in caverns

SEA CRAWLER
Westfall (94), C-2, D-2, Longshore

SEA ELEMENTAL
Feralas (46), C:(3, 4), D:(3, 4), E:(4-7), F-5, The Forgotten Coast

SEA SPRAY
Feralas (46), C:(3, 4), D:(3, 4), E:(4-7), F-5, The Forgotten Coast

"SEA WOLF" MACKINLEY
Stranglethorn Vale (74), B-8, Booty Bay (103), Building along the eastern side of bay near the hanging shark

SEARING BLADE CULTIST
Orgrimmar (60), F-5, Ragefire Chasm

SEARING BLADE ENFORCER
Orgrimmar (60), F-5, Ragefire Chasm

SEARING BLADE WARLOCK
Orgrimmar (60), F-5, Ragefire Chasm

SEARING GHOUL
Western Plaguelands (92), E:(6, 7), F:(6, 7), G:(6, 7), Ruins of Andorhal, Idle with Araj the Summoner in the center of city

SEARING HATCHLING
Dustwallow Marsh (38), E:(6-8), F:(6-8), G:(7, 8), The Dragonmurk

SEARING INFERNAL
Ashenvale (12), J:(6-8), K:(6, 7), Felfire Hill, Nightsong Woods, Dor'Danil Barrow Den, Warsong Labor Camp

SEARING LAVA SPIDER
Searing Gorge (64), F:(3, 6, 7), G:(2-4, 6-8), The Sea of Cinders

SEARING ROC
Tanaris (78), E:(6-8), F:(6, 7)

SEARING WHELP
Dustwallow Marsh (38), E:(6-8), F:(6-8), G:(7, 8), The Dragonmurk

SEARN FIREWARDER
Orgrimmar (60), D-5, Valley of Wisdom, Grommash Hold

SEARSCALE DRAKE
Burning Steppes (22), B:(2-4, 7), C:(4, 6), Blackrock Mountain

SEBASTIAN MELOCHE
Armorer, Silverpine Forest (68), F-4, The Sepulcher (124), Basement of inn

SECOND MATE SHANDRIL
Azshara (14), F-9, The Ruined Reaches, Kneeling on isle south of camp

SECURITY CHIEF BILGEWHIZZLE
Tanaris (78), J-3, Steamwheedle Port, Southern building

SEEKER AQUALON
Rare Spawn, Redridge Mountains (62), H-5, I-6, J-6, Lake Everstill, Stonewatch Falls, Lvl 21 Average Rare; Patrols the waterway connecting Lake Everstill with Stonewatch Falls

SEEKER CROMWELL
Undercity (88), I-5, K-7, The Trade Quarter, Roams Trade and Rogue Quarter

SEEKER THOMPSON
Undercity (88), I-5, L-2, The Trade Quarter, Roams Trade and Magic Quarter

SEER GRAYTONGUE
Mulgore (58), E-9, Red Cloud Mesa, Southern hills

SEER RAVENFEATHER
Mulgore (58), E-8, Camp Narache (105), Sitting by totem

SEER WISERUNNER
Mulgore (58), C-4, Cave

SEERETH STONEBREAK
Barrens (18), D-3, Camp at Stonetalon border

SEETH'REL
Burning Steppes (22), Searing Gorge (64), C-4/D-8, Blackrock Depths

SEIKWA
Stable Master, Mulgore (58), E-6, Bloodhoof Village (102), Outside inn

SE'JIB
Master Tribal Leatherworker, Stranglethorn Vale (74), D-4, Hut just south of Mizjah Ruins

SELENDRA
Cenarion Circle, Desolace (30), C-8, Sar'theris Strand, Under tree on beach

SELINA PICKMAN
Undercity (88), The Magic Quarter, Roams Magic Quarter

SELINA WESTON
Alchemy & Herbalism Supplies, Tirisfal Glades (86), H-5, Brill (104), In front of a half buried shed behind the Brill Town Hall

SELLANDUS
Expert Tailor, Stormwind (72), F-8, Mage Quarter, Larson Clothiers

SENANI THUNDERHEART
Ashenvale (12), I-6, Splintertree Post (126), Right of inn

SENATOR BARIN REDSTONE
Ironforge (52), E-5, The Great Forge, The High Seat

SENATOR MEHR STONEHALLOW
Dun Morogh (32), I-6, Gol'Bolar Quarry, Quarry camp by tent

SENIOR SURVEYOR FIZZLEDOWSER
Gadgetzan Water Co., Tanaris (78), G-3, Gadgetzan (111), Atop mound near far west wall

SENIR WHITEBEARD
Dun Morogh (32), F-5, Kharanos (114), In Caravan

SEN'JIN WATCHER
Durotar (34), H-7, Sen'jin Village (123)

SENTINEL AMARASSAN
Stonetalon Mountains (70), C-2, D:(1-2), Stonetalon Peak, Patrols path to Talon Den

SENTINEL ARYNIA CLOUDSBREAK
Teldrassil (80), D-3, The Oracle Glade, East of road next to moonwell

SENTINEL DALIA SUNBLADE
Darnassus (26), E-9, The Temple of the Moon, South of fountain

SENTINEL ELISSA STARBREEZE
Darkshore (24), F-4, Auberdine (101), Second floor of eastern building

SENTINEL FARSONG
Ashenvale (12), H-8, Silverwing Grove, Left of ramp

SENTINEL GLYNDA NAL'SHEA
Darkshore (24), F-4, Auberdine (101), Off path leading east out of town

SENTINEL KELDARA SUNBLADE
Azshara (14), B-6, Haldarr Encampment, Lying in tent atop temple ruins

SENTINEL KYRA STARSONG
Teldrassil (80), G-6, Dolanaar (109), Inn

SENTINEL MELYRIA FROSTSHADOW
Ashenvale (12), C-5, Shrine of Aessina, Center of Shrine

SENTINEL ONAEYA
Ashenvale (12), D-4, Maestra's Post, Left of ramp into main outpost

SENTINEL SELARIN
Darkshore (24), F-4, Auberdine (101), North of Auberdine

SENTINEL SHAYA
Teldrassil (80), G-6, Lake Al'Ameth, South of Dolanaar, near graveyard

SENTINEL SHAYLA NIGHTBREEZE
Teldrassil (80), D-5, E-5, Patrols road outside Darnassus

SENTINEL THENYSIL
Ashenvale (12), E-5, Astranaar (101), Entrance of northwest building

SENTINEL TYSHA MOONBLADE
Darkshore (24), F-6, Twilight Vale, Kneeling beside tree east of road

SENTINEL VELENE STARSTRIKE
Ashenvale (12), F-6, Silverwind Refuge, Right wing of building

SENTRY POINT CAPTAIN
Dustwallow Marsh (38), H-4, Sentry Point, Tower

SENTRY POINT GUARD
Dustwallow Marsh (38), H-4, Sentry Point

SEOMAN GRIFFITH
Leather Armor Merchant, Stormwind (72), J-5, Old Town, Protective Hide

SERENA BLOODFEATHER
Barrens (18), D-1, The Dry Hills, Far north

SERGE HINOTT
Expert Alchemist, Hillsbrad Foothills (48), G-2, Tarren Mill (128), House on the left

SERGEANT BA'SHA
Accessories Quartermaster, Orgrimmar (60), E-7, Valley of Strength, Standing outside Hall of Legends

SERGEANT BRASHCLAW
Rare Spawn, Westfall (94), D-3, Lvl 18 Uncommon; Guards gnoll camp in copse of trees

SERGEANT DE VRIES
Morale Officer, Elwynn Forest (42), C-7, Westbrook Garrison, First floor kitchen in garrison

SERGEANT DURGEN STORMPIKE
Alterac Mountains (8), E-8, Alterac Valley, Cave

SERGEANT HOUSER
Sergeant, Undercity (88), F-3, The War Quarter, Platform in front of Skull Building

SERGEANT MALTHUS
Stranglethorn Vale (74), E-1, The Stockpile, Idle near cauldron in the back of cave

SERGEANT RUTGAR
Sergeant, Undercity (88), F-3, The War Quarter, Platform in front of Skull Building

SERGEANT YOHWA
Stranglethorn Vale (74), D-1, Rebel Camp, Camp

SERGRA DARKTHORN
Barrens (18), F-3, The Crossroads (107), Eastern entrance

SERIADNE
Stable Master, Teldrassil (80), G-6, Dolanaar (109), East of inn

SERIL SCOURGEBANE
Winterspring (98), I-4, Everlook (110), Inside building directly north of inn

SERVANT OF ALLISTARJ
Blasted Lands (20), I:(3-5), Dark Portal, Serpent's Coil, 3 servants (one per location), each roaming a small area around spawn point

SERVANT OF ARKKOROC
Azshara (14), G:(4-7), H:(4-7), I:(4-7), J:(5-7), Bay of Storms, Hetaera's Clutch, Southridge Beach

SERVANT OF AZORA
Elwynn Forest (42), I-7, Tower of Azora

SERVANT OF GROL
Blasted Lands (20), F-1, G-4, Dreadmaul Hold, Dreadmaul Post, 3 servants (two at DH, one at DP)

SERVANT OF HORGUS
Eastern Plaguelands (40), E-8, Darrowshire

SERVANT OF ILGALAR
Redridge Mountains (62), K-5, Tower of Ilgalar

SERVANT OF RAZELIKH
Blasted Lands (20), H:(5, 6), I:(5, 6), Dark Portal, Situated along the outer lip of the Dark Portal

SERVANT OF SEVINE
Blasted Lands (20), F:(3, 4), Altar of Storms, 3 servants (two at BL, one at AoS)

SERVO
Badlands (16), H:(4, 5), The Dustbowl, Patrols around camp

SETHIR THE ANCIENT
Teldrassil (80), D-2, On branches north of The Oracle Glade

SETIS
Rare Spawn, Silithus (66), E-5, The Scarab Wall, Lvl 61 Uber-Rare; Spawns in front of the wall and roams the length of northern Silithus

SEVERED DREAMER
Ashenvale (12), J-7, Dor'Danil Barrow Den

SEVERED DRUID
Ashenvale (12), J-7, Dor'Danil Barrow Den

SEVERED KEEPER
Ashenvale (12), J-7, Dor'Danil Barrow Den

SEVERED SLEEPER
Ashenvale (12), J-7, Dor'Danil Barrow Den

SEWA MISTRUNNER
Fishing Supplier, Thunder Bluff (84), F-5, High rise, outside Mountaintop Bait & Tackle tent

SHADE OF AMBERMOON
Silithus (66), G-3, Southwind Village, Terrace of building

SHADE OF ELURA
Darkshore (24), E-5, The Long Wash, Underwater near shipwreck

SHADE OF ERANIKUS
Swamp of Sorrows (76), I-5, The Temple of Atal'Hakkar

SHADETHICKET BARK RIPPER
Ashenvale (12), H:(6-8), I:(5-8), J:(5-7), K:(6, 7)

SHADETHICKET MOSS EATER
Ashenvale (12), F:(4, 5), Iris Lake

SHADETHICKET ORACLE
Ashenvale (12), I-8, Fallen Sky Lake, Island in center of lake

SHADETHICKET RAINCALLER
Ashenvale (12), D:(6, 7), E-6, Ruins of Stardust

SHADETHICKET STONE MOVER
Ashenvale (12), H:(6-8), I:(5-8), J:(5-7), K:(6, 7)

SHADETHICKET WOOD SHAPER
Ashenvale (12), D:(6, 7), E-6, Ruins of Stardust

SHADI MISTRUNNER
Trade Goods Supplier, Thunder Bluff (84), D-6, Lower rise, in Trade Goods and Supplies tent

SHADOW
Dorion's Pet, Darnassus (26), E-1, Cenarion Enclave, Northeast structure, upper level

SHADOW CHARGER
Silverpine Forest (68), F-7, Shadowfang Keep

SHADOW HUNTER VOSH'GAJIN
Burning Steppes (22), Searing Gorge (64), C-4/D-8, Blackrock Spire

SHADOW LORD FEL'DAN
Felwood (44), E-6, Shadow Hold, Anteroom after spiral tunnel

SHADOW PANTHER
Swamp of Sorrows (76), H-6, I:(3, 7), J:(2, 3, 7, 8), K:(2, 3, 6, 7), L:(4-6), Sorrowmurk

SHADOW PRIEST ALLISTER
Silverpine Forest (68), G-4, The Sepulcher (124), In front of tombstone in graveyard

SHADOW PRIEST SARVIS
Tirisfal Glades (86), C-7, Deathknell (109), Church

SHADOW PRIESTESS VANDIS
Tirisfal Glades (86), K-7, The Bulwark, Camp on right side of road

SHADOW SPRITE
Teldrassil (80), G-5, Fel Rock

SHADOWCLAW
Rare Spawn, Darkshore (24), F-4, Lvl 13 Uncommon; Roams near Auberdine

SHADOWED SPIRIT
Western Plaguelands (92), I-7, Scholomance

SHADOWFANG DARKSOUL
Silverpine Forest (68), F-7, Shadowfang Keep

SHADOWFANG GLUTTON
Silverpine Forest (68), F-7, Shadowfang Keep

SHADOWFANG MOONWALKER
Silverpine Forest (68), F-7, Shadowfang Keep

SHADOWFANG RAGETOOTH
Silverpine Forest (68), F-7, Shadowfang Keep

SHADOWFANG WHITESCALP
Silverpine Forest (68), F-7, Shadowfang Keep

SHADOWFANG WOLFGUARD
Silverpine Forest (68), F-7, Shadowfang Keep

SHADOWFORGE AMBUSHER
Badlands (16), G-1, Uldaman

SHADOWFORGE ARCHAEOLOGIST
Badlands (16), G-1, Uldaman

SHADOWFORGE CHANTER
Badlands (16), F-3, G-3, Angor Fortress

SHADOWFORGE CITIZEN
Burning Steppes (22), Searing Gorge (64), C-4/D-8, Blackrock Depths

SHADOWFORGE COMMANDER
Rare Spawn, Badlands (16), F-3, Angor Fortress, Lvl 40 Semi-Rare; Patrols second floor of fortress

SHADOWFORGE DARKCASTER
Badlands (16), G-1, Uldaman

SHADOWFORGE DARKWEAVER
Badlands (16), H-3, Hammertoe's Digsite

SHADOWFORGE DIGGER
Badlands (16), G-1, Marker's Terrace

SHADOWFORGE DIGGER
Badlands (16), G-1, Uldaman

SHADOWFORGE FLAME KEEPER
Burning Steppes (22), Searing Gorge (64), C-4/D-8, Blackrock Depths

SHADOWFORGE GEOLOGIST
Badlands (16), G-1, Uldaman

SHADOWFORGE PEASANT
Burning Steppes (22), Searing Gorge (64), C-4/D-8, Blackrock Depths

SHADOWFORGE RELIC HUNTER
Badlands (16), G-1, Uldaman

SHADOWFORGE RUFFIAN
Badlands (16), G-1, Uldaman

SHADOWFORGE SENATOR
Burning Steppes (22), Searing Gorge (64), C-4/D-8, Blackrock Depths

SHADOWFORGE SHARPSHOOTER
Badlands (16), G-1, Uldaman

SHADOWFORGE SURVEYOR
Badlands (16), G-1, Marker's Terrace, Uldaman

SHADOWFORGE TUNNELER
Badlands (16), H-3, Hammertoe's Digsite

SHADOWFORGE WARRIOR
Badlands (16), F:(3, 4), G-3, Angor Fortress

SHADOWGLEN SENTINEL
Teldrassil (80), G-4, H:(4, 5), Shadowglen (124)

SHADOWHIDE ASSASSIN
Redridge Mountains (62), J:(4, 5), K:(4, 5), Galardell Valley

SHADOWHIDE BRUTE
Redridge Mountains (62), J:(3-5), K:(3, 4), Galardell Valley

SHADOWHIDE DARKWEAVER
Redridge Mountains (62), J:(3-5), K:(4-6), L:(5, 6), Galardell Valley

SHADOWHIDE GNOLL
Redridge Mountains (62), J:(4-6), Galardell Valley

SHADOWHIDE SLAYER
Redridge Mountains (62), J:(3-5), K:(4-6), L:(5, 6), Galardell Valley

SHADOWHIDE WARRIOR
Redridge Mountains (62), J:(3-5), K:(3-6), L:(5, 6), Galardell Valley

SHADOWHORN STAG
Ashenvale (12), E:(6, 7), F:(5, 6), G:(5-6)

SHADOWMAGE
Eastern Plaguelands (40), E-5, F-5, K:(4, 5), The Fungal Vale

SHADOWMAGE VIVIAN LAGRAVE
Badlands (16), A-5, Kargath (114), Bonfire left of orc burrow

SHADOWMAW PANTHER
Stranglethorn Vale (74), C-4, D:(3-5), E:(3, 4), F:(2, 3)

SHADOWPREY GUARDIAN
Desolace (30), B-7, C-7, Sar'theris Strand, Shadowprey Village (125)

SHADOWPRIEST SEZZ-ZIZ
Tanaris (78), E-1, Zul'Farrak

SHADOWSHARD RUMBLER
Desolace (30), D-5, Mauradon

SHADOWSHARD SMASHER
Desolace (30), D-5, Mauradon

SHADOWSILK POACHER
Searing Gorge (64), G-3

SHADOWSWORN ADEPT
Blasted Lands (20), I:(3-5), J:(3, 5), Dark
Portal, Serpent's Coil

SHADOWSWORN CULTIST
Blasted Lands (20), I:(3-5), J:(3, 5), Dark
Portal, Serpent's Coil

SHADOWSWORN DREADWEAVER
Blasted Lands (20), F:(3, 4), Altar of
Storms

SHADOWSWORN ENFORCER
Blasted Lands (20), F:(3, 4), Altar of
Storms

SHADOWSWORN THUG
Blasted Lands (20), I:(3-5), J:(3, 5), Dark
Portal, Serpent's Coil

SHADOWSWORN WARLOCK
Blasted Lands (20), F:(3, 4), Altar of
Storms

SHADOWY ASSASSIN
Hillsbrad Foothills (48), E:(5, 6), F:(5, 6),
Southshore (125), Spawn behind
Magistrate's building after warning to
protect the Magistrate

SHADRA
The Venom Queen, The Hinterlands
(50), E-7, Shadra'Alor, (Summon) Small
pond in center of village

SHADUMBRA
Ashenvale (12), H-5, Raynewood
Retreat, Spawns just north of
Raynewood Retreat and roams to a
clearing south of Howling Vale and back

SHAEL'DRYN
Ashenvale (12), G-5, Moonwell, Near
moonwell

SHAETHIS DARKOAK
Hippogryph Master, Silithus (66), I-1,
Valor's Rest, South of road

SHAHIAR
Loramus's Guardian, Azshara (14), H-7,
Bay of Storms, Patrols near Loramus

SHAILIEA
Stormwind (72), C-5, E-5, The Park,
Roams The Park

SHAINA FULLER
First Aid Trainer, Stormwind (72), F-3,
Cathedral Square, Cathedral of Light

SHAKES O'BREEN
Arathi Highlands (10), D-8, Faldir's
Cove, Dock

"SHAKY" PHILLIPE
Stranglethorn Vale (74), B-8, Booty Bay
(103), On dock near ship launch

SHALDYN
Clothier, Darkshore (24), F-4, Auberdine
(101), Right wing of northern building

SHALOMON
Weaponsmith, Teldrassil (80), G-6,
Dolanaar (109), Inn

SHALUMON
Tabard Vendor, Darnassus (26), I-2 ,
Craftsmen's Terrace, Southeast building,
second floor

SHAMBLING HORROR
Tirisfal Glades (86), I-4, Brightwater
Lake

SHAN'TI
Fruit Vendor, Orgrimmar (60), D-5,
Valley of Strength, Stranglethorn
Imported Fruits

SHANDA
Priest Trainer, Teldrassil (80), H-4,
Shadowglen (124), Third level of main
building

SHANDA THE SPINNER
Rare Spawn, Loch Modan (54), K-5, Lvl
19 Semi-Rare; Roams small area around
spawn point

SHANDRINA
Trade Goods, Ashenvale (12), F-6,
Silverwind Refuge, Right wing of
building

SHANDRIS FEATHERMOON
General of the Sentinel Army, Feralas
(46), C-5, Feathermoon Stronghold
(110), Southwest building

SHA'NI PROUDTUSK
Burning Steppes (22), J-5, Dreadmaul
Rock, (Summon) Altar with remains

SHANKYS
Fishing Supplier, Orgrimmar (60), I-3,
Valley of Honor, Lumak's Fishing

SHARA BLAZEN
Hillsbrad Foothills (48), H-2, Tarren Mill
(128), Church

SHARD OF MYZRAEL
Quest Item, Arathi Highlands (10), I-3,
West of Circle of East Binding

SHARDI
Wind Rider Master, Dustwallow Marsh
(38), D-3, Brackenwall Village (104),
Southwest part of village

SHARDTOOTH BEAR
Winterspring (98), E:(4, 5), F:(3, 4),
G:(3-5), H-4, Frostfire Hot Springs,
Timbermaw Post

SHARDTOOTH MAULER
Winterspring (98), H:(3-5), I:(3-5),
J:(3-5), Starfall Village, Everlook,
Winterfall Village

SHARLINDRA
Undercity (88), H-9, Royal Quarter, In
Throne room

SHARPBEAK
The Hinterlands (50), H-7, Jintha'Alor,
Cage on mountain northeast of altar

SHARPBEAK'S FATHER
The Hinterlands (50), G-6, The Altar of
Zul, (Summon) Flies to Sharpbeak

SHARPBEAK'S MOTHER
The Hinterlands (50), G-6, The Altar of
Zul, (Summon) Flies to Sharpbeak

SHARPTALON
Ashenvale (12), J-6, Nightsong Woods,
Spawns north of southern bridge and
roams southern side of road heading
west

SHARPTOOTH FRENZY
Stranglethorn Vale (74), C:(1, 4),
D:(1-4), C-7, D:(3, 4), River

SHAWN
Redridge Mountains (62), C-5,
Lakeshire (115), L-shaped dock west of
the bridge

SHAY LEAFRUNNER
Feralas (46), D-1, Ruins of Ravenwind,
In northwestern ruins along hill

SHAYIS STEELFURY
Armor Crafter, Orgrimmar (60), J-2,
Valley of Honor

SHAZZRAH
Burning Steppes (22), Searing Gorge
(64), C-4/D-8, The Molten Core

SHEAL RUNETOTEM
Druid Trainer, Thunder Bluff (84), J-3,
Elder Rise, Inside Hall of Elders

SHEENDRA TALLGRASS
Trade Supplies, Feralas (46), I-4, Camp
Mojache (105), Big western tent

SHELBY STONEFLINT
Stable Master, Dun Morogh (32), F-5,
Kharanos (114), Outside of distillery

SHELDON VAN CROY
Cloth Armor Merchant, Undercity (88),
J-3, The Magic Quarter

SHELDRAS MOONTREE
Druid Trainer, Stormwind (72), C-6, The
Park, By pool of water

SHELENE RHOBART
Journeyman Leatherworker, Tirisfal
Glades (86), I-6, In camp outside of
Undercity

SHELGRAYN
Stable Master, Desolace (30), I-1, Nijel's
Point (119), Outside inn

SHELLEI BRONDIR
Gryphon Master, Wetlands (96), A-6,
Menethil Harbor (117), South of keep

SHELLENE
Orphanage matron, Stormwind (72),
G-4, Cathedral Square, Orphanage

SHEN'DRALAR ANCIENT
Feralas (46), G-4, Dire Maul

SHEN'DRALAR PROVISIONER
Feralas (46), G-4, Dire Maul

SHEN'DRALAR SPIRIT
Feralas (46), G-4, Dire Maul

SHEN'DRALAR ZEALOT
Feralas (46), G-4, Dire Maul

SHENTHUL
Rogue Trainer, Orgrimmar (60), E-5,
The Cleft of Shadow, Shadowswift
Brotherhood

SHERI ZIPSTITCH
Tailoring Supplies, Duskwood (36), K-4,
Darkshire (108), Second floor of house

SHERMAN FEMMEL
Butcher, Redridge Mountains (62), C-4,
Lakeshire (115), First floor of Lakeshire
Inn

SHEZA WILDMANE
Thunder Bluff (84), H-3, Elder Rise, In
front of Elder Rise Drums

SHI'ALUNE
Kaerbrus' Pet, Felwood (44), H-3,
Talonbranch Glade, Near pond

SHIKRIK
Shaman Trainer, Durotar (34), F-7, Valley
of Trials (131)

SHILL DINGER
Burning Steppes (22), Searing Gorge
(64), C-4/D-8, Blackrock Depths

SHIM'LA
Orgrimmar (60), H-2, Valley of Honor,
Near Hunter's Hall entrance

SHIMRA
General Trade, Orgrimmar (60), E-8,
F-8, Valley of Strength, Orgrimmar
General Store

SHINDRELL SWIFTFIRE
Ashenvale (12), E-5, Astranaar (101),
Northern entrance

SHIZZLE
Un'Goro Crater (90), F-1, Marshal's
Refuge (116), South of cave

SHLEIPNARR
Rare Spawn, Searing Gorge (64), H-4,
Lvl 47 Very Rare; Patrols path near
spawn point

SHOJA'MY
Stable Master, Durotar (34), H-4, Razor
Hill (122), Outside inn

SHOMA
Weapon Vendor, Orgrimmar (60), J-2,
Valley of Honor, Arms of Legend

SHONI THE SHILENT
Stormwind (72), H-1, Dwarven District,
Next to well

SHORE CRAWLER
Westfall (94), B:(6-8), C:(8, 9), D-9,
Longshore

SHORE STRIDER
Feralas (46), C-3, D:(3-5), E:(5-7), The
Forgotten Coast

SHORT JOHN MITHRIL
Stranglethorn Vale (74), C-5, Gurubashi
Arena, (Summon) Spawns in the
western seats of the arena every 3
hours

SHREEV
Tanaris (78), G-3, Gadgetzan (111),
Outside northwestern hut

SHRIEKING BANSHEE
Eastern Plaguelands (40), D-2,
Stratholme

SHRIKE BAT
Badlands (16), G-1, Uldaman

SHYLAMIIR
Herbalism Trainer, Stormwind (72), B-5,
The Park, Northwest Building

SHYLENAI
Owl Trainer, Darnassus (26), K-4,
Warrior's Terrace, South of path just
after entrance to city

SHYN
Wind Rider Master, Feralas (46), I-4,
Camp Mojache (105), East of inn

SHYRKA WOLFRUNNER
Stable Master, Feralas (46), I-4, Camp
Mojache (105), Outside big western
tent

SHY-ROTAM
Winterspring (98), G-1, Frostsaber Rock,
On the rock (spawns for quest)

SIAN'DUR
Hunter Trainer, Orgrimmar (60), H-2,
Valley of Honor, Hunter's Hall

SIAN'TSU
Shaman Trainer, Orgrimmar (60), D-4,
Valley of Wisdom, Grommash Hold

SIAN-ROTAM
Winterspring (98), G-1, Frostsaber Rock,
On the rock (spawns for quest)

SICKLY REFUGEE
Silverpine Forest (68), G:(8, 9), The
Greymane Wall

SIDA
Wetlands (96), A-6, Menethil Harbor
(117), Outside house east of keep

SHEZA WILDMANE ...

SIEGE GOLEM
Rare Spawn, Badlands (16), F-4, Angor
Fortress, Lvl 40 Average Rare; Patrols
path to an area of Badlands just south
of Kargath (A-6)

SIGRUN IRONHEW
Badlands (16), H-4, Camp

SIKWA
Stable Master, Barrens (18), F-3, The
Crossroads (107), Behind inn

SILAS ZIMMER
Undercity (88), L-2, The Magic Quarter,
Outside of Skull Building

SILDANAIR
Warrior Trainer, Darnassus (26), H-4,
Warrior's Terrace, Middle of terrace

SILITHID CREEPER
Barrens (18), E-7, F-7, Field of Giants,
Southern Barrens

SILITHID GRUB
Barrens (18), E-7, F-7, Field of Giants,
Southern Barrens

SILITHID HARVESTER
Barrens (18), E-7, Field of Giants

SILITHID HIVE DRONE
Thousand Needles (82), H-8, I:(8, 9),
J-8, The Rustmaul Dig Site, The
Shimmering Flats

SILITHID INVADER
Thousand Needles (82), H-8, I:(8, 9),
The Rustmaul Dig Site

SILITHID RAVAGER
Thousand Needles (82), H-8, I:(8, 9),
The Rustmaul Dig Site

SILITHID SEARCHER
Thousand Needles (82), I:(8, 9), J-8, The
Rustmaul Dig Site, The Shimmering Flats

SILITHID SWARMER
Barrens (18), E-7, F-7, Field of Giants,
Southern Barrens

SILT CRAWLER
Swamp of Sorrows (76), J:(1, 9),
K:(1, 2, 7, 8), L:(2, 3, 7, 8), Misty Reed
Strand

SILVA FIL'NAVETH
Darnassus Flight Master, Moonglade
(56), F-4, Nighthaven (120), Southwest
side of town

SILVARIA
Pet Trainer, Darnassus (26), E-1,
Cenarion Enclave, Northeast structure,
upper level

SILVERBACK PATRIARCH
Stranglethorn Vale (74), C-7, D:(6, 7),
Mistvale Valley, Ruins of Aboraz, The
Crystal Shore

SILVERMANE HOWLER
The Hinterlands (50), E-6, F:(4-7),
G:(4-6), H:(4-6), The Hinterlands

SILVERMANE STALKER
The Hinterlands (50), H:(4-6), I:(4-6),
J:(4-6), K:(5, 6), L-5, Overlook Cliffs,
Along Hills

SILVERMANE WOLF
The Hinterlands (50), D:(5-7), E:(4-6),
F:(4, 5), The Hinterlands

SILVERPINE DEATHGUARD
Guard, Silverpine Forest (68), G-4, The
Sepulcher (124)

SILVERWING ELITE
Ashenvale (12), H-8, Fallen Sky Lake,
Silverwing Grove, Silverwing Outpost

SILVERWING SENTINEL
Ashenvale (12), H-7, Nightsong
Woods, Silverwing Outpost

SILVERWING WARRIOR
Ashenvale (12), H-7, Nightsong
Woods, Silverwing Outpost

SIMON TANNER
Expert Leatherworker, Stormwind (72),
J-5, Old Town, The Protective Hide

SIMONE CANTRELL
Landscape Architect, Hillsbrad Foothills
(48), J-2, Garden to the right of Chateau
Ravenholdt

SIMONE THE INCONSPICUOUS
Un'Goro Crater (90), E:(4-8), F-6, F-8,
G:(6-8), Golakka Hot Springs, The
Slithering Scar, Terror Run, Walks big
area from The Slithering Scar to north of
the springs

SINDA
Leather Armor Merchant, Teldrassil
(80), G-6, Dolanaar (109), Inn

SIN'DALL
Stranglethorn Vale (74), C-2, Tkashi
Ruins, Roams small area around spawn
point

SINDRAYL
Hippogryph Master, Moonglade (56),
G-7, East of small body of water, south
of lake

SINGE
Pet, Redridge Mountains (62),
I-5, Stonewatch, Second floor of
Stonewatch Keep

SINGED BASILISK
Stonetalon Mountains (70), C-6,
D:(6, 7), E-6, The Charred Vale

SINGER
Rare Spawn, Arathi Highlands (10), D-3,
Northfold Manor, Lvl 34 Uncommon;
Roams in farm

SIR S. J. ERLGADIN
Stranglethorn Vale (74), C-1,
Nesingwary's Expedition, Camp

SIRRA VON'INDI
Historian of Darkshire, Duskwood (36),
J-5, Darkshire (108), Darkshire Town
Hall

SISTER AQUINNE
Novice Priestess, Darnassus (26),
C-4, The Temple Gardens, South of
teleporter

SISTER HATELASH
Rare Spawn, Mulgore (58), D-1, Lvl 51
Uncommon; Northwest nest

SISTER OF CELEBRIAN
Desolace (30), D-5, Mauradon

SISTER RATHTALON
Barrens (18), D-1, The Dry Hills, Roams
the nest

SISTER RIVEN
Stonetalon Mountains (70), C-7,
D-7, The Charred Vale, Patrols across
Charred Vale

SKARR THE UNBREAKABLE
Rare Spawn, Feralas (46), G-4, Dire
Maul, Lvl 58 Rare

SKARR THE UNBREAKABLE
Feralas (46), G-4, The Maul, In arena

SKELETAL ACOLYTE
Western Plaguelands (92), E:(6, 7),
F:(6, 7), G:(6, 7), Ruins of Andorhal, Idle
with Araj the Summoner in the center
of city

SKELETAL BERSERKER
Eastern Plaguelands (40), D-2,
Stratholme

SKELETAL EXECUTIONER
Western Plaguelands (92), E:(6, 7),
F:(6, 7), G:(6, 7), Ruins of Andorhal, Idle
with Araj the Summoner in the center
of city

SKELETAL FIEND
Duskwood (36), B:(4, 5), C:(4, 5), Raven
Hill Cemetery (122)

SKELETAL FLAYER
Western Plaguelands (92), D:(5, 6),
E:(5, 6), F:(7, 8), G:(7, 8), Sorrow Hill

SKELETAL FROSTWEAVER
Barrens (18), F-9, Razorfen Downs

SKELETAL GUARDIAN
Eastern Plaguelands (40), D-2, Stratholme

SKELETAL HEALER
Duskwood (36), A-4, B:(3, 4), Raven Hill Cemetery (122)

SKELETAL HIGHBORNE
Feralas (46), G-4, Dire Maul

SKELETAL HORROR
Duskwood (36), A:(4, 5), B:(4, 5), C:(4, 5), K-6, Raven Hill Cemetery (122)

SKELETAL MAGE
Duskwood (36), K-7, Tranquil Gardens Cemetery

SKELETAL MINER
Westfall (94), D-7, E-7, The Deadmines

SKELETAL RAIDER
Duskwood (36), A:(3, 4), B:(3, 4), Raven Hill Cemetery (122)

SKELETAL SERVANT
Eastern Plaguelands (40), D-3, Stratholme

SKELETAL SHADOWCASTER
Barrens (18), F-9, Razorfen Downs

SKELETAL SORCERER
Western Plaguelands (92), D-6, E:(5, 6), G-8, Sorrow Hill

SKELETAL SUMMONER
Barrens (18), F-9, Razorfen Downs

SKELETAL TERROR
Western Plaguelands (92), F-5, Dalson's Tears

SKELETAL WARDER
Duskwood (36), A:(3, 4), B:(3, 4), Raven Hill Cemetery (122)

SKELETAL WARLORD
Western Plaguelands (92), E:(6, 7), F:(6, 7), Ruins of Andorhal, Idle with Araj the Summoner in the center of city

SKELETAL WARRIOR
Duskwood (36), K-7, Tranquil Gardens Cemetery

SKHOWL
Rare Spawn, Alterac Mountains (8), D:(5, 6), E-4, F-6, Growless Cave, Ruins of Alterac, Lvl 36 Semi-Rare; Roams small area around spawn point

SKITTERING CRUSTACEAN
Ashenvale (12), B-2, Blackfathom Deeps

SKOLMIN GOLDFURY
Bow Merchant, Ironforge (52), J-6, The Military Ward, Goldfury's Hunting Supplies

SKORN WHITECLOUD
Mulgore (58), E-6, Bloodhoof Village (102), Outside inn

SKUERTO
Arathi Highlands (10), F-5, Refuge Point, Camp

SKUL
Rare Spawn, Eastern Plaguelands (40), D-2, Stratholme, Lvl 58 Rare

SKULKING CORPSE
Western Plaguelands (92), I-7, Scholomance

SKULLSPLITTER AXE THROWER
Stranglethorn Vale (74), D-4, E:(3, 4), Ruins of Zul'Mamwe

SKULLSPLITTER BEASTMASTER
Stranglethorn Vale (74), E:(4, 5), Ruins of Zul'Mamwe

SKULLSPLITTER BERSERKER
Stranglethorn Vale (74), E-5, Ruins of Zul'Mamwe

SKULLSPLITTER HEADHUNTER
Stranglethorn Vale (74), E-5, Ruins of Zul'Mamwe

SKULLSPLITTER HUNTER
Stranglethorn Vale (74), E:(4, 5), Ruins of Zul'Mamwe

SKULLSPLITTER MYSTIC
Stranglethorn Vale (74), D-4, E:(3, 4), Ruins of Zul'Mamwe

SKULLSPLITTER SCOUT
Stranglethorn Vale (74), E:(4, 5), Ruins of Zul'Mamwe

SKULLSPLITTER SPIRITCHASER
Stranglethorn Vale (74), E-5, Ruins of Zul'Mamwe

SKULLSPLITTER WARRIOR
Stranglethorn Vale (74), D-4, E:(3, 4), Ruins of Zul'Mamwe

SKULLSPLITTER WITCH DOCTOR
Stranglethorn Vale (74), E:(4, 5), Ruins of Zul'Mamwe

SKUM
Barrens (18), E-4, Wailing Caverns

SKY SHADOW
Deadwind Pass (28), B-4, C:(3-6), D:(2, 4-6), E-5, Deadman's Crossing, Deadwind Ravine, Sleeping Gorge

SKYMANE GORILLA
Stranglethorn Vale (74), D:(8, 9), Jaguero Isle

SLAGG
Superior Butcher, Arathi Highlands (10), J-3, Hammerfall (113), Platform of north building

SLARK
Rare Spawn, Westfall (94), F-1, Longshore, Lvl 15 Uncommon; Runs entire Longshore coast

SLAUGHTERHOUSE PROTECTOR
Eastern Plaguelands (40), D-3, E-2, Plaguewood

SLAVE MASTER BLACKHEART
Rare Spawn, Searing Gorge (64), E:(2-4), The Slag Pit, Lvl 50 Uncommon; Roams small area around spawn point

SLAVE WORKER
Searing Gorge (64), D:(2-5), E:(2-5), F-4, The Cauldron, Mines

SLAVERING EMBER WORG
Burning Steppes (22), D:(5, 6), E-3, F:(3, 7), G:(2, 3, 6), H:(5, 6), I:(3-6), J-3

SLAVERING GHOUL
Western Plaguelands (92), D-6, E:(5, 6), F:(7, 8), G:(7, 8), Sorrow Hill

SLAVERING WORG
Silverpine Forest (68), F-7, Shadowfang Keep

SLEEBY
Arathi Highlands (10), I-3, Circle of East Binding, Patrols with Fozruck to each of the four Circles of Binding

SLIME MAGGOT
Swamp of Sorrows (76), I-5, The Temple of Atal'Hakkar

SLIMESHELL MAKRURA
Barrens (18), H:(4, 5), The Merchant Coast, The Tidus Stair

SLIN SKYCHASER
Shaman Trainer, Thunder Bluff (84), B-2, Spirit Rise, Inside Hall of Spirits

SLITHERBLADE MYRMIDON
Desolace (30), C:(1, 2), D:(1, 2), E:(1, 2), Sar'theris Strand

SLITHERBLADE NAGA
Desolace (30), D:(2, 3), E-2, Ethel Rethor, Sar'theris Strand

SLITHERBLADE ORACLE
Desolace (30), C:(1, 2), D:(1, 2), E:(1, 2), Sar'theris Strand

SLITHERBLADE RAZORTAIL
Desolace (30), C:(1, 2), D:(1, 2), Sar'theris Strand

SLITHERBLADE SEA WITCH
Desolace (30), C:(1, 2), D:(1, 2), Sar'theris Strand

SLITHERBLADE SORCERESS
Desolace (30), C-1, D:(1-3), E:(1, 2), Ethel Rethor, Sar'theris Strand

SLITHERBLADE TIDEHUNTER
Desolace (30), C:(1, 2), D-1, E-1, Sar'theris Strand

SLITHERBLADE WARRIOR
Desolace (30), C-1, D:(1-3), E:(1, 2), Ethel Rethor, Sar'theris Strand

SLOAN MCCOY
Poison Supplier, Stormwind (72), K-6, Old Town, SI:7

SLUDGE BEAST
Rare Spawn, Barrens (18), G-1, The Sludge Fen, Lvl 19 Semi-Rare; In sludge

SLUDGINN
Rare Spawn, Wetlands (96), A-7, B-7, Lvl 30 Average Rare; South of Menethil Harbor, in hills across water

SLY GARRETT
Shady Goods, Stranglethorn Vale (74), B-8, Booty Bay (103), Outside of fireworks shop on the eastern side of bay

SMALL CRAG BOAR
Dun Morogh (32), B:(7, 8), C:(7, 8), D-7, Coldridge Pass, Coldridge Valley (106)

SMEED SCRABBLESCREW
Desolace (30), H-6, Scrabblescrew's Camp, In front of hut

SMILING JIM
Dustwallow Marsh (38), I-5, Theramore Isle (130), Sitting outside inn to north

SMITH ARGUS
Journeyman Blacksmith, Elwynn Forest (42), E-6, Goldshire (112), Smithy

SMITH SLAGTREE
Blacksmithing Supplies, The Hinterlands (50), L-8, Revantusk Village, Makeshift smithy on right side of village

SMOKEY LARUE
Eastern Plaguelands (40), K-6, Light's Hope Chapel (116), Camp on left side of chapel

SMOLDAR
Rare Spawn, Searing Gorge (64), C-6, Lvl 50 Semi-Rare; Patrols the northwestern portion of the zone

SMOLDERTHORN AXE THROWER
Burning Steppes (22), Searing Gorge (64), C-4/D-8, Blackrock Spire

SMOLDERTHORN BERSERKER
Burning Steppes (22), Searing Gorge (64), C-4/D-8, Blackrock Spire

SMOLDERTHORN HEADHUNTER
Burning Steppes (22), Searing Gorge (64), C-4/D-8, Blackrock Spire

SMOLDERTHORN MYSTIC
Burning Steppes (22), Searing Gorge (64), C-4/D-8, Blackrock Spire

SMOLDERTHORN SEER
Burning Steppes (22), Searing Gorge (64), C-4/D-8, Blackrock Spire

SMOLDERTHORN SHADOW HUNTER
Burning Steppes (22), Searing Gorge (64), C-4/D-8, Blackrock Spire

SMOLDERTHORN SHADOW PRIEST
Burning Steppes (22), Searing Gorge (64), C-4/D-8, Blackrock Spire

SMOLDERTHORN WITCH DOCTOR
Burning Steppes (22), Searing Gorge (64), C-4/D-8, Blackrock Spire

SMUDGE THUNDERWOOD
Poison Vendor, Hillsbrad Foothills (48), K-2, Basement of Chateau Ravenholdt

SNAGGLESPEAR
Rare Spawn, Mulgore (58), F-7, Lvl 9 Uncommon; Camp

SNANG
Journeyman Tailor, Orgrimmar (60), H-5, The Drag, Magar's Cloth Goods

SNAP JAW
Alterac Mountains (8), K-6, Chillwind Point, River

SNAPJAW
Hillsbrad Foothills (48), G-5, River

SNAPJAW CROCOLISK
Stranglethorn Vale (74), D:(2-4)

SNAPPING CRUSTACEAN
Ashenvale (12), B-2, Blackfathom Deeps

SNARL
Expert Blacksmith, Orgrimmar (60), J-2, Valley of Honor, Across from Arms of Legend

SNARLER
Rare Spawn, Feralas (46), I-4, Lariss Pavilion, Lvl 42 Uncommon; Spawns near delta and roams southeast

SNARLFLARE
Rare Spawn, Redridge Mountains (62), D-6, E-3, F-3, Alther's Mill, Lvl 18 Uncommon; Roams small area around spawn point

SNARLMANE
Rare Spawn, Silverpine Forest (68), J:(2, 3), Fenris Keep, Lvl 23 Uncommon; Stands idle at spawn point

SNEED
Westfall (94), D-7, E-7, The Deadmines

SNEED'S SHREDDER
Westfall (94), D-7, E-7, The Deadmines

SNICKERFANG HYENA
Blasted Lands (20), I:(3, 4), Serpent's Coil

SNORT THE HECKLER
Rare Spawn, Barrens (18), D-3, Lvl 17 Uncommon; Roams southwest of Forgotten Pools

SNOW LEOPARD
Dun Morogh (32), C:(4, 5), D:(3-5), E:(3, 4), F:(3, 6), G:(5, 6), H:(5, 6), I-6, K-4

SNOW TRACKER WOLF
Dun Morogh (32), F-5, G:(4, 5), Kharanos (114)

SNURK BUCKSQUICK
Zeppelin Master, Durotar (34), H-1, Atop tower

SOARING RAZORBEAK
The Hinterlands (50), B-5, C-5, The Hinterlands

SOGNAR CLIFFBEARD
Meat Vendor, Ironforge (52), H-8, I-7, The Military Ward, Roams The Military Ward

SOLAKAR FLAMEWREATH
Burning Steppes (22), Searing Gorge (64), C-4/D-8, Blackrock Spire

SOLEIL STONEMANTLE
Banker, Ironforge (52), E-6, The Commons, Vault of Ironforge

SOLM HARGRIN
Rogue Trainer, Dun Morogh (32), D-7, Coldridge Valley (106), Anvilmar

SOMNUS
Swamp of Sorrows (76), J-7, Patrols a circular path around swamp land near the southeastern coast line

SON OF ARKKOROC
Azshara (14), G:(4-7), H:(4-7), I:(4-7), J:(5-7), Bay of Storms, Hetaera's Clutch, Southridge Beach

SON OF ARUGAL
Silverpine Forest (68), F-3, G:(3, 8), Roam

SON OF ARUGAL
Silverpine Forest (68), F-7, Shadowfang Keep

SON OF CENARIUS
Stonetalon Mountains (70), D:(1, 2), E:(1, 2), Stonetalon Peak

SON OF FLAME
Burning Steppes (22), Searing Gorge (64), C-4/D-8, The Molten Core

SOOLIE BERRYFIZZ
Alchemy Supplies, Ironforge (52), I-5, Tinker Town, Berryfizz's Potions and Mixed Drinks

SORAN
Banker, Orgrimmar (60), F-7, Valley of Strength

SORCERER ASHCROMBE
Silverpine Forest (68), F-7, Shadowfang Keep

SOREK
Warrior Trainer, Orgrimmar (60), J-3, Valley of Honor, Hall of the Brave

SORIID THE DEVOURER
Rare Spawn, Tanaris (78), E:(4, 5), The Noxious Lair, Lvl 50 Uncommon; Spawns in multiple chambers

SORROW SPINNER
Swamp of Sorrows (76), A-5, B-5, C:(4-6), D:(3, 5, 6), E:(3, 4), F-3, I-3

SOULLESS GHOUL
Western Plaguelands (92), E:(6, 7), F:(6, 7), G:(6, 7), Ruins of Andorhal, Idle with Araj the Summoner in the center of city

SOUTHERN SAND CRAWLER
Stranglethorn Vale (74), B:(8, 9), C:(7-9), D-7, Jaguero Isle, Wild Shore

SOUTHSEA BRIGAND
Barrens (18), H:(4, 5), The Merchant Coast, Northwatch Hold

SOUTHSEA CANNONEER
Barrens (18), H:(4, 5), The Merchant Coast, The Tidus Stair

SOUTHSEA CUTTHROAT
Barrens (18), G:(4, 5), H:(4, 5), The Merchant Coast

SOUTHSEA DOCK WORKER
Tanaris (78), J-5, K-5, Lost Rigger Cove

SOUTHSEA FREEBOOTER
Tanaris (78), J:(4, 5), K-5, Lost Rigger Cove

SOUTHSEA PIRATE
Tanaris (78), J:(4, 5), K-5, Lost Rigger Cove

SOUTHSEA PRIVATEER
Barrens (18), G:(4, 5), H:(4, 5), The Merchant Coast

SOUTHSEA SWASHBUCKLER
Tanaris (78), J-5, K-5, Lost Rigger Cove

SOUTHSHORE GUARD
Hillsbrad Foothills (48), E:(5, 6), F:(5, 6), Southshore (125)

SOVIK
Engineering Supplies, Orgrimmar (60), I-3, J-3, Valley of Honor, Nogg's Machine Shop

SPACKLE THORNBERRY
Demon Trainer, Stormwind (72), D-8, Mage Quarter, The Slaughtered Lamb

SPARK NILMINER
Un'Goro Crater (90), F-1, Marshal's Refuge (116), Entrance to cave

SPARKLESHELL BORER
Thousand Needles (82), J:(8, 9), K:(8, 9), Tahonda Ruins, The Rustmaul Dig Site, The Shimmering Flats

SPARKLESHELL SNAPPER
Thousand Needles (82), I-8, J:(7, 8), K:(5-8), L:(6-8), The Rustmaul Dig Site, The Shimmering Flats, Weazel's Crater

SPARKLESHELL TORTOISE
Thousand Needles (82), I:(6, 7), J:(5-7), K:(5, 6), Ironstone Camp, The Shimmering Flats, Weazel's Crater

SPAWN OF HAKKAR
Swamp of Sorrows (76), I-5, The Temple of Atal'Hakkar

SPECTRAL ATTENDANT
Western Plaguelands (92), F-7, Ruins of Andorhal, Idle with Araj the Summoner in the center of city

SPECTRAL BETRAYER
Eastern Plaguelands (40), G-5, Blackwood Lake

SPECTRAL CITIZEN
Eastern Plaguelands (40), D-2, Stratholme

SPECTRAL CORPSE
Eastern Plaguelands (40), G-6, The Infectis Scar, North near a sword with a glowing aura

SPECTRAL DEFENDER
Eastern Plaguelands (40), G-5, Blackwood Lake

SPECTRAL MARAUDER
Eastern Plaguelands (40), G-6, The Infectis Scar, North near a sword with a glowing aura

SPECTRAL PROJECTION
Western Plaguelands (92), I-7, Scholomance

SPECTRAL RESEARCHER
Western Plaguelands (92), I-7, Scholomance

SPECTRAL TEACHER
Western Plaguelands (92), I-7, Scholomance

SPECTRAL TUTOR
Western Plaguelands (92), I-7, Scholomance

SPELL EATER
Winterspring (98), H:(5, 6), I-5, Mazthoril

SPELLMAW
Winterspring (98), H-5, Mazthoril, Outside near entrance

SPEWED LARVA
Desolace (30), D-5, Mauradon

SPIGOT OPERATOR LUGLUNKET
Gadgetzan Water Co., Tanaris (78), H-3, Gadgetzan (111), Between bank and inn

SPIKED STEGODON
Un'Goro Crater (90), C:(5-7), D:(6-8), E:(6-8), Golakka Hot Springs, Terror Run

SPINED CRAWLER
Ashenvale (12), A:(2-4), B:(2-4), The Zoram Strand (131), Zoram'gar Outpost (131)

SPIRE SCARAB
Burning Steppes (22), Searing Gorge (64), C-4/D-8, Blackrock Spire

SPIRE SCORPID
Burning Steppes (22), Searing Gorge (64), C-4/D-8, Blackrock Spire

SPIRE SPIDER
Burning Steppes (22), Searing Gorge (64), C-4/D-8, Blackrock Spire

SPIRE SPIDERLING
Burning Steppes (22), Searing Gorge (64), C-4/D-8, Blackrock Spire

SPIRESTONE BATTLE LORD
Rare Spawn, Burning Steppes (22), Searing Gorge (64), C-4/D-8, Blackrock Spire, Lvl 58 Uncommon

SPIRESTONE BATTLE MAGE
Burning Steppes (22), Searing Gorge (64), C-4/D-8, Blackrock Spire

SPIRESTONE BUTCHER
Burning Steppes (22), Searing Gorge (64), C-4/D-8, Blackrock Spire

SPIRESTONE ENFORCER
Burning Steppes (22), Searing Gorge (64), C-4/D-8, Blackrock Spire

SPIRESTONE LORD MAGUS
Burning Steppes (22), Searing Gorge (64), C-4/D-8, Blackrock Spire

SPIRESTONE MYSTIC
Burning Steppes (22), Searing Gorge (64), C-4/D-8, Blackrock Spire

SPIRESTONE OGRE MAGUS
Burning Steppes (22), Searing Gorge (64), C-4/D-8, Blackrock Spire

SPIRESTONE REAVER
Burning Steppes (22), Searing Gorge (64), C-4/D-8, Blackrock Spire

SPIRESTONE WARLORD
Burning Steppes (22), Searing Gorge (64), C-4/D-8, Blackrock Spire

SPIRIT OF GELK
The Second Kahn, Desolace (30), C-6, Maraudon, Middle tier of purple section

SPIRIT OF KIRITH
Blasted Lands (20), J-3, Serpent's Coil, (Summon) Spawns upon killing Kirith the Damned

SPIRIT OF KOLK
The First Kahn, Desolace (30), C-6, Maraudon, Near entrance to purple section

SPIRIT OF MAGRA
The Third Kahn, Desolace (30), C-6, Maraudon, Crystal cave in orange section near giant crystal

SPIRIT OF MARAUDOS
The Fourth Khan, Desolace (30), D-5, Mauradon

SPIRIT OF MINSHINA
Durotar (34), H-7, Sen'jin Village (123), (Summon) Find his skull

SPIRIT OF TREY LIGHTFORGE
Felwood (44), E-6, Jaedenar, (Summon) Appears outside of Shadow Hold entrance

SPIRIT OF VENG
The Fifth Khan, Desolace (30), D-5, Mauradon

SPITEFLAYER
Rare Spawn, Blasted Lands (20), I-5, Dark Portal, Lvl 52 Semi-Rare; Patrols to tower ruins at the edge of Serpent's Coil (1-3)

SPITELASH BATTLEMASTER
Azshara (14), H:(8, 9), I:(8, 9), H:(8, 9), I:(8, 9), Ravencrest Monument

SPITELASH MYRMIDON
Azshara (14), E:(4-6), F:(4-7)

SPITELASH RAIDER
Azshara (14), F-9, The Ruined Reaches

SPITELASH SCREAMER
Azshara (14), B:(5, 6), C:(5, 6), D:(4-6)

SPITELASH SERPENT GUARD
Azshara (14), D:(5, 6), E:(5, 6), Ruins of Eldarath, Temple of Zin-Malor

SPITELASH SIREN
Azshara (14), D:(5, 6), E:(4-6), F:(4-7), Ruins of Eldarath, The Shattered Strand, Southridge Beach, Temple of Zin-Malor

SPITELASH WARRIOR
Azshara (14), B:(5, 6), C:(5, 6), D:(4-6)

SPITELASH WITCH
Azshara (14), F-9, The Ruined Reaches

SPLINTER FIST ENSLAVER
Duskwood (36), E-8, Vul'Gol Ogre Mound

SPLINTER FIST FIRE WEAVER
Duskwood (36), E-7, Vul'Gol Ogre Mound

SPLINTER FIST FIREMONGER
Duskwood (36), D-7, E-8, Vul'Gol Ogre Mound

SPLINTER FIST OGRE
Duskwood (36), E-7, Vul'Gol Ogre Mound

SPLINTER FIST TASKMASTER
Duskwood (36), D-7, E-7, Vul'Gol Ogre Mound

SPLINTER FIST WARRIOR
Duskwood (36), D:(7, 8), E-8, Vul'Gol Ogre Mound

SPLINTERBONE CAPTAIN
Barrens (18), F-9, Razorfen Downs

SPLINTERBONE CENTURIAN
Barrens (18), F-9, Razorfen Downs

SPLINTERBONE SKELETON
Barrens (18), F-9, Razorfen Downs

SPLINTERBONE WARRIOR
Barrens (18), F-9, Razorfen Downs

SPLINTERED SKELETON
Western Plaguelands (92), I-7, Scholomance

SPLINTERTREE GUARD
Ashenvale (12), B-4, I:(6, 7)

SPLINTERTREE RAIDER
Ashenvale (12), I-7, Nightsong Woods, Silverwing Outpost

SPOT
Dustwallow Marsh (38), I-5, Theramore Isle (130), Outside Foothold Citadel

SPRAGGLE FROCK
Un'Goro Crater (90), F-1, Marshal's Refuge (116), Near entrance to cave, next to sign

SPRINGSPINDLE FIZZLEGEAR
Artisan Engineer, Ironforge (52), I-4, Tinker Town, Springspindle's Gadgets

SPRINKLE
Tanaris (78), G-3, Gadgetzan (111), Outside northwestern hut

SPRITE DARTER
Feralas (46), H:(4, 5), I-5, Camp Mojache (105), Lower Wilds, Woodpaw Hills

SPRITE DRAGON
Feralas (46), D-2, E:(1, 3), F-3, Ruins of Ravenwind, The Twin Colossals

SPRITE JUMPSPROCKET
Journeyman Engineer, Stormwind (72), H-1, Dwarven District, North end of district, by tent

SPROGGER
Stranglethorn Vale (74), B-8, Booty Bay (103), On dock near ship launch on the northern side of bay

SPROK
Dun Morogh (32), C-4, Gnomeregan

SPUTTERVALVE
Tinkers' Union, Barrens (18), H-4, Ratchet (121), Stall near bank

"SQUEALER" THORNMANTLE
Mulgore (58), H-8, Brambleblade Ravine, Cave in center of ravine

SQUIDDIC
Rare Spawn, Redridge Mountains (62), G-7, Lake Everstill, Lvl 19 Uncommon; Patrols back and forth just offshore by the murloc camp

SQUIRE MALTRAKE
Searing Gorge (64), D-4, Patrols a semicircle around Kalaran Windblade

SRANDA
Light Armor & Weapons Merchant, Badlands (16), A-5, Kargath (114), Forge left of orc burrow

SRAZZ
Pie Vendor, Ironforge (52), E-4, The Great Forge, Circles Great Forge

SRI'SKULK
Rare Spawn, Tirisfal Glades (86), K-5, L:(4, 5), Venomweb Vale, Lvl 13 Uncommon; Roams small area around spawn point

STALVAN MISTMANTLE
Duskwood (36), K-4, Manor Mistmantle, House

STANLEY
Hillsbrad Foothills (48), C-3, Hillsbrad Fields (113), Dog house outside house at northern end of town

STARN
Gunsmith & Bowyer, Thousand Needles (82), F-5, Freewind Post, Next to hut, west of inn

STARVING BLISTERPAW
Tanaris (78), E:(2, 3), F:(2, 3), G:(2-4), H:(2-4), I:(2, 3), J-3

STARVING BONEPAW
Desolace (30), G-2, I-4, J:(3, 4), Thunder Axe Fortress

STARVING BUZZARD
Badlands (16), G-3, H-1, I:(2-4), Dustwind Gulch, Uldaman

STARVING DIRE WOLF
Duskwood (36), A:(3-7), B:(2, 3), C-3, D:(2, 3), E-2, F-2, G:(1, 2), H-2, I-2, J-2, K-2, L-2, The Darkened Bank

STARVING MOUNTAIN LION
Hillsbrad Foothills (48), D:(3, 4), E:(3-5), F:(3-5), G-4, Thoughout Hillsbrad

STARVING SNICKERFANG
Blasted Lands (20), F-3, G:(2, 3), H-3, Dreadmaul Hold, Rise of the Defiler

STARVING WINTER WOLF
Dun Morogh (32), D-4, Iceflow Lake

STEELJAW SNAPPER
Tanaris (78), I:(2, 3), J:(2-4), K-4

STEELSNAP
Thousand Needles (82), A:(2-3), B:(2-3), Camp E'thok, Spawns at Camp E'thok and roams around plateaus

STEGODON
Un'Goro Crater (90), C:(5-7), D:(6-8), E:(6-8), Golakka Hot Springs, Terror Run

STEN STOUTARM
Dun Morogh (32), D-7, Coldridge Valley (106), By keg on cart

STEPHANIE TURNER
Stormwind (72), I-6, Trade District, Outside Everyday Merchandise

STEPHEN BHARTEC
Tirisfal Glades (86), D-6, Deathknell (109)

STEPHEN RYBACK
Cooking Trainer, Stormwind (72), K-4, Old Town, Pig and Whistle Tavern

STEVEN
Stormwind (72), Roams city with Miss Danna

STEVEN BLACK
Stable Master, Duskwood (36), J-5, Darkshire (108), Outside of Scarlet Raven Inn

STEVEN LOHAN
Stormwind (72), F-9, Mage Quarter, The Blue Recluse

STINGLASHER
Feralas (46), I-6, The Writhing Deep, Spawns in center of west hive and travels to east hive and back

"STINKY" IGNATZ
Dustwallow Marsh (38), F-2, Kneeling near crate and barrels

STITCHED HORROR
Eastern Plaguelands (40), B-4, C:(2, 3), D:(3, 4), E:(2-4), F:(2-4), H:(6, 7), Plaguewood, Stratholme

STITCHES
Gift of the Embalmer, Duskwood (36), D-3, Raven Hill Cemetery (122), (Summon) Behind locked cage

STOLEY
Tanaris (78), J-3, Steamwheedle Port, Southern building

STOLID SNAPJAW
Desolace (30), D-5, Mauradon

STOMA THE ANCIENT
Felwood (44), G-3, Irontree Woods, (Summon) Talk to the ancients on the island

STOMPER KREEG
Feralas (46), G-4, Dire Maul

STONARD CARTOGRAPHER
Swamp of Sorrows (76), F-5, Stonard (126), Scaffolding northeast of camp just past orc borrows

STONARD EXPLORER
Swamp of Sorrows (76), F:(4, 5), J:(1, 7), Stonard (126)

STONARD GRUNT
Swamp of Sorrows (76), E-5, F:(5, 6), Stonard (126)

STONARD HUNTER
Swamp of Sorrows (76), J:(7, 8), K:(7, 8), Stonard (126)

STONARD ORC
Swamp of Sorrows (76), E-5, F-5, Stonard (126)

STONARD SCOUT
Swamp of Sorrows (76), B-5, D-6, E-5, Stonard (126)

STONARD SHAMAN
Swamp of Sorrows (76), K-8, Stonard (126)

STONARD WAYFINDER
Swamp of Sorrows (76), F-5, Stonard (126)

STONE BEHEMOTH
Darkshore (24), E:(8, 9), Remtravel's Excavation

STONE FURY
Alterac Mountains (8), H-4, K-4

STONE GOLEM
Badlands (16), F-3, Angor Fortress

STONE GUARDIAN
Un'Goro Crater (90), F-3, G-4, J:(4, 6-8), Fire Plume Ridge, Lakkari Tar Pits, The Marshlands

STONE KEEPER
Badlands (16), G-1, Uldaman

STONE MAW BASILISK
Stranglethorn Vale (74), C-1, D-1

STONE RUMBLER
Barrens (18), E-9, Razorfen Kraul

STONE STEWARD
Badlands (16), G-1, Uldaman

STONE WATCHER OF NORGANNON
Tanaris (78), F-8, Uldum, (Summon) Platinum discs from Uldaman are necessary

STONEARM
Rare Spawn, Barrens (18), E:(2-3), Lvl 15 Uncommon; Roams Kolkar villages around the pools

STONELASH FLAYER
Silithus (66), D:(4, 5), E:(4, 5), F:(4, 5), G:(4, 5), H-4, Southwind Village

STONELASH PINCER
Silithus (66), D:(2, 3), E:(2-4), F:(3, 4), G:(3, 4)

STONELASH SCORPID
Silithus (66), E:(1, 2), F:(1, 2), G:(1-3), H:(1-3), Southwind Village

STONESPINE
Rare Spawn, Eastern Plaguelands (40), D-2, Stratholme, Lvl 60 Rare

STONESPLINTER BONESNAPPER
Loch Modan (54), D-9, E:(8, 9), G:(2, 3), Stonesplinter Valley

STONESPLINTER DIGGER
Loch Modan (54), I:(6, 7), J:(6, 7), Ironband's Excavation Site

STONESPLINTER GEOMANCER
Loch Modan (54), I:(6, 7), J:(6, 7), Ironband's Excavation Site

STONESPLINTER SCOUT
Loch Modan (54), C:(5-7), D:(7, 8), Stonesplinter Valley

STONESPLINTER SEER
Loch Modan (54), C:(8, 9), D:(8, 9), E-8, F:(2, 3), G-2, Stonesplinter Valley

STONESPLINTER SHAMAN
Loch Modan (54), D-9, E:(8, 9), G:(2, 3), Stonesplinter Valley

STONESPLINTER SKULLTHUMPER
Loch Modan (54), C:(8, 9), D:(8, 9), E-8, F:(2, 3), G-2, Stonesplinter Valley

STONESPLINTER TROGG
Loch Modan (54), C:(5-7), D:(7, 8), Stonesplinter Valley

STONETALON GRUNT
Stonetalon Mountains (70), E-7, F-6, Sun Rock Retreat (127)

STONETUSK BOAR
Elwynn Forest (42), D:(8, 9), E:(7-9), F:(7-9), Fargodeep Mine, The Maclure Vineyards, The Stonefield Farm

STONEVAULT AMBUSHER
Badlands (16), G-1, Uldaman

STONEVAULT BASHER
Badlands (16), J:(4, 5), Dustwind Gulch

STONEVAULT BASHER
Badlands (16), G-1, Uldaman

STONEVAULT BONESNAPPER
Badlands (16), G:(6, 7), H:(6, 7), Agmond's End

STONEVAULT BRAWLER
Badlands (16), G-1, Uldaman

STONEVAULT CAVE HUNTER
Badlands (16), G-1, Uldaman

STONEVAULT CAVE LURKER
Badlands (16), G-1, Uldaman

STONEVAULT FLAMEWEAVER
Badlands (16), G-1, Uldaman

STONEVAULT GEOMANCER
Badlands (16), G-1, Uldaman

STONEVAULT MAULER
Badlands (16), G-1, Uldaman

STONEVAULT ORACLE
Badlands (16), G-1, Uldaman

STONEVAULT ROCKCHEWER
Badlands (16), G-1, Uldaman

STONEVAULT SEER
Badlands (16), J:(4, 5), Dustwind Gulch, Uldaman

STONEVAULT SHAMAN
Badlands (16), G-7, H-7, Agmond's End

STORM BAY ORACLE
Azshara (14), E-9, F:(7, 9), G:(7, 9), H:(7-9), I:(7-9), J:(7-9), K:(8, 9), The Ruined Reaches, Southridge Beach

STORM BAY WARRIOR
Azshara (14), E:(1, 2), F:(1, 2), G:(1, 4), H:(1, 3, 4), I:(1, 3, 4), J-1, K:(1-5), L:(1-4), Jagged Reef, The Shattered Strand, Tower of Eldara

STORM SHADOWHOOF
Felwood (44), E-5, Bloodvenom Post, Campfire

STORMHIDE
Barrens (18), E:(7, 8), F:(7, 8)

STORMPIKE BATTLEGUARD
Alterac Mountains (8), D-7, E-8, The Headland, Alliance entrance

STORMSCALE MYRMIDON
Darkshore (24), H-2, I:(1-3), Ruins of Mathystra

STORMSCALE SIREN
Darkshore (24), H:(3, 4), Cliffspring Falls, Cliffspring River

STORMSCALE SORCERESS
Darkshore (24), H-2, I-2, Ruins of Mathystra

STORMSCALE TOXICOLOGIST
Darkshore (24), H-3, Cliffspring Falls

STORMSCALE WARRIOR
Darkshore (24), I-2, Ruins of Mathystra

STORMSCALE WAVE RIDER
Darkshore (24), H:(3, 4), Cliffspring Falls, Cliffspring River

STORMSNOUT
Barrens (18), E:(4-6), F:(5, 6)

STORMWIND CITY GUARD
Elwynn Forest (42), D:(4, 5), Valley of Heroes

STORMWIND GUARD
Elwynn Forest (42), B-8, C:(7, 8), E-6, F:(5, 7), J-7, L-8

STRAHAD FARSAN
Barrens (18), H-3, Ratchet (121), Tower in eastern hills

STRANGLETHORN RAPTOR
Stranglethorn Vale (74), B-2, Ruins of Zul'Kunda, The Savage Coast

STRANGLETHORN TIGER
Stranglethorn Vale (74), B-1, C:(1, 2), D:(1, 2), E:(1, 2)

STRANGLETHORN TIGRESS
Stranglethorn Vale (74), C-4, D:(3-5), E:(2, 3), F:(2, 3)

STRASHAZ HYDRA
Dustwallow Marsh (38), I-2, J-2, Alcaz Island

STRASHAZ MYRMIDON
Dustwallow Marsh (38), J:(1, 2), K-2, Alcaz Island

STRASHAZ SIREN
Dustwallow Marsh (38), J:(1, 2), Alcaz Island

STRASHAZ SORCERESS
Dustwallow Marsh (38), J:(1, 2), K-2, Alcaz Island

STRASHAZ WARRIOR
Dustwallow Marsh (38), J:(1, 2), Alcaz Island

STRATHOLME COURIER
Eastern Plaguelands (40), D-2, Stratholme

STRIDER CLUTCHMOTHER
Darkshore (24), E-9, F-9, Remtravel's Excavation, Twilight Vale, Wanders with fledglings

STRIGID HUNTER
Teldrassil (80), D:(3, 4), E:(4, 5), F:(3, 4), The Oracle Glade, Wellspring Lake

STRIGID OWL
Teldrassil (80), F:(5, 6), G:(5-7), H:(5, 6), I:(5, 6), Dolanaar (109), Lake Al'Ameth, Starbreeze Village

STRIGID SCREECHER
Teldrassil (80), D-5, E:(5-8), F:(7, 8), G:(7, 8), H:(7, 8), Gnarlpine Hold, Lake Al'Ameth, Pools of Arlithrien

STROMGARDE CAVALRYMAN
Arathi Highlands (10), G-4, Stromgarde Keep (127),

STROMGARDE DEFENDER
Arathi Highlands (10), C-6, D-6, Stromgarde Keep (127)

STROMGARDE TROLL HUNTER
Arathi Highlands (10), C-6, Stromgarde Keep (127)

STROMGARDE VINDICATOR
Arathi Highlands (10), C-6, D-6, Stromgarde Keep (127)

STRUMNER FLINTHEEL
Armor Crafter, Blasted Lands (20), J-2, Nethergarde Keep (119), Smithy

STUART FLEMING
Fisherman, Wetlands (96), A-6, Menethil Harbor (117), Dock

SUBTERRANEAN DIEMETRADON
Desolace (30), D-5, Mauradon

SUCCUBUS MINION
Morgan's Minion, Redridge Mountains (62), K-5, Tower of Ilgalar, (Summon) Summoned by Morganth

SUFFERING HIGHBORNE
Winterspring (98), H:(4, 5), Lake Kel'Theril, The Ruins of Kel'Theril

SUFFERING VICTIM
Tirisfal Glades (86), K-3, L-3, Scarlet Monastery

SULFURON HARBINGER
Burning Steppes (22), Searing Gorge (64), C-4/D-8, The Molten Core

SULHASA
Wind Rider Master, Silithus (66), I-1, Valor's Rest, North of road

SUL'LITHUZ ABOMINATION
Tanaris (78), E-1, Zul'Farrak

SUL'LITHUZ BROODLING
Tanaris (78), E-1, Zul'Farrak

SUL'LITHUZ SANDCRAWLER
Tanaris (78), E-1, Zul'Farrak

SUMI
Blacksmithing Supplier, Orgrimmar (60), J-2, K-2, Valley of Honor, The Burning Anvil

SUMMONED BLACKHAND DREADWEAVER
Burning Steppes (22), Searing Gorge (64), C-4/D-8, Blackrock Spire

SUMMONED BLACKHAND VETERAN
Burning Steppes (22), Searing Gorge (64), C-4/D-8, Blackrock Spire

SUMMONED GUARDIAN
Arathi Highlands (10), B-7, Stromgarde Keep (127), (Summon) Base of tower

SUNN RAGETOTEM
Staff Merchant, Thunder Bluff (84), E-5, F-5, High rise, in Rainsticks tent

SUNSCALE LASHTAIL
Barrens (18), E:(1-4), F:(2, 3), G-3, The Crossroads (107), Gold Road, Thorn Hill

SUNSCALE SCREECHER
Barrens (18), D:(2, 3), E:(2-4), F:(1-5), G:(1-5), H:(1-4)

SUNSCALE SCYTHECLAW
Barrens (18), D:(2, 3), E:(1, 2, 4, 5), F-5, G:(1, 3-5), H-3

SUPER-SELLER 680
Desolace (30), E-8, North of road

SUPERVISOR FIZSPROCKET
Mulgore (58), G-3, H-5, The Venture Co. Mine, Deep in southern part of mine

SUPERVISOR LUGWIZZLE
Barrens (18), G-1, The Sludge Fen, Patrols derrick

SUPERVISOR RAELEN
Elwynn Forest (42), K-7, Eastvale Logging Camp, Next to carriage by logging operation

SURA WILDMANE
War Harness Vendor, Thunder Bluff (84), F-5, High rise, between Ragetotem Arms and Aska's Kitchen

SURENA CALEDON
Elwynn Forest (42), J-8, Brackwell Pumpkin Patch, In house with Morgan the Collector and Erlan Drudgemoor

SURF CRAWLER
Durotar (34), I:(2, 3, 7-9), J:(7-9), K-7

SURF GLIDER
Tanaris (78), I-6, J:(5, 6), Lost Rigger Cove, Southbreak Shore

SUSAN TILLINGHAST
Undercity (88), K-6, The Rogues' Quarter, Roams Rouge Quarter

SUZANNE
Stormwind (72), F-8, Mage Quarter, Roamer - sits by tower

SUZETTA GALLINA
Stormwind (72), H-7, The Canals, Gallina Winery

SVEN YORGEN
Duskwood (36), A-3, The Hushed Bank, Camp

"SWAMP EYE" JARL
Dustwallow Marsh (38), G-3, Swamplight Manor, In front of farmhouse

SWAMP JAGUAR
Swamp of Sorrows (76), A-6, B:(4-6), C:(3-6), D:(3-5), E:(3-5), F-4, G-4

SWAMP OOZE
Dustwallow Marsh (38), D:(5, 6), E:(5, 6), F:(5, 6), The Dragonmurk, Lost Point, The Quagmire

SWAMPWALKER
Swamp of Sorrows (76), A:(3, 4), B:(3, 4), F-4, G:(3, 4), Stagalbog Cave, Misty Valley

SWAMPWALKER ELDER
Swamp of Sorrows (76), A:(3, 4), B-3, Misty Valley

SWART
Shaman Trainer, Durotar (34), H-4, Razor Hill (122), Barracks

SWIFTMANE
Barrens (18), G-3, Runs across plateau northwest of Ratchet

SWINEGART SPEARHIDE
Barrens (18), E:(4-5), Agama'gor, Guards near hills

SWIRLING VORTEX
Thousand Needles (82), I:(5-7), J:(5-7, 9), K:(6-8), L:(6, 8), Tahonda Ruins, The Shimmering Flats

SWOOP
Mulgore (58), D:(4, 5), E:(4, 5), F:(3-5), G:(4-7)

SYDNEY UPTON
Staff Merchant, Undercity (88), J-3, The Magic Quarter

SYLISTA
Stable Master, Stormwind (72), D-5, The Park, By Owl Statue

SYLVANNA FORESTMOON
Expert Alchemist, Darnassus (26), G-2, Craftsmen's Terrace, First floor

SYNDICATE ASSASSIN
Alterac Mountains (8), E:(1, 2), F-2, Sofera's Naze

SYNDICATE CONJUROR
Arathi Highlands (10), C-6, D-6, Stromgarde Keep (127)

SYNDICATE ENFORCER
Alterac Mountains (8), E:(1, 2), F-2, Sofera's Naze

SYNDICATE FOOTPAD
Alterac Mountains (8), F-8, H:(6, 7), Sofera's Naze

SYNDICATE HIGHWAYMAN
Arathi Highlands (10), D:(2, 3), E-3, Northfold Manor

SYNDICATE MAGUS
Arathi Highlands (10), C-6, D-6, Stromgarde Keep (127)

SYNDICATE MERCENARY
Arathi Highlands (10), D-3, Northfold Manor

SYNDICATE PATHSTALKER
Arathi Highlands (10), D-3, Northfold Manor

SYNDICATE PROWLER
Arathi Highlands (10), C-6, D-6, Stromgarde Keep (127)

SYNDICATE ROGUE
Hillsbrad Foothills (48), H-5, I-4, J:(4, 5), Durnholde Keep

SYNDICATE SABOTEUR
Alterac Mountains (8), F-2, G:(2, 3), H-3, Dalaran

SYNDICATE SENTRY
Alterac Mountains (8), F-2, G:(2, 3), H:(3, 4), Sofera's Naze

SYNDICATE SHADOW MAGE
Hillsbrad Foothills (48), H-5, I-4, J:(4, 5), K-4, Durnholde Keep

SYNDICATE SPY
Alterac Mountains (8), H:(4, 5), I:(4, 5), Sofera's Naze

SYNDICATE THIEF
Alterac Mountains (8), F-8, H:(6, 7), Sofera's Naze

SYNDICATE WATCHMAN
Hillsbrad Foothills (48), H-5, I-4, J:(4, 5), K-4, Durnholde Keep

SYNDICATE WIZARD
Alterac Mountains (8), H:(4, 7), I-4, Sofera's Naze

SYNGE
Gun Merchant, Thousand Needles (82), K-8, Mirage Raceway (118), Inside racetrack, next to building

SYRAL BLADELEAF
Teldrassil (80), G-6, Dolanaar (109), Outside building north of road

SYURANA
Trade Goods, Winterspring (98), H-3, Starfall Village, Just inside main building

SYURNA
Rogue Trainer, Darnassus (26), D-2, E-2, Cenarion Enclave, Den, west of path

---

T

TABETHA
Dustwallow Marsh (38), F-6, The Quagmire, Farmhouse

TABLET OF THE SEVEN
Burning Steppes (22), F-4, Ruins of Thaurissan, Doodad at base of dwarven statue

TAGAIN
Cloth Armor Merchant, Thunder Bluff (84), E-4, Middle rise, inside Thunder Bluff Armorers tent

TAH WINTERHOOF
Thunder Bluff (84), F-5, High rise, inside Winterhoof Totems tent

TAI'TASI
Trade Supplies, Durotar (34), H-7, Sen'jin Village (123), Main floor of big hut

TAIGA WISEMANE
Desolace (30), C-7, Shadowprey Village (125), Up hill near gong

TAI'JIN
Priest Trainer, Durotar (34), H-4, Razor Hill (122), Barracks

TAIM RAGETOTEM
Alterac Valley Battlemaster, Thunder Bluff (84), G-8, Hunter Rise, Between bridges in a tent

TAINTED OOZE
Felwood (44), E:(5, 6), F:(5, 6), Felwood

TAJARRI
Moonglade (56), E-4, Shrine of Remulos, Northeast of tree

TAKAR THE SEER
Barrens (18), F-6, Southern Barrens, Northeast of Camp Taurajo

TAKATA STEELBLADE
Desolace (30), G-5, Ghost Walker Post (111), Near western end of bridge

TAKK THE LEAPER
Rare Spawn, Barrens (18), G-1, Lvl 19 Semi-Rare; Roams ridge southeast of Sludge Fen

TAKRIN PATHSEEKER
Durotar (34), H-4, Razor Hill (122), Western entrance

TAL
Wind Rider Master, Thunder Bluff (84), E-5, At the top of large circular staircase

TALADAN
Expert Enchanter, Darnassus (26), H-1, Craftsmen's Terrace, Enchanting shop

TALAELAR
Fish Vendor, Darnassus (26), F-5, Tradesmen's Terrace, Dock

TALDAN
Drink Vendor, Darkshore (24), F-4, Auberdine (101), First floor of inn

TALEN
Ashenvale (12), B-4, Campfire along hills

TALENDRIA
Desolace (30), I-1, Nijel's Point (119), Northwestern ruins

TALIN KEENEYE
Dun Morogh (32), C-7, Coldridge Valley (106), Small camp along road

TALLONKAI SWIFTROOT
Teldrassil (80), G-6, Dolanaar (109), Upper floor inside building north of road

TALLOW
Hillsbrad Foothills (48), G-2, Tarren Mill (128), In between the house and inn on the left

TALLY BERRYFIZZ
Expert Alchemist, Ironforge (52), I-5, Tinker Town, Berryfizz's Potions and Mixed Drinks

TALO THORNHOOF
Feralas (46), I-4, Camp Mojache (105), In tent, east of bridge

TALONED SWOOP
Mulgore (58), D:(1, 2), E:(1-3), F:(1-3), G:(2, 3), H:(6, 7)

TALVASH DEL KISSEL
Ironforge (52), E-1, The Mystic Ward, North of Maeva's

TAMAR
Leatherworking Supplies, Orgrimmar (60), H-4, The Drag, Kodohide Leatherworkers

TAMARO
Orgrimmar (60), G-5, The Drag, Building south of Jandi's Arboretum

TAMED BATTLE BOAR
Barrens (18), E-9, Razorfen Kraul

TAMED HYENA
Barrens (18), E-9, Razorfen Kraul

TAMMRA WINDFIELD
Stonetalon Mountains (70), F-6, Sun Rock Retreat (127), By bonfire, east of building

TAMRA STORMPIKE
Rare Spawn, Hillsbrad Foothills (48), I-8, Dun Garok, Lvl 28 Uncommon; Roams a small area around spawn point

TAND
Basket Weaver, Thunder Bluff (84), E-3, Middle rise, near elevators

TANDAAN LIGHTMANE
Leather Armor Merchant, Ashenvale (12), E-5, Astranaar (101), Northwest buildling (south of road)

TANEEL DARKWOOD
Ashenvale (12), J-7, Dor'Danil Barrow Den, Across first bridge and in a side room

TANGLED HORROR
Swamp of Sorrows (76), A:(3, 4), G:(4, 5), H:(4, 5), I:(3, 4, 7), J:(3, 7, 8), K:(6, 7), Misty Valley

TANNOK FROSTHAMMER
Innkeeper's Assistant, Dun Morogh (32), F-5, Kharanos (114), Thunderbrew Distillery

TANNYSA
Herbalism Trainer, Stormwind (72), F-8, G-8, Mage Quarter, Across from Alchemy Needs

TANSY PUDDLEFIZZ
Fishing Supplier, Ironforge (52), F-1, The Forlorn Cavern, Traveling Fisherman

TAPOKE "SLIM" JAHN
Wetlands (96), A-6, Deepwater Tavern, Northwest corner of first floor

TAR BEAST
Un'Goro Crater (90), F:(3, 4), H:(3, 4), I-3, Fungal Rock, Lakkari Tar Pits

TAR CREEPER
Un'Goro Crater (90), F:(3, 4), H:(3, 4), I-3, Fungal Rock, Lakkari Tar Pits

TAR LORD
Un'Goro Crater (90), E-2, F:(2, 3), G:(2, 3), Fungal Rock, Lakkari Tar Pits

TAR LURKER
Un'Goro Crater (90), E-2, F:(2, 3), G:(2, 3), Lakkari Tar Pits

TARA COLDGAZE
Hillsbrad Foothills (48), G-3, Tarren Mill (128)

TARAGAMAN THE HUNGERER
Orgrimmar (60), F-5, Ragefire Chasm

TARANTULA
Redridge Mountains (62), A:(7-9), B-7, C:(7, 8), D-7, Lakeridge Highway

TARBAN HEARTHGRAIN
Baker, Barrens (18), G-3, Outside hut east of Crossroads

TARG
Alterac Mountains (8), E-5, Ruins of Alterac, Church

TARGORR THE DREAD
Stormwind (72), F-6, The Stockade

TARHUS
Reagent Vendor, Feralas (46), I-4, Camp Mojache (105), Inn

TARHUS
Reagent Vendor, Feralas (46), G-4, Dire Maul

TARI'QA
Trade Supplies, Barrens (18), F-3, The Crossroads (107), Outside inn

TARINDRELLA
Teldrassil (80), G-4, Shadowglen (124), Spawns near big tree, west of Aldrassil and roams west of road

TARKREU SHADOWSTALKER
Thousand Needles (82), I-6, Ironstone Camp, Camp just west of Shimmering Flats

TARN
Expert Leatherworker, Thunder Bluff (84), E-4, Middle rise, inside Thunder Bluff Armorers tent

TARONN REDFEATHER
Emerald Circle, Felwood (44), G-8, Emerald Sanctuary, Tent

TARREL ROCKWEAVER
Wetlands (96), A-5, Menethil Harbor (117), Bridge to town

TARREN MILL DEATHGUARD
Hillsbrad Foothills (48), G:(2, 3), H:(2, 3), Tarren Mill (128)

TARSHAW JAGGEDSCAR
Warrior Trainer, Durotar (34), H-4, Razor Hill (122), Barracks

TASKMASTER FIZZULE
Barrens (18), G-1, Near tower northwest of Sludge Fen

TASKMASTER SCRANGE
The Thorium Brotherhood, Searing Gorge (64), D-3, Thorium Point, Right side of camp under scaffolding

TASKMASTER WHIPFANG
Stonetalon Mountains (70), H-5, Blackwolf River, Windshear Crag, Spawns around river, west of Windshear Crag

TATTERNACK STEELFORGE
Barrens (18), F-6, Camp Taurajo (106), North side of camp

TAUR STONEHOOF
Blacksmithing Supplies, Thunder Bluff (84), D-6, Lower rise, next to pond

TAVERNKEEP SMITTS
Duskwood (36), J-4, Darkshire (108), Scarlet Raven Inn

TAWNY GRISETTE
Mushroom Vendor, Undercity (88), I-5, The Trade Quarter, Roams - Upper Ring of Trade Quarter

TAZAN
Barrens (18), H-4, The Merchant Coast, Roams camp at Merchant Coast

TECHBOT
Dun Morogh (32), C-4, Gnomeregan

TEG DAWNSTRIDER
Expert Enchanter, Thunder Bluff (84), E-4, Middle rise, inside Dawnstrider Enchantments tent

TEL'ATHIR
Journeyman Alchemist, Stormwind (72), G-8, Mage Quarter, Alchemy Needs

TELDRASSIL SENTINEL
Teldrassil (80), D-3, E-3, F-4, G-6, Shadowglen (124)

TELEPORTER TO RUT'THERAN VILLAGE
Teleporter, Darnassus (26), C-4, D-4, The Temple Gardens, West of bank

TELF JOOLAM
Durotar (34), F-6, Shrine of the Dormant Flame, Atop the hill near the fire shrine

TELONIS
Artisan Leatherworker, Darnassus (26), I-2 , Craftsmen's Terrace, Leatherworking shop

TELOREN
Hippogryph Master, Stonetalon Mountains (70), D-1, Stonetalon Peak, Next to hippogryphs and moonwell

TELURINON MOONSHADOW
Herbalism Trainer, Wetlands (96), A-6, Menethil Harbor (117), Building west of keep

TEMPERED WAR GOLEM
Searing Gorge (64), H-6, I-3, Dustfire Valley

TENARON STORMGRIP
Teldrassil (80), G-4, H-4, Shadowglen (124), Second room at end of ramp up tree

TENDRIS WARPWOOD
Feralas (46), G-4, Dire Maul

TENELL LEAFRUNNER
Emerald Circle, Felwood (44), G-8, Emerald Sanctuary, Roams entry path

TEPA
Expert Tailor, Thunder Bluff (84), E-4, Middle rise, inside Thunder Bluff Armorers tent

TEREMUS THE DEVOURER
World Boss, Blasted Lands (20), J-5, Roams Blasted Lands (excluding The Tainted Scar)

TERENTHIS
Darkshore (24), F-4, Auberdine (101), First floor of eastern building

TERL ARAKOR
Wetlands (96), D-4, Next to wagon just north of main road

TERONIS' CORPSE
Ashenvale (12), C-4, Lake Falathim, North side of center island

TERRORSPARK
Rare Spawn, Burning Steppes (22), E-4, F-4, G-4, H-4, I-3, Lvl 55 Average Rare; Roams small area around spawn point

TERROWULF FLESHRIPPER
Ashenvale (12), F-4, G-4, Nightsong Woods, Howling Vale

TERROWULF PACKLORD
Rare Spawn, Ashenvale (12), G-4, Howling Vale, Lvl 32 Average Rare; In front of structure

TERROWULF SHADOW WEAVER
Ashenvale (12), F-4, G-4, Nightsong Woods, Howling Vale

TERRY PALIN
Lumberjack, Elwynn Forest (42), L-6, Eastvale Logging Camp, In logging operation

TETHIS
Stranglethorn Vale (74), B-5, C:(4, 5), Gurubashi Arena, The Cape of Stranglethorn, Roams small area around spawn point

THADDEUS WEBB
Enchanting Supplies, Undercity (88), I-6, The Apothecarium, Near Rogues' Quarter entry

THADIUS GRIMSHADE
Blasted Lands (20), J-2, Nethergarde Keep (119), Top floor of tower facing entrance of keep

THALGUS THUNDERFIST
Weapon Merchant, Ironforge (52), H-9, The Military Ward, Timberline Arms

THALIA AMBERHIDE
Thousand Needles (82), F-5, Freewind Post, Inn

THALON
Wind Rider Master, Desolace (30), B-7, Shadowprey Village (125), End of dock

THAL'TRAK PROUDTUSK
Badlands (16), A-5, Kargath (114), Group left of orc burrow

THAMARIAN
Darkshore (24), E-4, Auberdine (101), Dock

THAMNER POL
Physician, Dun Morogh (32), F-5, Kharanos (114), Thunderbrew Distillery

THANTHALDIS SNOWGLEAM
Rewards Vendor, Alterac Mountains (8), E-8, The Headland, Camp outside Alterac Valley

THAREK BLACKSTONE
Armorer, Dun Morogh (32), F-5, Kharanos (114), Smithy

THARG
Dustwallow Marsh (38), D-3, Brackenwall Village (104), East entrance

THARIL'ZUN
Redridge Mountains (62), I-6, Stonewatch, With several orcs in camp just inside defensive walls near the southern entrance to the fortification

THARLIDUN
Stable Master, Arathi Highlands (10), J-3, Hammerfall (113), Platform of north building

THARM
Wind Rider Master, Stonetalon Mountains (70), E-6, Sun Rock Retreat (127), South of western structure, next to water

THARNARIUN TREETENDER
Darkshore (24), F-4, Auberdine (101), Outside eastern building

THARYNN BOUDEN
Trade Supplies, Elwynn Forest (42), E-7, Goldshire (112), In caravan by road at the far end of town

THAURIS BALGARR
Rare Spawn, Burning Steppes (22), F-4, G-4, H-4, I-4, Ruins of Thaurissan, Lvl 57 Uncommon; Roams small area around spawn point

THAURISSAN AGENT
Burning Steppes (22), F-4, G-4, H-4, I-4, Ruins of Thourissan

THAURISSAN FIREWALKER
Burning Steppes (22), F-4, G-4, H-4, I-4, Ruins of Thourissan

THAURISSAN SPY
Burning Steppes (22), F-4, G-4, H-4, I-4, Ruins of Thourissan

THE BEAST
Burning Steppes (22), Searing Gorge (64), C-4/D-8, Blackrock Spire

THE CLEANER
Eastern Plaguelands (40), C-2, Plaguewood, (Summon) During Priest epic staff quest to "clean" area

THE EVALCHARR
Rare Spawn, Azshara (14), A-5, B-6, Haldarr Encampment, Lvl 48 Very Rare; Roams area east of Southfury River

THE HUSK
Rare Spawn, Western Plaguelands (92), H-4, I:(3, 4), The Weeping Cave, Lvl 62 Very Rare; Roams small area around spawn point

THE NAMELESS PROPHET
Desolace (30), C-6, Maraudon, Foot of entry stairwell

THE ONGAR
Rare Spawn, Felwood (44), E-5, Bloodvenom River, Lvl 51 Very Rare; Roams river near spawn point

THE PLAINS VISION
Mulgore (58), E-6, Bloodhoof Village (102), (Summon) Spawns and runs to a cave

THE RAKE
Mulgore (58), F-2, The Golden Plains, Prowls plains

THE RAVENIAN
Western Plaguelands (92), I-7, Scholomance

THE RAZZA
Rare Spawn, Feralas (46), G-4, Dire Maul, The Maul, Lvl 60 Rare; In arena

THE REAK
Rare Spawn, The Hinterlands (50), G:(4, 5), I-4, Agol'watha, Skulk Rock, The Creeping Ruin, Lvl 49 Very Rare; Roams small area around spawn point

THE ROT
Rare Spawn, Dustwallow Marsh (38), G-6, Beezil's Wreck, Lvl 43 Average Rare; Roams the area around the wreck

THE SCOURGE CAULDRON
Western Plaguelands (92), E-6, F-5, G-6, H-6, Dalson's Tears, Felstone Field, Gahrron's Withering, The Writhing Haunt, Large stationary cauldron

THE THRESHWACKONATOR 4100
The First Mate, Darkshore (24), H-2, Mist's Edge, On beach near little inlet

THE UNFORGIVEN
Raid Sub-Boss, Eastern Plaguelands (40), D-2, Stratholme

THE WINDREAVER
World Boss, Silithus (66), E-1, Hive'Ashi, Spawns north near hills and roams to Twilight Post

THEKA THE MARTYR
Tanaris (78), E-1, Zul'Farrak

THELDURIN THE LOST
Badlands (16), H-8, Agmond's End, Camp

THELGRUM STONEHAMMER
Mining Supplier, Darkshore (24), F-4, Auberdine (101), In front of northern building

THELMAN SLATEFIST
Alterac Valley Battlemaster, Stormwind (72), L-2, Stormwind Keep, East wing

THENAN
Arathi Highlands (10), E-6, Circle of Inner Binding, (Summon) Crcle of Inner Binding

THEOCRITUS
Mage of Tower Azora, Elwynn Forest (42), I-7, Tower of Azora, Top floor of tower

THEODORE GRIFFS
Undercity (88), F-7, The Apothecarium, In laboratory

THEODORE MONT CLAIRE
Stable Master, Hillsbrad Foothills (48), H-2, Tarren Mill (128), Next to mailbox outside inn

THEODRUS FROSTBEARD
Priest Trainer, Ironforge (52), C-1, The Mystic Ward, Hall of Mysteries

THERADRIM GUARDIAN
Desolace (30), D-5, Mauradon

THERADRIM SHARDLING
Desolace (30), D-5, Mauradon

THERAMORE DESERTER
Dustwallow Marsh (38), D-5, Lost Point, The Quagmire

THERAMORE GUARD
Dustwallow Marsh (38), H:(4, 5), I:(4-6), J:(5, 6), Theramore Isle (130)

THERAMORE INFILTRATOR
Dustwallow Marsh (38), D-4, E:(2-4), F-3, Bluefen

THERAMORE LIEUTENANT
Dustwallow Marsh (38), I-5, Theramore Isle (130)

THERAMORE PRACTICING GUARD
Dustwallow Marsh (38), I-5, Theramore Isle (130)

THERAMORE SENTRY
Dustwallow Marsh (38), E-3, F-2, North Point Tower

THERAMORE SKIRMISHER
Dustwallow Marsh (38), E-4

THERESA
Gerard's Mind Slave, Undercity (88), G-3, G-2, The War Quarter, Roams to Father Lankester

THERESA MOULAINE
Robe Vendor, Stormwind (72), F-4, Cathedral Square, Righteous Plates

THERIDRAN
Druid Trainer, Stormwind (72), C-5, The Park, By pool of water

THERSA WINDSONG
Undercity (88), G-7, The Apothecarium, In laboratory

THERUM DEEPFORGE
Expert Blacksmith, Stormwind (72), H-2, Dwarven District, At the Forge

THERYLUNE
Darkshore (24), F-9, The Master's Glaive, Center isle of lake

THERYSIL
Ashenvale (12), C-5, Shrine of Aessina, North, just outside of shrine

THERZOK
Orgrimmar (60), E-5, The Cleft of Shadow, Shadowswift Brotherhood

THESSALA HYDRA
Desolace (30), D-5, Mauradon

THIEF CATCHER FARMOUNTAIN
Ironforge (52), Roams between Military Ward and the Commons

THIEF CATCHER SHADOWDELVE
Ironforge (52), Roams between Mystic Ward and the Commons

THIEF CATCHER THUNDERBREW
Ironforge (52), Roams between the Commons and the Hall of Explorers via the Great Forge

THISTLE BEAR
Darkshore (24), F:(2-6), G:(2-6)

THISTLE BOAR
Teldrassil (80), G:(3, 4), H:(3, 4), Shadowglen (124)

THISTLE CUB
Darkshore (24), H-4

THISTLEFUR AVENGER
Ashenvale (12), D:(4, 5), E:(3-4), Astranaar (101), Thistlefur Village

THISTLEFUR DEN WATCHER
Ashenvale (12), E:(3, 4), Thistlefur Hold

THISTLEFUR PATHFINDER
Ashenvale (12), D-4, E:(3, 4), Thistlefur Hold, Thistlefur Village

THISTLEFUR SHAMAN
Ashenvale (12), D:(4, 5), E:(3, 4), Astranaar (101), Thistlefur Hold, Thistlefur Village

THISTLEFUR TOTEMIC
Ashenvale (12), E:(3, 4), F-4, Thistlefur Village

THISTLEFUR URSA
Ashenvale (12), E:(3, 4), F-4, Thistlefur Hold, Thistlefur Village

THISTLEHEART
Warlock Trainer, Ironforge (52), G-1, The Forlorn Cavern, Building to the right of Traveling Fisherman

THISTLESHRUB DEW COLLECTOR
Tanaris (78), D:(6, 7), E:(6, 7), Thistleshrub Valley

THISTLESHRUB ROOTSHAPER
Tanaris (78), D:(6, 7), E:(6, 7), Thistleshrub Valley

THOMAS
Altar Boy, Stormwind (72), F-3, Cathedral Square, Cathedral of Light

THOMAS ARLENTO
Tirisfal Glades (86), H-5, Brill (104)

THOMAS BOOKER
Wetlands (96), A-5, Menethil Harbor (117), Training horse outside stables

THOMAS MILLER
Baker, Stormwind (72), I-6, Trade District, Roamer of Trade District

THOMAS MORDAN
Reagent Vendor, Undercity (88), J-4, The Trade Quarter, Upper Ring of Trade Quarter

THONTEK RUMBLEHOOF
Mulgore (58), F-6, Bloodhoof Village (102), Combat ground east of village

THONYS PILLARSTONE
Journeyman Enchanter, Ironforge (52), H-4, The Great Forge, Thistlefuzz Arcanery

THOR
Gryphon Master, Westfall (94), G-5, Sentinel Hill (123)

THORA FEATHERMOON
Alliance Outrunner, Barrens (18), F-8, Southern Barrens, Spawns at border to Dustwallow Marsh and travels north to Lushwater Oasis

THORFIN STONESHIELD
Hunter Trainer, Stormwind (72), I-1, I-3, Dwarven District, Building south of tram entrance

THORGAS GRIMSON
Hunter Trainer, Dun Morogh (32), D-7, Coldridge Valley (106), Anvilmar

THORGRUM BORRELSON
Gryphon Master, Loch Modan (54), D-5, Thelsamar (129), Right side of path leading into town

THORIUM BROTHERHOOD LOOKOUT
Lookout, Searing Gorge (64), D-3, Thorium Point

THORK
Barrens (18), F-3, The Crossroads (107), Tower south of inn

THORKAF DRAGONEYE
Master Dragonscale Leatherworker, Badlands (16), I-6, Small camp to right of bone pile

THORN EATER GHOUL
Barrens (18), F-9, Razorfen Downs

THORVALD DEEPFORGE
Loch Modan (54), C-7, Valley of Kings, First floor of tower

THOTAR
Hunter Trainer, Durotar (34), H-4, Razor Hill (122), Bunker

THRAG STONEHOOF
Journeyman Blacksmith, Thunder Bluff (84), D-6, Lower rise, next to pond

THRAGOMM
Loch Modan (54), H-7, Patrols large circular paths with Gradok and Haren Swifthoof along the eastern side of the loch

THRALL
Orgrimmar (60), C:(3, 4), Valley of Wisdom, Grommash Hold

THRALOSH
Cloth & Leather Armor Merchant, Swamp of Sorrows (76), F-5, Stonard (126), Smithy

THRAN KHORMAN
Warrior Trainer, Dun Morogh (32), D-7, Coldridge Valley (106), Anvilmar

THRASHTAIL BASILISK
Stranglethorn Vale (74), D-5, Crystalvein Mine

THRAWN BOLTAR
Blacksmithing Supplies, Dun Morogh (32), F-5, Kharanos (114), Smithy

THREGGIL
Rare Spawn, Teldrassil (80), G-5, Fel Rock, Lvl 6 Uncommon; Runs around water in western section of cave

THRUMN
Tabard Vendor, Thunder Bluff (84), D-6, Lower rise, in front of Thunder Bluff Civic Information tent

THULE RAVENCLAW
Silverpine Forest (68), J-2, Fenris Keep, Second floor of keep

THULMAN FLINTCRAG
Guns Vendor, Stormwind (72), H:(1, 2), Dwarven District, Building west of forge

THULTASH
Food & Drink Vendor, Swamp of Sorrows (76), F-5, Stonard (126), Scaffolding right of entrance to main hall

THULTAZOR
Arcane Goods Vendor, Swamp of Sorrows (76), F-5, Stonard (126), Scaffolding by tree in the center of camp

THUND
Journeyman Engineer, Orgrimmar (60), I-3, J-3, Valley of Honor, Nogg's Machine Shop

THUNDER LIZARD
Durotar (34), F:(2, 3), Thunder Ridge

THUNDERHAWK CLOUDSCRAPER
Barrens (18), E:(6, 7), F-6, Camp Taurajo (106), Southern Barrens, Southern Gold Road

THUNDERHAWK HATCHLING
Barrens (18), E:(4-6), F:(5, 6), Agama'gor, Bramblescar, Southern Barrens

THUNDERHEAD
Barrens (18), E:(6, 7), F-6, Camp Taurajo (106), Field of Giants, Southern Barrens

THUNDERHEAD CONSORT
Azshara (14), E:(7, 8), F:(7, 8), G:(7-9), H:(2, 3, 8, 9), I:(1-3), J:(2, 3), K:(2, 3)

THUNDERHEAD HIPPOGRYPH
Azshara (14), A:(5, 6), B:(5-7), Haldarr Encampment, Valormok

THUNDERHEAD PATRIARCH
Azshara (14), E:(7, 8), F:(7, 8), G:(7-9), H:(2, 3, 8, 9), I:(1-3), J:(2, 3), K:(2, 3)

THUNDERHEAD SKYSTORMER
Azshara (14), F:(1-4), G:(2-4), H:(1, 2), Legash Encampment, Thalassian Base Camp, Ursolan

THUNDERHEAD STAGWING
Azshara (14), A-8, B-8, C-8, D:(4, 5, 8), E:(2-4), F:(3, 4)

THUNDERHEART
Badlands (16), A-5, Kargath (114), Group left of orc burrow

THUNDERING BOULDERKIN
Thousand Needles (82), A:(1-3), H:(5, 6), I:(5, 6), Ironstone Camp, Windbreak Canyon

THUNDERING EXILE
Arathi Highlands (10), G-5, Circle of Outer Binding

THUNDERING INVADER
Azshara (14), J:(2, 3), K:(2, 3), Bitter Reaches, The Shattered Strand

THUNDERSTOMP
Rare Spawn, Barrens (18), E-8, Southern Barrens, Lvl 24 Uncommon; Roams clearing near Dustwallow Marsh border

THUNDERSTOMP STEGODON
Un'Goro Crater (90), C:(5-7), D:(6-8), E:(6-8), Golakka Hot Springs, Terror Run

THUNDRIS WINDWEAVER
Darkshore (24), F-4, Auberdine (101), Back terrace of northern building

THUN'GRIM FIREGAZE
Barrens (18), G-3, Atop Thorn Hill

THURGRUM DEEPFORGE
Blacksmithing Supplies, Ironforge (52), G-4, The Great Forge, Next to anvils

THURMAN AGAMAND
Tirisfal Glades (86), E-3, Agamand Mills (100), Roams on the western side of mill near dropoff

THURMAN MULLBY
General Goods Vendor, Stormwind (72), I-6, Trade District, Everyday Merchandise

THURMAN SCHNEDIER
Stormwind (72), F-8, Mage Quarter, Larson Clothiers

THUROS LIGHTFINGERS
Rare Spawn, Elwynn Forest (42), D-6, G:(6, 8), L-8, Crystal Lake, Jerod's Landing, Mirror Lake, Lvl 11 Uncommon; Stands idle at spawn point

THURSTON XANE
Mage Trainer, Thunder Bluff (84), C-3, Spirit Rise, The Pools of Vision

THUUL
Portal Trainer, Orgrimmar (60), D:(8, 9), Valley of Spirit, Darkbriar Lodge, top floor

THUWD
Skinning Trainer, Orgrimmar (60), H-4, The Drag, Kodohide Leatherworkers

THUZADIN ACOLYTE
Eastern Plaguelands (40), D-2, Stratholme

THUZADIN NECROMANCER
Eastern Plaguelands (40), D-2, Stratholme

THUZADIN SHADOWCASTER
Eastern Plaguelands (40), D-2, Stratholme

THYN'TEL BLADEWEAVER
Darnassus (26), H-4, Warrior's Terrace, Middle of terrace

THYSSIANA
Hippogryph Master, Feralas (46), K-5, Thalanaar, North of well

THYSTA
Wind Rider Master, Stranglethorn Vale (74), C-3, Grom'gol Base Camp (112), Inside camp walls to the right of eastern entrance

TICK
Tanaris (78), I-5, Caverns of Time, Land bridge leading to cavern

TIDE CRAWLER
Darkshore (24), E:(6, 7), F:(2, 3, 7), Mist's Edge, Twilight Shore

TIDERESS
Ashenvale (12), F-7, Mystral Lake, Roams underwater and on center island

TIEV MORDUNE
Silverpine Forest (68), F-4, North Tide's Run, Crouched on coastal hill behind megalith

TIGOR SKYCHASER
Shaman Trainer, Thunder Bluff (84), B-2, Spirit Rise, Inside Hall of Spirits

TILLI THISTLEFUZZ
Enchanting Supplies, Ironforge (52), H-4, The Great Forge, Thistlefuzz Arcanery

TIMBER
Rare Spawn, Dun Morogh (32), D-4, Iceflow Lake, Lvl 10 Uncommon; Large island at center of lake

TIMBER WOLF
Elwynn Forest (42), F:(3-5), G:(4, 5), Echo Ridge Mine, Northshire Valley (120)

TIMBERLING
Teldrassil (80), G:(6, 7), H:(6, 7), Dolanaar (109), Lake Al'Ameth

TIMBERLING BARK RIPPER
Teldrassil (80), F-7, G-7, Lake Al'Ameth

TIMBERLING MIRE BEAST
Teldrassil (80), E:(3, 4), The Oracle Glade, Wellspring River

TIMBERLING TRAMPLER
Teldrassil (80), E-4, G-7, Lake Al'Ameth, Wellspring Lake, Wellspring River

TIMBERMAW DEN WATCHER
Azshara (14), D-3, E:(2, 3), F:(2, 3), Timbermaw Hold, Ursolan

TIMBERMAW PATHFINDER
Azshara (14), C:(4, 5), D:(4, 5), Bear's Head, Ruins of Eldarath

TIMBERMAW SHAMAN
Azshara (14), D-3, E:(2, 3), F:(2, 3), Timbermaw Hold, Ursolan

TIMBERMAW TOTEMIC
Azshara (14), C-5, D:(4, 5), Bear's Head, Timbermaw Hold

TIMBERMAW URSA
Azshara (14), E:(2, 3), F:(2, 3), Timbermaw Hold, Ursolan

TIMBERMAW WARRIOR
Azshara (14), C:(4, 5), D:(4, 5), Bear's Head, Ruins of Eldarath, Timbermaw Hold

TIMBERWEB RECLUSE
Azshara (14), B-5, C-5, D:(4, 5), E:(2-4), F-3

TIMMY THE CRUEL
Eastern Plaguelands (40), D-2, Stratholme

TIMOTHY CLARK
Wetlands (96), A-6, Menethil Harbor (117), Second floor of keep

TIMOTHY WELDON
Heavy Armor Merchant, Undercity (88), I-4, The Trade Quarter, Upper Ring of Trade Quarter

TIMOTHY WORTHINGTON
Master Tailor, Dustwallow Marsh (38), I-5, Theramore Isle (130), 2nd floor of building in south corner

TINK SPROCKETWHISTLE
Engineering Supplies, Dun Morogh (32), C-4, Gnomeregan

TINKEE STEAMBOIL
Burning Steppes (22), H-2, Flame Crest, Under scaffolding

TINKERER GIZLOCK
Desolace (30), D-5, Mauradon

TINKERER SNIGGLES
Barrens (18), F-1, Building southwest of Sludge Fen

TINKERWIZ
Journeyman Engineer, Barrens (18), H-4, Ratchet (121), Building northeast of town

TINKMASTER OVERSPARK
Master Gnome Engineer, Ironforge (52), J-5, Tinker Town, Outside tram entrance

TIRION FORDRING
Eastern Plaguelands (40), A-4, Thondroril River, In front of house on banks of Thondoril River

TIRISFAL FARMER
Tirisfal Glades (86), D-5, E-5, Solliden Farmstead

TIRISFAL FARMHAND
Tirisfal Glades (86), D-5, E-5, Solliden Farmstead

TISA MARTINE
Ironforge (52), J-7, The Military Ward, Bruuk's Corner

TIYANI
Food & Drink Vendor, Darkshore (24), G-8, Grove of the Ancients, Center of temple

TIZA BATTLEFORGE
Ironforge (52), C-1, The Mystic Ward, Hall of Mysteries

TOBIAS SEECHER
Burning Steppes (22), Searing Gorge (64), C-4/D-8, Blackrock Depths

TODDRICK
Butcher, Elwynn Forest (42), F-7, Goldshire (112), First floor of Lion's Pride Inn

TOG RUSTSPROCKET
Dun Morogh (32), F-5, Kharanos (114), Gnomish camp on right of distillery

TOGNUS FLINTFIRE
Journeyman Blacksmith, Dun Morogh (32), F-5, Kharanos (114), Smithy

TOG'THAR
Hillsbrad Foothills (48), J-4, Durnholde Keep, In ruins in the upper level of keep

TOK'KAR
Swamp of Sorrows (76), K-8, Misty Reed Post, Next to bonfire in camp

TOLDREN DEEPIRON
Priest Trainer, Ironforge (52), C-1, The Mystic Ward, Hall of Mysteries

TOMAS
Cook, Elwynn Forest (42), F-7, Goldshire (112), First floor of Lion's Pride Inn

TOMB FIEND
Barrens (18), F-9, Razorfen Downs

TOMB REAVER
Barrens (18), F-9, Razorfen Downs

TOMMY JOE STONEFIELD
Elwynn Forest (42), D-9, The Stonefield Farm, By river bank west of farm

TONGA RUNETOTEM
Barrens (18), F-3, The Crossroads (107), Southern entrance

TOOGA
Tanaris (78), D-6, E:(6, 7), Thistleshrub Valley, Roams valley and south

TOPPER MCNABB
Stormwind (72), H-6, Trade District, Northwest alley

TOR'PHAN
Cloth & Leather Armor Merchant, Orgrimmar (60), H-5, The Drag, Magar's Cloth Goods

TOREK
Ashenvale (12), I-7, Nightsong Woods, East of road leading to Barrens

TOR'GAN
Arathi Highlands (10), J-4, Hammerfall (113), Outside fence east building

TORM RAGETOTEM
Warrior Trainer, Thunder Bluff (84), G-9, Hunter Rise, Inside Hunter's Hall

TORMENTED OFFICER
Silverpine Forest (68), F-7, Shadowfang Keep

TORMENTED SPIRIT
Rare Spawn, Tirisfal Glades (86), E-3, Agamand Mills (100), Lvl 8 Uncommon; Patrols the northwestern edge of mill

TORMUS DEEPFORGE
Ironforge (52), F-4 , The Great Forge, The Great Anvil

TORN
Banker, Thunder Bluff (84), E-6, Thunder Bluff Bank

TORN FIN COASTRUNNER
Hillsbrad Foothills (48), B:(6, 7), C-7, D-7, Western Strand, Coast

TORN FIN MUCKDWELLER
Hillsbrad Foothills (48), A-6, B:(6, 7), C-7, Western Strand, Coast

TORN FIN ORACLE
Hillsbrad Foothills (48), D-7, E:(6, 7), F-6, Western Strand, Coast

TORN FIN TIDEHUNTER
Hillsbrad Foothills (48), C-7, D-7, E:(6, 7), F:(6, 7), Western Strand, Coast

TORN SCREAMER
Eastern Plaguelands (40), B:(3, 4), C:(2-4), D:(3, 4), E:(2-4), F:(2-4), Plaguewood

TORN SCROLL
Eastern Plaguelands (40), D-8, The Undercroft, Crypt

TORQ IRONBLAST
Gunsmith, Dustwallow Marsh (38), I-5, Theramore Isle (130), First floor of Foothold Citadel

TORREN SQUAREJAW
Explorers' League, Loch Modan (54), E-5, Thelsamar (129), Second house on right of path

TORTA
Tanaris (78), J-3, Steamwheedle Port, Small cove south of the port

TORTURED DRUID
Silithus (66), G-3, H-3, Southwind Village

TORTURED SENTINEL
Silithus (66), G-3, H-3, Southwind Village

TORWA PATHFINDER
Un'Goro Crater (90), J-7, On hill, next to waterfall

TOSAMINA
Orgrimmar (60), I-2 , Valley of Honor, In building with Horde orphans

TOWN CRIER
Duskwood (36), J-5

TOXIC HORROR
Felwood (44), G-3, Irontree Woods

TRACKMASTER ZHERIN
Thousand Needles (82), K-8, Mirage Raceway (118), Grandstands at drag strip

TRADE MASTER KOVIC
The Undermarket, Searing Gorge (64), D-5, The Cauldron, Next to Clunk in cave

TRAINED RAZORBEAK
The Hinterlands (50), B:(5, 6), C:(5, 6), The Hinterlands

TRAK'GEN
General Goods, Orgrimmar (60), F-8, Valley of Strength, Orgrimmar General Store

TRAN'REK
Tanaris (78), H-3, Gadgetzan (111), Near crane to north

TRAUGH
Expert Blacksmith, Barrens (18), F-3, The Crossroads (107), Western entrance

TRAVIST BOSK
Undercity (88), F-3, The War Quarter, Platform in front of Skull building

TRAYEXIR
Weapon Merchant, Durotar (34), H-7, Sen'jin Village (123), Main floor of big hut

TREANT SPIRIT
Felwood (44), G-3, Irontree Woods

TRENTON LIGHTHAMMER
The Mithril Order, Tanaris (78), H-3, Gadgetzan (111), Near southern entrance

TRESHALA FALLOWBROOK
Darnassus (26), I-7, Tradesmen's Terrace, Across second story bridge from Weapons shop

TRIANNA
Journeyman Tailor, Darnassus (26), I-2 , Craftsmen's Terrace, Tailoring shop

TRISTANE SHADOWSTONE
Dun Morogh (32), D-4, Brewnall Village, Patrols between scaffolding and half way along road heading south out of village

TRIXIE QUIKSWITCH
Expert Engineer, Ironforge (52), I-4, Tinker Town, Springspindle's Gadgets

TROYAS MOONBREEZE
Feralas (46), C-4, Feathermoon Stronghold (110), Southeastern building

TRUK WILDBEARD
Bartender, The Hinterlands (50), B-4, Aerie Peak (100), Wildhammer Keep

TRULL FAILBANE
Felwood (44), E-5, Bloodvenom Post, Campfire

TSUNAMAN
Stonetalon Mountains (70), F-6, Sun Rock Retreat (127), Outside hut on cliff south of inn

TSU'ZEE
Rare Spawn, Feralas (46), G-4, Dire Maul, Lvl 59 Rare

TUKK
General Goods Vendor, Desolace (30), C-7, Shadowprey Village (125), Near entrance

TUMI
Heavy Armor Merchant, Orgrimmar (60), J-2, K-2, Valley of Honor, The Burning Anvil

TUNDRA MACGRANN
Dun Morogh (32), D-5, Chill Breeze Valley, Camp in front of cave on hill

TUNKK
Leatherworking Supplies, Arathi Highlands (10), J-3, Hammerfall (113), Inside east building

TUNNEL RAT DIGGER
Loch Modan (54), D:(2, 3), Silver Stream Mine, Mine

TUNNEL RAT FORAGER
Loch Modan (54), C-4, D-2, E:(1, 2), Silver Stream Mine, Front of mine

TUNNEL RAT GEOMANCER
Loch Modan (54), D:(2, 3), Silver Stream Mine, Mine

TUNNEL RAT KOBOLD
Loch Modan (54), C-4, D-2, E:(1, 2), Silver Stream Mine, Mine

TUNNEL RAT SCOUT
Loch Modan (54), B-3, C:(3, 4), D:(2, 3), Silver Stream Mine, Mine

TUNNEL RAT SURVEYOR
Loch Modan (54), D:(2, 3), Silver Stream Mine, Mine

TUNNEL RAT VERMIN
Loch Modan (54), B-3, C:(3, 4), D:(1-3), E:(1-3), Silver Stream Mine, Front of mine

TURAK RUNETOTEM
Druid Trainer, Thunder Bluff (84), J-3, Elder Rise, Inside Hall of Elders

TURHAW
Butcher, Thousand Needles (82), F-5, Freewind Post, Next to hut, west of inn

TURIAN
Thrown Weapons Merchant, Darnassus (26), H-6, Tradesmen's Terrace, Thrown Weapons shop

TURUK AMBERSTILL
Dwarven Weaponsmith, Dun Morogh (32), I-5, Amberstill Ranch, On porch of building

TUTEN'KASH
Barrens (18), F-9, Razorfen Downs

TWAIN
Stormwind (72), Roams city with Miss Danna

TWIGGY FLATHEAD
The Announcer, Barrens (18), I-5, Fray Island, Bleechers

TWILIGHT ACOLYTE
Ashenvale (12), B-2, Blackfathom Deeps

TWILIGHT AQUAMANCER
Ashenvale (12), B-2, Blackfathom Deeps

TWILIGHT AVENGER
Silithus (66), D:(2, 4, 5), E:(2, 3), F:(2, 3), Twilight Base Camp, Twilight Outpost, Twilight Post

TWILIGHT BODYGUARD
Burning Steppes (22), Searing Gorge (64), C-4/D-8, Blackrock Depths

TWILIGHT DARK SHAMAN
Searing Gorge (64), A:(3, 4), B:(3, 4), Firewatch Ridge

TWILIGHT DISCIPLE
Darkshore (24), F:(8, 9), The Master's Glaive, Twilight Vale

TWILIGHT ELEMENTALIST
Ashenvale (12), B-2, Blackfathom Deeps

TWILIGHT EMISSARY
Burning Steppes (22), Searing Gorge (64), C-4/D-8, Blackrock Depths

TWILIGHT FIRE GUARD
Searing Gorge (64), A:(3, 4), B:(3, 4), C:(2, 3), Firewatch Ridge

TWILIGHT GEOLORD
Silithus (66), D:(2, 4, 5), E:(2, 3), F:(2, 3), Twilight Base Camp, Twilight Outpost, Twilight Post

TWILIGHT GEOMANCER
Searing Gorge (64), A:(3, 4), B:(3, 4), C:(2, 3), Firewatch Ridge

TWILIGHT IDOLATER
Searing Gorge (64), C-3, Firewatch Ridge

TWILIGHT LORD EVERUN
Rare Spawn, Silithus (66), D-5, E-2, F-3, Twilight Base Camp, Twilight Outpost, Twilight Post, Lvl 60 Uncommon; Roams respective camp

TWILIGHT LORD KELRIS
Ashenvale (12), B-2, Blackfathom Deeps

TWILIGHT LORESEEKER
Ashenvale (12), B-2, Blackfathom Deeps

TWILIGHT MASTER
Silithus (66), D:(4, 5), Twilight Outpost

TWILIGHT REAVER
Ashenvale (12), B-2, Blackfathom Deeps

TWILIGHT RUNNER
Stonetalon Mountains (70), D:(1, 2), E:(1, 2), Stonetalon Peak

TWILIGHT SHADOWMAGE
Ashenvale (12), B-2, Blackfathom Deeps

TWILIGHT STONECALLER
Silithus (66), D:(4, 5), E-2, F:(2, 3), Twilight Base Camp, Twilight Outpost

TWILIGHT THUG
Darkshore (24), F:(8, 9), H:(3, 4), The Master's Glaive, Twilight Vale

TWILIGHT'S HAMMER AMBASSADOR
Burning Steppes (22), Searing Gorge (64), C-4/D-8, Blackrock Depths

TWILIGHT'S HAMMER EXECUTIONER
Burning Steppes (22), Searing Gorge (64), C-4/D-8, Blackrock Depths

TWILIGHT'S HAMMER TORTURER
Burning Steppes (22), Searing Gorge (64), C-4/D-8, Blackrock Depths

TWIZWICK SPROCKETGRIND
Journeyman Engineer, Mulgore (58), H-3, In hills northeast of north entrance to Venture Co. Mine

TYLER
Undercity (88), G-2, The War Quarter, Fights captives in War Quarter

TYMOR
Ironforge (52), D-1, The Mystic Ward, Building to the right of Hall of Mysteries

TYNNUS VENOMSPROUT
Shady Dealer, Ironforge (52), G-1, The Forlorn Cavern, Top of steps, just inside east entrance

TYRANDE WHISPERWIND
High Priestess of Elune, Darnassus (26), E-8, The Temple of the Moon, Balcony, north of fountain

TYRANIS MALEM
Desolace (30), G-3, Thunder Axe Fortress, Center of smaller fortress

TYRANT DEVILSAUR
Un'Goro Crater (90), D:(3, 4), F-4, H:(3, 8), J-4

TYRION
Stormwind (72), K-1, Stormwind Keep, Courtyard

TYRION'S SPYBOT
Stormwind (72), K-1, Stormwind Keep, Courtyard

U

U'CHA
Un'Goro Crater (90), I-2, Fungal Rock, Northern section of cave

UG'THOK
Journeyman Blacksmith, Orgrimmar (60), J-2, Valley of Honor, Across from Arms of Legend

UHGAR
Weaponsmith, Durotar (34), H-4, Razor Hill (122), Northeast of inn

UHK'LOC
Rare Spawn, Un'Goro Crater (90), I-2, Fungal Rock, Lvl 53 Uncommon; Northern section of cave

UKOR
Durotar (34), H-7, Near signpost on road

UKRA'NOR
Staff Merchant, Orgrimmar (60), C-7, Valley of Spirit, Skyfury Staves

ULA'ELEK
Durotar (34), H-7, Sen'jin Village (123), Outside big hut

ULAG THE CLEAVER
Tirisfal Glades (86), H-5, Brill (104), (Summon) Spawns in front of the mausoleum in the graveyard

ULATHEK
Felwood (44), E-6, Shadow Hold, Northwest cave across bridge after spiral tunnel

ULBREK FIREHAND
Stable Master, Ironforge (52), I-8, The Military Ward, Hall of Arms

ULFIR IRONBEARD
Hunter Trainer, Stormwind (72), I-2, Dwarven District, Building south of tram entrance

ULLANNA
Trade Supplies, Darkshore (24), G-8, Grove of the Ancients, Center of temple

ULTHAM IRONHORN
Ram Riding Instructor, Dun Morogh (32), I-5, Amberstill Ranch, By hay bails in corral

ULTHIR
Alchemy Supplies, Darnassus (26), G-2, Craftsmen's Terrace, Alchemy shop

UMA BARTULM
Herbalism & Alchemy Supplies, Dustwallow Marsh (38), H-5, Theramore Isle (130), Hut in west corner

UMARON STRAGARELM
Winterspring (98), I-4, Everlook (110), Near the machinery along the east wall

UMBER
Moonglade (56), F-4, Nighthaven (120), Just outside northwest building on wooden walkway

UMBRANSE THE SPIRITSPEAKER
Winterspring (98), J-3, Inside small shack in hills

UMI RUMPLESNICKER
Winterspring (98), I-4, Everlook (110), Behind building directly north of entrance

UMPI
Hillsbrad Foothills (48), G-2, Tarren Mill (128), House on the left

UNA
Artisan Leatherworker, Thunder Bluff (84), D-4, Middle rise, inside Thunder Bluff Armorers tent

UNA JI'RO
Darkshore (24), J-2, Big structure, north of lake

UNDEAD DYNAMITER
Westfall (94), D-7, E-7, The Deadmines

UNDEAD EXCAVATOR
Westfall (94), D-7, E-7, The Deadmines

UNDEAD POSTMAN
Eastern Plaguelands (40), D-2, Stratholme

UNDEAD RAVAGER
Desolace (30), H:(8, 9), I:(8, 9), Valley of Bones

UNDEAD SCARAB
Eastern Plaguelands (40), D-2, Stratholme

UNDERTAKER MORDO
Tirisfal Glades (86), C-8, Deathknell (109), Outside of Shadow Grave

UNFETTERED SPIRIT
Tirisfal Glades (86), K-3, L-3, Scarlet Monastery

UNGER STATFORTH
Horse Breeder, Wetlands (96), A-5, Menethil Harbor (117), Outside stables

UN'GORO GORILLA
Un'Goro Crater (90), H-2, I-2, Fungal Rock, Lakkari Tar Pits

UN'GORO STOMPER
Un'Goro Crater (90), H-2, I-2, Fungal Rock, Lakkari Tar Pits

UN'GORO THUNDERER
Un'Goro Crater (90), I-2, Fungal Rock, Lakkari Tar Pits

UNLIVING ATAL'AI
Swamp of Sorrows (76), I-5, The Temple of Atal'Hakkar

UNLIVING CARETAKER
Deadwind Pass (28), C:(6-8), D:(7, 8), E:(7-9), F-8, Karazhan, Morgan's Plot

UNLIVING MOSSFLAYER
Eastern Plaguelands (40), D-8, The Undercroft

UNLIVING RESIDENT
Deadwind Pass (28), C:(6-8), D:(7, 8), E:(7-9), F-8, Karazhan, Morgan's Plot

UNSEEN SERVANT
Eastern Plaguelands (40), H:(6, 7), Corin's Crossing

UNSTABLE CORPSE
Western Plaguelands (92), I-7, Scholomance

UN'THUWA
Mage Trainer, Durotar (34), H-7, Sen'jin Village (123), Small hut to southeast

UR'KYO
Priest Trainer, Orgrimmar (60), D-9, Valley of Spirit, Spirit Lodge

URDA
Wind Rider Master, Arathi Highlands (10), J-3, Hammerfall (113), Camp

UR'DAN
Felwood (44), E-6, Shadow Hold, Top floor of the final area

UREK THUNDERHORN
Hunter Trainer, Thunder Bluff (84), G-9, Hunter Rise, Inside Hunter's Hall

UROK DOOMHOWL
Burning Steppes (22), Searing Gorge (64), C-4/D-8, Blackrock Spire

UROK ENFORCER
Burning Steppes (22), Searing Gorge (64), C-4/D-8, Blackrock Spire

UROK OGRE MAGUS
Burning Steppes (22), Searing Gorge (64), C-4/D-8, Blackrock Spire

URSAL THE MAULER
Teldrassil (80), E-8, Gnarlpine Hold, Patrols southwest camp

URSANGOUS
Ashenvale (12), I-7, Spawns west of Mystral Lake and roams in a loop to the northwest

URSIUS
Winterspring (98), H-3, Roams hills

URSOL'LOK
Rare Spawn, Ashenvale (12), J-5, K-6, Nightsong Woods, Satyrnaar, Warsong Lumber Camp, Lvl 31 Semi-Rare

URSULA DELINE
Warlock Trainer, Stormwind (72), D-8, Mage Quarter, The Slaughtered Lamb

URSYN GHULL
Priest Trainer, Thunder Bluff (84), C-3, Spirit Rise, The Pools of Vision

URTHARO
Weapon Merchant, Orgrimmar (60), E-7, Valley of Strength, The Shattered Axe

URTRAN CLANBRINGER
Guild Master, Orgrimmar (60), E-7, Valley of Strength, Horde Embassy

URUSON
Rare Spawn, Teldrassil (80), I-6, Starbreeze Village, Lvl 7 Uncommon; Patrols road in village

UTHAN STILLWATER
Fisherman, Mulgore (58), E-6, Stonebull Lake, North end of lake

UTHEK THE WISE
Desolace (30), D-8, Gelkis Village, Hut on hill

UTHEL'NAY
Mage Trainer, Orgrimmar (60), D:(8, 9), Valley of Spirit, Darkbriar Lodge

UTHIL MOONCALL
Ashenvale (12), J-7, Dor'Danil Barrow Den, Northeast cave at bottom of den

UTHOK
General Supplies, Stranglethorn Vale (74), C-3, Grom'gol Base Camp (112), By orcish carriage just inside camp walls to the right of western entrance

UTHRAR THREX
Journeyman Tailor, Ironforge (52), F-3, The Great Forge, Stonebrow's Clothier

UTHROK
Bowyer & Gunsmith, Barrens (18), F-3, The Crossroads (107), Western entrance

UTTNAR
Butcher, Arathi Highlands (10), J-3, Hammerfall (113), Platform of north building

UZZEK
Barrens (18), G-2, Camp near tree

V

VAEAN
Enchanting Supplies, Darnassus (26), H-1, Craftsmen's Terrace, Enchanting shop

VAELAN
Burning Steppes (22), Searing Gorge (64), C-4/D-8, Blackrock Spire

VAELASTRASZ THE RED
Burning Steppes (22), Searing Gorge (64), C-4/D-8, Blackrock Spire

VAGASH
Dun Morogh (32), H-5, I-5, Amberstill Ranch, Patrols in and around cave above ranch

VAHGRUK
Wind Rider Master, Burning Steppes (22), H-2, Flame Crest, Right of cave

VAHLARRIEL DEMONSLAYER
Desolace (30), I-1, Nijel's Point (119), Near entrance

VALDARON
Tailoring Supplies, Darkshore (24), F-4, Auberdine (101), Right wing of northern building

VALDRED MORAY
Silverpine Forest (68), G-8, The Greymane Wall, Patrols between the camps along right side of wall

VALE SCREECHER
Feralas (46), F-5, G:(5, 6)

VALGAR HIGHFORGE
Paladin Trainer, Ironforge (52), C-1, The Mystic Ward, Hall of Mysteries

VALSTAG IRONJAW
Wetlands (96), A-6, Menethil Harbor (117), Just inside keep

VAMPIRIC DUSKBAT
Tirisfal Glades (86), E:(6, 7), F:(6, 7), G-6, H:(3, 4), I:(3-6), J:(3-7), K:(4-7), L-4

VANCE UNDERGLOOM
Journeyman Enchanter, Tirisfal Glades (86), H-5, Brill (104), Second floor of Gallows' End Tavern

VARG WINDWHISPER
Leather Armor Merchant, Mulgore (58), E-6, Bloodhoof Village (102), Northeast tent

VARIA HARDHIDE
Armor Merchant, Mulgore (58), E-8, Camp Narache (105), Southwest tent

VARIAN WRYNN
King of Stormwind, Dustwallow Marsh (38), J-2, Alcaz Island, Underground dungeon in east camp

VARIMATHRAS
Boss, Undercity (88), H-9, Royal Quarter, In Throne room

VAR'JUN
Mulgore (58), E-6, Bloodhoof Village (102), Outside main tent

VARK BATTLESCAR
Skinning Trainer, Desolace (30), B-7, Shadowprey Village (125), Top of western structure

ARO'THEN'S GHOST
Rare Spawn, Azshara (14), A:(7-8), B-7, Lvl 48 Uncommon; Roams area north of road among ruins

ARTRUS THE ANCIENT
Felwood (44), G-3, Irontree Woods, (Summon) Talk to the ancients on the island

AULT WARDEN
Badlands (16), G-1, Uldaman

AZARIO LINKGREASE
Master Goblin Engineer, Barrens (18), H-4, Ratchet (121), Building northeast of town

ECTUS
Western Plaguelands (92), I-7, Scholomance

EENIX
Venture Co. Merchant, Stonetalon Mountains (70), G-5, Windshear Crag, In mountains, west of the river

EHENA
Horde Cloth Quartermaster, Orgrimmar (60), D:(8, 9), Valley of Spirit, Darkbriar Lodge

EJREK
Dun Morogh (32), C-6, Chill Breeze Valley, Outside troll hut

ELDAN LIGHTFOOT
Leather Armor Merchant, Elwynn Forest (42), C-7, Westbrook Garrison, First floor armory in garrison

ELINDE STARSONG
Duskwood (36), J-8, Roland's Doom, (Summon) Dirt pile

ELMA WARNAM
Undead Horse Riding Instructor, Tirisfal Glades (86), H-5, Brill (104), Stable

ELORA NITELY
Undercity (88), I-4, The Trade Quarter, Upper Ring of Trade Quarter

EL'RIN FANG
Durotar (34), H-7, Sen'jin Village (123), Structure left of big hut

ENDOR-TRON 1000
Desolace (30), H-4, Spawns when caravan is at Kormek's hut

ENGEFUL ANCIENT
Rare Spawn, Stonetalon Mountains (70), C-7, D-7, The Charred Vale, Lvl 29 Uncommon; Roams the vale

ENGEFUL SURGE
Arathi Highlands (10), E-8

ENOM BELCHER
Eastern Plaguelands (40), D-2, Stratholme

ENOM MIST LURKER
Western Plaguelands (92), C-6, D:(5-7), E:(6, 7), The Bulwark

ENOM WEB SPIDER
Duskwood (36), A:(3-7), B:(3, 7), C-3, D-3, E-2, F-2, G-2, H-2, I-2, J-2, K-2, The Darkened Bank

ENOMHIDE RAVASAUR
Un'Goro Crater (90), H:(5, 6), I:(5, 6), J:(5, 6), The Marshlands

ENOMLASH SCORPID
Badlands (16), G-1, Uldaman

ENOMOUS CLOUD SERPENT
Thousand Needles (82), B:(2, 4), C:(3-5), D-5, E:(5, 6), G:(5, 6), Camp E'thok, Darkcloud Pinnacle, The Screeching Canyon

ENOMTAIL SCORPID
Durotar (34), E:(3, 5, 6), F:(2, 3, 5), G-2, H:(1, 2)

ENOMTIP SCORPID
Burning Steppes (22), J-3, K:(2, 3, 5, 6), L:(3-6), Dreadmaul Rock

ENTURE CO. BUILDER
Stonetalon Mountains (70), H-4, Cragpool Lake

ENTURE CO. DEFORESTER
Stonetalon Mountains (70), H:(4, 5), I:(4-6), J:(5, 6), Blackwolf River, Cragpool Lake, Windshear Crag

ENTURE CO. DRONE
Westfall (94), I-7, Circles tower

ENTURE CO. DRONE
Barrens (18), F-1, Patrols outside tower northeast of Sludge Fen

VENTURE CO. DRUDGER
Barrens (18), F-1, G-1, The Sludge Fen

VENTURE CO. ENFORCER
Barrens (18), G-1, H-1, Boulder Lode Mine

VENTURE CO. ENGINEER
Stonetalon Mountains (70), H-4, Cragpool Lake

VENTURE CO. FOREMAN
Stranglethorn Vale (74), D:(4, 5)

VENTURE CO. GEOLOGIST
Stranglethorn Vale (74), B-1, D:(2, 3), E:(2, 3)

VENTURE CO. HIRELING
Mulgore (58), F:(6, 7), Winterhoof Water Well

VENTURE CO. LABORER
Mulgore (58), E:(4, 5), F:(5, 7), Ravaged Caravan, Thunderhorn Water Well, Winterhoof Water Well

VENTURE CO. LOGGER
Stonetalon Mountains (70), H:(4, 5), I:(4-6), J:(5, 6), Blackwolf River, Cragpool Lake, Windshear Crag

VENTURE CO. LOOKOUT
Barrens (18), F-1

VENTURE CO. LUMBERJACK
Stranglethorn Vale (74), E-2

VENTURE CO. MACHINE SMITH
Stonetalon Mountains (70), H-4, Cragpool Lake

VENTURE CO. MECHANIC
Stranglethorn Vale (74), B-1, D-2, E-2

VENTURE CO. MERCENARY
Barrens (18), G-1, The Sludge Fen

VENTURE CO. MINER
Stranglethorn Vale (74), B-1, C-1

VENTURE CO. OPERATOR
Stonetalon Mountains (70), H-5, I:(4, 5), J:(5, 6), Blackwolf River, Cragpool Lake, Windshear Crag

VENTURE CO. OVERSEER
Barrens (18), G-1, H-1, Boulder Lode Mine

VENTURE CO. PATROLLER
Barrens (18), F-1

VENTURE CO. PEON
Barrens (18), F-1

VENTURE CO. SHREDDER
Stranglethorn Vale (74), E:(2, 3)

VENTURE CO. STRIP MINER
Stranglethorn Vale (74), D:(4, 5)

VENTURE CO. SUPERVISOR
Mulgore (58), D-2, E-1, G:(3-5), H:(4, 5), The Venture Co. Mine, Wildmane Water Well

VENTURE CO. SURVEYOR
Stranglethorn Vale (74), D:(4, 5)

VENTURE CO. TASKMASTER
Mulgore (58), E:(4, 5), F-5, Ravaged Caravan, Stonebull Lake, Thunderhorn Water Well

VENTURE CO. TINKERER
Stranglethorn Vale (74), D:(4, 5)

VENTURE CO. WORKBOSS
Stranglethorn Vale (74), B-1, E-2

VENTURE CO. WORKER
Mulgore (58), D:(1, 2), E-1, G:(4, 5), H:(3-5), The Venture Co. Mine, Wildmane Water Well

VENYA MARTHAND
Tirisfal Glades (86), C-7, Deathknell (109), Church

VERA NIGHTSHADE
Ashenvale (12), I-6, Splintertree Post (126), Sitting in inn

VERDAN THE EVERLIVING
Barrens (18), E-4, Wailing Caverns

VERDANTINE BOUGHGUARD
The Hinterlands (50), I:(2, 3), J:(1-3), Seradane

VERDANTINE ORACLE
The Hinterlands (50), I:(2, 3), J:(1-3), Seradane

VERDANTINE TREE WARDER
The Hinterlands (50), I:(2, 3), J:(1-3), Seradane

VEREK
Burning Steppes (22), Searing Gorge (64), C-4/D-8, Blackrock Depths

VEREN TAILSTRIDER
Thunder Bluff (84), E-4, Middle rise, inside Thunder Bluff Armorers tent

VERIFONIX
Rare Spawn, Stranglethorn Vale (74), D-6, The Cape of Stranglethorn, Lvl 42 Average Rare; Patrols a circular path around ridgeline stopping periodically to mine

VERNA FURLBROW
Westfall (94), G-2, The Jansen Stead, Cart near Old Blanchy

VERNER OSGOOD
Redridge Mountains (62), D-5, Lakeshire (115), Stable

VERNON HALE
Bait and Tackle Supplier, Redridge Mountains (62), C-5, Lakeshire (115), Behind shed near docks on western side of town

VEROG THE DERVISH
Barrens (18), F-4, Spawns on structure west of Stagnant Oasis

VERON AMBERSTILL
Ram Breeder, Dun Morogh (32), I-5, Amberstill Ranch, By carriage in front of corral

VESPRYSTUS
Hippogryph Master, Teldrassil (80), G-9, Rut'theran Village, By Hipporgryphs

VEXSPINDLE
Cloth & Leather Armor Merchant, Barrens (18), H-4, Ratchet (121), Plate-n-Chain

VEYZHAK THE CANNIBAL
Rare Spawn, Swamp of Sorrows (76), I-5, The Temple of Atal'Hakkar, Lvl 48 Uncommon

VHAN
Journeyman Tailor, Thunder Bluff (84), E-4, Middle rise, inside Thunder Bluff Armorers tent

VHARR
Superior Weaponsmith, Stranglethorn Vale (74), C-3, Grom'gol Base Camp (112), Next to forge

VICIOUS FALLOUT
Dun Morogh (32), C-4, Gnomeregan

VICIOUS GRAY BEAR
Hillsbrad Foothills (48), D:(3, 4), E:(3-5), F:(3-5), G-4, H-4, I:(3-5), J-5, Thoughout Hillsbrad

VICIOUS GRELL
Teldrassil (80), F-5, G-5, Fel Rock

VICIOUS NIGHT WEB SPIDER
Tirisfal Glades (86), K:(5, 6), L:(5, 6), Venomweb Vale

VICIOUS OWLBEAST
The Hinterlands (50), D:(5-7), E:(4-6), F:(4, 5), The Hinterlands

VICTOR BARTHOLOMEW
Undercity (88), K-1, The Magic Quarter, Green circle west of Skull Building

VICTOR WARD
Journeyman Tailor, Undercity (88), J-3, The Magic Quarter

VIDRA HEARTHSTOVE
Loch Modan (54), D-5, Thelsamar (129), Stoutlager Inn

VIKKI LONSAV
General Goods, Arathi Highlands (10), F-5, Refuge Point, Camp

VIKTORI PRISM'ANTRAS
Duskwood (36), K-5, Darkshire (108), First house on left side of road heading into Darkshire from the east

VILE BAT
Silverpine Forest (68), F-7, Shadowfang Keep

VILE FAMILIAR
Durotar (34), F-5, G:(5, 6), Burning Blade Coven, Valley of Trials (131)

VILE FIN LAKESTALKER
Silverpine Forest (68), J:(2, 4, 5), K-2, The Dawning Isles

VILE FIN MINOR ORACLE
Tirisfal Glades (86), B-4, C:(4, 5), D-4, E-3, G-3, H-3, I:(2, 3), J-3, Whispering Shore, Coast

VILE FIN MUCKDWELLER
Tirisfal Glades (86), B-4, C:(4, 5), D-4, E-3, H-3, I:(2, 3), J-3

VILE FIN ORACLE
Silverpine Forest (68), J:(2, 4, 5), K-2, The Dawning Isles

VILE FIN PUDDLEJUMPER
Tirisfal Glades (86), C:(4, 5), D-4, G-3, H-3, Whispering Shore, Coast

VILE FIN SHORECREEPER
Silverpine Forest (68), K-3, L-3, The Dawning Isles

VILE FIN SHREDDER
Silverpine Forest (68), H:(2, 3), I:(1-3), J-1, The Shining Strand

VILE FIN TIDECALLER
Silverpine Forest (68), K-3, L-3, The Dawning Isles

VILE FIN TIDEHUNTER
Silverpine Forest (68), H:(2, 3), I:(1-3), J-1, The Shining Strand

VILE LARVA
Desolace (30), D-5, Mauradon

VILE OOZE
Felwood (44), E-5, Shadow Hold

VILE PRIESTESS HEXX
The Hinterlands (50), I-8, Jintha'Alor, Patrols between altar and cave entrance

VILE SLIME
Western Plaguelands (92), H-4, I:(3, 4), The Wheeping Cave

VILE SPRITE
Darkshore (24), G-4, Bashal'Aran

VILE STING
Thousand Needles (82), I-7, J-7, The Shimmering Flats, Roams west side of Shimmering Flats, near old camp

VILE TUTOR
Cult of the Damned, Eastern Plaguelands (40), H:(6, 7), Corin's Crossing

VILE'REL
Burning Steppes (22), Searing Gorge (64), C-4/D-8, Blackrock Depths

VILEBRANCH AMAN'ZASI GUARD
The Hinterlands (50), H:(7, 8), I-8, J-8, Jintha'Alor

VILEBRANCH AMBUSHER
The Hinterlands (50), J-6, Jintha'Alor

VILEBRANCH AXE THROWER
The Hinterlands (50), F:(6, 7), G:(6, 7), The Altar of Zul

VILEBRANCH BERSERKER
The Hinterlands (50), I:(6, 7), J-7, Jintha'Alor

VILEBRANCH BLOOD DRINKER
The Hinterlands (50), I:(6-8), J-8, Jintha'Alor

VILEBRANCH HEADHUNTER
The Hinterlands (50), J-7, Jintha'Alor

VILEBRANCH HIDESKINNER
The Hinterlands (50), I:(6-8), J:(7, 8), Jintha'Alor

VILEBRANCH KIDNAPPER
The Hinterlands (50), L-4, The Hinterlands, Island off coast

VILEBRANCH RAIDING WOLF
The Hinterlands (50), I:(6-8), Jintha'Alor

VILEBRANCH SCALPER
The Hinterlands (50), G:(6, 7), H:(4, 6), J:(4, 5), K-5, Shaol'Watha

VILEBRANCH SHADOW HUNTER
The Hinterlands (50), I:(6-8), J-7, Jintha'Alor

VILEBRANCH SHADOWCASTER
The Hinterlands (50), I:(6, 7), J:(6, 7), Jintha'Alor

VILEBRANCH SOOTHSAYER
The Hinterlands (50), G:(6, 7), H-4, J-4, K-5, Shaol'Watha

VILEBRANCH SOUL EATER
The Hinterlands (50), I:(6-8), J-8, Jintha'Alor

VILEBRANCH WARRIOR
The Hinterlands (50), I-6, J:(6, 7), Jintha'Alor

VILEBRANCH WITCH DOCTOR
The Hinterlands (50), G-7, I-6, J-7, Jintha'Alor

VILEBRANCH WOLF PUP
The Hinterlands (50), F-7, G:(6, 7), H-6, I:(6, 7), J-7, Jintha'Alor

VINASIA
Cloth Armor Merchant, Darnassus (26), H-7, Tradesmen's Terrace, Cloth Armor shop

VINCENT HYAL
Wetlands (96), A-6, Deepwater Tavern, First floor

VINNA WAYNE
Hillsbrad Foothills (48), H-2, Tarren Mill (128), Graveyard

VIRA YOUNGHOOF
First Aid Trainer, Mulgore (58), E-6, Bloodhoof Village (102), Inn

VIVIANNA
Trade Supplies, Feralas (46), C-4, Feathermoon Stronghold (110), Inn

VIZNIK GOLDGRUBBER
Banker, Stranglethorn Vale (74), B-8, Booty Bay (103), Stranglethorn Trust Bank

VIZZKLICK
Tailoring Supplies, Tanaris (78), G-3, Gadgetzan (111), Outside western structure

VOGGAH DEATHGRIP
Alterac Mountains (8), I-6, Camp outside Alterac Valley

VOICE OF ELUNE
Winterspring (98), J-6, Owl Wing Thicket, (Summon) Altar

VOL'JIN
Boss, Orgrimmar (60), C-4, Valley of Wisdom, Grommash Hold

VOLCHAN
Rare Spawn, Burning Steppes (22), K-6, Terror Wing Path, Lvl 60 Uncommon; Patrols a circular path around Dreadmaul Rock to the east

VOLCOR
Darkshore (24), G-8, Blackwood Den, Sitting in cave

VOLOREN
Fishing Supplier, Darnassus (26), F-5, Tradesmen's Terrace, Dock

VOODOO TROLL
Durotar (34), J:(8, 9), Echo Isles

VORLUS VILEHOOF
Teldrassil (80), F-6, Moonwell in hills

VORN SKYSEER
Mulgore (58), E-8, Camp Narache (105), Southwest tent

VORREL SENGUTZ
Tirisfal Glades (86), K-3, L-3, Scarlet Monastery

VORSHA THE LASHER
Ashenvale (12), A-3, The Zoram Strand (131), Off coast northwest of outpost

VOSUR BRAKTHEL
Journeyman Alchemist, Ironforge (52), I-5, Tinker Town, Berryfizz's Potions and Mixed Drinks

VRANG WILDGORE
Weaponsmith & Armorcrafter, Barrens (18), E-1, Small inlet among hills

VROK BLUNDERBLAST
Gunsmith, Loch Modan (54), D-4, Thelsamar (129), Porch of house on hill on left of path

VULTROS
Rare Spawn, Westfall (94), C-7, E-4, E-6, F-2, G-7, H-6, The Dead Acre, The Dust Plains, Furlbrow's Pumpkin Farm, Stendel's Pond, Westfall, Lvl 26 Average Rare; Roams around spawn points

VYRIN SWIFTWIND
Loch Modan (54), K-6, The Farstrider Lodge, Rear of lodge

W

WAILING ANCESTOR
Tirisfal Glades (86), F-3, G-3, Agamand Mills (100)

WAILING BANSHEE
Eastern Plaguelands (40), D-2, Stratholme

WAILING DEATH
Western Plaguelands (92), H:(5, 6), I:(5, 6), Gahrron's Withering

WAILING GUARDSMAN
Silverpine Forest (68), F-7, Shadowfang Keep

WAILING HIGHBORNE
Darkshore (24), F-6, G-6, Ameth'Aran

WAILING SPECTRE
Deadwind Pass (28), C:(6-8), D:(7, 8), E:(7-9), F-8, Karazhan, Morgan's Plot

WALDOR
Journeyman Leatherworker, Barrens (18), E-4, The Wailing Caverns, Right eye of cave above entrance

WALDOR
Journeyman Leatherworker, Barrens (18), E-4, Wailing Caverns

WALLACE THE BLIND
Weaponsmith, Silverpine Forest (68), G-8, The Greymane Wall, Under scaffolding along left side of wall

WALTER ELLINGSON
Heavy Armor Merchant, Undercity (88), I-4, The Magic Quarter, Upper Ring of Trade Quarter

WANDERING BARRENS GIRAFFE
Barrens (18), E:(4-6), F:(5, 6)

WANDERING EYE OF KILROGG
Feralas (46), G-4, Dire Maul

WANDERING PROTECTOR
Ashenvale (12), H-4

WANDERING SKELETON
Western Plaguelands (92), F-5, Dalson's Tears, Patrols path around outhouse

WANDERING SPIRIT
Tirisfal Glades (86), J-6, Balnir Farmstead

WAR GOLEM
Rare Spawn, Badlands (16), G:(1, 3), H-3, Angor Fortress, Hammertoe's Digsite, The Maker's Terrace, Lvl 36 Semi-Rare; Roams small area around spawn point

WAR MASTER VOONE
Burning Steppes (22), Searing Gorge (64), C-4/D-8, Blackrock Spire

WAR PARTY KODO
Thousand Needles (82), I-6, Ironstone Camp, Camp just west of Shimmering Flats

WAR REAVER
Burning Steppes (22), F-4, G:(3, 4), H:(3, 4), I-4, Ruins of Thourissan

WARBRINGER CONSTRUCT
Burning Steppes (22), Searing Gorge (64), C-4/D-8, Blackrock Depths

WARCALLER GORLACH
Orgrimmar (60), Valley of Wisdom, Roams most of Orgrimmar (except for Valley of Honor)

WARCHIEF REND BLACKHAND
Burning Steppes (22), Searing Gorge (64), C-4/D-8, Blackrock Spire

WARD GUARDIAN
Barrens (18), E-9, Razorfen Kraul

WARDEN BELAMOORE
Alterac Mountains (8), B-8, Lordamere Internment Camp, Third floor of building left of camp

WARDEN THELWATER
Stormwind (72), F-6, The Canals, Top of steps to stockade

WARDER STILGISS
Burning Steppes (22), Searing Gorge (64), C-4/D-8, Blackrock Depths

WARG DEEPWATER
Fisherman, Loch Modan (54), E-4, The Loch, In front of house on the western shore of loch

WARLEADER KRAZZILAK
Tanaris (78), F-3, Sandsorrow Watch, Atop watchtower

WARLORD GORETOOTH
Badlands (16), A-5, Kargath (114), Tower platform

WARLORD KOLKANIS
Rare Spawn, Durotar (34), F-8, Kolkar Crag, Lvl 9 Uncommon; Outside hut (left as you enter, middle of chasm to right, or in the back)

WARLORD KRELLIAN
Azshara (14), E-5, Temple of Zin-Malor, Dais in main temple

WARLORD KROM'ZAR
Barrens (18), E-3, Spawns near orc bunkers

WARLORD THRESH'JIN
Rare Spawn, Eastern Plaguelands (40), I-2, J-2, Mazra'Alor, Zul'Mashar, Lvl 58 Uncommon; Stands idle at spawn point

WARMASTER LAGGROND
Frostwolf Clan, Alterac Mountains (8), I-6, Alterac Valley, Cave

WAROSH
Burning Steppes (22), Searing Gorge (64), C-4/D-8, Blackrock Spire

WARPWOOD CRUSHER
Feralas (46), G-4, Dire Maul

WARPWOOD GUARDIAN
Feralas (46), G-4, Dire Maul

WARPWOOD MOSS FLAYER
Felwood (44), G-2, H:(2, 3), Irontree Cavern, Irontree Woods

WARPWOOD SHREDDER
Felwood (44), G-2, H:(2, 3), Irontree Cavern, Irontree Woods

WARPWOOD STOMPER
Feralas (46), G-4, Dire Maul

WARPWOOD TANGLER
Feralas (46), G-4, Dire Maul

WARPWOOD TREANT
Feralas (46), G-4, Dire Maul

WARSONG OUTRIDER
Ashenvale (12), L-5, Nightsong Woods, Southfury River, Warsong Lumber Camp

WARSONG RUNNER
Ashenvale (12), B-4, The Zoram Strand (131), Zoram'gar Outpost (131)

WARSONG SCOUT
Ashenvale (12), I-6, Nightsong Woods, Splintertree Post (126)

WARSONG SHREDDER
Ashenvale (12), I-7, K-5, Nightsong Woods, Warsong Labor Camp, Warsong Lumber Camp

WARUG
Desolace (30), J-7, Magram Village, Northeast of pool

WARUG'S BODYGUARD
Desolace (30), J-7, Magram Village, Northeast of pool

WASHTE PAWNE
Barrens (18), D-8, E:(7-8), Blackthorn Ridge, Southern Barrens, Roams clearing near Blackthorn Ridge

WASTEWANDER ASSASSIN
Tanaris (78), H-4, I:(3, 4), J-4, Waterspring Field, Wavestrider Beach

WASTEWANDER BANDIT
Tanaris (78), I:(2-4), Noonshade Ruins, Waterspring Field, Wavestrider Beach

WASTEWANDER ROGUE
Tanaris (78), H-4, I:(3, 4), Waterspring Field, Wavestrider Beach

WASTEWANDER SCOFFLAW
Tanaris (78), J-4, Wavestrider Beach

WASTEWANDER SHADOW MAGE
Tanaris (78), H-4, I:(2-4), J-4, Noonshade Ruins, Waterspring Field, Wavestrider Beach

WASTEWANDER THIEF
Tanaris (78), I:(2-4), Noonshade Ruins, Waterspring Field, Wavestrider Beach

WATCH COMMANDER ZALAPHIL
Rare Spawn, Durotar (34), I-6, Tiragarde Keep, Lvl 9 Uncommon; Receiving room of castle

WATCHER BACKUS
The Night Watch, Duskwood (36), J-4, Darkshire (108), Patrols between the north edge of Darkshire and the road up to the fork (J-3)

WATCHER BIGGS
Swamp of Sorrows (76), C-6, Idle next to carriage in southwestern swamp land

WATCHER BROWNELL
The Night Watch, Duskwood (36), J-4, Darkshire (108), Outside on the right of the Scarlet Raven Inn

WATCHER BUKOURIS
Duskwood (36), J-5

WATCHER CALLAHAN
The Night Watch, Duskwood (36), K-2, By carriage

WATCHER CORWIN
Duskwood (36), J-5, Darkshire (108)

WATCHER CUTFORD
Duskwood (36), J-5, F-6, Darkshire (108), Roams road

WATCHER DODDS
The Night Watch, Duskwood (36), F-7, By felled log in camp

WATCHER FRAZER
Duskwood (36), J-5, Darkshire (108)

WATCHER GELWIN
Duskwood (36), J-5, Darkshire (108), Patrols road from Darkshire to Rotting Orchard

WATCHER HARTIN
Duskwood (36), J-4, Darkshire (108)

WATCHER HUTCHINS
Duskwood (36), F-7, Darkshire (108)

WATCHER JAN
Duskwood (36), K-5, Darkshire (108)

WATCHER JORDEN
Duskwood (36), J-5, J-6, Darkshire (108), Roams road

WATCHER KEEFER
Duskwood (36), J-5, Darkshire (108)

WATCHER KELLER
Duskwood (36), K-4, Darkshire (108)

WATCHER LADIMORE
The Night Watch, Duskwood (36), J-5, Darkshire (108), Patrols around the center of town

WATCHER MAHAR BA
Blasted Lands (20), J-2, Nethergarde Keep (119), Top floor of tower facing entrance of keep

WATCHER MERANT
Duskwood (36), J-5, Darkshire (108), Patrols road from Darkshire to Rotting Orchard

WATCHER MOCARSKI
Duskwood (36), J-5, Darkshire (108)

WATCHER PAIGE
Duskwood (36), F-7, Darkshire (108), Crossroad south of Twilight Grove

WATCHER PETRAS
Duskwood (36), K-5, I-4, Darkshire (108), Roams road

WATCHER ROYCE
Duskwood (36), K-5, Darkshire (108)

WATCHER SARYS
Duskwood (36), J-5, Darkshire (108)

WATCHER SELKIN
Duskwood (36), J-5, Darkshire (108), Patrols road from Darkshire to Rotting Orchard

WATCHER THAYER
Duskwood (36), J-5, Darkshire (108), Patrols road from Darkshire to Rotting Orchard

WATCHER WOLLPERT
Duskwood (36), K-5, Darkshire (108)

WATCHMAN DOOMGRIP
Burning Steppes (22), Searing Gorge (64), C-4/D-8, Blackrock Depths

WATCHMASTER SORIGAL
Duskwood (36), K-5, Darkshire (108), By barrel filled carriage on the right side of road heading into Darkshire from the east

WATER SPIRIT
Silverpine Forest (68), F-4, The Tides Run, Coast of pond

WATERY INVADER
Winterspring (98), H-4, Lake Kel'Theril

WAVE STRIDER
Feralas (46), C-3, D:(3-5), E:(5-7), The Forgotten Coast

WAVETHRASHER
Azshara (14), G-4, H:(3, 4), I:(3, 4), J-4, K:(3, 4), L:(2-4)

WEAPON TECHNICIAN
Burning Steppes (22), Searing Gorge (64), C-4/D-8, Blackrock Depths

WEAVER
Swamp of Sorrows (76), I-5, The Temple of Atal'Hakkar

WEBWOOD LURKER
Teldrassil (80), F:(5, 6), G:(5, 6), H:(5, 6), I-6, Dolanaar (109), Lake Al'Ameth, Starbreeze Village

WEBWOOD SILKSPINNER
Teldrassil (80), D-3, E:(3-5), F:(3, 4), The Oracle Glade, Wellspring Lake, Wellspring River

WEBWOOD SPIDER
Teldrassil (80), G:(2, 3), H-3, Shadowglen (124), Shadowthread Cave

WEBWOOD VENOMFANG
Teldrassil (80), D-5, E:(5-8), F:(7, 8), G:(7, 8), H-7

WELDON BAROV
House of Barov, Western Plaguelands (92), F-8, Chillwind Camp, By well

WENDIGO
Dun Morogh (32), E:(4, 5), F-5, The Grizzled Den

WENIKEE BOLTBUCKET
Barrens (18), F-1, Outside tower near Ashenvale border

WENNA SILKBEARD
Special Goods Dealer, Wetlands (96), C-3, Sundown Marsh, Building next to windmill

WERG THICKBLADE
Leatherworking Supplies, Tirisfal Glades (86), K-7, The Bulwark, Camp on left side of road

WERG THICKBLADE
Western Plaguelands (92), C-6, The Bulwark

WESLEY
Stable Master, Hillsbrad Foothills (48), F-6, Southshore (125), Right of inn by mailbox

WESTFALL WOODWORKER
Westfall (94), F-5, Sentinel Hill (123)

WETLANDS CROCOLISK
Wetlands (96), B:(3, 5, 6), C:(3, 4, 6), D:(2, 3), E:(3, 4), F:(3, 4), G-4

WHARFMASTER DIZZYWIG
Barrens (18), H-4, Ratchet (121), Dock

WHARFMASTER LOZGIL
Stranglethorn Vale (74), B-8, Booty Bay (103), On dock near ship launch on the northern side of bay

WHIP LASHER
Feralas (46), G-4, Dire Maul

WHIRLING INVADER
Silithus (66), D:(1, 2), E:(1, 2), The Crystal Vale, Ravaged Twilight Base Camp

WHIRLWIND RIPPER
Desolace (30), D-7, E:(2-4, 6-8), F:(1-4, 7), G:(2-4, 6, 7), H:(3, 4, 6), I:(5-7), J:(5, 6)

WHIRLWIND SHREDDER
Desolace (30), C:(7, 8), D:(7, 8), E-8, F-9, G:(8, 9), H:(7-9), Gelkis Village, Mannoroc Coven, Sar'theris Strand

WHIRLWIND STORMWALKER
Desolace (30), D-4, E:(4-6), F:(4-6), G:(4, 5), H:(4-6), J:(1, 4, 5), K:(2, 4, 5)

WHISKEY SLIM
Blackwater Raiders, Stranglethorn Vale (74), B-8, Booty Bay (103), First floor of The Salty Sailor Tavern

WHIT WANTMAL
Duskwood (36), K-4, Darkshire (108), First house on the right side of road heading into Darkshire from the east

WHUUT
Journeyman Alchemist, Orgrimmar (60), G-3, The Drag, Yelmak's Alchemy and Potions

WIGCIK
Superior Fisherman, Stranglethorn Vale (74), B-8, Booty Bay (103), In building on first level along the southern side of the bay

WIK'TAR
Fish Merchant & Supplies, Ashenvale (12), B-4, Zoram'gar Outpost (131), Outside western structure

WILD BUCK
Ashenvale (12), B:(2-4), C:(2-4), D:(2-4)

WILD GRELL
Darkshore (24), G-4, Bashal'Aran

WILD GRYPHON
Hillsbrad Foothills (48), J-3, K:(3, 4), Durnholde Keep, Behind keep

WILDER THISTLENETTLE
Stormwind (72), J-2, Dwarven District, Tavern

WILDHAMMER SENTRY
The Hinterlands (50), B-5, Aerie Peak (100)

WILDSPAWN BETRAYER
Feralas (46), G-4, Dire Maul

WILDSPAWN FELSWORN
Feralas (46), G-4, Dire Maul

WILDSPAWN HELLCALLER
Feralas (46), G-4, Dire Maul

WILDSPAWN IMP
Feralas (46), G-4, Dire Maul

WILDSPAWN ROGUE
Feralas (46), G-4, Dire Maul

WILDSPAWN SATYR
Feralas (46), G-4, Dire Maul

WILDSPAWN SHADOWSTALKER
Feralas (46), G-4, Dire Maul

WILDSPAWN TRICKSTER
Feralas (46), G-4, Dire Maul

WILDTHORN LURKER
Ashenvale (12), J:(5, 6), K:(4-6), L:(5, 6)

WILDTHORN STALKER
Ashenvale (12), B-5, C:(4-6), D:(4-6), E:(3-6), F:(4, 5), H:(7, 8), I:(7, 8), J:(6, 7)

WILDTHORN VENOMSPITTER
Ashenvale (12), G:(6, 7), H:(5-7), I:(5, 6)

WILEY THE BLACK
Redridge Mountains (62), C-4, Lakeshire (115), Second floor of Lakeshire Inn

WILHELM STRANG
Mail Armor Merchant, Stormwind (72), K-5, Old Town, Limited Immunity

WILLIAM MACGREGOR
Bowyer, Westfall (94), G-5, Sentinel Hill (123), At intersection east of the Sentinel Tower

WILLIAM MONTAGUE
Banker, Undercity (88), I-4, The Trade Quarter

WILLIAM PESTLE
Elwynn Forest (42), F-7, Goldshire (112), First floor of Lion's Pride Inn

WILLIDEN MARSHAL
Un'Goro Crater (90), F-1, Marshal's Refuge (116), Entrance to cave

WILLIX THE IMPORTER
Barrens (18), E-9, Razorfen Kraul

WILLOW
Twilight's Hammer, Desolace (30), H-4, Kormek's Hut, Inside hut

WILMA RANTHAL
Skinning Trainer, Redridge Mountains (62), L-7, Camp

WIND HOWLER
Barrens (18), E-9, Razorfen Kraul

WINDFURY HARPY
Mulgore (58), C-4, D-4, H-7, The Rolling Plains

WINDFURY MATRIARCH
Mulgore (58), C:(2, 3), D-1, F-1, G:(1, 2), The Golden Plains, Windfury Ridge

WINDFURY SORCERESS
Mulgore (58), C:(2, 3), D-1, F-1, G:(1, 2), The Golden Plains, Windfury Ridge

WINDFURY WIND WITCH
Mulgore (58), C-4, D-4, H-7, The Rolling Plains

WINDSHEAR DIGGER
Stonetalon Mountains (70), I-6, J-6, Blackwolf River, Windshear Crag, Windshear Mine

WINDSHEAR GEOMANCER
Stonetalon Mountains (70), I-6, J-6, Blackwolf River, Windshear Crag, Windshear Mine

WINDSHEAR OVERLORD
Stonetalon Mountains (70), I-6, J-6, Blackwolf River, Windshear Crag, Windshear Mine

WINDSHEAR STONECUTTER
Stonetalon Mountains (70), I-6, Windshear Mine

WINDSHEAR TUNNEL RAT
Stonetalon Mountains (70), I-6, Windshear Mine

WINDSHEAR VERMIN
Stonetalon Mountains (70), I-6, Windshear Mine

WINIFRED KERWIN
Undercity (88), K-1, The Magic Quarter, Green circle west of Skull Building

WINKEY
Tanaris (78), I-6, Southbreak Shore, Small island off coast

WINNA HAZZARD
Felwood (44), E-5, Bloodvenom Post, Up hill

WINSTONE WOLFE
, Hillsbrad Foothills (48), K-2, , First floor of Chateau Ravenholdt

WINTER WOLF
Dun Morogh (32), D-4, E-5, F:(4, 5), G:(4, 5), Iceflow Lake, Kharanos (114), Steelgrill's Depot

WINTERFALL AMBUSHER
Winterspring (98), E-4, Timbermaw Post

WINTERFALL DEN WATCHER
Winterspring (98), D-4, E-4, F-4, J:(3, 4), Timbermaw Post, Timbermaw Village

WINTERFALL PATHFINDER
Winterspring (98), E:(3, 4), F-4, Timbermaw Post

WINTERFALL RUNNER
Felwood (44), H-1, Felpaw Village, Northwest camp

WINTERFALL RUNNER
Winterspring (98), D-3, Roams between Felwood entrance and Winterfall Village

WINTERFALL SHAMAN
Winterspring (98), J:(3, 4), Winterspring Village

WINTERFALL TOTEMIC
Winterspring (98), D-4, E-4, F-4, Timbermaw Post

WINTERFALL URSA
Winterspring (98), J-4, Winterspring Village

WINTERSPRING OWL
Winterspring (98), H:(3, 5), I:(3-5), J:(3-5)

WINTERSPRING SCREECHER
Winterspring (98), H-2, I:(1-3, 5, 6)

WIRY SWOOP
Mulgore (58), D:(5-8), E-7, F:(6, 7), G:(6, 7), Palemane Rock, Stonebull Lake, Winterhoof Water Well

WITCH DOCTOR JIN'ZIL
Stonetalon Mountains (70), J-9, Malaka'jin, Inside den

WITCH DOCTOR MAU'RI
Orgrimmar (60), D-8, Valley of Spirit, On center stepping stone in pond

WITCH DOCTOR UNBAGWA
Stranglethorn Vale (74), C-6, Spirit Den, Cave

WITCH DOCTOR UZER'I
Feralas (46), I-4, Camp Mojache (105), Outside big western tent

WITCH DOCTOR ZUM'RAH
Tanaris (78), E-1, Zul'Farrak

WITCHWING AMBUSHER
Barrens (18), D:(1, 2), The Dry Hills

WITCHWING HARPY
Barrens (18), D:(1, 2), E:(1, 2), The Dry Hills

WITCHWING ROGUEFEATHER
Barrens (18), D:(1, 2), E:(1, 2), The Dry Hills

WITCHWING SLAYER
Barrens (18), D:(1, 2), The Dry Hills

WITCHWING WINDCALLER
Barrens (18), D:(1, 2), The Dry Hills

WITHERBARK AXE THROWER
Arathi Highlands (10), H-7, I:(6, 7), J-6, Witherbark Village

WITHERBARK BERSERKER
Arathi Highlands (10), C:(6, 7)

WITHERBARK BROODGUARD
The Hinterlands (50), D-7, E:(6, 7), F:(6, 7), Shadra'Alor

WITHERBARK CALLER
The Hinterlands (50), E:(7, 8), F:(6, 7), Shadra'Alor

WITHERBARK HEADHUNTER
Arathi Highlands (10), H-7, I:(7, 8), J:(4, 6-8), K-4, Witherbark Village

WITHERBARK HIDESKINNER
The Hinterlands (50), D-6, E-6, Hiri'Watha

WITHERBARK SADIST
The Hinterlands (50), E:(6, 7), F-7, Shadra'Alor

WITHERBARK SCALPER
The Hinterlands (50), C:(5, 6), D:(5, 6), Zan'Watha

WITHERBARK SHADOW HUNTER
Arathi Highlands (10), I-8, J:(7, 8), Witherbark Village

WITHERBARK SHADOWCASTER
Arathi Highlands (10), D:(4-5), E:(4-5), J-4, K-4, Witherbark Village

WITHERBARK TROLL
Arathi Highlands (10), D:(4, 5), E:(4, 5), J-4, K-4, Witherbark Village

WITHERBARK VENOMBLOOD
The Hinterlands (50), D-6, E-6, Hiri'Watha

WITHERBARK WITCH DOCTOR
Arathi Highlands (10), D:(4, 5), H-7, I:(6, 7), J:(6, 7), Witherbark Village

WITHERBARK ZEALOT
The Hinterlands (50), C-6, D:(5, 6), Zan'Watha

WITHERED ANCIENT
Ashenvale (12), G:(3, 4), H:(4, 5), Nightsong Woods, Raynewood Retreat

WITHERED BATTLE BOAR
Barrens (18), F-9, Razorfen Downs

WITHERED PROTECTOR
Felwood (44), G-3, Irontree Woods

WITHERED QUILGUARD
Barrens (18), F-9, Razorfen Downs

WITHERED REAVER
Barrens (18), F-9, Razorfen Downs

WITHERED SPEARHIDE
Barrens (18), F-9, Razorfen Downs

WITHERED WARRIOR
Barrens (18), F-9, Razorfen Downs

WITHERHEART THE STALKER
Rare Spawn, The Hinterlands (50), E-7, Shadra'Alor, Lvl 45 Semi-Rare; Patrols while stealthed around small pond

WITHERVINE BARK RIPPER
Dustwallow Marsh (38), D:(2, 3, 5), E:(2-4), F-2, G:(2, 3), H-2, Bluefen, Brackenwall Village (104), The Quagmire

WITHERVINE CREEPER
Dustwallow Marsh (38), D-2, E-2, F-2, G:(2, 3), H-2, Bluefen

WITHERVINE MIRE BEAST
Dustwallow Marsh (38), D:(3, 5), E:(3-6), F:(5, 6), The Dragonmurk, The Quagmire

WITHERVINE RAGER
Dustwallow Marsh (38), D-5, E:(5, 6), F:(5, 6), The Dragonmurk, The Quagmire

WIXXRAK
Weaponsmith & Gunsmith, Winterspring (98), I-4, Everlook (110), Inside northeast building

WIZBANG CRANKTOGGLE
Darkshore (24), F-4, Auberdine (101), Third floor of inn

WIZLO BEARINGSHINER
Thousand Needles (82), B-3, Whitereach Post, Next to hut

WIZZLE BRASSBOLTS
Thousand Needles (82), K-8, Mirage Raceway (118), West of racetrack

WIZZLECRANK'S SHREDDER
Barrens (18), G-1, The Sludge Fen, North side of Sludge Fen

WOLF MASTER NANDOS
Silverpine Forest (68), F-7, Shadowfang Keep

WOLFGUARD WORG
Silverpine Forest (68), F-7, Shadowfang Keep

WOO PING
Weapon Master, Stormwind (72), H-6, Trade District, Weller's Arsenal, Trains: Crossbows, Daggers, Polearms, Staves, 1H Swords, & 2H Swords

WOOD LURKER
Loch Modan (54), H:(2, 3), J:(3, 4), K-4

WOODPAW ALPHA
Feralas (46), E-4, H:(5, 6), I:(5, 6), J-6

WOODPAW BRUTE
Feralas (46), E-4, H-5, I:(4, 5), J-5

WOODPAW MONGREL
Feralas (46), H-5, I:(4, 5), J-5, Grimtotem Compound, Lower Wilds, Woodpaw Hills

WOODPAW MYSTIC
Feralas (46), E-4, H:(5, 6), I:(5, 6), J-6

WOODPAW REAVER
Feralas (46), E-4, H:(5, 6), I:(5, 6), J-6

WOODPAW TRAPPER
Feralas (46), H-5, I:(4, 5), J-5, Grimtotem Compound, Lower Wilds, Woodpaw Hills

WOODSMAN
Eastern Plaguelands (40), G-2, Quel'Lithien Lodge

WOOLY KODO
Barrens (18), E:(6, 8), Wooly Kodo

WORB STRONGSTITCH
Light Armor Merchant, Feralas (46), I-4, Camp Mojache (105), Big western tent

WORG
Silverpine Forest (68), F-5, G:(4, 5), I-1, J-1, Throughout Silverpine

WRAHK
Tailoring Supplies, Barrens (18), F-3, The Crossroads (107), Southern entrance

WRATH HAMMER CONSTRUCT
Burning Steppes (22), Searing Gorge (64), C-4/D-8, Blackrock Depths

WRATHTAIL MYRMIDON
Ashenvale (12), A:(2, 3), B-3, The Zoram Strand (131), Zoram'gar Outpost (131)

WRATHTAIL PRIESTESS
Ashenvale (12), A:(2, 3), B-3, The Zoram Strand (131), Zoram'gar Outpost (131)

WRATHTAIL RAZORTAIL
Ashenvale (12), A-3, B:(2, 3), The Zoram Strand (131), Zoram'gar Outpost (131)

WRATHTAIL SEA WITCH
Ashenvale (12), A:(2, 3), B:(2, 3), The Zoram Strand (131), Zoram'gar Outpost (131)

WRATHTAIL SORCERESS
Ashenvale (12), A:(2, 3), B:(2, 3), The Zoram Strand (131)

WRATHTAIL WAVE RIDER
Ashenvale (12), A:(2, 3), B:(2, 3), The Zoram Strand (131), Zoram'gar Outpost (131)

WREN DARKSPRING
Demon Trainer, Dun Morogh (32), D-7, Coldridge Valley (106), Anvilmar

WRENIX THE WRETCHED
Barrens (18), H-4, Ratchet (121), Shack northeast of town

WRENIX'S GIZMOTRONIC APPARATUS
Barrens (18), H-4, Ratchet (121), Shack northeast of town

WRETCHED ZOMBIE
Tirisfal Glades (86), C-6, D-6, Deathknell (109)

WRINKLE GOODSTEEL
Superior Armor Crafter, Tanaris (78), G-3, Gadgetzan (111), Western structure

WRITHING HIGHBORNE
Darkshore (24), F-6, G-6, Ameth'Aran

WRITHING MAGE
Hillsbrad Foothills (48), A-8, Purgation Isle, Island

WU SHEN
Warrior Trainer, Stormwind (72), L:(4, 5), Old Town, Command Center

WUARK
Armorer & Shieldcrafter, Durotar (34), H-4, Razor Hill (122), Northeast of inn

WULAN
Cooking Supplies, Desolace (30), C-7, Shadowprey Village (125), Top of tall eastern structure

WUNNA DARKMANE
Trade Goods, Mulgore (58), E-6, Bloodhoof Village (102), Northeast tent

WYND NIGHTCHASER
Winterspring (98), H-3, Starfall Village, Terrace of main building

WYNNE LARSON
Robe Merchant, Stormwind (72), F-8, Mage Quarter, Larson Clothiers

WYRMKIN DREAMWALKER
Swamp of Sorrows (76), H:(5, 6), I:(6, 7), K:(5-7), L:(5, 6)

WYRMKIN FIREBRAND
Wetlands (96), L:(5, 6), Grim Batol

X

XABRAXXIS
Darkshore (24), H-3, Cliffspring Falls, South of river

XAI'ANDER
Weaponsmith, Ashenvale (12), E-5, Astranaar (101), Left as you enter southwest building

XANDAR GOODBEARD
General Supplies, Loch Modan (54), K-6, The Farstrider Lodge, Center of lodge

XANIS FLAMEWEAVER
Thunder Bluff (84), B-2, Spirit Rise, Sitting in front of Hall of Spirits

XAN'TIS
Snake Vendor, Orgrimmar (60), A-6, C-8, Valley of Spirit, Roams Valley of Spirits

XAR'TI
Raptor Riding Trainer, Durotar (34), H-7, Sen'jin Village (123), Among raptors south of village

XAVARIC
Felwood (44), E:(2-3), Jadefire Run, Western camp in hills

XAVATHRAS
Felwood (44), E-7, Ruins of Constellas, Western camp near cliff edge

XAVIAN BETRAYER
Ashenvale (12), J:(4, 5), Satyrnaar, Xavian

XAVIAN FELSWORN
Ashenvale (12), J:(4, 5), Satyrnaar, Xavian

XAVIAN ROGUE
Ashenvale (12), J:(4, 5), Satyrnaar, Xavian

XEN'TO
Cooking Supplier, Orgrimmar (60), G-5, The Drag, Borstan's Firepit

XEN'ZILLA
Stonetalon Mountains (70), I-9, Malaka'jin, Small structure

XIGGS FUSELIGHTER
Ironforge (52), J-9, The Military Ward, Hall of Arms

XIGGS FUSELIGHTER'S FLYINGMACHINE
Azshara (14), K-9, The Ruined Reaches, East of landing pad

XIZK GOODSTITCH
Tailoring Supplies, Stranglethorn Vale (74), B-8, Booty Bay (103), A Tailor to Cities (shop)

XIZZER FIZZBOLT
Engineering Supplies, Winterspring (98), I-4, Everlook (110), Inside building directly south of entrance

XOA'TSU
Pet Trainer, Orgrimmar (60), H:(1, 2), Valley of Honor, Behind Hunter's Hall

XON'CHA
Stable Master, Orgrimmar (60), I:(1-2), Valley of Honor, Outside o Hunter's Hall

XOR'JUUL
Hunter Trainer, Orgrimmar (60), H-2, Valley of Honor, Hunter's Hall

XOROTHIAN DREADSTEED
Feralas (46), G-4, Dire Maul

XOROTHIAN IMP
Feralas (46), G-4, Dire Maul

XT:4
Stonetalon Mountains (70), I-5, Windshear Crag, East of logging camp

XT:9
Stonetalon Mountains (70), G-5, H:(5-6), Windshear Crag, West and south of turn in river

X'YERA
Priest Trainer, Orgrimmar (60), D-9, Valley of Spirit, Spirit Lodge, top floor

XYLINNIA STARSHINE
Expert Enchanter, Feralas (46), C-4, Feathermoon Stronghold (110), Southeast of inn

Y

YALDA
Darkshore (24), F-4, Auberdine (101), House on hill

YAMA SNOWHOOF
Ashenvale (12), I-6, Splintertree Post (126), Inn

YANNI STOUTHEART
General Supplies, Loch Modan (54), D-5, Thelsamar (129), Stoutlager Inn

YARLYN AMBERSTILL
Pet Vendor, Dun Morogh (32), I-5, Amberstill Ranch, Patrols circular path around ranch

YARR HAMMERSTONE
Mining Trainer, Dun Morogh (32), G-5, Steelgrill's Depot, Basement of right building

YARROG BANESHADOW
Durotar (34), G-6, Burning Blade Coven, On ledge in back of cave

YAW SHARPMANE
Hunter Trainer, Mulgore (58), E-6, Bloodhoof Village (102), North tents

YEH'KINYA
Tanaris (78), J-2, Steamwheedle Port, Outside northern building

YELMAK
Expert Alchemist, Orgrimmar (60), G-3, The Drag, Yelmak's Alchemy and Potions

YELNAGI BLACKARM
Durotar (34), H-4, Razor Hill (122), Inn

YENNIKU
Darkspear Hostage, Stranglethorn Vale (74), D-6, Ruins of Aboraz, Northwestern corner of ruins

YLDAN
Bag Merchant, Darnassus (26), I-5, Tradesmen's Terrace, Bags shop

YONADA
Tailoring & Leatherworking Supplies, Barrens (18), F-6, Camp Taurajo (106), Southern building

YONN DEEPCUT
Skinner, Mulgore (58), E-6, Bloodhoof Village (102), Northeast tent

YORBA SCREWSPIGOT
Tanaris (78), J-3, Steamwheedle Port, Southern building

YORI CRACKHELM
Dun Morogh (32), D-7, Coldridge Valley (106), Next to caravan

YORUS BARLEYBREW
Redridge Mountains (62), C-4, Lakeshire (115), First floor of Lakeshire Inn

YOUNG ARIKARA
Thousand Needles (82), F-5, Freewind Post, Next to western bridge

YOUNG BLACK BEAR
Dun Morogh (32), D-6, E:(6, 7), F:(4-7), G-5, I-1, Kharanos (114), Steelgrill's Depot, The Grizzled Den

YOUNG BLACK RAVAGER
Duskwood (36), B:(6-8), C:(6-8), D-6, E-6, F:(6-8), G:(6, 7), H-6, I-3, J-3, Brightwood Grove

YOUNG CHIMAERA
Stonetalon Mountains (70), C-6, D-6, E-6, The Charred Vale

YOUNG DIEMETRADON
Un'Goro Crater (90), G-2, H:(3, 4), I:(3, 4), J:(2-4, 6, 7), Lakkari Tar Pits, The Marshlands

YOUNG FLESHRIPPER
Westfall (94), D:(2, 3), E:(2-4), F:(2-4), G:(1-4)

YOUNG FOREST BEAR
Elwynn Forest (42), C:(7-9), E-9, F:(7-9), G:(7, 8), H:(7, 8), I:(6-8), J:(6-8), K:(6, 8), L:(6-8)

YOUNG GORETUSK
Westfall (94), C:(3, 4), D:(2-4), E:(2-4), F:(2-5), G:(1-4)

YOUNG JUNGLE STALKER
Stranglethorn Vale (74), C-5, Gurubashi Arena, The Cape of Stranglethorn

YOUNG LASHTAIL RAPTOR
Stranglethorn Vale (74), C-3, Grom'gol Base Camp (112), The Savage Coast

YOUNG MESA BUZZARD
Arathi Highlands (10), B:(4, 5), C:(2, 4), D:(2, 3), E:(4, 6), F-6, G:(4, 5), I:(4, 5), J-5, Along hills

YOUNG MOONKIN
Darkshore (24), F:(4, 5), G:(4, 5)

YOUNG MURK THRESHER
Dustwallow Marsh (38), F:(3, 4), G:(4, 5), H:(4, 5), Dustwallow Bay

YOUNG NIGHT WEB SPIDER
Tirisfal Glades (86), C:(5, 6), Deathknell (109)

YOUNG NIGHTSABER
Teldrassil (80), G-4, H:(4, 5), Shadowglen (124)

YOUNG PANTHER
Stranglethorn Vale (74), C-2, D:(1, 2), E:(1, 2), Kurzen's Compound, Tkashi Ruins

YOUNG PRIDEWING
Stonetalon Mountains (70), H-6, J:(4, 5), The Talondeep Path, Windshear Crag

YOUNG REEF CRAWLER
Darkshore (24), E:(5, 6), F:(3, 5), Mist's Edge, The Long Wash, Twilight Shore

YOUNG SAWTOOTH CROCOLISK
Swamp of Sorrows (76), C:(4, 5), D:(3-5), E:(3-5)

YOUNG SCAVENGER
Tirisfal Glades (86), C:(6, 7), D:(6, 7), Deathknell (109)

YOUNG STRANGLETHORN RAPTOR
Stranglethorn Vale (74), B-2, Ruins of Zul'Kunda, The Savage Coast

YOUNG STRANGLETHORN TIGER
Stranglethorn Vale (74), C:(1, 2), D:(1, 2), Nesingwary's Expedition, Rebel Camp, Tkashi Ruins

YOUNG THISTLE BOAR
Teldrassil (80), G-4, H:(4, 5), Shadowglen (124)

YOUNG THRESHADON
Loch Modan (54), F:(3-6), H:(4, 5), The Loch

YOUNG WAVETHRASHER
Azshara (14), E:(1, 2), F:(1, 2), G-1, H-1, I-1, J-1, K:(1, 2), L:(1, 2), Jagged Reef

YOUNG WENDIGO
Dun Morogh (32), E-5, F-5, The Grizzled Den

YOUNG WETLANDS CROCOLISK
Wetlands (96), A-5, B:(4-6), C:(3, 4), D:(3, 4), E-4, G:(3, 4), H:(4-7), I:(6, 7)

YOUNG WOLF
Elwynn Forest (42), E-6, F:(4-6), G-4, Echo Ridge Mine, Northshire Valley (120)

YOWLER
Redridge Mountains (62), B-3, Redridge Canyons, With several gnolls in camp

YUGREK
Wind Rider Master, Winterspring (98), I-4, Everlook (110), Northwest of town

YUKA SCREWSPIGOT
Burning Steppes (22), H-2, Flame Crest, Cave

YVETTE FARTHING
Tirisfal Glades (86), H-5, Brill (104), First floor of Gallows' End Tavern

Z

ZACHARIAH POST
Undead Horse Merchant, Tirisfal Glades (86), H-5, Brill (104), Stable

ZAELDARR THE OUTCAST
Eastern Plaguelands (40), D-8, The Undercroft, Crypt

ZAETAR'S SPIRIT
Desolace (30), D-5, Mauradon

ZALAS WITHERBARK
Rare Spawn, Arathi Highlands (10), J-8, Witherbark Village, Lvl 40 Uber-Rare; Cave south of village

ZALASHJI
Tanaris (78), J-3, Zalashji's Den, Cave on coast

ZALAZANE
Durotar (34), J-9, Echo Isles, Roams southern part of village

ZALDIMAR WEFHELLT
Mage Trainer, Elwynn Forest (42), F-7, Goldshire (112), Second floor of Lion's Pride Inn

ZAMAEL LUNTHISTLE
Searing Gorge (64), C-3, Firewatch Ridge, Cage next to lava pool

ZAMAN
Loramus's Guardian, Azshara (14), H-7, Bay of Storms, Patrols near Loramus

ZAMEK
Thousand Needles (82), K-8, Mirage Raceway (118), Inside racetrack, next to building

ZAMJA
Cooking Trainer, Orgrimmar (60), G-5, The Drag, Borstan's Firepit

ZAN SHIVSPROKET
Speciality Engineer, Hillsbrad Foothills (48), K-2, Basement of Chateau Ravenholdt

ZANARA
Bowyer, Dustwallow Marsh (38), D-3, Brackenwall Village (104), West entrance

ZANDALAR ENFORCER
Stranglethorn Vale (74), A-2, Yojamba Isle

ZANDALAR HEADSHRINKER
Stranglethorn Vale (74), A-2, Yojamba Isle

ZANDO'ZAN
Orgrimmar (60), E-5, The Cleft of Shadow, Shadowswift Brotherhood

ZANE BRADFORD
Wand Vendor, Undercity (88), J-3, The Magic Quarter

ZANGEN STONEHOOF
Thunder Bluff (84), F-5, High rise, in the center of the rise

ZANKAJA
Orgrimmar (60), D-6, Valley of Strength, Near highest bridge from Skytower

ZANNOK HIDEPIERCER
Leatherworking Supplies, Silithus (66), I-1, Valor's Rest, South of road

ZANSOA
Fishing Supplies, Durotar (34), H-7, Sen'jin Village (123), Main floor of big hut

ZANZIL HUNTER
Stranglethorn Vale (74), C-5, D-6, Ruins of Jubuwal

ZANZIL NAGA
Stranglethorn Vale (74), C-5, D-6, Ruins of Jubuwal

ZANZIL THE OUTCAST
Stranglethorn Vale (74), D-6, Ruins of Aboraz, By bonfire in ruins

ZANZIL WITCH DOCTOR
Stranglethorn Vale (74), C-5, D-6, Ruins of Jubuwal

ZANZIL ZOMBIE
Stranglethorn Vale (74), C-5, D-6, Ruins of Jubuwal

ZAP FARFLINGER
Unbalanced Engineer, Winterspring (98), I-4, Everlook (110), Transporter outside of bank

ZAPETTA
Zeppelin Master, Tirisfal Glades (86), H-6, Zepplin tower just north of Undercity

ZARDETH OF THE BLACK CLAW
Stormwind (72), D-8, Mage Quarter, The Slaughtered Lamb

ZARENA CROMWIND
Superior Weaponsmith, Stranglethorn Vale (74), B-8, Booty Bay (103), Cuts-n-Bruises Incorporated (shop) on the southern side of The Old Port Authority

ZARGH
Butcher, Barrens (18), F-3, The Crossroads (107), East of inn

ZARICOTL
Rare Spawn, Badlands (16), E:(5, 6), H-6, The Dustbowl, Mirage Flats, Lvl 55 Uncommon; Roams small area around spawn point

ZARISE
Bat Handler, Hillsbrad Foothills (48), G-2, Tarren Mill (128), To the left just outside town

ZARLMAN TWO-MOONS
Mulgore (58), E-6, Bloodhoof Village (102), Northern clearing

ZARRIN
Cook, Teldrassil (80), G-6, Dolanaar (109), Next to cauldron southeast of inn

ZARUK
Arathi Highlands (10), J-4, Hammerfall (113), Inside fence east building

ZAYUS
High Priest, Orgrimmar (60), D-9, Valley of Spirit, Spirit Lodge, top floor

ZAZO
Orgrimmar (60), G-7, Valley of Strength, Inn

ZEAL'AYA
Herbalism Supplier, Orgrimmar (60), F-4, G-4, The Drag, Jandi's Arboretum

ZEKKIS
Swamp of Sorrows (76), I-5, The Temple of Atal'Hakkar

ZEL'MAK
Warrior Trainer, Orgrimmar (60), J-3, Valley of Honor, Hall of the Brave

ZEM LEEWARD
Redridge Mountains (62), C-5, Lakeshire (115), Straight dock west of the bridge

ZENDO'JIAN
Weapon Vendor, Orgrimmar (60), J-2, Valley of Honor, Arms of Legend

ZENGU
Arathi Highlands (10), J-3, Hammerfall (113), Platform of north building

ZENN FOULHOOF
Teldrassil (80), H-6, West of main road, south of intersection to Starbreeze Village

ZERILLIS
Rare Spawn, Wetlands (96), E-1, Zul'Farrak, Lvl 45 Rare

ZERILLIS
Tanaris (78), E-1, Zul'Farrak

ZEVRIM THORNHOOF
Feralas (46), G-4, Dire Maul

ZEVROST
Warlock Trainer, Orgrimmar (60), F-5, The Cleft of Shadow, Darkfire Enclave

ZGGI
Zardeth's Minion, Stormwind (72), D-8, Mage Quarter, The Slaughtered Lamb

ZHEVRA CHARGER
Barrens (18), D:(2, 3), E:(1, 2, 4-7), F:(5, 6), G:(1, 3, 5), H:(3, 5)

ZHEVRA RUNNER
Barrens (18), E:(2-5), F:(1-4), G:(2-4), H:(2-4)

ZIGGURAT PROTECTOR
Eastern Plaguelands (40), C-2, D:(3, 4), E-4, F-3, Plaguewood

ZIKKEL
Banker, Barrens (18), H-4, Ratchet (121), Bank

ZILZIBIN DRUMLORE
Orgrimmar (60), G-5, The Drag, Building south of Jandi's Arboretum

ZIXIL
Merchant Supreme, Hillsbrad Foothills (48), G-3, Patrols with Overwatch Mark I between Tarren Mill and Southshore

ZIZ FIZZIKS
Stonetalon Mountains (70), G-6, Windshear Crag, In small house in mountains, just north of Webwinder Path

ZIZZEK
Fisherman, Barrens (18), H-4, Ratchet (121), Front of inn

ZJOLNIR
Raptor Handler, Durotar (34), H-7, Sen'jin Village (123), Among raptors south of village

ZLAGK
Butcher, Durotar (34), F-7, Valley of Trials (131), Northwest structure

ZNORT
Arathi Highlands (10), I-3, Circle of East Binding, Patrols with Fozruck to each of the four Circles of Binding

ZOLO
Swamp of Sorrows (76), I-5, The Temple of Atal'Hakkar

ZOR LONETREE
Elder Far Seer, Orgrimmar (60), D-4, Valley of Wisdom, Grommash Hold

ZORA
Rare Spawn, Silithus (66), D-4, Hive'Zora, Lvl 59 Average Rare; Roams hive

ZORBIN FANDAZZLE
Feralas (46), E-4, The Forgotten Coast, Tent near dock

ZUDD
Pet Trainer, Stranglethorn Vale (74), C-3, Grom'gol Base Camp (112), By crates inside camp walls to the left of western entrance

ZUKK'ASH STINGER
Feralas (46), I-6, J-6, The Writhing Deep

ZUKK'ASH TUNNELER
Feralas (46), I:(6, 7), J-6, The Writhing Deep

ZUKK'ASH WASP
Feralas (46), I-6, The Writhing Deep

ZUKK'ASH WORKER
Feralas (46), I-6, The Writhing Deep

ZUL'AREK HATEFOWLER
Rare Spawn, The Hinterlands (50), D-6, E-6, Hiri'Watha, Zun'Watha, Lvl 43 Uncommon; Roams small area around spawn point

ZUL'BRIN WARPBRANCH
Rare Spawn, Eastern Plaguelands (40), I-2, J-2, Mazra'Alor, Zul'Mashar, Lvl 59 Semi-Rare; Stands idle at spawn point

ZUL'FARRAK DEAD HERO
Tanaris (78), E-1, Zul'Farrak

ZUL'FARRAK ZOMBIE
Tanaris (78), E-1, Zul'Farrak

ZUL'LOR
Swamp of Sorrows (76), I-5, The Temple of Atal'Hakkar

ZULRG
Weaponsmith, Dustwallow Marsh (38), D-3, Brackenwall Village (104), Center of village

ZUN'DARTHA
Swamp of Sorrows (76), F-5, Stonard, Right of entrance to inn

ZUREETHA FARGAZE
Durotar (34), F-7, Valley of Trials (131), Structure to south

ZUZUBEE
Race Announcer, Thousand Needles (82), K-8, Mirage Raceway (118), Grandstands at drag strip

ZZARC' VUL
Duskwood (36), E-8, Vul'Gol Ogre Mound, Roams small area around spawn point

WEAPON MASTERS

REGION	MINI REGION	GRID LOC	NAME	NOTES
Darnassus (26)	Warrior's Terrace	H-5	Ilyenia Moonfire	Lower southwest platform, Trains: Bows, Daggers, Fist, Thrown, & Staves
Ironforge (52)	The Military Ward	H-9	Bixi Wobblebonk	Timberline Arms, Trains: Crossbows, Daggers, & Throwing Weapons
Ironforge (52)	The Military Ward	H-9	Buliwyf Stonehand	Timberline Arms, Trains: Crossbows, Daggers, Fist, Guns, 1H Mace, & 2H Mace
Orgrimmar (60)	Valley of Honor	J-2	Hanashi	Arms of Legend, Trains: Bows, 1H Axe, 2H Axe, Staves, & Thrown
Orgrimmar (60)	Valley of Strength	J-2	Sayoc	Arms of Legend, Trains: Bows, Daggers, Fist Weapons, 1H Axe, 2H Axe, Thrown
Stormwind (72)	Trade District	H-6	Woo Ping	Weller's Arsenal, Trains: Crossbows, Daggers, Polearms, Staves, 1H Swords, & 2H Swords
Thunder Bluff (84)		D-6	Ansekhwa	Lower rise, Trains: 1H Mace, 2H Mace, Staves, & Guns
Undercity (88)	The War Quarter	H-3	Archibald	Trains: Crossbows, Daggers, 1H Sword, 2H Sword, & Polearms

INNKEEPERS

REGION	MINI REGION	GRID LOC
Arathi Highlands (10)	Hammerfall (113)	J-3
Ashenvale (12)	Splintertree Post (126)	I-6
Ashenvale (12)	Astranaar (101)	E-5
Badlands (16)	Kargath (114)	A-5
Barrens (18)	The Crossroads (107)	F-3
Barrens (18)	Camp Taurajo (106)	F-6
Barrens (18)	Ratchet (121)	H-4
Darkshore (24)	Auberdine (101)	F-4
Darnassus (26)	Craftsmen's Terrace	I:(1, 2)
Desolace (30)	Nijel's Point (119)	I-1
Desolace (30)	Shadowprey Village (125)	C-7
Dun Morogh (32)	Kharanos (114)	F-5
Durotar (34)	Razor Hill (122)	H-4
Duskwood (36)	Darkshire (108)	J-4
Dustwallow Marsh (38)	Theramore Isle (130)	I-5
Elwynn Forest (42)	Goldshire (112)	F-7
Feralas (46)	Camp Mojache (105)	I-4
Feralas (46)	Feathermoon Stronghold (110)	C-4
Hillsbrad Foothills (48)	Southshore (125)	F-6
Hillsbrad Foothills (48)	Tarren Mill (128)	H-2
Ironforge (52)	The Commons	B-5
Loch Modan (54)	Thelsamar (129)	D-5
Mulgore (58)	Bloodhoof Village (102)	E-6
Orgrimmar (60)	Valley of Strength	G-7
Redridge Mountains (62)	Lakeshire (115)	C-4
Silverpine Forest (68)	The Sepulcher (124)	F-4
Stonetalon Mountains (70)	Sun Rock Retreat (127)	F-6
Stormwind (72)	Trade District	H:(6, 7)
Stranglethorn Vale (74)	Booty Bay (103)	B-8
Swamp of Sorrows (76)	Stonard (126)	F-5
Tanaris (78)	Gadgetzan (111)	H-3
Teldrassil (80)	Dolanaar (109)	G-6
The Hinterlands (50)	Aerie Peak (100)	B-4
The Hinterlands (50)	Revantusk Village	L-8
Thousand Needles (82)	Freewind Post	F-5
Thunder Bluff (84)		E-6
Tirisfal Glades (86)	Brill (104)	H-5
Undercity (88)	The Trade Quarter	I-4, J-4
Westfall (94)	Sentinel Hill (123)	F-5
Wetlands (96)	Deepwater Tavern	A-6
Winterspring (98)	Everlook (110)	I-4

MOUNT TRAINERS

TITLE	NAME	REGION	MINI REGION	GRID LOC	NOTES
Horse Riding Instructor	Randal Hunter	Elwynn Forest (42)	Eastvale Logging Camp	L-6	Corral
Kodo Riding Instructor	Kar Stormsinger	Mulgore (58)	Bloodhoof Village (102)	E-6	Northern clearing
Mechanostrider Pilot	Binjy Featherwhistle	Dun Morogh (32)	Steelgrill's Depot	G-5	By mechanostrider's outside of depot
Nightsaber Riding Instructor	Jartsam	Darnassus (26)	Cenarion Enclave	E-1	Intersection of paths
Ram Riding Instructor	Ultham Ironhorn	Dun Morogh (32)	Amberstill Ranch	I-5	By hay bails in corral
Raptor Riding Trainer	Xar'Ti	Durotar (34)	Sen'jin Village (123)	H-7	Among raptors south of village
Undead Horse Riding Instructor	Velma Warnam	Tirisfal Glades (86)	Brill (104)	H-5	Stable
Wintersaber Trainers	Chal Fairwind	Winterspring (98)		J-3	Outside small shack in hills
Wintersaber Trainers	Rivern Frostwind	Winterspring (98)	Frostsaber Rock	G-1	Atop Frostsaber Rock
Wolf Riding Instructor	Kildar	Orgrimmar (60)	Valley of Honor	I-1	Outside of Hunter's Hall

FLIGHT MASTERS

ALLIANCE

REGION	MINI REGION	GRID LOC
Arathi Highlands (10)	Refuge Pointe	F-5
Ashenvale (12)	Astranaar (101)	E-5
Azshara (14)	Talrendis Point	A-8
Blasted Lands (20)	Nethergarde Keep (119)	J-2
Burning Steppes (22)	Morgan's Vigil (118)	K-7
Darkshore (24)	Auberdine (101)	F-4
Desolace (30)	Nijel's Point (119)	H-1
Duskwood (36)	Darkshire (108)	K-4
Dustwallow Marsh (38)	Theramore Isle (130)	I-5
Eastern Plaguelands (40)	Light's Hope Chapel (116)	K-6
Felwood (44)	Talonbranch Glade	H-3
Feralas (46)	Feathermoon Stronghold (110)	C-4
Feralas (46)	Thalanaar	K-5
Hillsbrad Foothills (48)	Southshore (125)	F-5
Ironforge (52)	The Great Forge	G-5
Loch Modan (54)	Thelsamar (129)	D-5
Moonglade (56)		G-7
Redridge Mountains (62)		D-6
Searing Gorge (64)	Thorium Point	D-3
Silithus (66)	Valor's Rest	I-1
Stonetalon Mountains (70)	Stonetalon Peak	D-1
Stormwind (72)	Trade District	J-6
Stranglethorn Vale (74)	Booty Bay (103)	B-8
Tanaris (78)	Gadgetzan (111)	H-3
Teldrassil (80)	Rut'theran Village	G-9
The Hinterlands (50)	Aerie Peak (100)	B-5
Western Plaguelands (92)	Chillwind Camp	F-8
Westfall (94)	Sentinel Hill (123)	G-5
Wetlands (96)	Menethil Harbor (117)	A-6
Winterspring (98)	Everlook (110)	I-4

HORDE

REGION	MINI REGION	GRID LOC
Arathi Highlands (10)	Hammerfall (113)	J-3
Ashenvale (12)	Zoram'gar Outpost (131)	B-4
Azshara (14)	Valormok	B-5
Badlands (16)	Kargath (114)	A-5
Barrens (18)	Camp Taurajo (106)	F-6
Barrens (18)	The Crossroads (107)	F-3
Burning Steppes (22)	Flame Crest	H-2
Desolace (30)	Shadowprey Village (125)	B-7
Dustwallow Marsh (38)	Brackenwall Village (104)	D-3
Eastern Plaguelands (40)	Light's Hope Chapel (116)	K-5
Felwood (44)	Bloodvenom Post	E-5
Feralas (46)	Camp Mojache (105)	I-4
Hillsbrad Foothills (48)	Tarren Mill (128)	G-2
Moonglade (56)		D-7
Orgrimmar (60)	Valley of Strength	E-6
Searing Gorge (64)	Thorium Point	D-3
Silithus (66)	Valor's Rest	I-1
Silverpine Forest (68)	The Sepulcher (124)	G-4
Stonetalon Mountains (70)	Sun Rock Retreat (127)	E-6
Stranglethorn Vale (74)	Booty Bay (103)	B-8
Stranglethorn Vale (74)	Grom'gol Base Camp (112)	C-3
Swamp of Sorrows (76)	Stonard (126)	F-5
Tanaris (78)	Gadgetzan (111)	H-3
The Hinterlands (50)	Revantusk Village	L-8
Thousand Needles (82)	Freewind Post	F-5
Thunder Bluff (84)		E-5
Undercity (88)	The Trade Quarter	I-5
Winterspring (98)	Everlook (110)	I-4

CLASS TRAINERS

DRUID TRAINERS

REGION	MINI REGION	GRID LOC	NAME	NOTES
Darnassus (26)	Cenarion Enclave	D-1	Denatharion	Northwest structure
Darnassus (26)	Cenarion Enclave	D-1	Fylerian Nightwing	Northwest structure
Darnassus (26)	Cenarion Enclave	D-1	Mathrengyl Bearwalker	Northwest structure, on balcony
Felwood (44)	Talonbranch Glade	H-3	Golhine the Hooded	Front of building
Feralas (46)	Camp Mojache (105)	I-4	Jannos Lighthoof	In tent, east of water
Moonglade (56)	Nighthaven (120)	G-4	Loganaar	Next to moonwell, by northern section of lake
Mulgore (58)	Bloodhoof Village (102)	F-6	Gennia Runetotem	East tent
Mulgore (58)	Camp Narache (105)	E-8	Gart Mistrunner	North tent
Stormwind (72)	The Park	C-5	Maldryn	By pool of water
Stormwind (72)	The Park	C-6	Sheldras Moontree	By pool of water
Stormwind (72)	The Park	C-5	Theridran	By pool of water
Teldrassil (80)	Dolanaar (109)	G-6	Kal	Moonwell south side of Dolanaar
Teldrassil (80)	Shadowglen (124)	G-4	Mardant Strongoak	First room off of ramp up tree
Thunder Bluff (84)	Elder Rise	I-3	Kym Wildmane	Inside Hall of Elders
Thunder Bluff (84)	Elder Rise	J-3	Sheal Runetotem	Inside Hall of Elders
Thunder Bluff (84)	Elder Rise	J-3	Turak Runetotem	Inside Hall of Elders

HUNTER TRAINERS

REGION	MINI REGION	GRID LOC	NAME	NOTES
Ashenvale (12)	Shrine of Aessina	C-6	Alenndaar Lapidaar	Hidden in a camp near mountains in far southwest of region
Ashenvale (12)	Silverwind Refuge	F-6, G-6	Danlaar Nightshade	Back of building
Darnassus (26)	Cenarion Enclave	E-1	Dorion	Northeast structure, upper level
Darnassus (26)	Cenarion Enclave	E-1	Jeen'ra Nightrunner	Top of structure, connected to the northeast structure
Darnassus (26)	Cenarion Enclave	E-1	Jocaste	Northeast structure
Dun Morogh (32)	Coldridge Valley (106)	D-7	Thorgas Grimson	Anvilmar
Dun Morogh (32)	Kharanos (114)	F-5	Grif Wildheart	On hill at southwest end of town
Durotar (34)	Valley of Trials (131)	F-7	Jen'shan	Structure to south
Durotar (34)	Razor Hill (122)	H-4	Thotar	Bunker
Felwood (44)	Talonbranch Glade	H-3	Kaerbrus	Near pond
Ironforge (52)	The Military Ward	J-9	Daera Brightspear	Hall of Arms
Ironforge (52)	The Military Ward	J-8	Olmin Burningbeard	Hall of Arms
Ironforge (52)	The Military Ward	I-8	Regnus Thundergranite	Hall of Arms
Loch Modan (54)	The Farstrider Lodge	K-6	Dargh Trueaim	In right hall of lodge
Mulgore (58)	Camp Narache (105)	E-8	Lanka Farshot	Main tent (north)
Mulgore (58)	Bloodhoof Village (102)	E-6	Yaw Sharpmane	North tents
Orgrimmar (60)	Valley of Honor	H-2	Ormak Grimshot	Hunter's Hall
Orgrimmar (60)	Valley of Honor	H-2	Sian'dur	Hunter's Hall
Orgrimmar (60)	Valley of Honor	H-2	Xor'Juul	Hunter's Hall
Stormwind (72)	Dwarven District	I-2, J-2	Einris Brightspear	Building south of tram entrance
Stormwind (72)	Dwarven District	I-1, I-3	Thorfin Stoneshield	Building south of tram entrance
Stormwind (72)	Dwarven District	I-2	Ulfir Ironbeard	Building south of tram entrance
Stranglethorn Vale (74)	Grom'gol Base Camp (112)	C-3	Kragg	Just inside camp walls to the left of western entrance
Swamp of Sorrows (76)	Stonard (126)	F-5	Ogromm	Behind orcish carriage left of entrance to main hall
Teldrassil (80)	Shadowglen (124)	G-4	Ayanna Everstride	First room off of ramp up tree
Teldrassil (80)	Dolanaar (109)	G-6	Dazalar	East of inn
Thunder Bluff (84)	Hunter Rise	G-9	Holt Thunderhorn	Inside Hunter's Hall
Thunder Bluff (84)	Hunter Rise	G-9	Kary Thunderhorn	Inside Hunter's Hall
Thunder Bluff (84)	Hunter Rise	G-9	Urek Thunderhorn	Inside Hunter's Hall

PET TRAINERS

REGION	MINI REGION	GRID LOC	NAME	NOTES
Ashenvale (12)	Shrine of Aessina	C-6	Bolyun	Hidden in a camp near mountains in far southwest of region
Ashenvale (12)	Silverwind Refuge	F-6	Caelyb	Right wing of building
Darnassus (26)	Cenarion Enclave	E-1	Silvaria	Northeast structure, upper level
Dun Morogh (32)	Kharanos (114)	F-5	Peria Lamenur	In caravan
Durotar (34)	Razor Hill (122)	H-4	Harruk	Bunker
Felwood (44)	Talonbranch Glade	H-3	Nalesette Wildbringer	Front of building
Ironforge (52)	The Military Ward	J-8	Belia Thundergranite	Hall of Arms
Loch Modan (54)	The Farstrider Lodge	K-6	Claude Erksine	In right hall of lodge
Mulgore (58)	Bloodhoof Village (102)	E-6	Reban Freerunner	North tents
Orgrimmar (60)	Valley of Honor	H:(1, 2)	Xoa'tsu	Behind Hunter's Hall
Stormwind (72)	Dwarven District	I-2	Karrina Mekenda	Building south of tram entrance
Stranglethorn Vale (74)	Grom'gol Base Camp (112)	C-3	Zudd	By crates inside camp walls to the left of western entrance
Swamp of Sorrows (76)	Stonard (126)	F-5	Grokor	Behind orcish carriage left of entrance to main hall
Teldrassil (80)	Dolanaar (109)	G-6	Keldas	East of inn
Thunder Bluff (84)	Hunter Rise	F-8	Hesuwa Thunderhorn	In building west of Hunter's Hall

MAGE TRAINERS

REGION	MINI REGION	GRID LOC	NAME	NOTES
Dun Morogh (32)	Kharanos (114)	F-5	Magis Sparkmantle	Thunderbrew Distillery
Dun Morogh (32)	Coldridge Valley (106)	D-7	Marryk Nurribit	Back room of Anvilmar (first floor)
Durotar (34)	Valley of Trials (131)	F-7	Mai'ah	Structure to south
Durotar (34)	Sen'jin Village (123)	H-7	Un'Thuwa	Small hut to southeast
Elwynn Forest (42)	Northshire Valley (120)	G-4	Khelden Bremen	Second floor of abbey
Elwynn Forest (42)	Goldshire (112)	F-7	Zaldimar Wefhellt	Second floor of Lion's Pride Inn
Ironforge (52)	The Mystic Ward	C-1	Bink	Hall of Mysteries
Ironforge (52)	The Mystic Ward	C-1	Dink	Hall of Mysteries
Ironforge (52)	The Mystic Ward	C-1	Juli Stormkettle	Hall of Mysteries
Ironforge (52)	The Mystic Ward	C-1	Nittlebur Sparkfizzle	Hall of Mysteries
Orgrimmar (60)	Valley of Spirit	D-8	Deino	Darkbriar Lodge
Orgrimmar (60)	Valley of Spirit	D:(8, 9)	Enyo	Darkbriar Lodge
Orgrimmar (60)	Valley of Spirit	D:(8, 9)	Pephredo	Darkbriar Lodge
Orgrimmar (60)	Valley of Spirit	D:(8, 9)	Uthel'nay	Darkbriar Lodge
Stormwind (72)	Mage Quarter	F-8	Elsharin	Wizard's Sanctum
Stormwind (72)	Mage Quarter	F-8	Jennea Cannon	Wizard's Sanctum
Stormwind (72)	Mage Quarter	F-8	Maginor Dumas (Master Mage)	Wizard's Sanctum
Thunder Bluff (84)	Spirit Rise	C-3	Archmage Shymm	The Pools of Vision
Thunder Bluff (84)	Spirit Rise	C-3	Thurston Xane	The Pools of Vision
Tirisfal Glades (86)	Brill (104)	H-5	Cain Firesong	Second floor of Gallows' End Tavern
Tirisfal Glades (86)	Deathknell (109)	C-7	Isabella	Church
Undercity (88)	The Magic Quarter	L-1	Anastasia Hartwell	Northwest corner of Skull Building
Undercity (88)	The Magic Quarter	L-1	Kaelystia Hatebringer	Inside Skull Building
Undercity (88)	The Magic Quarter	L-1	Pierce Shackleton	Inside Skull Building

PORTAL TRAINERS

REGION	MINI REGION	GRID LOC	NAME	NOTES
Darnassus (26)	The Temple of the Moon	E-8	Elissa Dumas	Northeast of fountain
Ironforge (52)	The Mystic Ward	C-1	Milstaff Stormeye	Hall of Mysteries
Orgrimmar (60)	Valley of Spirit	D:(8, 9)	Thuul	Darkbriar Lodge, top floor
Stormwind (72)	Mage Quarter	F-8	Larimaine Purdue	Wizard's Sanctum
Thunder Bluff (84)	Spirit Rise	C-3	Brigitte Cranston	The Pools of Vision
Undercity (88)	The Magic Quarter	L-1	Lexington Mortaim	On Skull Building

PALADIN TRAINERS

REGION	MINI REGION	GRID LOC	NAME	NOTES
Dun Morogh (32)	Kharanos (114)	F-5	Azar Stronghammer	Thunderbrew Distillery
Dun Morogh (32)	Coldridge Valley (106)	D-7	Bromos Grummner	Anvilmar
Dustwallow Marsh (38)	Theramore Isle (130)	I-5	Brother Karman	Outside Foothold Citadel
Elwynn Forest (42)	Northshire Valley (120)	G-4	Brother Sammuel	Hall of Arms of abbey
Elwynn Forest (42)	Goldshire (112)	E-7	Brother Wilhelm	Rear entrance of smith
Ironforge (52)	The Mystic Ward	C-1	Beldruk Doombrow	Hall of Mysteries
Ironforge (52)	The Mystic Ward	C-1	Brandur Ironhammer	Hall of Mysteries
Ironforge (52)	The Mystic Ward	C-1	Valgar Highforge	Hall of Mysteries
Stormwind (72)	Cathedral Square	F-3	Arthur the Faithful	Cathedral of Light
Stormwind (72)	Cathedral Square	F-3	Katherine the Pure	Cathedral of Light
Stormwind (72)	Cathedral Square	F-3	Lord Grayson Shadowbreaker	Cathedral of Light

PRIEST TRAINERS

REGION	MINI REGION	GRID LOC	NAME	NOTES
Darnassus (26)	The Temple Gardens	E-8	Astarii Starseeker	Balcony, north of fountain
Darnassus (26)	The Temple of the Moon	E-8	Priestess Alathea	Balcony, north of fountain
Darnassus (26)	The Temple of the Moon	E-8	Jandria	Just inside temple, north of fountain
Darnassus (26)	The Temple of the Moon	E-9	Lariia	South of fountain
Dun Morogh (32)	Coldridge Valley (106)	D-7	Branstock Khalder	Anvilmar
Dun Morogh (32)	Kharanos (114)	F-5	Maxan Anvol	Thunderbrew Distillery
Durotar (34)	Razor Hill (122)	H-4	Tai'jin	Barracks
Durotar (34)	Valley of Trials (131)	F-7	Ken'jai	
Elwynn Forest (42)	Goldshire (112)	F-7	Priestess Josetta	Second floor of Lion's Pride Inn
Elwynn Forest (42)	Northshire Valley (120)	G-4	Priestess Anetta	Room behind the Library Wing of abbey
Ironforge (52)	The Mystic Ward	C-1	Braenna Flintcrag	Hall of Mysteries
Ironforge (52)	The Mystic Ward	C-1	High Priest Rohan	Hall of Mysteries
Ironforge (52)	The Mystic Ward	C-1	Theodrus Frostbeard	Hall of Mysteries
Ironforge (52)	The Mystic Ward	C-1	Toldren Deepiron	Hall of Mysteries
Orgrimmar (60)	Valley of Spirit	D-9	Ur'kyo	Spirit Lodge
Orgrimmar (60)	Valley of Spirit	D-9	X'Yera	Spirit Lodge, top floor
Stormwind (72)	Cathedral Square	F-3	Brother Benjamin	Cathedral of Light
Stormwind (72)	Cathedral Square	F-3	Brother Joshua	Cathedral of Light
Stormwind (72)	Cathedral Square	F-3	High Priestess Laurena	Cathedral of Light
Stormwind (72)	The Park	C-5	Nara Meideros	By pool of water
Teldrassil (80)	Dolanaar (109)	G-6	Laurna Morninglight	Bottom floor inside building north of road
Teldrassil (80)	Shadowglen (124)	H-4	Shanda	Third level of main building
Thunder Bluff (84)	Spirit Rise	C-3	Father Cobb	The Pools of Vision
Thunder Bluff (84)	Spirit Rise	C-3	Malakai Cross	The Pools of Vision
Thunder Bluff (84)	Spirit Rise	C-3	Miles Welsh	The Pools of Vision
Thunder Bluff (84)	Spirit Rise	C-3	Ursyn Ghull	The Pools of Vision
Tirisfal Glades (86)	Brill (104)	H-5	Dark Cleric Beryl	Second floor of Gallows' End Tavern
Tirisfal Glades (86)	Deathknell (109)	C-7	Dark Cleric Duesten	Church
Undercity (88)	The War Quarter	G-2	Aelthalyste	Outside Skull Building
Undercity (88)	The War Quarter	G-2	Father Lankester	Outside Skull Building
Undercity (88)	The War Quarter	F-2	Father Lazarus	Outside Skull Building

ROGUE TRAINERS

REGION	MINI REGION	GRID LOC	NAME	NOTES
Darnassus (26)	Cenarion Enclave	E-2	Anishar	Den, bottom of ramp
Darnassus (26)	Cenarion Enclave	D-2	Erion Shadewhisper	Den, small room on lower level
Darnassus (26)	Cenarion Enclave	D-2, E-2	Syurna	Den, west of path
Dun Morogh (32)	Coldridge Valley (106)	D-7	Solm Hargrin	Anvilmar
Dun Morogh (32)	Kharanos (114)	F-5	Hogral Bakkan	Thunderbrew Distillery
Durotar (34)	Razor Hill (122)	H-4	Kaplak	Bunker
Durotar (34)	Valley of Trials (131)	F-7	Rwag	
Elwynn Forest (42)	Goldshire (112)	F-7	Keryn Sylvius	Second floor of Lion's Pride Inn
Elwynn Forest (42)	Northshire Valley (120)	G-4	Jorik Kerridan	Abbey stable
Hillsbrad Foothills (48)		K-2	Fahrad (Grand Master Rogue)	Balcony of Chateau Ravenholdt
Ironforge (52)	The Forlorn Cavern	G-1	Fenthwick	South building, inside east entrance
Ironforge (52)	The Forlorn Cavern	G-1	Hulfdan Blackbeard	South building, inside east entrance
Ironforge (52)	The Forlorn Cavern	G-1	Ormyr Flinteye	South building, inside east entrance
Orgrimmar (60)	The Cleft of Shadow	E-5	Gest	Shadowswift Brotherhood
Orgrimmar (60)	The Cleft of Shadow	E-5	Ormok	Next to Shadowswift Brotherhood building
Orgrimmar (60)	The Cleft of Shadow	E-5	Shenthul	Shadowswift Brotherhood
Stormwind (72)	Old Town	L-6	Lord Tony Romano	SI:7
Stormwind (72)	Old Town	K-5	Osborne the Night Man	Outside SI:7
Stranglethorn Vale (74)	Booty Bay (103)	B-8	Ian Strom	Second floor of The Salty Sailor Tavern
Teldrassil (80)	Dolanaar (109)	G-6	Jannok Breezesong	Inn
Teldrassil (80)	Shadowglen (124)	H-4	Frahun Shadewhisper	In northeast room inside main building
Tirisfal Glades (86)	Brill (104)	H-5	Marion Call	Second floor of Gallows' End Tavern
Tirisfal Glades (86)	Deathknell (109)	D-6	David Trias	First floor of second house on right side of road
Undercity (88)	The Rogues' Quarter	L-7	Carolyn Ward	Inside Skull Building
Undercity (88)	The Rogues' Quarter	L-7	Gregory Charles	Inside Skull Building
Undercity (88)	The Rogues' Quarter	L-7	Miles Dexter	Inside Skull Building

SHAMAN TRAINERS

REGION	MINI REGION	GRID LOC	NAME	NOTES
Durotar (34)	Razor Hill (122)	H-4	Swart	Barracks
Durotar (34)	Valley of Trials (131)	F-7	Shikrik	
Mulgore (58)	Bloodhoof Village (102)	F-6	Narm Skychaser	East tent
Mulgore (58)	Camp Narache (105)	E-8	Meela Dawnstrider	North tent
Orgrimmar (60)	Valley of Wisdom	D-4	Kandris Dreamseeker	Grommash Hold
Orgrimmar (60)	Valley of Wisdom	D-4	Sagorne Crestrider	Grommash Hold
Orgrimmar (60)	Valley of Wisdom	D-4	Sian'tsu	Grommash Hold
Swamp of Sorrows (76)	Stonard (126)	F-6	Haromm	Scaffolding just inside camp walls left of southern entrance
Thunder Bluff (84)	Spirit Rise	B-2	Beram Skychaser	Inside Hall of Spirits
Thunder Bluff (84)	Spirit Rise	B-2	Slin Bloodhaze	Inside Hall of Spirits
Thunder Bluff (84)	Spirit Rise	B-2	Tigor Skychaser	Inside Hall of Spirits

WARLOCK TRAINERS

REGION	MINI REGION	GRID LOC	NAME	NOTES
Dun Morogh (32)	Coldridge Valley (106)	D-7	Alamar Grimm	Anvilmar
Dun Morogh (32)	Kharanos (114)	F-5	Gimrizz Shadowcog	Gnomish camp on right of distillery
Durotar (34)	Razor Hill (122)	H-4	Dhugru Gorelust	Behind barracks
Durotar (34)	Valley of Trials (131)	F-7	Nartok	Back of cave
Elwynn Forest (42)	Goldshire (112)	F-7	Maximillian Crowe	Basement of Lion's Pride Inn
Elwynn Forest (42)	Northshire Valley (120)	G-4	Drusilla La Salle	Graveyard on right side of abbey
Ironforge (52)	The Forlorn Cavern	G-1	Alexander Calder	Building to the right of Traveling Fisherman
Ironforge (52)	The Forlorn Cavern	G-1	Briarthorn	Building to the right of Traveling Fisherman
Ironforge (52)	The Forlorn Cavern	G-1	Thistleheart	Building to the right of Traveling Fisherman
Orgrimmar (60)	The Cleft of Shadow	E-5, F-5	Grol'dar	Darkfire Enclave
Orgrimmar (60)	The Cleft of Shadow	F-5	Mirket	Darkfire Enclave
Orgrimmar (60)	The Cleft of Shadow	F-5	Zevrost	Darkfire Enclave
Stormwind (72)	Mage Quarter	D-8	Demisette Cloyce	The Slaughtered Lamb
Stormwind (72)	Mage Quarter	D-8	Sandahl	The Slaughtered Lamb
Stormwind (72)	Mage Quarter	D-8	Ursula Deline	The Slaughtered Lamb
Swamp of Sorrows (76)	Stonard (126)	F-5	Kartosh	Second floor of main hall
Tirisfal Glades (86)	Brill (104)	H-5	Rupert Boch	Second floor of Gallows' End Tavern
Tirisfal Glades (86)	Deathknell (109)	D-6	Maximillion	Church
Undercity (88)	The Magic Quarter	L-2	Kaal Soulreaper	Inside Skull Building
Undercity (88)	The Magic Quarter	L-2	Luther Pickman	Inside Skull Building
Undercity (88)	The Magic Quarter	L:(1, 2)	Richard Kerwin	Northeast corner of Skull Building

DEMON TRAINERS

REGION	MINI REGION	GRID LOC	NAME	NOTES
Dun Morogh (32)	Coldridge Valley (106)	D-7	Wren Darkspring	Anvilmar
Dun Morogh (32)	Kharanos (114)	F-5	Dannie Fizzwizzle	Gnomish camp on right of distillery
Durotar (34)	Razor Hill (122)	H-4	Kitha	Behind barracks
Durotar (34)	Valley of Trials (131)	F-7	Hraug	Back of cave
Elwynn Forest (42)	Goldshire (112)	F-7	Cylina Darkheart	Basement of Lion's Pride Inn
Elwynn Forest (42)	Northshire Valley (120)	G-4	Dane Winslow	Graveyard on right side of abbey
Ironforge (52)	The Forlorn Cavern	G-1	Jubahl Corpseseeker	First building on north from east entrance
Orgrimmar (60)	The Cleft of Shadow	E-5, F-5	Kurgul	Darkfire Enclave
Stormwind (72)	Mage Quarter	D-8	Spackle Thornberry	The Slaughtered Lamb
Swamp of Sorrows (76)	Stonard (126)	F-5	Greshka	Second floor of main hall
Tirisfal Glades (86)	Brill (104)	H-5	Gina Lang	Second floor of Gallows' End Tavern
Tirisfal Glades (86)	Deathknell (109)	C-7	Kayla Smithe	Church
Undercity (88)	The Magic Quarter	L:(1, 2)	Martha Strain	Inside Skull Building

WARRIOR TRAINERS

REGION	MINI REGION	GRID LOC	NAME	NOTES
Darnassus (26)	Warrior's Terrace	H-3	Arias'ta Bladesinger	Lower northwest platform
Darnassus (26)	Warrior's Terrace	H-3	Darnath Bladesinger	Lower northwest platform
Darnassus (26)	Warrior's Terrace	H-4	Sildanair	Middle of terrace
Dun Morogh (32)	Coldridge Valley (106)	D-7	Thran Khorman	Anvilmar
Dun Morogh (32)	Kharanos (114)	F-5	Granis Swiftaxe	Thunderbrew Distillery
Durotar (34)	Razor Hill (122)	H-4	Tarshaw Jaggedscar	Barracks
Durotar (34)	Valley of Trials (131)	F-7	Frang	Structure to south
Dustwallow Marsh (38)	Theramore Isle (130)	I-5	Captain Evencane	2nd floor of Foothold Citadel
Elwynn Forest (42)	Goldshire (112)	E-7	Lyria Du Lac	Rear entrance of smith
Elwynn Forest (42)	Northshire Valley (120)	G-4	Llane Beshere	Hall of Arms of abbey
Ironforge (52)	The Military Ward	I-9	Bilban Tosslespanner	Hall of Arms
Ironforge (52)	The Military Ward	I-9	Kelstrum Stonebreaker	Hall of Arms
Ironforge (52)	The Military Ward	J-9	Kelv Sternhammer	Hall of Arms
Mulgore (58)	Bloodhoof Village (102)	F-6	Krang Stonehoof	Combat ground east of village
Mulgore (58)	Camp Narache (105)	E-8	Harutt Thunderhorn	Main tent (north)
Orgrimmar (60)	Valley of Honor	J-3	Grezz Razorfist	Hall of the Brave
Orgrimmar (60)	Valley of Honor	J-3	Sorek	Hall of the Brave
Orgrimmar (60)	Valley of Honor	J-3	Zel'mak	Hall of the Brave
Stormwind (72)	Old Town	L-5	Ander Germaine	Command Center
Stormwind (72)	Old Town	L:(4, 5)	Ilsa Corbin	Command Center
Stormwind (72)	Old Town	L:(4, 5)	Wu Shen	Command Center
Swamp of Sorrows (76)	Stonard (126)	F-5	Malosh	First floor of inn
Teldrassil (80)	Dolanaar (109)	G-6	Kyra Windblade	Inn
Teldrassil (80)	Shadowglen (124)	H-4	Alyissia	In northeast room inside main building
Thunder Bluff (84)	Hunter Rise	G-8	Ker Ragetotem	Inside Hunter's Hall
Thunder Bluff (84)	Hunter Rise	G-9	Sark Ragetotem	Inside Hunter's Hall
Thunder Bluff (84)	Hunter Rise	G-9	Torm Ragetotem	Inside Hunter's Hall
Tirisfal Glades (86)	Brill (104)	H-5	Austil de Mon	First floor of Gallows' End Tavern
Tirisfal Glades (86)	Deathknell (109)	D-6	Dannal Stern	First floor of second house on right side of road
Undercity (88)	The War Quarter	G-1	Angela Curthas	In Skull Building
Undercity (88)	The War Quarter	F-2	Baltus Fowler	In Skull Building
Undercity (88)	The War Quarter	F-2	Christoph Walker	In Skull Building

PROFESSION TRAINERS

ALCHEMY

TITLE/DESCRIPTION	REGION	MINI REGION	GRID LOC	NAME
Artisan Alchemist	Darnassus (26)	Craftsmen's Terrace	G-2	Ainethil
Artisan Alchemist	Undercity (88)	The Apothecarium	F-7	Doctor Herbert Halsey
Expert Alchemist	Ashenvale (12)	Silverwind Refuge	G-6	Kylanna
Expert Alchemist	Darnassus (26)	Craftsmen's Terrace	G-2	Sylvanna Forestmoon
Expert Alchemist	Dustwallow Marsh (38)	Theramore Isle (130)	H-5	Alchemist Narett
Expert Alchemist	Hillsbrad Foothills (48)	Tarren Mill (128)	G-2	Serge Hinott
Expert Alchemist	Ironforge (52)	Tinker Town	I-5	Tally Berryfizz
Expert Alchemist	Orgrimmar (60)	The Drag	G-3	Yelmak
Expert Alchemist	Stormwind (72)	Mage Quarter	G-8	Lilyssia Nightbreeze
Expert Alchemist	Stranglethorn Vale (74)	Booty Bay (103)	B-8	Jaxin Chong
Expert Alchemist	Thunder Bluff (84)		E-3	Bena Winterhoof
Expert Alchemist	Undercity (88)	The Apothecarium	G-7	Doctor Marsh
Journeyman Alchemist	Darnassus (26)	Craftsmen's Terrace	G-2	Milla Fairancora
Journeyman Alchemist	Durotar (34)	Sen'jin Village (123)	H-7	Miao'zan
Journeyman Alchemist	Elwynn Forest (42)		E-5	Alchemist Mallory
Journeyman Alchemist	Ironforge (52)	Tinker Town	I-5	Vosur Brakthel
Journeyman Alchemist	Loch Modan (54)	Thelsamar (129)	E-5	Ghak Healtouch
Journeyman Alchemist	Orgrimmar (60)	The Drag	G-3	Whuut
Journeyman Alchemist	Stormwind (72)	Mage Quarter	G-8	Tel'Athir
Journeyman Alchemist	Teldrassil (80)	Dolanaar (109)	G-6	Cyndra Kindwhisper
Journeyman Alchemist	Thunder Bluff (84)		E-3	Kray
Journeyman Alchemist	Tirisfal Glades (86)	Brill (104)	H-5	Carolai Anise
Journeyman Alchemist	Undercity (88)	The Apothecarium	F-7	Doctor Martin Felben
Master Alchemist	Feralas (46)	Feathermoon Stronghold (110)	C-4	Kylanna Windwhisper
Master Alchemist	Swamp of Sorrows (76)	Stonard (126)	F-5	Rogvar

BLACKSMITHING

TITLE/DESCRIPTION	REGION	MINI REGION	GRID LOC	NAME
Armorsmith	Orgrimmar (60)	Valley of Honor	J-2	Okothos Ironrager
Artisan Blacksmith	Ironforge (52)	The Great Forge	G-4	Bengus Deepforge
Artisan Blacksmith	Orgrimmar (60)	Valley of Honor	J-2, K-2	Saru Steelfury
Artisan Blacksmith of the Mithril Order	Stranglethorn Vale (74)		F-2	Galvan the Ancient
Expert Blacksmith	Barrens (18)	The Crossroads (107)	F-3	Traugh
Expert Blacksmith	Duskwood (36)	Darkshire (108)	J-5	Clarise Gnarltree
Expert Blacksmith	Ironforge (52)	The Great Forge	G-4	Rotgath Stonebeard
Expert Blacksmith	Orgrimmar (60)	Valley of Honor	J-2	Snarl
Expert Blacksmith	Stormwind (72)	Dwarven District	H-2	Therum Deepforge
Expert Blacksmith	Thunder Bluff (84)		D-6	Karn Stonehoof
Expert Blacksmith	Undercity (88)	The War Quarter	I-3	James Van Brunt
Journeyman Blacksmith	Darkshore (24)	Auberdine (101)	F-4	Delfrum Flintbeard
Journeyman Blacksmith	Dun Morogh (32)	Kharanos (114)	F-5	Tognus Flintfire
Journeyman Blacksmith	Durotar (34)	Razor Hill (122)	H-4	Dwukk
Journeyman Blacksmith	Elwynn Forest (42)	Goldshire (112)	E-6	Smith Argus
Journeyman Blacksmith	Ironforge (52)	The Great Forge	G-4	Groum Stonebeard
Journeyman Blacksmith	Orgrimmar (60)	Valley of Honor	J-2	Ug'thok
Journeyman Blacksmith	Silverpine Forest (68)	The Sepulcher (124)	F-4	Guillaume Sorouy
Journeyman Blacksmith	Stormwind (72)	Dwarven District	I-2, J-2	Dane Lindgren
Journeyman Blacksmith	Thunder Bluff (84)		D-6	Thrag Stonehoof
Journeyman Blacksmith	Undercity (88)	The War Quarter	H-3	Basil Frye
Master Blacksmith	Stranglethorn Vale (74)	Booty Bay (103)	C-8	Brikk Keencraft
Weaponsmith	Orgrimmar (60)	Valley of Honor	J-2	Borgosh Corebender

ENCHANTING

TITLE/DESCRIPTION	REGION	MINI REGION	GRID LOC	NAME
Artisan Enchanter	Elwynn Forest (42)	Tower of Azora	I-7	Kitta Firewind
Artisan Enchanter	Stonetalon Mountains (70)	Sun Rock Retreat (127)	F-6	Hgarth
Expert Enchanter	Darnassus (26)	Craftsmen's Terrace	H-1	Taladan
Expert Enchanter	Feralas (46)	Feathermoon Stronghold (110)	C-4	Xylinnia Starshine
Expert Enchanter	Ironforge (52)	The Great Forge	H-4	Gimble Thistlefuzz
Expert Enchanter	Orgrimmar (60)	The Drag	F-4	Godan
Expert Enchanter	Stormwind (72)	The Canals	F-6	Lucan Cordell
Expert Enchanter	Thunder Bluff (84)		E-4	Teg Dawnstrider
Expert Enchanter	Undercity (88)	The Apothecarium	I-6	Lavinia Crowe
Journeyman Enchanter	Darnassus (26)	Craftsmen's Terrace	H-1	Lalina Summermoon
Journeyman Enchanter	Ironforge (52)	The Great Forge	H-4	Thonys Pillarstone
Journeyman Enchanter	Orgrimmar (60)	The Drag	F-4	Jhag
Journeyman Enchanter	Stormwind (72)	The Canals	F-6	Betty Quin
Journeyman Enchanter	Teldrassil (80)	The Oracle Glade	D-3	Alanna Raveneye
Journeyman Enchanter	Thunder Bluff (84)		E-4	Mot Dawnstrider
Journeyman Enchanter	Tirisfal Glades (86)	Brill (104)	H-5	Vance Undergloom
Journeyman Enchanter	Undercity (88)	The Apothecarium	I-6	Malcomb Wynn
Master Enchanter	Badlands (16)	Uldaman	G-1	Annora

ENGINEERING

TITLE/DESCRIPTION	REGION	MINI REGION	GRID LOC	NAME
Artisan Engineer	Ironforge (52)	Tinker Town	I-4	Springspindle Fizzlegear
Artisan Engineer	Orgrimmar (60)	Valley of Honor	I-3, J-3	Roxxik
Expert Engineer	Duskwood (36)	Darkshire (108)	K-5	Finbus Geargrind
Expert Engineer	Ironforge (52)	Tinker Town	I-4	Trixie Quikswitch
Expert Engineer	Orgrimmar (60)	Valley of Honor	I-3, J-3	Nogg
Expert Engineer	Stormwind (72)	Dwarven District	H-1	Lilliam Sparkspindle
Expert Engineer	Undercity (88)	The Rogues' Quarter	K-7	Franklin Lloyd
Journeyman Engineer	Barrens (18)	Ratchet (121)	H-4	Tinkerwiz
Journeyman Engineer	Darkshore (24)	Auberdine (101)	F-4	Jenna Lemkenilli
Journeyman Engineer	Dun Morogh (32)	Steelgrill's Depot	G-5	Bronk Guzzlegear
Journeyman Engineer	Durotar (34)	Razor Hill (122)	H-4	Mukdrak
Journeyman Engineer	Ironforge (52)	Tinker Town	I-4	Jemma Quikswitch
Journeyman Engineer	Loch Modan (54)	Stonewrought Dam	F-1	Deek Fizzlebizz
Journeyman Engineer	Mulgore (58)		H-3	Twizwick Sprocketgrind
Journeyman Engineer	Orgrimmar (60)	Valley of Honor	I-3, J-3	Thund
Journeyman Engineer	Stormwind (72)	Dwarven District	H-1	Sprite Jumpsprocket
Journeyman Engineer	Undercity (88)	The Rogues' Quarter	K-7	Graham Van Talen
Master Engineer	Tanaris (78)	Gadgetzan (111)	H-3	Buzzek Bracketswing
Master Gnome Engineer	Ironforge (52)	Tinker Town	J-5	Tinkmaster Overspark
Master Gnome Engineer	Stranglethorn Vale (74)	Booty Bay (103)	B-8	Oglethorpe Obnoticus
Master Goblin Engineer	Barrens (18)	Ratchet (121)	H-4	Vazario Linkgrease
Master Goblin Engineer	Tanaris (78)	Gadgetzan (111)	H-3	Nixx Sprocketspring

HERBALISM

TITLE/DESCRIPTION	REGION	MINI REGION	GRID LOC	NAME
Apprentice Herbalist	Tirisfal Glades (86)	Brill (104)	H-5	Faruza
Herbalism Trainer	Darnassus (26)	The Temple Gardens	F-7	Firodren Mooncaller
Herbalism Trainer	Elwynn Forest (42)		E-5	Herbalist Pomeroy
Herbalism Trainer	Feralas (46)	Camp Mojache (105)	I-4	Ruw
Herbalism Trainer	Ironforge (52)	The Great Forge	G-6	Reyna Stonebranch
Herbalism Trainer	Orgrimmar (60)	The Drag	F-4, G-4	Jandi
Herbalism Trainer	Redridge Mountains (62)	Lakeshire (115)	B-4	Alma Jainrose
Herbalism Trainer	Stormwind (72)	The Park	B-5	Shylamiir
Herbalism Trainer	Stormwind (72)	Mage Quarter	F-8, G-8	Tannysa
Herbalism Trainer	Thunder Bluff (84)		F-4	Komin Winterhoof
Herbalism Trainer	Undercity (88)	The Apothecarium	H-5	Martha Alliestar
Herbalism Trainer	Wetlands (96)	Menethil Harbor (117)	A-6	Telurinon Moonshadow
Herbalist	Ashenvale (12)	Silverwind Refuge	G-6	Cylania Rootstalker
Herbalist	Durotar (34)	Sen'jin Village (123)	H-7	Mishiki
Herbalist	Dustwallow Marsh (38)	Theramore Isle (130)	H-5	Brant Jasperbloom
Herbalist	Hillsbrad Foothills (48)	Tarren Mill (128)	G-2	Aranae Venomblood
Herbalist	Loch Modan (54)	Thelsamar (129)	D-5	Kali Healtouch
Herbalist	Moonglade (56)	Nighthaven (120)	F-5	Malvor
Herbalist	Teldrassil (80)	Dolanaar (109)	G-6	Malorne Bladeleaf
Superior Herbalist	Stranglethorn Vale (74)	Grom'gol Base Camp (112)	C-3	Angrun
Superior Herbalist	Stranglethorn Vale (74)	Booty Bay (103)	B-8	Flora Silverwind

LEATHERWORKING

TITLE/DESCRIPTION	REGION	MINI REGION	GRID LOC	NAME
Artisan Leatherworker	Darnassus (26)	Craftsmen's Terrace	I-2	Telonis
Artisan Leatherworker	Thunder Bluff (84)		D-4	Una
Expert Leathercrafter	Desolace (30)	Ghost Walker Post (111)	G-6	Narv Hidecrafter
Expert Leatherworker	Ashenvale (12)	Astranaar (101)	E-5	Aayndia Floralwind
Expert Leatherworker	Barrens (18)	Camp Taurajo (106)	F-6	Krulmoo Fullmoon
Expert Leatherworker	Darnassus (26)	Craftsmen's Terrace	I-2	Faldron
Expert Leatherworker	Ironforge (52)	The Great Forge	E-3	Fimble Finespindle
Expert Leatherworker	Orgrimmar (60)	The Drag	H-4	Karolek
Expert Leatherworker	Stormwind (72)	Old Town	J-5	Simon Tanner
Expert Leatherworker	Stranglethorn Vale (74)	Grom'gol Base Camp (112)	C-3	Brawn
Expert Leatherworker	Thunder Bluff (84)		E-4	Tarn
Expert Leatherworker	Undercity (88)	The Rogues' Quarter	I-6	Arthur Moore
Journeyman Leatherworker	Barrens (18)	The Wailing Caverns	E-4	Waldor
Journeyman Leatherworker	Barrens (18)	Wailing Caverns	E-4	Waldor
Journeyman Leatherworker	Darnassus (26)	Craftsmen's Terrace	I-2	Darianna
Journeyman Leatherworker	Elwynn Forest (42)	Goldshire (112)	F-6	Adele Fielder
Journeyman Leatherworker	Ironforge (52)	The Great Forge	E-3	Gretta Finespindle
Journeyman Leatherworker	Mulgore (58)	Bloodhoof Village (102)	E-6	Chaw Stronghide
Journeyman Leatherworker	Orgrimmar (60)	The Drag	H-4	Kamari
Journeyman Leatherworker	Stormwind (72)	Old Town	J-5	Randal Worth
Journeyman Leatherworker	Teldrassil (80)		E-5	Nadyia Maneweaver
Journeyman Leatherworker	Thunder Bluff (84)		D-4	Mak
Journeyman Leatherworker	Tirisfal Glades (86)		I-6	Shelene Rhobart
Journeyman Leatherworker	Undercity (88)	The Rogues' Quarter	J-6	Dan Golthas
Master Dragonscale Leatherworker	Azshara (14)	Ruins of Eldarath	D-6	Peter Galen
Master Dragonscale Leatherworker	Badlands (16)		I-6	Thorkaf Dragoneye
Master Elemental Leatherworker	Searing Gorge (64)	Tanner Camp	H-7	Sarah Tanner
Master Leatherworker	Feralas (46)	Camp Mojache (105)	I-4	Hahrana Ironhide
Master Leatherworking Trainer	The Hinterlands (50)	Aerie Peak (100)	B-4	Drakk Stonehand
Master Tribal Leatherworker	Stranglethorn Vale (74)		D-4	Se'Jib
Tribal Leatherworking Trainer	Feralas (46)	Thalanaar	K-5	Caryssia Moonhunter

MINING

TITLE/DESCRIPTION	REGION	MINI REGION	GRID LOC	NAME
Miner	Durotar (34)	Razor Hill (122)	H-4	Krunn
Miner	Silverpine Forest (68)	The Sepulcher (124)	F-4	Johan Focht
Miner	Tanaris (78)	Gadgetzan (111)	G-3	Pikkle
Mining Trainer	Darkshore (24)	Auberdine (101)	F-4	Kurdram Stonehammer
Mining Trainer	Dun Morogh (32)	Gol'Bolar Quarry	J-6	Dank Drizzlecut
Mining Trainer	Dun Morogh (32)	Steelgrill's Depot	G-5	Yarr Hammerstone
Mining Trainer	Duskwood (36)	Darkshire (108)	J-5	Matt Johnson
Mining Trainer	Ironforge (52)	The Great Forge	G-3	Geofram Bouldertoe
Mining Trainer	Loch Modan (54)	Thelsamar (129)	E-5	Brock Stoneseeker
Mining Trainer	Orgrimmar (60)	Valley of Honor	I-3	Makaru
Mining Trainer	Stormwind (72)	Dwarven District	H-2	Gelman Stonehand
Mining Trainer	Thunder Bluff (84)		C-6	Brek Stonehoof
Mining Trainer	Undercity (88)	The War Quarter	H-4	Brom Killian

SKINNING

TITLE/DESCRIPTION	REGION	MINI REGION	GRID LOC	NAME
Skinner	Ashenvale (12)	Silverwind Refuge	F-6	Jayla
Skinner	Barrens (18)	Camp Taurajo (106)	F-6	Dranh
Skinner	Elwynn Forest (42)	Goldshire (112)	F-6	Helene Peltskinner
Skinner	Mulgore (58)	Bloodhoof Village (102)	E-6	Yonn Deepcut
Skinner	Teldrassil (80)		E-5	Radnaal Maneweaver
Skinner	Tirisfal Glades (86)		I-6	Rand Rhobart
Skinning Trainer	Darnassus (26)	Craftsmen's Terrace	I-2	Eladriel
Skinning Trainer	Desolace (30)	Shadowprey Village (125)	B-7	Malux
Skinning Trainer	Desolace (30)	Shadowprey Village (125)	B-7	Vark Battlescar
Skinning Trainer	Feralas (46)	Camp Mojache (105)	I-4	Kulleg Stonehorn
Skinning Trainer	Ironforge (52)	The Great Forge	E-3	Balthus Stoneflayer
Skinning Trainer	Orgrimmar (60)	The Drag	H-4	Thuwd
Skinning Trainer	Redridge Mountains (62)		L-7	Wilma Ranthal
Skinning Trainer	Stormwind (72)	Old Town	J-5	Maris Granger
Skinning Trainer	Thunder Bluff (84)		E-4	Mooranta
Skinning Trainer	Undercity (88)	The Rogues' Quarter	J-6	Killian Hagey

TAILORING

TITLE/DESCRIPTION	REGION	MINI REGION	GRID LOC	NAME
Artisan Tailor	Stormwind (72)	Mage Quarter	G-7	Georgio Bolero
Artisan Tailor	Undercity (88)	The Magic Quarter	J-3	Josef Gregorian
Expert Tailor	Barrens (18)	Camp Taurajo (106)	F-6	Mahani
Expert Tailor	Darnassus (26)	Craftsmen's Terrace	H-2	Me'lynn
Expert Tailor	Ironforge (52)	The Great Forge	F-3	Jormund Stonebrow
Expert Tailor	Orgrimmar (60)	The Drag	H-5	Magar
Expert Tailor	Stormwind (72)	Mage Quarter	F-8	Sellandus
Expert Tailor	Stranglethorn Vale (74)	Booty Bay (103)	B-8	Grarnik Goodstitch
Expert Tailor	Thunder Bluff (84)		E-4	Tepa
Expert Tailor	Undercity (88)	The Magic Quarter	J-3	Rhiannon Davis
Journeyman Tailor	Barrens (18)	The Crossroads (107)	F-3	Kil'hala
Journeyman Tailor	Darkshore (24)	Auberdine (101)	F-4	Grondal Moonbreeze
Journeyman Tailor	Darnassus (26)	Craftsmen's Terrace	I-2	Trianna
Journeyman Tailor	Elwynn Forest (42)	Eastvale Logging Camp	K-7	Eldrin
Journeyman Tailor	Ironforge (52)	The Great Forge	F-3	Uthrar Threx
Journeyman Tailor	Orgrimmar (60)	The Drag	H-5	Snang
Journeyman Tailor	Stormwind (72)	Mage Quarter	G-7	Lawrence Schneider
Journeyman Tailor	Thunder Bluff (84)		E-4	Vhan
Journeyman Tailor	Tirisfal Glades (86)	Cold Hearth Manor	G-5	Bowen Brisboise
Journeyman Tailor	Undercity (88)	The Magic Quarter	J-3	Victor Ward
Master Shadoweave Tailor	Stormwind (72)	Mage Quarter	D-8	Jalane Ayrole
Master Shadoweave Tailor	Undercity (88)	The Magic Quarter	L-2	Josephine Lister
Master Tailor	Dustwallow Marsh (38)	Theramore Isle (130)	I-5	Timothy Worthington
Master Tailor	Hillsbrad Foothills (48)	Tarren Mill (128)	H-2	Daryl Stack

HERBALISM

Herb Name	Herbalism Skill Requirement	Alterac Mountains	Arathi Highlands	Ashenvale	Azshara	Badlands	Barrens	Blasted Lands	Burning Steppes	Darkshore	Deadwind Pass	Desolace	Dun Morogh	Durotar	Duskwood	Dustwallow Marsh	Eastern Plaguelands	Elwynn Forest	Felwood	Feralas	Hillsbrad	Hinterlands	Loch Modan	Moonglade	Mulgore	Redridge Mountains	Searing Gorge	Silithus	Silverpine Forest	Stonetalon Mountains	Stranglethorn Vale	Swamp of Sorrows	Tanaris	Teldrassil	Thousand Needles	Tirisfal Glades	Un'Goro Crater	Western Plaguelands	Westfall	Wetlands
Arthas' Tears	220																●		●																			●		
Black Lotus	300								●								●																							
Blindweed	235																															●					●			
Briarthorn	70			●			●			●					●						●		●			●			●	●									●	●
Bruiseweed	100	●	●	●			●			●		●			●						●		●			●			●	●					●				●	●
Dreamfoil	270				●					●									●	●																	●		●	●
Earthroot	15						●			●		●	●	●							●				●				●					●	●				●	
Fadeleaf	160	●	●			●									●							●									●	●								
Firebloom	205					●		●																			●						●							
Ghost Mushroom	245											●										●																		
Golden Sansam	260			●					●								●		●	●		●																●		
Goldthorn	170	●	●			●									●						●		●								●	●								
Grave Moss	120	●	●				●					●			●																									●
Gromsblood	250							●				●							●																					
Icecap	290																																							
Khadgar's Whisker	185	●	●		●	●									●						●	●	●								●	●								
Kingsblood	125	●	●	●		●	●					●			●						●									●	●	●			●					●
Liferoot	150	●	●	●								●			●						●	●								●	●	●								●
Mageroyal	50				●		●			●					●						●		●			●			●	●						●			●	●
Mountain Silversage	280					●			●								●		●																		●	●		●
Peacebloom	1						●			●			●	●		●		●			●		●		●				●					●		●			●	
Plaguebloom	285																●		●																			●		
Purple Lotus	210			●	●	●													●	●		●									●		●							
Silverleaf	1						●			●			●	●				●			●		●			●			●					●		●			●	●
Stranglekelp	85	●	●	●	●					●						●						●							●	●	●								●	●
Sungrass	230					●		●							●	●			●	●		●							●										●	●
Swiftthistle*																																								
Wild Steelbloom	115	●	●	●		●						●			●							●							●	●					●					●
Wildvine**																																								
Wintersbite	195	●																																						

* Found with Mageroyal or Briarthorn

** Found with Purple Lotus and off Trolls in Hinterlands and Stranglethorn Vale

MINING

Ore Name	Mining Skill Requirement	Alterac Mountains	Arathi Highlands	Ashenvale	Azshara	Badlands	Barrens	Blasted Lands	Burning Steppes	Darkshore	Deadwind Pass	Desolace	Dun Morogh	Durotar	Duskwood	Dustwallow Marsh	Eastern Plaguelands	Elwynn Forest	Felwood	Feralas	Hillsbrad	Hinterlands	Loch Modan	Moonglade	Mulgore	Redridge Mountains	Searing Gorge	Silithus	Silverpine Forest	Stonetalon Mountains	Stranglethorn Vale	Swamp of Sorrows	Tanaris	Teldrassil	Thousand Needles	Tirisfal Glades	Un'Goro Crater	Western Plaguelands	Westfall	Wetlands	Winterspring
Copper	1	●		●			●			●		●	●	●				●			●				●	●			●	●					●	●			●	●	
Dark Iron	230								●																		●														
Gold	155	●	●	●	●	●		●	●			●				●	●		●	●	●	●					●	●		●	●	●	●				●		●	●	●
Incendicite	65																																								●
Indurium	150					●																																			
Iron	125	●		●		●		●	●			●			●	●				●						●	●			●	●		●		●		●				
Lesser Bloodstone	75		●																																						
Mithril	175	●		●		●		●	●						●						●					●	●			●	●		●		●		●				●
Rich Thorium	270					●			●								●																		●			●	●		●
Silver	75	●		●		●	●			●			●	●	●						●					●	●			●					●	●			●	●	●
Small Thorium	250								●							●											●								●						
Tin	65	●		●		●		●		●		●		●	●						●		●			●	●			●					●				●	●	●
Truesilver	230	●		●		●		●	●							●					●						●			●	●		●		●				●	●	●

SKINNING

Leather Type	Skinning Requirement
Light Leather	1–150
Light Hide	51–150
Medium Leather	65–225
Medium Hide	75–225
Heavy Leather	125–300
Heavy Hide	125–300
Thick Leather	175–300
Thick Hide	175–300
Rugged Leather	225–300
Rugged Hide	225–300

Specialty Leather Type	Skinning Requirement	Location(s)
Black Dragonscale	250–300	Skinning Level 50-60 Elite Whelps and Wyrmkin in Blackrock Spire and Burning Steppes
Black Whelp Scale	85–125	Skinning Level 17-25 Whelps in Redridge Mountains and Wetlands
Blue Dragonscale	250–300	Skinning Level 50-60 Elite Whelps and Wyrmkin in Azshara and Winterspring
Chimera Leather	250–275	Skinning Level 50-55 Chimeras in Winterspring
Core Leather	310 (Use Finkle's Skinner from Blackrock Spire)	Skinning Ancient Core Hounds in Molten Core (310 Skinning Req.)
Deviate Scale	75–110	Skinning and Looting Level 15-22 Beasts in and around Wailing Caverns (Barrens)
Devilsaur Leather	275–300	Skinning Level 55-60 Elite Devilsaurs in Un'Goro Crater
Enchanted Leather	Enchanter with 250 Skill	Created by Enchanters (Skill 250)
Frostsaber Leather	275–300	Skinning Level 55-60 Frostsabers in Winterspring
Green Dragonscale	200–300	Skinning Level 40-60 Elite Whelps and Wyrmkin in Swamp of Sorrows & Temple of Atal'Hakkar
Green Whelp Scale	170–180	Skinning Level 34-36 Whelps in Swamp of Sorrows
Heavy Scorpid Scale	250–275	Skinning Level 50-55 Scorpids in Blackrock Spire, Burning Steppes, and Silithus
Perfect Deviate Scale	75–110	Skinning and Looting Level 15-22 Beasts in and around Wailing Caverns (Barrens)
Red Dragonscale	250–300	Skinning Level 50-60 Elite Whelps and Wyrmkin in Blackrock Spire and Wetlands
Red Whelp Scale	120–135	Skinning Level 24-27 Whelps in Wetlands
Scorpid Scale	200–250	Skinning Level 40-50 Scorpids in Blasted Lands, Tanaris, and Uldaman
Shadowcat Hide	185–215	Skinning Level 37-43 Shadow Panthers in Stranglethorn Vale and Swamp of Sorrows
Slimy Murloc Scale	75–125	Looting Level 15-25 Murlocs (Many Locations)
Thick Murloc Scale	150–175	Looting Level 30-35 Murlocs in Dustwallow Marsh, Hillsbrad Foothills, and Stranglethorn Vale
Thick Wolfhide	200–250	Skinning Level 40-50 Wolves in Burning Steppes, Feralas, and Hinterlands
Thin Kodo Leather	50–100	Skinning Level 10-20 Kodos in Barrens and Mulgore
Turtle Scale	190–265	Skinning Level 38-53 Turtles in Dustwallow Marsh, Hinterlands and Tanaris
Warbear Leather	250–275	Skinning Level 50-55 Bears in Felwood, Western Plaguelands, and Winterspring
Worm Dragonscale	200–300	Skinning Level 40-60 Whelps/Wyrmkin in Azshara, Burning Steppes, Swamp of Sorrows, and Winterspring

RARE MOBS

Rare Mob Spawn Times

Level	Uncommon	Semi-Rare	Avgerage Rare	Very Rare	Uber-Rare
6-9	~1 - 2 hrs	X	X	X	X
11-15	~1.5 - 2.5 hrs	X	X	X	X
16-20	~2 - 3 hrs	~4 - 6 hrs	X	X	X
21-25	~4 - 6 hrs	~8.5 - 12.5 hrs	~17 - 25.5 hrs	X	X
26-30	~5 - 8 hrs	~10.5 - 16 hrs	~21 - 32 hrs	X	X
31-35	~5 - 8 hrs	~10.5 - 16 hrs	~21 - 32 hrs	32 - 48 hrs	X
36+	~5 - 8 hrs	~10.5 - 16 hrs	~21 - 32 hrs	32 - 48 hrs	48 - 72 hrs

ALTERAC MOUNTAINS, PAGE 8

ARAGA
Dalaran, Sofera's Naze, The Headland, D:(7, 8), E-9, Lvl 35 Average Rare; Roams small area around spawn point

CRANKY BENJ
Lordamere Lake, A-5, Lvl 32 Very Rare; Patrols eastern coast of lake

GRANDPA VISHAS
The Uplands, D-3, Lvl 34 Common; Inside house

GRAVIS SLIPKNOT
Strahnbrad, H-4, Lvl 36 Uncommon; Windmill on western side of town

JIMMY THE BLEEDER
Corrahn's Dagger, Sofera's Naze, F-8, H-7, Lvl 27 Average Rare; Roams around camp

LO'GROSH
Crushridge Hold, Slaughter Hollow, F-3, G-5, Lvl 39 Average Rare; Roams small area around spawn point

NARILLASANZ
Chillwind Point, J:(5, 6), K:(4-6), Lvl 44 Semi-Rare; Patrols area between lake and road

SKHOWL
Growless Cave, Ruins of Alterac, D:(5, 6), E-4, F-6, Lvl 36 Semi-Rare; Roams small area around spawn point

ARATHI HIGHLANDS, PAGE 10

DARBEL MONTROSE
Stromgarde Keep (127), C-7, D-6, Lvl 39 Semi-Rare; Roams with minion near spawn point

FOULBELLY
Stromgarde Keep (127), B-6, Lvl 42 Very Rare; Stands to the right of tower in ogre quarter of keep

KOVORK
Boulderfist Outpost, D-5, Lvl 36 Uncommon; Inside cave at Boulder'gor

MOLOK THE CRUSHER
Boulderfist Hall, G-8, Lvl 39 Semi-Rare; Westernmost point in cave

NIMAR THE SLAYER
Witherbark Village, I:(6, 7), J-6, Lvl 37 Uncommon; Roams in village

PRINCE NAZJAK
The Drowned Reef, C:(8, 9), Lvl 41 Very Rare; Roams in the reef

RUUL ONESTONE
The Tower of Arathor, B-7, Lvl 39 Average Rare; Roams the top floor of tower

SINGER
Northfold Manor, D-3, Lvl 34 Uncommon; Roams in farm

ZALAS WITHERBARK
Witherbark Village, J-8, Lvl 40 Uber-Rare; Cave south of village

ASHENVALE, PAGE 12

AKKRILUS
Fire Scar Shrine, C-6, D-6, Lvl 26 Average Rare; Close to northern entrance to Fire Scar Shrine

APOTHECARY FALTHIS
Bathran's Haunt, D-3, Lvl 22 Uncommon; Within haunt to the east

ECK'ALOM
Mystral Lake, F-7, G-7, Lvl 27 Average Rare; Spawns in areas around lake

LADY VESPIA
The Zoram Strand (131), B:(2-3), Lvl 22 Uncommon; Roams coastline

MIST HOWLER
C:(2-3), D-1, Lvl 22 Uncommon; Roams forest near spawn points

MUGGLEFIN
Lake Falathim, C-4, Lvl 23 Semi-Rare; Roams near spawn points

OAKPAW
Greenpaw Village, F-6, G-6, Lvl 27 Semi-Rare; Roams throughout village

PRINCE RAZE
Xavian, J:(4-5), Lvl 32 Uncommon; Can be found near delta, next to a totem in middle of camp, or next to Geltharis

RORGISH JOWL
Thistlefur Village, E-4, Lvl 25 Uncommon; Roams camp near spawn locations

TERROWULF PACKLORD
Howling Vale, G-4, Lvl 32 Average Rare; In front of structure

URSOL'LOK
Nightsong Woods, Satyrnaar, Warsong Lumber Camp, J-5, K-6, Lvl 31 Semi-Rare

AZSHARA, PAGE 14

ANTILOS
Legashi Encampment, A-5, I-2, Lvl 50 Very Rare; Roams south from first spawnpoint and around second

GATEKEEPER RAGEROAR
Timbermaw Hold, D-3, Lvl 49 Semi-Rare; Guards gate

GENERAL FANGFERROR
Temple of Zin-Malor, E-5, Lvl 50 Semi-Rare; Top of main temple

LADY SESSPIRA
Ruins of Eldarath, D-5, Lvl 51 Uncommon; Patrols the ruins

MAGISTER HAWKHELM
Thalassian Base Camp, G-3, Lvl 52 Average Rare; Roams close to spawn points

MASTER FEARDRED
Legash Encampment, H:(2-3), Lvl 51 Average Rare

MONNOS THE ELDER
Bitter Reaches, H-9, K-2, Lvl 54 Uber-Rare; Roams across northern and southern peninsulas

SCALEBEARD
Bay of Storms, G-5, Lvl 52 Uncommon; Spawns in Scalebeard's Cave and roams

THE EVALCHARR
Haldarr Encampment, A-5, B-6, Lvl 48 Very Rare; Roams area east of Southfury River

VARO'THEN'S GHOST
A:(7-8), B-7, Lvl 48 Uncommon; Roams area north of road among ruins

BADLANDS, PAGE 16

7:XT
Camp Boff, Camp Cagg, The Dustbowl, Mirage Flats, A-8, B-7, C-8, D:(5, 7), H-8, I-7, Lvl 41 Very Rare; Roams small area around spawn point

ANATHEMUS
C-7, Lvl 45 Uncommon; Patrols large radius around entire region

BARNABUS
Agmond's End, Badlands, Mirage Flats, F-7, G-7, H:(6, 7), Lvl 38 Average Rare; Roams small area around spawn point

BROKEN TOOTH
Angor Fortress, Dustwind Gulch, G-4, H-2, I-3, Lvl 37 Uncommon; Roams small area around spawn point

DIGMASTER SHOVELPHLANGE
Uldaman, G-1, Lvl 38 Semi-Rare

RUMBLER
Camp Cagg, A-8, B-9, Lvl 45 Uncommon; Roams small area around spawn point

SHADOWFORGE COMMANDER
Angor Fortress, F-3, Lvl 40 Semi-Rare; Patrols second floor of fortress

SIEGE GOLEM
Angor Fortress, F-4, Lvl 40 Average Rare; Patrols path to an area of Badlands just south of Kargath (A-6)

WAR GOLEM
Angor Fortress, Hammertoe's Digsite, The Maker's Terrace, G:(1, 3), H-3, Lvl 36 Semi-Rare; Roams small area around spawn point

ZARICOTL
The Dustbowl, Mirage Flats, E:(5, 6), H-6, Lvl 55 Uncommon; Roams small area around spawn point

BARRENS, PAGE 18

AMBASSADOR BLOODRAGE
Razorfen Downs, F-9, Lvl 36 Semi-Rare; Spawns in/near huts

AZZERE THE SKYBLADE
Southern Barrens, E-6, Lvl 25 Uncommon; Patrols area south of Camp Taurajo

BLIND HUNTER
Razorfen Kraul, E-9, Lvl 32 Rare

BROKESPEAR
The Stagnant Oasis, F:(4-5), G-4, Lvl 17 Uncommon; Stays near spawn points

BRONTUS
Blackthorn Ridge, E-8, Lvl 27 Average Rare; Spawns near center hut and roams ridge

CAPTAIN GEROGG HAMMERTOE
Bael'dun Keep, F-8, Lvl 27 Average Rare; Second floor of keep

DIGGER FLAMEFORGE
Bael Modan, E-8, Lvl 24 Uncommon; In excavation site tent

DISHU
F:(2-3), Lvl 13 Uncommon; Patrols close to spawn points

ELDER MYSTIC RAZORSNOUT
Thorn Hill, G:(2, 3), Lvl 15 Uncommon; Eastern Razormane camp

ENGINEER WHIRLEYGIG
The Sludge Fen, G-1, Lvl 19 Uncommon; Control room

FOREMAN GRILLS
The Sludge Fen, G-1, Lvl 19 Uncommon; Patrols derrick

GEOPRIEST GUKK'ROK
Agama'gor, E:(4-5), Lvl 19 Uncommon; Guards Bristleback den

GESHARAHAN
Lushwater Oasis, E-4, Lvl 20 Average Rare; Swims in the oasis

HAGG TAURENBANE
Blackthorn Ridge, D-8, E-8, Lvl 26 Uncommon

HEGGIN STONEWHISKER
Bael Modan, E-8, Lvl 24 Uncommon; Crane

RATHORIAN
Dreadmist Den, E-2, F-2, Lvl 15 Uncommon; In cave atop Dreadmist Peak

SLUDGE BEAST
The Sludge Fen, G-1, Lvl 19 Semi-Rare; In sludge

SNORT THE HECKLER
D-3, Lvl 17 Uncommon; Roams southwest of Forgotten Pools

STONEARM
E:(2-3), Lvl 15 Uncommon; Roams Kolkar villages around the pools

TAKK THE LEAPER
G-1, Lvl 19 Semi-Rare; Roams ridge southeast of Sludge Fen

THUNDERSTOMP
Southern Barrens, E-8, Lvl 24 Uncommon; Roams clearing near Dustwallow Marsh border

BLASTED LANDS, PAGE 20

AKUBAR THE SEER
Dark Portal, G-5, H-5, I-5, Lvl 54 Uncommon; Roams small area around spawn point

CLACK THE REAVER
Dreadmaul Post, G-4, Lvl 53 Semi-Rare; Patrols to tower ruins at the edge of Serpent's Coil (I-3)

DEATHEYE
Dreadmaul Hold, G:(2, 3), Lvl 49 Average Rare; Roams small area around spawn point

DREADSCORN
Altar of Storms, F-3, Lvl 57 Uncommon; Patrols to foot of hill in Blasted Lands (F-4)

GRUNTER
Serpent's Coil, H-3, I-3, Lvl 50 Very Rare; Roams small area around spawn point

MAGRONOS THE UNYIELDING
Dreadmaul Post, G-4, Lvl 56 Average Rare; Roams small area around spawn point

MOJO THE TWISTED
Dreadmaul Hold, F-1, G-2, Lvl 48 Uncommon; Roams small area around spawn point

RAVAGE
G-4, I-4, Lvl 51 Semi-Rare; Roams small area around spawn point

SPITEFLAYER
Dark Portal, I-5, Lvl 52 Semi-Rare; Patrols to tower ruins at the edge of Serpent's Coil (I-3)

BLACKROCK MOUNTAIN, PAGES 22 & 64

CRYSTAL FANG
Blackrock Spire, C-4/D-8, Lvl 60 Rare

GHOK BASHGUUD
Blackrock Spire, C-4/D-8, Lvl 59 Uncommon

JED RUNEWATCHER
Blackrock Spire, C-4/D-8, Lvl 59 Uncommon

LORD ROCCOR
Blackrock Depths, C-4/D-8, Lvl 51 Rare

PANZOR THE INVINCIBLE
Blackrock Depths, C-4/D-8, Lvl 57 Rare

QUARTERMASTER ZIGRIS
Blackrock Spire, C-4/D-8, Lvl 59 Uncommon

SPIRESTONE BATTLE LORD
Blackrock Spire, C-4/D-8, Lvl 58 Uncommon

Burning Steppes, Page 22

DEATHMAW
Dreadmaul Rock, Terror Wing Path, I-3, J-6, K:(3, 5), Lvl 53 Uncommon; Roams small area around spawn point

GORGON'OCH
Dreadmaul Rock, J-4, Lvl 54 Average Rare

GRUKLASH
Altar of Storms, Blackrock Stronghold, A-3, D-3, E-5, Lvl 59 Uncommon

HAHK'ZOR
Dreadmaul Rock, J:(4, 5), K-4, Lvl 54 Semi-Rare; Roams small area around spawn point

HEMATOS
Blackrock Mountain, D-3, Lvl 60 Very Rare; Patrol circular path around Draco'dar

KROM'GRUL
Dreadmaul Rock, J:(4, 5), K:(4, 5), Lvl 54 Common; Roams small area around spawn point

MALFUNCTIONING REAVER
Dreadmaul Rock, Terror Wing Path, J-3, K:(3, 6), Lvl 56 Semi-Rare; Roams small area around spawn point

TERRORSPARK
E-4, F-4, G-4, H-4, I-3, Lvl 55 Average Rare; Roams small area around spawn point

THAURIS BALGARR
Ruins of Thaurissan, F-4, G-4, H-4, I-4, Lvl 57 Uncommon; Roams small area around spawn point

VOLCHAN
Terror Wing Path, K-6, Lvl 60 Uncommon; Patrols circular path around Dreadmaul Rock to the east

DARKSHORE, PAGE 24

CARNIVOUS THE BREAKER
Twilight Vale, F-5, F-8, Lvl 16 Uncommon; Roams close to spawn point

FIRECALLER RADISON
The Master's Glaive, F-9, Lvl 19 Semi-Rare; Wander center isle

FLAGGLEMURK THE CRUEL
Mist's Edge, Twilight Shore, E:(6-7), G-2, Lvl 16 Uncommon; Roams the shore close to spawn point

LADY VESPIRA
Ruins of Mathystra, I-2, Lvl 22 Semi-Rare; Roams throughout ruins

LICILLIN
Bashal'Aran, G-4, Lvl 14 Uncommon; Wanders through ruins

LORD SINSLAYER
Cliffspring Falls, H-3, Lvl 15 Uncommon; In caves

SHADOWCLAW
F-4, Lvl 13 Uncommon; Roams near Auberdine

DESOLACE, PAGE 30

ACCURSED SLITHERBLADE
Sar'theris Strand, C-2, D:(1-2), E-1, Lvl 35 Average Rare; Swims area between Ranzajar Isle and shore

GIGGLER
Tethris Aran, F-1, G-1, H:(2-3), I:(2-3), Lvl 34 Semi-Rare; Roams near spawn points

HISSPERAK
Kodo Graveyard, E:(4-6), F-5, G-5, Lvl 37 Semi-Rare; Roams area northwest of the Kodo Graveyard

KASKK
Mannoroc Coven, F-7, G:(7-8), Lvl 40 Very Rare; Patrols spawn points

MESHLOK THE HARVESTER
Mauradon, D-5, Lvl 48 Rare

PRINCE KELLEN
Sargeron, J-2, Lvl 33 Average Rare; Top of hill or east by hill

RAVENCLAW REGENT
Sargeron, J-2, Lvl 22 Uncommon; Southwest of Nijel's Point

DUN MOROGH, PAGE 32

BJARN
The Tundrid Hills, G-6, H-6, I-6, Lvl 12 Uncommon; Roams small area around spawn point

CAPTAIN BELD
Ironband's Compound, K-6, Lvl 11 Common; Basement of compound

DAN THE HOWLER
The Grizzled Den, E-5, F-5, Lvl 9 Uncommon; In cave

IBBLEWILT
Gnomeregan, C-4, Lvl 11 Uncommon; Roams small area around spawn point

GREAT FATHER ARCTIKUS
Frostmane Hold, B-5, C-5, Lvl 11 Uncommon; Cave at Frostmane Hold

HAMMERSPINE
Gol'Bolar Quarry, J-5, Lvl 12 Uncommon; Roams small area around spawn point

TIMBER
Iceflow Lake, D-4, Lvl 10 Uncommon; Large island at center of lake

DUROTAR, PAGE 34

CAPTAIN FLAT TUSK
Durotar, Razormane Grounds, F:(4, 5), G-5, Lvl 11 Uncommon; Near huts

DEATH FLAYER
E-5, F-5, Lvl 11 Uncommon; Roams clearing south of road

GEOLORD MOTTLE
Razormane Grounds, F-4, G-5, Lvl 9 Uncommon; Found near huts

WARLORD KOLKANIS
Kolkar Crag, F-8, Lvl 9 Uncommon; Outside hut (left as you enter, middle of chasm to right, or in the back)

WATCH COMMANDER ZALAPHIL
Tiragarde Keep, I-6, Lvl 9 Uncommon; Receiving room of castle

DUSKWOOD, PAGE 36

COMMANDER FELSTROM
Dawning Wood Catacombs, A-3, B-4, Lvl 32 Uncommon; Stands at spawn point

ENROS
Brightwood Grove, H-4, Lvl 32 Uncommon; Patrols to two additional worgen camps (I-6, H-3)

LORD MALATHROM
Dawning Wood Catacombs, C:(2, 3), Lvl 31 Uncommon; Roams small area around spawn point

LUPOS
Brightwood Grove, The Darkened Bank, C-3, D-3, E-3, H-3, I-3, J-3, Lvl 23 Uncommon; Roams small area around spawn point

MARAXIS
L-5, Lvl 27 Uncommon; Cave

NEFARU
Roland's Doom, I-8, J-8, Lvl 34 Uncommon; Roams small area around spawn point

DUSTWALLOW MARSH, PAGE 38

BURGLE EYE
Dreadmurk Shore, H:(1-3), Lvl 38 Uncommon; Spawns on the five isles

DARKMIST WIDOW
Darkmist Cavern, D-2, Lvl 40 Uncommon; Back of cavern

DART
F-2, Lvl 38 Uncommon; Runs in a circle near spawn point

DROGOTH THE ROAMER
Bluefen, D-1, Lvl 37 Uncommon; Roams throughout Bluefen

LORD ANGLER
Tidefury Cove, G-6, Lvl 44 Average Rare; Roams the cove

OOZEWORM
The Den of Flame, The Dragonmurk, D:(6-7), E-6, Lvl 42 Very Rare; Roams spawn points

RIPSCALE
The Quagmire, E-5. F:(5-6), Lvl 39 Semi-Rare; Roams swamp

THE ROT
Beezil's Wreck, G-6, Lvl 43 Average Rare; Roams the area around the wreck

EASTERN PLAGUELANDS, PAGE 40

DEATHSPEAKER SELENDRE
The Fungal Vale, The Noxious Glade, E-5, K:(4, 5), Lvl 56 Uncommon; In camp

DUGGAN WILDHAMMER
The Undercroft, B-7, C-6, D-8, E-7, Lvl 55 Semi-Rare; Roams small area around spawn point

GISH THE UNMOVING
Pestilent Scar, F-4, J-6, Lvl 56 Average Rare; Patrols between its two spawn points

HEARTHSINGER FORRESTEN
Stratholme, D-2, Lvl 57 Rare

HED'MUSH THE ROTTING
Crown Guard Tower, Eastwall Tower, Northpass Tower, E-7, G-3, I-5, Lvl 57 Very Rare; Roams small area around spawn point

HIGH GENERAL ABBENDIS
Tyr's Hand, K-8, L-8, Lvl 59 Uncommon; Second floor of castle or in The Scarlet Basilica

LORD DARKSCYTHE
Plaguewood, D-3, E:(3, 4), F-3, Lvl 57 Average Rare; Roams small area around spawn point

RANGER LORD HAWKSPEAR
Quel'Lithien Lodge, G-2, Lvl 60 Uncommon; Patrols lodge

SKUL
Stratholme, D-2, Lvl 58 Rare

STONESPINE
Stratholme, D-2, Lvl 60 Rare

WARLORD THRESH'JIN
Mazra'Alor, Zul'Mashar, I-2, J-2, Lvl 58 Uncommon; Stands idle at spawn point

ZUL'BRIN WARPBRANCH
Mazra'Alor, Zul'Mashar, I-2, J-2, Lvl 59 Semi-Rare; Stands idle at spawn point

ELWYNN FOREST, PAGE 42

FEDFENNEL
Stone Cairn Lake, I-4, Lvl 12 Uncommon; Stands idle at spawn point

GRUFF SWIFTBITE
Forest's Edge, C-9, Lvl 12 Uncommon; Patrols small area around spawn point

MORGAINE THE SLY
Mirror Lake Orchard, D-6, Lvl 10 Uncommon; House next to lake

MOTHER FANG
Jasperlode Mine, H-5, Lvl 10 Uncommon; Roams in mine

NARG THE TASKMASTER
Fargodeep Mine, E-8, Lvl 10 Uncommon; Roams in mine

THUROS LIGHTFINGERS
Crystal Lake, Jerod's Landing, Mirror Lake, D-6, G:(6, 8), L-8, Lvl 11 Uncommon; Stands idle at spawn point

FELWOOD, PAGE 44

ALSHIRR BANEBREATH
Jadefire Glen, F-8, Lvl 54 Uncommon; Roams Jadefire Glen

DEATH HOWL
Felwood, Morlos'Aran, G:(7-8), H-9, Lvl 49 Average Rare; Roams near spawn points

DESSECUS
Irontree Cavern, H-2, Lvl 56 Semi-Rare; Bottom cave

IMMOLATUS
Shatter Scar Vale, F-4, Lvl 56 Semi-Rare; Roams eastern craters

MONGRESS
F:(7-8), Lvl 50 Very Rare; Roams near spawn points

OLM THE WISE
Irontree Woods, G:(2-3), H:(1-3), Lvl 52 Average Rare; Roams near spawn points

RAGEPAW
Deadwood Village, G-9, Lvl 51 Uncommon; Roams southern area of camp

THE ONGAR
Bloodvenom River, E-5, Lvl 51 Very Rare; Roams river near spawn point

FERALAS, PAGE 46

ARASH-ETHIS
The Twin Colossals, D-2, E-2, Lvl 49 Uncommon; Patrols area west of road near mountains

DIAMOND HEAD
Sardor Isle, A:(5-6), C:(5-6), Lvl 45 Semi-Rare; Seabed off coast of isle

GNARL LEAFBROTHER
The Writhing Deep, I-6, Lvl 44 Very Rare; Roams west to the Woodpaw Hills

LADY SZALLAH
Isle of Dread, B-7, Lvl 46 Uncommon; Roams various areas outside of Shalzaru's Lair

MUSHGOG
Dire Maul, G-4, Lvl 60 Rare

OLD GRIZZLEGUT
Lower Wilds, Ruins of Isildien, G-6, H-4, Lvl 43 Very Rare; Roams in a wide area

QIROT
The Writhing Deep, I-6, Lvl 47 Uncommon; In hive

SKARR THE UNBREAKABLE
Dire Maul, G-4, Lvl 58 Rare

SNARLER
Lariss Pavilion, I-4, Lvl 42 Uncommon; Spawns near delta and roams southeast

THE RAZZA
Dire Maul, The Maul, G-4, Lvl 60 Rare; In arena

TSU'ZEE
Dire Maul, G-4, Lvl 59 Rare

HILLSBRAD FOOTHILLS, PAGE 48

BIG SAMRAS
Durnholde Keep, I-3, K:(4, 5), Lvl 27 Semi-Rare; Roams small area around spawn point

CREEPTHESS
Azurelode Mine, B-5, C-6, D:(5, 6), Lvl 24 Semi-Rare; Roams small area around spawn point

LADY ZEPHRIS
Eastern Strand, H-9, Lvl 33 Uncommon; Patrols southeastern coastline

RO'BARK
Nethander Stead, H-6, Lvl 28 Uncommon; Patrols crop field

SCARGIL
Western Strand, B-7, C-7, Lvl 30 Uncommon

TAMRA STORMPIKE
Dun Garok, I-8, Lvl 28 Uncommon; Roams a small area around spawn point

HINTERLANDS, PAGE 50

GRIMUNGOUS
The Overlook Cliffs, K-5, Lvl 50 Very Rare; Patrols the southeastern ridgeline

IRONBACK
The Overlook Cliffs, L:(5, 6), Lvl 51 Semi-Rare; Roams small area around spawn point

JALINDE SUMMERDRAKE
Quel'Danil Lodge, D-5, E:(4, 5), Lvl 49 Uncommon; Roams small area around spawn point

MITH'RETHIS THE ENCHANTER
Jintha'Alor, I-8, J-8, Lvl 52 Average Rare; Roams from camp to camp

OLD CLIFF JUMPER
The Hinterlands, C:(5, 6), Lvl 42 Semi-Rare; Patrols small area around spawn point

RAZORTALON
Bogen's Ledge, D:(5, 7), E-5, F-5, Lvl 44 Average Rare; Roams small area around spawn point

RETHEROKK THE BERSERKER
The Altar of Zul, G:(6, 7), H-6, Lvl 48 Uncommon; Roams around base of altar

THE REAK
Agol'watha, Skulk Rock, The Creeping Ruin, G:(4, 5), I-4, Lvl 49 Very Rare; Roams small area around spawn point

WITHERHEART THE STALKER
Shadra'Alor, E-7, Lvl 45 Uncommon; Patrols while stealthed around small pond

ZUL'AREK HATEFOWLER
Hiri'Watha, Zun'Watha, D-6, E-6, Lvl 43 Uncommon; Roams small area around spawn point

LOCH MODAN, PAGE 54

BOSS GALGOSH
Ironband's Excavation Site, I-6, Lvl 22 Uncommon; On excavation platform with a Stonesplitter Geomancer and Berserk Trogg

GRIZLAK
Silver Stream Mine, D-3, Lvl 15 Uncommon; Roams small area around spawn point

LORD CONDAR
Ironband's Excavation Site, The Farstrider Lodge, H-8, J-7, K-7, Lvl 15 Semi-Rare; Roams small area around spawn point

MAGOSH
Ironband's Excavation Site, I-7, Lvl 21 Uncommon; With two Stonesplitter Diggers on hilltop in center excavation site

SHANDA THE SPINNER
K-5, Lvl 19 Semi-Rare; Roams small area around spawn point

MULGORE, PAGE 58

ENFORCER EMILGUND
D-2, Lvl 11 Uncommon; Venture Co. camp

GHOST HOWL
C-2, D:(1, 4), F-1, Lvl 12 Uncommon; Roams plains in multiple areas

SISTER HATELASH
D-1, Lvl 11 Uncommon; Northwest nest

SNAGGLESPEAR
F-7, Lvl 9 Uncommon; Camp

REDRIDGE MOUNTAINS, PAGE 62

BOULDERHEART
L-6, Lvl 25 Semi-Rare; Roams small area around spawn point

CHATTER
Alther's Mill, G-4, H-5, Lvl 23 Uncommon; Roams small area around spawn point

KAZON
Render's Camp, D-1, Lvl 27 Uncommon; Idle by hut

RIBCHASER
Lakeridge Highway, Three Corners, A-6, D-8, Lvl 17 Uncommon; Patrols around gnoll camp

ROHH THE SILENT
Galardell Valley, Stonewatch Falls, Tower of Ilgalar, J:(3, 4), K:(5, 6), Lvl 26 Semi-Rare; Stands idle at spawn point

SEEKER AQUALON
Lake Everstill, Stonewatch Falls, H-5, I-6, J-6, Lvl 21 Average Rare; Patrols the waterway connecting Lake Everstill with Stonewatch Falls

SNARLFLARE
Alther's Mill, D-6, E-3, F-3, Lvl 18 Uncommon; Roams small area around spawn point

SQUIDDIC
Lake Everstill, G-7, Lvl 19 Uncommon; Patrols back and forth just offshore by the murloc camp

SEARING GORGE, PAGE 64

FAULTY WAR GOLEM
The Sea of Cinders, C-6, D-5, E-4, F-7, G-6, Lvl 46 Semi-Rare; Roams small area around spawn point

HIGHLORD MASTROGONDE
Firewatch Ridge, A-4, C-3, Lvl 51 Uncommon; Roams small area around spawn point

REKK'TILAC
Tanner Camp, The Sea of Cinders, Thorium Point, C-7, D-3, F-7, G-3, H-7, I-7, Lvl 48 Average Rare; Stands idle at spawn point

SCALD
The Cauldron, D-5, G-4, Lvl 49 Average Rare; Patrols path near spawn point

SHLEIPNARR
H-4, Lvl 47 Very Rare; Patrols path near spawn point

SLAVE MASTER BLACKHEART
The Slag Pit, E:(2-4), Lvl 50 Uncommon; Roams small area around spawn point

SMOLDAR
C-6, Lvl 50 Semi-Rare; Patrols the northwestern portion of the zone

RARE MOBS

SILITHUS, PAGE 66

GRETHEER
Hive'Regal, E-2, F-3, G-4, Lvl 57 Very Rare; Roams close to spawn points

GRUBTHOR
E-4, Lvl 58 Semi-Rare; Roams close to spawn points

HURICANIAN
The Crystal Vale, D-1, Lvl 58 Uncommon; Roams vale

KRELLACK
Southwind Village, G-2, Lvl 56 Semi-Rare; Roams close to spawn points

LAPRESS
Hive'Regal, G-5, Lvl 60 Very Rare; Spawns in far southeast of hive and roams hive

REX ASHIL
Hive'Ashi, F-2, Lvl 57 Average Rare; Patrols above and within hive

SETIS
The Scarab Wall, E-5, Lvl 61 Uber-Rare; Spawns in front of the wall and roams the length of northern Silithus

TWILIGHT LORD EVERUN
Twilight Base Camp, Twilight Outpost, Twilight Post, D-5, E-2, F-3, Lvl 60 Uncommon; Roams respective camp

ZORA
Hive'Zora, D-4, Lvl 59 Average Rare; Roams hive

SILVERPINE FOREST, PAGE 68

DEATHSWORN CAPTAIN
Shadowfang Keep, F-7, Lvl 25 Rare

GOREFANG
Malden's Orchard, Silverpine Forest, G:(2, 3), H-2, I-1, Lvl 13 Uncommon; Roams small area around spawn point

KRETHIS SHADOWSPINNER
The Skittering Dark, E-1, Lvl 15 Uncommon; Roaming in or around cave

OLD VICEJAW
H:(5, 6), Lvl 14 Uncommon; Roams small area around spawn point

SNARLMANE
Fenris Keep, J:(2, 3), Lvl 23 Uncommon; Stands idle at spawn point

STONETALON MOUNTAINS, PAGE 70

FOREMAN RIGGER
Blackwolf River, Windshear Crag, H-5, I-5, Lvl 24 Uncommon; West end of the crag

PRIDEWING PATRIARCH
Mirkfallon Lake, F:(4-5), G-4, Lvl 25 Uncommon; Spawns in mountains east or south of Mirkfallon Lake

VENGEFUL ANCIENT
The Charred Vale, C-7, D-7, Lvl 29 Uncommon; Roams the vale

STORMWIND, PAGE 72

BRUEGAL IRONKNUCKLE
The Stockade, F-6, Lvl 26 Rare

STRANGLETHORN VALE, PAGE 74

GLUGGLE
Kal'ai Ruins, C-3, Lvl 37 Semi-Rare; Patrols between ruins and path heading north

HIGH PRIESTESS HAI'WATNA
Zul'Gurub, F-2, Lvl 57 Semi-Rare; Ruins just before the entrance to Zul'Gurub

KURMOKK
Ruins of Aboraz, D-6, Lvl 42 Very Rare; Patrols through Mistvale Valley toward the road heading into Booty Bay

LORD SAKRASIS
Nek'Mani Wellspring, B-6, Lvl 45 Uncommon; Far end of bridge in front of altar

RIPPA
Southern Savage Coast, B-6, Lvl 44 Very Rare; Patrols the cove on the northern side of The Cape of Stranglethorn

ROLOCH
Mizjah Ruins, D-3, Lvl 38 Average Rare; Patrols between ruins and the path to the north

SCALE BELLY
Crystalvein Mine, F-5, Lvl 45 Uncommon; Mine

VERIFONIX
The Cape of Stranglethorn, D-6, Lvl 42 Average Rare; Patrols a circular path around ridgeline stopping periodically to mine

SWAMP OF SORROWS, PAGE 76

FINGAT
Stagalbog Cave, H-8, Lvl 43 Semi-Rare; Patrols cave

GILMORIAN
The Forbidding Sea, J-9, Lvl 43 Average Rare; Patrols up and down the eastern coastline

JADE
Temple of Atal'Hakkar, I-5, Lvl 47 Very Rare; Entrance to the Temple of Atal'Hakkar

LORD CAPTAIN WYRMAK
H-4, Lvl 45 Uncommon; Patrols the upper right portion of swampland surrounding the Temple of Atal'Hakkar

LOST ONE CHIEFTAIN
Fallow Sanctuary, H-2, Lvl 39 Semi-Rare; Idle near huts in the northwest corner of camp

LOST ONE COOK
Fallow Sanctuary, H-2, Lvl 37 Uncommon; Idle by one of the two cauldrons in camp

MOLT THORN
The Shifting Mire, C-5, D-4, Lvl 42 Average Rare; Patrols back and forth between connecting bridges along the western waterways

VEYZHAK THE CANNIBAL
The Temple of Atal'Hakkar, I-5, Lvl 48 Uncommon

TANARIS, PAGE 78

CYCLOK THE MAD
Dunemaul Compound, Eastmoon Ruins, Southmoon Ruins, F:(5-7), G:(6, 7), Lvl 48 Very Rare; Spawns in ruins or compound and sticks close to spawn point

GREATER FIREBIRD
Abyssal Sands, F-4, Lvl 46 Average Rare; Flies throughout northern sands

HAARKA THE RAVENOUS
The Gaping Chasm, H-7, Lvl 50 Average Rare; Spawns in one of the chambers and sticks close to spawn point

KREGG KEELHAUL
Lost Rigger Cove, J-5, K-5, Lvl 47 Uncommon; In west building, ship being built, or far ship at dock

MURDEROUS BLISTERPAW
H-4, Lvl 43 Very Rare; Roams from one set of hills to the other

OMGORN THE LOST
Dunemaul Compound, Eastmoon Ruins, Southmoon Ruins, F:(6, 7), G:(6, 7), Lvl 50 Semi-Rare; Roams a wide path around spawn point

SORIID THE DEVOURER
The Noxious Lair, E:(4, 5), Lvl 50 Uncommon; Spawns in multiple chambers

TELDRASSIL, PAGE 80

BLACKMOSS THE FETID
Wellspring River, E:(3-4), Lvl 13 Uncommon; Patrols up and down river

DUSKSTALKER
F-8, G-8, Lvl 9 Uncommon; Patrols south of Lake Al'Ameth

FURY SHELDA
The Oracle Glade, D:(3-4), Lvl 8 Uncommon; Patrols near harpy camps west of road

GRIMMAW
Gnarlpine Hold, E-8, Lvl 11 Uncommon; Patrols Gnarlpine camps

THREGGIL
Fel Rock, G-5, Lvl 6 Uncommon; Runs around water in western section of cave

URUSON
Starbreeze Village, I-6, Lvl 7 Uncommon; Patrols road in village

THOUSAND NEEDLES, PAGE 82

ACHELLIOS THE BANISHED
Whitereach Post, B:(3-4), C-4, Lvl 31 Uncommon; Circles a couple plateaus in southwestern region

GIBBLESNIK
Windbreak Canyon, G:(4-5), H:(5-6), Lvl 28 Semi-Rare; Several spawn points around Windbreak Canyons

HARB FOULMOUNTAIN
Darkcloud Pinnacle, D-3, E-3, Lvl 27 Uncommon; Patrols across three small plateaus, north of pinnacle

TIRISFAL GLADES, PAGE 86

BAYNE
Stillwater Pond, E:(4, 5), F-5, G-4, Lvl 10 Uncommon; Roams small area around spawn point

DEEB
The North Coast, G-3, H-3, Lvl 12 Uncommon; Stands idle at spawn point

FARMER SOLLIDEN
Solliden Farmstead, D-5, E-5, Lvl 8 Uncommon; Stands idle at spawn point

FELLICENT'S SHADE
Balnir Farmstead, J-6, Lvl 12 Uncommon; Patrols a circular path around crop field

LOST SOUL
Agamand Mills (100), F-4, G-5, Lvl 6 Uncommon; Roams small area around spawn point

MUAD
Whispering Shore, D-4, Lvl 10 Uncommon; Patrols in and along shoreline

RESSAN THE NEEDLER
Nightmare Vale, E-7, F:(6, 7), G-6, Lvl 11 Uncommon; Roams a small area around spawn point

SRI'SKULK
Venomweb Vale, K-5, L:(4, 5), Lvl 13 Uncommon; Roams small area around spawn point

TORMENTED SPIRIT
Agamand Mills (100), E-3, Lvl 8 Uncommon; Patrols the northwestern edge of mill

UN'GORO CRATER, PAGE 90

CLUTCHMOTHER ZAVAS
The Slithering Scar, G-8, Lvl 54 Semi-Rare; Inside The Slighering Scar

UHK'LOC
Fungal Rock, I-2, Lvl 53 Uncommon; Northern section of cave

WESTERN PLAGUELANDS, PAGE 92

DREADWHISPER
Gahrron's Withering, H-6, Lvl 58 Semi-Rare; Roams small area around spawn point

FOREMAN JERRIS
Hearthglen, F:(1, 2), Lvl 62 Uncommon; Roams small area around spawn point

FOREMAN MARCRID
Northridge Lumber Camp, F-3, Lvl 58 Average Rare; Roams small area around spawn point

FOULMANE
Dalson's Tears, F-5, Lvl 52 Semi-Rare; Patrols around cauldron

LORD MALDAZZAR
Sorrow Hill, F-8, G:(7, 8), Lvl 56 Uncommon; Roams small area around spawn point

PUTRIDIUS
Ruins of Andorhal, F-7, Lvl 58 Uber-Rare; Roamd around city

SCARLET EXECUTIONER
Hearthglen, F-2, Lvl 60 Very Rare; Roams in tower on the southern end of city

SCARLET HIGH CLERIST
G-2, Lvl 63 Average Rare; Spawns inside or on top of tower south of Hearthglen

SCARLET INTERROGATOR
Hearthglen, F-1, Lvl 61 Uncommon; Spawns on the first or second floor of tower in the northeast corner of city

SCARLET JUDGE
Hearthglen, E-2, Lvl 60 Semi-Rare; Roams in town hall

SCARLET SMITH
Hearthglen, F-1, Lvl 58 Uncommon; Spawns in around to the right of smithy

THE HUSK
The Weeping Cave, H-4, I:(3, 4), Lvl 62 Very Rare; Roams small area around spawn point

WESTFALL, PAGE 94

BRACK
Longshore, C-8, Lvl 19 Uncommon; Runs entire Longshore coast

FOE REAPER 4000
Alexston Farmstead, The Dead Acre, Fulbrow's Pumpkin Farm, The Molsen Farm, Moonbrook, D-5, E-4, F-2, F-7, G-6, Lvl 20 Semi-Rare; Roams around spawn points

LEPRITHUS
The Dust Plains, D-3, G-8, Lvl 19 Uncommon; Appears near coffin/tombstones under tree

MASTER DIGGER
Jangolode Mine, E-2, Lvl 15 Uncommon; In back of mine

SERGEANT BRASHCLAW
D-3, Lvl 18 Uncommon; Guards gnoll camp in copse of trees

SLARK
Longshore, F-1, Lvl 15 Uncommon; Runs entire Longshore coast

VULTROS
The Dead Acre, The Dust Plains, Furlbrow's Pumpki Farm, Stendel's Pond, Westfall, C-7, E-4, E-6, F-2, G-7, H-6, Lvl 26 Average Rare; Roams around spawn points

WETLANDS, PAGE 96

GARNEG CHARSKULL
Angerfang Encampment, E-5, F:(4, 5), Lvl 29 Uncommon; Spawns in a few different camps

GNAWBONE
Sundown Marsh, D-3, E-3, Lvl 24 Average Rare; Patrols mosshide camps north of road across from excavation site

LEECH WIDOW
Thelgen Rock, G-6, Lvl 24 Uncommon; Patrols southwest area of cave

MA'RUK WYRMSCALE
Dun Algaz, G-7, Lvl 25 Uncommon; Patrols water south of windmill

MIRELOW
Bluegill Marsh, Sundown Marsh, B:(3, 4), C:(2-4), Lvl 25 Semi-Rare; Patrols water west and south of windmill and around bluegill camps

RAZORMAW MATRIARCH
Raptor Ridge, I-3, J-3, Lvl 31 Uncommon; Spawns western or northeastern chamber of cave

SLUDGINN
A-7, B-7, Lvl 30 Average Rare; South of Menethil Harbor, in hills across water

ZERILLIS
Zul'Farrak, E-1, Lvl 45 Rare

WINTERSPRING, PAGE 98

AZUROUS
Ice Thistle Hills, J-5, Lvl 59 Average Rare; Wanders hills east of road

GENERAL COLBATANN
Mazthoril, H-5, Lvl 57 Semi-Rare; Central cavern

GRIZZLE SNOWPAW
Winterfall Village, J-4, Lvl 59 Uncommon; Patrols village

KASHOCH THE REAVER
Frostwhisper Gorge, I-7, Lvl 60 Average Rare; Guards tower in gorge

LADY HEDERINE
Darkwhisper Gorge, H-8, Lvl 61 Very Rare; Deep within the gorge

MEZZIR THE HOWLER
Frostfire Hot Springs, E-4, Lvl 55 Uncommon; Roams to the west

RAK'SHIRI
Frostsaber Rock, G:(1, 2), H-1, Lvl 57 Semi-Rare; Roams base of rock

SKILL TRAINERS

COOKING

TITLE/DESCRIPTION	NAME	REGION	MINI REGION	GRID LOC
...utcher	Sherman Femmel	Redridge Mountains (62)	Lakeshire (115)	C-4
...utcher	Dirge Quikcleave	Tanaris (78)	Gadgetzan (111)	H-3
...ook	Duhng	Barrens (18)		G-3
...ook	Tomas	Elwynn Forest (42)	Goldshire (112)	F-7
...ook	Pyall Silentstride	Mulgore (58)	Bloodhoof Village (102)	E-6
...ook	Zarrin	Teldrassil (80)	Dolanaar (109)	G-6
...ooking Trainer	Alegorn	Darnassus (26)	Craftsmen's Terrace	F-2
Cooking Trainer	Cook Ghilm	Dun Morogh (32)	Gol'Bolar Quarry	I-5
...ooking Trainer	Gremlock Pilsnor	Dun Morogh (32)	Kharanos (114)	F-5
...ooking Trainer	Daryl Riknussun	Ironforge (52)	The Great Forge	H-4
...ooking Trainer	Zamja	Orgrimmar (60)	The Drag	G-5
...ooking Trainer	Crystal Boughman	Redridge Mountains (62)	Lakeshire (115)	B-4
...ooking Trainer	Stephen Ryback	Stormwind (72)	Old Town	K-4
...ooking Trainer	Aska Mistrunner	Thunder Bluff (84)		F-5
...ecipe Trainer	Eunice Burch	Undercity (88)	The Trade Quarter	H-4, I-4
Recipe Trainer	Henry Stern	Barrens (18)	Razorfen Downs	F-9
...uperior Butcher	Slagg	Arathi Highlands (10)	Hammerfall (113)	J-3

FIRST AID

TITLE/DESCRIPTION	NAME	REGION	MINI REGION	GRID LOC
...st Aid Trainer	Dannelor	Darnassus (26)	Craftsmen's Terrace	G-1
...st Aid Trainer	Rawrk	Durotar (34)	Razor Hill (122)	H-4
...st Aid Trainer	Nissa Firestone	Ironforge (52)	The Great Forge	G-6
...st Aid Trainer	Vira Younghoof	Mulgore (58)	Bloodhoof Village (102)	E-6
...st Aid Trainer	Arnok	Orgrimmar (60)	Valley of Spirit	C-8
...st Aid Trainer	Shaina Fuller	Stormwind (72)	Cathedral Square	F-3
...st Aid Trainer	Byancie	Teldrassil (80)	Dolanaar (109)	G-6
...st Aid Trainer	Pand Stonebinder	Thunder Bluff (84)	Spirit Rise	C-2
...st Aid Trainer	Nurse Neela	Tirisfal Glades (86)	Brill (104)	H-5
...st Aid Trainer	Mary Edras	Undercity (88)	The Rogues' Quarter	J-5
...st Aid Trainer	Fremal Doohickey	Wetlands (96)	Deepwater Tavern	A-6
...ysician	Thamner Pol	Dun Morogh (32)	Kharanos (114)	F-5
...ysician	Michelle Belle	Elwynn Forest (42)	Goldshire (112)	F-7
...auma Surgeon (First Aid)	Doctor Gregory Victor	Arathi Highlands (10)	Hammerfall (113)	J-4
...auma Surgeon (First Aid)	Doctor Gustaf VanHowzen	Dustwallow Marsh (38)	Theramore Isle (130)	I-5

FISHING

TITLE/DESCRIPTION	NAME	REGION	MINI REGION	GRID LOC
...rtisan Fisherman	Nat Pagle	Dustwallow Marsh (38)	Tidefury Cove	H-6
...tcher	Sherman Femmel	Redridge Mountains (62)	Lakeshire (115)	C-4
...herman	Kil'Hiwana	Ashenvale (12)	Zoram'gar Outpost (131)	B-4
...herman	Kilxx	Barrens (18)	Ratchet (121)	H-4
...herman	Zizzek	Barrens (18)	Ratchet (121)	H-4
...herman	Heldan Galesong	Darkshore (24)	Twilight Shore	E-6
...herman	Lui'Mala	Desolace (30)	Shadowprey Village (125)	B-7
...herman	Paxton Ganter	Dun Morogh (32)	Iceflow Lake	E-4
...herman	Lau'Tiki	Durotar (34)	Darkspear Strand	H-8
...herman	Lee Brown	Elwynn Forest (42)	Crystal Lake	F-6
...herman	Brannock	Feralas (46)	Feathermoon Stronghold (110)	C-4
...herman	Donald Rabonne	Hillsbrad Foothills (48)	Southshore (125)	F-6
...herman	Warg Deepwater	Loch Modan (54)	The Loch	E-4
...herman	Uthan Stillwater	Mulgore (58)	Stonebull Lake	E-6

SPECIALTY VENDORS

ARCANE TRINKETS VENDOR
Stormwind (72), Mage Quarter, E-8, Charys Yserian, Ancient Curios

BAEL'DUN MORALE OFFICER
Barrens (18), Bael'dun Keep, F-8, Malgin Barleybrew, Back of right wing

BLUE MOON ODDS AND ENDS
Undercity (88), The Apothecarium, H-5, Allesandro Luca,

BOY WITH KITTENS
Stormwind (72), Cathedral Square, The Canals, Lil Timmy, Roams Cathedral Square and The Canals

COCKROACH VENDOR
Undercity (88), The Trade Quarter, I:(4, 5), Jeremiah Payson, Under Bridge in Trade Quarter

CRAZY CAT LADY
Elwynn Forest (42), F-5, Donni Anthania, House southwest of Northshire Valley

FIREWORKS MERCHANT
Stranglethorn Vale (74), Booty Bay (103), B-8, Crazk Sparks, Shop on the back side of building near the overturned boat and hanging shark on the eastern side of bay

FIREWORKS VENDOR
Stormwind (72), Mage Quarter, D-7, Darian Singh, Pyrotechnics

FIREWORKS VENDOR
Ironforge (52), Tinker Town, J-5, Fizzlebang Booms, Things That Go Boom

FREEWHEELING MERCHANT
Westfall (94), Moonbrook, E-7, Defias Profiteer, Top floor of Moonbrook inn

FREEWHEELING TRADESWOMAN
Hillsbrad Foothills (48), Durnholde Keep, J-4, Kris Legace, Just below rear of ruins in the upper level of keep

GUILD TABARD VENDOR
Ironforge (52), The Commons, D-8, Lyesa Steelbrow, Ironforge Visitor's Center

HORSE BREEDER
Dustwallow Marsh (38), Theramore Isle (130), I-5, Gregor MacVince, Stables to southwest

HORSE BREEDER
Elwynn Forest (42), Eastvale Logging Camp, L-6, Katie Hunter, Corale

HORSE BREEDER
Hillsbrad Foothills (48), Southshore (125), F-6, Merideth Carlson, Stable

HORSE BREEDER
Wetlands (96), Menethil Harbor (117), A-5, Unger Statforth, Outside stables

ICE CREAM VENDOR
Thousand Needles (82), Mirage Raceway (118), J-8, Brivelthwerp, Next to building west of racetrack

KODO MOUNTS
Mulgore (58), Bloodhoof Village (102), E-6, Harb Clawhoof, Northern clearing

MASTER OF COOKING RECIPES
Stormwind (72), Old Town, J-5, Kendor Kabonka, Pig and Whistle Tavern

MECHANOSTRIDER MERCHANT
Dun Morogh (32), Steelgrill's Depot, G-5, Milli Featherwhistle, By mechanostrider's outside of depot

MERCHANT SUPREME
Hillsbrad Foothills (48), G-3, Zixil, Patrols with Overwatch Mark I between Tarren Mill and Southshore

OWL TRAINER
Darnassus (26), Warrior's Terrace, K-4, Shylenai, South of path just after entrance to city

PET VENDOR
Dun Morogh (32), Amberstill Ranch, I-5, Yarlyn Amberstill, Patrols circular path around ranch

PIRATE SUPPLES
Stranglethorn Vale (74), Booty Bay (103), B-8, Narkk, Nautical Needs (shop) on the northern side of The Old Port Authority

POTIONS & HERBS
Wetlands (96), G-4, Kixxle, Next to road to Dun Modr, by bridge

POTIONS, SCROLLS AND REAGENTS
Dustwallow Marsh (38), Brackenwall Village (104), D-3, Balai Lok'Wein, Northern part of village

QUARTERMASTER
Westfall (94), Sentinel Tower, G-5, Quartermaster Lewis, Sentinel Tower

RAM BREEDER
Dun Morogh (32), Amberstill Ranch, I-5, Veron Amberstill, By carriage in front of corral

RAPTOR HANDLER
Durotar (34), Sen'jin Village (123), H-7, Zjolnir, Among raptors south of village

RARE GOODS
Duskwood (36), K-2, Kzixx, By carriage

REWARDS VENDOR
Alterac Mountains (8), I-6, Jekyll Flandring, Left camp outside Alterac Valley (Horde)

REWARDS VENDOR
Alterac Mountains (8), The Headland, E-8, Thanthaldis Snowgleam, Camp outside Alterac Valley

RIDING WOLF (KENNEL MASTER)
Orgrimmar (60), Valley of Honor, I-1, Ogunaro Wolfrunner, Outside of Hunter's Hall

SABER HANDLER
Darnassus (26), Cenarion Enclave, E-1, Lelanai, Intersection of paths

SCROLLS AND POTIONS
Arathi Highlands (10), Stromgarde Keep (127), C-6, Deneb Walker, Well near church

SHADY DEALER
Stormwind (72), Old Town, L-6, Jasper Fel, SI:7

SHADY DEALER
Wetlands (96), Deepwater Tavern, A-6, Samor Festivus, Northwest, upstairs room

SHADY DEALER
Ironforge (52), The Forlorn Cavern, G-1, Tynnus Venomsprout, Top of steps, just inside east entrance

SHADY GOODS
Stranglethorn Vale (74), Booty Bay (103), B-8, Sly Garrett, Outside of fireworks shop on the eastern side of bay

SILVERWING SUPPLY OFFICER
Ashenvale (12), Silverwing Grove, H-8, Illiyana Moonblaze, In tent to the right of ramp

SMOKYWOOD PASTURES
Barrens (18), Mor'shan Base Camp, E-1, Hecht Copperpinch, Outside entrance to Warsong Gulch

SNAKE VENDOR
Orgrimmar (60), Valley of Spirit, A-6, C-8, Xan'tis, Roams Valley of Spirits

SPECIAL GOODS DEALER
Wetlands (96), Sundown Marsh, C-3, Wenna Silkbeard, Building next to windmill

SPECIAL WEAPON CRAFTER
Ironforge (52), The Great Forge, G-5, H-5, Ironus Coldsteel, The Great Anvil

SPECIALIST LEATHERWORKING SUPPLIES
Barrens (18), Wailing Caverns, E-4, Kaldan Felmoon,

SPECIALIST LEATHERWORKING SUPPLIES
Barrens (18), The Wailing Caverns, E-4, Kalldan Felmoon, Right eye of cave above entrance

SPECIALIST TAILORING SUPPLIES
Redridge Mountains (62), Render's Valley, J-8, Captured Servant of Azora, By cages in camp

SPECIALITY DRESS MAKER
Moonglade (56), Nighthaven (120), G-3, Geenia Sunshadow, First floor of northeast building

SPECIALITY ENGINEER
Hillsbrad Foothills (48), , K-2, Zan Shivsproket, Basement of Chateau Ravenholdt

SPECIALITY TAILORING SUPPLIES
Ironforge (52), The Great Forge, F-3, Outfitter Eric, Stonebrow's Clothier

SPECIALTY GOODS
Wetlands (96), Dun Modr, F-2, Dark Iron Entrepreneur, Behind bar in southern building

STYLISH CLOTHIER
Barrens (18), E-4, Kiknikle, Near mountains west of oasis

SWEET TREATS
Orgrimmar (60), Valley of Strength, E-7, Alowicious Czervik,

TABARD VENDOR
Orgrimmar (60), Valley of Strength, E-7, Garyl, Horde Embassy

TABARD VENDOR
Undercity (88), The Trade Quarter, J-4, Merill Pleasance, East spoke from bank

TABARD VENDOR
Stormwind (72), Trade District, H-7, I-7, Rebecca Laughlin, Stormwind Visitor's Center

TABARD VENDOR
Darnassus (26), Craftsmen's Terrace, I-2 , Shalumon, Southeast building, second floor

TABARD VENDOR
Thunder Bluff (84), D-6, Thrumn, Lower rise, in front of Thunder Bluff Civic Information tent

UNDEAD HORSE MERCHANT
Tirisfal Glades (86), Brill (104), H-5, Zachariah Post, Stable

WAR HARNESS MAKER
Orgrimmar (60), Valley of Honor, I-4, Kiro, Kiro's Harnesses

WAR HARNESS VENDOR
Thunder Bluff (84), F-5, Sura Wildmane, High rise, between Ragetotem Arms and Aska's Kitchen

WARSONG SUPPLY OFFICER
Barrens (18), Mor'shan Base Camp, E-1, Kelm Hargunth, Outside entrance to Warsong Gulch

World of WarCraft

ATLAS

LEGAL

BRADYGAMES STAFF

Publisher
David Waybright

Licensing Manager
Mike Degler

Director of Marketing
Steve Escalante

Editor-In-Chief
H. Leigh Davis

Creative Director
Robin Lasek

Assistant Marketing Manager
Susie Nieman

Assistant Marketing Manager, Online
Rachel Wolfe

Marketing Coordinator
Autumne Bruce

Team Coordinator
Stacey Beheler

CREDITS

Senior Development Editor
Christian Sumner

Editorial Intern
Matt Berner

Lead Designer
Dan Caparo

Designer
Rob Floyd

Data Gatherers
Edwin Kern
Michael Lummis

Special Contributor
Leon Whitney

Brady Census Takers
Michael Owen
Ken Schmidt

Cartography: Town & Encampment Maps
Argosy Publishing

ACKNOWLEDGMENTS

This project is a collaboration of so many talented people that we feel it's important to recognize them all.

From Argosy Publishing
Thanks to Rob Kneebone and Kevin Haley for providing such an awesome team. Chris Scalici's devotion to pumping out killer maps in almost no time was phenomenal and Mike Bedar saved the project by providing that crucial piece of the puzzle. Thanks all!

From Blizzard
First off, we have to thank everyone at Blizzard (especially the QA teams) for their hospitality while we spent weeks in-house gathering data. Specifically, we'd like to thank Scott Army for his help compiling data, Brian Hsieh for just being a fantastic front man, and Ben Brode for keeping us up and running and for providing that little application that made things so much easier. Kaéo Milker and Carlos Guerrero made sure to keep us fed—thanks to you both. A very special thank you goes to Gloria Soto for handling such a massive project with style, and Lisa Pearce for helping to whip us through the approvals. Finally, this book would be nothing without the guidance and assistance from Chris Metzen. Just working with this team was an honor.

From BradyGames
A bunch of people pitched in to help out on a project simply because of their knowledge of, and enthusiasm for, the **World of Warcraft**. Michael Owen took time out of his schedule to fly out to Blizzard and partake in the fun that is data entry. Ken Schmidt was an eternal source of information and just about everyone else mentioned in the staff/credits went beyond their normal duties to help on this project. Thanks to you all for helping to create such a wonderful product.